The Reshaping of
Ancient Israelite History in Chronicles

The Reshaping of Ancient Israelite History in Chronicles

ISAAC KALIMI

Winona Lake, Indiana
EISENBRAUNS
2005

Cataloging in Publication Data

Kalimi, Isaac.
  The reshaping of ancient Israelite history in Chronicles / by Isaac Kalimi.
    p. cm.
  Includes bibliographical references and index.
  ISBN 1-57506-058-2 (hardback : alk. paper)
  1. Bible. O.T. Chronicles—Historiography. 2. Bible. O.T. Chronicles—
Language, style. 3. Bible. O.T. Chronicles—Comparative studies.
4. Bible. O.T. Samuel—Comparative studies. 5. Bible. O.T. Kings—
Comparative studies. I. Title.
BS1345.52.K35   2004
222′.606—dc22

                                                          2004017730

ונתתי להם בביתי ובחומתי יד ושם טוב מבנים ומבנות

Isaiah 56:5

To the blessed memory of the beloved members of my family,

Rabbi Rahamim and Sarah Kalimi
Naomi Kalimi and Rivka
Miriam and Mordechai Sarṣi
Rabbe and Hannah Cohen
Benjamin and Rahman Oheb-Zion

All זכרונם לברכה

Contents

Preface xiii

Introduction 1
  1. Literary-Historiographical Elements That
      Differentiate the Parallel Texts   1
  2. The Creation of the Parallel Texts and the
      Differences between Them   2
    A. The State of Research   2
    B. Are the Differences between Chronicles and
       Samuel–Kings Exegetical Only?   6
    C. Conclusion   10
  3. The Sources upon Which the Study Is Based
      and Research Methods   11
  4. Methodological Problems   12
  5. The Structure of the Study   16

Chapter 1.   Literary-Chronological Proximity 18
  1. The Creation of Literary or Chronological Proximity
      between Unconnected Historical Events   18
  2. The Creation of Literary Proximity
      between Separate Issues   27
  3. The Transformation of Literary Proximity into
      Chronological-Topical Proximity   29
  4. Conclusion   33
  5. Appendix: The "Stronghold" (2 Samuel 5:17)   34

Chapter 2.   Historiographical Revision................... 36
  1. The Removal of Internal Contradictions
      in Samuel–Kings   38
  2. Preventing the Formation of a Contradiction
      between an Early Text and an "Addition"
      and/or Any Other Biblical Passage   47
  3. Removal of the Contradictions between
      Contemporary Reality and the Earlier Text   50
  4. Adjusting the Description in the Early Text
      to the Chronicler's Mood   52
  5. Verse Precision   57

Chapter 3.   Completions and Additions 59
  1. Textual Completions Based on Other Texts   59
    A. Completing a Description Adduced in a
       Certain Context Resembling a Description
       Adduced Elsewhere in a Similar Context   59

      B. Adding Details alongside a General Expression in
          Light of the Details in Another Occurrence
          of the Same Expression 63
      C. Adding a Name Parallel to a Place-Name in Light
          of the Content of Another Biblical Text 64
      D. Addition of Information to the Text in Light of
          Another Part of the Narrative 67
   2. Completion of an "Ellipsis" 68
   3. Attribution of Names to Unnamed Figures 74
   4. Addition of the Site of Events 77

Chapter 4.   Omissions 85
   1. Omission of Secondary Information 85
      A. Omission of the Names of Foreign Rulers'
          Relatives or Gods 85
      B. Omission of a Foreign Ruler's Name and/or Title 87
      C. Omission of Information concerning the
          History of Foreign Kingdoms 89
      D. Omission of Information Secondary to the
          Main Sequence of the Narrative 91
   2. Omission of Allusions to Narrations That Appear in
      Other Texts but Do Not Appear in Chronicles 93
   3. Omission of a "Numerical Inclusio" 97

Chapter 5.   Given Name – Equivalent Name Interchanges . . 99
   1. Geographical Names 100
   2. Names of Individuals or Peoples 104

Chapter 6.   Treatment of Problematic Texts 108
   1. Changing a Problematic Text in Order
      to Attribute Meaning to It 108
   2. Removing a Difficulty by Inverting the
      Order of the Text Components 114
   3. Omitting an Unintelligible Text 119

Chapter 7.   Harmonizations 123
   1. Textual Harmonization 123
   2. Content Harmonization 140
   3. Harmonizing Divine Word and Divine Action 159

Chapter 8.   Character Creation 166
   1. Rendering Characters More Significant 166
      A. David in the Census Narrative 166
         I. Reshaping of David's Figure in the Census Narrative 167
         (1) Using a Personal Name in Place of a General Title 167
         (2) Adding a Personal Name to a General Title 168
         (3) Changing Direct Speech to Indirect Speech,
         Thus Requiring the Use of a Name 168

(4) Omitting the General Title המלך 'the King'   168
(5) Using the Personal Name דויד in "Additions"   169
II. Transforming General Formulations into
Personal Ones   170
B. "Israel" (People and Land) in the
Census Narrative   170
C. Jehoiada the Priest   171
(1) Using a Personal Name in Place of a
General Title   173
(2) Adding a Personal Name alongside a
Title in the Text   173
(3) Adding a Personal Name Wherever
He Saw Fit   174
2. Rendering Characters Less Significant   174
A. Joash/Jehoash, King of Judah   174
(1) Increased Use of the General Title
המלך 'the King'   175
(2) Mentioning a Personal Name in
Uncomfortable Situations   175
(3) Omitting the Name "Joash" from the Text and
Then Alluding to It   176
B. Necho, King of Egypt   177
(1) Omitting the Title "Pharaoh"   177
(2) Referring to an Egyptian Ruler by
His General Title Only   178
(3) Mentioning "Necho" with No Title Whatever   178
(4) Limiting the Number of Times an Egyptian Ruler
Is Mentioned   179
(5) Denoting a Personal Name in
Difficult Situations   179
3. Excursus: Nathan before David   180
4. Creating Hierarchical Balance   182

Chapter 9.   "Measure for Measure"   186

Chapter 10. Allusion   194
1. Integrating Allusions into an Earlier Text   195
A. In Concluding Formulas   195
B. In Other Texts   199
2. Adducing an Entire Narrative in an
Allusion to an Earlier Text   205
3. Integrating Allusions into "Additions"   208
A. In Genealogical Lists   208
B. In Other Additions   209

Chapter 11. Chiasmus 215
   1. Chiasmus in the Hebrew Bible and in the Book of
       Chronicles: The State of the Research   216
   2. Chiastic Structures   218
     A. Chiastic Structures in Limited Literary Units   218
     B. Chiastic Structures in Larger Literary Units   223

Chapter 12. Chiasmus between Parallel Texts 232
   1. Chiasmus between Parallel Texts:
       Using the Words of the Earlier Text   234
       Two-Member Structures   234
       Three-Member Structures   246
   2. Chiasmus between Parallel Texts:
       Using Alternate Words   247
       Two-Member Structures   247
       A Three-Member Structure   251
   3. Chiasmus between Parallel Texts from
       Other Biblical Books and Chronicles   252
     A. Texts from Other Biblical Books   252
       Two-Member Structures   252
       A Three-Member Structure   254
       Literary Units in the Order of Chiasmus
         between Parallel Texts   254
     B. Chiasmus between Parallel Texts in "Additions"   255
   4. Chiastic Parallelism with Samuel–Kings
       and Internal Chiasmus between Parallel Texts   256
     A. Inverted Word Order plus Original Word Order
       in the Parallel Texts   257
     B. Original Word Order plus Inverted Word Order
       in an "Addition"   260
       Two-Member Structures   260
       Structures of Three or More Members   264
   Appendix: Diachronic Chiasmus   269
     A. The Inverse Recording of a Cardinal Number
       and Its Noun   269
       Two-Member Structures   270
       Three-Member Structures   271
     B. The Inverse Recording of Word Pairs   272

Chapter 13. Repetitions 275
   1. Resumptive Repetition   275
   2. Repetitive Introductions   289

Chapter 14. Inclusio 295
   1. Inclusios in Narrative Texts   297
     A. Comprehensive Literary Units   297
     B. Limited Literary Units   307

C. Perfecting an Existing Inclusio   313
D. Literary Inclusios in "Additions"   314
2. Literary and/or Numerical Inclusios in
      Lists or Collections of Lists   315
A. The List of David's Offspring   315
B. The List of Zerah's Sons   318
C. The List of Judah's Sons   318
D. The List of the Inhabitants of Jerusalem   320
E. The List of Issachar's Children   321
F. Genealogical Lists That Have No Parallel   322

Chapter 15. Antithesis   325
1. Contrasting the Deeds of Persons and Groups   326
2. Contrasting the Fate of Kings and Leaders   336
3. Relying on the Lord Contrasted with
      Relying on Flesh and Blood   341
4. Perfecting an Existing "Antithesis"
      in the Earlier Text   345

Chapter 16. Simile   350

Chapter 17. Key Words.   356

Chapter 18. Numerical Patterns   362
1. Shaping a Text in a "Three-Four"
      Numerical Pattern   362
2. Creating an Alternate Tradition and Formulating It
      in a "Six-Seven" Numerical Pattern   365

Chapter 19. Generalization and Specification   369
1. From General to Specific   369
2. From Specific to General   377
3. From General to Specific and
      Back to General   378

Chapter 20. Inconsistency, Disharmony,
      and Historical Mistakes   381
1. Inconsistency in Adapting an Earlier Text   381
A. Inconsistency in the "Revision" of Early History   381
B. Inconsistency in Harmonizing the Contents   383
C. Inconsistency in the Completion of
      "Elliptical Verses"   384
2. Changes in the Earlier Text Leading to Disharmony   385
A. Changes Leading to Disharmony
      Elsewhere in the Bible   385
B. Deviations and Contradictions between
      Chronicles and Torah Legislation   392
3. Historical Mistakes   392

Conclusion 404
       1. In General   404
       2. The Textual Aspect   405
       3. The Ideological-Theological Aspect   406
       4. The Uniformity of Chronicles   406
       5. The Image of the Writer and of His Book   407
       6. The Chronicler as Redactor and Author   409
       7. History and Historiography   409
       8. A "Critical" Aspect of Chronicles   410
       9. Research Model   411

Bibliography 413

Indexes 445
       Index of Authors 445
       Index of Scripture 449
       Index of Ancient Sources 468

Preface

Several reviewers of my Hebrew book, *The Book of Chronicles: Historical Writing and Literary Devices* (Biblical Encyclopaedia Library 18; Jerusalem, 2000), have articulated their hope that it would also appear in English. This volume not only fulfills the friendly wishes of those scholars but offers much more. It is not just an English translation of the Hebrew book but goes far beyond it, because I have expanded, updated, and revised numerous sections and notes throughout. A number of new examples have also been added to the 20 chapters of the book. Obviously, this study represents my latest research and opinion on the subject.

In this volume, abbreviations of books of the Bible, ancient sources, and rabbinic literature follow the *Society of Biblical Literature Handbook*. The abbreviations of less well-known sources are cited following their full form in the Index of Ancient Sources (pp. 469ff.). Bibliographic citations in the footnotes use the author's last name and a short title of the item referenced; complete information for each is found in the bibliography. In citations of the Hebrew text of Scripture, 'ה is used as an abbreviation for the Tetragrammaton / YHWH.

Special thanks go to Mr. James Eisenbraun, Publisher of Eisenbrauns, and to Mrs. Beverly McCoy, Editor, for their excellent work, personal encouragement all along the way, and fine design and production.

Isaac Kalimi
Case Western Reserve University
Cleveland, Summer 2004

Introduction

1. Literary-Historiographical Elements That Differentiate the Parallel Texts

Chronicles is the only comprehensive book of the Bible whose sources are, for the most part, available to us. A comparison of Chronicles with other books of the Bible reveals that almost half the text of Chronicles has parallels in the books of Samuel and Kings.[1] Some of these parallel passages (henceforth: "the parallel texts") are virtually identical; in other cases, the text in Chronicles has been wholly or partially edited and adapted in various ways and degrees of intensity and from various points of view.

Despite differences of opinion among scholars regarding the precise dating of the book of Chronicles,[2] it is generally accepted that the book was compiled in the Second Temple Period.[3] Since the books of Samuel–Kings were largely composed during the First Temple Period and certainly no later than the Babylonian Exile,[4] the text of Chronicles and its earlier parallels provide an extensive and enlightening example of a later biblical author's editing and adaptation of earlier literary-historiographical sources available to him. The parallel texts thus offer

---

1. To a minor extent, in the Pentateuch and the books of Joshua, Psalms, Ruth, Ezra and Nehemiah as well. For a comparative list of parallel texts, see Keil, *Manual*, 49–54; Driver, *Introduction*, 519–25; Kittel, *Chronik*, 82; Curtis-Madsen, *Chronicles*, 17–19. For anthologies of parallel texts, see: Mosiman, *Zusammenstellung*; Vannutelli, *Libri Synoptici*; Crocket, *Harmony*; Bendavid, *Parallels in the Bible*; Kegler-Augustin, *Synopse*; Endres-Millar-Burns, *Synoptic Parallels*. For a list of bibliographical abbreviations, see pp. 413ff.

2. See Kalimi, "Abfassungszeit"; idem, "Aramäische Grabinschrift"; idem, "Date of Chronicles."

3. Apparent first and foremost from the late language of the book, including the use of Persian words, the influence of Imperial Aramaic, and even first signs of Mishnaic Hebrew, from its style and from its orthography. To this must be added the mention of characters and events from the Persian period (e.g., 1 Chr 3:19 and 2 Chr 36:22–23); and see Zunz, *Vorträge der Juden*, 32–34; Kropat, *Syntax*; Curtis-Madsen, *Chronicles*, 27–36; Elmslie, *Chronicles* (1916) xxi; Polzin, *Late Biblical Hebrew*; Hurvitz, *Transition Period*, 15–16; idem, *Hebrew Language*, 214–15; Kalimi, "Abfassungszeit," 223; idem, "Date of Chronicles."

4. Despite the basic differences in historiographical method of the books of Samuel and Kings, the nature of the sources integrated into them, the historical background of their composition, their purpose, the site and date of their composition—I will refer to them as representative of a single historiographical type ("the Deuteronomistic historiography") contrasting with that of Chronicles ("the Chronistic historiography").

1

a wealth of material for diachronic research in various fields: linguistic (vocabulary, syntax, morphology, and orthography),[5] textual, and theological-ideological.[6]

The present study focuses on the literary-historiographical elements differentiating the earlier and later parallel texts.[7] Its chief objectives are to identify and define the literary and historiographical forms and techniques by which the author of Chronicles (henceforth: "the Chronicler") shaped the texts that he took from the books of Samuel–Kings and to examine his use of these devices in recounting the history of the Davidic kingdom. Special attention is paid to the distribution of these devices in the parallel texts; to the frequency of their appearance in the passages exclusive to Chronicles—that is, the texts without parallels in the other books of the Bible (henceforth: "additions")[8]; as well as to the place and uniqueness of these devices in the context of biblical literature and historiography as a whole. An effort is made to understand the foremost principles and motives that may have guided the Chronicler in his various literary-historiographical modifications and their significance in our interpretation of the text of Chronicles from various standpoints.

2. The Creation of the Parallel Texts and the Differences between Them

A. The State of Research

As already mentioned, nearly half of the book of Chronicles has parallel texts in the books of Samuel–Kings. How is this fact to be interpreted? How can one explain the variations that distinguish the parallel texts? These basic questions (of paramount importance for an understanding of the historiography of Chronicles and for an assessment of the reliability of the description of the monarchy) engaged the scholars of Chronicles from the very beginning of such research in the nineteenth

---

5. See, for example, the examples and discussion in the studies listed above in n. 3. See also Bendavid, *Biblical Hebrew and Mishnaic Hebrew*, 1.67–73; Japhet, "Interchanges of Verbal Roots," 9–50. For lists of orthographic variants and linguistic modifications, see also Keil, *Manual*, 56–59 nn. 6–7 (though some of the examples adduced by Keil are imprecise).

6. See, for example, the examples adduced in Japhet, *Ideology*.

7. I regard the books of Samuel–Kings on the one hand and the book of Chronicles on the other first and foremost as a form of literature. Their genre is characterized as biblical historical writing. Hence, the term "literary-historiographical" is used in this study. In order to be more precise, I differentiate between proper "literary changes" and "historiographical changes." This is explained in detail below.

8. For a list of the "additions" in Chronicles, see Keil, *Manual*, 54–55 n. 4 ("matters not mentioned at all in the early books"); 55–56 n. 5 ("additions to matter mentioned in the early books").

century.[9] It is universally agreed that the books of Samuel–Kings, as well as the books of the Pentateuch and of the Former Prophets relevant to our study, were composed many years before the recording of the book of Chronicles and that the Chronicler was aware of their existence.

The problem of the source of the parallel texts in Chronicles may thus be solved in either of the following ways: (a) the Chronicler used the parallel texts from the books of Samuel–Kings to which he had immediate access; (b) the Chronicler took the parallel texts from a third "common source" (*gemeinschaftliche Quelle*), that is, from an earlier independent source (or sources), that had first served the writers of Samuel–Kings (assuming, of course, that these sources survived to his day). The problem of the differences between the parallel texts may also be solved in these two ways: in the case of (a), the changes stem primarily from the Chronicler's deliberate and purposeful reworking of the earlier sources, while in the case of (b), they reflect divergent emphases and usages employed by the authors of Samuel and Kings, on the one hand, and the Chronicler, on the other, in editing the earlier, detailed "third common source" to which they both had access.

These approaches were developed with precision by scholars of the nineteenth century. The second was preferred by a number of researchers and interpreters[10] and is to be found in its best form in the writings of C. F. Keil.[11] It has, however, been rejected by scholars for a variety of

---

9. The differences between the parallel texts in the book of Chronicles and the books of Samuel–Kings were familiar in antiquity as well. It was not by accident that the Midrash says: "Chronicles was composed in order to be studied" (*Lev. Rab.* 1:3 // *Ruth Rab.* 2:1; *b. Meg.* 13a). In the introduction to his commentary on Chronicles, R. David Kimḥi (ca. 1160–1235) writes: "This book contains very obscure passages as well as passages disagreeing with texts in Samuel and Kings." In medieval days, however, no serious attempt was made to understand their nature; at the most, homilies were drawn from them, as Kimḥi relates: "I have found no commentator who tries to explain them. However, in Narbonna I found anonymous commentaries on this book, most of which are of the homily type." Some 250 years later, in the introduction to his commentary on the book of Samuel, Don Isaac Abarbanel (1437–1508) raises various questions concerning the relationship between Chronicles and the books of Samuel–Kings, noting: "I alone seek an answer and an explanation, there being no one else showing an interest in these, for I have found no reference large or small, good or bad, to these points in the writings of our sages, neither those of early Talmudic scholars nor of later writers and commentators. No one shows any doubt at all, nor has any of them provided a method of answering. Yet God has added agony to my pain in that nowhere in this land is there a commentary to Chronicles, other than a few insignificant comments made by R. David Kimḥi, who has made no profound study of this at all. The very book of Chronicles itself does not appear often in the Midrashim of the Jews. . . ." On this issue, see in detail Kalimi, "History of Interpretation," 5–41, esp. 22–38; idem, *Jewish Tradition and Exegesis*.

10. For Example, Eichhorn, *Einleitung*, 2.529–50, esp. 537, 540, 548–49; Bertholdt, *Einleitung*, 3.965–66, 972–88; Bertheau, *Chronik*, xxix–xlv, esp. xli–xlv.

11. See Keil, *Apologetischer Versuch*, 159, 199–235, esp. 206, 235; idem, *Chronicles*, 28–38, esp. 38; idem, *Manual*, 49–75, esp. 50, 63, 65 n. 2, 67, 69, 70–71. Keil

reasons: it was part of the conservative-orthodox school of nineteenth-century Bible study, which aimed at defending first the historical reliability of Chronicles in its narration of the period of the Monarchy and then the early dating and the authority of the Pentateuch, against the campaign waged by W. L. M. de Wette and his followers. It is indeed difficult to assume the existence of a third "common source" that served the authors of Samuel–Kings (or of even earlier writings upon which the later authors relied), on the one hand, and the Chronicler, on the other. This is so because of the considerable period of time separating these works from one another and because of the innumerable historical vicissitudes, devastations, and exiles visited in the meantime upon the people and the land. It is no less difficult to assume that the Chronicler made no (or, alternately, only limited) use of the existing ancient historical biblical books, despite the fact that his book contains many texts paralleling them, on occasion word for word. De Wette[12] had already noted that the parallel texts in Chronicles link up naturally and with no difficulty whatever with the passages in Samuel–Kings that were omitted from Chronicles (henceforth, "the omissions"), for example: 1 Chronicles 10 (// 1 Samuel 31) with 1 Samuel 28–30; 1 Chr 11:1–3 (// 2 Sam 5:1–3) with 2 Sam 2:1; 1 Chr 14:3 (// 2 Sam 5:13) with 2 Sam 3:2–5; and 1 Chr 15:29 (// 2 Sam 6:16) with 2 Sam 6:20–23. Textual errors and irrelevant expressions appearing in the books of Samuel–Kings reappear in the parallel texts in Chronicles.[13] Furthermore, many passages in the book of Kings that show signs of Deuteronomistic editing appear word for word in Chronicles, neither in their archaic, pre-Deuteronomistic form nor in some new form determined by the Chronicler. It will be seen that the Chronicler often alludes to the narration in Samuel–Kings, and in many cases it is impossible to understand his allusions without first being familiar with the narration in those books (see below, chap. 10). It will also be seen that many passages in Chronicles are related to their counterparts in Samuel–Kings by "chiasmus between parallel texts," indicating the direct use made by the Chronicler of those writings (see below, chap.12).

On the other hand, the first approach was already formulated in de Wette's book[14] and was reevaluated and improved in the writings of

---

himself also refers to other scholars of the same opinion, for example, A. Dillmann and H. A. C. Havenick. This approach is artificially revived by Auld, *Kings without Privilege*. Auld's arguments, however, are not convincing; see also McKenzie, "Chronicler as Redactor," 70–90.

12. De Wette, *Lehrbuch*, 278–79 (= idem, *Introduction*, 306–7).

13. Cf. Curtis-Madsen, *Chronicles*, 19 and the examples adduced there.

14. De Wette, *Beiträge*, 1–132; and cf. de Wette, *Lehrbuch*, 278–84, esp. 278–79 (= idem, *Introduction*, 306–15, esp. 306–7).

C. P. W. Gramberg and K. H. Graf,[15] attaining its peak in the hands of J. Wellhausen.[16] Henceforth, it became almost universally accepted by experts and has been accepted in principle (sometimes with minor shifts and emphases, as will be demonstrated below) ever since.

Proponents of this approach assume initially that, in principle, the version of the books of Samuel–Kings to which the Chronicler had access—his *Vorlage*—was identical with the one available to us. This assumption (taken for granted) is basic to the greater part of the exegetical and research literature relating to Chronicles. In 1948, however, G. Gerleman came out strongly against this assumption.[17] Though Gerleman also attributed the creation of the parallel texts to the Chronicler's utilization of the books of the Pentateuch and Former Prophets, his opinion was that the differences between the parallel texts did not result from the Chronicler's purposeful adaptation of the ancient material but, rather, reflect the differences in wording between the unredacted, "erratic, vulgar text" of the Pentateuch and Former Prophets, to which he had access, and the Masoretic version that is available to us, after having been redacted by the sages during the period subsequent to the destruction of the Second Temple ("textus receptus"). The book of Chronicles, because of its lower level of sanctity in the biblical hierarchy and because of its lesser significance in national life, as well as the lack of liturgical use made of it in the synagogue, was never edited, nor was it subjected to linguistic-textual archaization—at least, not to the extent that the Pentateuch and the books of the Former Prophets were archaized. In this way, Chronicles came to retain excerpts from the early, vulgar, unedited books of the Pentateuch and Former Prophets, which differ in many details from the Masoretic version of the edited books to which we have access, on the one hand, and are more reminiscent of the unedited Samaritan version of the Pentateuch, on the other.[18] However,

---

15. Gramberg, *Chronik*; Graf, *Geschichtlichen Bücher*, 114–247.

16. Wellhausen, *Prolegomena*, 165–223 (= ET, pp. 171–227).

17. Gerleman, *Synoptic Studies*, 3–35.

18. According to Gerleman (ibid., 13–14, and see also pp. 12, 15–22), the differences between the parallel texts in Chronicles and Samuel–Kings resemble in various details the linguistic differences between the Samaritan Pentateuch and that of the Masoretes. He also claims that there exists a morphological and orthographic similarity in the writing and arrangement of the material between Chronicles and the Samaritan Pentateuch, a similarity differentiating them from Samuel–Kings and the Masoretic Pentateuch. In his opinion, no modernization of the Pentateuch by the editor of the Samaritan Pentateuch or of passages from Samuel–Kings by the Chronicler ever took place; rather "we are concerned with a critically restored text, on the one hand, and a vulgar text on the other." Gerleman postulates as well that, had the Former Prophets been preserved in the Samaritan canon, the parallel texts in "the Samaritan version of Samuel–Kings" would undoubtedly match, from a linguistic point of view, the passages in the MT of Chronicles, and would resemble the Samaritan Pentateuch (ibid., 19–20)!

the initial assumptions upon which Gerleman based his claims do not hold up under close scrutiny (as demonstrated by S. Talmon), and his approach has not been accepted by the scholarly world. Gerleman over-looks the early linguistic characters of the books of Samuel (particu-larly) and Kings compared to Chronicles, which is dominated by late Biblical Hebrew. His perspective—that the Samaritan Pentateuch is unedited (erratic)—is inaccurate. The Samaritan version of the Torah is edited and archaized much more than its Masoretic version. The latter contains many ancient linguistic phrases.[19]

At the present time, the number of scholars who believe that the vast majority of differences between the parallel texts result from the Chron-icler's purposefully tendentious adaptation of the text is steadily grow-ing. Nevertheless, it is not considered impossible that some of the variations stem from textual differences between the books of the Pen-tateuch and Former Prophets that were available to the Chronicler and the versions of the books that are available to us,[20] while others result from scribal errors that have occurred throughout the generations in the Pentateuch and Former Prophets, as well as in Chronicles itself.

B. Are the Differences between Chronicles and Samuel–Kings Exegetical Only?

In 1972, T. Willi published his book *Die Chronik als Auslegung*,[21] in which he compares portions of the parallel texts in Chronicles and Samuel–Kings and views the variants distinguishing them as exegeti-cal modifications. He defines the literary nature of Chronicles as a "com-mentary" and views the Chronicler as an "exegete" interpreting the texts. As he puts it, this is the purpose for which the book was com-posed.[22] Willi's basic assumption is that the Chronicler viewed all of the

---

19. See Talmon, "Samaritan Pentateuch," 124–28; idem, "Tanach, Text," 626–27, 630.

20. See, for example, von Rad, *Geschichtsbild*, 63 and n. 106; Rudolph, *Chronik*, xv; Japhet, *Ideology*, 244 n. 149—regarding the Pentateuch to which the Chronicler had access; Cross, "Qumran and Septuagint," 15–26; idem, "Oldest Manuscript," 147–72; idem, "Report," 11; idem, *Ancient Library*, 30–33, 140–43 (and see also in his works adduced below, pp. 12–13, nn. 44, 47); Ulrich, *Qumran Text of Samuel*, 257–59; Segal, *Samuel*, 46–47, regarding the book of Samuel that was available to the Chron-icler; Lemke, "Synoptic Problem," 349–63, esp. 362; Japhet, *Ideology*, 8; Williamson, *Chronicles*, 2–3, 19, regarding the books of Samuel–Kings to which the Chronicler had access. McKenzie, *Chronicler*, 119, 154–55, has claimed that the Chronicler's *Vorlage* of Samuel differed from the *Vorlage* of the MT of Samuel, but his *Vorlage* of Kings was of the same type as the MT of Kings.

21. See Willi, *Chronik*.

22. See ibid., 48–66 (esp. pp. 53–54, 55–56, 66), 193. On p. 54, Willi writes: "Wenn der Chronist der Nötigung, Geschichte der vorexilischen Zeit zu schreiben, nach-geben wollte, so blieb ihm schon aus diesem Grunde nur ein Weg: der Interpretation

books of the Pentateuch and the Former Prophets as canonical.[23] Furthermore, it is Willi's view that Chronicles and Ezra–Nehemiah are two independent works by the same author.[24] Most of the material included in 1 Chronicles 1–9, 15:2–16 as well as 23:2b–27:34, and several passages in 2 Chronicles are additions made by later editor(s),[25] whereas Willi's definition of the literary type of Chronicles and of the purpose of its composition automatically implies a negation of Chronicles as a historical source for the events of the period of the Israelite Monarchy. Willi also does not consider engaging in the study of the period during which the book was compiled to be of any value.

Willi's approach is accepted by some scholars, such as R. Smend, J. Becker, and I. Gabriel. This approach, however, is unlikely, as I argued in detail in another study.[26] It is noteworthy to mention here that I consider the Chronicler to be a creative artist, a *historian* who selected the material he desired out of his sources and edited it in the order, the context, and the form he found fitting, thus creating a literary composition comprising part of late biblical historiography. The Chronicler's "exegesis" finds its expression first and foremost in the definition of the ancient historiographical data that was available to him at the time that he carried out his selection. Nevertheless, the purpose of the composition of the book of Chronicles was not merely to clarify early sources. The books of Samuel–Kings were not simply canonical for the Chronicler, who did not treat them as immutable, sealed books that one could only strive to explain and to comprehend in their given form. On the contrary, these books served him as raw material to be manipulated as he saw fit: he adapted them, adding to them and deleting from them in accordance with his ideological-theological outlook, his literary and historiographical methods, and his linguistic and stylistic taste. The interpretive and exegetical changes appearing in his book stem primarily from his particular use of early sources (which occasionally contain difficulties of various types or contradict some other biblical verse) and from his being a historian, providing his sources with evaluations and explanations. All of these are subsumed within a broad scale of modifications differentiating his work from Deuteronomistic historiography.[27]

---

des überlieferten Materials, mithin der Auslegung des deuteronomistischen Geschichtswerkes."

23. See ibid., 176ff. 241–44; and following him, Smend, *Entstehung*, 228–29.

24. See Willi, *Chronik*, 180. Claims of this kind were already made by de Wette, *Lehrbuch*, 290–91 (= *Introduction*, 328–30); Keil, *Chronicles*, 23–25.

25. See Willi, *Chronik*, 194–204 and also Noth and Rudolph.

26. See Kalimi, "Characterization of the Chronicler," 19–39, and references there to the scholars mentioned above and others.

27. See also Mosis, *Untersuchungen*, 12–13.

The books of Chronicles and Ezra–Nehemiah[28] seem to comprise, at least in their present form, two separate historiographical units as they appear in the Hebrew canon and in all of the early translations. The significant differences—and this is the decisive factor, in the long run—in the outlooks, the historiosophy, the historiography, the language, and the style of differentiating the two aforesaid units, as well as the duplication caused by combining them into a single unit—all make it likely that they were penned by different authors at different times. The similarity between the works is a natural result of their having been composed in mutually adjacent periods and of their common religious, cultural, social, political, geographical, and linguistic background, since it would seem from the books of Ezra and Nehemiah that both Ezra and Nehemiah were active (together and/or separately) during the reign of Artaxerxes I, king of Persia (464–424 B.C.E.).[29] According to Neh 5:14 and 13:6, Nehemiah composed his memoirs some time after the 32d year of Artaxerxes' reign (433/432 B.C.E.). The genealogical list appearing in Neh 12:10–11 ends with Yadduaʿ, son of Yoḥanan,[30] who (according to the Elephantine manuscripts) served as high priest in 407 B.C.E.[31] The memoirs of Nehemiah thus seems to have been written near the end of the fifth century, and the memoirs of Ezra at almost the same time.[32] The Chronicler, who apparently composed his work toward the end of the fifth century or during the first quarter of the fourth century B.C.E.,[33] was aware of the activity of these individuals and was familiar with their memoirs, for the list of inhabitants of Jerusalem

28. For the purposes of our discussion here, I shall view Ezra and Nehemiah as a single book, together with scholars who have considered this issue. This is clear, too, in *b. B. Bat.* 15a (and see also *b. Sanh.* 93b, where the following question is raised: "Why was no book named after Nehemiah, son of Hilkiah?" In other words, the book of Nehemiah was included under the title of the book of *Ezra*, rather than under its own title—*Nehemiah*); Josephus, *Ag. Ap.* 1.8; Eusebius; the Alexandrinus codex of the Septuagint; the Peshiṭta and a few medieval commentaries. Moreover, no Masoretic scribe commented at the end of Ezra. In contrast, however, the Masoretes noted at the end of Nehemiah: "the sum of the verses of Ezra and Nehemiah is 688."

29. In Ezra 4:7, 8, 11; 7:1; 8:1; Neh 2:1; 13:6, the king is Artaxerxes I; cf. Tadmor, "Chronology," 304, 305–6; Segal, "Books of Ezra–Nehemiah," 97; idem, "Nehemiah," 817–20; idem, "Ezra–Nehemiah," 151; Harrison, *Introduction*, 1157. For another opinion see, for example, Ackroyd, *Israel*, 191–96; idem, *Chronicles*, 24–26 and further references there.

30. "Jonathan," the MT, is a scribal error; cf. Neh 12:22, 23.

31. See Cowley, *Aramaic Papyri*, no. 30, lines 18, 30 // no. 31, lines 17–18, 29 (pp. 112, 120).

32. Cf. Segal, "Ezra–Nehemiah," 151. For the dating of these books, cf. also Rudolph, *Esra und Nehemia*, xxiv–xxv.

33. See Kalimi, "Abfassungszeit"; idem, "Aramäische Grabinschrift"; idem, "Date of Chronicles."

appearing in 1 Chr 9:2–17 was taken from Neh 11:3–19.[34] Furthermore, from the examples of various literary phenomena adduced in the present study, conclusions may be drawn concerning the use that the Chronicler made of Ezra–Nehemiah.[35] The tradition regarding the order of the books of the Bible found in the Babylonian Talmud (b. B. Bat. 14b–15a), a tradition that puts the books of Ezra–Nehemiah before Chronicles, may indeed indicate that Ezra and Nehemiah were compiled and arranged in order before the book of Chronicles.[36] The view that Chronicles was an independent work, separate from the books of Ezra and Nehemiah, has been accepted by a number of scholars.[37]

---

34. For this, see below, example 14.22 (pp. 320–321); Kalimi, "Ethnographical Introduction," pp. 556–62, esp. 559–61.

35. For example, example 3.3 (pp. 62–63); example 3.20 (pp. 79–81); and example 7.7 (pp. 129–130).

36. In principle, this conclusion is accepted by Harrison, Introduction, 1150, and also by Japhet: "Though the book of Ezra–Nehemiah describes a later period in the history of Israel, with regard to the date of its compilation it would seem to be the earlier of the two [i.e., of the books of Chronicles and Ezra–Nehemiah]"; see Japhet, "Biblical Historiography," 176, 186.

37. Cf. König, Einleitung, 285; Welch, Judaism, 185, 186–87; idem, Chronicler, 1; Segal, "Books of Ezra and Nehemiah," 81–88, 93; idem, Introduction to the Bible, 3.776–78, 801; idem, "Ezra–Nehemiah," 150; Mazar, "Chronicles," 605; Elmslie, Chronicles (1954), 345, 547–48; Liver, "History and Historiography," 154–56 (= Studies in Bible, 225–26), and see also his criticism of Rudolph, Chronikbücher, in Beth Mikra 1 (1956) 33; Grintz, "High Priesthood," Early Biblical Ethnology, 275–77 (= Zion 23 [1958/59] 138–40); Uffenheimer, Visions of Zechariah, 172–77; Harrison, Introduction, 1149–50, 1157; Japhet, "Authorship," 330–71; idem, Ideology, 4, 269; idem, "Biblical Historiography," 176; Williamson, Israel, 5–82; idem, Chronicles, 5–11; similarly, see also Welten, Geschichte, 4 n. 15, 172; Newsome, "Understanding," 202 n. 10, 215; Porter, "Historiography," 152–54; Seeligmann, "Beginnings of Midrash," 14 n. 1; Braun, "Solomonic Apologetic," 516; idem, "Chronicles, Ezra and Nehemiah," 52–64, esp. p. 63. However, contrary to the scholars listed above, most scholarly opinion views the books of Chronicles and Ezra–Nehemiah as originally a single, great work, the results of the work of a single writer who wanted to describe the history of Israel from its earliest period to the days of Ezra and Nehemiah, as a single historical unit. This opinion was expressed in the commentary by R. Levi ben Gershon (1288–1344) to 2 Chr 36:22: "This book and that of Ezra were written by a single author, for their language is similar." See Mortara, Commentaries by RaLBaG, 86; and cf. Naḥmanides' commentary on Exod 1:1. The scientific basis for this opinion was finally provided by Zunz, Vorträge der Juden, 13–36. Two years after Zunz's study was completed (Berlin, 1832), that of Movers (see Movers, Kritische Untersuchung) was published. In it the writer drew a similar conclusion. Ever since, it has served as a kind of fundamental assumption in the vast majority of introductory writings, commentaries, and scientific analyses of the books dealt with. See, for example: McKenzie, Chronicler, 25–26; Haran, "Catch-Lines," 124–29; idem, "Identical Lines," 18–20; Hanson, "Israelite Religion," 488–99 (Cross, McKenzie, and Hanson feel that the entire book of Chronicles developed in three different "editions": Chr[1], Chr[2], and Chr[3]); Ackroyd, "Concept of Unity," 189–201; Blenkinsopp, Ezra–Nehemiah, 47–54;

The material found in 1 Chr 1:1–2 Chr 36:23 is apparently a single literary unit penned by the Chronicler.[38] The extent to which the descriptions in the book are credible and dependable must be assessed on their own merits, separately with regard to each point. Moreover, despite the difficulty of determining the exact time of the Chronicler's activity and our meager knowledge of the Persian period to which he is ascribed, one must acknowledge the possible influences on the Chronicler's writing of his temporal and spatial environment. The Chronicler was not active in a vacuum: he related to his period and place and cannot be considered to have been cut off from the historical context of his environment and time. It would thus be good to attempt to read the book of Chronicles in light of the cultural and historical background against which it was composed, for only thus can one appreciate the unique value of the work.

C. Conclusion

Despite the great importance attributed to the study of the parallel texts in general and to the literary-historiographical modifications distinguishing them in particular, they have not been analyzed comprehensively and systematically until now.[39] Of course, commentaries and monographs dealing with Chronicles have on occasion pinpointed various changes of detail, even indicating types of literary and historiographical variants, as the result of a discussion of some of the problems encountered in the book. Yet, on the whole, reaction has been restricted

---

Smend, *Entstehung*, 226; Delcor, "Jewish Literature," 368–69; Gelston, "End of Chronicles," 53–60; Koch, "Weltordnung und Reichsidee," 220–39; Tuell, *First and Second Chronicles*, 9.

38. For this, see below, in the conclusion, §4, pp. 406–407.

39. In 1977, S. Japhet published *The Ideology of the Book of Chronicles and Its Place in Biblical Thought* (= her Ph.D. dissertation, 1973 [both in Hebrew]; ET, 1989). As its title indicates, the book deals primarily with a description of the varying components and divergent world outlooks found in Chronicles and the extent to which they occupy a unique niche in the complex web of biblical thoughts and beliefs. The author attempts to uncover the Chronicler's national-theological message (such as the essence of God and the principles guiding him; the essence of the nation; the essence of the relationship between God and nation; the land and the links between it and all sectors of the nation), while trying to refute the accepted ways of analyzing the book of Chronicles (for example, viewing the book as a polemic directed against the Samaritans, pp. 325–34; seeking the messianic-eschatological aspirations in Chronicles, pp. 493–504). This leads her to deal with the elements making up the book of Chronicles as a whole, including the variegated additional material found in it and the parallel texts appearing in other biblical books, such as in parts of Samuel–Kings, from which one can learn of the Chronicler's opinions and intentions. Japhet, however, treats very little of the new literary-historiographical form given to the parallel texts or of the literary-historiographical techniques that the Chronicler employed—because this exceeded the parameters of her research.

to incidental comments or marginal polemics (sometimes expressing a particular bias). Be that as it may, the full dimensions of the phenomenon have not as yet been thoroughly studied. As a consequence, not only have scholars and commentators failed to encompass the entire concept of recurring literary-historiographical variants characterizing the parallel texts and distinguishing them, thus leaving considerable room for innovative study in this field; it has even been deemed necessary to reexamine independently all pertinent manifestations of the subject and then to bind these into a single, consistent research unit in order to cast new light on the conclusions drawn by earlier scholars regarding various aspects of the entire topic.

3. The Sources upon Which the Study Is Based and Research Methods

This study is based in the main upon the Masoretic version of the book of Chronicles and of the books of Samuel–Kings.

Although the main topic of this study is not a textual phenomenon per se but an editorial/revision phenomenon, it nevertheless deals with several textual issues. It is worth noting that the Masoretic version of these books was preferred to all alternative possibilities as a basis for research, not only because of its status as a *textus receptus*, but largely because it provides the only complete text of these books transmitted directly and consecutively in their original—Hebrew—language and jealously preserved by the Masoretes. Biblical criticism has indeed demonstrated that the reading of the Masoretic version is generally to be preferred to that of the alternatives, every deviation from it or preference of an alternate version requiring well-founded justification.[40] It must, nevertheless, be stressed that my preference for the Masoretic Text is merely a statistical datum and has, consequently, no influence on decisions made in individual cases, for it is impossible to predict exceptions to this impression.[41]

Special attention has been given to optimal usage of the epigraphical and archaeological sources discovered in the Land of Israel and other biblical lands, on the one hand, and to the postbiblical Jewish sources as well as the classical sources, on the other. All of these sources were used intentionally to achieve a better understanding of the biblical texts and in order to illustrate them by topological examples.

---

40. Cf. Würthwein, *Text of OT*, 112, 113–14; Noth, *Welt*, 286–87 (= *OT World*, 359–60); Thompson, "Textual Criticism," 888; Roberts, *OT Text*, 270; Seeligmann, "Editorial Alteration," 279; Tov, "Textual Evaluation," 120, and n. 23 there, for additional bibliography. The superiority of the MT over the alternatives is clear, too, from the majority of the examples adduced by Brin, "Working Methods," 445–49.

41. See Tov, "Textual Evaluation," 120.

The present study has been carried out in accordance with literary and historiographical criteria in an attempt to exploit advances in both biblical and extrabiblical scholarship in these areas. The study takes into consideration the diverse legacy of biblical literature and its various strata, to which the Chronicler almost certainly had access, as well as the historical-political, social, religious, cultural, and material realities of what was, to the best of our knowledge, his time and place.

4. Methodological Problems

A number of methodological problems were encountered.

(A) Were the Samuel–Kings texts used by the Chronicler (his *Vorlage*) identical to the Masoretic Text of these books in our possession? On the other hand, is our text of the book of Chronicles identical to the text penned by the Chronicler?

There seem to be grounds to believe that both the Chronicler's *Vorlage* and the text that he wrote differed to some extent from our versions of these texts.[42] How, then, can we distinguish between the Chronicler's deliberate modifications of the Samuel–Kings texts (which undoubtedly account for the decisive majority of the differences between the two texts) and the discrepancies between his *Vorlage* and our version of the books of Samuel–Kings or the intentional or unintentional changes introduced by copiers as the text of Chronicles was copied and recopied and passed along from one generation to the next?[43] These problems cannot be resolved unequivocally. I have thus exercised great caution in determining which changes were intentionally made by the Chronicler and which are to be otherwise interpreted. In this respect, I have relied on relevant fragments of the Samuel–Kings scrolls discovered in the Judean Desert and published,[44] as well as the early translations of the books of Samuel, Kings, and Chronicles. My purpose in this was both to become acquainted with earlier versions of the texts and to identify

---

42. In this regard, see above, §2 (pp. 2ff.).

43. The MT of Chronicles has been well preserved in general, and it seems likely that the relatively late compilation of the book, its restricted distribution among broad sectors of the nation and the limited use made of it contributed to this. Yet, naturally enough, this book, too, copied and passed along over a period of hundreds of years, is not entirely free of error, especially in its lists of names.

44. For the publication of the scroll fragments, see in the main the works by Cross adduced in this study and those of his pupils, for example, Ulrich, *Qumran Text of Samuel*; McKenzie, *Chronicler*; as well as the newer commentaries to these books, for example, McCarter, *I Samuel*; idem, *II Samuel*; Gray, *Kings*. A single fragment of Chronicles (4QChr = 4Q118) was found in Qumran Cave 4; it contains sections of six lines in two columns. Unfortunately, these too have been damaged by worms, only four words remaining; see Cross, "Report," 11; idem, *Ancient Library*, 32. On the attitude of the Qumran community toward the book of Chronicles, see Kalimi, "History of Interpretation," 19–22; idem, *Jewish Tradition and Exegesis*.

errors and emendations incorporated into the Masoretic Text over the course of generations. Careful examination of these texts; awareness of how scribal modifications and copiers' errors originate; a careful, balanced, positive attitude toward the authenticity of the Masoretic Text, based on the ancient textual tradition, the Masoretes' extreme conservatism and precise preservation of the text; reliance on criteria important in the study of the biblical text and in the determination of the most authentic version, together with an awareness of the limitations of these criteria;[45] attention to the consistency of a given text with its linguistic and stylistic context, as well as its content and immediate and expanded literary structure; the book's underlying concepts and historical and geographical background—all of these helped in coping with the aforesaid methodological problems.

(B) The wording of certain sections of the Septuagint of Samuel–Kings differs from the wording of the Masoretic Text of these books, while closely resembling the parallel passages in the Masoretic Text of Chronicles.[46] Though a comparison of the Septuagint with the Masoretic Text was not within the scope of this study, there were cases where I felt it vital to take this problem into consideration, according to the guidelines for determining the preferred version outlined above. It is to be noted that, in some instances, the similarity between the Septuagint version of Samuel and the Masoretic Text of the parallel passages in Chronicles may be ascribed to the similarity of the Chronicler's *Vorlage* to both the Septuagint translators' *Vorlage* and the Qumran version of Samuel (4QSam[a]),[47] whereas other instances of identity between the

---

45. For the criteria and their limitations, see Tov, "Textual Evaluation," 112–32.

46. The LXX version most relevant to Chronicles (Codex B) strongly resembles the MT, to such an extent that the possibility of the MT's having been before the translator(s) has been seriously considered, the translation being attributed to Theodotion (ca. 200 C.E.); see, for example, Torrey, *Ezra Studies*, 63, 66–82 (and the list there of other scholars of his opinion); Olmstead, "Biblical Text," 3–4; Curtis-Madsen, *Chronicles*, 38–39; Elmslie, *Chronicles* (1916) lviii–lx. In 1946, Gerleman came out in opposition to this school of thought, expressing his opinion that the LXX version of Chronicles had been composed no later than the middle of the second century B.C.E., as demonstrated by the use made of it by Eupolemus and Josephus (in addition to the linguistic and stylistic considerations pointing in the same direction), and by the indications of Ptolemaic hellenization found in it. Moreover, Gerleman claims that a parallel text comparison of the LXX version of Chronicles with that of Samuel–Kings shows that assimilation took place between them and that the LXX version of Chronicles was adapted to the MT of the parallel text in Samuel–Kings; see Gerleman, *Septuagint*, 3–45. Shenkel has recently shown that the translator of LXX[B] to 1 Chronicles used the parallel texts of LXX[B] to Samuel, adapting them to the MT of 1 Chronicles; see Shenkel, "Synoptic Parallels," 63–85.

47. Gerleman, *Synoptic Studies*, 34 and see also pp. 10, 23, 25–26, 30–32, believes that the version of Samuel–Kings that was in front of the LXX translators was still in "the same vulgar textual tradition" as the version that was in the hands of the

Septuagint of Samuel–Kings and the parallel passages in Masoretic Chronicles may derive from other factors: either the harmonization of the parallel texts by the authors of the Hebrew text behind the Septuagint or the harmonization rendered by the Septuagint translators themselves, such as by combining two parallel passages.[48] This practice was rather widespread among ancient writers and translators in general and among the translators of the Septuagint in particular.[49] Moreover, certain passages in the MT of Samuel that appear in modified form in Chronicles (and the religious and literary consonance of the modifications with the rest of the book clearly mark them as the work of the Chronicler) appear in the same modified form in the Septuagint of Samuel–Kings. Some examples:

(1) We read in 2 Sam 8:8 of David's taking "exceeding much brass" from the cities of Hadadezer. In 1 Chr 18:8 the Chronicler added to the early text: "wherewith Solomon made the brazen sea and the pillars and the vessels of brass." This addition was apparently intended to generate a kind of uniformity and wholeness in the description of the Davidic and Solomonic monarchy: what the father wanted to do but could not was carried out by the son; and, were it not for the preparations made by the father, the son would not have been able to complete and execute his father's desire.[50] It is also possible that by means of this addition the Chronicler wanted to indicate his interest in the Temple rites.[51] The Septuagint of Samuel has here: ἐν αὐτῷ ἐποίησεν Σαλωμὼν τὴν θάλασσαν τὴν χαλκῆν, καὶ τοὺς στύλους, καὶ τοὺς λουτῆρας, καὶ πάντα τὰ σκεύη ('wherewith Solomon made the brazen sea and the pillars and the lavers and all the vessels'). These words were added here by the

---

Chronicler when he took from it the parallel texts for his own work—hence the similarity between the LXX of Samuel–Kings and the MT of Chronicles. The fundamental assumptions made by Gerleman in his study do not stand up in the light of criticism, as shown by Talmon, "Samaritan Pentateuch," 124–28. Cross believes that the Chronicler used an early Palestinian version that was available at the time in Jerusalem, so that his *Vorlage* in 1 Samuel 1–2 Sam 11:1 closely resembled LXX[B, L] and 4QSam[a]; and in 2 Sam 11:2–24:25 closely resembled LXX[L] (but not LXX[B]) and 4QSam[a]; see Cross, "Biblical Text," 294–95; idem, "Contribution," 81–95, esp. 88; and also Lemke, "Synoptic Problem," 362–63, as well as the bibliography adduced above in connection with the creation of the parallel texts.

48. Examples of this are to be found in various places in the notes to this study.

49. See Tov, "Harmonizations," 3–29. The textual considerations of the translator(s) were not restricted to single words or phrases; they were "likely to weigh ideological and textual considerations as well, regarding the relations between the translated passage and other texts in the same book or even in other books"; see Brin, "Working Methods," 449, and the examples he adduces, pp. 445–48.

50. See Williamson, "Accession of Solomon," 356–59 and additional examples there; cf. also Braun, *1 Chronicles*, 204–5.

51. Cf. Brunet, "Chroniste," 506; Ackroyd, *Chronicles*, 70.

translator (or earlier, by the copier of his *Vorlage*), according to the parallel text in Chronicles, with the apparent aim of "completing" the earlier text or harmonizing it with its parallel passage. The word גם ('also') in v. 11 ("These *also* did King David dedicate, etc.") is no indication that the phrase under consideration ("wherewith Solomon made, etc.") was unintentionally omitted from the Masoretic Text of Samuel, as claimed by Rudolph.[52] This word may well be connected with the continuation of our verse: "with the silver and gold that he dedicated of all the nations which he subdued."[53]

(2) There are grounds for reasoning that the narrative of the census and of the construction of the altar in the threshing floor of Araunah were not originally to be found where they are at present—in 2 Samuel 24—but elsewhere in the description of the Davidic monarchy.[54] Inserting the narrative in its present position, at the end of the book, took place at a certain stage in the development of the literary structure of Samuel–Kings (apparently while the Deuteronomistic history was being formulated) so as to link as much as possible the narrative of David's erection of the altar with the narrative of Solomon's construction of the Temple in Kings, thereby indicating the relationship of the two events. Explicit linkage between them is to be found in 1 Chr 21:28–22:1, where the Chronicler added to the earlier text from Samuel "At that time, when David saw that the Lord had answered him in the threshing floor of Ornan the Jebusite, then he sacrificed there. . . . Then David said: 'This is the house of the Lord God, and this is the altar of burnt-offering for Israel'" (1 Chr 22:1). Thereupon, he indeed begins to

---

52. Rudolph, *Chronik*, 135.

53. Cf. Smith, *Samuel*, 307–8; Budde, *Samuel*, 240–41; Curtis-Madsen, *Chronicles*, 234; Rehm, *Untersuchungen*, 25; Williamson, "Accession of Solomon," 357–58 n. 17; Braun, *1 Chronicles*, 204–5; Pisano, *Additions*, 47–48, as against Thenius, *Samuel*, 163–64; Lemke, "Synoptic Problem," 355; McKenzie, *Chronicler*, 65. The "evidence" adduced by the last two scholars from the fact that the phrase under consideration is to be found in *Ant.* 7.106 cannot be brought in support of their hypothesis; that is, the Chronicler and the LXX of Samuel here reflect their own *Vorlage*, for Josephus had before him both texts, Samuel and Chronicles, and he chose the expanded of the two, Chronicles, incidentally making whatever modifications he felt suitable. McKenzie also concludes from the occurrence of the words καὶ τοὺς λουτῆρας ('and the lavers') in the LXX of Samuel, taken together with their omission in Chronicles, that the two texts are mutually independent. However, this conclusion, too, first drawn by Klostermann, *Samuel–Könige*, 166, is groundless. It is very possible that the translator (or the author of his *Vorlage*) felt himself free to expand the phrase in Chronicles in accordance with the description of the Temple vessels appearing in 1 Kgs 7:38 (// 2 Chr 4:6): "And he made ten lavers of brass . . . ," or according to the description of the vessels of the Tabernacle in Exod 30:18, 28; 31:9, etc.

54. The precise original place of 2 Samuel 24 has not been agreed on by scholars. See, in detail, Kalimi, "Land/Mount Moriah," 9–32, esp. pp. 24–25 n. 43.

tell of the preparations made by David for the building of the Temple
(1 Chr 22:2ff.). Now, explicit linkage of the type found in the aforesaid
"addition" in Chronicles occurs in the Septuagint of 2 Sam 24:25: καὶ
προσέθηκεν Σαλωμων ἐπὶ τὸ θυσιαστήριον ἐπ ἐσχάτῳ, ὅτι μικρὸν ἦν ἐν πρώτοις
('And after this, Solomon enlarged the altar, for originally it was small').
This verse does not occur in the Masoretic Text of Samuel.[55]

(3) Another instance, this time from a textual viewpoint: occasionally, an erroneous phrase in Chronicles appears in its distorted form in
the Septuagint of Samuel–Kings as well, while the Masoretic Text of
Samuel–Kings displays the undistorted form of that phrase. Thus, for
example, the name "Hadarezer" occurs in the MT of 1 Chr 18:3, 5, 7–10;
19:16, 19 and in the parallel passages in the Septuagint of Samuel
(Ἀδρααξαρ). Yet this is merely the distorted form of the theophoric name
"Hadadezer" occurring in the MT of Samuel and 1 Kgs 11:23. This is an
instance of an interchange of the graphically similar ד and ר. Contrast
1 Chr 1:6 רודנים with Gen 10:4 דדנים; 1 Chr 1:41 חמרן with Gen 36:26:
חמדן.[56] A name identical with הדדעזר is found in the Shalmaneser III inscription: "Adad-ʾidri."[57] This form of the name "Hadad" also appears in
the Aramaic iniscription uncovered in the archaeological excavations at
Tel Dan.[58] Does not this instance also illustrate the fact that the form
of a word in the Septuagint of Samuel–Kings sometimes follows the Hebrew form found in Chronicles?

5. The Structure of the Study

This study reflects the historical and editorial work of the Chronicler.
The first nineteen chapters deal with the various recurrences of literary
and historiographical changes found primarily in the parallel texts of
Chronicles. The chapters are arranged in such a way as to treat first of
historiographical emendations and last of literary ones, with features
closely related to both types considered between them.

Chapter twenty relates to yet another aspect of the Chronicler's
work, an aspect supplementing the general impression of his literary-
historiographical activity: there is a certain lack of systemization in the
literary-historiographical reworking of the early texts; certain modifications introduced by the Chronicler into the early texts generated a disharmony with other verses in his book or in other biblical books; certain

---

55. In this regard, see Kalimi, "Land/Mount Moriah," 25 n. 47.

56. For additional instances of this feature in biblical literature, see Sperber, "Hebrew," 167, §21.

57. See Michel, "Die Assur-Texte," 257, 259; Luckenbill, *ARAB*, vol. 1, §608; Pritchard, *ANET*, 278–79.

58. See Biran-Naveh, "Aramaic Stele," 81–98, esp. p. 87; idem, "Tel Dan Inscription," 1–18, esp. p. 9.

historiographical emendations apparently have their origin in lacunae in the Chronicler's knowledge of the history and culture of monarchic Israel.

Basically similar literary-historiographical changes will be treated together, though separated into subsections that stress their unique nature. It will occasionally be necessary to compare side-by-side features dealt with in separate chapters (such as chapters 11 and 12), in order to indicate their basically unique character and the differences between them.

The chapters of this study begin with a general definition of the feature; its distribution in biblical literature in general and in Chronicles in particular (occasionally noting the status of the research into the topic being considered); adducing typological examples from the various kinds of biblical and/or extrabiblical literature—both from ancient Near Eastern literatures and from the variegated literature of the Jewish-Hellenistic type.

The number of examples adduced for each feature reflects the distribution of the feature in the parallel texts of Chronicles and its place in the methods and techniques of the Chronicler's writing and editing activity. The examples are organized not in canonical order of the biblical texts/themes but according to their contribution to illustrating the topic in Chronicles.

Chapter 1
Literary-Chronological Proximity

The Chronicler creates literary or chronological proximity between two unconnected historical events recorded in the earlier text from the books of Samuel and Kings (1); he creates a literary proximity between separate issues (2); finally, he exploits an already-existing literary proximity in the earlier text, transforming it into topical-chronological proximity (3).

Most of the following examples are original. Some of them have already been recognized by scholars. However, bringing them together is new; it is my attempt to show the extent of this recurrence in the Chronicler's work. The technique is also known from Assyrian royal inscriptions—for example, from Tiglath-pileser III's summation inscription[1] and from Sennacherib's inscriptions.[2]

1. The Creation of Literary or Chronological Proximity between Unconnected Historical Events

1.1 According to the Deuteronomistic history, David was anointed king only over the tribe of Judah after the death of Saul (1 Samuel 31), while Abner installed Ish-bosheth (= Esh-baal), Saul's son, as king over the Northern tribes (2 Sam 2:1–4, 8–10). Two years later, after the assassination of Abner and Ish-bosheth (3:12–39 and chap. 4), the elders of Northern Israel approached David in Hebron, made a covenant with him, and anointed him "king over Israel" (5:1–3).

The Chronicler omits from his narrative the passages describing the period from the death of Saul to the installing of David in Hebron by the elders of the Northern Israelite tribes (2 Samuel 1–4), that is, the description of the events occurring during the period of David's reign over Judah, which coincides with the reign of Ish-bosheth over the Northern tribes. He places the story of David's coronation in Hebron over all Israel (1 Chr 11:1–3 // 2 Sam 5:1–3) next to the story of the death of Saul (1 Chronicles 10 // 1 Samuel 31), thus creating the impression that the two events occurred one after the other without any time having elapsed between them. This impression is strengthened in the mind of the reader by the verse "therefore he (God) slew him (Saul) and turned the

---

1. See Eph'al, *Arabs*, 29 n. 76.
2. See Levin, "Neo-Assyrian Royal Inscriptions," 63.

kingdom unto David, the son of Jesse" (1 Chr 10:14b, an "addition"), which bridges the gap between the story of the death of Saul (1 Chr 10:1–14a) and the story of the installing of David (1 Chr 11:1–3). This literary-chronological proximity thus aims to erase the two-year interval between the two events in order to portray David as the king who ruled over all of the tribes of Israel, both Northern and Southern, throughout his reign.[3]

A close scrutiny of the text shows that, whereas the expressions "all the tribes of Israel" and "all the elders of Israel" in 2 Sam 5:1, 3 refer to the representatives of the Northern tribes only (David had already been installed as king over Judah; see 2 Sam 2:4), the parallel phrases "all Israel" and "all the elders of Israel" in 1 Chr 11:1, 3 do indeed refer to the representatives of all of the Israelite tribes, those of the North together with those of the South, for the Chronicler says nothing of David's reign over Judah alone. A similar distinction exists between the phrase "and they anointed David king over Israel" in 2 Sam 5:3b and the identical phrase in the parallel text in 1 Chr 11:3b: while in Samuel "Israel" is a term referring only to the Northern tribes of Israel, in Chronicles it refers to all of the tribes of Israel.[4]

1.2 The story of the conquest of Jerusalem in 2 Sam 5:6–9 appears between two events of central importance: on the one hand, the installing of David as king over the Northern tribes (vv. 1–3); on the other, the Philistines' military campaigns against David (vv. 17–25). In vv. 4–5, the author summarized David's reign in Hebron (over Judah only) and in Jerusalem (over Judah and Israel).

It seems that David's wars against the Philistines broke out directly after his becoming king over the Northern tribes of Israel, as shown clearly by v. 17: "And when the Philistines heard that David had been

---

3. Indeed, in 1 Chr 3:4 the Chronicler mentions the seven-year reign of David in Hebron, but along with this he omits the expressions "over Judah" and "over all Israel and Judah," which appear in the earlier text (2 Sam 5:5) and which hint about the separate reign of David over Judah only. Also, in 1 Chr 29:27 he prefaces his statement about the number of years David reigned in Hebron (7 years) and in Jerusalem (33 years) with the words: "Thus David, the son of Jesse, reigned over *all Israel*" (v. 26). Incidentally, 2 Sam 5:5, "at Hebron he reigned over Judah seven years and six months" (cf. also 2:11), is problematic. According to 2 Sam 2:10, Ish-bosheth, son of Saul, reigned over Israel for only 2 years, and it is difficult to accept that David was installed as king over the Northern tribes 5 1/2 years after the death of Ish-bosheth. Solving this problem was the task of the Deuteronomistic historian (and of the modern historian). The Chronicler, who did not mention the reign of Ish-bosheth, avoided the problem; see example 4.17 (p. 96).

4. This example is mentioned generally in the commentaries; for example, Curtis-Madsen, *Chronicles*, 184; Myers, *I Chronicles*, 85; Williamson, *Chronicles*, 96, 97. I have developed and improved it with a few nuances.

anointed king over Israel, they went up to seek David." This verse is
merely the continuation of the narrative appearing in v. 3: "and King
David made a covenant with them in Hebron before the Lord, and they
anointed David king over Israel."[5] Only after David had defeated the
Philistines did he attempt to conquer Jerusalem.[6] Thus, the order in
which these three narratives appear in 2 Samuel does not reflect their
chronological order of occurrence[7] but the intention of the redactor of
the book to portray the capture of Jerusalem as the first royal act em-
barked on by David after he had been accepted as king over all of the
tribes of Israel and as a jumping-off point for his steadily increasing
might (see v. 10).

This aim is far more apparent in Chronicles: in order to create optimal proximity between the story of David's anointing in Hebron (1 Chr
11:1–3 // 2 Sam 5:1–3) and that of his campaign to conquer Jerusalem
(1 Chr 11:4–8 // 2 Sam 5:6–9), the Chronicler relocates the intervening
section that records the years of David's reign (2 Sam 5:4–5) elsewhere
in his book, modifying it somewhat in the process (1 Chr 3:4b).[8] Moreover, the Chronicler ignores the years during which David reigned over
Judah alone while Ish-bosheth reigned over the tribes of Israel. According to his version, David was anointed king over all Israel immediately
after the death of Saul (1 Chr 10:13–14, 11:1–3).[9] Chronicles presents
the story of the conquest of Jerusalem (1 Chr 11:4–8) between the story
of David's anointing in Hebron (vv. 1–3 // 2 Sam 5:1–3) and the description of the various sectors of the nation that "came to Hebron to install
David as king over all Israel" and celebrated with him there for three

---

5. The view of Hauer ("Jerusalem," 574) that the anointing of David over all Israel was "an internal Israelite event" that "escaped notice until a trickle of Jebusite
refugees heralded" it is unacceptable. It is more likely that news of this important
event spread quickly not only to the Israelite tribes but also to the close neighbors of
the Israelites, primarily to the Philistines, as the biblical tradition testified. It seems
that Hauer's assumption is based on his presupposition that the "order of the text in
2 Samuel 5 may imply a chronology," and he then claims that "the capture of Jerusalem was prior to the Philistine wars" (pp. 574–75).

6. Cf. Smith, *Samuel*, 287; Noth, *Geschichte Israels*, 163 (= *History of Israel*, 187);
Bright, *History*, 194 n. 33; Lemaire, "United Monarchy," 94; see also the appendix
below (§5, pp. 34–35).

7. Contra Hauer ("Jerusalem," 575–78), Yeivin ("Wars of David," 151–52), Aharoni
(*Land of the Bible,* 292–93); Garsiel (*Kingdom of David,* 42–43), and Oded ("Israel
and Judah," 118), who regard the three events mentioned in 2 Samuel 5 as being arranged chronologically. Neither can I accept the opinion of Japhet, "Conquest," 208
n. 12: "The order of the events in 2 Samuel 2–5 bears such a strong stamp of political
logic, that it is unanimously accepted as historical."

8. For this relocation and the use made of it in 1 Chr 3:4b, see in detail below, example 14.19 (pp. 315–317).

9. For a discussion of this, see above, example 1.1 (pp. 18–19).

days (1 Chr 11:9–12:41). This presentation of the order of events creates the impression that "all Israel" (11:1, in place of "all the tribes of Israel," 2 Sam 5:1), who gathered together "to David unto Hebron and installed him as king over them," went with him immediately after his coronation, before the celebration of the event, to conquer Jerusalem: "And David and all Israel went to Jerusalem" (1 Chr 11:4, in place of "And the king and his men went to Jerusalem" in 2 Sam 5:6).[10]

Presenting the capture of Jerusalem as David's first act immediately after his installation,[11] even before the celebration of this event, as well as involving "David and all Israel" (i.e., all sectors of the nation) and not just some of the people ("the king and his men")[12] in this conquest, as told in Samuel, reflects the great significance that the Chronicler attributes to the conquest of Jerusalem, while relying on the earlier text in Samuel.[13] In this way, he apparently tries to hint at the future centrality of Jerusalem in national life, as the seat of the Davidic monarchy and the site of the Temple—subjects that are very dear to him.[14]

The future significance of Jerusalem in the life of the Israelite nation seems also to have been indicated by the description of the special difficulty involved in its capture and the need to award a special prize

---

10. The Greek translation of 1 Chr 11:4 (A. Rahlfs edition) combines the two parallel texts: καὶ ἐπορεύθη ὁ βασιλεὺς καὶ ἄνδρες Ισραηλ ('and the king and men of Israel marched'). In H. B. Swete's edition of the LXX, the version of the text is identical to that of the MT of 2 Sam 5:6, that is, "and the king and his men marched to. . . ."

11. Contrary to Japhet ("Conquest," 208), who claims that the Chronicler describes it [bringing the Ark to Jerusalem] as the first act of David after his coronation and a direct continuation of it. She views the conquest of Jerusalem as a part of the celebration of David's coronation in Hebron and considers this the only way of interpreting the present literary structure of 1 Chronicles 11 (p. 208 n. 13). Also contrary to Cogan ("Chronology," 206–7), who views the bringing of the Ark as David's "first royal act," according to Chronicles.

12. "His men" are in all likelihood the men of the band that accompanied him, as shown clearly by the following verses: 1 Sam 23:13; 27:2–3, 8; 29:2; 2 Sam 2:3.

13. Hence, Gilad's conclusion is groundless: "From the phrase 'And all Israel' we conclude that David's army was not composed of a group of 'select fighters,' as some commentators would have it, but was rather a large army properly deployed for the conquest of the militarily and topographically well-fortified and defended stronghold of Jebus" ("Conquest of Jerusalem," 99–107, esp. p. 101).

14. Williamson suggests another consideration that may have played a part in the arrangement of the material here: "Since both the start of 1 Chronicles 11 and the close of 1 Chronicles 12 are dealing with David's coronation at Hebron, it is clear that the Chronicler's account of the capture of Jerusalem in 11:4–9 must be out of order. His purpose in this case may well have been to develop his ideal portrayal, already begun in 11:1–3, of a united Israel centered by David on Jerusalem" ("We Are Yours," 168). For this reasons, in his opinion, the Chronicler regarded 11:4–9 "as an integral part of the opening paragraph [e.g., David's coronation at Hebron—I. K.]" (p. 169 n. 17).

to whoever would attack the Jebusites and bring about the fall of the city.[15]

After the coronation celebrations (1 Chr 12:39–41), David did not tarry for even a moment. Since Jerusalem had already been conquered, he attempted to bring the Ark of the Covenant up to Jerusalem from Kiriat-jearim (1 Chronicles 13 // 2 Sam 6:1–12). The building of the palace, the list of "those born to him in Jerusalem," and David's battle against the Philistines (2 Sam 5:11–12, 13–16, 17–25) were all moved to 1 Chronicles 14 (1–2, 3–7, 8–17), to the three-month interval between the first attempt to bring the Ark up (from Kiriat-jearim, v. 13) and the second attempt to bring it up (from the home of Obed-Edom the Gittite, chaps. 15–16).

1.3 According to 2 Kgs 22:3 // 2 Chr 34:8, the cult reforms instituted by Josiah were carried out in the 18th year of his reign, the year they celebrated the Passover (2 Kgs 23:23 // 2 Chr 35:19). Josiah reigned 31 years (2 Kgs 22:1, which the Chronicler stereotypically rewrote in 2 Chr 34:1). It may thus be concluded that, according to Kings and Chronicles, Josiah's cult reforms and Passover celebration took place some 13 years before his death at Megiddo (609 B.C.E.). In spite of this, the Chronicler attempts to ignore this time interval and create a chronological link between the cult reform and Passover celebration, on the one hand, and Josiah's death at Megiddo, on the other. He concludes the narrative of the Passover sacrifice with the words "In the eighteenth year of the reign of Josiah was this Passover kept" (2 Chr 35:19 // 2 Kgs 23:23) and immediately begins v. 20 with the words "After all this,[16] when Josiah had prepared the Temple, Necho, king of Egypt, went up to fight at Carchemish on the Euphrates, and Josiah went out against him . . ." (in place of "In his days[17] Pharaoh Necho, king of Egypt, went up . . . ," in 2 Kgs 23:29). This creation of explicit chronological proximity is reinforced by the existing literary proximity between the story of the cult reform and the Passover celebration, on the one hand, and Josiah's clash with Necho, on the other. This is so because the Chronicler has omitted

---

15. See Kalimi, "Capture of Jerusalem," 66–79.

16. For the use of this phrase to define the time of an event within a chain of events, see 2 Chr 21:18: "And after all this [i.e., after the capture of the sons, wives, and property of King Jehoram by the Philistines and the Arabians, as described in vv. 16–17] the Lord smote him in his bowels with an incurable disease" (as prophesied by Elijah in his letter to Jehoram, vv. 14–15); and for the use of the phrase "after . . . that . . . ," see Josh 7:8: "after that Israel hath turned their backs"; see Josh 9:16; 23:1; 24:20; Judg 11:36; 19:23; 2 Sam 19:31.

17. For the phrase "in his days," see 2 Kgs 8:20: "In his days Edom revolted." This phrase is similar to "then," "in those days," and "at that time," and so on. See below for this, example 1.9 (pp. 29–32); and Cogan-Tadmor, *II Kings*, 291.

the text in 2 Kgs 23:24–27 (the evaluation of Josiah's religious image), while transferring v. 28 from its place and relocating it (with certain modifications) after the story of Josiah's death (2 Chr 35:26–27).[18]

The literary and chronological proximity seems to contrast the fate of Josiah with the fate of Hezekiah: Hezekiah, who reinstated Temple worship, carried out a cult reform and celebrated the Passover, succeeded in his struggle against Sennacherib, king of Assyria; whereas Josiah, who performed similar acts—that is, a comprehensive cult reform and a Passover celebration—failed in his struggle against Pharaoh Necho and was himself killed. This contrast is also stressed by the stylistic-literary affinity found in the Chronicler's introductions to these events:

> *After these things and these faithful acts,*[19] Sennacherib, the king of Assyria, came and invaded Judah and laid siege to the fortified cities with the thought of conquering them. (2 Chr 32:1)
>
> *After all this, when Josiah had provided for the Temple*, Necho, king of Egypt, went up to fight . . . , and Josiah went out against him. (2 Chr 35:20)

This is explained precisely in the commentary attributed to Rashi on 2 Chr 35:20: "The verse mourns and laments the fate of Josiah, who was not saved by a miracle like Hezekiah, where it says, 'After these things and these faithful acts' Sennacherib came up against Hezekiah and a miracle saved him."[20]

Moreover, the fate of the most faithful king, Josiah (2 Kgs 23:25; 2 Chr 34:1 // 2 Kgs 22:1), is described very like the fate of Ahab, king of Israel (compare 2 Chr 35:22–24 with 1 Kgs 22:30, 34–37), the most wicked king of Israel (1 Kgs 16:29–33). The Chronicler's justification for this is "He did not listen to the words of Necho from the mouth of God, and he sallied out to join battle in the plain of Megiddo" (2 Chr 35:21–22). In other words, Josiah acted like Ahab, who did not listen to the words of God given through Micaiah, son of Imlah, and marched against Ramoth-gilead to make war. The Chronicler presumably wished to lead his potential audience to the conclusion that disobeying God's word ultimately brings death: the sinner may be either a wicked king (Ahab) or even a king with an extremely positive record (Josiah).

---

18. Contra Williamson (*Chronicles*, 408–9), who states: "the Chronicler does not follow precisely the order of his *Vorlage* as regards his source citation formula (contrast vv. 26–27 and 2 Kgs 23:28 . . .). There is no apparent reason for this quite exceptional circumstance. It is thus reasonable to suppose that the form of Kings which he was following, and which we know was not always identical with our Masoretic Text, already reflected this change of order."

19. This phrase refers to earlier verses in chap. 31; and see the following example.

20. See Ehrlich, *Mikrâ ki-Pheschutô*, 469; Elmslie, *Chronicles* (1916), 343–44.

1.4 The author of the books of Kings gives a precise date for Sennacherib king of Assyria's invasion of the kingdom of Judah: "Now in the fourteenth year of King Hezekiah did Sennacherib king of Assyria come up against all the fortified cities of Judah and took them" (2 Kgs 18:13 // Isa 36:1).[21] The Chronicler, for his part, replaced the precise dating of the earlier text with a fossilized connecting phrase that determines the relative position of the event within the chain of events that he ascribes to the reign of Hezekiah king of Judah: "After these things[22] and these faithful acts, Sennacherib king of Assyria came and entered Judah and encamped against the fortified cities and thought to make a breach therein for himself" (2 Chr 32:1). The purpose of the phrase "After these things and these faithful acts" is to forge a clear literary and "chronological" link between the failure of Sennacherib's campaign against Judah described in chap. 32 and Hezekiah's religious-ritual activity recounted in chaps. 29–31 (reinstating Temple worship, celebrating the Passover, and comprehensive cult reforms). This link was created not merely by means of the standard formula "after these things," where "these things" refer to events previously recounted, but also by inserting into the formula the Hebrew word 'and these faithful acts' (והאמת), employing the definite article.[23] This word is related to the word that the Chronicler added to yet another formula concluding a description of religious-ritual activity: "and he wrought that which was good and right and faithful before the Lord his God" (2 Chr 31:20).[24] The wording of 2 Chr 31:20 may have been influenced by Hezekiah's prayer "Then he turned his face to the wall and prayed unto the Lord, saying: 'Remember now, I beseech You, how I have walked before You in truth

---

21. For the problems raised by this date in comparison with chronological data provided elsewhere in the Bible and in the inscription of Sennacherib, as well as for proposed solutions, see Montgomery, *Kings*, 483; Tadmor, "Chronology," cols. 278–79; Cogan-Tadmor, *II Kings*, 228.

22. Montgomery ("Archival Data," 49) hypothesized that the redactor of Kings inserted the word אז 'then' instead of the precise date, which was written in the early archival sources that were available to him (see, e.g., 1 Kgs 9:24). The example dealt with here strengthens Montgomery's hypothesis and shows that it is also possible for the expression "after these things" to have replaced a precise date found in the earlier text: "in the fourteenth year of King Hezekiah" (2 Kgs 18:13).

23. The formula common in the biblical narrative is "after these things" (e.g., Gen 15:1; Esth 2:1, 3:1; Ezra 7:1) or the formula with the word ויהי at its head: "And it came to pass after these things" (e.g., Gen 22:1, 20; 39:7; 40:1; 48:1; 1 Kgs 17:17; 21:1). The formula "after these things and these faithful acts" occurs in the Bible only in 2 Chr 32:1.

24. The usual formula is "and you shall do that which is right and good in the sight of the Lord"; for example, Deut 6:18; 12:28. In accordance with these verses in the book of Deuteronomy, the Chronicler in 2 Chr 14:1 also modified the text in 2 Kgs 15:11.

and with a whole heart, and have done that which is good in Your sight'"
(2 Kgs 20:3 // Isa 38:3).

The literary and "chronological" connection in Chronicles now being
discussed was intended to explain the success of Hezekiah, on the one
hand, and the failure of Sennacherib, on the other, and to inculcate into
the reader's mind the message that when a king follows in the paths of
God no enemy—not even the mighty Assyrian emperor—can overcome
him. As Ehrlich puts it: "'After these things and these faithful acts'—
this phrase tells you right away that Sennacherib must eventually fail,
for he came at the wrong time—after Hezekiah performed all these good
deeds, the Lord his God would surely save him from the hands of his
enemies."[25] Indeed, the Chronicler wrote the rest of this verse in accordance with the same intention: "and (he) entered into Judah and encamped against the fortified cities and *thought to make a breach therein
for himself.*" In other words, Sennacherib planned to conquer the fortified cities of Judah, but in the end he was not successful (just as he did
not succeed in taking Jerusalem). In contrast, 2 Kgs 18:13 states explicitly: "Sennacherib, king of Assyria, camped up against all the fortified
cities of Judah and took them." The admission of the author of Kings
that the cities of Judah were captured is supported by other biblical
sources, such as Mic 1:8–16 and apparently Isa 10:28–32, and by extrabiblical sources, especially the description of Sennacherib's third campaign (col. III, 18–23; 701 B.C.E.):

> And Hezekiah (from) the land of Judah, who did not surrender to my
> yoke, his 46 fortified cities, walled cities and innumerable small
> towns around them—with trampled ramparts, sacks moved up (to the
> wall) and infantry assaults, in tunnels (under the walls) and with
> breaches (of the walls), I encircled them (and) conquered them.[26]

It is also supported by the reliefs describing the taking of Lachish that
were found along a wall of one of the central halls in Sennacherib's palace in Nineveh, and by the Lachish excavations, stratum III.[27] The
Chronicler thus deviated from historical truth regarding the conquest
by Sennacherib of the cities of Judah in favor of the theological message
he desired to convey to his readers.

W. Rudolph[28] lists 2 Chr 32:1ff. among the exceptions to the rule of
divine reward, according to which the Chronicler described events that
took place in the period of the Monarchy: the Chronicler made no earlier

---

25. Ehrlich, *Mikrâ ki-Pheschutô*, 467.
26. See Luckenbill, *Annals of Sennacherib*, 32–33; Pritchard, *ANET*, 288.
27. See Ussishkin, *Conquest of Lachish*; idem, "Lachish," 42–56; Eph'al, "Assyrian
Ramp," 333–47.
28. Rudolph, *Chronik*, xix.

attempt to ascribe sin to Hezekiah, despite the fact that Sennacherib's campaign against Judah was, indeed, a punitive measure. The rabbis sensed this and explained it away in whatever manner they could.[29] Indeed, the Chronicler did not ascribe sin to Hezekiah as he did, for example, to Asa and Jehoshaphat (2 Chr 16:10–12, 20:35–37), yet he did not omit the "punitive measure" from his book: Sennacherib's campaign against Judah. Nevertheless, he attempted to cope with this theological problem by integrating this event, too, into the sequence of events already suiting his rule of divine reward: he depicted the Assyrian campaign against Judah as one destined to fail because of Hezekiah's righteousness (2 Chr 32:1). True, eventually Sennacherib did "return with shame of face to his own land" (v. 21, an "addition" to the earlier text in 2 Kgs 19:36 // Isa 37:37). Furthermore, he portrayed righteous Hezekiah not only as someone who was saved by the Lord and not merely as someone undamaged by the Assyrian campaign (once again, for his part, Hezekiah's cities were not captured by Sennacherib), but rather as someone who even gained from the Assyrian campaign: "And many brought gifts unto the Lord to Jerusalem, and precious things to Hezekiah king of Judah, so that he was exalted in the sight of all nations from thenceforth" (2 Chr 32:23, an "addition").

Another explanation of the question under consideration was offered by S. Japhet. In her opinion, Sennacherib's campaign belongs to the category of "a trial" that is part of the system of divine regard, according to which the Chronicler explains certain events.[30]

1.5 The narrative unit concerning David's rescue from the hands of the Philistine and his men's oath that "you shall go no more out with us to battle" (2 Sam 21:15–17) is linked with the narrative unit concerning the slaying of Saph, a descendant of the giant, by Sibbechai the Husha-thite (v. 18b) by means of the connective formula "after this" (v. 18a). The Chronicler omitted all of the stories recounted in 2 Sam 13:1–21:17—that is, the stories of Amnon and Tamar, the revolt of Absalom, the revolt of Sheba ben Bichri, and the revenge of the Gibeonites against the sons of Saul. In this way, the connective formula "after this" in 1 Chr 20:4a (// 2 Sam 21:18a) actually links the story of the slaying of Saph (in Chronicles: Sippai), descendant of the giant, by Sibbechai the Husha-thite (1 Chr 20:4b) and the story of the conquest and enslavement of Rabbah of the Ammonites by Joab and David (20:1–3 // 2 Sam 12:26–31).

---

29. See *b. Sanh.* 94b: "Is such a reward deserving for such a gift?" (Rashi: "Did Sennacherib come because of Hezekiah's faithfulness?") and see also R. David Kimḥi on 2 Chr 32:1.

30. Japhet, *Ideology*, 154 n. 453, 193ff.

Did the Chronicler create this literary proximity purposely, to create continuity of war stories, or was it a chance result of his omissions? It is hard to decide. The subject under discussion describes the situation that we find in the literary tract of Chronicles as it appears before us, and this is the main determining factor.

1.6 The word אז 'then' occurring at the beginning of 1 Kgs 9:24b connects the story of Pharaoh's daughter being brought up "out of the city of David unto her house which (Solomon) had built for her" (v. 24a) with the building of the Millo (v. 24b). In 2 Chronicles 8 the Chronicler omitted the building of the Millo mentioned in 1 Kgs 9:24b but not the word אז. Here this word serves to link the story of Pharaoh's daughter being brought up from the city of David to the house Solomon had built for her (2 Chr 8:11) and the verse relating to Solomon's ritual customs (8:12–16 // 1 Kgs 9:25).[31] In this example as well, it is hard to determine the meaning of the literary-chronological proximity, but we cannot overlook its existence in the Chronicler's composition as it is presented to us.

1.7 The narrative of Solomon's ritual custom (2 Chr 8:12–16 // 1 Kgs 9:25, partially) is linked in Chronicles with the story of the journey to Ophir (vv. 17–18 // 1 Kgs 9:26–28) by means of the word אז added by the Chronicler to the earlier text, at the beginning of v. 17. The word אז seems to occur in Chronicles in the sense of 'at that time' rather than in the sense it has in various verses in Kings, where it denotes the exact time of an event (that presumably appeared in an archival source that was used by the author of Kings) not connected to the events discussed before.[32]

2. The Creation of Literary Proximity between Separate Issues

1.8 In 2 Chr 32:20, the Chronicler hints at the prayer uttered by Hezekiah, king of Judah, during the Assyrian crisis, a prayer presented in detail in 2 Kgs 19:15–19 (// Isa 37:15–20).[33] This is surprising when we consider 2 Chr 30:18–19, where the Chronicler himself places a prayer in the mouth of Hezekiah (though for an entirely different purpose). Moreover, in a similar situation elsewhere he composed a prayer

---

31. Curtis and Madsen (*Chronicles*, 354) believe that the word אז relates here to the dedication of the Temple, whereas Williamson claims that the word introduces Solomon's custom in making sacrifice ("Chronicles," 231). Neither of these explanations is likely.

32. For the significance of the word אז in Kings, see Montgomery, "Archival Data," 46–52.

33. For this, see below, example 10.15 (p. 205).

and placed it in the mouth of a king in a crisis: the prayer of Jehoshaphat, king of Judah, at the time of the invasion of Judah by the
kingdoms on the eastern bank of the Jordan (2 Chr 20:1–13).[34] The
Chronicler even omitted the prophecy of Isaiah and his reaction to
Hezekiah's prayer (2 Kgs 19:20–34 // Isa 37:21–35)—this, too, contrary
to his policy in 2 Chr 20:14–17, where he placed a prophecy in the
mouth of Jahaziel, the son of Zechariah, in response to Jehoshaphat's
prayer. It is especially surprising, because presenting the prophecy announcing in advance the defeat of Sennacherib (2 Kgs 19:32–33 // Isa
37:33–35), which the Chronicler records (2 Chr 32:21), would have demonstrated clearly the fulfilling of God's word as well as his control of the
ways of history—beliefs stressed by the Chronicler elsewhere by means
of "additions" to the earlier text.[35] Instead, he added "Isaiah, son of
Amoz, the prophet" to Hezekiah, noting that together they "cried to
heaven" (2 Chr 32:20).[36]

The Chronicler seems to have had to mention Hezekiah's prayer by
implication only and even to omit Isaiah's reaction to this prayer and
his prophecy in order to create literary proximity between the prayer of
prophet and king, on the one hand, and the Lord's salvation, on the
other. In this way, the Lord's salvation of Hezekiah is mentioned immediately after his prayer (2 Chr 32:20–21). This proximity becomes even
more pronounced with the omission of the temporal phrase "that very
night" preceding the description of the salvation in the earlier text
(2 Kgs 19:35), as if he wanted to say that the salvation came immediately, without even waiting until "that very night": "And Hezekiah the
king and Isaiah the prophet, the son of Amoz, prayed because of this

---

34. Not to mention other prayers the Chronicler put in the mouths of various persons in other situations, for example, 1 Chr 29:10–19 (David); or his custom of repeating (generally speaking) the prayers that he found in Samuel–Kings; for example,
1 Chr 17:16–27 // 2 Sam 7:18–29 (David's prayer); 2 Chr 6:1–42 // 1 Kgs 8:12–53 (Solomon's prayer).

35. For this, see below, chap. 7, §3 (pp. 159–165).

36. Note the way he mentions Isaiah: "Isaiah, son of Amoz, the prophet," exactly
as he was mentioned earlier, when Hezekiah sent Shebna the scribe and the priestly
elders to "Isaiah, son of Amoz, the prophet" (Isa 37:2 // 2 Kgs 19:2: "Isaiah the prophet,
son of Amoz") to request of him, among other things: "make prayer for the remnant
that is left" (2 Kgs 19:4 // Isa 37:4). Isaiah calmed Hezekiah down and even prophesied concerning the retreat and defeat of Sennacherib, but nowhere is it related that
he "made a prayer," as the king had requested. The Chronicler notes here that "Isaiah, son of Amoz, the prophet" did indeed pray with King Hezekiah himself. Childs
(*Isaiah*, 108) already recognized that the Chronicler tried here to harmonize a complexity in the earlier text: "in II Kings 19.3ff. (B[1]) Hezekiah is *reticent* to pray directly
and requests Isaiah to pray on his behalf. In 19.14ff. (B[2]) Hezekiah confidently offers
a lengthy prayer with no reference to Isaiah's intercession. The Chronicler harmonizes the difficulty by having both Hezekiah and Isaiah pray (32.20)."

and cried to heaven. And the Lord sent an angel, who cut off all the mighty men, and commanders and captains, in the camp of Assyria. . . ." By means of this proximity the Chronicler apparently wanted to create a sense of the Lord's responding immediately to the prayer of Hezekiah and Isaiah, saving them from the king of Assyria; "And we will cry unto You in our affliction, and You will hear and save" (2 Chr 20:9b), as it were.[37] This emphasizes the great righteousness and the power of the prayer of these persons.[38] On the other hand, in Kings (and in the book of Isaiah), 20 verses intervene between the mention of Hezekiah's prayer and the description of the Lord's salvation from the hands of Assyria (2 Kgs 19:15–35 // Isa 37:15–36).

3. The Transformation of Literary Proximity into Chronological-Topical Proximity

1.9 According to the synchronism in Kings, Jehoahaz, son of Jehu, king of Israel, ascended the throne in the twenty-third year of the reign of Joash, king of Judah, and died in the thirty-seventh year of Joash's reign (2 Kgs 13:1, 10). Joash, king of Judah, died in the second year of the reign of Joash, son of Jehoahaz, king of Israel (14:1). Consequently, Joash, king of Judah, outlived Jehoahaz, son of Jehu, by two years.

According to 2 Kgs 13:2–3, Jehoahaz, son of Jehu, sinned against God, and therefore God repeatedly delivered him "into the hand of Hazael, king of Aram, and into the hand of Ben-hadad, son of Hazael." That is to say, Hazael passed away in the lifetime of Jehoahaz, son of Jehu: part of the reign of his son, Ben-hadad, overlapped the reign of Jehoahaz; and Ben-hadad continued his battle with Jehoahaz after the death of his father, Hazael. This may be deduced, too, from the verse in 2 Kgs 13:25 relating to Jehoash, son of Jehoahaz: "And Jehoash, the son of Jehoahaz, took again out of the hand of Ben-hadad, the son of Hazael, the cities that he had taken out of the hand of Jehoahaz, his father, by war."

---

37. See also 2 Chr 18:31 (an "addition" within a parallel passage, 1 Kgs 22:32): "but *Jehoshaphat cried out, and the Lord helped him*; and God moved them to depart from him"; 2 Chr 13:14–15 (has no parallel in 1 Kings): "they cried unto the Lord, and the priests sounded the trumpets. Then *as the men of Judah shouted, it came to pass that God smote Jeroboam and all Israel* before Abijah and Judah."

38. This was expressed sharply and explicitly later in *Lam. Rabbati, Pethiḥta* 30 (ed. S. Buber, p. 32): "Hezekiah stood up and said: 'I have the strength neither to slay nor to pursue, nor to utter a song, but I will sleep upon my bed and You perform (all these things).' The Holy One, blessed be He, replied, 'I will do so'; as it is said, 'And it came to pass that night, that the angel of the Lord went forth etc.' (2 Kgs 19:35)." This resembles the well-known motif in the Hasidic story: the righteous man decrees—and the Almighty carries out the decree!

We may conclude from this that Hazael died in the lifetime of Jehoahaz, king of Israel, and that Jehoahaz died in the lifetime of Joash, king of Judah. Consequently, Hazael, king of Aram, died a number of years before the death of Joash, king of Judah.

2 Kgs 12:18–19 tells of Hazael's campaign against the land of Israel, during which Joash, king of Judah, was forced to pay him heavy tribute in order to remove the threat hanging over Jerusalem. From our conclusion above, it is obvious that this Aramean campaign took place several years before Joash was assassinated by his servants (vv. 21–22a). B. Mazar claims: "The story told in Ch. 12 of 2 Kgs makes it quite clear that it [i.e., Hazael's campaign against the land of Israel—I. K.] refers to the twenty-third year of Joash, king of Judah, the year in which Jehu died," and that "these events must be fixed between Tishri 814 and Nisan 813; according to other calculations, they took placed in 815–814 B.C.E."[39] In this way he explains the use of אז at the beginning of the story of Hazael's campaign in 2 Kgs 12:18–19 as referring to the precise dating of "the twenty-third year of the reign of Joash," which opens the narrative of the Temple repairs in vv. 7–17. In similar fashion, he presents the story relating to Jehu here, "and Hazael smote them in all the borders of Israel: from the Jordan eastward, all the land of Gilead . . . from Aroer which is by the valley of Arnon, that is Gilead and Bashan" (2 Kgs 10:32–33), and the story relating to Jehoahaz, "And the anger of the Lord was kindled against Israel, and He delivered them into the hand of Hazael . . ." (13:3). Mazar's approach has been adopted by a number of scholars.[40]

However, no chronological sense is to be ascribed to the general term אז. The redactor of Kings made use of this indefinite term in place of the precise dating that appeared in the early archival sources to which he had access.[41] It seems that he did so in order to provide literary uniformity in a narrative about a given king. Furthermore, it is difficult to link the campaign conducted by Hazael on the eastern bank of the Jordan, described in 2 Kgs 10:31–34, with the one he conducted on its western bank, recorded in in 2 Kgs 12:18–19. These verses refer to the routes of two entirely different campaigns, routes that followed central yet different roads ("the king's road" and "the coastal road"), spaced far apart

---

39. Mazar, "Samaria Ostraca," 180.

40. For example, Loewenstamm, "Hazael," 88; Tadmor, "Jehu," 477: "At the end of the days of Jehu, Hazael had already invaded the western bank of the Jordan . . . he had reached as far as Gath and was paid tribute by Joash, king of Judah. This campaign, which took place according to 2 Kgs 12:7, 18 in the twenty-third year of the reign of Joash, occurred in the twenty-eighth year of Jehu's reign—the year 814/5."

41. See Montgomery "Archival Data," 49, and the example adduced there; also Cogan-Tadmor, "Ahaz and Tiglath-Pileser," 55–61, esp. p. 57.

from one another. Nevertheless, for our purposes, even according to Mazar and the supporters of his approach, Hazael's campaign to the western bank of the Jordan River took place many years before the assassination of Joash, king of Judah.[42] Indeed, the story of Joash's murder appears in 2 Kings within the closing remarks of the Deuteronomistic historian on the period of Joash's reign (vv. 20–22).[43] These remarks were placed next to the narrative of Hazael's invasion of the land of Israel and his acceptance of tribute from Joash but without creating a cause-and-effect relationship between the latter and the story of the assassination. This historian does not hint in any way that Hazael's campaign against Jerusalem and the tribute that Joash was compelled to bring him were a punishment for any sin. On the contrary, he states that Joash did what "was right in the eyes of the Lord all his days, as Jehoiada the priest instructed him" (v. 3).

A different picture emerges from the parallel descriptions in 2 Chronicles 24. According to the Chronicler, after the death of Jehoiada the priest, Joash abandoned the Temple and worshiped *asherim*. When Zechariah, son of Jehoiada the priest, warned against this, he was stoned "at the commandment of the king in the court of the house of the Lord" (vv. 17–22). These sins of Joash caused "the army of the Arameans to come up against him, and they came to Judah and Jerusalem, and destroyed all the princes of the people from among the people, and sent all their spoil to the king of Damascus . . ." (vv. 23ff.). Moreover, this historian made use of the already existing literary proximity in Kings between the narrative of the Aramean campaign against the land of Israel and the narrative of the assassination of Joash at the hands of his servants, and created a chronological-topical proximity between the two events by erasing the considerable time interval separating them (or, alternatively, by virtue of his unawareness of this time span). According to the Chronicler, the Aramean army struck the king down: "So they executed judgment on Joash. When they had departed from him, leaving him severely wounded, his servants conspired against him because of the blood of the son(s) of Jehoiada the priest, and slew him on his bed" (vv. 24c–25a).

---

42. About sixteen years: 815/14 and 798 B.C.E., respectively.

43. This is true, too, in connection with Josiah (2 Kgs 23:28–30): the story of his death near Megiddo appears within the closing remarks of the Deuteronomistic historian of the period of the reign of Josiah: "Now the rest of the acts of Josiah and all that he did, are they not written in the book of the chronicles of the kings of Judah? In his days Pharaoh Necho, king of Egypt, went up . . . [the story of Josiah's death— vv. 29–30a]. And the people of the land took Jehoahaz, son of Josiah, and anointed him and installed him as king in his father's stead." This feature itself is common in the book of Kings.

This chronological-topical proximity has no factual basis,[44] its sole objective being to adapt the narrative in the earlier text to the strict system of rewards and consequences that guided the Chronicler's historiography; that is, the Aramean campaign against Judah was a punishment inflicted upon the people, the princes, and the king of Judah. During this campaign Joash was wounded bodily as a punishment for having abandoned the Temple and for having worshiped the asherim, and this is also the background for his subsequent assassination by his servants, a deliberate punishment by the Lord for having murdered Zechariah, son of Jehoiada.[45]

1.10 A case similar to the previous one concerns the murder of Sennacherib, king of Assyria: 2 Kgs 19:35–36 (// Isa 37:36–37) tells of the defeat of the Assyrian army and of Sennacherib's return to Nineveh. Nearby (v. 37 // Isa 37:38) we learn of Sennacherib's assassination at the hands of his sons:

> The angel of the Lord went forth and smote in the camp of the Assyrians. . . . So Sennacherib, king of Assyria, departed and went and returned, and resided at Nineveh [vv. 35–36]. And it came to pass, as he was worshiping in the house of Nisroch his god, that Adram-melech and Sarezer [*Qere*: his sons] smote him with the sword . . . [v. 37].

---

44. The literary proximity between the story of Hazael's campaign against the land of Israel and the tribute paid to him by Joash, on the one hand, and the narrative of Joash's assassination, on the other, together with the unambiguous topical-chronological proximity created by the Chronicler between the two events seem to have led several historians to link the two stories together. Thus, for example, Reviv, *From Clan to Monarchy,* 204: "the diminished temple income and treasures [which had been turned over to Hazael, together with the treasures of the royal palace— I. K.] aroused once again the anger of the priesthood. A plot was conceived against Joash . . ."; Oded, "Israel and Judah," 149–50: "Joash's collapse in the Aramean campaign *and his disease* may have provided the opportunity for plots to be woven within the royal court and outside of it. The assassins of the king were 'his servants'. . . ." Tadmor ("First Temple and Restoration," 126) linked them: "Jehoash was assassinated by two of his servants as a result of the internal conflicts in Judah and the conditions of (Judah's) subjugation to Aram." See also n. 45.

45. Contra Mazar ("Samaria Ostraca," 181), who considers 2 Chr 24:23–25 an independent reliable narrative rather than a reworked version of the story of Hazael's campaign in the parallel text in 2 Kgs 12:18–19. On the basis of this assumption, Mazar concludes that the Aramean campaign described in 2 Chr 24:23ff. was a different one, headed by Ben-hadad, in 798 B.C.E.: "Ben-hadad attacked the kingdom of Israel and Jehoahaz perished in this war or as a consequence of it. The army of Aram continued southward, invaded Judah and perpetrated a great massacre in Jerusalem and Judah. This caused a revolt in Jerusalem and Joash perished during this revolt about a year after the Aramean invasion" (in 797/796).

The Deuteronomistic historian does not, in fact, link these two events explicitly. Placing them one after the other, however, creates an impression that Sennacherib was assassinated by his sons upon his return from his unsuccessful campaign against Judah. This impression is greatly strengthened by Isaiah's prophecy: "Behold, I shall put a spirit in him, and he shall hear a rumor and shall return to his own land; and I will strike him down by the sword in his own land" (2 Kgs 19:7 // Isa 37:7).[46]

The message that the Deuteronomistic historian tried to put in the minds of his potential readers covertly ("between the lines") was conveyed by the Chronicler overtly. He linked Sennacherib's embarrassing return from Judah with his assassination in Nineveh and presented the two events as a single unit: "So he returned with shame of face to his own land, and when he had come into the house of his god, they that came forth of his own bowels slew him there with the sword" (2 Chr 32:21b). The Chronicler seems to have desired by means of this explicit linkage not to leave any doubt about the fulfillment of Isaiah's prophecy that Sennacherib would retreat from the gates of Jerusalem and be assassinated in his own country (2 Kgs 19:7 // Isa 37:7).[47]

The Assyrian and Babylonian documentation shows that in fact there was no connection whatever between Sennacherib's unsuccessful campaign against Judah in 701 B.C.E. and his assassination by his son some 20 years later, in 681 B.C.E.[48]

4. Conclusion

A comparison of the texts in the books of Chronicles with the parallel texts in Samuel and Kings shows how the Chronicler uses literary and chronological proximity. He places the anointing of David over the

---

46. Compare Eph'al, "Sennacherib," 1065. As in the Bible, the assassination of Sennacherib by his son is explained in an inscription dated to the beginning of the reign of Nabonidus, king of Babylon, as a punishment meted out by Marduk for having destroyed the city of Babylon (689 B.C.E.); see Langdon, *Neu-babylonischen*, 270–72, I. 7–40.

47. In this regard, see below, example 7.27 (p. 161). The affair was depicted in the same way by later generations; for example, by Josephus, *Ant.* 10.21–22: "God had visited a pestilential sickness upon his army, and on the first night of the siege one hundred and eighty-five thousand men had perished with their commanders and officers [this is a combination of the narrative in 2 Kgs 19:35 and the one in 2 Chr 32:21—I. K.]. By this calamity he was thrown into a state of alarm and terrible anxiety, and, fearing for his entire army, he fled with the rest of his force to his own realm, called the kingdom of Ninos [Nineveh]. And, after remaining there a short while, he was treacherously attacked by his elder sons."

48. For a detailed discussion of the circumstance of the Sennacherib assassination, see Parpola, "Murderer of Sennacherib," 171–82; Zawadzki, "Death of Sennacherib," 69–72.

Northern tribes close to the death of Saul and portrays David as king over all Israel throughout his reign. The capture of Jerusalem is presented as David's first act immediately after his installation—a hint at the future centrality of this city in the life of the nation. The Chronicler creates literary and chronological proximity between the cult reform, the passover celebration, and Josiah's clash with Necho to contrast the destiny of Josiah with that of Hezekiah (to stress this contrast, he describes the fate of Josiah in terms similar to the fate of Ahab).

He replaces the precise dating of Sennacherib's invasion of Judah (2 Kgs 18:13 // Isa 36:1) with a phrase that determines the relative position of the event within the chain of events in the reign of Hezekiah (2 Chr 32:1). Therefore, he forges a literary and "chronological" link between Hezekiah's ritual activity and the failure of Sennacherib's campaign in Judah. Literary proximity is also created between Hezekiah's prayer and the Lord's salvation of Hezekiah to show the Lord's immediate response to the prayer of the king and the prophet. The Chronicler also transforms literary proximity into chronological-topical proximity: in 2 Chronicles 24 he makes use of the already existing literary proximity in 2 Kings 12–13 between the story of the Aramean campaign against the land of Israel and the story of the murder of Joash by his servants. He creates a chronological-topical proximity between the two events by overlooking the considerable time interval separating them and adapts the narrative in the earlier text to the strict system of rewards that motivates his writing. The Chronicler makes explicit linkage between Sennacherib's unsuccessful campaign against Judah and his assassination in Nineveh, as prophesied by Isaiah.

The Chronicler makes use of this literary technique to express various historiosophical and historiographical concepts and to advance his own views and beliefs. Thus, the historical credibility of the descriptions formulated in Chronicles by this means would indeed seem to be highly questionable.

5. Appendix: The "Stronghold" (2 Samuel 5:17)

If Jerusalem was indeed conquered after David's Philistine wars (2 Sam 5:17–25), המצודה 'the stronghold' mentioned in 2 Sam 5:17 to which David withdrew under Philistine pressure cannot be identified with the stronghold (of Zion) mentioned in vv. 7, 9. The 'stronghold' of 2 Sam 5:17 is apparently the cave of Adullam, which is called 'the stronghold' in 1 Sam 22:4–5 (for a cave termed a 'stronghold', see also 1 Sam 23:14; Job 39:27–28). This seems to be the case in 2 Sam 23:13–14 (// 1 Chr 11:15–16): "And three of the thirty chiefs *went down*, and came to David at harvest time [the version in Chronicles, "*went down* among the *crags* to David," is preferable] unto the cave of Adullam; and the Philistine troops *were encamped in the valley of Rephaim*, and David was then in the stronghold. . . ." This story and that telling of the Philistine campaign in 2 Sam 5:17–18 have a common background: "When David heard of this, he went down to the stronghold. *The Philistines came and deployed in the valley of Rephaim.*" Moreover, the phrase *"he went down* to the stronghold" is more suited to a context relating to the cave of Adullam than it is to Jerusalem, to which one ascends. Similarly, the question David puts to the Lord, "Shall I *go up* against the Philistines?" and the Lord's reply, *"go up*, for I will certainly deliver the Philistines into thy hand" (v. 19), are more suited to the geographical location of the cave of Adullam, from which one goes up, to that of Jerusalem, from where one descends to the valley of Rephaim. Though Hauer and Yeivin hold that the conquest of Jerusalem preceded David's wars against the Philistines, they identify the "stronghold" of 2 Sam 5:17 with Adullam.[49] Yeivin thinks that "it is difficult to assume that the reference here is to the stronghold of the City of David, for he was occupying it. . . ."[50] Here the question arises: if the "stronghold" of 2 Sam 5:17 really refers to the cave of Adullam, why were the Philistines encamped in the distant valley of Rephaim (v. 18)? During the campaign, were they not informed where David really was? Or perhaps first of all they attempted to cut off the tribes of Judah from those of the North in order to keep from David the assistance of the tribes of the North, who had just accepted him as their king? The reason is difficult to determine with any degree of certainty.

B. Mazar has a different opinion.[51] He moves David's conquest of Jerusalem up to the very beginning of his reign in Hebron—that is, prior to the union with the tribes of the North and his Philistine wars—and identifies the "stronghold" with the "stronghold of Zion." This identification is also accepted by some other scholars,[52] though it seems implausible.[53]

---

49. Hauer, "Jerusalem," 575–78; Yeivin, "Wars of David," 152.

50. See also Bright, *History*, 194.

51. Mazar, "David's Reign," 242 n. 2.

52. Aharoni, *Land of the Bible*, 292, 318; Garsiel, *Kingdom of David*, 43; Reviv, *From Clan to Monarchy*, 123–24. For these scholars' starting-point, see also n. 7 above.

53. See Kalimi, "Capture of Jerusalem," 66–79.

Chapter 2
Historiographical Revision

The term *historiographical revision* refers to a change introduced by a later historian into an earlier historical work in order to overcome an internal contradiction in that work or in order to prevent the creation of a contradiction between that work and an "addition" that he has made to it. Sometimes the "revision" is intended to adapt a description presented in the early work to the outlook, taste, or contemporary reality of a later historian or to different historical information that he had access to.

The examples of this phenomenon found in Chronicles indicate that the Chronicler would make use of a technique of omitting words or expressions from the text of Samuel–Kings in order to overcome contradictions of one sort or another found in the descriptive flow of these historiographical works, or contradictions between these works and "additions" he made to them. Rare are cases of the "revision" having been made by adding or changing the words of the early text so as to adapt the description presented in it to the outlook of the Chronicler himself.

The "revision" carried out by Josephus when he cites biblical texts can serve as typological examples of this feature. For example:

(a) In 1 Sam 18:14–27 we find Saul requesting that David provide "a hundred Philistine foreskins" (v. 25) before he will agree to David's marriage to his daughter Michal. David brings twice that number of foreskins and wins the princess (v. 27). Josephus, who designed his work first and foremost for uncircumcised Hellenistic readers, revised the early text and wrote: "I engage myself to marry my daughter to him, if he will bring me six hundred *heads* of the enemy" (*Ant.* 6.197, and see 6.201), "and David did so" (6.203).

(b) In 1 Samuel 27 we read of David's having received Ziklag from Achish, king of Gath. After this, David raided the tribes of Geshur, the Girzites, and the Amalekites, "and he took away the sheep, and the oxen, and the asses and the camels" as booty, and "*David* left neither *man nor woman* alive, to bring them to Gath, saying: 'Lest they tell on us, saying: "So did David . . ."'" (vv. 5–11). The brutality displayed by the founder of the Davidic dynasty was not acceptable to Josephus; as a result, in *Ant.* 6.323 he revised the biblical text and wrote: "[David] made clandestine raids on the neighbours of the Philistines . . . and returning with abundant booty of cattle and camels; *he refrained from* (taking captive) *any men*, for fear that they would denounce him to King Achish." Josephus related only the part of the biblical text that he felt comfortable with—that is, the fact that David refrained from taking people captive. He omitted the parts of the biblical story that he was uncomfortable with—that is, that David killed the people. From the account in *Antiquities*, it is difficult to fathom just what happened to the people that David did not take captive.

(c) According to Ezra 4:7ff., "Rehum the official and Shimshai the scribe wrote a letter against Jerusalem to Artaxerxes the king, as follows. . . ." According to the chronology that Josephus had, however, the inimical letter was written not in the days of Artaxerxes, king of Persia, but earlier, in the days of Cambyses, Cyrus's son and heir.[1] When Josephus cited the letter in his work, he refrained from spelling out the name of the king, "Artaxerxes," explicitly; he simply wrote "our sovereign" in a general form: "To our sovereign from (δέσποτα) Rathymos, the recorder of all things that happen, Samelios, the scribe, who records everything that transpires, and the judges" (*Ant.* 11.21–22).

Nicholas of Damascus acted similarly. For example, in Josephus's *Ant.* 14.8–9, we read that "there was a certain friend of Hyrcanus, an Idumaean called Antipater, who, having a large fortune and being by nature a man of action and a troublemaker. . . . Nicholas of Damascus, to be sure, says that his family belonged to the leading Jews who came to Judaea from Babylon. But he says this in order to please Antipater's son Herod, who became king of the Jews by a certain turn of fortune." On the other hand, in *J.W.* 1.6.2, Josephus quotes from the work of Nicholas of Damascus, while amending its text according to the reliable historical information available to him: "[Antipater was] an Idumaean by race, his ancestry, wealth, and other advantages put him in the front rank of his nation." This means that Nicholas of Damascus "revised" the reliable historical information he had access to concerning Antipater's Idumean origins in order to satisfy Herod. At a later date, when Josephus referred to this, he "revised" Nicholas's text and related the historical truth concerning Antipater's origins.

It should also be noted that the early Alexandrians "revised" certain texts in Homer's writing "whenever [they were] not in conformity with the manners of the court of the Ptolemies or the customs of certain Greeks."[2]

The "revisions" made in the Samaritan Pentateuch as compared with its Masoretic counterpart can serve as close typological examples that

---

1. For Josephus's relevant chronological calculations, see Tuland, "Josephus," 176–92.

2. See Lieberman, *Hellenism*, 37.

are not results of a comprehensive historical writing like those of the
Chronicler and Josephus. Thus, for example:

(a) In Exod 13:4 we find: היום אתם יצאים בחדש האביב 'This day you are
going forth in the month of Abib'. This verse seems to contradict Deut
16:1: כי בחדש האביב הוציאך ה׳ אלהיך ממצרים לילה 'for in the month of Abib the
Lord thy God brought you forth out of Egypt by *night*'. To prevent this
contradiction, the Samaritan Pentateuch omits the expression 'this day'
in Exod 13:4, writing instead "_____ and you are going forth in the
month of Abib."

(b) An example of another type is to be found in Exod 20:18: וכל העם
ראים את הקולת ואת הלפידם ואת קול השפר ואת ההר עשן 'And all the people saw
the sounds and the torches *and the voice of the horn* and the mountain
smoking'. Since the claim that the people saw *the sounds and the voice
of the horn* contradicts the very nature of man and the abilities of his
senses, however, the text was "revised" in the Samaritan Pentateuch as
follows: "And all the people heard *the sounds and the voice of the horn*
and saw the torches and the mountain smoking."

1. The Removal of Internal Contradictions in Samuel–Kings

2.1 In 2 Sam 7:1 we are told that, when David was settled in his
house "and the Lord had given him rest from all his enemies round
about," he expressed his desire to establish a permanent house for the
Lord. However, the description "*and the Lord had given him rest from
all his enemies* round about"[3] does not match the text further on concerning the Lord's promise to David (v. 11) "*and I shall give you rest
from all your enemies*," where it seems that David had not yet been
given rest from all his enemies. Moreover, from v. 12, "I shall set up your
seed after you, that shall proceed out of your body . . . ," it seems that
Nathan's prophecy to David was uttered before the birth of Solomon—
that is, prior to David's wars with Aram and the Ammonites that are recounted in 2 Sam 8:3–8; chap. 10; 11:1; 12:26–31. It is thus difficult to
say that the Lord had given David rest from all of his enemies at the
time of Nathan's prophecy. Furthermore, from the standpoint of the or-
dering of the verses, the declaration in 2 Sam 7:1b, "and the Lord gave
him [David] rest from all his enemies," does not fit well with the narratives following close by in chap. 8, which are linked by means of the expression ויהי אחרי כן 'And after this it came to pass' to Nathan's prophecy
and to David's prayer: "*And after this it came to pass that David smote
the Philistines. . . . And he smote Moab. . . . David smote* also Hadad-

---

3. Compare this expression with the phrase in v. 11 and Deut 12:10–11, "and He
shall give you rest from all your enemies round about," and Deut 25:19; Josh 21:44;
23:1; 1 Kgs 5:18, etc.

ezer . . ." (8:1ff.). Neither does the declaration in 2 Sam 7:1b fit comfortably with Solomon's message to Hiram in 1 Kgs 5:17–18, according to which David had been unable to build the Temple because of the wars that encompassed him while, as for Solomon, *"the Lord my God has given me rest on every side*; there is neither adversary nor evil occurrence." It seems that for these reasons the Chronicler omitted the declaration "and the Lord had given him rest from all his enemies round about" in 1 Chr 17:1.[4] In fact, on this point Solomon is presented in Chronicles as a figure antitypical to that of his father: Solomon is a *"man of rest,"* and the Lord promised that *"I would give him rest from all his enemies about him,* for Solomon will be his name, and peace and quiet I shall give unto Israel in his days" (1 Chr 22:9–10). In contrast, David is a *"man of war* . . . , and you have shed much blood" (1 Chr 28:3).[5]

2.2 In 1 Kgs 5:27–28 we are told that for the establishment of the Temple Solomon raised *"a levy out of all Israel,"* 30,000 men, and organized them in labor-gangs, each consisting of 10,000 men, that were sent alternately for a month to Lebanon. This information[6] contradicts what we are told in 1 Kgs 9:20–22: *"But of the children of Israel did Solomon make no bondservants*; but they were the men of war and his servants and his princes and his captains and leaders of his chariot corps and of his horsemen." To meet the needs of the various construction projects, Solomon raised a levy of workers from among the foreign peoples who remained at the time in the land "of the Amorites, the Hittites, the Perizzites, the Hivites, and the Jebusites, *who were not of the children of Israel."*

In order to remove this contradiction, the Chronicler omitted the narrative in 1 Kgs 5:27–28 regarding the raising of a levy of the children of Israel (see the parallel passage in 2 Chronicles 2) and adduced only the text that tells of the raising of the laborers from among the non-Israelite residents who remained in the land (2 Chr 8:7–9).[7] Likewise, before the

---

4. On this point, see Curtis-Madsen, *Chronicles*, 226.

5. See also 1 Chr 22:8: "You have shed blood abundantly and have waged great wars . . . because you have shed much blood upon the earth before me"; Dirksen, "David Disqualified," 51–56; Kelly, "David's Disqualification," 53–61.

6. Similarly, the information in 1 Kgs 11:28 regarding "the labor of the house of Joseph."

7. As he puts it, these strangers remained in the land because "the children of Israel did not consume them" (2 Chr 8:8). On the other hand, in the earlier text in 1 Kgs 9:21, we find that they remained in the land because "the children of Israel *were not able* utterly to destroy them." And it seems to be as Seeligmann puts it: "The deliberate change may well be as follows: the Chronicler was no longer prepared to admit the possibility that the Israelites were unable to destroy utterly the Canaanite foe. Not destroying them was, in his eyes, a transgression against a divine precept" ("From Historic Reality," 287–88 n. 33).

narrative further along in the text (in 1 Kgs 5:29–30) regarding "70,000 that bore burdens and 80,000 hewers in the mountains," and so forth, who labored in building the Temple, he made sure to bring up the fact that these were "all the *strangers* that were in the land of Israel" (2 Chr 2:16–17);[8] in other words, "*all the people* that were left of the Amorites, the Hittites, the Perizzites, the Hivites, and the Jebusites, *who were not of the children of Israel*" (2 Chr 8:7–8 // 1 Kgs 9:10–21).[9]

2.3 In 1 Kgs 9:11–14 we find that Solomon granted Hiram 20 cities in the land of Galilee, apparently in return for wood for construction, gold, and experts provided by the king of Tyre:[10]

Now Hiram, king of Tyre, had furnished Solomon with cedar trees and cypress trees, and with gold, according to all his desire. Then King Solomon gave Hiram twenty cities in the land of Galilee.

But when Hiram came from Tyre to see the cities that Solomon had given him, they did not please him.

And he said: "What cities are these that you have given me, my brother?"

So they are called the land of Cabul[11] unto this day.[12]

---

8. For a detailed discussion of this addition, see example 14.3 (pp. 301–302). The belief that the construction of the Temple was carried out by means of foreign workers made its way to yet another Second Temple writer: the Jewish-Hellenistic writer Eupolemus ben Yohanan (ca. 157 B.C.E.) relates that Suron, the King of Tyre, Sidon, and Phoenicia, and Vaphres, the King of Egypt, responded to Solomon's request, each sending 80,000 laborers to Jerusalem in order to build the Temple. For an English version of Eupolemus's work, see Fallon, "Eupolemus," 865–70 (Fragment 2).

9. For the identification of "the strangers" with "all the people that were left of the Amorites . . . who were not of the children of Israel," see Japhet, *Ideology*, 335.

10. Note the verbs נתן . . . נשא (v. 11), which serve as terms in barter trade; for this, see De Vries, *1 Kings*, 131–32.

11. For the meaning of the name כבול 'Cabul' and, for the geographical position of "the land of Cabul," see Katzenstein, *Tyre*, 104–5, and the references to earlier literature there.

12. Noth views the narrative in 1 Kgs 9:10–14 as a late etiological account aimed at explaining the name ארץ כבול 'the land of Cabul' and casts doubt on its historical authenticity (*Geschichte Israels*, 194 n. 2, 195 n. 3 = *History of Israel*, 212 n. 1, 213 n. 3). However, as Liver says: "Even assuming that the explanation of the name, phrased in so typical a fashion ויקרא להם ארץ כבול עד היום הזה, is etiological, the item itself is not to be doubted, as it contains a certain dimming of the image of Solomon and was certainly not contrived by the Israelite scribe" ("Hiram of Tyre," 189–90 n. 3). It is to be noted that it is doubtful that the author of the book of Kings considered the sale of the cities to Hiram to be faulty, the narrative thus not containing "a certain dimming of the image of Solomon." The sale of the cities was not an exceptional step in the ancient Near East. Similar events are known to have transpired (though in an earlier period) from documents from Alalakh; see Fensham, "Treaty between Solomon and Hiram," 59–60, and references to earlier bibliography there.

But Hiram had sent one hundred twenty talents of gold to the king.[13]

This information in the book of Kings, showing Solomon to have been in such economic distress that only by conceding a province of the land of Israel was he able to pay the king of Tyre for the goods he received, completely contradicts the Lord's promise to Solomon concerning the great wealth he would acquire: "I have also given you what you have not asked for, *both riches* and honor—so that there has not been any king like you—*all your days*" (1 Kgs 3:13). The Chronicler went even further in the parallel text in 2 Chr 1:12: "and I will give you *riches, wealth*, and honor, *such as none of the kings have had that have been before you; neither shall any after you have the like.*" This presentation does not even match the description of Solomon's extreme wealth, for example, in 1 Kgs 10:27: "And the king made silver to be in Jerusalem as stones, and cedars made he to be as the sycamore-trees that are in the Lowland, for abundance" (// 2 Chr 9:27 and see also 1:15: "And the king made silver and gold to be as common in Jerusalem as stones . . .").[14]

Because of these contradictions and apparently also because the Chronicler considered it wrong to hand over cities of the land of Israel to foreign rule, thus narrowing the borders of the kingdom of Israel in return for the goods Solomon had received, he "touched up" the narrative contained in the early historiography and wrote precisely the opposite: Solomon expanded the borders of Israel—he received cities from Hiram, king of Tyre, rebuilt them (indicating his wealth) and settled Israelites in them (2 Chr 8:2): "and the cities that Hiram had given to Solomon, Solomon built them, and caused the children of Israel to dwell there."

To reinforce this historiographical picture, the Chronicler went into additional detail: "And Solomon went to Hamath-zobah, and prevailed against it. And he built Tadmor in the wilderness[15] and all the store-cities that he built in Hamath" (vv. 3–4; an "addition"). In other words, not only did Solomon not reduce the borders of the kingdom of David, he even expanded them, built, and settled up to the farthest border of his kingdom. In this way, the Chronicler glorified the name of King Solomon in his work,[16] something he would not have achieved had he simply

---

13. In the Septuagint, the Peshiṭta, and the Vulgate, the name "Solomon" appears at this point.

14. And see also 1 Kgs 10:21 // 2 Chr 9:20, which stresses the king's wealth in gold.

15. Instead of "and Tamar in the wilderness, in the land" in 1 Kgs 9:18b, "Tamar" apparently referring to a settlement in the south of the Judean Desert.

16. For the verse in 2 Chr 8:2 glorifying Solomon, see Ehrlich, *Mikrâ ki-Pheschutô*, 451; Liver, "Hiram of Tyre," 189–90 n. 3. For an explanation from a different direction, see Rudolph, *Chronik*, 219; Bickerman, *Ezra*, 22; and Japhet, *Ideology*, 480: "Apparently, considerations of 'historical probability' led to the change in Chronicles. The Chronicler could not even conceive of the possibility that Solomon might have been unable to pay Hiram for his assistance and therefore had to hand over part of his

omitted the earlier text from the book of Kings.[17]

It thus seems that 2 Chr 8:2 is not to be viewed as an "early historical
tradition," as a number of scholars claim,[18] nor is it to be added to the
narrative of 1 Kgs 9:10–14 and the two writings viewed as supple-
mentary portions of a single ancient accounting.[19] This combination is
nothing but an attempt to create harmony between two mutually contradictory passages.

2.4 2 Kgs 8:20–22a recounts an expedition undertaken by Joram of
Judea against Edom in order to restore it to Judean control. From the
account that we have, the description of the results of the war contradicts the description of the military campaign: if indeed Joram smote
the Edomites and the captains of the chariots, why then did "the people"
flee[20] to their tents? This wonder leads us to surmise that some error entered the text, and a number of possible emendations have been put forward: for example, Stade[21] turns the word order around, reading: ויקם
אדום לילה ויסב אליו ויך אתו ואת שרי הרכב וינס העם לאהליו 'Edom rose up by
night and pivoted toward him, and smote him and the captains of the

---

territory. It seemed to him that the reverse situation rang much truer." Rudolph
notes that the narrative of the preparations made by David for the erection of the
Temple and the very fact that the expenditures involved in building the Temple led
to a concession of some of the lands of the Holy Land were some of the motives for the
revision (though, in his opinion, unlike that of Bickerman and Japhet, the version of
the text in Chronicles reflects an alternate ancient tradition opposing the tradition of
the version in Kings, which the Chronicler preferred to the tradition of Kings and adduced it in his book).

17. Disagreeing with Williamson, *Chronicles*, 228.

18. So, for example, Katzenstein, *Tyre*, 104; Williamson, *Chronicles*, 229: "little
historical weight should be afforded the Chronicler's version here." Williamson and
Willi (*Chronik*, 75–78) claim that the Chronicler's *Vorlage* was faulty here and that
the verses in 2 Chr 8:1–6 represent the best reconstruction it was possible to carry
out. This claim, however, is groundless. See also the next note.

19. So, for example, Myers joins the passage in Chronicles with that in Kings and
surmises: "The cities may have been collateral until the time when payment could be
made in gold" (*II Chronicles*, 47)! The similar opinions of other scholars, such as
A. Noordtzij, A. van Selms, and J. Goettsberger (and even earlier, Josephus, *Ant.*
8.5, and Pseudo-Hieronymus), were already rejected by Rudolph, *Chronik*, 219. For the
same reason, one should also reject the explanation adopted by Stern, who argues
that 2 Chr 8:1–2 refers to the first half of Solomon's reign, when "the northern border
of his kingdom extended all the way to the southern border of Phoenicia proper." On
the other hand, 1 Kgs 9:11 refers to the "second half of his reign, [when] he ceded back
to Phoenicia everything north of [the] Carmel coast"; see Stern, "Many Masters of
Dor," 20–21.

20. The word "people" seems to refer here to Joram's soldiers; cf. 2 Sam 20:15;
1 Kgs 20:15, etc.

21. Stade, *Kings*, 218; idem, "König Joram," 337–40; and in his wake, also Curtis-
Madsen, *Chronicles*, 415.

chariots, and the people fled to their tents'. Kittel proposed reading: ויהי הוא קם לילה ויכהו אדום 'And it came to pass that when he rose up at night Edom smote him . . .'.[22] Jepsen and Rudolph read ויכה אתו אדום 'and Edom smote him' instead of ויכה אֶת אֱדוֹם 'and he smote Edom'.[23]

It is reasonable to assume that the fault in the text before us in the book of Kings had already made its way into the Chronicler's Vorlage. Otherwise, it is difficult to explain why the Chronicler emended the earlier text, which presented the campaign headed by the evil Joram as a defeat—a presentation suiting his views on retribution. At any rate, he attempted to eliminate the aforesaid contradiction/discord by omitting the phrase וינס העם לאהליו:[24]

2 Kgs 8:20–22a		2 Chr 21:8–10a	
בימיו *פשע* אדום מתחת יד	20.	בימיו *פשע* אדום מתחת יד	8.
יהודה וימלכו עליהם מלך		יהודה וימליכו עליהם מלך	
ויעבר יורם צעירה	21.	ויעבר יהורם עם שריו[25]	9.
וכל הרכב עמו[26]		וכל הרכב עמו	
ויהי הוא קם לילה		ויהי הוא קם לילה	
ויכה את אדום הסביב אליו		ויך את אדום הסובב אליו	
ואת שרי הרכב		ואת שרי הרכב	
וינס העם לאהליו			
ויפשע אדום מתחת יד יהודה	22a.	ויפשע אדום מתחת יד יהודה	
עד היום הזה.		עד היום הזה.	

The words closing the account of the campaign in 2 Chr 21:10a (// 2 Kgs 8:22a), "So Edom has revolted against the rule of Judah to this day," generate a disharmony with Joram's victory in the war as presented in v. 9.[27] However, the Chronicler may have thought that, although Joram attacked Edom, he failed to defeat the Edomites and failed to impose his

---

22. Kittel, *BH*, 571.

23. A. Jepsen, *BHS*, 633; Rudolph, *Chronik*, 264 (following Šanda); and for a similar idea, see also the New English Bible (NEB) of 2 Chr 21:9.

24. Thus in all the early translations except for the Septuagint, in which the phrase appears, apparently influenced by the verse in the parallel text in Kings.

25. Compare the style of this passage with that of Josh 10:29: ויעבר יהושע וכל ישראל עמו ממקדה לבנה . . ., and also with that of v. 31 there.

26. עם שריו 'with his princes' instead of צעירה 'to Zair' in Kings. The word צעירה is a hapax legomenon in the Bible, perhaps an error for שעירה 'to Sair' (ש/צ, dental consonantal interchanges); see Rudolph, *Chronik*, 264; Liver, "Israel and Edom," 200 (also there, a discussion of other proposed ways of interpreting this word). Even accepting Liver's assumption (p. 205 n. 29) that the version to which the Chronicler had access was שעירה, there is still place for an explanation of the emendation שעירה / עם שריו; for this, see Japhet, *Ideology*, 418.

27. From a purely literary point of view, the expressions בימיו פשע אדום מתחת יד יהודה . . . ויפשע אדום מתחת יד יהודה (8a, 10a // 2 Kgs 8:20a, 22a) form the structure of an *inclusio*.

authority over them, as occurred on other occasions in the ancient world. For example: (a) Jehoram, king of Israel, and his allies attacked Mesha, king of Moab, who had rebelled against Israel, yet they were not successful in defeating him, in capturing Kir-Hareseth, or in restoring Moab to Israelite domination (2 Kgs 1:1; chap. 3). The words of 2 Kgs 8:21 resemble 2 Kgs 3:24: ויבאו אל מחנה ישראל ויקמו ישראל ויכו את מואב וינסו מפניהם 'When they came to the camp of Israel, the Israelites rose up and attacked the Moabites, so that they fled before them'. (b) Sennacherib, king of Assyria, struck the Egyptian force sent by Shabtekha the Kush-ite to help Hezekiah and his allies (Eltekeh, 701 B.C.E.) but could not defeat Egypt because apparently the Assyrian army was incapable of pursuing the Egyptians.[28] (c) Sennacherib wreaked havoc in Judah, captured her fortified cities with Lachish at their head, tore much terri-tory[29] from her—yet could neither capture Jerusalem nor do away with the kingdom of Hezekiah.

2.5 1 Kgs 15:18 relates that Asa, king of Judah, sent "all the silver and gold *that was left* in the treasure of the House of the Lord and the treasures of the king's house" to Ben-Hadad (I), king of Aram. "That was left" here apparently refers to what was left after the campaign of robbery carried out by Shishak, king of Egypt, in Jerusalem during Re-hoboam's reign. This phrase, however, contradicts what we are told there: "and (Shishak) took away the treasures of the House of the Lord and the treasures of the king's house; *he even took away all . . .*" (1 Kgs 14:26 = 2 Chr 12:9b). If Shishak "took away *all*" during the reign of Re-hoboam, how can one speak of what was left during Asa's reign? This may be at the root of the omission of the word הנותרים in the account of the dispatching of the treasures to Ben-Hadad in 2 Chr 16:2: "Then Asa brought silver and gold _____ out of the treasures of the House of the Lord and of the king's house and sent to Ben-Hadad."[30]

2.6 In 1 Kgs 5:1[4:21] we read: "And Solomon ruled over all the king-doms from the river to the land of the Philistines and to the border of Egypt;[31] *they brought tribute and served Solomon all the days of his*

28. See, in this connection, Tadmor, "Assyrian Campaigns," 227; Eph'al, "Sen-nacherib," 1066.

29. See 2 Kings 18–19 // Isaiah 36–37, the Prism of Sennacherib, the Lachish re-liefs, and the archaeological excavations at Lachish.

30. Curtis and Madsen (*Chronicles*, 388) provided an alternate explanation for this omission: "This statement is omitted, doubtless, because such a reference to de-pleted treasuries would have been quite inappropriate after the prosperity of Asa mentioned above."

31. For the difficulty in this passage and the Chronicler's attempt to deal with it, see example 6.1 (pp. 108–110).

life." The conclusion of this passage does not match the account in 1 Kgs 11:14–25 of the rebellions of Hadad, the Edomite, and Rezon ben-Eliada, who was "an adversary to Israel *all the days of Solomon*" (v. 25).[32] These rebellions show that they did not bring him tribute and serve him in all the kingdoms "from the river to the land of the Philistines and to the border of Egypt"[33] "all the days" of Solomon's life. While the Chronicler does not use the narrative in 1 Kgs 11:14–25 in his work,[34] he does apparently make the fundamental assumption that his readers are familiar with it.[35] He therefore borrows the text of 1 Kgs 5:1 for 2 Chr 9:26, finding it proper to "revise" its contents—that is, to omit the words מגשים מנחה ועבדים את שלמה כל ימי חייו 'they brought tribute and served Solomon all the days of his life' (although, in his eyes, these words glorify King Solomon's success).

2.7 In 2 Kgs 23:34, we are informed that Pharaoh Necho installed "Eliakim, son of Josiah, *in place of Josiah, his father,*" and then changed his name to Jehoiakim. Since, however, it was "Jehoahaz, son of Josiah," whom they had installed "*in place of his father*" (2 Kgs 23:30 // 2 Chr 36:1), the Chronicler saw fit to omit the words "in place of Josiah, his father," from the account in 2 Kgs 23:34 and instead wrote: "And the king of Egypt made Eliakim, his brother, king _____ over Judah and Jerusalem, and changed his name to Jehoiakim" (2 Chr 36:4).[36]

The expression "in place of Josiah, his father," in 2 Kgs 23:34 can be justified by saying that Pharaoh Necho did not recognize the legitimacy of the installation of Jehoahaz as king "in place of his father" by the people of the land and viewed the pro-Egyptian Eliakim/Jehoiakim as the rightful ruler in place of his father.

2.8 1 Kgs 3:14 speaks of the Lord's promise to Solomon: "If you walk in my ways, to keep my statutes and my commandments, as your father

---

32. Add to these the revolt of Jeroboam ben-Nebat (1 Kgs 11:26–41).

33. The historical reliability of the account in 1 Kgs 5:1 and 4, regarding the extent of Solomon's rule is doubtful in light of 1 Kgs 11:14–24; see Miller-Hayes, *History of Ancient Israel*, 214. For another opinion, see Malamat, "Foreign Policies," 195–222.

34. The accounts of these rebellions might well have detracted from the magnificence of Solomon and indicated that it was as if his dominion had been reduced; see Abramsky, "King Solomon," 8. Furthermore, these accounts seem to stress Solomon's sins, which the Chronicler was interested in obscuring.

35. This assumption is clearly expressed in the various allusions that the Chronicler makes throughout his work to verses in the books of the Pentateuch and the Former Prophets—verses that he does not include in his work. For this, see chap. 10, "Allusion" (pp. 194ff.).

36. The Greek translation of Chronicles combined 2 Chr 36:4 with 2 Kgs 23:34–35; see Curtis-Madsen, *Chronicles*, 520.

David did, then I will lengthen your days."[37] In the parallel text of 2 Chronicles 1, the Chronicler omitted this verse. Now, the omission of the condition "if you will walk in my ways . . ." is understandable in light of the Chronicler's design to omit every allusion to Solomon's sins (1 Kgs 11:1–13), including even potential texts. But why did he omit the expression והארכתי את ימיך 'then I will lengthen your days'?[38]

In 1 Chr 29:1 (and compare 22:5), the Chronicler portrays Solomon as "young and tender" when he assumed the throne.[39] This statement by the Chronicler is apparently rooted in 1 Kgs 3:7, "and I am but a young lad; I know not how to go out or come in."[40] Since Solomon reigned 40 years (2 Chr 9:30 // 1 Kgs 11:42), it seems that he was not particularly long-lived.[41] The use of the phrase והארכתי את ימיך 'then I will lengthen your days' would thus have depicted either the Lord as one who did not keep his promise or Solomon as a sinner whose days were shortened because of sin[42]—possibilities that did not serve the Chronicler's designs. Moreover, because the life of Solomon was short despite his wisdom (1 Kgs 5:9–14), for the Chronicler to retain 1 Kgs 3:14b would certainly call into question the ultimate statement of Prov 3:16, which praises wisdom as resulting in long life: "In her (= wisdom's) right hand is *length of days* / in her left, riches and honor."

---

37. This verse meets the spiritual requirements of the Deuteronomistic source in Deut 17:20. For another opinion, see Malamat, "Longevity," 222 n. 29 and earlier relevant bibliography there. For the motif, the longevity of kings and its connection with their righteousness and honesty in the ancient Near East, see there, pp. 221–24.

38. Rudolph (*Chronik*, 197) thinks that the Chronicler omitted the topic of longevity because Solomon did not live up to its condition. However, as already noted, he could have omitted the condition and left the expression "and I will lengthen your days" as the absolute statement.

39. Solomon's installation as king is described further on in this chapter in vv. 22–25 (his second installation); see also 1 Chr 23:1 (the first installation).

40. Yeivin ("Solomon," 693) postulated that Solomon was 16 years old at his accession to the throne. Malamat ("Longevity," 223–24 n. 32) is less decisive, assuming that he was under the age of 20. Contrasting with the expression נער ורך, which denotes age in 1 Chr 29:1, the Chronicler's language contains the phrase נער ורך־לבב, which denotes character; see 2 Chr 13:7 and 12:13 (in connection with Rehoboam, Solomon's son).

41. Josephus, *Ant.* 8.211, was not of that opinion: "And Solomon attained a good old age and died, after having reigned eighty years and lived ninety-four years." Josephus seems to have believed that Solomon met the condition of observing the precepts of the Lord and so enjoyed longevity, but *when already elderly* he sinned (1 Kgs 11:4: "For it came to pass, when Solomon was old").

42. Similarly Zalewski, *Solomon*, 257ff.

2. Preventing the Formation of a Contradiction
between an Early Text and an "Addition"
and/or Any Other Biblical Passage

2.9 In 2 Kgs 23:22, expressing his evaluation of Josiah's Passover, the Deuteronomistic historian wrote: "for such a Passover had not been kept since the days of the judges that judged Israel, not even during the days of the kings of Israel *or the kings of Judah.*" In the parallel 2 Chr 35:18, the Chronicler omitted the words ומלכי יהודה 'or the kings of Judah' because they contradict what was previously said in 2 Chronicles 30 (an "addition") about Hezekiah, *king of Judah*, Josiah's grandfather, who celebrated the Passover (although, admittedly, in the second month) publicly, in the Temple in Jerusalem.[43]

2.10 In his evaluation of Amaziah, the Deuteronomistic historian wrote in 2 Kgs 14:3: "And he did that which was right in the eyes of the Lord, yet not like David his father; *he did according to all that Joash his father had done.*" The Chronicler wrote "yet not with a whole heart" instead of "yet not like David his father," omitting completely the comparison with Joash (2 Chr 25:2): "And he did what was right in the eyes of the Lord, yet not with a whole heart[44] _____." The significance of this omission becomes apparent in light of the Chronicler's account of Joash, who forsook the Temple after the death of Jehoiada the priest, worshiped the Asherahs and the idols (2 Chr 24:18, "addition") and had Zechariah, son of Jehoiada the priest, stoned (2 Chr 24:20–22, "addition"). Since Amaziah, his son, did nothing like this but conducted himself in accordance with Torah precepts ("he slew his servants who had killed the king, his father. But he did not put their children to death but did according to what is written in the Torah, in the book of Moses," 2 Chr 25:3–4 // 2 Kgs 14:5–6), it would be incorrect to say that "he did according to all that Joash his father had done." On the other hand, according to the book of Kings, Amaziah did "what was right in the sight of the Lord" (2 Kgs 14:3a), just as Joash his father did "what was right in the sight of the Lord" (2 Kgs 12:3).

2.11 In 2 Kgs 24:19 (// Jer 52:2) we are told about Zedekiah, king of Judah: "He did what was evil in the sight of the Lord, *according to all that Jehoiakim had done.*" In 2 Chr 36:12, the Chronicler adduced this passage and omitted the phrase "according to all that Jehoiakim had

---

43. Williamson (*Chronicles*, 407) thinks that the Chronicler's concern for "the unity of the people of God" was behind this omission.

44. "Yet not with a whole heart" alludes, apparently, to the sins of Amaziah that the Chronicler recounts in 2 Chr 25:14–16 ("addition").

done" for, in the books of Kings and Jeremiah, no mention is made of Zedekiah's building himself a house unjustly or oppressing and persecuting a prophet of the Lord until he died, as in the accounts of Jehoiakim, king of Judah (Jer 22:13–17; 26:20–23).[45] The portrait of Jehoiachin is similarly evaluated in 2 Chr 36:9a. Here, the Chronicler omitted the words "according to all that his father (= Jehoiakim) had done," which appear in 2 Kgs 24:9, presumably for the same reason that I detailed concerned King Zedekiah.

2.12 In 2 Chronicles 32, the Chronicler omitted the passage found in 2 Kgs 18:21 (// Isa 36:6), "Now, behold, *you are relying on the staff of this bruised reed—on Egypt,*" and so forth, as well as vv. 23–24 (// Isa 36:8–9), where we find, among other things: "How then can you repulse a single satrap among the least of my master's servants, when you rely on Egypt for chariots and horsemen?"[46] The omission of these passages stems from the fact that they contradict statements that the Chronicler had previously had Hezekiah say, statements indicating that the king of Judah had put his faith in the Lord: "And he gathered them together to him in the square at the city gate and encouraged them, saying: 'Be strong and of good courage. Do not be afraid or dismayed at the king of Assyria or at all the multitude that is with him, for there is a greater one with us than with him. With him is an arm of flesh. *With us is the Lord our God to help us and to fight our battles.' And the people relied* on the words of Hezekiah, king of Judah" (2 Chr 32:6–8).[47]

2.13 In 2 Kgs 10:13–14 an account is given of the slaughter of אחי אחזיהו 'the brothers of Ahaziahu' carried out by Jehu. In 2 Chr 22:8 the Chronicler writes that Jehu killed בני אחי אחזיהו 'the *offspring* of the brothers of Ahaziah', for from his viewpoint the brothers of Ahaziah (themselves the offspring of Jehoram, king of Judah) had been taken captive by the Arabs and the Philistines (2 Chr 21:17, "addition"):[48] ". . . and they came up against Judah . . . and carried away all the substance

---

45. See also 2 Chr 36:8, "Now the rest of the acts of Jehoiakim, and his *abominations* which he did . . . ," instead of "Now the rest of the acts of Jehoiakim, and *all* that he did . . . ," in 2 Kgs 24:5.

46. The dependence of the kingdom of Judah on the aid of Egypt in 701 B.C.E. is also apparent from the narrative in 2 Kgs 19:9 (// Isa 37:9) and from the story of the third campaign of Sennacherib, king of Assyria.

47. In a similar vein, see Curtis-Madsen, *Chronicles*, 487–88; Williamson, *Chronicles*, 383. This passage is a literary imitation of Josh 1:9: "Have not I commanded you? Be strong and of good courage; be not afraid, neither be dismayed: for the Lord your God is with you wherever you go."

48. The Chronicler seems to have interpreted the word אחי here in its most limited sense; see Japhet, *Ideology*, 466 n. 57.

... and *his sons* also and his wives; so that there was never a son left him, save Jehoahaz, the smallest of his sons."

2.14 2 Kgs 12:21 relates that the servants of Joash, king of Judah, conspired against him and assassinated him in בית מלא היורד סלא 'Beth-Millo, on the way that goes down to Silla'.[49] The Chronicler revised 2 Chr 24:25b to match a section that he had related before in an "addition" he made to the text (vv. 24–25a). According to this "addition," the army of the Arameans "executed judgment" on Joash and "left him with great wounds." Now, since the natural place to find a sick/wounded man is in bed, the Chronicler wrote that the place of the assassination was "on his [Joash's] bed":

2 Kgs 12:21	2 Chr 24:25
	ובלכתם ממנו כי עזבו אתו במחליים רבים
ויקמו עבדיו ויקשרו קשר	התקשרו עליו עבדיו . . .
ויכו את יואש בית מלא היורד סלא	ויהרגהו[50] על מטתו

This revision in the book of Chronicles provides a suitable end to the life-span of Joash, king of Judah: Joash was saved from the sword of Athaliah by virtue of having been hidden "in the bedroom" (2 Chr 22:11 // 2 Kgs 11:2), and he met his death "on his bed."

In this revision, the Chronicler removed the obscure geographical expression about Beth-Millo from his work, a step that renders a more fluent reading of the story. However, this was achieved quite incidentally, as a part of the main purpose discussed above, not as an independent goal, as some scholars believe.[51]

2.15 The Deuteronomistic historiographer concludes his description of the history of Jehoiakim, king of Judah, with the commonplace formula (2 Kgs 24:6) וישכב יהויקם עם אבתיו וימלך יהויכין בנו תחתיו 'So Jehoiakim slept with his fathers; and Jehoiachin his son reigned in his stead'. Now the words וישכב יהויקם עם אבותיו contradict Jeremiah's prophecy concerning Jehoiakim: "He shall be buried with the burial of an ass, dragged off and cast out beyond the gates of Jerusalem" (Jer 22:19). This seems to be the reason that the Chronicler omitted the words וישכב יהויקים עם אבתיו

---

49. This geographical location is not sufficiently clear. For the attempts made by the early translators and by modern scholars to clarify it, on occasion with proposals for emendation, see Montgomery, *Kings*, 433; Gray, *Kings*, 590 note a, 590–91; Cogan-Tadmor, *II Kings*, 139.

50. For the reason for the exchange ויהרגהו / ויכו את יואש, see the discussion in examples 9.2 and 9.3 (pp. 188–190).

51. For example, Willi, *Chronik*, 122; Williamson, *Chronicles*, 326.

'Jehoiakim slept with his fathers', stating only "Jehoiachin his son reigned in his stead" (2 Chr 36:8).[52]

An additional reason for the aforesaid omission may be discerned in the fact that, according to the Chronicler, Jehoiakim was exiled to Babylon (2 Chr 36:6b, "addition"), though no mention is made of his return from there. If he did not return, then from the Chronicler's viewpoint it would have been impossible to claim that he slept "with his fathers."[53] Nevertheless, from the text ויאסרהו בנחשתים להליכו בבלה "and bound him in bronze shackles to take him to Babylon" (2 Chr 36:6b), one can deduce that, in fact, Jehoiakim was not exiled to Babylon but merely bound and released, as an act intended to frighten. If so, then the latter explanation for the omission of the expression וישכב יהויקים עם אבתיו is invalid.

3. Removal of the Contradictions between Contemporary Reality and the Earlier Text

2.16 1 Sam 31:12–13 relates that the men of Jabesh-Gilead burned the bodies of Saul and his sons:

> and they took the body of Saul and the bodies of his sons from the wall of Beth-shan; they came to Jabesh and burned them there. They took their bones and buried them under the tamarisk tree in Jabesh.

The incineration of bodies is known not to have been customary in Israel.[54] In certain cases, such an act is depicted in the Bible as an unusually severe punishment for sin that merited it (Gen 38:24; Lev 20:14—wickedness; 21:9—fornication by the daughter of a priest; Josh 7:15, 25—partaking of the devoted thing; and perhaps also Isa 30:33).

Under normal circumstances, however, the burning of a body was considered a severe crime, as seems to be understood from Amos's prophecy against Moab (Amos 2:1). This prohibition was perpetuated in Israel, and Tacitus listed it as a characteristic of the Jews: "They bury

---

52. In the Greek translation of 2 Chr 36:8, we find: "And Jehoiakim slept with his fathers, and was buried in the garden of Uzza with his fathers." Here we have a combination of the parallel text in 2 Kgs 24:6a, "And Jehoiakim slept with his fathers," and 2 Kgs 21:18, in the context of Manasseh: "And he was buried in the garden of his house, in the garden of Uzza" (cf. also v. 26). And in fact this verse does not appear in the parallel, 1 Esdras (= Greek Ezra = Vulgate 3 Esdras = 3 Ezra, the Apocryphal Ezra) 1:40–41.

53. See Williamson, *Chronicles*, 414.

54. Burials by fire were the custom, apparently, with the Hittites in Anatolia and northern Syria, as well as in countries bordering on the Aegean Sea. A single case of burial by fire has been uncovered in Azor and is ascribed to settlers of "the sea peoples," in the 12th or 11th century B.C.E.; see Dothan, "Cremation Burial," who also provides bibliography.

the body and do not burn it, and in this they continue the custom of the Egyptians" (*History* 5.5).

Apparently, because of the foreign nature of the custom of incinerating bodies in Israel, because of the fact that such an act was considered criminal by the prophet Amos,[55] and because the ancient sources depicted incineration as a punishment for circumstances of severe transgression, circumstances that did not fit the context of 1 Chronicles 10, in which the intention of the men of Jabesh-Gilead was to perform deeds of kindness and mercy to King Saul, who had treated them well (1 Sam 11:1–11)—because of these things, the Chronicler omitted the words "and burned them there" from the earlier text and wrote (1 Chr 10:12):

> and took away the body of Saul, and the bodies of his sons, and brought them to Jabesh, _____ and buried their bones under the terebinth in Jabesh.[56]

Translators and commentators throughout the generations have attempted to deal with this passage in the book of Samuel, some by correcting the Masoretic Text[57] and others by means of a variety of explanations.[58]

---

55. For this point, see Curtis-Madsen, *Chronicles*, 182.

56. Contrary to Budde (*Samuel*, 192), who believes that here the wording of Chronicles reflects his *Vorlage*. According to Budde, the matter of incinerating bodies in Samuel is a gloss by some late scribe who hated Saul and tried to besmirch his memory. However, without the words "and burned them there," the rest of v. 13, "and took *their bones* and buried," appears strange and incomprehensible—why did the men of Jabesh bury only the bones? What happened to the other parts of the bodies? Indeed, the omission of the words "and burned them there" in Chronicles involves the omission of the exposition in the clause "and buried their bones."

57. Thus, for example, *Tg. Jonathan* emended the text and wrote: "and they burned them up as they burn up the kings there"; and see also Rashi, ad loc. The text, however, reads "and burned them," rather than "and burned for/upon them," which is the wording of the account in Jer 34:5: "they shall make a burning for you"; 2 Chr 16:14: "they made a burning for him" (cf. also 21:19); *b. ʿAbod. Zar.* 11a: "Just as they burn *for* the kings, so they burn *for* the princes . . . there was a case where Rabban Gamaliel the elder died and Onkelos the Proselyte burnt for him seventy talents of flint." Among the more recent commentators, note, for example, Klostermann (*Samuelis–Könige*, 128–29) who proposed amending the text to read: וישפדו להם 'and they stabbed them'. Smith (*Samuel*, 254) properly rejected this emendation. For, were we to accept it, the passage would not become part of the following narrative concerning the mourning customs practiced by the men of Jabesh-gilead, since the episode of the interment of the bones interrupts the sections on mourning customs.

58. For example, R. David Kimḥi proposed: "One may interpret this (as meaning) that they burned the flesh, for it had become corrupt and they did not desire to bury them with the worms, for this was not honorable, and so they burned the flesh and buried the bones." Driver proposed translating the words וישרפו אתם שם 'and anointed them there with resinous' matter ("Burial Custom," 315). In his opinion, the word וישרפו here is to be derived from שרף; thus, they anointed them with seraph.

2.17 In 1 Kgs 10:11–12 an account is given of the importing of a large quantity of sandalwood for Solomon, and the narrator notes: *"No such sandalwood has come or been seen to this day."* There may have been sandalwood trees or trees that the Chronicler identified as sandalwood trees in the land of Judah, and the words of the ancient narrator may have seemed to be contradicting this reality. Accordingly, the Chronicler reworked and shortened the early text to match the reality of his time and place, stating: ולא נראו כהם לפנים בארץ יהודה 'But there were none like this seen before in the land of Judah' (2 Chr 9:10–11).

While, according to the book of Kings, Solomon's era was unique among all generations in the importing of sandalwood, according to the book of Chronicles, sandalwood trees were not seen in Judah before the Solomonic era but were present in the subsequent period.

4. Adjusting the Description in the Early Text to the Chronicler's Mood

2.18 According to the account in 2 Sam 5:6–9, David captured Jerusalem, settled there, reconstructed the city, and changed its name to "City of David." This custom—conquering a city, rebuilding it, and changing its name to that of its leader/conqueror—is familiar from other biblical passages and from documents from the ancient Near East. Thus, for example, the book of Numbers speaks of Sihon, king of the Amorites, who took Heshbon from the first king of Moab and renamed it after himself עיר סיחון or קרית סיחון 'the city of Sihon' (21:26–28). Jair, son of Manasseh, conducted himself in the same way: "he went and took their fortresses[59] and called them Havvoth-jair" (Num 32:41; compare with Deut 3:14). One also thinks of Nobah, who took "Kenath and its fortresses and called it Nobah, after his own name" (Num 32:42). In the Kurkh Monolith Inscription, Shalmaneser III, king of Assyria, describes his conquest of the Aramean kingdom of Bīt Adini (the biblical Beth-Eden; see Amos 1:5; Ezek 27:23; 2 Kgs 19:12 // Isa 37:12) on the banks of the Euphrates, founding a city on the ruins of its center, Til-Barsip, and naming it after himself "Kar Shalmaneser" (853 B.C.E.).[60] On his second campaign (702 B.C.E.), Sennacherib, king of Assyria, captured the city of Elenzaš in the land of Ellipi (in the Zagros Mountain Range), rebuilt it, and changed its name to "Kar Sennacherib."[61] In 676 B.C.E.,

---

59. The meaning of the word חַוֹּתֵיהֶם may be 'their fortresses'; see Gray, *Numbers*, 440. "Their fortresses" is connected with the collective noun "the Amorites" in v. 39. Bergman (= Biran) proposed reading "the villages of Ham" (Gen 14:5) instead of "their fortresses" ("Occupation," 176).

60. See Luckenbill, *ARAB*, vol. 1, §610; Pritchard, *ANET*, 278b.

61. See Luckenbill, *ARAB*, vol. 2, §237.

Esarhaddon, king of Assyria, conquered Sidon and destroyed it. In the vicinity of the ruins of the conquered city, he set up a new city and named it "Kar Esarhaddon."[62] Naming a city after a king glorified his name and victory, eternalized them, and perhaps even denoted his ownership of the site.

The account in 2 Sam 5:9, "David resided in the stronghold *and called it* 'the City of David,'" did not appeal to the Chronicler but not necessarily because the custom discussed above was no longer in use in the later period. While we have no evidence that this custom dated to the Chronicler's own era, the many examples from the subsequent Hellenistic period show that it had never come to an end in the ancient world. Plutarch relates that, when he was still a lad of 16 (340 B.C.E.), Alexander of Macedonia waged war against the tribe of Maids (who lived on the Satrimon River), captured their city, and changed its name to Alexandropolis (Plutarch, *Alexander* 9.1). Even better known is his conquest of the Egyptian village of Rhacotis in the year 332 B.C.E. and its transformation into the harbor town bearing the name of its captor: Alexandria.[63]

It seems that, from the Chronicler's point of view, it was not fitting for King David to name the city of Jerusalem after himself, especially since, according to the account in the previous verse (1 Chr 11:6, "addition"), it was Joab, son of Zeruiah, who first smote the Jebusites, thus leading to the fall of the city. For this reason, he amended the text and wrote: "And David resided in the stronghold;[64] *accordingly, they* [those who did so, not David himself] *called it* 'City of David'" (1 Chr 11:7). In other words, the Chronicler attempted to overcome the syntactical ambiguity of the verb ויקרא in the earlier text, which was not vowel-pointed and could have borne either a personal subject ('a certain person וַיִּקְרָא called it', as in the accepted reading tradition) or an impersonal one ('any person, people קוּרָא called it'). By so doing, the Chronicler presented yet another aspect of David's piety and humility and of the affection that the nation felt for him.

2.19 In 1 Kings 3 we are told of the Lord's revelation to Solomon "in a dream by night" (v. 5a), and the narrator also concludes his narrative with the words: "Solomon awoke, and behold, it was a dream" (v. 15a).

---

62. See Borger, *Asarhaddon*, Prism A, I, p. 48; Luckenbill, *ARAB*, vol. 2, §§527–28; Pritchard, *ANET*, 290b, 291a.

63. See Golan, *Hellenistic World*, 27–28. There are additional examples of this custom's being practiced by Alexander the Great in the east; see Bury-Meiggs, *History of Greece*, 457, 462, 473, 474, 489, 491.

64. Hurvitz believes that the word במצד 'in the stronghold' appears "in an Aramaic grammatical pattern" corresponding to the word במצדה, which is used in 2 Sam 5:9 (*Transition Period*, 59 n. 158).

Divine revelation by means of a dream is legitimate and commonplace in biblical literature (see Gen 20:3; 31:10–13; Deut 13:2, 4, 6; 1 Sam 28:6, 15; Joel 3:1; Job 33:14–18). However, it appears that, since according to Num 12:6–8 prophetic dreams are ranked low in the hierarchy of divine revelation, the account in Kings—that Solomon had had a divine revelation in a dream—was not attractive to the Chronicler; he thus decided to omit the words "in a dream" and "Solomon awoke and, behold, it was a dream" from the earlier text. By means of these omissions, the Chronicler also attempted to prevent his reader from wondering whether Solomon was perhaps unworthy of a higher prophetic level—a thought that would diminish Solomon's personal image.[65] These omissions generate a direct and immediate divine revelation to Solomon,[66] a fact that glorifies him:

1 Kgs 3:5–15a	*2 Chr 1:7–12*
5a. In Gibeon the Lord appeared to Solomon *in a dream* by night	7a. In that night did God appear unto Solomon
5b–14. (The narrative of the prophetic dream at Gibeon)	7b–12. (The narrative of the revelation at Gibeon)
15a. *And Solomon awoke, and* behold, it was a dream.	

2.20 The book of Kings relates that, after the death of Josiah, king of Judah, at Megiddo, "the people of the land took Jehoahaz, the son of Josiah, *and anointed him*, and made him king in his father's stead" (2 Kgs 23:30).[67] In 2 Chr 36:1 the Chronicler omitted the expression "and

---

65. Coggins (*Chronicles*, 148) ascribes these omissions to the influence of Jer 23:25–32, where reservations are given about prophetic dreams. It is reasonable, however, to assume that the Chronicler realized that Jeremiah's words were intended for "*the prophets who prophesy falsely in My name*, saying: I have dreamed, I have dreamed . . . the prophets who prophesy lies and the deceit of their hearts, who plan to cause My people forget My name by their dreams. . . ." Solomon certainly did not fall into this category. Rudolph (*Chronik*, 197) proposed an alternate explanation. In his opinion, the omissions stem from the Chronicler's desire to shorten the length of the text, especially since dreams as a means of revelation do not always work out well.

66. See Curtis-Madsen, *Chronicles*, 316–17; Myers, *II Chronicles*, 6.

67. For a similar intervention on the part of "the people of the land" in the process of anointing a king in Judah, see 2 Kgs 14:21 // 2 Chr 26:1 ("the people of Judah" but in the Greek translation, ὁ λαὸς τῆς γῆς 'the people of the land'); 2 Kgs 21:24 // 2 Chr 33:25. For עם הארץ 'people of the land', see Talmon, "Judaean *Am Haʾaretz*"; Ishida, "People of the Land," 23–38, and the bibliography of earlier works cited there; Reviv, *Society*, 149–56, and see also pp. 31, 160, 163, 164, 175.

anointed him": "the people of the land took Jehoahaz, the son of Josiah, _____ and made him king in his father's stead in Jerusalem."[68]

From the other accession narratives in the books of Samuel–Kings, it seems that the anointing of a king was carried out by a priest and/or by a prophet (or one of the young prophets in training): the prophet Samuel, who served in the temple at Shilo for a number of years (1 Samuel 1–3),[69] anointed Saul as king (1 Sam 9:16; 10:1) and, later, David (1 Sam 16:13);[70] Zadok the priest (and apparently Nathan the prophet as well) anointed Solomon king in his father's stead (1 Kgs 1:34, 45, but compare v. 39);[71] Elijah the prophet was commanded "and when you come, you shall anoint Hazael to be king over Aram; and Jehu, the son of Nimshi, you shall anoint to be king over Israel" (1 Kgs 19:15–16), and in the end, Jehu was anointed to be king over Israel by one of the apprentice prophets whom Elisha the prophet had sent (2 Kgs 9:1–6).[72]

The anointing, which in itself was a sacral deed that dedicated a person to a certain role, was not used exclusively for kings.[73] In the other cases as well, the anointer was a prophet or priest: Moses (the greatest of the prophets) anointed Aaron the priest with the oil of anointing (Exod 29:7, and compare with v. 21; 30:30; Lev 8:12). He also anointed various ritual implements: the Tent of Meeting, the Ark of the Covenant, the table, the candlestick, the altar and all of the other implements in the Tent (Exod 30:22–29; Lev 8:11)—that is, he sanctified them and dedicated them to their function. "The oil of anointing" was in

---

68. This is the wording in the parallel text in 1 Esd 1:32. The Greek translation here adds: καὶ ἔχρισαν αὐτόν 'and anointed him', apparently in accordance with the text in Kings.

69. According to the Chronicler, Samuel was a Levite (1 Chr 6:1–12), and for this, see example 7.21 (pp. 151–153).

70. For the early nature of the tradition in this passage, see Smith, *Samuel*, 143–47. In 2 Sam 2:4 we are told: "And the men of Judah came, and there they anointed David king over the house of Judah"; and in 2 Sam 5:3 we are told: "So all the elders of Israel came . . . and anointed David king over Israel." In these verses the root משח is a general verb of making someone king rather than a verb of anointing with oil; in this regard, see Ben-Barak, "Coronation Ceremony," 44 n. 7, 47 n. 26.

71. See Šanda, *Könige*, 20; Noth, *Könige*, 24. There are, however, some who feel that v. 39, telling only of the anointing of Solomon by Zadok the priest, reflects historical reality, whereas the mention of Nathan alongside Zadok in vv. 34 and 45 is secondary, its purpose being to show that Solomon, too, like Saul and David, was anointed by a prophet. So, for example, Benzinger, *Könige*, 7–9; Jepsen, *BH*, 559, 560. On the other hand, some claim that it is the mention of Zadok the priest that is secondary, the only purpose of which was to ascribe importance to the house of Zadok; see Schoors, "Isaiah," 93.

72. In 2 Chr 22:7 the Chronicler referred to this subject and wrote, "Jehu, son of Nimshi, whom *the Lord anointed.*"

73. See Liver, "Kings, Monarchy," 1100.

the possession of Phinehas, son of Eleazar *the priest*, perhaps an indication that the anointing was the prerogative of a high priest. Indeed, in
1 Kgs 1:39, we are told that the horn of the oil from which Zadok the
priest anointed Solomon was placed "in the tent"—apparently the tent
set up by David for the Ark of the Covenant (2 Sam 6:17).

The Chronicler seems to have deduced from these narratives that the
anointing of a king cannot be performed by simple Israelites, "people of
the land," as related in 2 Kgs 23:30, but only by a priest and/or a prophet
(or one of the prophets in training). Consequently, the expression "and
anointed him" (by a layperson—Jehoahaz) did not suit his way of thinking; he omitted it from the earlier text that lay in front of him.

2.21 The following textual change must be viewed in the same light:
2 Kgs 11:12 relates, "Then he brought out the king's son and put the
crown and insignia on him. They proclaimed him king, *and anointed
him.* They clapped their hands and said, 'Long live the king.'" No explicit subject of the clause "and anointed him" is named here.[74] In any
case, the Chronicler left no room for doubt: he stated explicitly that it
was done by *Jehoiada and his sons*, the priests: "Then they brought out
the king's son, put the crown and insignia on him, and proclaimed him
king. *Jehoiada and his sons anointed him* and said: 'Long live the king'"
(2 Chr 23:11).

2.22 After he failed in his attempt to bring the Ark of the Lord up to
the City of David, David extended the Ark's stay with Obed-edom the
Gittite by three months (1 Chr 13:13–14 // 2 Sam 6:10–11). Obed-edom
seems to have been a man of Philistine origin (from the Philistine city of
Gath; compare Josh 13:3; as was Ittai the Gittite, 2 Sam 15:19), who
lived in the area of the Gibeonites, near Israelite Kiriath-jearim (compare with Josh 9:17). At any rate, in Samuel there is no evidence whatever that his origin was Levite. However, the Chronicler found the idea
of leaving the Ark with a man who was not a Levite (and very likely not
even an Israelite) ideologically faulty—all the more so because the Torah makes no reference to this topic at all. It merely requires *the bearing of* the Ark to be undertaken by the Levites (Num 3:28–31; 4:4–15
[P]; Deut 10:8 [D]).[75] The Chronicler transformed Obed-edom into a

---

74. The MT וימשחהו 'and they anointed him' (plural) is to be preferred to the LXX
καὶ ἔχρισαν αὐτόν 'and he anointed him' (singular); see Montgomery, *Kings*, 425,
against Gray, *Kings*, 571 note f. The translator may have attempted in this way to allude to its having been Jehoiada the priest who anointed Joash king, like the Chronicler's explicit attempt to do so and perhaps under the influence of this attempt; see
the continuation of the discussion.

75. For this, see example 7.20 (pp. 149–151).

Levite, a keeper of the gates of the Ark of the Lord (1 Chr 15:18, 24; 16:38 as well as 26:1–5; 2 Chr 25:24), and also a Levite who played on harps and stringed instruments before the Ark in Jerusalem (1 Chr 15:21; 16:4–5).[76]

According to the Chronicler, Obed-edom thus served in two distinct levitical functions: a gatekeeper and an instrument-player at one and the same time! This presentation of Obed-edom stresses even further the lack of reliability of the Chronicler's artificial descriptions.[77]

5. Verse Precision

There are cases when the Chronicler thought that the early narrator had not been linguistically precise in denoting or describing an event or an object. As a result, he altered the text in order to render the passage more precisely, whether or not this had any significance from a general viewpoint or from the standpoint of content.

A typical example of this sort is found in the historiography of the Hasmonean revolt. 1 Macc 2:28 says of Mattathias: "And he fled with his sons to the hills, and they left all they had in the city (ἐν τῇ πόλει)." Later, in *Ant.* 12.271, Josephus renders the language of the ancient source more precisely, adjusting it to the natural dimensions of the place (the small town Modiʿin), and wrote: "And he left with his sons for the desert, leaving behind all his property in the village (ἐν τῇ κώμῃ)."[78]

2.23 2 Kgs 22:14–16 tells what Hulda the prophetess replied to the messengers who had arrived from Josiah to ask of the Lord regarding "the words of the book" found in the Temple:

Thus says the Lord:
"I will indeed bring disaster on this place and its inhabitants,

---

76. For the view that the transformation of Obed-edom was the intention of the Chronicler, see Curtis-Madsen, *Chronicles*, 215; Segal, *Samuel*, 272–73; Haran, "Priests and Levites," 157. Of a different opinion are Jawitz, *History of Israel*, 2.14; Hoffman, *Decisive Evidence*, 138 note a; Klein, "Priests' and Levites' Cities," 86; Young, *Introduction*, 399. These scholars accept the Chronicler's words as truth and believe that Obed-edom was indeed a Levite from the Levite city of Gath-rimmon (Josh 19:45; 21:24); so did Josephus, *Ant.* 7.83, and R. David Kimḥi in his commentary on 1 Chr 13:13.

77. As opposed to Young (*Introduction*, 399), who believes that in these passages the Chronicler was describing two different persons from the tribe of Levi with the same name, Obed-edom, but with two different occupations: the one in 1 Chr 15:18, 24 was a gatekeeper, and the other, in 1 Chr 15:21, was a musician. However, according to an interpretation of 1 Chr 15:18–24 that is dependent on the literary and historical context of the verses, we are dealing with only one person.

78. See Melam[m]ed, "Josephus and Maccabees I," 124.

all *the words of* the book
that the king of Judah *has read*."

According to this passage, fulfilling "all the words of the book" is equivalent to bringing "disaster on this place and its inhabitants." The
phrase "the words of the book" apparently refers, first and foremost, to
the series of curses in Deut 28:15–68, as well as to 27:15–26; 29:19–28.
Thus, it seems that in 2 Chr 34:24 the Chronicler was more precise in
denoting the details: instead of "all *the words of* the book" used in the
ancient text, he wrote, "all the curses[79] written in the book"[80] (resembling Deut 29:19: "*all the curses written* in this book").

2.24 In Ps 105:6, the phrase "the seed of *Abraham* His servant" is
parallel to the phrase "the sons of *Jacob* His chosen ones." Reference to
the name "Jacob" in parallelism with the name "Abraham" is familiar
from Mic 7:20 and Isa 63:16. However, in order to generate full congru-
ence between the two phrases, the Chronicler replaced "Abraham" in
the earlier text with "Israel," the synonymous equivalent of "Jacob";
thus, "the seed of Israel[81] his servant"[82] / "the sons of *Jacob* his chosen
ones" (1 Chr 16:13). This change also creates harmony with similar
verses in Isaiah, for example, 41:8, "And you, *Israel* my servant / *Jacob*
whom I have chosen" (and see also 45:4); and also approaches the continuation, "He set it up *for Jacob* as law, / *for Israel* an everlasting covenant" (1 Chr 16:17 // Ps 105:10). To this we must add Rudolph's topical
explanation, according to which the Chronicler made this textual correction because "the seed of Abraham" also includes non-Israelites—
Ishmael (Gen 25:1ff.).[83]

---

79. In the LXX (2 Chr 34:24), τοὺς πάντας λόγους 'all the words', apparently to create textual harmonization with the parallel text in Kings.

80. Compare Benzinger, *Chronik*, 131; Rudolph, *Chronik*, 324. McKenzie (*Chronicler*, 166) believes that the aforesaid emendation in Chronicles either reflects the
Chronicler's *Vorlage* or was introduced by a later scribe. There is, however, no evidence in support of his opinion.

81. The Peshiṭta's "Abraham" is secondary, appearing to have resulted from textual harmonization with the verse in Psalms.

82. The Greek translation has παῖδες 'his servants' (plural) like the parallel "his
chosen ones." Some believe that the word בחיריו was written plural by mistake and
that the correct reading is בחירו (singular), like the parallel עבדו 'his servant'. See, for
example, Briggs and Briggs, *Psalms*, 2.344; Ehrlich, *Mikrâ ki-Pheschutô*, 442 (based
on the two MSS of Psalms!).

83. Rudolph, *Chronik*, 120. R. David Kimḥi already interpreted the verse thus:
"for Abraham had other seed, but the seed of Israel is unique in us. And when he said
'the seed of Abraham' he actually meant 'the seed of Israel.'"

Chapter 3
Completions and Additions

1. Textual Completions Based on Other Texts

On occasion, the Chronicler "completed" the text appearing in Samuel–Kings on the basis of a passage or passages elsewhere in the same book or in another book of the Bible. This phenomenon is expressed in the parallel texts of Chronicles in various ways: (1A) the Chronicler may complete a description adduced in connection with a certain hero or event with information gleaned from a description occurring elsewhere in a similar context; (1B) he may add details to a general expression, in accordance with the details he found used with the same expression elsewhere in the Bible; (1C) he may add a name in parallelism with a given name, according to the content of some other biblical passage; (1D) and he may add information to the text based on conclusions that he has drawn from the narrative elsewhere in the book.

A. Completing a Description Adduced in a Certain Context Resembling a Description Adduced Elsewhere in a Similar Context

3.1 2 Sam 23:21 says about Benaiah, son of Jehoiada:

והוא הכה את איש מצרי

אשר (*Qere*) איש: (²איש) מראה¹

וביד המצרי חנית

He killed an Egyptian,
a handsome man,
and the Egyptian had a spear in his hand.

---

1. The correct reading is apparently that of the parallel text in 1 Chr 11:23 (מדה), the word מראה merely being an erroneous spelling of מדה, which it resembles graphically. An איש מדה is a tall man; compare 2 Sam 21:20, איש מדין // 1 Chr 20:6, איש מדה; and see Segal, *Samuel*, 372, 392. Furthermore, the narrator was undoubtedly interested in describing the height and girth of the Egyptian hero in order to stress the bravery and conquest of Benaiah, son of Jehoiada, rather than his good looks or his beauty (such as in the Peshiṭta and the Vulgate: יפה מראה 'of beautiful appearance').

2. Thus, in the LXX[B, L] ἄνδρα and in the parallel text of 1 Chr 11:23 (see below), and this is apparently the original version.

59

In 1 Chr 11:23, the Chronicler expanded his description of the Egyptian on the basis of the description adduced for the Philistine hero Goliath in 1 Sam 17:4, 7:

<table>
<tr><td align="center">1 Sam 17:4, 7</td><td align="center">1 Chr 11:23</td></tr>
<tr><td></td><td align="center" dir="rtl">והוא הכה את האיש המצרי</td></tr>
<tr><td align="center" dir="rtl">ויצא איש הבנים ממחנות פלשתים</td><td></td></tr>
<tr><td align="center" dir="rtl">גלית שמו מגת גבהו שש אמות וזרת³</td><td align="center" dir="rtl">איש מדה חמש באמה</td></tr>
<tr><td align="center" dir="rtl">. . . וחץ⁴ חניתו כמנור ארגים</td><td align="center" dir="rtl">וביד המצרי חנית כמנור ארגים⁵</td></tr>
</table>

And he killed an Egyptian.

There went out from the camp of the Philistines a champion named Goliath, of Gath, whose *height was six cubits* and a span. . . . and the shaft of *his spear was like a weaver's beam.*	a man of great stature, *five cubits high,* and in the Egyptian's hand *was a spear like a weaver's beam.*

In this way, an analogy was generated between the Egyptian hero who was struck down by Benaiah, son of Jehoiada, and the Philistine hero who was struck down by David or Elhanan, thus glorifying the bravery of Benaiah (in addition to the space generously devoted to him in the description of David's heroes in 1 Chr 11:22–25 // 2 Sam 23:20–23).

3.2 In describing the procession that led the Ark from the home of Obed-edom the Gittite to Jerusalem (below: the story of the second ascent), 2 Sam 6:15 relates: "So David and all the house of Israel brought up the Ark of the Lord with shouting and with the sound of the horn." The Chronicler adduced this text in 1 Chr 15:28, adding to it in accordance with a similar narration—that of leading the Ark out of Kiriath-jearim (1 Chr 13:8 // 2 Sam 6:5; below, the story of the first ascent):

<table>
<tr>
<td align="center">2 Sam 6:15</td><td align="center">//</td><td align="center">1 Chr 15:28</td>
<td align="center">1 Chr 13:8</td><td align="center">//</td><td align="center">2 Sam 6:5</td>
</tr>
<tr>
<td align="center" dir="rtl">ודוד וכל בית</td><td></td><td align="center" dir="rtl">וכל</td>
<td align="center" dir="rtl">ודויד וכל</td><td></td><td align="center" dir="rtl">ודוד וכל בית</td>
</tr>
<tr>
<td align="center" dir="rtl">ישראל</td><td></td><td align="center" dir="rtl">ישראל</td>
<td align="center" dir="rtl">ישראל</td><td></td><td align="center" dir="rtl">ישראל</td>
</tr>
</table>

---

3. In LXX^B, L, in 4QSam^a, and in *Ant.* 6.171: ארבע אמות וזרת 'four cubits and a span'; but in the LXX^A, we fine: שש אמות וזרת 'six cubits and a span'.

4. וחץ, according to the *Qere* and *Targum Jonathan*: ועץ; and see 2 Sam 21:19 = 1 Chr 20:5, ועץ חניתו כמנור ארגים 'and the shaft of his spear was like a weaver's beam', as in 2 Sam 23:7, ואיש יגע בהם ימלא ברזל ועץ חנית 'but the man that touches them must be armed with iron and the staff of a spear'. For ח / ע interchanges, see also Gen 10:23 (MT) ערן; LXX חורן; 2 Kgs 20:13 וישמע // Isa 39:2 וישמח.

5. For a discussion of this verse, see also chapter 16 for the LXX version of 2 Sam 23:21.

מעלים את	מעלים את ארון .	משחקים לפני	משחקים לפני ה'
ארון ה'	ברית ה'	האלהים	
בתרועה	בתרועה	בכל עז ובשירים	בכל עצי ברושים[6]
ובקול שופר	ובקול שופר	וכנרות ובנבלים	בכנרות ובנבלים
	ובחצצרות ו<u>במצלתים</u>	ובתפים	ובתפים
	משמעים[7]	<u>ובמצלתים</u> ובחצצרות	ובמנענעים
	<u>בנבלים</u> וכנרות		ובצלצלים[8]

2 Sam 6:15: So David and all the house of Israel brought up the Ark of the Lord with shouting and with the sound of the horn.

1 Chr 15:28: So all Israel brought up the Ark of the Covenant of the Lord with shouting and with the sound of the horn, *trumpets*, and **cymbals** and made loud music with HARPS and *lyres*.

1 Chr 13:8: David and all Israel danced before God with all their might, with songs, *lyres*, HARPS, tambourines, **cymbals**, and *trumpets*.

2 Sam 6:5: David and all the house of Israel danced before the Lord with all manner of instruments made of cypress wood and with *lyres*, HARPS, tambourines, castanets, and paired percussion instruments.

The fact that the text taken from 2 Sam 6:15 was added to according to the reading in 1 Chr 13:8 // 2 Sam 6:5 is also evident from the chiastic structures the Chronicler set up between the lists of musical instruments in 1 Chr 15:28 and 1 Chr 13:8.[9]

In transferring the list of musical instruments from the story of the Ark's first ascent to the story of its second ascent, the Chronicler may have wanted to indicate that the rejoicing and the magnificence of the second ascent were no less pronounced than those of the first.[10]

---

6. "It seems to me that there is a scribal error here, and this ובכל is really בכלי" (Ehrlich, *Mikrâ ki-Pheschutô*, 198). The verse apparently intends to mention all kinds of musical instruments made of cypress wood; see also Segal, *Samuel*, 271. The LXX here reads like the parallel text in Chronicles, בכל עז 'with all their might' (and compare v. 14: ודוד מכרכר בכל עז 'David danced with all his might'), and some scholars prefer this reading (Segal, ibid.; Curtis-Madsen, *Chronicles*, 207). The MT, however, by virtue of its being the *lectio difficilior*, seems to be the more ancient, especially since the context requires musical instruments.

7. For the instruments called מצלתים משמיעים 'cymbals sounding aloud', see Evenari, "Cymbals," 24–25. The attribute משמיעים referring to cymbals appears (five times) only in 1 Chronicles 15–16.

8. Some identify צלצלים (apparently a paired percussion instrument) with מצלתים 'cymbals'; see Evenari, "Cymbals," 25.

9. For this, see in detail chap. 12, "Chiasmus between Parallel Texts" (pp. 232ff.).

10. In the story of the first ascent, the musical instruments are found in the hands of "David and all of Israel" (1 Chr 13:8) while, in the story of the second ascent, the Chronicler has placed them in the hands of musicians of the tribe of Levi (in Samuel,

3.3 In 1 Kgs 5:24–25[10–11], we are informed that in return for the construction lumber supplied by Hiram, king of Tyre, Solomon gave Hiram חטים מכלת לביתו 'wheat as food for his household' and oil. In 2 Chr 2:9, the Chronicler has expanded the list of agricultural products Solomon supplied to Hiram, adding יין 'wine', apparently on the basis of the narrative of the establishment of Zerubabel's Temple in Ezra 3:7. In other words, what took place in the building of the Second Temple had already taken place in the building of the First Temple:[11]

1 Kgs 5:24–25[10–11]	2 Chr 2:9	Ezra 3:7
ויהי חירום נתן לשלמה	והנה לחטבים לכרתי	ויתנו כסף לחצבים
עצי ארזים ועצי ברושים	העצים[12]	ולחרשים
כל חפצו		
ושלמה נתן לחירם . . .	נתתי	
. . . חטים מכלת לביתו	חטים מכות[13] לעבדיך . . .	ומאכל
	ושערים . . .	

in both narratives of the Ark's ascent, the musical instruments are found in the hands of "David and all the house of Israel," 2 Sam 6:5, 15). In 1 Chr 15:16 (an "addition"), the Chronicler tells of the preparations made by David with "the princes of the *Levites* to appoint their kindred the singers *with instruments of music: psalteries and harps and cymbals sounding aloud*—to lift up the voice with joy." He goes on to link each of the musical instruments listed in vv. 16 and 28 with singer-Levites: "So the singers Heman, Asaph, and Ethan with *cymbals* of brass to sound aloud" (v. 19); "and Zechariah and Aziel . . . with *psalteries* set to Alamoth" (v. 20); "and Mattithiah and Eliphelehu . . . with *harps* on the Sheminith, to lead" (v. 21). "And Shebaniah and Joshaphat . . . did blow with the *trumpets* before the Ark of God" (v. 24). It seems that placing the musical instruments in the hands of the singer-Levites is anachronistic, according to the norm in the Chronicler's period, in the days of the Second Temple; and see, for example, Neh 12:27: "And at the dedication of the wall of Jerusalem, they sought the Levites out of all their places to bring them to Jerusalem to perform the dedication and the rejoicing with thanksgiving and with song, with cymbals, psalteries, and harps." This point is added to the Levites' bearing the Ark upon their shoulders, which led, in his opinion, to the success of the second ascent.

11. Williamson, on the basis of the LXX of Kings, wonders whether the Chronicler had a different *Vorlage* here (*Chronicles*, 200). The LXX of Kings, however, mentions neither "wine" nor "barley." The identical amount of oil occurring in the LXX of Kings and in Chronicles is an insufficient basis for such an hypothesis.

12. The phrase לחטבים לכרתי העצים is a hendiadys or a twofold version; compare Deut 19:5: לכרת העץ . . . . לחטב עצים 'to hew wood . . . to cut down the tree'.

13. The word מכות 'beating' does not suit its present context and seems to be a distortion of מכלת 'food', as in Kings. This, indeed, is the reading here of both the Aramaic translation and the Vulgate. The word מכלת is an abbreviated form of מאכלת (see Isa 9:4), derived from מאכל; compare Ezra 3:7: ומאכל 'and food'. The words "Solomon gave Hiram . . . *food for his household*" (v. 25) are a continuation and an answer to Hiram's request: "You will meet my needs by providing *food for my household*" (v. 23). See also 2 Chr 2:14 and the rest of the discussion here.

	... וייין	וּמִשְׁתֶּה 14
שמן כתית	רשמן ...	וְשֶׁמֶן
		לצדנים ולצרים
		להביא עצי ארזים
		מן הלבנון

1 Kgs 5:24–25[10–11]: So Hiram gave Solomon timber of cedar and timber of cypress as much as he desired. And Solomon gave Hiram . . . **wheat as food** for his household . . . beaten **oil**.

2 Chr 2:9: Behold, I will give your servants, the hewers, the cutters of timber, . . . **beaten wheat** . . . , barley . . . , *wine* . . . , and **oil**.

Ezra 3:7: They gave money to the hewers and carpenters and **food**, *banquet*, and **oil** to the Sidonians and Tyrians to bring cedar trees from Lebanon.

The Chronicler repeated the list of products later on as well, in v. 14, although in the opposite order: "Now, therefore, *the wheat, barley, oil, and wine* that my lord has spoken of—let him send it to his servants."

B. Adding Details alongside a General Expression in Light of the Details in Another Occurrence of the Same Expression

3.4 1 Kgs 9:25 tells of Solomon's offering up sacrifices "three times a year" on the altar in the Temple. The expression 'three times a year' here almost certainly refers to the main festivals of Israel—שלוש רגלים (פעמים=)—mentioned in the Pentateuch (Exod 23:14–17; 34:23, 24; Deut 16:16). The Chronicler was not satisfied with this general expression; he thus listed alongside it the names of the festivals as he found them in Deut 16:16:

1 Kgs 9:25	*2 Chr 8:12–13*	*Deut 16:16*
והעלה שלמה	אז 15 העלה שלמה	
	עלות לה׳ על מזבח ה׳	
	אשר בנה לפני האולם	
	ובדבר יום ביום ...	
שלש פעמים בשנה	ולמועדות שלש פעמים בשנה	שלש פעמים בשנה
	בחג המצות	בחג המצות
	ובחג השבעות	ובחג השבעות
	ובחג הסכות	ובחג הסכות

---

14. For the words יין 'wine' / משתה 'banquet', see Isa 5:12: "The harp . . . and *wine are their banquets*"; Dan 1:5: "a portion of the king's food and of the wine *of his banquet*," and see also vv. 8 and 16; similarly, Esth 5:6; 7:2, 7, 8 (משתה יין 'banquet of wine').

15. The word אז 'then' is here a remnant of 1 Kgs 9:24b: אז בנה את המלוא 'then he built Millo'. For this, see example 1.7 (p. 27).

1 Kgs 9:25: **Three times a year** Solomon offered. . . .

2 Chr 8:12–13: Then Solomon offered burnt-offerings to the Lord on the altar of the Lord that he built in front of the porch, according to the requirement of each day . . . and during the appointed seasons, **three times a year**: *the Feast of Unleavened Bread, Feast of Weeks, and Feast of Tabernacles.*

Deut 16:16: **Three times a year** . . . *the Feast of Unleavened Bread, Feast of Weeks, and Feast of Tabernacles.*

The expression "three times a year" along with the details of the festivals, expressed in this form and in these terms, appear in the Bible only in Deut 16:16 and 2 Chr 8:12–13.[16] This would thus indicate the connection between the verse in Chronicles and the verse in Deuteronomy.

C. Adding a Name Parallel to a Place-Name in Light of the Content of Another Biblical Text

3.5 In the narrative of the conquest of Jerusalem (2 Sam 5:6), we read: וילך המלך ואנשיו ירושלם 'the king and his men went to Jerusalem'. The Chronicler adduced this text in 1 Chr 11:4, adding to it according to Judg 19:10 in regard to Jerusalem:

2 Sam 5:6	*1 Chr 11:4*	*Judg 19:10*
וילך המלך ואנשיו	וילך דויד וכל ישראל	ויקם וילך ויבא עד־נכח
ירושלם	**ירושלם היא יבוס**	**יבוס היא ירושלם** [17]
אל היבסי יושב הארץ	ושם היבוסי ישבי הארץ	

2 Sam 5:6: The king and his men went to *Jerusalem* against the Jebusites, the inhabitants of the land.

1 Chr 11:4: David and all Israel went to *Jerusalem, that is Jebus*, and the Jebusites, the inhabitants of the land, were there.

Judg 19:10: He got up, departed, and arrived at *Jebus—that is, Jerusalem.*

---

16. In Exod 23:14–17: שלש רגלים תחג לי בשנה את חג המצות . . . וחג הקציר . . . וחג האסף 'Three times a year you shall hold a feast for me: the Feast of Unleavened Bread . . . and the Feast of Harvest . . . and the Feast of Ingathering'; and in Exod 34:18–24: את חג המצות תשמר . . . וחג השבעת תעשה לך . . . וחג האסיף . . . שלש פעמים בשנה יראה . . . 'The Feast of Unleavened Bread you shall keep . . . and you shall observe the Feast of Weeks . . . and the Feast of Ingathering. . . . Three times a year shall appear . . .' (note also the structure, from the specific to the general, whereas in the verses in the table above the structure is from the general to the specific).

17. Compare with the text further on, in v. 11, and with Josh 18:28 in the LXX, the Peshiṭṭa, and the Vulgate. The wording ירושלם היא יבוס in Chronicles appears in chiastic order in comparison with Judg 19:10: יבוס היא ירושלם.

Thus, we have before us a kind of geographical-historical comment on the early text made by the Chronicler, according to the text in Judg 19:10 and resembling a verse later in the text: וילכד דוד את מצדת ציון היא עיר דוד 'And David took the stronghold of Zion—that is, the City of David' (2 Sam 5:7 // 1 Chr 11:5).[18] For the practice of referring to a city by the name of a kingdom or a nation that inhabited it, compare 2 Chr 25:28, עיר יהודה 'city of Judah'; 1 Sam 15:5, עיר עמלק 'city of Amalek'; Isa 15:1, קיר מואב (1QIsaᵃ: עיר מואב) 'city of Moab'.

3.6 In 2 Sam 6:2 we are told:

ויקם וילך דוד וכל העם אשר אתו מבעלי יהודה להעלות משם את ארון האלהים

David rose and went with all the people that were with him, from Baale-judah, to bring the Ark of God from there.

The Masoretic Text reading מבעלי יהודה and the similar reading in the Septuagint τῶν ἀρχόντων Ἰούδα 'the lords' or 'notables of Judah' are problematic, for the continuation of the verse, להעלות *משם* את ארון האלהים 'to bring the Ark of God *from there*' indicates that what we are looking at is a place-name. The phrase מבעלי יהודה seems to be a distorted form of בעלת יהודה / בעל יהודה (or even of אל בעלת/בעלת or אל בעלה/בעלת, as seems likely from the reading of the *Samuel Scroll* (4QSamᵃ) and from the parallel text in 1 Chr 13:6 (see the continuation of our discussion). Moreover, "even though we find in the Bible בעלי יריחו (Josh 24:11), בעלי שכם (Judg 9;22), בעלי קעילה (1 Sam 23:12), and בעלי הגבעה (Judg 20:5), יבש גלעד (2 Sam 21:12)—all these are towns while Judah is a country; the expression 'the lords of the land' is not to be found, unlike the expression 'the lords of the town' (Judg 9:51)."[19]

In 1 Chr 13:6, the Chronicler introduced an explanatory gloss to the ancient name בעלתה (= 'to Baalah'): בעלתה, אל קרית יערים *אשר ליהודה*. This is apparent from the description of the northern boundary of Judah's inheritance in the book of Joshua, ותאר הגבול בעלה היא קרית יערים (Josh 15:9):[20]

2 Sam 6:2	1 Chr 13:6
ויקם וילך דוד וכל העם אשר אתו	ויעל דויד וכל ישראל
*בעלתה	**בעלתה**, אל קרית יערים אשר ליהודה
להעלות משם את ארון האלהים	להעלות משם את ארון האלהים

18. For the opposite order, see מעיר דוד היא ציון (1 Kgs 8:1 // 2 Chr 5:2).

19. Ehrlich, *Mikrâ ki-Pheschutô*, 197; and see Curtis-Madsen, *Chronicles*, 207; McCarter, *II Samuel*, 162; contrary to Feigin, "Transferring the Ark," 84–85; and Blenkinsopp, "Kiriath-Jearim," 152. For a detailed discussion of this issue, see Kalimi, "Paronomasia," 27–41, esp. pp. 32–33.

20. Compare with קרית בעל היא קרית יערים 'Kiriath-baal—that is, Kiriath-jearim' (Josh 15:60; 18:14).

The writer of 4QSam[a] acted like the Chronicler, perhaps under his influence: בעלה היא קר[ית יערים אשר] ליהודה.[21]

The apparent aim of this explicit identification of בעלה with קרית יערים
was to link the narrative with the earlier one in v. 5 ("addition"),

ויקהל דויד את כל ישראל . . . להביא את ארון האלהים מקרית יערים

So David assembled all Israel together . . . to bring the Ark of God
from Kiriath-jearim,

and perhaps with the narrative in 1 Sam 6:21–7:2 as well, according to
which the people of Kiriath-jearim were those who brought the Ark up
from the field of Joshua of Beth-shemesh, bringing it to the home of Abinadab on the hill in their town. In other words, בעלה is not another place
but merely the ancient name of קרית יערים, where the Ark had been for 20
years, until David took it to Jerusalem, as related further on.[22] 2 Sam
6:2 and 1 Chr 13:6 are thus parallel passages and are not mutually com-
plementary, as Naor believes, for example.[23]

3.7 The Chronicler acts in this fashion with other names as well. For
example, in 1 Chronicles 1 he adduces the genealogical list of the descendants of Shem according to Gen 11:10–26. Upon reaching the tenth
generation, Abram, he adds alongside it the parallel, more common,
name אברם הוא אברהם 'Abram—that is, Abraham' (v. 27), on the basis of
Gen 17:5: ולא יקרא עוד את שמך אברם והיה שמך אברהם 'Neither shall your
name anymore be called Abram, but your name shall be Abraham'.[24]
Similarly we find in 2 Chr 20:2 ("addition"), והנם בחצצון־תמר היא עין גדי
'and behold, they are in Hazazon-Tamar—that is, Ein-gedi', but here it
is not clear what the basis for the identification was.

This feature is well known from other places in late biblical literature; for example, Neh 8:9: נחמיה הוא התרשתא 'And Nehemiah, who was
the Tirshatha'; Esth 2:7: הדסה היא אסתר 'Hadassah, that is Esther'. It appears in the early biblical historiography as well, and see (in addition to
the verses adduced above in example 3.5, p. 64) also: בלע היא צער 'Bela,
which is Zoar' (Gen 14:2, 8); עמק השדים הוא ים המלח 'the Valley of Siddim—
that is, the Dead Sea' (14:3); עמק שוה הוא עמק המלך 'the Valley of Shaveh—

---

21. The Qumran text is adduced by McCarter, *II Samuel*, 162.

22. Yet the identification of Baalah with Kiriath-jearim is not self-evident from a
study of biblical geography. For this, see McCarter, *II Samuel*, 168 and the bibliography that appears there.

23. See Naor, "Solomon and Hiram," 100.

24. And cf. Neh 9:7: אתה הוא ה׳ האלהים אשר בחרת באברם והוצאתו מאור כשדים ושמת שמו
אברהם 'You are the Lord, the God who chose Abram and brought him out of Ur of the
Chaldees and gave him the name of Abraham'. For the meaning of the names and the
possible relationship between them, see Curtis-Madsen, *Chronicles*, 70–71.

that is, the King's Valley' (14:17); עין משפט הוא קדש 'En-mishpat—that is, Kadesh' (14:7); and Judg 1:10, 11.

The feature can be seen in postbiblical literature as well; for example, in Gen 14:18 we are told: ... ומלכי־צדק מלך שלם הוציא לחם ויין 'And Melchizedek, king of Salem, brought forth bread and wine ...'. The compiler of the *Genesis Apocryphon* (1QGenAp) wrote: ירושלים היא שלם ... 'Jerusalem—that is, Salem', apparently on the basis of Ps 76:3: ויהי בשלם סכו / ומעונתו בציון 'His abode has been established in Salem / and His dwelling place in Zion'.[25] Josephus also relates about Agrippa: "[And he] came to the city of Caesarea, which had previously been called Strato's Tower" (*Ant.* 19.343, and see also 14.76).

D. Addition of Information to the Text in Light of Another Part of the Narrative

3.8 In 1 Kgs 5:29–30 there is an account of a number of porters who were quarrying stone in the mountains and were in charge of the building of Solomon's Temple, without denoting their ethnic origin. In contrast, in the parallel text in 2 Chr 2:16–17, the Chronicler added that the laborers were כל האנשים הגירים אשר בארץ־ישראל 'all the aliens that were in the land of Israel':[26]

1 Kgs 5:29–30	2 Chr 2:16–17
ויהי לשלמה	ויספר שלמה
	כל האנשים הגירים אשר בארץ־ישראל
	אחרי הספר אשר ספרם דויד אביו[27]
	וימצאו מאה וחמישים אלף ושלש אלפים
	ושש מאות
שבעים אלף נשא סבל	ויעש מהם שבעים אלף סבל
ושמנים אלף חצב בהר ...	ושמנים אלף חצב בהר
שלשת אלפים ושלש מאות	ושלשת אלפים ושש מאות מנצחים
הרדים בעם העושים במלאכה	להעביד את העם

---

25. For the identification of Salem with Jerusalem, see *Ant.* 1.180; *Targum Onkelos* and *Targum Yerushalmi* (= *Pseudo-Jonathan*) on Gen 14:18; *Gen. Rab.* 43:7; and so on. This identification seems to contradict the Samaritans, who identified שלם with שכם; for this, see Kalimi, "Affiliation of Abraham," 33–58.

26. For the foreigners and aliens mentioned in Chronicles, see Japhet, *Ideology*, 334–51.

27. See 1 Chr 22:2, ויאמר דויד לכנוס את הגרים אשר בארץ־ישראל ויעמד חצבים לחצוב אבני גזית לבנות בית האלהים 'David commanded to gather together the aliens who were in the land of Israel, and he set masons to hew dressed stones to build the House of God'; and for the phrase itself, see also 2 Chr 30:25, הגרים הבאים מארץ־ישראל 'the aliens that came out of the land of Israel'.

Solomon had	Solomon numbered all the aliens that were in the land of Israel, after the census that David his father had taken; and there were found 153,600.
70,000 that bore burdens, and	And he assigned 70,000 of them to bear burdens,
80,000 that were hewers in the mountains . . . 3,300 who oversaw the people that did the work.	80,000 to be hewers in the mountains, and 3,600 overseers to set the people to work.

The Chronicler deduced the foreign origin of the laborers engaged in building the Temple from the narrative concerning the establishment of Solomon's cities of provisions and his cities of chariots and horsemen. There it is said explicitly that the laborers were of the ancient inhabitants of the land, not of the Israelites:

כל העם הנותר מן האמרי החתי הפרזי החוי והיבוסי אשר לא מבני־ישראל המה,
בניהם אשר נתרו אחריהם בארץ אשר לא יכלו בני־שראל להחרימם, ויעלם שלמה
למס־עבד עד היום הזה: ומבני ישראל לא נתן שלמה עבד כי הם אנשי המלחמה
ועבדיו ושריו ושלשיו ושרי רכבו ופרשיו

All of the people who were left of the Amorites, Hittites, Perizzites, Hivites, and Jebusites, who were not of the children of Israel—their descendants who were still left in the land, whom the children of Israel were not able to destroy utterly. From these, Solomon raised a levy of bondservants, as is still the case today. But Solomon made no slaves of the Israelites. They were his soldiers, officers, commanders, and chief officers of his chariots and horsemen. (1 Kgs 9:20–22 ∥ 2 Chr 8:7–9)[28]

2. Completion of an "Ellipsis"

An *ellipsis* is an omission of a word or an informative phrase that is clear from the context.[29] There are several sections in the books of

---

28. The Chronicler omitted the item concerning the drafting of a levy of 30,000 men of all Israel (1 Kgs 5:27–28); for this, see example 2.2 (pp. 39–40).

29. Cf. Gesenius-Kautzsch, *Hebrew Grammar*, §117g/pp. 364–65, and the examples there from throughout the Bible; and Watson, *Hebrew Poetry*, 303–6, and the additional references there. This feature is already mentioned in the *beraitha* of 32 virtues of R. Eliezer, son of R. Yose Ha-Gelilee ("ellipsis"), and see also *b. Sanh.* 93a; R. Abraham ibn Ezra on Deut 20:19: "One may shorten any expression for the sake of brevity, as in חמור לחם [i.e., משא חמור לחם 'an ass laden with bread', 1 Sam 16:20—I.K.]," and similarly in his commentary on Gen 43:20; Exod 4:10 (in the name of R. Judah Halevi); 9:30; 13:15; 14:4; Lev 5:1; R. David Kimḥi on Ps 21:13: "תכונן וכן במיתריך על פני הם 'you shall make ready with your bowstrings against their face'—this is in short, for such is the custom of the Bible where the matter is clearly understood" (for further

Samuel–Kings that are "elliptical." Despite the fact that the brevity adopted by the compilers of these books does no damage to the content and the meaning of these sections, the Chronicler saw fit to complete these elipses according to their contexts, in order to clarify the texts to an even greater degree. For example:

3.9 In the narrative of the conquest of Jerusalem in the book of Samuel, we find: ויאמר לדוד לאמר: לא תבוא הנה 'He said to David: "You shall not come in here"' (2 Sam 5:6). From the syntactical standpoint, the subject of the sentence is obviously missing: who is the person speaking to David? From the context, it seems that the speaker is one of the people in the besieged city—someone who was authorized to speak to the enemy. In 1 Chr 11:5a, the Chronicler has completed the missing item on the assumption that more than one speaker was involved—the defenders of the besieged city:

2 Sam 5:6b	*1 Chr 11:5a*
לדוד ויאמר	ויאמרו *ישבי יבוס* לדויד
לאמר לא תבוא הנה . . .	לא תבוא הנה . . . [30]
He said to David:	The *inhabitants of Jebus* said to David:
"You shall not come in here. . . ."	"You shall not come in here. . . ."

3.10 In the narrative of the heroism of Eleazar, son of Dodo, in 2 Sam 23:9, we read:

ואחרו אלעזר בן דדי (*Qere*) דדו) בן אחחי בשלשה גברים (*Qere*) הגברים)[31]

עם דוד בחרפם בפלשתים נאספו שם למלחמה _____   _____

Next to him was Eleazar, the son of Dodo, the son of an Ahohite, one of the three warriors with David, when they jeopardized their lives against the Philistines who were there gathered together for battle.

---

examples, see Melamed, *Bible Commentators*, 2.838–43). Similarly, Rashi (see Melamed, 1.427–28) and R. Isaiah of Teranni (see Melamed, "Commentary of R. Isaiah," 285–88).

30. The word לאמר does not appear in the LXX of Samuel either, and it may not have appeared in the Chronicler's *Vorlage*. According to Segal, it is repeated in the MT of 2 Sam 5:6 from the following phrase in the verse (Segal, *Samuel*, 260).

31. The letter ה beginning the word גברים was omitted because of haplography with the letter closing the previous word, שלשה. It is also possible that this is a remnant of a "shortened spelling" characteristic of the ancient period of the textual tradition—that is, a single ה served here instead of two consecutive ones. The phenomenon is known from the Lachish ostraca; for example: in ostracon #3, line 8, וכיאמר = וכי יאמר; line 9, חיהוה = חי יהוה. For a transliteration of the ostracon, see Tur-Sinai, *Lachish Ostraca*, 53.

The expression עם דוד בחרפם (v. 9b) is apparently elliptical: the subject and predicate of the sentence are missing. In 1 Chr 11:13a, the Chronicler has completed all that is necessary:

הוא (אלעזר בן דדו) היה עם דויד בפס דמים, והפלשתים נאספו שם למלחמה
He was with David at Pas-dammim when the Philistines were gathered together for battle.

3.11 When David's three warriors had fulfilled his request and had drawn water from the well/pit of Bethlehem, which was under Philistine rule, David realized the jeopardy in which he had placed his heroes and viewed the water as the equivalent of blood, which must not be drunk but spilled on the ground instead.[32] And so he poured out the water to the Lord, saying:

חלילה לי ה׳ [33] מעשתי זאת, הדם האנשים ההלכים בנפשתם?
Be it far from me, O Lord, that I should do this; the blood of men who went at the risk of their lives? (2 Sam 23:15–17)

After the word בנפשותם 'in jeopardy of their lives', one expects to find the word אשתה 'shall I drink', a word nonexistent in the earlier text. The Chronicler completed the missing word and wrote: הדם האנשים האלה אשתה בנפשותם?[34]. Furthermore, he expanded the text while explaining בנפשותם: כי בנפשותם הביאום 'for at the risk of their lives they brought it [the water]' (1 Chr 11:19):

2 Sam 23:17	1 Chr 11:19
ויאמר (דוד) חלילה לי ה׳	ויאמר (דויד) חלילה לי מאלהי
מעשתי זאת	מעשות זאת
הדם האנשים ההלכים בנפשתם	הדם האנשים האלה *אשתה* בנפשותם
	כי בנפשותם הביאום
ולא אבה לשתותם	ולא אבה לשתותם[35]

---

32. See Lev 17:10–14; Deut 12:16, 23–25; 15:23; and see also Gen 9:4.

33. In the Lucianic version of the LXX, in the Peshiṭta, and in *Targum Jonathan*, and in a number of manuscripts of the MT of the Bible: מֶה, as in the parallel text in 1 Chr 11:19: מֵאלֹהי.

34. The passage is completed in a similar fashion in the LXX and the Vulgate of the book of Samuel. McCarter (*II Samuel*, 491) comments correctly: "But if this was the primitive text, it is difficult to see how *'šth* was lost in MT."

35. David's action and statement regarding the water from the well of Bethlehem in the book of Samuel are in a "literary inclusio," beginning and ending with the phrase ולא אבה לשתותם 'and he did not want to drink it' (2 Sam 23:16b, 17b). The Chronicler transferred this "literary inclusio" to his own work: . . . . ולא אבה דויד לשתותם ולא אבה לשתותם (1 Chr 11:18b, 19b), while stressing דויד. It is possible, however, that

And he said: "Be it far from me,	And said: "God forbid that
O Lord, that I should do this;	I should do this; *shall I drink*
the blood of the men who	the blood of these men that
went at the risk of their lives?"	have put their lives in
	jeopardy? *for at the risk of*
	their lives they brought it."
Therefore he would not drink it.	Therefore he would not drink it.

3.12 In response to David's desire to build a temple, the Lord said:

כי לא ישבתי בבית למיום העלתי את בני ישראל ממצרים ועד היום הזה *ואהיה*
מתהלך באהל ובמשכן

For I have not resided in a house since the day that I brought up the
children of Israel out of Egypt, even to this day, *but have been moving
about in a Tent and in a Tabernacle.* (2 Sam 7:6)

The clause ואהיה מתהלך באהל ובמשכן seems to be elliptical, as was already
sensed in the *beraitha* on the 32 virtues: "Elliptical—how is that? ואהיה
מתהלך באהל ובמשכן (2 Sam 7:6)—this should read מאהל אל אהל ואהיה מתהלך
וממשכן אל משכן 'but have been moving from tent to tent and from tabernacle to tabernacle', but the text reads elliptically."[36]

The Chronicler preceded the Tannaim in this understanding of the
verse under discussion and completed it as follows: ואהיה [מתהלך][37] מאהל
אל אהל וממשכן [אל משכן][38] 'but I have [moved] from tent to tent and from
tabernacle [to tabernacle]' (1 Chr 17:5).[39]

The passages considered here can be explained otherwise as well: the
words אהל and משכן are parallels in both biblical and Ugaritic literature;
for example, ויטש *משכן* שלו / *אהל* שכן באדם 'He forsook the *Tabernacle* of

---

the name "David" already existed in Samuel, as it exists in a number of manuscripts
of the MT and in the Lucianic recension of the LXX.

36. See Melamed, "Beraitha of Thirty-Two *Midot*," 43 (= idem, *Bible Commentators*, 2.1070); Zucker, "Solution of Thirty-Two *Midot*," 19.

37. The word מתהלך is to be expected here, given the context and given the continuation בכל אשר התהלכתי 'wherever I walked' (v. 6 // 2 Sam 7:7); similarly, it appears in
the Peshiṭta; and see the Aramaic translation, ad situ. What seems to have occurred
here is a kind of haplography: מתהלך מאהל.

38. The words אל משכן are to be expected here, given the context, and seem probable on the basis of the Aramaic translation. What transpired here may have been a
case of homoioteleuton: וממשכן אל משכן. See Rudolph, *Chronik*, 130; idem, *BHS*, 1492;
Segal, *Samuel*, 277. It is quite possible, however, that here the Chronicler himself
adopted an elliptical style, as R. David Kimḥi posits: "וממשכן—this should be וממשכן
אל משכן, but as he has already said מאהל אל אהל, he relies on the reader's understanding"; see also the commentary attributed to Rashi.

39. For the style of this verse, see 1 Chr 16:20 // Ps 105:13: ויתהלכו מגוי אל גוי ומממלכה
אל עם אחר 'they went about from nation to nation and from one kingdom to another'.

Shiloh, the *Tent* where he lived among human beings' (Ps 78:60), ויכס
המשכן את מלא ה' וכבוד / מועד אהל את הענן 'Then the cloud covered the Tent
of Meeting, and the glory of the Lord filled the *Tabernacle*' (Exod 40:34),
יחנו שם הענן ישכן אשר ובמקום ישראל בני יסעו כן ואחרי האהל מעל הענן העלות ולפי
יחנו המשכן על הענן ישכן אשר ימי כל ... 'Whenever *the cloud was taken up*
from over the Tent, then after that the children of Israel journeyed; and
in the place where the cloud stayed, there the children of Israel encamped ... as long as *the cloud stayed on the Tabernacle*, they remained encamped' (Num 9:17–18), and in Ugaritic literature: *taʾty*
aʾlm laʾhlhm / dr aʾl lmšknthm 'the gods will come into their *tents* / a
generation enters its *tabernacles*'.[40] It is thus possible for the phrase
ובמשכן באהל in 2 Sam 7:6 to be a case of hendiadys.[41] If it is, the Chronicler may have taken the phrase apart and enlarged it in light of the
narrative of the wanderings of the Ark in the Former Prophets.[42]

3.13 The narrative in 2 Sam 24:16 is itself elliptical, for some kind of
informative completion is expected of the reader between the first part
of the verse (16a) and the second part (16b):

16a. לשחתה ירושלם המלאך ידו וישלח[43]

And when the angel stretched out his hand to Jerusalem to destroy
it,

16b. ידך! הרף עתה רב! בעם: המשחית למלאך ויאמר הרעה, אל ה' וינחם
the Lord repented of the evil and said to the angel destroying the
people: "It is enough! Now stay your hand!"

Whereupon the Chronicler completed 1 Chr 21:15 with the words
ה': ראה וכהשחית

---

40. See Gordon, *Ugaritic Textbook*, 195, text 128, III 18–19; the translation follows
Loewenstamm, "Expanded Limb," 116–17. Similarly *tbʿ ktr lʾahlh / hyn tbʿ lmšknth*
'Ktr turned *to his tents* / Hyn turned *to his tabernacles*' (2 Aqht, V 31–33); and see
Cassuto, *Goddess Anath*, 28–29.

41. And see also מועד אהל משכן (Exod 39:32; 40:2, 6, 29—P; 1 Chr 6:17).

42. The LXX Chronicles, "in a tent and in a tabernacle," seems to be an attempt to
create textual harmonization with the early text in Samuel.

43. The order of the words המלאך ידו is problematic. It would be more correct to say
ידו את המלאך. In fact, the word המלאך with the definite article is itself problematic, for
this is the first mention of the angel in the narrative. It is thus reasonable to assume
that the letters ידו ה־ are a distortion of the word יהוה and that in the early version the
verse read ירושלם מלאך יהוה וישלח, as we find in the parallel text of 1 Chr 21:15. See
Budde, *Samuel*, 333; Smith, *Samuel*, 391; Rofé, *Belief in Angels*, 191 n. 17. For other
explanations, see Ehrlich, *Mikrâ ki-Pheschutô*, 260–61 (המלאך being an additional explanation of ידו); Segal, *Samuel*, 401 ("Perhaps our version includes some omission
which told of an angel").

וישלח האלהים מלאך לירושלם להשחיתה
וכהשחית ראה ה'
וינחם על הרעה ויאמר למלאך המשחית: רב! עתה הרף ידך![44]

God sent an angel to Jerusalem to destroy it;
and *as he was about to destroy it, the Lord beheld,*
and He repented of the evil, and said to the destroying angel:
"It is enough; now stay your hand!"

3.14 In 2 Sam 6:6 we are told: וישלח עזה אל ארון האלהים ויאחז בו כי שמטו
הבקר 'Uzzah put forth his hand to the Ark of God and took hold of it; for
the oxen stumbled'. This verse is elliptical and, after the words וישלח עזה,
the reader is expected to add: את ידו.[45] In 1 Chr 13:9 the Chronicler has
completed the text, writing: [46] וישלח עזא *את ידו* לאחז את הארון כי שמטו הבקר
'Uzza put forth *his hand* to hold the Ark, for the oxen stumbled'.

3.15 In 1 Kgs 6:2, the measurements of Solomon's Temple are
adduced: ... רחבו _____ ששים אמה ארכו ועשרים 'sixty cubits long, and
twenty _____ wide'. In describing the breadth of the Temple, the word
אמה 'cubit' is expected—just as it appears in the description of the length
of the building. The Chronicler viewed this passage as elliptical and
completed it, in 2 Chr 3:3: אמות ששים ורחב *אמות עשרים* ... הארך 'the length
... was sixty and its width was twenty'. The translators of the Septuagint, Peshiṭta, and Vulgate of 1 Kgs 6:2 did the same: they added the
word אמה to the ancient text. The assumption that the word under consideration was in the Chronicler's Vorlage but was omitted from the

---

44. Japhet holds a different opinion: "According to the description in Samuel, the
angel does not harm Jerusalem: God changes His mind and stops him just as he
stretches out his hand. But in 1 Chr 2:15 the word וכהשחית (= 'when he was about to
destroy it') has been added, indicating clearly that the process of destruction had already begun when God repented of the evil" (*Ideology*, 140). This opinion leads her to
raise a question: "This change appears most odd: why would the Chronicler wish to
increase the damage described in Samuel?" According to the above explanation, there
is no justification for this question.

45. Something similar can be seen in 2 Sam 22:17 // Ps 18:17: ישלח ממרום יקחני 'He
sent from on high; he took me'. The poet clearly intends to say 'He sent *his hand* from
on high; he took me'; and compare ממרום, פצני והצילני 'דך in some MSS] שלח ידיך 'Stretch
forth your hands from on high, rescue me and deliver me' (Ps 144:7).

46. Like the Chronicler, and perhaps according to his book, the writer of 4QSam[a]
completed the text: [את] וישלח עזא ידו אל ארון ה[אלהים] 'Uzzah put forth his hand to the
Ark of God'. The translators of the LXX did the same: καὶ ἐξέτεινεν Ὀζὰ τὴν χεῖρα
αὐτοῦ ἐπὶ τὴν κιβωτὸν τοῦ θεοῦ, as did Targum Jonathan, the Peshiṭta, and the Vulgate. Nevertheless, it is also possible (as in McCarter, *II Samuel*, 164) that a technical
copyist's error occurred in the book of Samuel, a kind of homoioarcton: וישלח עזה את ידו
אל ארון. If this assumption is correct, the Chronicler did not complete the text under
review in Samuel; instead, he reflects his *Vorlage*.

Masoretic Text of the book of Kings—for unknown reasons—is less likely, if only because this phenomenon is so widespread in Chronicles.[47]

3. Attribution of Names to Unnamed Figures

There are cases in which the Chronicler attributed names to figures that the compilers of the early historical books chose to present anonymously. In the examples adduced below, the Chronicler did not identify the unnamed figures with figures known from other places in the Bible but instead, apparently, gave them names of his own invention. This device is thus the completion of a "lacuna" in the early text in an imaginative manner in order to meet the natural curiosity of a reader who might well ask, for example, what the names of David's other brothers were.

This phenomenon is familiar from other Second Temple period works as well, as in the literature of the period after the destruction of the Temple. For example, the compiler of the book of *Jubilees* provided names for Noah's wife: אמזרה (4:33); for his son's wives: נאלתמאוך, the wife of Ham, אדתנסס, the wife of Japhet, and סדקתלבב, the wife of Shem (7:13–16); the wife of Arpachshad (Gen 10:22): ראסואיה (8:1); the wives of the sons of Jacob: "the name of Reuben's wife, Ada; the name of Simeon's wife, Adiba the Canaanite; the name of Levi's wife, Milka," and so on (34:20); and of the daughter of Pharaoh (Exod 2:15): תרמות (47:5). The name of Micah's mother is not mentioned in Judges 17. The author of *Biblical Antiquities* (Pseudo-Philo) calls her: דדילה (44:1, 2). The "old man" who took the Levite and his concubine into his home (Judg 19:16, 20) is here called בתק, and the Levite himself, בהל (45:2). The Amalekite (young) man is unnamed in 2 Sam 1:1, 5, 6, 13. Pseudo-Philo named him "Edabus, son of Agag, king of the Amalekites" (65:4). In Midrash Psalms 'Shocher-Tov' 7:2 we read: "'There ran a man of Benjamin out of the army, and came to Shiloh. . . .' (1 Sam 4:12), the *man of Benjamin* being Saul."

The "daughter of Pharaoh" (Exod 2:5) is called תרמותיס by Josephus (*Ant.* 2.224).[48] The names of the mothers of Abraham, Haman, and David do not appear in the Bible, but according to the Sages "Abraham's mother, Amatlai, daughter of Karnebo; Haman's mother, Amatlai, daughter of Orabti . . . ; David's mother, Nisbat, daughter of 'Ada'el" (*b. B. Bat.* 91a). Samson's mother appears in the Bible as "the woman" (Judg 13:3, 6, 10). The Sages referred to her as צללפונית[49] and to the "daughter of Pharaoh" as בתיה.[50] *Targum Pseudo-Jonathan* on Gen

---

47. For "ellipsis" in Chronicles, see also below, chap. 20, §1C (pp. 384–385).
48. Apparently on the basis of *Jub* 47:5, and see also below in our discussion.
49. *B. B. Bat.* 91a and *Num. Rab.* 10:5: הצללפוני.
50. *Deut. Rab.* 87:5; *Midrash Proverbs* 31:15; *b. Meg.* 13a; *Pirqe R. El.* chap. 48.

21:21 (ותקח לו אמו אשה מארץ מצרים) 'and his mother took him a wife out of the land of Egypt') lists the names of Ishmael's wives! The wise woman who saved Abel of Beth-Maacah from the attack of Joab (2 Sam 20:16) is identified by *Targum Pseudo-Jonathan* on Gen 46:17 as Asher's daughter, Serah (cf. *Gen. Rab.* 94:6). An "angel of the Lord" in Judg 2:1 was identified with Phinehas (Num 25:7; see *Lev. Rab.* 1:1; *Seder Olam Rabbah* 20).

3.16 Gen 38:2 reports that Judah's wife, the mother of Er, Onan, and Shelah, was the "daughter" of a Canaanite man, "Shua," but her name is not cited in this verse. In 1 Chr 2:3, the Chronicler combined the attribute בת 'daughter' with the proper noun שוע 'Shua', thus creating a name for Judah's wife, Bath-shua. He also changed the masculine adjective הכנעני 'Canaanite' to its feminine form הכנענית 'Canaanitess' and added it to the newly-formed name. However, he may also have been following Gen 38:12, where Judah's wife is already called Bath-shua.

3.17 According to 1 Sam 16:6–13 and 17:12, Jesse had seven sons besides his youngest son, David. Of the seven, the text lists the names of only the first three: אליאב הבכור ומשנהו אבינדב והשלישי שמה 'Eliab the first-born, and next to him Abinadab, and the third Shammah" (17:13, and see 16:6–9), while the names of the other brothers were not handed down to us. However, according to 1 Chr 2:13–15, Jesse had seven sons including David,[51] and the Chronicler lists the names of all seven:

ואישי הוליד את בכרו את אליאב ואבינדב השני ושמעא השלישי נתנאל הרביעי
רַדַּי הַחֲמִישִׁי אֹצֶם הַשִּׁשִּׁי דָּוִיד הַשְּׁבִיעִי

Jesse became the father of his firstborn Eliab, his second Abinadab, his third Shimea, his fourth Nethanel, his fifth Raddai, his sixth Osem, and his seventh David.

The first three names match the names in Samuel, whereas the other names—Nethanel, Raddai, and Osem—are names added to the earlier text by the Chronicler in order to redeem David's brothers from eternal anonymity.[52] The name Raddai is not found anywhere else in the Bible; the name Osem appears only one other time, in 1 Chr 5:25 ("addition"); and the name Nethanel appears another 13 times in the biblical text, 8 times in literature from the Persian period (1 Chr 15:24; 24:6; 2 Chr

---

51. For the various traditions regarding the number of Jesse's sons in 1 Samuel 16–17 and in 1 Chr 2:13–15, see the discussion below, example 18.5 (pp. 365–368) and Kalimi, "Transmission of Tradition," 1–9.

52. See Zakovitch, *Numerical Sequence*, 47. Opposed are Noth (*Chronicler's History*, 52, 151 n. 27); also Braun (*1 Chronicles*, 34), who think that the names of David's brothers were taken from a temple or from royal archives that did not survive.

17:7; 35:9—"additions"; Ezra 10:22; Neh 12:21, 36) and 5 times in the Priestly source of the Pentateuch (Num 1:8; 2:5; 7:18, 23; 10:15).

3.18 In 2 Kgs 11:4, we are informed that in the seventh year Jehoiada summoned the captains of the Carites and the captains of the guards of the House of the Lord and made a covenant with them. The Deuteronomistic historian did not list the names of the captains, and they are not given elsewhere in the Bible. In contrast, the Chronicler lists the names of these 5 captains:

2 Kgs 11:4	2 Chr 23:1
ובשנה השביעית שלח יהוידע	ובשנה השבעית התחזק יהוידע
ויקח את *שרי המאיות* (Qere) המאות:	ותקח את *שרי המאות*
לכרי ולרצים	
	לעזריה בן ירחם
	ולישמעאל בן יהוחנן
	ולעזריהו בן עובד
	ואת מעשיהו בן עדיהו
	ואת אלישפט בן זכרי
ויבא אתם אליו בית ה׳	עמו בברית
ויכרת להם ברית	

In the seventh year, Jehoiada	In the seventh year, Jehoiada
sent and summoned	strengthened himself and took
the captains of hundreds,	*the captains of hundreds,*
of the Carites and of the guard,	
	Azariah son of Jeroham,
	Ishmael son of Jehohanan,
	Azariahu son of Obed,
	Maaseiah son of Adaiahu
	and Elishaphat son of Zichri
and brought them to him in the	into covenant with him.
House of the Lord; and he	
made a covenant with them.	

The form of the name אלישפט is unlike any in the Bible (although the names יהושפט and שפטיה resemble it). Zichri, the name of Elishaphat's father, is apparently a late name. It appears in the Bible 12 times: 9 times in Chronicles (1 Chr 8:19, 23, 27; 9:15; 26:25; 27:16; 2 Chr 17:6; 23:1; 28:7), 2 times in Nehemiah (11:9; 12:17), and once in the Priestly source of the Pentateuch (Exod 6:21). This name as well as the rest of the names are known, first and foremost, as the names of priests and Levites from the genealogical lists in Chronicles: עזריהו occurs in the list of Aaron's sons in 1 Chr 5:40 (and see also vv. 35–37, and 6:21; 9:11); ירחם appears in the list of Levites in 1 Chr 6:12 (as well as in the list of Benjaminites in 1 Chr 8:27; 9:8; and in the list of David's helpers in

1 Chr 12:8); יהוחנן appears among Aaron's sons in 1 Chr 5:35 and among the gatekeepers in 1 Chr 26:3 (and see also Neh 12:22); מעשיהו is mentioned in the list of singers in 1 Chr 15:18, 20 (and see also Jer 21:1: מעשיהו הכהן); עדיהו appears in the list of priests in 1 Chr 9:12 // Neh 11:12 (and also in the list of Benjaminites in 1 Chr 8:22); the name זכרי is mentioned in the lists of Levites in 1 Chr 9:15; 26:25 (and in Exod 6:21 [P] in the list of the sons of Izhar of the tribe of Levi and in Neh 12:17 as the head of a family of priests in the days of Jehoiakim). The name עזריהו appears in our list as the name of 2 captains—the 1st and the 3d. There is a certain resemblance between עזריהו בן ירחם (Azariahu son of Jeroham, above) and עזראל בן ירחם, the prince of the tribe of Dan (1 Chr 27:22), and between עזריהו בן עובד (Azariahu son of Obed, above) and עובד and עזריה (the grandfather and the grandson of the family of Jerahmeel of the tribe of Judah, 1 Chr 2:38), who appear only in Chronicles. Contrary to a number of scholars,[53] I find it difficult to assume that the Chronicler had in front of him an original list of the names of the captains of hundreds in the days of Athaliah. It is more reasonable to view this list as a selection of names of priests and Levites mentioned in earlier lists in the book of Chronicles. The mention of the names of priests and Levites becomes clear in light of the claim that Jehoiada took "the captains of hundreds . . . with him to the house (of the Lord)"[54] (instead of the parallel text in 2 Kgs 11:4a: ויבא אתם אליו בית ה׳ . . . . וישבע אתם בבית ה׳ 'And he brought them to him *in the House of the Lord* . . . and he took an oath with them *in the House of the Lord*'). This fits the Chronicler's understanding, which is expressed further on:

> אל יבוא בית ה׳ כי אם הכהנים והמשרתים ללוים המה יבאו כי קדש המה
> וכל העם ישמרו את משמרת ה׳

But let none come into the House of the Lord, except the priests and those of the Levites who minister. They may come in, for they are holy, but all the people shall keep the instructions of the Lord. (2 Chr 23:6; and see also v. 7)

4. Addition of the Site of Events

In a number of cases in the books of Samuel–Kings, the precise geographical site of the event described was not given. In such cases, the Chronicler saw fit to add a place-name to the earlier text: sometimes the addition of the place-name is based on the mention of that name in a

---

53. Such as Keil, *Chronicles*, 408; Curtis-Madsen, *Chronicles*, 425.

54. Thus, according to the Greek translation: εἰς οἶκον [κυρίου] 'to the House [of the Lord]'. κυρίου appears only in versions A and L and is missing in version B; see also the parallel text in 2 Kgs 11:4a: ויבא אתם אליו בית ה׳ 'And he brought them to him in the House of the Lord'. The MT: בברית is apparently erroneous for לבית.

similar context in another biblical book, and on other occasions the information concerning the location is gleaned from the continuation of the narrative in the given text. However, in at least one case there is no way to determine just how the Chronicler decided on the precise location of the event.

3.19 In the book of Kings, we are told that two of the kings of Judah, Ahaz and Manasseh, passed their sons through fire without being told the precise location of the deed (2 Kgs 16:3; 21:6). From 2 Kgs 23:10 and a number of verses in the book of Jeremiah (7:31; 19:5–6; 32:35), it is clear that the Topheth where boys and girls were passed through / burned in fire[55] was located to the south of Jerusalem, in a valley called גי(א) בן־הנם. Sure enough, the Chronicler deduces from these verses that this was the case with Ahaz and Manasseh as well and adds the name גי(א) בן־הנם to the earlier texts:

2 Kings		2 Chronicles	
	16:3	והוא הקטיר בגיא בן־הנם	28:3
וגם את בנו העביר באש		ויבער את בניו באש	
כתועבות הגוים		כתעבות הגוים	
אשר הוריש ה׳ אתם		אשר הוריש ה׳	
מפני בני־ישראל		מפני בני־ישראל	
והעביר את בנו באש	21:6	והוא העביר את בניו באש	33:6
		בגי בן הנם	

16:3

and made his son pass through the fire, according to the abominations of the heathen, whom the Lord cast out before the children of Israel. 21:6: And he made his son pass through the fire.

28:3 Moreover he offered *in the valley of the son of Hinnom* and burned his children in the fire, according to the abominations of the heathen whom the Lord cast out before the children of Israel. 33:6: He also made his children pass through the fire *in the valley of the son of Hinnom.*

---

55. Some think that no real burning was involved and that the act was only symbolic, involving passing the child between two bonfires or torches in order to dedicate the child to a rite or to purification or as a symbol of sacrifice (like the narrative in *b. Sanh.* 64a); so, for example, Licht, "Molech," 1114; Weinfeld, "Molech Worship," 37–61, 152; Snaith, "Cult of Molech," 123–24. However, Stager has adduced strong archaeological evidence from the excavations in Carthage for the actual burning of children, as related explicitly in classical sources, such as: Diodorus Siculus 20.14.4–7; Plutarch, *Moralia* 171C–D, 175A; and see Stager, "Rite of Child Sacrifice," 1–11; idem, "Phoenician Carthage," 39–49; Mosca, "Child Sacrifice." It seems that the law in Deut 12:31 prohibiting the burning of children leaves no room for doubt that there was actual burning. See also Jer 7:31, and compare 19:5–6; 32:35. Day has come to the identical conclusion (*Molech,* 82–85).

3.20 Hiram, king of Tyre, agreed to Solomon's request to supply him with cedar and cypress trees for the construction of the Temple in Jerusalem. He stated that the trees would be transported from Phoenicia to the land of Israel by sea:

ואני אשימם דברות בים עד *המקום* אשר תשלח אלי ונפצתם שם ואתה תשא

I will make them into rafts to go by sea *to the place* that you indicate. I will have them broken up there for you to take away.

(1 Kgs 5:23[9])[56]

In this passage, no mention is made of the name or the precise location of "the place"—that is, the target port on the coast of the land of Israel where the trees were to be unloaded. In 2 Chr 2:15 the Chronicler has added to the earlier text the name of "the place," על ים יפו 'on the sea at Joppa', apparently in light of Ezra 3:7, which describes the preparations for the building of Zerubabel's Temple:

1 Kgs 5:22–23[8–9]	2 Chr 2:15	Ezra 3:7
אני אעשה את כל חפצך	ואנחנו נכרת עצים	ויתנו כסף לחצבים ולחרשים
בעצי ארזים ובעצי ברושים		ומאכל ומשתה ושמן
עבדי ירדו מן הלבנון ימה	מן הלבנון	לצדנים ולצרים [57]
ואני אשימם דברות בים	ונביאם לך רפסדות	להביא עצי ארזים
עד המקום אשר תשלח אלי	*על ים יפו*	מן הלבנון אל *ים יפוא*
ונפצתם שם ואתה תשא	ואתה תעלה אתם	כרשיון כורש מלך
	ירושלם	פרס עליהם
I will do all your	We will cut	They gave money to
desire concerning	wood	the hewers and
cedar and cypress.	from Lebanon,	carpenters; and food,
My servants will	and we will	banquet, and oil to
bring them down	bring it to you	the Sidonians and
from Lebanon to the sea,	as rafts *by sea*	Tyrians, to bring
and I will make them into	*to Joppa*, and	cedar trees from Lebanon
rafts to go by sea *to the*	you will take	*to the sea, to Joppa*,
place you indicate.	it up to	according to the grant
I will have them	Jerusalem.	that they had from Cyrus,
broken up there for you		king of Persia.
to take away.		

---

56. Arranging for the transfer of trees and/or other building materials from their place of origin to the construction site is known from royal inscriptions and commercial letters from Mesopotamia as well; for this, see Horowitz, *Temple Building*, 191–94.

57. For the introduction of the Sidonians before the Tyrians, see also 1 Chr 22:4: כי הביאו הצידנים והצרים עצי ארזים לרב לדויד 'the Sidonians and Tyrians brought cedar trees in abundance to David'; and similarly, Herodotus 7.98; see also 8.67.

It is reasonable to assume that the addition of the place-name here was
not merely a technical completion produced by matching a narrative in
a similar context in another book of the Bible. It also resulted from the
geographical proximity of the port of Joppa to Jerusalem,[58] closer than
any other port along the shores of the land of Israel.

It is also possible that this emendation reveals a certain degree of
anachronism that reflects the geopolitical reality of the Chronicler's
own day (about 400–375 B.C.E.), for during the Persian period Joppa
was controlled by Sidon, as shown by the following data:

1. The inscription of Eshmun‘azar, king of the Sidonians (dating, apparently, to the middle of the fifth century B.C.E.),[59] relates the following (lines 18–19): שא תרדאה ןגד תצרא יפיו ראד תיא םיכלמ ןדא ןל ןתי
   ןרש דשב 'The Lord of Kings [= the king of Persia] has given us Dor
   and Joppa, the great lands of grain that are in the field of Sharon.'
2. Joppa may be mentioned in a Sidonite context in the guide to sailors known as Pseudo-Scylax, which was compiled between 361
   and 357 B.C.E.[60]
3. The Phoenician devotion inscription to the god ʾsmn (the chief god
   in the Sidonite pantheon)[61] found in the vicinity of Joppa seems to
   testify to Sidonite control of the city.[62]

The Chronicler thus assumed that Joppa was also under the control of
Sidon when Solomon's Temple was being built, and it seemed only natural for the people to unload the wood for construction in a port under
their control.[63]

---

58. This is true, whether ופי םי 'the sea of/at Joppa' is referring to the actual Joppa
shore or to the shore in the vicinity of Joppa—for example, the Yarkon Delta, with a
port near the Yarkon Fortress (Tell el-Kedadi), or at Tell-Qasile, as claimed by Maisler (= Mazar), "Tell Qasile," 46; idem, "Jaffa and the Yarkon Area," 163.

59. For the inscription, see Donner-Röllig, *KAI*, no. 14; Pritchard, *ANET*, 662; for
a comprehensive discussion of the date of the inscription, see Gibson, *Phoenician Inscriptions*, 101–2; Eph‘al, "Syria–Palestine," 143–44, and the references to earlier literature there.

60. Codex Parisinus 443, the only manuscript remaining of Pseudo-Scylax; and see
Stern, *Greek and Latin Authors*, 3.10; for the likelihood of Joppa's being mentioned in
this fragment, see p. 12, and a discussion of the writer and his period on pp. 8–9.

61. See Katzenstein, "Phoenicia," 474.

62. For this inscription, see Conder, "Temple of Joppa," 170–74.

63. During the days of the Chronicler, Joppa was apparently inhabited, as revealed by Stratum II of the Jaffa excavations (the first half of the fourth century
B.C.E.); and see Kaplan, "Excavations," 193; idem, *Archaeology*, 77–78; and see Stern,
Material Culture, 22. It is reasonable to assume that Sidonians settled in the town;
see Eph‘al, "Syria–Palestine," 150.

The addition of the phrase על ים יפו 'by sea to Joppa' in 2 Chr 2:15[64]
expands the analogy between the passage on the preparations for the
construction of the Solomonic Temple and the passage on the preparations for the building of the Temple of Zerubabel.

3.21 2 Kgs 23:29 tells about Pharaoh Necho, king of Egypt, who went
up "against[65] the king of Assyria to the Euphrates River." In 2 Chr 35:20
(and compare 1 Esdr 1:23), the Chronicler has added the precise geographical aim of Pharaoh Necho's campaign on the shores of the Euphrates, "at Carchemish by the Euphrates,"[66] apparently by analogy
with the narrative about the very same king in a similar context—Jer
46:2.[67]

2 Kgs 23:29	*2 Chr 35:20*	*Jer 46:2*
עלה פרעה נכה	עלה נכו	על חיל פרעה נכו
מלך מצרים	מלך מצרים להלחם	מלך מצרים
על מלך אשור		אשר היה
על נהר פרת	בכרכמיש על פרת	*על נהר פרת בכרכמיש*[68]
Pharaoh Necho, king	Necho, king of Egypt,	Concerning the army
of Egypt, went up	went up to fight	of Pharaoh Necho, king
against the king of		of Egypt, which was by
Assyria	*at Carchemish*	the Euphrates River,
by the Euphrates River.	by the Euphrates.	*at Carchemish.* . . .

This analogy came about due to an ignorance of historical facts,[69] for
2 Kgs 24:29 and Jer 46:2 speak of two different battles that occurred at
separate times: Jeremiah speaks of the battle of Carchemish, which
took place in 605 B.C.E., where Pharaoh Necho was soundly defeated by
the Babylonian crown prince, Nebuchadnezzar II, as related in the

---

64. This also applies to the addition of the word "wine" to the list of agricultural
products that Solomon supplied to Hiram in return for the Temple construction materials, according to the text in Ezra 3:7. For this, see above, example 3.3 (pp. 62–63).

65. The word על 'against' appears here instead of אל, such interchanges being common in biblical literature. See, for example, 2 Kgs 22:16: הנני מביא רעה אל המקום הזה
'Behold, I will bring evil upon this place' with a parallel text four verses later (v. 20):
הרעה אשר אני מביא על המקום הזה בכל 'all the evil that I will bring upon this place'; and see
BDB 757a.

66. Contrary to Myers, who believes that the word כרכמיש was left out of Kings
(*II Chronicles*, 215). There is no textual support for Myers's explanation.

67. Cf. Montgomery, *Kings*, 537.

68. The words בכרכמיש על פרת 'at Carchemish by the Euphrates' in 2 Chr 35:20 appear in a sort of chiastic parallelism with the words in Jer 46:2, על נהר פרת בכרכמיש 'by
the Euphrates River, at Carchemish'.

69. For this feature in the book of Chronicles, see below, chap. 20, §3 (pp. 392ff.).

Babylonian Chronicles of that year and in the Bible;[70] whereas 2 Kgs
23:29 (the confrontation at Megiddo) concerns the events of 609 B.C.E.—
the Assyrian-Egyptian attack on the Babylonian expeditionary force at
Haran, reported in the Babylonian Chronicles of the year 609.[71]

Now, from the discovery of the seal ring belonging to Psamtik I, father of Necho II, in the excavations of Carchemish (House D),[72] one may
conclude that the Egyptians had been in Carchemish long before Necho
came to power (610 B.C.E.).[73] It would be more reasonable, however, to
assume that the Chronicler completed the text of Kings on the basis of
Jer 46:2, rather than on the basis of earlier information to which he had
access.[74] Also the language of 2 Chr 35:20, "Necho king of Egypt went
up to fight at Carchemish," cannot be reconciled with the Babylonian
Chronicles from the year 609, which say that the Egyptian-Assyrian
attack on the Babylonian expeditionary force took place *in Haran*. Furthermore, the analogy of 2 Kgs 23:28 with Jer 46:2 was apparently what
led the Chronicler to omit the words על מלך אשור 'to the king of Assyria'
in Kings and to add the word להלחם 'to fight' which does not appear in
the earlier text. This means that while, according to the book of Kings,
Pharaoh Necho joined the king of Assyria near the Euphrates for an un-
defined purpose, in the book of Chronicles (as a result of the aforesaid
analogy) the Chronicler represents Necho as having gone up *to fight* at
Carchemish near the Euphrates River. This is just like Jeremiah 46,
which states that Necho went up *to fight* at Carchemish near the Euphrates River. The Chronicler did not bother to note the name of the enemy against whom Necho fought, because the analogy makes it clear
that it was Babylon. "The king of Assyria" was not mentioned here, just
as he was not mentioned in Jeremiah 46.

3.22 In the narrative of the building of the Temple in 1 Kgs 5:15–
9:25, there is no mention of the precise location of the site of Solomon's
Temple. The biblical scribe apparently wrote in the same style as the
Mesopotamian (especially the Assyrian) and Northwest Semitic construction narratives, to which the thematic structure of 1 Kgs 5:15–9:25
is integrally related. Furthermore, it is probable that the precise location of temples under construction or already standing was so well

---

70. See Wiseman, *Chronicles of Chaldean*, 66–69 (B.M. 21946, obv. 1–8); see also
pp. 23–28, 46; Grayson, *ABC*, 99. In Jer 46:2 the event is dated, truly enough, to the
fourth year of the reign of Jehoiakim, son of Josiah, king of Judah (ca. 605 B.C.E.).

71. See Wiseman, *Chronicles of Chaldean*, 62–65 (B.M. 21906, rev. 66–78); see
also pp. 18–20, 45; Grayson, *ABC*, 95–96.

72. Regarding this discovery, see Woolley, *Carchemish*, plate 26c, no. 8.

73. This may be what should be deduced from the Babylonian Chronicles from the
year 610; see Malamat, "Historical Background," 236.

74. Against Williamson, *Chronicles*, 410.

known to the public that it was deemed unnecessary to note it explicitly.[75] However, in the narrative of the building of the Temple in Chronicles, the Chronicler has noted the precise location of the Temple site
with maximum detail (2 Chr 3:1):

ויחל שלמה לבנות את בית ה׳
בירושלם
בהר המוריה, אשר נראה [ה׳][76] לדויד אביהו
אשר הכין במקום דויד בגורן ארנן היבוסי

Then Solomon began to build the House of the Lord
at Jerusalem
on Mount Moriah, where [the Lord] appeared to David his father,
for which provision had been made in the Place of David,
on the threshing floor of Ornan the Jebusite.[77]

The fact that Solomon's Temple had been erected on the site of the
Akedah, the binding of Isaac, the Chronicler deduces from the verses in
Gen 22:14b, altering the name מֹרִיָה from the name of the land (Gen 22:2)
to the name of the mountain. This site was also chosen by the Lord for
the establishment of David's altar, on the threshing floor of Araunah/
Ornan the Jebusite, and in 1 Chr 22:1 there is clear indication that the
site of the threshing floor is also the site of the Temple.[78]

Mentioning the precise site of the Temple is natural in a narrative
specifying its construction, the date of its erection (given three times:
once according to the number of years after the exodus from Egypt
[1 Kgs 6:1a] and twice according to the number of years of Solomon's
reign [6:1b, 37]), its measurements, the construction materials needed
for its erection, its vessels, and so forth. The Chronicler thus felt the
lack of information specifying the site of the Temple in the earlier text
of Kings and saw fit to supply it. It is possible that the references to the
story of the Akeda and to the story of Araunah's threshing floor were intended to ascribe a special sanctity to the Temple *of the Chronicler's
own time*—the Temple of Zerubabel, which could not compare with Solomon's Temple in its dimensions, its wealth, and its ritual vessels.[79] It is
also possible that this verse covertly reflects the dispute with the Samaritan holy site on Mount Gerizim, which they claimed was the place
where Abraham bound his son, Isaac.[80]

---

75. For this topic, see in detail Kalimi, "Land/Mount Moriah," 9–32.

76. The context here demands the addition of the word "the Lord." The Greek version has κύριος here, and see also the Aramaic version.

77. The translation here follows the LXX, Vulgate, and Peshiṭta, rather than the
confused Masoretic Text.

78. See Kalimi, "Land/Mount Moriah," 9–15, 23–25.

79. See ibid., 25–31.

80. See Kalimi, "Affiliation of Abraham," 33–58.

3.23 1 Kgs 22:2 reads וירד יהושפט מלך יהודה אל מלך ישראל 'Jehoshaphat king of Judah came down to the king of Israel' but does not reveal just where the king of Israel was at the time. In 2 Chr 18:2, the Chronicler has added the name שמרון 'Samaria' to the ancient text: וירד [יהושפט] לקץ שנים אל אחאב לשמרון 'And after a lapse of years [Jehoshaphat] went down to Ahab *in Samaria*'. The information that Ahab was at the time in Samaria was undoubtedly drawn from the continuation of the text: ומלך ישראל ויהושפט מלך יהודה ישבים איש על כסאו מלבשים בגדים בגרן פתח שער שמרון 'Now the king of Israel and Jehoshaphat, king of Judah, sat each on his throne, arrayed in their robes, on a threshing floor at the entrance of the gate *of Samaria*' (1 Kgs 22:10 // 2 Chr 18:9).[81]

3.24 2 Sam 10:6 speaks of the Ammonites who hired Aramean armies to assist them, but no reference is made to the place where these armies encamped when they reached the land of the Ammonites. In 1 Chr 19:7 the Chronicler has noted the place where they encamped: ויבאו ויחנו לפני מידבא 'They came and encamped near Medeba'. It is difficult to determine what the Chronicler's source was for the site of the Aramean encampment. At any rate, Medeba is located in the heart of the plateau bearing its name, in the land of Moab[82]—that is, far to the south of the land of the Ammonites. It is doubtful whether the Aramean armies passed by Rabbat-Ammon and continued south to Medeba,[83] though it is not completely impossible, if Yadin's hypothesis is accepted. Yadin regarded this information in Chronicles to be reliable information and posited that the Aramean armies did indeed go south as far as Medeba in order to surprise David's army, which was headed for Rabbat-Ammon from the south, along the road that passes through Heshbon.[84]

---

81. For the location of the threshing floor at the entrance to the city, see Jer 15:7: ואזרם במזרה בשערי הארץ 'And I fan them with a fan in the gates of the land [= 'city'— I.K.]'.

82. According to Num 21:30, it was one of the Moabite cities captured by Sihon. Medeba and its plateau was included in the territory assigned to the tribe of Reuben (Josh 13:16; and compare Joshua 9; Num 33:3).

83. For this reason, apparently, some scholars emend the text of Chronicles and read: מי רבה 'the waters of Rabbah' (cf. 2 Sam 12:27); see, for example, Rothstein-Hänel, *Chronik*, 351–52; Rudolph, *Chronik*, 137; as well as in his marginal notes to this verse, *BHS*, 1495.

84. See Yadin, "Strategy," 347, 349–50.

Chapter 4
Omissions

1. Omission of Secondary Information

The Chronicler strove to omit from the earlier text any information extraneous to the direct narration of the history of the Israelite nation during the period of the monarchy, for example, he omitted the names of foreign rulers' relatives (father, sons, and so on) or gods; the names and/or titles of foreign rulers or princes who had headed a military-diplomatic campaign or mission against the kingdom of Judah; historical information found incidentally in the book of Kings, in a context relevant to the history of foreign kingdoms in the ancient Near East but lacking any direct relevance to the history of the kingdom of Judah. The Chronicler also omitted information secondary to the central descriptive theme in a given literary-historiographic unit. These omissions narrow the scope of the text and avoid tiring the reader with information unnecessary to the main sequence of the report on the history of Israel and/or of the literary unit.

A. Omission of the Names of Foreign Rulers' Relatives or Gods

4.1 The expression בֶּן רְחֹב in 2 Sam 8:3 (and see also v. 12) may denote either Hadadezer's familial origins, that is, his father's name,[1] or his country of origin, that is, that he was from אֲרַם בֵּית רְחוֹב 'Aram Beth-rehob' (see 2 Sam 10:6).[2] Either way, the Chronicler viewed this expression as secondary information and dropped it from the earlier text:

2 Sam 8:3	1 Chr 18:3
ויך דוד את הדדעזר	ויך דויד את הדרעזר[3]
בן רחב מלך צובה	מלך צובה חמתה
בלכתו להשיב ידו בנהר	בלכתו להציב ידו בנהר פרת

---

1. The word רחוב as a proper noun appears in Neh 10:12 as well, and perhaps in Shalmaneser III's monolith-inscription from Kurkh, which lists the allies he fought with at Karkar (853 B.C.E.): "[. . .],000 infantrymen of *Ba'sa mār Ruḫubi* KUR *Amanā*" (= 'Ba'sa, son of Reḫob, from Taurus Ammanus' / or: 'the Ammonite').

2. For this and its possible conclusions, see Malamat, "Foreign Policies," 197; Pitard, *Ancient Damascus*, 90.

3. The name Hadarezer here and in vv. 5, 7–10; 19:16, 19, as well as in the LXX of Samuel ('Αδρααζαρ) is a mistaken form of the name הדדעזר as it occurs in the Masoretic text of Samuel and in 1 Kgs 11:23; for this, see above, p. 16.

David struck down	David struck down
Hadadezer,	Hadarezer,
the son of Rehob, king of Zobah,	king of Zobah, at Hamath
as he went to establish his	as he went to establish
dominion at the River.	his dominion at the Euphrates River.

It is possible, however, that the expression under discussion was not merely "secondary information" but actually "embarrassing information": if רחב is interpreted as the name of a land, the Chronicler may have found it difficult to explain how Hadadezer was both king of Zobah and a native of the land of Rehob at the same time.

4.2 In 1 Kgs 15:18 the names of both the father and the grandfather of Ben-hadad, king of Aram, are given.[4] The Chronicler omitted these names, since they were secondary to the rest of the narrative, in particular, and to the description of the history of Israel, in general:

1 Kgs 15:18	*2 Chr 16:2*
וישלח המלך אסא	וישלח
אל בן־הדד	אל בן־הדד
בן טברמן	
בן חזיון [5]	
מלך ארם	מלך ארם
היושב בדמשק	היושב בדרמשק[6]

---

4. This was Ben-hadad I, who came to the throne ca. 900 B.C.E.

5. Regarding the identification of חזיון (1 Kgs 15:18) with רזון (1 Kgs 11:23), see Pitard, *Ancient Damascus*, 100–104, and the review of previous literature on this subject adduced there. Albright ("Votive Stele," 25–26) proposed this reading of the Aramaic stele dedicated to Melqart, found in 1939 at Breidj (some 7 km north of Aleppo): בר הדד בר טבר[מ]ן בֹּר [חז]יֹן מלך ארם 'Bar-Hadad, son of Tabri[mm]on, son of [Ḥez]ion, king of Aram' (lines 1–3). It is doubtful that this proposal, accepted by a number of scholars (for example, Unger, *Israel and the Arameans*, 56–60; Gibson, *Textbook*, 2.1–4; F. Rosenthal, in Pritchard, *ANET*, 655) reflects the truth. In fact, it is merely a completion of the lines on the basis of the genealogy here in 1 Kgs 15:18. Since Albright's proposal, other proposed readings have been suggested. See the review in Pitard, *Ancient Damascus*, 139–41. Pitard has recently reexamined the stele and reads: בר הדד בר עתרהמך מלך ארם. He claims that there is no connection whatever between this stele and the kingdom of Aram Damascus; see pp. 141–44, and also pp. 100, 111, 155.

6. The form דרמשק appears 6 times in the Hebrew Bible, all of them in Chronicles: 1 Chr 18:5, 6; 2 Chr 16:2; 24:23; 28:5, 23. Unlike the several scholars who think that דרמשק is the ancient form, made up of דר and משק (that is, the site of Dar's trade and economy; cf., e.g., Halevy, "Notes geographiques," 280–83), or of דר and משקה (that is, a land located in a region rich in water; cf. Haupt, "Midian und Sinai," 528); and unlike Ashbel ("דמשק or דרמשק," 108): "In the days of David in the 10th century (B.C.E.) and subsequently, in those of Asa, it was customary to call the city by the

Then King Asa sent them	And Asa sent them
to Ben-hadad,	to Ben-hadad,
son of Tabrimmon,	
son of Ḥezion,	
king of Aram,	king of Aram,
who lived in Damascus.	who lived in Damascus.

4.3 2 Kgs 19:37 (= Isa 37:38) describes the assassination of Sennacherib, king of Assyria, by his sons אדרמלך and שראצר 'Adrammelech and Sharezer', while he was worshiping in the בית נסרך אלהיו 'house of Nisroch his god'. In 2 Chr 32:21 the Chronicler has omitted the name of Sennacherib's god and the names of his sons, noting in brief only the main part of the narrative in the early text:

2 Kgs 19:37	*2 Chr 32:21*
ויהי הוא משתחוה	ויבא
בית נסרך אלהיו	בית אלהיו
ואדרמלך ושראצר	
בניו	ומיציאו (Qere: ומיציאי) מעיו
הכהו בחרב[7]	שם הפילהו בחרב
It came to pass, as he	When he had come into
was worshiping in the house	the house of his god,
of *Nisroch*, his god, that	those who had come forth of his
Adrammelech and Sharezer,	own bowels
his sons,	cut him down there
smote him with the sword.	with the sword.

The Chronicler appears to have viewed these names as information secondary to the description of the history of Hezekiah's period. In contrast, in 1 Chronicles 3, he supplied Jesse's anonymous sons with names![8]

B. Omission of a Foreign Ruler's Name and/or Title

4.4 2 Kgs 12:18–19 recounts the campaign of Hazael, king of Aram, in the land of Israel. The name of the king heading this campaign is

name printed in Chronicles"—I think that it is probable that the name דרמשק is a late form of the name דמשק, as shown by Kutscher, *Language*, 3–4, 102; and see also Hurvitz, *Transition Period*, 17–18; Pitard, *Ancient Damascus*, 9–10. This form was used in the Chronicler's days (ca. 400–375 B.C.E.) but not in the 13th century B.C.E. by the Aramean settlers in the area, as claimed by Kraeling, *Aram and Israel*, 47.

7. Parpola ("Murderer of Sennacherib," 171–82) considers the name אדרמלך an erroneous form of the name Arda-Mulišša/Arad-Ninlil, who is mentioned in a Neo-Assyrian letter (see Harper, *ABL*, part 11, no. 1091) and was apparently the second son and assassin of Sennacherib. The word בניו 'his sons' is *Qere* rather than *Kethiv*, but in a number of manuscripts of the Masoretic Text and the parallel text in Isa 37:38 it is *Kethiv*.

8. For details, see example 3.17 above (pp. 75–76).

mentioned three times in an episode taking no more than two verses: twice in the form חזאל מלך ארם 'Hazael, king of Aram' (vv. 18a, 19) and once in the form חזאל 'Hazael', without any title (v. 18b). In 2 Chr 24:23–24, the Chronicler reworked this episode in accordance with his belief in the concept of divine reward and judgment,[9] while omitting the name and title of the man heading the campaign:

2 Kgs 12:18–19	2 Chr 24:23–24
אז יעלה *חזאל מלך ארם* . . .	ויהי לתקופת השנה עלה
וישם *חזאל* פניו לעלות	עליו *חיל ארם* ויבאו אל יהודה
על ירושלם [10]	וירושלם
ויקח יהואש מלך יהודה את כל	וישחיתו את כל שרי העם מעם וכל
הקדשים . . . *וישלח לחזאל מלך ארם*	שללם . . . ואת יואש עשו שפטים
Then *Hazael, king of Aram*, went	It came to pass, at the end of
up . . . and *Hazael* set his face	the year, that *the army of*
to go up to Jerusalem. And	*the Arameans* came up against
Jehoash king of Judah took all	him. They came to Judah
the sacred things . . . and sent	and Jerusalem and destroyed
them to *Hazael, king of Aram.*	all their officials and sent
	all their spoil. . . . Thus, they
	executed judgment on Joash.

From the Chronicler's point of view, it makes no difference who actually headed the "army of the Arameans" that went up against Joash. This information is secondary to the description of the history of the kingdom of Judah. What is important is the fact that the "army of the Arameans" actually did go and served as מטה זעם 'a staff of wrath' in the hand of God to punish sinful groups in Judah.

4.5 In 2 Kgs 18:17, the titles of the three Assyrian ministers sent by Sennacherib, king of Assyria, to Hezekiah are detailed. The Chronicler omitted these adjectival titles, using a single word instead, עבדיו 'his servants':

2 Kgs 18:17	2 Chr 32:9
וישלח מלך אשור	שלח סנחריב מלך אשור
את תרתן	
ואת רב־סריס	*עבדיו* . . .
ואת רב־שקה	
אל המלך חזקיהו	על חזקיהו מלך יהודה

---

9. For this, see example 1.9 (pp. 29–32) and the relevant bibliography adduced there.

10. For the formula וישם פלוני פניו ל 'And X set his face toward', a formula used to denote the direction of the traveler's journey, see: וישם (יעקב) את פניו הר הגלעד (Gen 31:21); and, in a borrowed sense: ויתן יהושפט את פניו לדרוש לה' (2 Chr 20:3).

The king of Assyria sent	Sennacherib, king of Assyria, sent
the Tartan,	*his servants . . .*
the Rabsaris,	
and the Rabshakeh . . .	
to King Hezekiah.	to Hezekiah, king of Judah.

This omission avoids tiring the reader with unnecessary information about the main sequence of the narrative,[11] especially since the original significance of these titles, or at least the first two of them, apparently puzzled the Chronicler, just as they also puzzled interpreters and investigators up until the discovery of the Assyrian documents in the last century.[12]

C. Omission of Information concerning the History of Foreign Kingdoms

4.6 2 Kgs 12:18–19 tells about Hazael's campaign against the land of Israel. According to this source, during his campaign the king of Aram fought the town of Gath and captured it and then decided to go up against Jerusalem as well. The "Gath" mentioned here was apparently the Gath in the northern part of the inland plain, which was at this time "an important town in the state of Ashdod, near where one branch of 'the sea road' crossed the road leading eastwards to the mountainous district and to Jerusalem."[13] The Chronicler omitted the battle and conquest of Gath, apparently because it was information extraneous to the history of the kingdom of Judah:

---

11. It was for this reason, apparently, that the names were omitted in the parallel text in Isa 30:21 as well, except for that of Rabshakeh, whose voice is heard later on in the narrative (Isa 36:4, 11, 12 // 2 Kgs 18:19, 26, 27). Indeed, in the second narrative (2 Kgs 19:9b–35 = Isa 37:9b–36) the narrator does not mention the names of the emissaries of the king of Assyria; he prefers to use the term מלאכים 'emissaries' (2 Kgs 19:9b = Isa 37:9b), as may be seen, for example, in the narrative about "the servants of David," who were sent to comfort Hanun, king of the Ammonites (2 Sam 10:1–5 // 1 Chr 19:1–5), without mentioning either their names or their titles.

12. This is true, for example, for Josephus: "he left behind his general Rapsakēs . . . and also two other commanding officers. . . . The *names* of these men were Tharata and Aracharis" (*Ant.* 10.4). It has now become clear that these names are actually *titles* of Assyrian nobles: ^{lú}*ta/urtannu* = the Assyrian general (this title is mentioned in Isa 20:1 as well: אשדודה [תורתן 1QIsaª] :בשנת בוא תרתן 1QIsaª] 'In the year that Tartan [1QIsaª: Turtan] came to Ashdod'; see Ephʿal, "Tartan," 946–48). The word רב־סריס = *rab ša rēši* (perhaps the commander of the king's bodyguard, also mentioned as the title of one of the ministers of Nebuchadnezzar, king of Babylon, in Jer 39:3, 13; and see also Dan 1:3); see Fenton, "Saris, Rab-Saris," 1126–27. *Rab-šāqê* = the chief butler, who enjoyed a prominent position in the royal court; see Tadmor, "Rabshakeh," 323–25.

13. See Mazar, "Gath and Gittites," 105.

2 Kgs 12:18–19	*2 Chr 24:23–25a*
אז יעלה חזאל מלך ארם	ויהי לתקופת השנה עלה
וילחם על גת וילכדה	
וישם חזאל פניו לעלות	עליו (על יואש) חיל ארם
על ירושלם	ויבאו אל יהודה וירושלם
Then Hazael, king of Aram,	It came to pass, at the end of
went up,	the year,
fought against Gath, and took it;	
and Hazael set his face to go	that the army of Aram came up
against Jerusalem.	against him [Joash]. They came
	to Judah and Jerusalem.

According to the Chronicler's historiography, the Aramean campaign
was aimed only at the kingdom of Judah, and the reader is not informed
about whether the campaign harmed any other kingdoms in the land of
Israel or not.[14]

4.7 2 Kgs 19:37 (= Isa 37:38) describes the assassination of Sennacherib by his sons: והמה נמלטו ארץ אררט וימלך אסר־חדן בנו תחתיו 'they escaped
into the land of Ararat. Esarhaddon, his son, reigned in his stead'.[15] The
Chronicler omitted this information from his work, apparently because
he viewed it as extraneous to his description of the life of Hezekiah, in
particular, and of the history of Israel during the period of the kingdom,
in general. A reader of Chronicles thus does not know the names of Sennacherib's assassins, their fate, or the successor to the throne.

4.8 2 Kgs 23:29 tells about Pharaoh Necho, king of Egypt, who went
על מלך אשור על נהר פרת 'toward the king of Assyria* at the Euphrates
River'. In the parallel text, 2 Chr 35:20, the Chronicler omitted the
words מלך אשור על, that is, the political-military aim of Necho's campaign—joining up with the king of Assyria, Ashur-uballit, in order to assist him in his war against Nabopolassar, king of Babylon, as indicated
by extrabiblical sources.[16] He apparently considered this information
extraneous to his narrative of the history of Israel.

4.9 The book of Kings relates that Pharaoh Necho II (610–595 B.C.E.)
removed Jehoahaz, king of Judah, from his throne, installing Jehoiakim

---

14. For a discussion of these texts from another viewpoint, see above, example 4.4
(pp. 87–88), and below, example 9.1 (pp. 187–188).

15. For this affair, its historical background, and the identification of the assassin
and his motives, see Parpola, "Murderer of Sennacherib," 171–82.

16. B.M. 21901, rev. 61–71, and see Wiseman, *Chronicles of Chaldean*, 62–63;
Grayson, *ABC*, 95–96; Pritchard, *ANET*, 305; as well as Josephus, *Ant.* 10.74.

in his stead (2 Kgs 23:31–34). After describing the history of Jehoiakim's kingdom (2 Kgs 23:36–24:6), the author of the book noted (24:7):

ולא הוסיף עוד מלך מצרים לצאת מארצו
כי לקח מלך בבל מנחל מצרים עד נהר פרת
כל אשר היתה למלך מצרים

The king of Egypt did not leave his country anymore,
for the king of Babylon had taken—from the Wadi of Egypt to
the River Euphrates—all that pertained to the king of Egypt.

This verse apparently refers to the period following the defeat of Pharaoh Necho at the battle of Carchemish in 605 B.C.E. by the Babylonian
crown prince, Nebuchadnezzar II.[17] In 2 Chr 36:3–8, the Chronicler recounted (with slight emendations) that the king of Egypt removed Jehoahaz, king of Judah, from his throne and crowned Jehoiakim instead
of him. He omitted, however, the note about the Egyptian king as told in
2 Kgs 24:7, probably because he considered this description extraneous
to the history of the Judean kingdom.

*D. Omission of Information Secondary to the
   Main Sequence of the Narrative*

4.10 In 1 Chronicles 21, the Chronicler omitted the description of the
route taken by Joab at the time of the census (2 Sam 24:5–7) as well as
the time his journey took, מקצה תשעה חדשים ועשרים יום 'at the end of nine
months and twenty days' (24:8b), settling for the summarizing ויתהלך
בכל ישראל ויבא ירושלם 'he went throughout all Israel and came to Jerusalem' (1 Chr 21:4b // 2 Sam 24:8a+c). The Chronicler may have viewed the
description of Joab's route and the period of time it took as minor details
impeding the reader, who is trying to grasp the main issues in the continuation of the text: putting an end to the plague in Jerusalem and
building the altar on the threshing floor belonging to Arauna, the Jebusite—the site of the future Temple.[18]

4.11 In 2 Kgs 18:17 (// Isa 36:2) reference is made to the site of the
meeting between the three emissaries of the king of Assyria and the
three representatives of the king of Judah, near the walls of Jerusalem.
In 2 Chr 32:9, the Chronicler omitted this information:[19]

---

17. B.M. 21946, obv. 1–8, and see Wiseman, *Chronicles of Chaldean*, 66–69; as
well as pp. 23–28, 46; Grayson, *ABC*, 99; Pritchard, *ANET*, 307; Jer 46:2.
18. For another possible explanation of the omission of the description of this
route (2 Sam 24:5–7), see example 6.9 (p. 122).
19. For the omission of the titles of the Assyrian emissaries, see above, example
4.5 (pp. 88–89).

2 Chr 32:9	*2 Kgs 18:17*

אחר זה שלח סנחריב מלך אשור
עבדיו

ירושלימה והוא על לכיש . . .

וישלח מלך אשור
את תרתן . . .
מן לכיש אל המלך חזקיהו
בחיל כבד ירושלם ויעלו ויבאו
ירושלם ויעלו ויבאו²⁰
ויעמדו בתעלת הברכה העליונה
²¹*אשר במסלת שדה כובס*
ויקראו אל המלך
ויצא אלהם אליקים בן חלקיהו . . .

After this Sennacherib, king
of Assyria, sent his servants to
Jerusalem while he was at
Lachish.

The king of Assyria sent the
Tartan . . . with a great army
from Lachish to King Hezekiah
at Jerusalem. They went
up and came to Jerusalem . . .
and stood by the conduit of the
upper pool, which is on the
highway to the fuller's field. And
when they called for the king,
there came out to them Eliakim,
the son of Hilkiah.

The omission of the information under consideration stems, apparently,
from its lack of importance to the main sequence of the narrative. The
omission also contributes to an emphasis on the content of the message
borne by the servants of the king of Assyria and to a shortening of the
text itself, a practice that is typical of the Chronicler's handling of the
narrative of Sennacherib's campaign.

---

20. The words ירושלם ויעלו ויבאו are erroneously repeated in Kings. The second
phrase, ויעלו ויבאו, does not appear in the LXX, Syriac, or Vulgate. An example of duplication in the book of Kings is found in 2 Kgs 5:18, והשתחותי בית רמן בהשתחותי בית רמן
'I prostrate myself in the house of Rimmon, when I prostrate myself in the house of
Rimmon'; and in 2 Kgs 10:27, ויתצו את מצבת הבעל ויתצו את בית הבעל 'they broke down the
pillar of Baal, and they broke down the house of Baal'. For further examples of this in
biblical and extrabiblical literature, see Kalimi, "New Cart," 61. Though the words
under consideration do not appear even once in the parallel text in the book of Isaiah,
it is difficult to accept the explanation offered by Montgomery (*Kings*, 486) that these
words are not part of the original text, for they fit in well with the narrative from the
standpoint of meaning, language, and literary style (as far as style is concerned, see
2 Kgs 19:36 // Isa 37:37, וַיֵּשֶׁב בנינוה . . . וַיֵּלֶךְ וַיָּשָׁב ויסע 'he departed and went and returned
. . . and resided in Nineveh').
    21. For this meeting site, see Isa 7:3: אל קצה . . . צא נא לקראת אחז ויאמר ה׳ אל ישעיהו
תעלת הברכה העליונה אל מסלת שדה כובס 'Then the Lord said to Isaiah: "Go forth now to
meet Ahaz . . . to the end of the conduit of the upper pool, on the highway to the
fuller's field" '.

2. Omission of Allusions to Narrations That Appear in Other Texts but Do Not Appear in Chronicles

Occasionally the Chronicler omitted from his work a certain text that appeared in the books of Samuel–Kings, for various reasons. As a result, when he came across words and expressions indicating that text elsewhere, he omitted them as well. Thus, for example:

4.12 In Samuel, Abigail appears four times in a list of David's wives, always with the formula: אביגיל אשת נבל הכרמלי 'Abigail the Carmelitess, Nabal's wife' (1 Sam 27:3;[22] 30:5; 2 Sam 2:2; 3:3). The expression הכרמלי אשת נבל 'the wife of Nabal the Carmelite' hints at the narrative in 1 Sam 25:2–43 concerning the quarrel that broke out between David and Nabal the Carmelite, the circumstances of the meeting of "Abigail the wife of Nabal" (v. 14) and David, and her marriage to him after her husband's death. In Chronicles, Abigail appears only once (1 Chr 3:1), parallel to the list of David's sons in 2 Sam 3:3. Here the Chronicler omitted the phrase אשת נבל 'wife of Nabal' and changed the attribute הכרמלי, 'the Carmelite', referring to Nabal, to its feminine form: הכרמלית 'the Carmelitess', attributing it to Abigail:

2 Sam 3:3	כלאב לאביגל (*Qere*) לאביגיל: *אשת נבל הכרמלי*[23]
	Chileab, of Abigail *the wife of Nabal* the Carmelite.
1 Chr 3:1	דניאל לאביגיל _____ _____ *הכרמלית*
	Daniel, by Abigail _____ _____ the Carmeli*tess*.

The Chronicler seems to have omitted the expression אשת נבל, which hints at the narrative in 1 Sam 25:2–43, because he had not included this narrative, which was disrespectful to David, in his work. There is, however, another possible reason for this omission: the Chronicler found fault with David's marriage to Nabal's widow, because it was not fitting for a king to wed a widow (it must be stressed that she was not the widow of a previous king!). It was in fact customary to look for נערה בתולה 'a young virgin' for a king (1 Kgs 1:2, for David; Esth 2:2, 3, for Ahasuerus).[24]

---

22. Indeed, the MT here reads אביגיל אשת נבל הכרמלית, but the LXX and Vulgate have הכרמלי, as in the other cases where she is mentioned.

23. The LXX reflects a Hebrew *Vorlage* לאביגיל הכרמלית, and this is apparently true of 4QSam[a] as well: [ ] לאביגיל הל. These readings seem to have been influenced by the parallel text in 1 Chr 3:1. Indeed, in the other three cases the LXX is identical with the MT: אביגיל אשת נבל הכרמלי. For another opinion, see McCarter, *II Samuel*, 101.

24. The Pentateuch prohibited only the high priest from marrying אלמנה וגרושה וחללה זנה . . . כי אם בתולה מעמיו יקח אשה 'a widow, divorcee, profaned woman, or a harlot . . . ; instead, he shall take a virgin from his own people for a wife' (Lev 21:14, P). Ezekiel extended this prohibition to include regular priests as well (Ezek 44:22), but as a matter of principle the prohibition does not apply to Israelites who are not *cohens*.

4.13 2 Sam 7:14b, which reads אשר בהעותו והכחתיו בשבט אנשים ובנגעי בני אדם 'if he commits iniquity, I will chasten him with a rod such as mortals use and with punishments inflicted by human beings', is apparently an advance indication of Solomon's sins and of the rebellions against him, as related in 1 Kings 11.[25] But since the Chronicler omitted Solomon's sins and the rebellions against him, he also omitted the present verse, which hints at them. Thus, he left in his work no trace of Solomon's sins or of the tremors that beset his kingdom:

2 Sam 7:14–15	*1 Chr 17:13*
14a. אני אהיה לו לאב	אני אהיה לו לאב
והוא יהיה לי לבן	והוא יהיה לי לבן
14b. *אשר בהעותו*	
והכחתיו בשבט אנשים	
ובנגעי בני אדם	
15. וחסדי לא יסור ממנו כאשר	וחסדי לא אסיר מעמו כאשר
הסרתי . . . [26]	הסירותי . . . [27]
I will be his father	I will be his father
and he will be My son.	and he will be My son.
If he commits iniquity,	
I will punish him with a	
rod such as humans use	
and the strokes of human beings.	
But My mercy will not depart	I will not remove my mercy
from him, as I removed it from	from him, as I removed it from
Saul. . . .	Saul. . . .

The purpose of omitting Solomon's sins and any indication of them was to glorify his name.

---

25. This was already grasped by the Sages: "אשר בהעותו והוכחתיו בשבט אנשים"—this refers to Hadad and Razon son of Eliada, as was said: ויקם ה' לו שטן 'and God raised up as an antagonist to him'" (*Yal.* 2.146), and similarly Rashi, Radak, and a number of modern commentators, such as Segal, *Samuel*, 266, 280; Rothstein-Hänel, *Chronik*, 326; Rudolph, *Chronik*, 135; Coggins, *Chronicles*, 94–95; Mosis, *Untersuchungen*, 90.

26. Compare Ps 89:31–34: וחסדי, אם יעזבו בניו תורתי . . . ופקדתי בשבט פשעם ובנגעים עונם, וחסדי לא אפיר מעמו 'If his children forsake my law . . . , then I will punish their transgression with the rod and their iniquity with scourges, but my mercy will not depart from him'. See also Prov 13:24; 23:13; and see Segal, *Samuel*, 280.

27. Japhet provides another explanation for this omission (*Ideology*, 464). In her opinion, the Chronicler's outlook made this omission vital: the guarantee of the dynasty does not apply in all circumstances, the sins of the king cancel it in the main. However, this outlook would have required the Chronicler to include only the conditional section in Nathan's words, for the Davidic dynasty lasted some 400 years!

4.14 In 2 Kgs 21:3, the Deuteronomistic historian compares the deeds of Manasseh, king of Judah, to the deeds of Ahab, king of Israel: ויקם מזבחת[28] לבעל ויעש אשרה כאשר עשה אחאב מלך ישראל 'He raised altars to Baal and made an Asherah, *as did Ahab, king of Israel*'. The simile כאשר עשה אחאב 'as did Ahab' apparently refers to 1 Kgs 16:32–33: ויקם מזבח לבעל בית הבעל אשר בנה בשמרון ויעש אחאב את האשרה 'He raised an altar to Baal in the house of Baal, which he had built in Samaria. *Ahab also made an Asherah*'.

In his work, the Chronicler omitted the narrative referring to Ahab in 1 Kgs 16:32–33 and thus also the comparison of the sins of Manasseh with the sins of Ahab in the parallel text in 2 Chr 33:3 and merely wrote: ויקם מזבחות לבעלים ויעש אשרות _____ 'He raised altars to the Baals and made Asherahs'.

4.15 1 Kgs 22:1–2 reads as follows: וישבו שלש שנים אין מלחמה בין ארם ובין ישראל. ויהי בשנה השלישית וירד יהושפט מלך יהודה אל מלך ישראל 'Three years passed without war between Aram and Israel. And it came to pass in the third year that Jehoshaphat, king of Judah, came down to the king of Israel'. These "three years" of tranquility seem to have begun with the covenant made between the king of Israel and the king of Aram after the battle of Aphek (1 Kgs 20:26–34).[29] Since the Chronicler omitted the narrative in 1 Kgs 20:26–34, he also omitted the narrative in 1 Kgs 22:1 referring to the same events. Similarly, instead of the definitive date stated in the text (1 Kgs 22:2), ויהי בשנה השלישית 'it came to pass in the third year', he used a general, indefinite expression (2 Chr 18:2), וירד לקץ שנים 'And after a lapse of years he went down'.

4.16 1 Kgs 12:32–13:34 tells about the establishment of the religious ritual in the kingdom of Israel by Jeroboam, son of Nebat, the prophecy made by the man of God from Judah regarding this ritual, and what happened to the man of God from Judah when he ate with the prophet from Bethel. The Chronicler omitted this passage from his book because it dealt mainly with the kingdom of Israel rather than the Davidic dynasty, which is the concern of most of his book. This omission apparently also led to the omission of the narrative concerning the fulfillment of the prophecy of the man of God from Judah and concerning what

---

28. The LXX has מזבח, in the singular, which seems more reasonable; see 1 Kgs 16:32 adduced below, which is compared to it. The plural form מזבחת in the MT apparently developed under the influence of the parallel text in 2 Chr 33:3; cf. Montgomery, *Kings*, 519, 522; Gray, *Kings*, 705 note a.

29. For the identifications of the kings of Israel and Aram in 1 Kings 20 and 22 with Jehoahaz, son of Joash, and Ben-hadad, son of Hazael, see Pitard, *Ancient Damascus*, 115–25.

happened to him when he ate with the prophet of Bethel (2 Kgs 23:15–
20), in the parallel place in 2 Chronicles 34.[30]

4.17 According to the Chronicler, David reigned over all the tribes of
Israel, that is, over the Northern and the Southern tribes, immediately
after the death of Saul (1 Chr 10:14; 11–12). Consequently, he omitted
from his book the narrative about Ish-bosheth's reign over the Northern
tribes and David's reign over the Southern tribes only (2 Samuel 2–4).[31]
He also omitted any indications that David reigned only over Judah. For
example, 2 Sam 5:5 says of David:

בחברון מלך *על יהודה* שבע שנים וששה חדשים, ובירושלם מלך שלשים ושלש
שנה על כל ישראל ויהודה

In Hebron he reigned over Judah seven years and six months, and in
Jerusalem he reigned thirty-three years over *all Israel and Judah*.

In 1 Chr 3:4b, the Chronicler adduced this text after omitting the expressions *על יהודה, על כל ישראל ויהודה*, which hint at David's separate
reign over Judah, and wrote:

וימלך שם (בחברון) שבע שנים וששה חדשים ושלשים ושלוש שנה מלך בירושלם

There [in Hebron] he reigned seven years and six months; and in Jerusalem he reigned thirty-three years.

It should be noted that 1 Chr 29:27 // 1 Kgs 2:11, "The time that he
reigned over Israel was forty years: *seven years he reigned in Hebron*,
and thirty-three years he reigned in Jerusalem," and 1 Chr 3:4 (above)
mention the years of David's reign in Hebron but do not even hint at his
reign over Judah alone. In fact, in 1 Chr 29:26 the Chronicler preceded
his denoting of the number of years that David reigned in Hebron and
in Jerusalem with this sentence: *ודויד בן ישי מלך על כל ישראל* 'Thus David,
the son of Jesse, reigned *over all Israel*'.[32]

---

30. Except for v. 16b; for this, see p. 159.

31. Japhet believes that there is a hint at the period of Ish-bosheth's reign over Israel at Mahanaim and David's reign over Judah at Hebron in 1 Chr 26:26–28: "The
list mentions David and then goes back to an earlier period, referring to spoils from
the wars before David's reign. Four men appear: Samuel, Saul, Abner, and Joab. The
chronological listing of Samuel and Saul, followed by the pairing of Joab and Abner,
suggests an allusion to the period between Saul and David, which is known by the
names of the army commanders" (*Ideology*, 410 n. 41; see also idem, *Chronicles*, 463).
In actual fact, there is no need to assume that the reference is to the period of Ish-
bosheth's reign: Abner, son of Ner, Saul's military leader, is mentioned in this verse
along with Saul, son of Kish, just as Joab, son of Zeruiah, who was David's army commander, is mentioned.

32. On this issue, see also above, example 1.1 (pp. 18–19) and p. 19 n. 3.

3. Omission of a "Numerical Inclusio"

There are instances in which the Chronicler omitted a "numerical inclusio" from the earlier text because he had reduced or extended its scope. For example:

4.18 2 Sam 21:15–21 tells of the four sons of the giant who fell at the hands of David and his men. The narrator concludes (21:22): את ארבעת אלה ילדו להרפה בגת, ויפלו ביד דוד וביד עבדיו 'These *four* were born to the giant in Gath; and they fell by the hand of David and by the hand of his servants'. In his book, the Chronicler adduced only three of the four narratives found in the earlier text (1 Chr 20:4–7 // 2 Sam 21:18–21). For this reason he omitted the "numerical inclusio" in the text and concluded (1 Chr 20:8): אל[33] נולדו להרפא בגת ויפלו ביד דויד וביד עבדיו 'These   were descended from the giants in Gath, and they fell by the hand of David and by the hand of his servants'.

4.19 2 Samuel 23 includes the adventures of the chief warriors (23:8–23) and a list of David's warriors (23:24–39a). This list begins with the words (23:24) עשהאל אחי יואב בשלשים 'Asahel, the brother of Joab, was *of the thirty*', that is, he was one of the thirty warriors,[34] and ends with the words (23:39b) וכל שלשים ושבעה 'all thirty-seven', the total number of warriors and their chiefs presented in 23:8–39a.[35]

In 1 Chr 11:11–41a, the Chronicler adduced these lists while omitting the "numerical inclusio" phrases: שלשים, כל שלשים ושבעה 'thirty' and 'all thirty-seven' (see 11:26, 41). The omissions stem from the extension of the list in Chronicles by 16 warriors (11:41b–47),[36] an extension

---

33. The word אל is a variation of the אלה appearing in the text; it appears eight times in the Pentateuch: Gen 19:8, 25; 26:3, 4; Lev 18:27; Deut 4:42; 7:22; 19:11; and compare BDB, 41a; Curtis-Madsen, *Chronicles*, 244; Rudolph, *Chronik*, 140.

34. One text actually lists 31 warriors, and see n. 35 below.

35. A precise accounting reveals only 36 names: the three (23:8–17); the two (23:18–23); and 31 (23:24–39a). Perhaps Segal has the best solution (*Samuel*, 395): "The name of one mighty man has been omitted . . . and we have thirty-two names in the list of thirty. The two additional names are certainly those of mighty men who took the place of dead heroes like Asahel and Uriah the Hittite." Mazar believes: "The missing name erroneously omitted is preserved in 1 Chronicles—Zabad, son of Ahlai" ("Military Elite," 96 n. 62). It seems impossible, however, to decide whether this name begins the list of additional names found in Chronicles or belongs to the list of names adduced from 2 Samuel 23.

36. For the historical reliability of the list of 16 mighty men, see Benzinger, *Chronik*, 43; Rothstein-Hänel, *Chronik*, 240ff.; Klein, "David's Mighty Men," 95–106, especially p. 105 (= *Yedioth*, 304–15). On the other hand, Elliger ("Die dreissig Helden Davids," 79) believes that the list is a complete invention of the Chronicler's; cf. Noth, *ÜS*, 136–37 (= *Chronicler's History*, 54–55); Williamson, *Chronicles*, 103–4.

shattering the "numerical inclusio" of the text. In fact, the list in Chronicles contains 47 warriors (31 + 16), and if the number of chiefs (11:11–18) and the 2 (11:20–25) are added to them, the total is, of course, even greater.

In both cases, the Chronicler has not provided a new "numerical inclusio" corresponding to the scope and content of the passages in their new form. This is noteworthy, especially in light of his habit of adding "numerical inclusio" phrases to texts that lack them.[37]

---

37. See the examples adduced below, chap. 14, §2 (pp. 315–324).

Chapter 5
Given Name – Equivalent Name Interchanges

The Chronicler sometimes entered an equivalent name or a parallel or synonymous name to the name that occurs in the earlier text. This feature is found in the book of Chronicles both with regard to the names of geographical sites and with regard to the personal names of various individuals or peoples.

From a typological standpoint, this feature is reminiscent of the use of the parallel names of Jacob and Israel in the narrative of Joseph, for example, in Gen 37:1–3: in two consecutive verses the name יעקב appears, while in the very next verse it is the name ישראל that appears; occasionally both names are used in the very same verse: ויאמר אלהים לישראל במראת הלילה, ויאמר: יעקב יעקב . . . 'God spoke to *Israel* in visions of the night, and said: *Jacob, Jacob* . . .' (Gen 46:2).[1] A similar feature occurs in parallel expressions in poetry, for example, אל תירא עבדי יעקב / ואל תחת ישראל 'Fear you not, O *Jacob* my servant, and be not dismayed, O *Israel*' (Jer 30:10);[2] הנשאר בציון / והנותר בירושלם 'he that is left in *Zion*, and he that remains in *Jerusalem*' (Isa 4:3);[3] The Assyrian king Tukultī-apil-Ešarra is denoted by this name in Assyrian documents, while in Babylonian sources he is called by the name Pūlu. This is the situation in the book of Kings as well: in 2 Kgs 15:19, the king of Assyria is called פול 'Pūl', while further on (15:29) he appears under the name תגלת־פלאסר 'Tiglath-pileser'.[4] A Hittite source, the "Telepinus Declaration," reports the campaign of Mursili I against *Bābili* ('Babylon'), while later on a Neo-Hittite document reports the same king and the same campaign but uses the name ᵘʳᵘŠa-an-ḫa-ra ('Shinar').[5] Similarly, in the Hebrew Bible, 2 Chr 36:7 reports that Nebuchadnezzar, king of Babylon, carried part of the vessels of the house of the Lord and put them in his palace 'in *Babylon*'. Dan 1:2, which uses the text of Chronicles, relates that Nebuchadnezzar carried part of the vessels of the

---

1. Cf. also Gen 43:6, 8, 11; 45:28; 46:1 (Israel) in contrast to 45:25, 27 (Jacob).
2. And cf. Isa 40:27; 43:1; 48:12, etc.
3. And cf. Isa 10:32; 40:9; 62:1; Mic 3:12, etc.
4. In this regard see below, example 20.17 (pp. 402–403).
5. See Kalimi, "Shinar," 1213; Zadok, "Origin of the Name Shinar."

99

house of God and brought them to 'the land of *Shinar*', to the house of his god.[6]

In still another example from Jewish-Hellenistic historical writing, in 1 Macc 16:19, 20, 23, the son of Simon the Hasmonean is called יוחנן 'Yohanan' (or 'John'). In the parallel position, in the wars of the Jews against the Romans, Josephus notes: "John known also as Hyrcanus" (*J.W.* 2.1.3), and further on he sometimes uses Hyrcanus (e.g., *J.W.* 2.1.4), while on other occasions he uses John (e.g., *J.W.* 2.1.8). In *Ant.* 13.229 Josephus writes: "John, also called Hyrcanus," and thereafter only uses the name Hyrcanus (13.229, 230, 231, 233, 235, etc.).

The use of this device indicates the writer's active involvement in the historical source, without introducing any substantial change in the content of the source. The interchange also provides for literary variation in the use of the names.

1. Geographical Names

5.1 In 2 Kgs 14:20, Amaziah, king of Judah, is reported to have been buried בעיר דוד 'in the City of David', whereas in the parallel text in 2 Chr 25:28 he is said to have been buried בעיר יהודה 'in the city of Judah'. Some commentators and scholars of the book of Chronicles view the name עיר יהודה as a scribal error (without defining the nature of the error), and propose reading בעיר דוד as in the earlier text.[7] The Greek translator of Chronicles was the first to correct the text and write: ἐν πόλει Δαυὶδ ('in the City of David'), according to the reading in Kings. This seems, however, to be a deliberate replacement on the part of the Chronicler of the name 'City of David' with the synonymous 'City of Judah'. The term 'City of Judah' does not appear elsewhere in the Bible as the name of the 'City of David' or of 'Jerusalem', but it has a parallel in Mesopotamian literature: "In the seventh year, the month of Kislev, the king of Akkad collected up his armies and advanced into the land of Ḫatti and encamped at the city of Judah (*āl Ia-a-ḫu-du*)"—that is, at Jerusalem.[8] On occasion, then, writers in Israel and in Mesopotamia used

---

6. See Kalimi, "History of Interpretation," 8–10. For the interchange of the names Babylon/Shinar, see also Gen 11:2; Isa 11:11; Zech 5:11 (and see the LXX in each case).

7. Cf., e.g., Curtis-Madsen, *Chronicles*, 447; Rehm, *Untersuchungen*, 71; Rudolph, *Chronikbücher*, 280 (and cf. his suggestion in *BHS*, 1553); Williamson, *Chronicles*, 331—though Williamson does not reject the MT out of hand.

8. B.M. 21946, rev. 11–13; see Wiseman, *Chaldean Chronicles*, 72–73; Grayson, *ABC*, 102; Pritchard, *ANET*, 564. Indeed, Esarhaddon, king of Assyria, lists ᵐ*Me-nas-si-i šàr* ᵘʳᵘ*Ia-ú-di* 'Manasseh, king of the city of Judah', among the kings of Phoenicia, Israel, and Cyprus who brought him tribute; see Borger, *Asarhaddon*, Ninive A, V 55, 60; *ANET*, 291. Ephʿal has already shown, however, that the Assyrian scribes of the

the term 'City of Judah' instead of 'Jerusalem' / 'City of David', from the
period of the Judean monarchy onward.

A typological parallel of this feature is found in the book of Isaiah: the
ancient Moabite capital קיר־חרש 'Kir-heres' (Isa 16:11; compare with Jer
48:31, 36) or קיר־חרשת 'Kir-hareseth' (Isa 16:7; compare with 2 Kgs 3:25)
is also known as קיר מואב 'Kir Moab' (Isa 15:1). The word קיר in the Moabite language means 'city', as can be seen in the Mesha Stele (lines 10–
12): *wybn lh mlk ysrʾl ʾt ʿṭrt wʾltḥm bqr wʾḥzh wʾhrb ʾt kl hʿ(m m)hqr*
'When the king of Israel built up ʿAtereth, I waged war against the city,
I captured it, and I killed all the people of the city'.[9] Indeed, the phrase
עיר מואב 'city of Moab' appears in 1QIsaᵃ.

5.2 2 Kgs 16:20 reports that Ahaz was buried בעיר דוד 'in the city of
David'. In place of the name עיר דוד, the Chronicler wrote the early and
more common name of the city—ירושלים 'Jerusalem':[10]

2 Kgs 16:20	*2 Chr 28:27*
וישכב אחז עם אבתיו	וישכב אחז עם אבתיו
ויקבר עם אבתיו	ויקברהו[11]
בעיר דוד	*בעיר בירושלם*[12]
Ahaz slept with his fathers,	Ahaz slept with his fathers,
and was buried with his fathers	and they buried him
in the *City of David*.	in the *city, in Jerusalem*.

The Greek translation of the book of Chronicles has here: καὶ ἐτάφη ἐν
πόλει Δαυίδ 'and he was buried in the City of David'. It is reasonable to
assume that this version was formulated under the influence of 2 Kgs
16:20, in order to create harmony between the two parallel texts. Another example of this is found in the translation of 2 Chr 25:28.[13]

period were not always precise in their use of the determinatives URU (= 'city') and
KUR (= 'country') with the names of cities and countries in the western part of the Assyrian Empire (*Arabs*, 150 n. 514).

9. See Donner-Röllig, *KAI*, no. 181.

10. For these and other names of the city, see Mazar, "Jerusalem in the Biblical
Period," 11–15. The name עיר דוד 'City of David' was given to Jerusalem (especially to
the Zion fortress) after the city was taken by David (2 Sam 5:6–9 // 1 Chr 11:4–7) and
became accepted as the city became the center of David and Davidic dominion.

11. The Chronicler omitted the expression עם אבתיו 'with his fathers' because further on in the verse he says of Ahaz: "they did not bring him into the tombs of the
kings of Israel."

12. For the repetition of the preposition בָעיר בירושלם 'in the city, in Jerusalem', see:
2 Chr 6:17 לעבדך לדויד 'to your servant, to David' instead of לעבדך דוד 'to your servant,
David' in 1 Kgs 8:26; השתכחת בה בדניאל '[there] were found in Daniel'; בה בליליא קטיל
בלאשצר מלכא כשדיא 'on that very night, Belshazzar, the Chaldean king, was slain' (Dan
5:12, 30).

13. See example 5.1, above, p. 100, with n. 1.

5.3 2 Kings 23 relates that the religious reform instituted by Josiah, king of Judah, was carried out beyond the borders of Judah as well (23:19): וגם את כל בתי הבמות אשר *בערי שמרון*, אשר עשו מלכי ישראל להכעיס הסיר יאשיהו, ויעש להם ככל המעשים אשר עשה בבית אל 'Josiah also took away all the shrines of the high places that were *in the cities of Samaria* that the kings of Israel had made, provoking [the Lord], and did to them just as he had done in Bethel'. Instead of the words בערי שמרון 'in the cities of Samaria', the Chronicler wrote in 2 Chr 34:5–6: ויטהר את יהודה ואת ירושלם *ובערי מנשה ואפרים ושמעון* ועד נפתלי בחר בתיהם[14] סביב 'and purged Judah and Jerusalem. Also *in the cities of Manasseh, Ephraim, and Simeon*, even as far as Naphtali, in ruins all around'. The phrase בערי שמרון also occurs in 2 Kgs 17:24: ויבא מלך אשור מבבל ומכותה . . . וישב *בערי שמרון* תחת בני־ישראל וירשו את *שמרון וישבו בעריה*[15] 'The king of Assyria brought people from Babylon and from Cuthah . . . and placed them *in the cities of Samaria* in place of the Israelites. They possessed *Samaria and lived in its cities*'. It seems that the term שמרון here refers neither to the Northern Kingdom—a usage that can be found in various Assyrian inscriptions such as ᵐIa'su ᵐᵃᵗSamerinâ in the stele from Tell al-Rimah[16] or Minihimmi ᵃˡSamirināi in the annals of Tiglath-pileser III (line 8)[17]—nor to the shrunken kingdom of Israel, for when the exiles were brought in, and certainly when Josiah's reform was carried out, that kingdom was no longer in existence, even in its shrunken form. "Samaria" thus refers here to the satrapy of Samaria. Instead of the words ערי שמרון, the Chronicler used tribal names: "the cities of Manasseh, Ephraim, and Simeon." "Simeon" here (and in 2 Chr 15:9: ויקבץ את כל יהודה ובנימין והגרים עמהם מאפרים ומנשה *ומשמעון* . . . 'he gathered all Judah and Benjamin, and those who lived as aliens in Ephraim, Manasseh, *and Simeon*') does not refer to the tribe of Simeon that resided south of Judah (1 Chr 4:24–43; Josh 19:1–9), as several commentators and students of the book of Chronicles believe.[18] This name is apparently identical with Συμοων

---

14. *Qere*: בחרבותיהם 'with their axes'. Two words, בחר בתיהם, based on the reading בער בתיהם 'destroyed their holy places' (ע/ח interchange), may have been joined together here; see Seeligmann, "Editorial Alteration," 280 n. 2.

15. And see also v. 26. For the connection between 2 Kgs 23:15–20 and 2 Kgs 17:24–33, see Cogan-Tadmor, *II Kings*, 299.

16. See Page, "Stela of Adad-Nirari III," 142.

17. See Luckenbill, *ARAB*, vol. 1, §772; Pritchard, *ANET*, 283. And see also Hos 7:1: "Then is the iniquity of *Ephraim* uncovered / And the wickedness of *Samaria*."

18. See Curtis-Madsen, *Chronicles*, 504: "The mention of *Simeon*, whose territory was south of Judah (1 Ch. 4,28ff.), with the northern tribes is due to the fact that it was reckoned as one of the ten tribes forming the N. Kingdom." And see Elmslie, *Chronicles* (1916), 229–30, 332; Williamson, *Israel*, 104; idem, *Chronicles*, 270; Japhet, *Ideology*, 295; idem, *Chronicles*, 724; Coggins, *Chronicles*, 292. Coggins concludes from this that "the Chronicler knew very little of the historical reality of the affairs described."

'Simeon', which appears in the LXX^B of Josh 11:1; 12:20; 19:15 (and similarly in Vetus Latina and Vulgate),[19] and which is also the Simonia/ Simonias that appear in the writings of Josephus and in rabbinic literature, as well as today's Simonia ruins (Tell Shimron) in the tribal inheritance of Zebulun in the Valley of Jezreel.[20]

5.4 The name גבעון 'Gibeon' appears on occasion in the Bible in the form גבע 'Geba', for example, Ezra 2:20, גבר 'Gibbar' // Neh 7:25, 'Gibeon'.[21] In 2 Sam 5:22–25, the narrative of David's victory over the Philistines concludes with the words (v. 25): ויך את פלשתים מגבע עד באך גזר 'and struck down the Philistines *from Geba* all the way to Gezer'. In Isa 28:21, the prophet hints at, among other things, this victory of David, using the parallel, more common name Gibeon, instead of the name Geba, in the earlier text: כי כהר פרצים יקום ה', כעמק בגבעון ירגז לעשות מעשהו 'For the Lord will rise up as on Mount Perazim, he will rage as in the valley of *Gibeon* to do his deed'. The Chronicler, in the parallel text in 1 Chr 14:16, acted like Isaiah, writing Gibeon in place of Geba: ויכו את מחנה פלשתים מגבעון ועד גזרה 'And they struck down the camp of the Philistines *from Gibeon* to Gezer'.[22]

As far as content is concerned, there is thus no difference between the version reading "and he struck down the Philistines from *Geba* all the way to Gezer" (2 Sam 5:25) and the parallel text, "and they struck down the camp of the Philistines from *Gibeon* to Gezer" (1 Chr 14:16), for they both refer to the same geographical location. The logical conclusion is, then, that the disagreement among modern commentators and historians over the question of which of these versions should be preferred is an artificial one.[23]

---

19. In the MT the name is preserved as שמרון. It is difficult to determine just how this form developed. Rainey ("Shimron," 140) adduces support for the reading "Simeon" from Egyptian documents, the El-Amarna letters, testimony from the period of the Second Temple, and from the Mishnah and Talmud. See also the following note.

20. See Rainey, "Shimʿon/Shimron," *TA* 3.57–69; *TA* 8.149–50.

21. For ע/ר interchanges, compare Josh 11:1; 12:20; 19:15, MT שמרון, with LXX: Συμοων = שמעון (the "Simeon" that appears in 2 Chr 15:9; 34:6), and see further in this matter above, example 5.3 (p. 102), and Rainey's articles adduced there. For the form of the names (with *-on* ending) Geba/Gibeon, see, for example, Shemer/ Shomron (1 Kgs 16:24).

22. For a detailed discussion of these texts and for the Chronicler's preference, see example 7.13 (p. 134). Demsky comments on this interchange in Chronicles but does not notice that Isaiah preceded the Chronicler in this respect (Demsky, "Geba," 30).

23. Thus, e.g., Curtis-Madsen, *Chronicles*, 210; Rudolph, *Chronik*, 114; Mazar, "David and Solomon," 63; Garsiel, *Kingdom of David*, 46 n. 13—all believe that the reading in Chronicles is to be preferred. In contrast, Abramsky believes that the reading in Samuel is preferable (*Saul and David*, 382, 383 n. 3).

5.5 Instead of the place-name גבע בנימין 'Geba of Benjamin' (1 Kgs 15:22), the Chronicler wrote the parallel, shortened form of the name, גבע 'Geba':

1 Kgs 15:22	*2 Chr 16:6*
and with them King Asa built	and with them he built
Geba of Benjamin and Mizpah.[24]	*Geba* and Mizpah.

The interchange גבע(ת) בנימין / גבע is also found in the narratives concerning Saul in the book of Samuel.[25]

2. Names of Individuals or Peoples

5.6 2 Kgs 14:7 says of Amaziah, king of Judah: הוא הכה את אדום בגיא־ המלח (*Qere*) מלח: [26]עשרת אלפים 'He killed ten thousand of *Edom* in the Valley of Salt'. In 2 Chr 25:11, the Chronicler has replaced "Edom" with the parallel term בני־שעיר 'men of Seir': ואמציהו התחזק וינהג את עמו וילך גיא המלח ויך את בני־שעיר עשרת אלפים 'Amaziah took courage and led forth his people. He went to the Valley of Salt and struck down ten thousand *men of Seir*.' Further on in the passage, the Chronicler uses the name אדומים 'Edomites' in parallelism with בני שעיר 'men of Seir' (v. 14, "addition"), as well as in the expression אלהי אדום 'the gods of Edom' (v. 20, "addition"), which parallels "the gods of the men of Seir" (v. 14b).

14. Now it came to pass, after Amaziah had come from the slaughter of *the Edomites*, that he brought *the gods of the men of Seir* and set them up to be his gods. He prostrated himself before them and made offerings to them.
20. But Amaziah would not hear, for it was of God to deliver them into the hand [of their enemies], for they had sought *the gods of Edom*.[27]

5.7 Gen 36:40ff. lists "the names of the chiefs of *Esau*." In 1 Chr 1:51b the Chronicler exchanged the name *Esau* for the parallel name *Edom*, "the chiefs of *Edom* were," on the basis of Gen 36:1, "*Esau*—that is, *Edom*."[28] Furthermore, the Genesis list ends with the words, "These

---

24. In the LXX: גבעת בנימין in place of גבע בנימין. For the form גבע בנימין, see 1 Sam 13:16 and Judg 20:10.

25. See Mazar, "Geba," 411–12; idem, "Hill of God," 80–83.

26. The *Kethiv* form of this name appears in the parallel text 2 Chr 25:11 and also in 1 Chr 18:12. For the *Qere* form, see 2 Sam 8:13 and Ps 60:2.

27. For the interchanging names שעיר / אדום, see also ארצה . . . וישלח יעקב מלאכים שעיר / שדה אדום 'Jacob sent messengers . . . to the land of *Seir*, the field of *Edom*' (Gen 32:3); "O Lord, when You went forth out of *Seir* / When you marched out of the field of *Edom*" (Judg 5:4).

28. See also Gen 36:43: "This is Esau, the father of Edom."

are the chiefs of *Edom*" (Gen 36:43). By this exchange the Chronicler harmonized the name at the beginning of the list with the name at the end (a kind of textual harmonization).

5.8 In 1 Chr 3:15 the Chronicler lists the four sons of Josiah, king of Judah. Instead of the name *"Jehoahaz*, son of Josiah," that appears in Kings and in the parallel texts of his own work (2 Kgs 23:30, 31, 34 // 2 Chr 36:1, 2, 4—יואחז 'Joahaz'), he wrote the parallel name שלום *'Shallum'*, which appears in Jer 22:11: "Thus says the Lord regarding *Shallum*, the son of Josiah, king of Judah, who reigned in place of Josiah, his father."

We may conclude that "Shallum, the son of Josiah, king of Judah" is "Jehoahaz, son of Josiah," king of Judah, from the words *"who reigned in place of Josiah his father*," because Jehoahaz reigned in Judah immediately after the death of his father (2 Kgs 23:30 // 2 Chr 36:1). Jeremiah had prophesied the exile of *Shallum* and his death in exile. In 2 Kgs 23:33 // 2 Chr 36:3–4 Jehoahaz was exiled to Egypt, where he died.[29]

5.9 The son of Amaziah, king of Judah, and Jecoliah is generally known in Kings as עזריה(ו) 'Azariah(u)' (2 Kgs 14:21; 15:1, 6, 7, 17, 23, 27; 15:8), and only twice is he called עזיה(ו) 'Uzziah(u)' (2 Kgs 15:30, 32). In contrast, in the parallel texts in Chronicles (2 Chr 26:1, 3, 8, 9, 11, 14, 18, 19, 21, 22, 23; 27:2) the Chronicler wrote *Uzziah* instead of *Azariah*.[30] Only once, in the genealogy of the House of David, did he write *Azariah* (1 Chr 3:12).

---

29. This identification is accepted by most scholars. Ben-Yashar ("Last Kings of Judah," 111–23) had claimed that Jehoahaz was the Johanan mentioned in 1 Chr 3:15, whereas Shallum was the crown prince that Josiah had intended to succeed him—an intention never realized. In Jer 22:11, however, Shallum is explicitly called "king of Judah"! Some are of the opinion that Shallum was the proper name given to him at birth, while Jehoahaz was the name conferred at his coronation (e.g., Curtis-Madsen, *Chronicles*, 519; Montgomery, *Kings*, 550); or the reverse—that Jehoahaz was his birth name and Shallum his regnal name (e.g., Coggins, *Chronicles*, 25). It is doubtful, however, that such a custom—giving a new name at coronation—existed in Israel, certainly not systematically. In these cases: אליקים / יהויקים (Eliakim / Jehoiakim; 2 Kgs 23:34) and מתניה / צדקיהו (Mattaniah / Zedekiah; 2 Kgs 24:17), the names were changed by a foreign ruler to stress lordship over a vassal king; and see Liver, "King, Monarchy," 1102–3; Ben-Yashar, "Last Kings of Judah," 114–17, 129–30 and the additional literature cited there.

30. The words of Seeligmann ("Beginnings of Midrash," 16), "Uzziah is called [in Chronicles] Azariah consistently, and the text says of him: ויעזרהו האלהים 'And God helped him', כי הפליא להעזר עד כי חזק 'for he was marvelously helped till he was strong' (2 Chr 26:7, 15)," are imprecise, for an examination of the text reveals the exact opposite: the name Uzziah(u) is the common one in Chronicles, whereas Azariah(u) occurs in Kings.

The exchange of the names עזריה(ו) 'Azariah' / עזיה 'Uzziah' stems from
the similarity in meaning of the roots עזר 'help' / עזז 'shelter'.[31] Biblical
writers considered themselves free to substitute either of these roots for
the other, both in verse and in proper nouns. For example, instead of
ואלהי היה עזי 'my God has become my shelter' (Isa 49:5) we find ואלהי היה
עזרי 'my God has become my help' in 1QIsaᵃ. The name עזיאל 'Uzziel' in
1 Chr 25:4 is spelled עזראל 'Azarel' for the same person in 25:18; the
name עזיה 'Uzziah' appears in 1 Chr 6:9[24], the very same person who
was called עזריה 'Azariah' in 6:21[36]; Ezra 10:21 mentions Uzziah, the
very same person who appears in the apocryphal book of 1 Esdr 9:21 in
the form of Azariah.[32] The interchange of these names can thus not be
linked with differing historical circumstances in the life and reign of
this king of Judah, as several scholars have proposed.[33]

On the basis of epigraphic evidence dated to the period of this Judean king, as well as on the basis of early biblical texts and an Aramaic
inscription from the Second Temple period, it may reasonably be assumed that he was usually called Uzziah (or its full form, Uzziahu): on
two seals he is called עזיו 'Uzziahu': לאביו עבד עזיו 'to Abijah, servant of
Uzziah', לשבניו ע/בד עזיו 'to Shebaniah, servant of Uzziah'.[34] In the su-
perscription of the books of Isaiah, Hosea, and Amos, who prophesied
during his reign, the form of his name is עזיה(ו) 'Uzziah(u)' (Isa 1:1; Hos
1:1; and Amos 1:1). This is also true of the superscriptions at the beginning of chaps. 6 and 7 of Isaiah and of the chronological-historical notation in Zech 14:5. It is the case, too, with the stone on this king's grave
(the end of the Hasmonean period): לכה התית / טמי עוזיה / מלך יהודה / ולא
למפתח 'Here were brought the bones of Uzziah, king of Judah; it is not to
be opened'.[35] It is thus difficult to accept Cook's statement,[36] "The form
'Azariah' is more precise, and 'Uzziah' may be a popular, distorted
form," or even that of Whitehouse,[37] "It is very possible that the king
bore only the name 'Azariah', and that the name 'Uzziah' arose out of a
textual error."

---

31. See Brin, "The Roots עזז-עזר," 8–14.

32. For these examples and others, see ibid., 12–14, most of which were already
adduced by Meek, "Uzziah," 1021.

33. For example, Mazar and Yeivin have attempted to draw historical conclusions
from these name interchanges; see Yeivin, "'Uzziah," 126. On p. 127, Yeivin mentioned his reservations concerning these conclusions, in light of Brin's article (n. 28).

34. See Diringer, *Iscrizioni*, 221, 223.

35. See Sukenik, "Epitaph of Uzziahu," 290; in contrast to Yeivin, "Uzziah," 126;
Meek, "Uzziah," 1021.

36. See Cook, "Uzziah," 5241.

37. See Whitehouse, "Uzziah (Azariah)," 843.

5.10 2 Chronicles 25 says that Amaziah, king of Judah, hired soldiers from "Israel" in order to fight Edom (v. 6). Alongside the name *Israel* the Chronicler added the equivalent name "all *the children of Ephraim*" (v. 7),[38] apparently in order to make it clear that Israel here means the Northern Kingdom only and not the kingdom of Judah, which also is occasionally called Israel.[39] Further along in the narrative (v. 10), he uses the phrase להגדוד אשר בא אליו מאפרים 'to the army which had come to him from *Ephraim*', paralleling the phrase לגדוד ישראל 'to the army of *Israel*' (v. 9). It is thus not justifiable to view the phrase להגדוד אשר בא אליו מאפרים as a late gloss, as was claimed for example by Delitzsch.[40]

5.11 There are several more cases in which a name in the book of Chronicles differs from the one in Samuel–Kings. For example:

2 Sam 3:3: כלאב 'Chileab' // 1 Chr 3:1: דניאל 'Daniel'

1 Kgs 7:46: צרתן 'Zarethan' // 2 Chr 4:17: צרדתה 'Zeredah'

2 Kgs 11:19: שער הרצים 'the gate of the guards' // 2 Chr 23:20: שער העליון 'the upper gate'

1 Kgs 15:20: אבל בית-מעכה 'Abel-beth-maacah' // 2 Chr 16:4: אבל מים 'Abel-maim'

In these cases, insufficient data is available for us to decide if the names involved are parallel. However, the possibility exists and must be taken into account in considering these names.[41]

---

38. For denoting the Northern Kingdom by the name "Ephraim," see, for example, Isa 7:5, 8, 9, 17; Hos 5:3, 5; 7:1.

39. See, for example, 2 Chr 12:1; 21:4, and see Curtis-Madsen, *Chronicles*, 442; Williamson, *Chronicles*, 329.

40. See Delitzsch, *Schreibfehler*, 136.

41. The Jewish sages and medieval commentators taught that Chileab was a name assumed by Daniel; see *b. Ber.* 4a; the Aramaic translation ad loc.; R. David Kimḥi in his commentary on 2 Sam 3:3 and 1 Chr 3:1; Rashi on 2 Sam 3:3 and the commentary attributed to Rashi on 1 Chr 3:1. For the wording of the verses in the ancient translations, see Ed(itorial), *Encyclopaedia Biblica* 4.124 [Heb.]. At any rate, it is difficult to accept Williamson's opinion that the כלאב / דניאל interchange is the result of a scribal error (*Chronicles*, 56; what type of error?); but there is a possibility that this interchange already existed in the Chronicler's *Vorlage*.

Chapter 6
Treatment of Problematic Texts

In several passages in the books of Samuel and Kings, the text is problematic or completely unintelligible. In some of these places, a serious textual error may have been introduced at a very early stage in its transmission. It seems that the Chronicler attempted to ascribe some meaning to these passages or to overcome difficulties in them, either (1) by introducing changes into the text or (2) by rearranging its component parts. On occasion, however, the early text was so unintelligible and fragmentary that he saw fit (3) to omit it from his work, for having such a text in his work could not be helpful to the reader in any way; in fact, it would only interfere with the fluent reading of the narrative.

1. Changing a Problematic Text in Order to Attribute Meaning to It

6.1 The text in 1 Kgs 5:1 is problematic and unclear.

ושלמה היה מושל בכל הממלכות מן־הנהר   ארץ פלשתים ועד גבול מצרים

And Solomon ruled over all the kingdoms from the River   land of the Philistines and to the border of Egypt.

Various explanations have been proposed to clarify it; for example, Ehrlich thought that "the word ועד 'and unto' was omitted before ארץ 'the land of' in a scribal error";[1] Albright claimed that the wording of the text was fragmentary, the original passage containing a list of vassal kingdoms under Israelite domination, and the words ארץ פלשתים being the only ones to come down to us from this list;[2] Montgomery viewed the words ארץ פלשתים as a gloss.[3]

It is, indeed, possible that the word ועד was erroneously omitted from the book of Kings but was preserved in the parallel text in 2 Chr 9:26. In this case, therefore, the structure of the verse is like that in Num 21:24: ויכה ישראל לפי חרב ויירש את ארצו מארנן עד יבק עד בני עמון כי עז גבול בני

---

1. Ehrlich, *Mikrâ ki-Pheschutô*, 277; see also Gray, *Kings*, 141; and cf. Kittel, *BH*, 510.

2. See Albright, *Archaeology*, 213 n. 29; and subsequently Malamat, "Foreign Policies," 221 n. 82.

3. Montgomery, *Kings*, 131 and see also p. 127; and cf. Gray, *Kings*, 141 note b.

עמון 'And Israel put them to the sword, and took possession of their land, *from* the Arnon *to* the Jabbok *to* the Ammonites, for strong (LXX: Jazer) is the border of the children of Ammon'. However, it is more likely that the text under consideration in Kings (a version reflected in *Targum Jonathan*,[4] the Peshiṭta, the Vulgate, and the Hexapla) is a *lectio difficilior*, being even earlier than the parallel text in 2 Chr 9:26.[5] In other words, the version in 2 Chr 9:26 does not reflect the Chronicler's Vorlage but is the result of his labors to remove the difficulty found in the earlier text, as will be seen below.

Further along, 1 Kgs 5:4[4:24] relates that Solomon "had dominion over all the region across the River, from Tiphsah to Gaza, over all the kings across the River." This verse clearly marks the boundaries of Solomon's kingdom: from the border town of Tiphsah on the banks of the Euphrates River, at the northeastern edge of the kingdom, to the border town of Gaza in the land of the Philistines, at the southwestern edge. This entire geographical region is referred to in abbreviated form as עבר הנהר 'across the River'.[6]

The region referred to as עבר הנהר 'across the River' (or עבר נהרא/ה in Aramaic—Ezra 4:10, 11, 17, 20; 8:36, and so on)[7] was a satrapy of the Persian Empire. It extended from the Euphrates River in northeast Syria to the Egyptian border (that is, the Besor/Gaza stream or Wadi El-Arish) and included Syria, Phoenicia, the land of Israel, and Cyprus.[8]

---

4. According to the Sperber edition, *Targum Jonathan*, 2.221.

5. Cf. Montgomery, *Kings*, 131; Malamat, "Foreign Policies," 221 n. 82. This difficult text seems to have been already in front of the writer of the Septuagint, who wrote (2[46k]): ὅτι ἦν ἄρχων ἐν παντὶ πέραν τοῦ ποταμοῦ ἀπὸ Ῥαφὶ ἕως Γάζης 'on this side of the River, from Raphi unto Gaza'.

6. The use of the term עבר הנהר here is anachronistic: it does not fit in with the territorial-administrative realities of Solomonic days but, rather, that of the period when the Land of Israel was subjugated to kingdoms whose centers were to the east of the Euphrates.

7. The parallel term in Akkadian, *ebir-nāri*, first appears in a letter dating to the days of Sargon II (722–705 B.C.E.), recently republished by Parpola (*Correspondence of Sargon*, 204, line 10 [p. 160]) and not, as previously believed by scholars, in the inscriptions of Esarhaddon (680–669 B.C.E.); see, e.g., Rainey ("Eber-Hanahar"; "Satrapy of 'Eber-Hanahar'") and Stern ("Geographic-Historical Background," 230); or possibly not before the days of Assurbanipal (668–627[?] B.C.E.); see, e.g., Montgomery, *Kings*, 128.

8. Prior to the Babylonian revolt (482 B.C.E.), Babylon itself was included in this satrapy. Herodotus (3.89) attributes this administrative division (that is, the exclusion of Babylon from the satrapy of Eber-Hanahar) to Darius I (522–486 B.C.E.), but this is an anachronism stemming from the administrative arrangements in the Persian Empire of Herodotus's day (ca. 450 B.C.E.). Cf. Stern, "Geographic-Historical Background," 230. For עבר־הנהר and its boundaries at various times, see also Rainey, "Eber-Hanahar," 43–48; idem, "Satrapy of 'Eber-Hanahar,'" 105–16, 277–80.

The term הנהר 'the river', using the definite article ה, normally refers to the Euphrates,[9] and, in 1 Kgs 5:1 and 4 [4:21 and 24], the Chronicler understood the phrase מן הנהר . . . ועד גבול מצרים 'from the River . . . to the border of Egypt' as a description of the boundaries of "Eber-Hanahar," or 'across the River'.[10] Hence, he concluded that the borders of the Solomonic kingdom were identical with the borders of the satrapy of "Eber-Hanahar" in his own day (ca. 400–375 B.C.E.). Since "the land of the Philistines" was included in the satrapy of "Eber-Hanahar" and was the closest populated region to the Egyptian border, he introduced the word ועד 'to' before ארץ פלשתים, thus clearly demarcating the boundaries of Solomon's kingdom in 2 Chr 9:26:

ויהי (שלמה) מושל בכל המלכים

מן־הנהר ועד ארץ פלשתים ועד גבול מצרים[11]

He [Solomon] ruled over all the kings,
from the River *to* the land of the Philistines and to the border of Egypt.

Thus, the addition of the word ועד removed the difficulty in the earlier text by creating two parallel geographic defining characteristics of the southwest border of the kingdom of Solomon: *'to* the land of Philistines' (inclusive!) 'and to the border of Egypt'.

6.2 After Solomon's prayer dedicating the Temple, the Lord revealed himself to him and promised that, if he led Israel along the straight path, "My eyes and my heart shall be there perpetually" (1 Kgs 9:3 // 2 Chr 7:16); but if not, then ruin would befall him (1 Kgs 9:8), והבית הזה יהיה עליון, כל עבר עליו ישם[13] ושרק[12] 'and this house that is so high—everyone who passes by will be astonished at it and will hiss'. The words יהיה עליון 'that is so high' do not fit in the context of a catastrophe that was liable to befall the Temple, people, and land to such an extent that it would cause passersby to be astonished. Instead of עליון one would expect a word expressing ruin or destruction.

---

9. See, e.g., Exod 23:31; Deut 11:24; Isa 11:15; 27:12; as well as Josh 24:2, 3, 14, 15; and of course 1 Kgs 5:4.

10. At the close of the fifth century (402 B.C.E.), Egypt threw off the Persian yoke until the year 358 B.C.E.; see Ephʿal, "Syria–Palestine," 145. In other words, the border of the fifth satrapy was at that time also the international border between the Persian Empire and Egypt.

11. For the structure מ(ן) . . . (ו)עד . . . ועד in a description of the boundaries of a geographical unit, see, for example: Josh 1:4; 10:41; 16:3; Judg 11:33; 1 Sam 6:18.

12. The word ישם means 'will be astonished'; cf., e.g., Isa 52:14 and Job 16:7.

13. In several manuscripts, this passage reads וישרק.

Probably, the original reading of this text was יהיה לעיין 'will turn into heaps', reminiscent of a verse in a similar context, Mic 3:12: ירושלם עיין תהיה, והר הבית לבמות יער 'Jerusalem *shall become heaps*, and the mountain of the House as the high places of a forest', and in the parallel text in Jer 26:18: וירושלים עיים תהיה והר הבית לבמות יער.[14] This is also the conclusion to be drawn from the Vetus Latina/Old Latin, from Aquila, and from the Peshiṭta to Kings.[15] It is thus possible that the word עליון that appears in the Masoretic Text is an error for לעיין (an interchange of the letters ל/ע and a substitution of ו for י).[16] It is also possible that here we have a deliberate change made by the editor of the book of Kings or an early "scribal emendation,"[17] intended to temper a harsh expression concerning the House of the Lord (והבית הזה יהיה לעיין 'this house will turn into heaps') that disturbed the readers of Kings, just as, for example, the prophecy of Jeremiah (כשלו יהיה הבית הזה 'this House shall be as Shiloh') so disturbed the people gathered in the Temple that they sought to put him to death.[18] At any rate, it seems that the Chronicler's Vorlage had

---

14. For the form עיים, see Ps 89:1. Jer 49:17 has a similar form: "Edom *will become an astonishment*; everyone that passes by shall be astonished and shall hiss at all her plagues"; and also 18:16; 19:8; 50:13; Zeph 2:15; Lam 2:15.

15. *Targum Jonathan* has a combination of the original and the MT: וביתא הדין דהוה עילאי יהא חריב 'and this House that was so high shall be destroyed'; see also his translation of Isa 19:18, עיר ההרס (erroneous for עיר החרס 'city of the sun', Heliopolis; cf. Job 9:7): קרתא בית שמש דעתידא למחרב 'the town Beth-Shemesh (house of the sun) which will be destroyed'. This contrasts with Thenius (*Könige*, 144) and Klostermann (*Samuelis–Könige*, 326–27), who accept the reading of *Tg. Jonathan* as the original reading: והבית הזה אשר היה עליון יהיה לעיין.

16. These features are known from the history of the transmission of the biblical text, and see the examples in Sperber, "Parallel Transmission," 169–70. Cf., e.g., Elmslie, *Chronicles* (1916), 198; Stade, *Kings*, 110; Šanda, *Könige*, 247; Montgomery, *Kings*, 204; Gray, *Kings*, 236; and Rehm, *Könige*, 101; Jones, *Kings*, 1.211. And see also Seeligmann, "Editorial Alteration," 283–84. Benzinger (*Könige*, 66) and Noth (*Könige*, 194) prefer the reading of the Septuagint: καὶ ὁ οἶκος οὗτος ἔσται ὁ ὑψηλός 'and this most high house / which is most high'.

17. For this point, see Segal, *Introduction to the Bible*, 4.859–61; and especially Lieberman, *Hellenism*, 28–37.

18. Uriah, son of Shemaiah, the prophet from Kiriath-jearim, who prophesied "against this city and against this land *in words just like the words of Jeremiah*," was indeed put to death by Jehoiakim, king of Judah (Jer 26:20–23). Here I should note that there is apparently no connection between the narrative concerning Uriah son of Shemaiah in Jeremiah 26 and the text mentioning "the prophet" in Ostracon #3 of the Lachish Ostraca. Uriah, son of Shemaiah, is not mentioned in the Lachish Ostraca. Tur-Sinai's reading of Ostracon #6 line 10: אר(יהו) is unfounded. There is a "General K( )yahu, son of Elnathan" who is mentioned in Ostracon #3, but none of the ostraca says that he went down to Egypt to capture and fetch the "prophet." According to Jer 26:22, Jehoiakim sent "Elnathan son of Achbor" to Egypt, not "K( )yahu son of Elnathan." The event involving Uriah, son of Shemaiah, occurred during the reign of

the word עליון 'so high', like the Masoretic Text of Kings. He, for his part, in his attempt to attribute some meaning to the problematic text, changed the text and wrote: עליו ישם והבית הזה אשר היה עליון לכל עבר 'And this house, *which was* so high to every passerby, will be desolate' (2 Chr 7:21). Thus, instead of עבר עליו 'passerby', ישם 'will be desolate' now becomes central.[19]

6.3 The text of 2 Sam 8:1–2 says of David, who smote the Philistines ויכניעם ויקח דוד את מתג האמה מיד פלשתים 'and subdued them; and David took *Metheg-ha-ammah* from the hand of the Philistines'. The phrase מתג האמה 'Metheg-ha-ammah' is problematic and, because it apparently results from some error, no suitable solution has yet been offered.[20] This version of the expression seems to have been in the Chronicler's Vorlage,[21] and he attempted to explain it as a geographical site (1 Chr 18:1): ויקח את גת ובנתיה מיד פלשתים 'and took *Gath and its towns* out of the hand of the Philistines'. The Chronicler, it seems, did not take into account the narrative in 1 Kgs 2:39–41, for it indicates that at the outset of the reign of Solomon the city of Gath existed as a kingdom ruled by Achish.[22] At any rate, even if Gath had been linked with King David in some kind of alliance (a possibility not noted anywhere in the Bible) the text "David *took Gath* and its towns *from the hand of the Philistines*" cannot be reconciled with the narrative in Kings.[23] It is thus doubtful whether this verse in Chronicles can be relied on in describing David's relations with the Philistines.[24]

6.4 2 Kgs 15:5 refers to Uzziah, king of Judah:

וינגע ה' את המלך ויהי מצרע עד יום מתו וישב *בבית החפשית* ויותם בן המלך
על הבית

The Lord smote the king so that he was a leper until the day of his death and resided *in a house set apart*. And Jotham, the son of the king, was over the house.

Jehoiakim (Jer 26:21, 22, 23), whereas the story of "the prophet" in the Lachish Ostraca apparently took place during the reign of Zedekiah, king of Judah (against Tur-Sinai, *Lachish Ostraca*, 93–103, 138, 166, 172; and see also the table he adduces on pp. 230–31).

19. See Seeligmann, "Editorial Alteration," 284.

20. For the various interpretations proposed to explain the phrase, see the review and the literature adduced in Malamat, "Foreign Policies," 218 n. 73; McCarter, *II Samuel*, 243.

21. Cf. Williamson, *Chronicles*, 138.

22. "Neither would the conquest of Gath-Gittaim west of Gezer exhaust David's achievements in that area," Aharoni, *Land of the Bible*, 294; cf. also Rainey, "Philistine Gath," 72*.

23. Against Kassis, "Gath," 268–69; and Williamson, *Chronicles*, 138.

24. Against Oded, "Israel and Judah," 118; Kassis, "Gath," 268–69.

Translators, commentators, and researchers throughout the generations have pondered the interpretation of the expression בבית החפשית.
For example, the Septuagint had trouble translating the word החפשית
and merely transliterated it: ἐν οἴκῳ ἀφφουσώθ.[25] The Aramaic translation has ויתיב בר מן ירושלם 'and he lived outside of Jerusalem', apparently
in accordance with Lev 13:46 (and see also Num 5:1–4; 12:10–15; 2 Kgs
7:3). So also Josephus (*Ant.* 9.227): "And so for a time *he dwelt outside
the city*, living the life of a private citizen." The Vulgate translated it: *in
domo libera* 'in a free house'. Modern scholars assumed that this was a
distorted phrase and proposed a number of alternate readings to correct it; for example, בית החבשית, בית המספחת,[26] בביתה חפשית,[27] בבית החרף[28]
(that is, a place of detention or of bandaging).[28] Those scholars, too,
who retained the reading of the Masoretic Text could not agree on its
meaning; for example, Thenius explained it as a 'house of the sick' (*das
Siechhaus*);[29] Rudolph viewed the phrase as an empty cliche actually
meaning a house of confinement (*Haus der Unfreiheit*) and proposed
explaining it as 'a blocked, closed off house' (*Haus der Absperrung*);[30]
Willi felt that the expression referred to 'a house of retirement (from
a job)' (*Haus des Ruhestands*).[31] However, ever since the discovery of
the parallel expression *bt ḥptt* in the Ugaritic Baal legends (I*AB v 15;
IIAB viii 7), it is generally assumed that the expression is an early
Hebrew-Canaanite phrase denoting an isolated place for lepers, perhaps outside the city.[32]

The Chronicler seems already to have found the earlier expression,
בית החפשית, problematic. He attempted to clarify the phrase to some extent by expanding the text (2 Chr 26:21):

וישב בית החפשות (*Qere*) החפשית: *מצרע כי נגזר מבית ה'* ויותם בנו על
בית המלך

---

25. The Greek translators of the parallel texts in Chronicles did something
similar: ἐν οἴκῳ ἀφφουσώθ.

26. See Stade, "Anmerkungen," 156–59; and also his commentary, *Kings*, 250.

27. Klostermann (*Samuelis–Könige*, 444) proposed this, and his proposal was accepted by a broad range of researchers (e.g., Burney, *Kings*, 321; Gray, *Kings*, 618
note b).

28. The two last suggestions are presented by H. Graetz and P. Haupt, respectively, cited in Curtis-Madsen, *Chronicles*, 453.

29. See Thenius, *Könige*, 349.

30. See Rudolph, *Chronik*, 284; and also his article, "Haus der Freiheit," 418.

31. See Willi, "Die Freiheit Israels," 536.

32. See Ginsberg, *Ugarit Texts*, 42, 53, 142; Cassuto, "Death of Baal," 160–61;
idem, *Goddess Anath*, 22–23, 49; Gordon, *Ugaritic Textbook*, 179, Text 67: V 15; see
also p. 404 no. 995; Hobbs, *2 Kings*, 194; Cogan-Tadmor, *II Kings*, 166–67 and the review and additional literature adduced there.

resided in a house set apart, *being a leper, for he was cut off from the house of the Lord*. Jotham, his son, was over the king's house.

In other words, dwelling in בית החפשית meant isolation or confinement[33] from the Temple, the Temple being where the king of Judah had attempted to take over an important responsibility—offering up incense.

2. Removing a Difficulty by Inverting the Order of the Text Components

6.5 The text in 2 Kgs 11:13 speaks of Athaliah, who heard את קול הרצין העם 'the noise of the guard and of the people'. The phrase קול הרצין העם is a problematic one, and it may already have become distorted at an early stage in the transmission of the text. Some claim that the word הרצין is actually a gloss, viewing the plural ending ן- as a sign of Aramaic influence.[34] It is possible, however, that this is merely a scribal error of substituting the letter נ for the letter ם, instances of which are plentiful in the biblical text.[35] It seems, as Talmon puts it, that two variant readings have come together here: "according to the one, הרצים announced the time of the revolution in the courtyard (11:4, 6, 11); according to the other, this act is attributed to the 'people of the land' (11:14) known in brief as העם, further on in the very same text (11:13)."[36]

At any rate, it seems that the present form of the phrase under consideration was the form known to the Chronicler who, in order to attribute some meaning to the phrase, inverted the order of its component parts and presented the word (!)רצים 'running' as an adjective referring to העם 'the people' (2 Chr 23:12): ותשמע עתליה את קול העם הרצים 'Athaliah heard the noise of the people running'.[37]

6.6 The component parts of 1 Kgs 6:1b, which notes the date of the start of construction on the Temple, were adduced in 2 Chr 3:2 in inverted order:

---

33. For this sense of the phrase נגזר מ-, see, for example, Isa 53:8; and BDB, 160b.

34. Cf., e.g., Burney, *Kings*, 311; Stade, *Kings*, 236; Curtis-Madsen, *Chronicles*, 430; Montgomery, *Kings*, 425.

35. Cf. Gray, *Kings*, 520.

36. Talmon, *Transmission of OT Text*, 42. Later he defined the feature as a "style doublet" (in "Textual Study," 143 n. 131).

37. After the period of the Chronicler, attempts continued to be made to clarify the meaning of the problematic phrase in 2 Kgs 11:13. Thus, for example, the Greek translator wrote καὶ ἤκουσεν Γοθολια τὴν φωνὴν τῶν τρεχόντων τοῦ λαοῦ 'Athaliah heard the sound of the people's guards'.

1 Kgs 6:1b	למלך ³⁸ השני הַחֹדֶשׁ הוא זו בחדש *הרביעית בשנה* . . . ויהי
	ישראל על שלמה
	And it came to pass . . . *in the fourth year*, in the
	month of Ziv, which is the second month
	of Solomon's reign over Israel.
2 Chr 3:2	למלכותו ארבע בשנת ³⁹ בשני השני בחדש
	in the second day *of the second month*,
	in the fourth year *of his reign.*

The Chronicler seems to have inverted the order of the components of
the earlier text in order to overcome its syntactic complexity, for the direct continuation of the words הרביעית בשנה 'in the fourth year' is למלך
ישראל על שלמה 'of Solomon's reign over Israel'. The intermediate words
השני הַחֹדֶשׁ הוא זו בחדש 'in the month of Ziv, which was the second month'
interrupt the smooth flow between the two sentence components and
render the reading awkward.

Examples similar to the syntactic structure of the text in 2 Chr 3:2
are found in Phoenician inscriptions of the fifth through fourth centuries B.C.E. For instance,

צדנם מלך אשמנעזר מלך למלכי [14] וארבע עסר בשנת בל בירח
In the month of Bul, in the fourteenth year *of the reign of King Eshmun'azar, king of the Sidonians*

ואדיל כתי על למלכי 2 בשנת בל בירח
In the month of Bul, in the second year *of his reign* over Kty and 'dyl

(אדיל ו) כתי מלך פמייתן למ(לך 21 בשנת בל ליֹרח 6 בימם
On the sixth day *of the month of Bul*, in the twenty-first year *of the
reign of (Pmyytn, king of Kty and) 'dyl.*⁴⁰

The change in Chronicles of the order of components of the earlier text
thus matches the custom of denoting time according to the number of
years of the king's reign during the approximate period of the writing of
the Chronicles.

6.7 The following example indicates that the Chronicler inverted the
order of the components of the text in order to overcome theological

---

38. The phrase השני הַחֹדֶשׁ הוא is an explanatory gloss referring to the expression
זו בחדש 'in the month of Ziv', which appears to be the Phoenician name of the month
under consideration. See also 1 Kgs 6:37.

39. The word בשני probably appears due to dittography with the preceding השני or
with the following word, בשנת. It does not appear in the LXX, Vulgate, or Peshiṭta.

40. Donner-Röllig, *KAI*, no. 14, line 1 (fifth century B.C.E.); no. 38, line 1 (391 B.C.E.);
no. 32, line 1 (341 B.C.E.).

difficulties as well: in 1 Kgs 22:49–50, the Deuteronomistic historiographer wrote that Jehoshaphat, king of Judah, built ships of Tarshish to sail to Ophir in order to bring back gold. In this he was unsuccessful, for the ships floundered at Ezion-geber for some reason that the text does not see fit to reveal (22:49).

Many hazards await shipping in the Gulf of Elath/Aqaba and in the Red Sea, more so than in the Mediterranean Sea: the Red Sea is dominated by unstable gusts of wind and

> a complex set of streams excelling in instability and in frequent shifts in the direction of flow. . . . Sailing conditions in the Gulf of Aqaba/Eilath were far more difficult than in the Red Sea. While the winds in the gulf are undoubtedly more stable, nevertheless they blow strongly from the northeast. . . . Ships heading south from Eilath were in danger of breaking up because of the force of the north wind blowing them toward the coral barriers in the Tiran Straits.[41]

It is thus possible that Jehoshaphat's ships broke up in the midst of one of the sudden violent storms that visit the gulf; the poet of Ps 48:8 may have been hinting at this: וברוח קדים תשבר אניות תרשש 'With an easterly wind shall you break the ships of Tarshish'. It is possible, too, that the ships broke up because no one knew how to build them properly and/or because no one was sufficiently familiar with the art of navigating on an open sea. At any rate, after what had happened at Ezion-geber, Ahaziah, king of Israel, expressed his readiness for cooperation between the two kingdoms[42] in matters of shipping and maritime trade, but Jehoshaphat rejected his overtures (1 Kgs 22:50).

In 2 Chr 20:35–37, the Chronicler adduced the order of events as presented in the earlier texts in inverted fashion, thus creating between them a connection of cause and effect while expanding and altering the narrative. Contrary to 1 Kings 22, he wrote that Jehoshaphat, king of Judah, collaborated—on his own initiative—with Ahaziah, king of Israel, in shipping and maritime trade. They built ships at Ezion-geber in order to reach Tarshish (20:35–36).[43] Because of this cooperation with the king of Israel, "the Lord broke up what Jehoshaphat had made." The

---

41. See Karmon, "Geopolitical Position," 55, 57.

42. The kingdom of Israel was able to offer assistance in this matter mainly by virtue of its good relations with the kingdom of Tyre. The men of Tyre were skilled in building ships, sailing them, and navigating on an open sea. They assisted Solomon in this (1 Kgs 9:27; 10:11, 22; 2 Chr 8:18) and, later, the kings of Assyria and Persia.

43. For the change אניות תרשיש / אניות ללכת תרשיש 'ships of Tarshish / ships to go to Tarshish' and for the change in destination—"Tarshish" instead of "Ophir"—see below, example 20.12 (pp. 393–396).

ships broke up, thus preventing the two kings from setting sail for Tarshish (20:37):

1 Kgs 22:49–50	2 Chr 20:35–37
A. יהושפט עשר⁴⁴ אניות תרשיש	B. ואחרי־כן⁴⁵ אתחבר יהושפט
ללכת אופירה לזהב	מלך יהודה עם אחזיה מלך ישראל
ולא הלך כי נשברה	הוא הרשיע לעשות
(נשברו :Qere)	ויחברהו עמו לעשות אניות
אניות בעציון־גבר	ללכת תרשיש
B. אז אמר אחזיהו בן אחאב	A. ויעשר אניות בעציון גבר
אל יהושפט	ויתנבא אליעזר בן דדוהו
ילכו עבדי עם עבדיך באניות	(דֹדָיָהוּ ממרשה :Qere)
ולא אבה יהושפט	על יהושפט לאמר
	כהתחברך עם אחזיהו
	פרץ ה׳ את מעשיך
	וישברו אניות ולא עצרו
	ללכת אל תרשיש

A. Jehoshaphat made ships of Tarshish to go to Ophir for gold; but they did not go, for the ships broke up at Ezion-geber.
to make ships
to go to Tarshish.

B. Then Ahaziah, son of Ahab, said to Jehoshaphat: "Let my servants go with your servants in the ships"; but Jehoshaphat would not.

B. And after this Jehoshaphat, king of Judah, joined himself with Ahaziah, king of Israel, who did very wickedly; and he joined him

A. And they made the ships in Ezion-geber; then Eliezer, the son of Dodavahu of Mareshah prophesied against Jehoshaphat saying: "Because you have joined with Ahaziah, the Lord has made a breach in your work." And the ships broke up and were not able to go to Tarshish.

From the purely literary/stylistic point of view, inverting the order of the Kings passage created a chiastic parallelism between Chronicles

---

44. *Qere*: עשה 'built', and so also in many manuscripts of the MT.

45. The words ואחרי־כן appear here in place of the word אז in Kings. However, while the word אז in Kings indicates that Ahaziah's proposal was made subsequent to the breaking up of the ships at Ezion-geber, the words ואחרי־כן in Chronicles have no meaning whatsoever, since because of the inverted order of events in Chronicles they follow directly after v. 34, which sums up, "Now the rest of the acts of Jehoshaphat, first and last. . . ."

and Kings. Yet the Chronicler's main purpose in inverting the order of
the narrative here and creating a cause-and-effect connection between
them, while introducing a religious-theological explanation for the
breaking up of the ships at Ezion-geber, is rooted in his view of retribution. He grasped the breaking up of the ships of the righteous king of
Judah, not as the result of pure chance or a mere lack of fortune, but as
a punitive step taken by the Lord (it made no difference whatever what
the real historical path was in which the hand of the Lord was expressed). This punishment would not have befallen Jehoshaphat had he
not sinned.

Since the book of Kings does not attribute any sin to Jehoshaphat,
the Chronicler's grasp of retribution forced him to invent a "sin."[46] He
therefore altered the narrative in Kings—according to which "Jehoshaphat would not" accept Ahaziah's proposal of interkingdom cooperation in matters of shipping and trade (1 Kgs 22:50). The Chronicler
wrote that Jehoshaphat did indeed join with Ahaziah in making "ships
to go to Tarshish" (2 Chr 20:35).[47] Since Ahaziah was wicked (1 Kgs
22:52–54), in the Chronicler's opinion, cooperating with him was a serious sin: "he did wickedly" (2 Chr 20:35b).[48] This sin was what led to the
punitive measure of wrecking the ships, as the Chronicler voiced it
through Eliezer, son of Dodavahu, the prophet: "Because you have
joined with Ahaziah, the Lord will break up what you have made! And
the ships broke up and were not able to go to Tarshish" (20:37). In this
light, the inversion of the order of events is understandable: justice re-

---

46. For a detailed description of the Chronicler's understanding of retribution, see
Japhet, *Ideology*, 165–68; Kelly, *Retribution*, 13–133. This underlying thinking about
retribution that led the Chronicler to create a link of cause and effect between events
is evident quite often in Chronicles; see also 2 Chr 12:7, 12; 13:18; 14:6; 15:15; 25:27,
and so on. And see Japhet, *Ideology*, 168.

47. Hence Japhet's postulate (ibid.)—"in all these instances [i.e., in the cases adduced on pp. 166–68, including this case of ours in 2 Chr 20:35–37, dealt with there
in n. 489] the Chronicler does not alter *the historical facts in his sources*; he merely
explains them according to his system"—is imprecise.

48. See also 2 Chr 19:1–3 ("addition"): after Jehoshaphat returned from the battle
of Ramoth-gilead, where together with the king of Israel he had waged a formidable
fight against the Arameans (2 Chronicles 18 // 1 Kings 22), Jehu, son of Hanani the
seer, spoke up against him: "Do you help the wicked and love those who hate the
Lord? For this, wrath from the Lord is upon you." The concept that an alliance with
the Northern Kingdom was sinful also arises from the narrative about Amaziah, king
of Judah, the mercenaries from Ephraim (2 Chr 25:6–10), and perhaps from the very
assassination of Ahaziah, king of Judah, in Samaria during the Jehu revolt (2 Chr
22:7–9). One should remember that the very birth and survival of the Northern Kingdom of Israel were considered a serious sin by the Chronicler—as serious as rebelling
against the Lord's will (2 Chr 13:4–12), though the book of Chronicles does contain
another outlook as well (see 2 Chr 10:15). For the tension between the two views, see
Japhet, *Ideology*, 308–24.

quires that the "sin" (joining with Ahaziah) precede the "punishment" (wrecking the ships).

In general, the reworking of a given text and the inversion of the order of its component parts stemmed from the Chronicler's intention of adapting the narrative of Kings to the principle of divine retribution that guided him in his historiographical work (and from this viewpoint, the example under consideration could fall under the framework of chap. 2, §4 as well). There is thus no justification for preferring the reworked narrative in 2 Chr 20:35–37 to the earlier text, 1 Kgs 22:49–50, or researching the economic ties (shipping and maritime trade) between the kingdoms of Judah and Israel in the days of Jehoshaphat and Ahaziah[49] or drawing any historical conclusions whatever. The Chronicler's use of the technical term חבר (a term that occurs in similar contexts in other sources)[50] cannot justify preferring the narrative of Chronicles to the narrative of Kings. It is well known that a later historian sometimes may make use of early term(s) in his work. As a matter of fact, borrowed terms are occasionally used to style a later work in a way that is reminiscent of the earlier text in order to gain the reader's confidence.

3. Omitting an Unintelligible Text

6.8 The narrative concerning the capture of Jerusalem in 2 Sam 5:6–9 contains a number of unintelligible and fragmentary phrases, and gleaning a fluent, undisputed description from the passage is difficult. Generations of copyists, translators, commentators, and scholars have puzzled over interpreting the conditional clause (5:6b): כי אם הסירך העורים והפסחים 'unless you take away the blind and the lame';[51] the comment

---

49. Several scholars did this; for example, Elat claims: "Of the existence of economic ties (of the kingdom of Israel) with the kingdom of Judah . . . one may learn from the tradition of the book of Chronicles of the participation of Ahaziahu, king of Israel, in the attempt made by Jehoshaphat, king of Judah, to build a fleet to set sail for Ophir (2 Chr 20:35–37 and cf. 1 Kgs 22:49–50)" (*Economic Relations*, 204). See also Elat, "Trade," 129. Reviv writes similarly: "The text in 2 Chr 20:35–36 reads: . . . ואחרי כן אתחבר יהושפט 'And afterward, Jehoshaphat joined . . .'. This indicates that the kings of Israel and Judah had entered into a partnership for trade, this time also by sea" (*From Clan to Monarchy*, 180). Similarly, Ahituv ("Shipping," 1072) and Oded ("Israel and Judah," 144) treat the text in 2 Chr 20:35–37 as a completely reliable historical source. Ahituv even believes that of the two "the more complete narrative is in 2 Chr 20:36–37."

50. For a detailed discussion of this term and of its repetition here, see example 13.10 (pp. 287–288).

51. 4QSam[a] reads: כי הסיתו העורים והפסחים לאמר לא יבוא] דויד הנה 'For [the blind and the lame incited, saying:] David [will not come in] here' (presented in McKenzie, *Chronicler*, 43). This, however, seems to be reflecting not an early version but an attempt by the scribe of the scroll to explain the basis for David's hatred of the blind and the lame.

regarding David's unexplained hatred for the unfortunate (5:8b): ואת
הפסחים ואת העורים שנאו (Qere) שנאי) נפש דוד; על כן יאמרו: עור ופסח לא יבוא אל
הבית 'and (takes away) the lame and the blind, that are hated of David's
soul; therefore they say: "a blind man and a lame man shall not come
into the House"'; and also the obscure phrase in 5:8: ויגע בצנור 'and he
touches the gutter'. In fact, a satisfactory comprehensive explanation
for these unintelligible passages has yet to be found. Not one of the
many explanations that have been proposed is more than a hypothesis
of a fairly low degree of probability.[52]

It seems that the Chronicler himself already had difficulty understanding the passages under consideration, and to save his potential
audience such difficulties, he simply omitted them from his own work
(1 Chr 11:4–5):

2 Sam 5:6, 8	1 Chr 11:4, 6
6. And the king and his men went to Jerusalem against the Jebusites, the inhabitants of the land, who spoke to David, saying: "You shall not come in here *except you take away the blind and the lame*," thinking: David cannot come in here. . . .	4. And David and all Israel went to Jerusalem—that is, Jebus—and the Jebusites, the inhabitants of the land, were there. And the inhabitants of Jebus said to David: "You shall not come in here"
8. And David said on that day: "Whoever smites the Jebusites *and touches the gutter, and (takes away) the lame and the blind, that are hated of David's soul—.*" Therefore, they say: "A blind man and a lame man shall not come into the House."	6. And David said: "Whoever smites the Jebusites first shall be. . . ."

Actually, it is possible to explain the absence of the words כי אם הסירך
העורים והפסחים לאמר: לא יבוא דוד הנה in Chronicles as homoioteleuton committed either by the Chronicler himself or by a scribe-copyist at some

52. For various explanations of the matter of the blind and the lame, see, for example, Josephus, *Ant.* 7.61–64; *Tg. Jonathan*, ad loc.; *Pirqe R. El.*, chap. 36; R. David
Kimḥi (who gives the opinion of R. Abraham ibn Ezra). For explanations of ויגע בצנור,
see also the LXX, the Vulgate and the commentaries of Rashi, R. David Kimḥi, and
R. Levi ben Gershon. For the various opinions proposed in scholarly literature in
these matters, see Sukenik (= Yadin), "Blind and Lame," 222–25 (and cf. Yadin, *Art
of Warfare*, 267–70); Segal, *Samuel*, 260, 261–62; Mazar, "Jerusalem in the Biblical
Period," 28–29; for additional literature on this subject, see Kalimi, *Bibliography*,
139–41, items 1272–95; idem, "Capture of Jerusalem," 66–79.

stage in the transmission of the work, mainly because of the repetition of the word הנה:

2 Sam 5:6–7	1 Chr 11:5
. . . וַיאמר לדוד	ויאמרו ישבי יבוס לדויד
לאמר לא תבוא הנה	*לא תבוא הנה*
כי אם הסירך העורים והפסחים	
לאמר לא יבוא דוד הנה	
. . . וילכד דוד את מצודת ציון	. . . וילכד דויד את מצודת ציון

Moreover, the omission of the words: (*Qere*) שנאו (שנאי את העורים ואת הפסחים: נפש דוד; על כן יאמר: עור ופסח לא יבוא אל הבית can be attributed to the Chronicler's desire to prevent the denigration of David as one who hated handicapped people for no known reason. However, since my solution proposed above includes a comprehensive explanation for all the unintelligible phrases in the early narrative that do not occur in Chronicles (including: ויגע בצנור), it seems that it is to be preferred.

6.9 The phrase: וְהִקְטִיר אִתּוֹ אֲשֶׁר לִפְנֵי ה׳ 'offering thereby (on the altar) that was before the Lord' (1 Kgs 9:25) is problematic and completely obscure. In modern research, various solutions have been proposed to emend the phrase, in order to give it meaning. The most common proposed emendation is Klostermann's: ה׳ והקטיר את אשו לפני 'offering his fire before the Lord'.[53] Stade[54] wrote concerning this phrase: "והקטיר אתו אשר . . . is beyond translation and probably consists of a haphazard conglomeration of marginal glosses," preferring this explanation to Klostermann's proposed emendation.

The difficulty in comprehending the phrase under consideration may have led to its being omitted from its parallel text in 2 Chr 8:12:

1 Kgs 9:25	2 Chr 8:12
והעלה שלמה שלש פעמים בשנה	אז העלה שלמה
עלות ושלמים על המזבח	עלות לה׳ על מזבח ה׳
אשר בנה לה׳	אשר בנה לפני האולם
והקטיר אתו אשר לפני ה׳	
And three times in a year did	Then Solomon offered burnt-
Solomon offer burnt-offerings	offerings unto the Lord on
and peace-offerings upon the	the altar of the Lord which
alter which he built unto the	he had built before the porch.

---

53. See Klostermann, *Samuelis-Könige*, 331; and following him, Burney, *Kings*, 141–42; Tur-Sinai, *Meaning*, 23; Noth, *Könige*, 220; Jones, *1 Kings*, 219. For other proposals, see Gray, *Kings*, 254.

54. Stade, *Kings*, 113.

Lord, *offering thereby (on*
the altar) that was before the
Lord.

It was apparently for this reason that in the Septuagint (both the Codex
Vaticanus and the Lucianic recension) of Kings, the words אתו אשר were
omitted. These translations therefore simply read והקטיר לפני ה' 'offering
before the Lord'.

6.10 The description of the route taken by Joab at the time of the
census (2 Sam 24:5–7) is replete with difficult phrases and words. For
example, the phrase ויחנו בערוער 'they camped in Aroer' at the beginning
of the description is problematic, for in order to hold a census it would
have been necessary to move from one settlement to the next and not
make camp. The expression ארץ תחתים חדשי 'the land of Taḥtim-Ḥodshi'
(v. 6) "is extremely surprising and the translations and commentators
have grown tired in seeking to understand it."[55] Moreover, a place called
"Yaʿan" (v. 6) is not known from any other source. The phrase הנחל הגד
'the valley of Gad' is also difficult to explain. It may be that the Chronicler omitted the description of the journey from 1 Chronicles 21 because
it was obscure.[56]

---

55. Segal, *Samuel*, 398.

56. Cf. ibid., and see also the various solutions Segal suggests; further, Driver,
Samuel, 373–75; Smith, *Samuel*, 389–90. For another possible explanation of this
omission, see above, example 4.10 (p. 91).

Chapter 7
Harmonizations

1. Textual Harmonization

Textual harmonization is the use of textual elements in one text that harmonize with elements in a parallel text elsewhere. Unlike content harmonization, which is, in the main, an attempt to bring about *thematic equivalence* between mutually contradictory passages dealing with a common subject, textual harmonization is mainly an attempt to generate *equivalence in wording* between parallel texts.

The Chronicler adduced elements from texts in Samuel–Kings in harmony with elements in parallel texts found in these very same books, in some other biblical work, or in his own composition. For this purpose, he adopted various literary techniques: he sometimes *added* a word or a number of words to a Samuel–Kings text in accordance with the passage in the parallel text; he sometimes *omitted* a word or a number of words from the Samuel–Kings text in accordance with the passage in the parallel text; he sometimes *changed* or *replaced* a word or a number of words in Samuel–Kings in accordance with the parallel passage; on occasion, he made use of a number of these techniques at once or even all of them together.

The example closing the first section of this chapter (example 7.17, p. 139) shows that on certain occasions the Chronicler *combined* the language of the narrative in Samuel with the language of the law established in the Pentateuch, creating textual harmonization between the two.

In the examples from Chronicles presented below, the weight of passages from Kings used to harmonize with parallel texts in Deuteronomy is also clearly felt. This is understandable in light of the Deuteronomistic editor's integration of passages from Deuteronomy into the book of Kings from beginning to end.

The parallel texts in Chronicles that were used by the Chronicler to provide textual harmonizations cannot be used as a basis for drawing historical, ideological, or other conclusions concerning the period of the Monarchy.

Typical examples of textual harmonization generated by a *creative writer*, such as the Chronicler, can be found by comparing the Samaritan Pentateuch with the Masoretic Torah.[1] Textual harmonizations

---

1. For this, see Weiss, "Synonymous Variants," 132–58.

arising from the activities of a *transmitter* are evident in biblical manuscripts, the form of which has since been finalized.[2]

7.1 In his evaluation of the reign of Asa, king of Judah, the Deuteronomistic historian wrote (1 Kgs 15:11):

ויעש אסא . . . . . . הישר בעיני ה׳ . . . . . . כדוד אביו

And Asa did what was _____ right in the eyes of the Lord, _____ *as
did David his father.*

The Chronicler adduced this passage by creating textual harmonization
between it and the parallel text in Deuteronomy:

ויעש אסא הטוב בעיני ה׳ אלהיו . . . . . .

כי תעשה הטוב בעיני ה׳ אלהיך

2 Chr 14:1: And Asa did what was *good and* right in the eyes of
the Lord *his God.*
Deut 12:28: When you do what is *good and* right in the eyes of the
Lord *your God.*[3]

The phrase ה׳ (מלפני/) בעיני *הטוב והישר* עשה 'did what was *good and right*
in the eyes of the Lord' appears in the Bible only four times:[4] twice in
Deuteronomy (6:18; 12:28) and twice in Chronicles. Once it is used in
the text under consideration, in the evaluation of Asa. The other time is
in 2 Chr 31:20 (an "addition") in the evaluation of the righteous king,
Hezekiah. This verse was composed by the Chronicler by altering and
strengthening the relevant phrase: ויעש הטוב והישר *והאמת* לפני ה׳ אלהיו
'and he did what was good and right *and faithful* before the Lord his
God'.[5] The fact that this phrase appears only in Deuteronomy and

2. See Tov, "Harmonizations," 3–29. On pp. 19–23 he adduces examples of textual
harmonization for early biblical translations.

3. Cf. also Deut 6:18: ה׳ בעיני והטוב הישר ועשית 'and you shall do that which is right
and good in the eyes of the Lord' (in the Samaritan Pentateuch, Peshiṭta, and in some
manuscripts of the LXX, the wording here is אלהיך ה׳ בעיני 'in the eyes of the Lord your
God', apparently to bring about harmonization with the parallel text in Deut 12:28).

4. Yet without connection with ה׳ (מלפני/) עיני; see also Josh 19:25; Jer 26:14, 40:4;
and cf. 2 Kgs 10:3.

5. On the basis of these words, the Chronicler immediately introduced Sennacherib's campaign against Hezekiah: . . . . אשור מלך סנחריב בא האלה והאמת הדברים אחרי 'After
these things and this faithfulness, Sennacherib, king of Assyria, came . . .' (2 Chr
32:1). The evaluation in 2 Chr 31:20 is an addition to that adduced in 2 Chr 29:2 =
2 Kgs 18:3, ה׳ בעיני הישר ויעש 'And he did what was right in the eyes of the Lord', wording that occurs in connection with other kings of Judah (see following note).

Chronicles stresses the use made by the Chronicler of the earlier book, Deuteronomy.

It should be noted that, in general, in evaluating the character of the other kings of Judah, the Chronicler adduces the wording of the same text in Kings without any change: "And (. . .) did what was right in the eyes of the Lord." So, for example 2 Chr 24:2 = 2 Kgs 12:3 (Jehoash); 2 Chr 25:2 = 2 Kgs 14:3 (Amaziah); 2 Chr 26:4 = 2 Kgs 15:3 (Uzziah); 2 Chr 27:2 = 2 Kgs 15:34 (Jotham); 2 Chr 34:2 = 2 Kgs 22:2 (Josiah).[6]

7.2 In 2 Chr 33:8, part of the narrative about the reign of Mannaseh, the Chronicler uses a Deuteronomistic phrase from the parallel 2 Kgs 21:8, thus creating textual harmony with Deuteronomy and other biblical books:

רק אם ישמרו לעשות *ככל* אשר צויתם ולכל התורה ‎_____ _____ :2 Kgs 21:8
אשר צוה אתם *עבדי* משה

If only they will observe to do *according to all* that I have commanded them and according to all the law _____ _____ that my *servant* Moses commanded them.

רק אם ישמרו לעשות את כל אשר צויתים לכל התורה והחקים :2 Chr 33:8
והמשפטים ביד משה

If only they will observe to do *all* that I have commanded them, even all the law *and the statutes and the ordinances, by the hand of* Moses.[7]

ושמרתם לעשות את כל החקים *והמשפטים* אשר אנכי נתן לפניכם :Deut 11:32
היום

And you shall observe to do all the statutes *and the ordinances* that I set before you this day.[8]

אלה *החקים והמשפטים* והתורת אשר נתן ה' . . . *ביד* משה :Lev 26:46

These are *the statutes and the ordinances* and the laws that the Lord established . . . *by the hand of* Moses.

ללכת בתורת האלהים אשר נתנה *ביד* משה עבד האלהים ולשמור :Neh 10:30
ולעשות *את כל* מצות ה' אדנינו *ומשפטיו וחקיו*

to walk in God's law, which was given *by the hand of* Moses the servant of God, and to observe and do *all* the commandments of the Lord our Lord, *and His ordinances and His statutes*.

---

6. Indeed, this phrase is more frequent in the Bible, and see also, for example, Exod 15:26; Deut 12:25; 13:19; 1 Kgs 11:38; and cf. Judg 17:6; 21:25. The opposite phrase to ה' בעיני הישר (. . .) ויעש in Kings and Chronicles is ה' בעיני הרע (. . .) ויעש.

7. The Peshiṭta has here: משה עבדי אתם צוה אשר 'that My servant Moses commanded them' in place of the MT משה ביד 'by the hand of Moses', apparently a result of the influence of Kings: cf. Curtis-Madsen, *Chronicles*, 497.

8. Cf. also Deut 4:8; 5:28; 26:17; et al.

Note that in a number of places in Kings the words חק(ים) ומשפט(ים) 'statute(s) and ordinance(s)' are used in similar phrases. For example:

ככל אשר צויתיך חוקי ומשפטי תשמר

according to all that I have commanded you, keeping my statutes
and my ordinances (1 Kgs 9:4 = 2 Chr 7:17);

ללכת בכל דרכיו ולשמור מצוותיו וחקיו ומשפטיו אשר צוה את אבותינו

. . . to walk in his ways and to observe his commandments and
statutes which he imposed on our fathers (1 Kgs 8:58).

And also 1 Chr 22:13:

תשמור לעשות את החקים ואת המשפטים אשר צוה ה' את משה על ישראל

. . . to observe the statutes and the ordinances which the Lord commanded Moses for Israel.

(And compare 1 Chr 28:8; 29:19, "addition.") This fact sufficed to moti-
vate the Chronicler to add the words to similar texts in his Vorlage in
which the words were, so to speak, "missing."

7.3 The verse in 2 Kgs 18:4 says of Hezekiah, king of Judah:

He *removed* the high places	הוא *הסיר* את הבמות .a
and *dashed in pieces* the pillars	*ושבר* את המצבת
and *cut down* the Asherah	*וכרת* את האשרה
and broke in pieces the bronze	וכתת נחש הנחשת אשר עשה משה .b
serpent that Moses had made,	כי עד הימים ההמה היו בני ישראל
for until those days the children	מקטרים לו ויקראו לו נחשתן
of Israel had burned incense to	
it and called it Nehushtan.	

In 2 Chr 31:1, the Chronicler copied the text of 2 Kgs 18:4a and created
textual harmony with the parallel passage in Deut 7:5 (cf. also Deut
12:3):[9]

2 Chr 31:1	*Deut 7:5*
<div dir="rtl">וככלות כל זאת יצאו כל ישראל</div>	<div dir="rtl">כי כה תעשו להם</div>
<div dir="rtl">הנמצאים לערי יהודה</div>	
<div dir="rtl">וישברו המצבות</div>	<div dir="rtl">מזבחתיהם *תתצו*</div>

---

9. The Chronicler omitted 2 Kgs 18:4b—regarding "the bronze serpent that Moses
had made"—because it stains the honor of Moses our Teacher; cf. Rudolph, *Chronik*,
305. For bronze serpent rites in Israel and in the ancient Near East, see Joines,
"Bronze Serpent," 245–56.

ויגדעו האשרים
וינתצו את הבמות ואת המזבחות

Now when all this was over,
all Israel who were present
went out to the cities of
Judah and *dashed in pieces*
the pillars
and *hewed down* the Asherim,
and *broke down*
the high places and the altars.

ומצבתם תשברו
ואשירהם תגדעון 10

But this is how you shall deal with
them:

you shall *break down*
their altars
and *dash in pieces* their pillars
and *hew down*
their Asherim.

This harmonization is not limited to the exchange of verbs, הסיר . . . כרת in Kings for the verbs גדע . . . נתץ in Deuteronomy; it is also attuned to the spirit of the Torah commandment. The Torah imposes the responsibility for the uprooting of foreign rituals on *the people*: כי כה תעשו להם 'but thus *shall you (pl.) deal* with them'. The Chronicler, accordingly, ascribes the uprooting of the rites not to the king, as in 2 Kgs 18:4, but to *the people*—"*all Israel* who were present *went out* to the cities of Judah"—and then shifts from the singular forms הסיר . . . שבר . . . כרת in the earlier text to the plural forms וישברו . . . ויגדעו . . . וינתצו, to match those in the Torah.

The addition of the phrase ואת המזבחות 'and the altars' to the earlier text may itself be influenced by the wording of Deuteronomy, which requires מזבחתיהם תתצו 'you shall break down their altars'.

7.4 2 Kgs 21:3 describes Manasseh, king of Judah, in this way: וישב וִיבן את הבמות אשר אבד חזקיהו אביו 'For he rebuilt the high places that Hezekiah, his father, had destroyed'. In 2 Chr 33:3, the Chronicler used נתץ instead of אבד, which is found in the earlier text, apparently to create textual harmonization with the narrative of Hezekiah's reign in 2 Chr 31:1: וינתצו את הבמות 'and broke down the high places':

	2 Kings		*2 Chronicles*	
Hezekiah:	הוא הסיר את הבמות	18:4	וינתצו את הבמות	31:1
	He *removed* the high places		(they) *broke down* the high places	
Manasseh:	וישב ויבן את הבמות	21:3	וישב ויבן את הבמות	33:3
	אשר אבד חזקיהו אביו[11]		אשר נתץ יחזקיהו אביו	
	He rebuilt the high places		He rebuilt the high places	
	that Hezekiah his father had		that Hezekiah his father had	
	destroyed.		*broken down.*	

---

10. The Samaritan Pentateuch has ואשריהם, as do also in a number of manuscripts of the MT.

11. The Lucianic recension changed the wording here, writing κατέσκαψεν 'and broke down', as in the parallel text in Chronicles.

Indeed, the root נתץ often appears in the Bible to denote the destruction of an altar or a high place; see, for example, 2 Kgs 23:8: ונתץ את במות השערים 'and he broke down the high places of the gates'; 23:12, 15; Exod 34:13; Deut 7:5; 12:3; Judg 2:2; 6:28, 30–32; 2 Chr 34:7.

7.5 In 2 Kgs 21:2 the Deuteronomistic historian writes about Manasseh: ויעש הרע בעיני ה׳ כתועבת הגוים אשר הוריש ה׳ מפני בני ישראל 'And he did what was evil in the sight of the Lord, following the abominations of the nations that the Lord cast out before the children of Israel'. Further along in the text, he lists these abominations one by one (21:6): והעביר את בנו באש ועונן ונחש _ _ _ ועשה אוב וידענים 'And he passed his son through the fire and practiced soothsaying and sorcery and dealt with persons who consulted ghosts and spirits'. These verses resemble the Deuteronomistic commandment in Deut 18:9–12 linguistically and stylistically but are in opposition to its injunction:

כי אתה בא אל הארץ אשר ה׳ אלהיך נתן לך, לא תלמד לעשות כתועבת הגוים
ההם, לא ימצא בך מעביר בנו ובתו באש קסמים מעונן ומנחש *ומכשף* וחבר חבר
ושאל אוב וידעני_ . . . , כי תועבת ה׳ כל עשה אלה ובגלל התועבת האלה ה׳
אלהיך מוריש אותם מפניך

When you come into the land that the Lord your God has given
you, you shall not learn to follow the abominations of those
nations; there shall not be found among you anyone who passes
his son or his daughter through the fire, one who uses divination,
a soothsayer or an enchanter or a sorcerer or a charmer or one who
consults a ghost or a spirit . . . , for whoever does these things is an
abomination to the Lord; and because of these abominations the
Lord your God is driving them out before you.

This linguistic-stylistic similarity led the Chronicler to copy the text from Kings, while completing and matching certain details to the text in Deuteronomy (2 Chr 33:2, 6):

ויעש הרע בעיני ה׳ כתועבות הגוים אשר הוריש ה׳ מפני בני ישראל . . . והוא
העביר את בניו[12] באש בגי בן-הנם ועונן ונחש *וכשף* ועשה אוב וידעוני

And he did what was evil in the sight of the Lord, just like the
abominations of the nations whom the Lord drove out before the
children of Israel . . . , and he passed his sons through the fire in
the valley of Ben Hinnom; and practiced soothsaying and used
enchantments and practiced sorcery and consulted ghosts and
spirits.

---

12. In the Peshiṭta, the wording here has been attuned to the MT reading of the parallel text in Kings: בנו 'his son'. Cf. Curtis-Madsen, *Chronicles*, 497. In the LXX of 2 Kgs 21:6, one reads: בניו 'his sons', as in Chronicles.

It should be stressed that the phrase וּ(מְ)עוֹנֵן וּ(מְ)נַחֵשׁ וּ(מְ)כַשֵּׁף 'and practices/d soothsaying and uses/d enchantments and practices/d sorcery', with its three component parts, only appears in the Bible twice—in the text under consideration in Chronicles and in Deut 18:10—a fact that underlines the connection between the two passages.

7.6 In reply to Solomon's prayer, the Lord stresses that, if the children of Israel do not observe his laws and commandments or if they worship other gods, they will be removed—they will be exiled from their land (1 Kgs 9:6–7): והכרתי את ישראל מעל פני האדמה אשר נתתי להם 'then will I *remove*[13] Israel from the land that I have given them'. Instead of this, the Chronicler wrote in 2 Chr 7:20: ונתשתים מעל אדמתי אשר נתתי להם 'then will I *uproot* them out of my land that I have given them'. Avishur[14] lists the כרת/נתש interchange in the above texts as a word pair alternating in parallel texts. He does not, however, explain why the Chronicler chose at this particular point to use the word נתש instead of the word כרת, used in the earlier text. Japhet[15] writes: "נתש is rarer than כרת, and is found mainly in Jeremiah. It may be the influence of this book that led to the selection of the alternate verb."

It seems, however, that the explanation for this change in Chronicles is as follows: the passage in 1 Kgs 9:6–9 is part of a speech that the Deuteronomistic editor of Kings has put in God's mouth. In fact, it has clearly been influenced to a considerable extent by the passage in Deut 29:21–27, both with regard to its content and to its phraseology, style, and literary structure. Indeed, according to the passage in Deuteronomy, the punishment for forsaking the Covenant of the Lord and for worshiping other gods (vv. 24–25) is this (Deut 21:27): ויתשם ה' מעל אדמתם 'And the Lord *uprooted* them from their land'. In 2 Chr 7:20, the Chronicler matched the text in 1 Kgs 9:7 with that of Deut 29:27 and wrote: ונתשתים מעל אדמתי אשר נתתי להם.

7.7 In 2 Chr 6:40, the Chronicler has, to all appearances, attempted to match up the text of Solomon's prayer (1 Kgs 8:52) with the text of Nehemiah's prayer (Neh 1:6): he has added the phrase ואזניך קשובות 'and Your ears attentive', according to the text in Nehemiah, to the expression עיניך פתחות 'let your eyes be open', which he adduced from Kings;[16]

---

13. That the root כרת here means 'remove, exile' is clear from the rest of the passage: והיה ישראל למשל ולשנינה בכל העמים 'and Israel shall be a proverb and a byword among all peoples'.

14. See Avishur, *Word Pairs*, 531.

15. Japhet, "Interchanges," 20.

16. For the phrase ואזניך קשובות, see also Neh 1:11, אנא ה', תהי נא אזנך קשבת אל תפלת עבדך 'Please, O Lord, let your ear be attentive to the prayer of your servant', as well

and, in place of the words לִהְיוֹת . . . אֶל תְּחִנַּת in Kings, he has written תְּחִי נָא . . . יִהְיוּ נָא, similar to the text in Nehemiah—אֶל תְּפִלַּת . . . לִתְפִלַּת:

1 Kgs 8:52	2 Chr 6:40	Neh 1:6
להיות	יִהְיוּ נָא	תְּהִי נָא
עיניך פתחות	עיניך פתחות	*אָזְנְךָ קַשֶּׁבֶת*
	ואזניך קשבות	וְעֵינֶיךָ פְתֻחוֹת
אל תחנת עבדך	לתפלת המקום הזה	לשמע *אל תפלת עבדך*
ואל תחנת עמך ישראל . . .		
that your eyes may	please let	please let
be open to the	*your eyes be open*	*your ear be attentive*
supplication of	*and your ears be*	*and your eyes open*
your servant and	*attentive* to the	to listen to the
to the supplication	prayer (made) in	prayer of your servant
of your people Israel.	this place	

The phrases אזניך קשבות and ועיניך פתחות are adduced in Chronicles in the order characteristic of chiastic parallelism, strengthening our assumption that the Chronicler had in mind the text in Neh 1:6 ("the Seidel rule").[17] Note also that in 2 Chr 7:15 the Chronicler inserted this verse into the Lord's reply to Solomon: עתה עיני יהיו פתחת ואזני קשבות לתפלת המקום הזה 'Now my eyes shall be open and my ears attentive to the prayer (made) in this place (that is, to the prayers "that they shall pray toward this place," 6:20)'.

7.8 With the ascension of Rehoboam son of Solomon to the throne, the tribes of the North made their demands (1 Kgs 12:4 // 2 Chr 10:4): הקל מעבדת אביך הקשה ומעלו הכבד אשר נתן עלינו ונעבדך 'Now lighten the grievous service of your father and his heavy yoke that he put on us, and we will serve you'. Rehoboam, however, not only refused to respond to their demands, he informed them that he would make his yoke heavier than his father's (1 Kgs 12:12–14 // 2 Chr 10:12–14). Accordingly, the tribes of the North rebelled against him, announcing (1 Kgs 12:16): מה לנו חלק בדוד ולא נחלה בבן ישי לאהליך ישראל 'What portion have we in David? We have no inheritance in the son of Jesse. To your tents, O Israel!' The Chronicler used this text in 2 Chr 10:16, adding the word איש between the phrases בבן ישי and לאהליך ישראל, in accordance with the parallel text about the rebellion of Sheba, son of Bichri, against David (2 Sam 20:1):[18]

as Ps 130:2: תהיינה אזניך קשבות לקול תחנוני 'Let your ears be attentive to the voice of my supplications'.

17. See chap. 12, p. 232.

18. Opposing Curtis and Madsen, who believe that the word איש 'man' resulted from dittography with the word ישי 'Jesse' (*Chronicles*, 364).

1 Kgs 12:16	2 Chr 10:16	2 Sam 20:1
מה לנו חלק בדוד	מה לנו חלק בדויד	אין לנו חלק בדוד
ולא נחלה בבן ישי	ולא נחלה בבן ישי	ולא נחלה (לנו)[19] בבן ישי
לאהליך ישראל	איש לאהליך ישראל	איש[20] לאהליו ישראל
What portion have	What portion have	We have no portion
we in David? We	we in David? We	in David, no
have no inheritance	have no inheritance	inheritance
in the son of Jesse.	in the son of Jesse.	in the son of Jesse.
To your	*Each of you* to your	*Everyone* to your
tents, O Israel!	tents, O Israel!	tents, O Israel!

This addition broadens the base of the analogy existing between the Northern tribes' declaration of rebellion against Solomon's son and their declaration of rebellion against Solomon's father, an analogy that portrays them as recidivist rebels against the Davidic dynasty.

7.9 Nathan's prophecy to David in 2 Sam 7:15a includes the following phrase: וחסדי לא יסור ממנו 'but my mercy shall not depart *from him*', whereas the parallel text in 1 Chr 17:13b has וחסדי לא אסיר מעמו 'and I will not take my mercy *away from him*'. The word אסיר 'take' in Chronicles may indeed reflect the Chronicler's *Vorlage*, and the Septuagint, Vulgate, and Peshiṭta of Samuel do have the equivalent wording. This version also fits well into the Lord's statement to David, worded as it is with a first-person future form, and even parallels the form הסירותי, which appears further along in the passage.

However, despite the fact that the words ממנו and מעמו are of similar meaning and occur in both early and later Hebrew, the Chronicler found it necessary to adjust the wording of the passage in Samuel to that of

---

19. The (second occurrence of the) word לנו does not appear in seven manuscripts of the MT of Samuel or in the Peshiṭta, the Old Latin, and the Vulgate version. It also does not appear in the parallel verse in 1 Kgs 12:16 and in 2 Chr 10:16. It is thus possible that the word is secondary in our text, having been erroneously written into it from the beginning of the verse: . . . אין לנו. There is a similar phenomenon, for example, in the phrase יערי ארגים in 2 Sam 21:19: the word ארגים was erroneously transposed from the end of the verse, which concludes with the words כמנור ארגים 'like a weaver's beam', to its beginning—in the parallel text in 1 Chr 20:5 the name, indeed, appears in its original form: בן יעור.

20. The word איש is stressed further on in the text as well: ויעל כל איש ישראל מאחרי דוד אחרי שבע בן בכרי ואיש יהודה דבקו במלכם . . . 'So all the men of Israel went up from following David and they followed Sheba, son of Bichri; but the men of Judah did cleave unto their king" (2 Sam 20:2). For the expression איש לאהליו/לאהליך 'each man to your/his tents'; cf. also 2 Sam 18:17: וכל ישראל נס איש לאהליו 'and all Israel fled, each man to his tent'.

the parallel text in Ps 89:34a: וחסדי לא אפיר [21] מעמו 'but my mercy will I not remove from him',[22] and wrote מעמו instead of ממנו. Indeed, the roots סור and חסד do appear in similar contexts specifically with מעמ(ו), as can be seen, for example, in the following verses:

סור:	1 Sam 16:14	ורוח ה׳ סרה מעם שאול
		The spirit of the Lord had departed from Saul
	1 Sam 18:12	כי היה ה׳ עמו ומעם שאול סר
		for the Lord was with him and had departed from Saul
	1 Sam 18:13	ויסירהו שאול מעמו
		Thus, Saul removed him from him
חסד:	1 Sam 20:15	ולא תכרית את חסדך מעם ביתי
		and do not cut off your kindness from my house
	Gen 24:27	אשר לא עזב חסדו ואמתו מעם אדני
		who has not forsaken his mercy and his truth
		toward my master

7.10 2 Kgs 22:20 relates that Hulda prophesied concerning Josiah: ולא תראינה עיניך בכל הרעה אשר אני מביא על המקום הזה 'neither shall your eyes see all the evil that I will bring upon this place'. In 2 Chr 34:28 the Chronicler adduced this verse and added the words ועל ישביו 'and upon the inhabitants thereof', apparently in order to harmonize the Lord's word in v. 24 (// 2 Kgs 22:16) with the words that Josiah heard, על המקום הזה ועל ישביו 'upon this place and the inhabitants thereof' (v. 27 // 2 Kgs 22:19):

2 Kings 22	*2 Chronicles 34*
16. Thus says the Lord: "Behold, I shall bring evil *upon this place and upon the inhabitants thereof.*"	24. Thus says the Lord: "Behold, I shall bring evil *upon this place and upon the inhabitants thereof.*"
19. Because your heart was tender, and you humbled yourself before the Lord when you heard what I spoke *against this place and against the inhabitants thereof.*	27. Because your heart was tender, and you humbled yourself before God when you heard his words *against this place and against the inhabitants thereof.*
20. Thus, behold, I will gather you to your fathers, and you will be	28. Behold, I will gather you to your fathers, and you will be

21. The initial version of this verse may well have been אסיר, as in the Peshitta, the Vulgate, and a number of MT manuscripts; and cf. Briggs and Briggs, *Psalms*, 2.261; F. Buhl, in *BH*, 1054; Tur-Sinai, *Peshutô*, 4.190.

22. This psalm is a later elaboration on Nathan's original prophecy in Samuel; see Sarna, "Psalm 89," 29–46.

gathered to your grave in peace; neither shall your eyes see all the evil that I will bring *on this place.* [23]	gathered to your grave in peace: neither shall your eyes see all the evil that I will bring *upon this place and the inhabitants thereof.*

7.11 1 Kgs 3:11–14 relates that, in reply to Solomon's request for wisdom, the Lord said to him, among other things:

יען אשר שאלת את הדבר הזה . . .
ולא שאלת לך עשר _ _ _ _
ולא שאלת נפש איביך
ושאלת לך הבין לשמע משפט
הנה עשיתי כדברך
הנה נתתי לך לב חכם ונבון . . .
וגם אשר לא שאלת נתתי לך גם *עשר* גם כַבוד

Because you have asked this thing . . .
and have not asked for riches for yourself,
nor have asked for the life of your enemies;
but have asked for understanding to discern justice;
behold, I have done according to your word:
I have given you a wise and understanding heart; . . .
and I have also given you what you have not asked for,
    both *riches* and ho<u>no</u>r.

The phrase *ולא שאלת לך עשר* appears twice in the Lord's reply: once in quoting from Solomon's own statement regarding the things that he did not request (v. 11c) and once in noting the items that he promises to Solomon, despite his not having requested them—with the addition of the words גם כבוד 'and honor' (v. 13a): וגם אשר *לא שאלת נתתי לך, גם עשר גם* כבוד 'and I have also given you what *you have not asked for,* both *riches* and honor'. In 2 Chr 1:11–12, the Chronicler has created harmony between the two parallel phrases in the text by mentioning the word כבוד the first time as well:

לא שאלת עשר , נכסים [24] *וכבוד*
11b. and *you have not asked riches,* wealth, or *honor*
ועשר ונכסים וכבוד אתן לך
12b. and I will give you *riches* and wealth and *honor*

---

23. Here Lucian added the words "and the inhabitants thereof," whether in accordance with the parallel text in Chronicles or in accordance with the previous vv. 16, 19—or both.

24. For the word נכסים, which is characteristic of the later stratum of Biblical Hebrew, see the thorough discussion in Hurvitz, *Transition Period,* 24–26.

The phrase עשר ונכסים וכבוד seems to have been transferred from here to
Qoh 6:2: איש אשר יתן לו האלהים עשר ונכסים וכבוד ואיננו חסר לנפשו מכל אשר
יתאוה[25] 'a man to whom God gives *riches, wealth,* and honor so that he
wants nothing for his soul of all that he desires'. The purpose of this
quotation in Qohelet may well be to strengthen the impression that the
speaker is King Solomon.

7.12 1 Kgs 15:13 speaks of Asa, king of Judah, who deposed his
mother the queen, cut down the image she had set up as an Asherah,
and burned it in the Kidron Valley: ויכרת אסא את מפלצתה וישרף בנחל קדרון
'And Asa cut down her image and *burned* it *in the Kidron Valley*'. In
2 Chr 15:16, the Chronicler used this text, having harmonized the narratives of Asa's burning of the Asherah image in the Kidron Valley,
Josiah's burning of the Asherah in the Kidron Valley, and the burning
of the golden calf by Moses:

2 Chr 15:16b	2 Kgs 23:6	Exod 32:20
ויכרת אסא את מפלצתה	ויצא את האשרה מבית ה׳	ויקח את העגל אשר עשו
וידק וישרף	וישרף אתה בנחל קדרון	וישרף באש
בנחל קדרון	וידק לעפר . . .	ויטחן עד אשר דק[26]
and Asa cut down her	and he brought the	and he took the calf
image	Asherah out of the	that they had made,
and *stamped it down*	House of the Lord . . .	and *burned* it *in fire*
and burned it in	and burned it in the	and *ground it to dust.*
the Kidron Valley.	Kidron Valley, *and*	
	stamped it into dust.	

It seems that the word וידק 'and stamped it down' in 2 Chr 15:16b is the
Chronicler's[27] and not "a late addition to his work."[28] The fact that this
word does not appear in the Greek translation, the Peshiṭta, or the Vulgate of 2 Chr 15:16b stems, apparently, from an inverse process: an attempt to harmonize the verse in the later Chronicles text with the verse
in the earlier Kings text.

7.13 In 1 Chr 14:11, 13b, 16b, the Chronicler adjusted 2 Sam 5:20,
22b, and 25b to match Isa 28:21. This prophetic source may be alluding
to David's triumphs over the Philistines as related in 2 Sam 5:17–25, using them as an example of the Lord's intervention on behalf of his

---

25. See also Qoh 5:18. Qohelet was apparently written in the Hellenistic period
(3rd century B.C.E.); see Fox, "Ecclesiastes," 71; Crenshaw, "Ecclesiastes," 275; as well
as many other commentators.

26. See also 2 Chr 34:4, 7 ("addition").

27. Cf. Curtis-Madsen, *Chronicles*, 386; Rudolph, *Chronik*, 246.

28. Against Benzinger, *Chronik*, 102; Elmslie, *Chronicles* (1916) xxiii.

people: כי כהר פרצים יקום ה׳, כעמק[29] בגבעון ירגז לעשות מעשהו 'For the Lord will rise up as on Mount Perazim, he will rage as in the valley of Gibeon to do his work' (Isa 28:21). Though the connection between this verse and the verses preceding and following it is not sufficiently clear, the considerable linguistic similarity between it and the narrative in 2 Samuel 5, as well as the fact that references to historical events appear in the book of Isaiah in particular (for example, Isa 9:3: החתת כיום מדין 'You have broken as on the day of Midian' is apparently referring to Gideon's war against the Midianites as described in Judges 6–8; and see also Isa 10:26 ועורר עליו ה׳ צבאות שוט כמכת מדין בצור עורב 'and the Lord of Hosts shall wield a scourge against him, as in the slaughter of Midian at the rock of Oreb') and in prophetic literature in general[30] make my assumption quite likely.

The phrase כהר פרצים יקום ה׳ 'the Lord will rise up as on Mount Perazim' is a reference to David's victory at Baal-perazim, פרץ ה׳ את איבי לפני כפרץ מים 'the Lord has broken my enemies before me like a breach of waters' (2 Sam 5:20);[31] while כעמק בגבעון ירגז 'he will rage in the valley of Gibeon' alludes to David's second victory over the Philistines, who had raided the valley of Rephaim but were defeated מגבע עד באך גזר 'from Geba to the approach to Gezer' (2 Sam 5:22–25). There are indeed scholars who feel that כעמק בגבעון ירגז relates to Joshua's victory over the Canaanites at *Gibeon* (Josh 10:10–11) rather than to David's victory over the Philistines "from *Geba* to the approach to Gezer" (2 Sam 5:25b).[32] It is more reasonable, however, to assume that the prophet is referring to David's two victories over the Philistines, victories described one after the other in 2 Sam 5:17–25, rather than to two victories by two different military leaders over different foes in different periods, which are described in different anthologies. That the phrase כעמק בגבעון ירגז refers to מגבע עד באך גזר can also be concluded from the wordplay ירגז – גזר. Furthermore, Demsky[33] has already shown that in the books of Samuel the name גבע often appears in place of the more common גבעון. Thus, we probably should not conclude from the גבע/גבעון interchange that two separate events are being referred to.[34]

---

29. The wording of 1QIsaᵃ, . . . בהר . . . בעמק, seems secondary (the substitution of graphically similar ב for כ, which denotes resemblance), for the prophet is comparing the Lord's future actions with actions in the past, which serve him as examples.

30. For this, see below, chap. 10, "Allusion," pp. 194–195.

31. In this respect, commentators on Isaiah agree with commentators on the books of Samuel and Chronicles: see, e.g., Curtis-Madsen, *Chronicles*, 209; Smith, *Samuel*, 290; Wildberger, *Jesaja*, 1079; Watts, *Isaiah*, 371.

32. Thus, e.g., Luzzatto, *Isaiah*, 219; Clements, *Isaiah*, 232; Driver, *Samuel*, 265; Segal, *Samuel*, 268; Williamson, *Chronicles*, 119.

33. Demsky, "Geba," 26–31.

34. For this, see also example 5.4 (p. 103).

In describing the first war, the Chronicler equated בעל פרצים 'Baal-perazim' in Samuel with הר פרצים 'Mount Perazim' in Isaiah, and as a result wrote ויעלו בבעל פרצים 'So they *ascended* to Baal-perazim' (1 Chr 14:11) in place of ויבא דוד בבעל פרצים 'And David *came* to Baal-perazim' (2 Sam 5:20), because the use of the verb עלה is more suited to contexts involving high places—mountains or hills.[35] In his description of the second war he wrote ויפשטו בעמק 'And (they) made a raid in the valley' (1 Chr 14:13b) in place of וינטשו בעמק רפאים 'and spread themselves out in the valley of Rephaim' (2 Sam 5:22b). Similarly, the Chronicler preferred to use the name Gibeon ויכו את מחנה פלשתים מגבעון עד גזרה 'And they smote the camp of the Philistines *from Gibeon* even to Gezer' (1 Chr 14:16b) instead of the name Geba: ויך את פלשתים מגבע עד באך גזר 'and he smote the Philistines *from Geba* to the approach to Gezer' (2 Sam 5:25b).[36] These emendations were apparently intended to create textual harmonization between the passage in Samuel and the verse alluding to it in Isaiah, כעמק בגבעון ירגז,[37] in order to expand the base of analogy between an allusive text and the text alluded to and to tighten the links between them.[38]

7.14 2 Sam 5:2 says that the Northern tribes of Israel, when asking David to reign over them, quoted a prophecy predicting that David would reign over Israel. In 1 Chr 11:2, the Chronicler used this quotation to harmonize his text with the parallel text of Nathan's prophecy to David:

---

35. Cf. Williamson, *Chronicles*, 118. For another explanation of this change, see below, §3, "Harmonizing Divine Word with Divine Action." The place בעל / הר פרצים is identified with a mountain or a hill adjoining the valley of Rephaim, though there are differences of opinion concerning the precise identification of the site. For the various opinions, see Kallai, "Baal Perazim," 290–91. A. Mazar ("An Early Israelite Site," 37–38) has suggested that Baal-perazim be identified with a site in the Gilo neighborhood of southern Jerusalem, at the peak of the mountain ridge between the valley of Rephaim and Beit-Jala. B. Mazar ("Israelite Settlement," 153–54) accepted this identification, in the belief "that Baal Perazim, being adjacent to Bethlehem, the town where David was born, was merely the ritual center of the clan whose 'father' was Perez, Judah's firstborn."

36. The LXX reading here, מגבעון, is apparently the work of the translator who tried to harmonize the text with those in Chronicles and in Isaiah. However, the possibility that this translation reflects an early version cannot be ruled out. Driver postulated, following Thenius, that the Masoretic reading מגבע is an abbreviated form—that is, מגבע = מגבעון (Driver, "Abbreviations," 123).

37. Cf. in general terms Rudolph, *Chronik*, 114; Segal, *Samuel*, 268.

38. Another explanation is provided by Abramsky (*Saul and David*, 383 n. 3): "The Chronicler, because of the respect he accorded Gibeon, relied on the passage in Isaiah."

2 Sam 5:2	*1 Chr 11:2*	*1 Chr 17:7 (// 2 Sam 7:9)*
ויאמר ה׳ לך	ויאמר ה׳ אלהיך לך	כה אמר ה׳ צבאות
אתה תרעה את עמי	אתה תרעה את עמי	אני לקחתיך מן הנוה
את ישראל	את ישראל	מן אחרי הצאן
ואתה תהיה לנגיד	ואתה תהיה _נגיד	להיות _נגיד
על ישראל	על *עמי* ישראל	על *עמי* 39 ישראל
And the Lord said to you: "You shall feed my people Israel, and you shall be prince over Israel."	And the Lord your God said to you: "You shall feed my people Israel, and you shall be prince over *my people* Israel."	Thus says the Lord of hosts: "I took you from the pasture, from following the flock, to be prince over *my people* Israel."

The addition of the word עמי 'my people' in 1 Chr 11:2 actually perfects the symmetry between the first part of God's statement to David, *אתה תרעה את עמי את ישראל* 'You shall feed my people Israel', and the end of the statement, *ואתה תהיה נגיד על עמי ישראל* 'and you shall be prince over my people Israel'. In this way, the word of the Lord is presented with a more complete literary design.

7.15 Solomon's statement to the Lord in 1 Kgs 8:26 parallels David's statement to the Lord in 2 Sam 7:25. The Chronicler attempted to create as broad a harmony as possible between these two texts—that is, between the original words used by the father and the words quoted by the son. Instead of the word הקם in Samuel, he wrote יאמן, as in Kings; he introduced the word ה׳, which is in David's statement, into Solomon's statement; and he omitted the word נא, which appears only in Solomon's speech:[40]

2 Sam 7:25	//	*1 Chr 17:23*		*2 Chr 6:17*	//	*1 Kgs 8:26*
ועתה ה׳ אלהים		ועתה ה׳		ועתה ה׳ אלהי ישראל		ועתה __ אלהי ישראל
הדבר אשר דברת		הדבר אשר דברת				
על עבדך ועל ביתו		על עבדך ועל ביתו				

---

39. In 2 Sam 7:9, the word על is repeated, though it is actually unnecessary and could have been omitted. The omission of the word in 1 Chr 17:7 expands the harmony between this passage and its parallel text in 1 Chr 11:2.

40. The word נא 'please' appears in manuscripts of the Greek and Syriac translations to 2 Chr 6:17, but these readings are secondary, as shown by the fact that the word is missing in this very text that the Chronicler introduced into 2 Chr 1:9a: עתה ה׳ אלהים יאמן דברך . . . 'Now, O Lord God, let your promise . . . be established'.

הקם	יאמן	יאמן	יאמן נא
		דברך אשר	‏(Qere): דבריך
		דברת	‏דברך) אשר דברת
		לעבדך לדויד[41]	לעבדך דו ד אבי[42]
And now, O Lord God, confirm the word that you have spoken concerning your servant and concerning his House.	And now, O Lord, let the word that you have spoken concerning your servant and concerning his House, be *verified*.	And now, O Lord, God of Israel, let your word be *verified* that you spoke to your servant David.	And now, God of Israel, let your word be *verified* that you spoke unto your servant David, my father.

7.16 In descriptions of the making of the Temple vessels in the book of Kings, the expression "X (את) ויעש" is regularly used. For example:

And he made the molten sea (1 Kgs 7:23)	ויעש את הים
And he made the bases (1 Kgs 7:27)	ויעש את המכנות
And he made ten lavers (1 Kgs 7:38)	ויעש עשרה כירות

ויעש חירום את הכירות ואת היעים ואת המזרקות ויכל חירם לעשות את כל
המלאכה אשר עשה למלך שלמה בית ה׳

And Hiram made the lavers and the shovels and the basins. So Hiram finished all the work that he did for King Solomon in the House of the Lord (1 Kgs 7:40)

ואת כל הכלים האהל (Qere): האלה) אשר עשה חירם למלך שלמה בית ה׳

even all these vessels that Hiram made for King Solomon in the House of the Lord (1 Kgs 7:45)

ויעש שלמה את כל הכלים אשר בית ה׳ את מזבח הזהב ואת השלחן

And Solomon made all the vessels that were in the House of the Lord: the golden altar and the table (1 Kgs 7:48)

ותשלם כל המלאכה עשר עשה המלך שלמה בית ה׳

Thus, all the work that King Solomon did in the House of the Lord was finished (1 Kgs 7:51)

---

41. The reasoning of Japhet ("Interchanges," 36–37) is difficult to accept, as if the interchange stemmed from the Chronicler's desire to avoid using imperative mood forms toward God. This is so since, immediately thereafter, the text is adduced precisely, despite the imperative form in it: ועשה כאשר דברת 'and do as you have said' (1 Chr 17:23 // 2 Sam 7:25). Yet, as she puts it, the interchange does not stem from linguistic considerations for "the phrase הקים ברית, דבר, שבועה is very common in the Bible."

42. The passage in 2 Sam 7:25 is quoted in 1 Kgs 8:26 by Solomon in the order of chiastic parallelism.

The exception to this rule is the verse dealing with the pillars of brass. Here the verb used is ויצר:נחשת העמודים שני את [43]ויצר 'Thus he fashioned the two pillars of brass' (1 Kgs 7:15).

In 2 Chr 3:15, the Chronicler adjusted the language of this passage to match that of the other verses, writing: [44]שנים עמדים הבית לפני ויעש '*And he made* two pillars in front of the House'. Indeed, 1 Kgs 7:18, which has no parallel text in Chronicles, uses the verb ויעש in connection with the pillars: העמודים את ויעש.

7.17 The Chronicler also harmonizes the language of one narrative in the book of Samuel with a law in the Torah by combining both expressions into one. In 1 Chr 10:13–14 he adds a short summary to the earlier text, 1 Samuel 31, in order to explain the circumstances of the death of Saul and the transfer of the monarchy to David, son of Jesse. One of the reasons that he gives for Saul's death and the loss of the monarchy is: וימיתהו בה׳ דרש ולא לדרוש באוב לשאול וגם 'and also because he *consulted* a ghost *for guidance* and did not inquire of the Lord, and so he killed him' (1 Chr 10:13b–14a). Some consider the word לדרוש superfluous, added by dittography with the continuation of the verse, ולא דרש.[45] Some consider it a late gloss on the word לשאול, which appears earlier.[46] But why would it be deemed necessary to add a "gloss" alongside the common, clear word לשאול? Weiss is of the opinion that the word לדרוש is original: "ולא דרש is nothing but an explanatory gloss to לדרוש."[47] An explanation of a different sort has been proposed by Talmon: "the main part of the text, two synonymous versions—וגם לשאול / לדרש באוב."[48]

The wording seems to be neither dittography nor a gloss. That is to say, the double reading was not created while the text was being handed down, sometime after the Chronicler's own day. It is not the case that one manuscript of Chronicles did read וגם לשאול באוב while another manuscript had וגם לדרוש באוב, with the result that the transmitter did not know how to decide or did not want to decide between the various

---

43. In the LXX: καὶ ἐχώνευσε 'and he poured'.

44. The verb ויעש is used in all of the verses in Chronicles, including the paralleling passages adduced above from Kings; and see 2 Chr 3:16 (twice); 4:1, 2, 6, 11, 13, 16, 19.

45. See Ehrlich, *Randglossen*, 333; Begrich, *BH*, 1346; Rudolph, *Chronik*, 94; Braun, *1 Chronicles*, 148. The word לדרוש does not appear in the Peshiṭta.

46. See Rudolph and Braun in the previous note; Ackroyd, "Chronicler as Exegete," 8.

47. Weiss, "Negative לא," 36. Weiss indicates additional possible examples of the ל = לא phenomenon; see pp. 33–36.

48. Talmon, *Double Readings*, 22. According to him, the one reading reflects the wording in 1 Sam 28:7, while "the other adopts synonymous language similar to the synonymity of the parallel texts."

readings and therefore wrote both down. Instead, it seems that 1 Chr 10:13–14 was created by the Chronicler. He attempted to create textual harmonization between the language of the text in Deut 18:10–11— שאל אוב וידעני ודרש אל המתים . . . לא ימצא בך 'There shall not be found among you . . . one who *consults* a ghost or a familiar spirit or a necromancer'—and the language of the narrative of Saul and the woman who divined by means of a ghost in 1 Sam 28:7—ויאמר שאול לעבדיו: בקשו לי אשת בעלת־אוב ואלכה אליה ואדרשה בה 'Then said Saul to his servants: "Seek me a woman who divines by a ghost that I may go to her and *inquire* of her"'.[49] In this way the Chronicler combined the two phrases and brought them together, creating a double reading in his work.[50]

The legal terminology in Lev 19:31; 20:6 is פנה אל האבת 'appealing to the ghosts', but the Chronicler here added the language of the law as it appears in Deuteronomy, שאל אוב 'consult a ghost', apparently to facilitate the exegetical use of the name שאול 'Saul'.

2. Content Harmonization

Harmonization of content is the process of reconciling two mutually contradictory texts by adjusting the content of one to match the other. The Deuteronomistic historian generally used the earlier sources available to him without altering their content, even when they affronted his views. This was true, for example, of the narrative in which Elijah repaired "the altar of the Lord that was thrown down" (1 Kgs 18:30–32) and of Elijah's complaint before the Lord, את מזבחתיך הרסו 'they have thrown down your altars' (1 Kgs 19:10, 14), both of which contradict the rule in Deut 12:4–14 about limiting the performance of rituals to one place; and the story of David, who took away the idols of the Philistines (2 Sam 5:21) and thereby contradicted the demands of Deut 7:25 and 12:3 to destroy the idols of the Gentiles.[51] The Deuteronomist's views were expressed mainly in speeches or editorials located between his sources, like links, rather than inserted into his sources.[52]

---

49. The root דרש also appears in Isaiah's prophecies speaking of the ghosts: וכי יאמרו אליכם דרשו אל האבות ואל הידענים המצפצפים והמהגים הלוא עם אל אלהיו ידרש . . . 'And when they say unto you: "Seek unto the ghosts and the familiar spirits that chirp and that mutter; should not a people seek under their God?"' (Isa 8:19); ודרשו אל האלילים ואל האטים ואל האבות ואל הידענים 'And they shall seek unto the idols and to the whisperers, and to the ghosts, and to the familiar spirits' (Isa 29:3b). The stylistic and content similarity between the text in Chronicles ולא דרש כה' and that in Isaiah: עם אל אלהיו ידרש is worthy of note.

50. The roots שאל and דרש appear in parallel in Deut 18:11: . . . ושאל אוב וידעני ודרש אל המתים 'inquiring of a ghost and a familiar spirit, and asking of the dead'; and cf. Talmon, "Double Readings," 22 n. 153.

51. For this, see example 7.6 above (p. 129).

52. For this feature of Deuteronomistic historiography, see Wellhausen, *Prolegomena*, 224, 292 (ET, pp. 228, 294).

In contrast, the author of Chronicles mixed his views with the early sources. In other words, generally speaking, he reworked the sources and inserted his beliefs and opinions into them. He read the books of Samuel–Kings in light of the text of the Pentateuch, his starting point being his belief that all five books of the Torah preceded the historiographical books and that the national heroes had known the Torah, he himself being incapable of imagining that they had not observed its laws fastidiously. As a result, when the Chronicler encountered a contradiction between the description of the lives of certain persons in the books of Samuel–Kings and the requirements of the Torah, he attempted to reconcile them by adjusting the contents of the text in Samuel–Kings to the relevant Torah passage.[53] The presentation of national heroes in this way apparently stems from the existence of all sections of the Torah in the Chronicler's own day and its having become a first-rate normative force in individual and public life in Israel. We must remember that the book of Chronicles was almost certainly compiled during the period after the attempts made by Ezra and Nehemiah to have the Torah accepted in everyday life and the signing of the Covenant "to walk in God's law, which was given by Moses, . . . and to observe all the commandments of the Lord our master and his ordinances and his statutes" (Neh 10:30; and see also Ezra 9–10; Nehemiah 8–10; 13).

It seems that the main purpose of the harmonizations in the book of Chronicles is to portray as worthy of emulation the figures who carefully observed the commandments of the Torah in the history of the nation. The harmonizations were also intended to soothe the average reader, who encountered contradictions between the narratives in Samuel–Kings concerning the activities of national heroes and others who shaped national history and the demands of the Torah and the standards operative in his own day. This reader, lacking the knowledge and the instruments needed for the research and the study to reconcile the contradictions, was liable to lose his self-confidence.

This phenomenon has many typological examples in Josephus's *Jewish Antiquities*, in the ancient biblical translations, and in rabbinic literature. For instance, Gen 18:8 speaks of Abraham, who "took *butter and milk*, and the calf he had prepared and set them before them, and he stood by them under the tree while they ate." Since the consumption of butter and milk and a calf cannot be reconciled with the Torah requirement not to "seethe a kid in its mother's milk" (Exod 23:19; 34:26; Deut 14:21), Josephus wrote: "He ordered loaves of fine flour to be made forthwith and killed a calf and cooked it and brought it to them as they reclined under the oak" (*Ant.* 1.197). Josephus omitted the reference to "butter and milk" that was found in the early narrative.

---

53. Cf. ibid., 184, 292; von Rad, *Geschichtsbild*, 1; Kaufmann, *Religion of Israel*, 8.455–56.

The Chronicler attempted to harmonize contradictory passages within the book of Kings as well. Similarly, he created harmony between the contradictory requirements of laws that appear in different collections in the Torah when he referred to them in "additions" in his work (for instance, examples 7.30 [p. 164] and 7.31 [p. 164]) regarding Josiah's Passover).[54] However, most of the cases of content harmonization in Chronicles are between passages from Samuel–Kings and the Priestly source in the Pentateuch (P). The freshness and special influence of this source intertwined with earlier Torah sources (J, E, D) may well be the reason for this.

The adducing of early historiographical texts in harmony with Torah verses, sometimes to the extent of creating verbal analogies between them, distorts the realistic historical description of both characters and events. It portrays the narratives along lines that the later historian tried to draw for his potential readers in the Second Temple era. However, the Chronicler did not use this editorial-exegetical technique in a systematic fashion, as can be seen in chap. 20, §1 (below, pp. 381ff.).

7.18 Despite the fact that Solomon's ritual behavior at the onset of his reign was not acceptable to the Deuteronomistic historian, he refrained from condemning him. He did not even avoid a positive evaluation (1 Kgs 3:3): ויאהב שלמה את ה' ללכת בחקות דוד אביו 'and Solomon loved the Lord, walking in the statutes of David his father', though he expressed some reserve: רק בבמות הוא מזבח ומקטיר 'except that he sacrificed and offered incense on the high places', for this was the period prior to the establishment of the central Temple in Jerusalem. This was noted explicitly in connection with the ritual behavior of the people (1 Kgs 3:2): רק העם מזבחים בבמות, כי לא נבנה בית לשם ה' עד הימים ההם 'However, the people were sacrificing on the high places, because there was not yet a House built for the name of the Lord.'[55] Accordingly, this historian's understanding of the sacrifices offered up by Solomon on the great high place at Gibeon and afterward, in Jerusalem (vv. 4, 15), becomes evident to us, as well as his refusal to rule on this behavior.

The Chronicler's methodology was different. He would not accept the fact that Solomon, one of the more significant kings of Israel, worshiped the Lord at the high places, though this was in the period prior to the establishment of the Temple, for this ritual behavior contradicts

---

54. This is similar to the harmonizations found in the Samaritan Pentateuch between stories in the books of Exodus and Numbers and stories in Deuteronomy; for example, Exod 18:24–26 was adjusted to match Deut 1:9–18; for this and other examples, see Purvis, "Samaritan Pentateuch," 408–9.

55. This verse is a kind of interpretation of the principle of ritual concentration in Deut 12:8ff.; cf. Kaufmann, *Religion of Israel*, 1.86.

the Torah commandment: under all conditions (Lev 17:8–9, Holiness Code—H):

איש איש מבית ישראל ומן הגר אשר יגור בתוכם אשר יעלה עלה או זבח, ואל פתח
אהל־מועד לא יביאנו לעשות אתו לה', ונכרת האיש ההוא מעמיו

Anyone of the house of Israel or of the aliens who live among them who offers a burnt offering or a sacrifice and does not bring it to the entrance of the Tent of Meeting to sacrifice it to the Lord—that person shall be cut off from his people.

In the Chronicler's mind, apparently, it was not to be assumed that Solomon was unfamiliar with the entire Law of Moses, just as it was not to be assumed that King Solomon, chosen by the Lord to "sit on the throne of the Lord as king in place of David, his father" (1 Chr 29:23),[56] was familiar with a commandment of the Torah yet deliberately deviated from it.[57] For this reason, the Chronicler reworked the text of 1 Kings 3 in an attempt to harmonize it with the commandments of the Torah. According to him, the reason that Solomon went to sacrifice in Gibeon was not "that it was the great high place," as the Deuteronomist had presented it, but because "the Tent of Meeting of God that Moses, the servant of the Lord, had made in the wilderness was there, . . . and the bronze altar that Bezalel, the son of Uri, the son of Hur, had made had been placed in front of the Tabernacle of the Lord" (2 Chr 1:3, 5). In other words, the Chronicler identified "the high place that was in Gibeon" (1:3a) with the bronze altar created by Bezalel in front of the Tabernacle of the Lord, which in his opinion stood in Gibeon at the time.[58] Consequently, the conclusion to be drawn by the reader is that

---

56. See 1 Chr 28:5: "He has chosen Solomon my son to sit on the throne of the kingdom of the Lord over Israel"; 2 Chr 9:8: "who delighted in you, to set you on his throne, to be king for the Lord your God" (replacing "to set you on the throne of Israel" in 1 Kgs 10:9); 1 Chr 22:9–10; 28:10, etc. For Solomon sitting on the throne of the Lord, see North, "Religious Aspects," 24, 28; Wilda, *Königsbild*, 32; Poulssen, *König und Tempel*, 170, 172; Abramsky, "King Solomon," 4–5.

57. And, because the system of Divine retribution was one of the central pillars of the Chronicler's work, if Solomon really had deliberately transgressed a Torah commandment, he would have had to provide a punishment and would have had to explain why Solomon the sinner was worthy of divine revelation and beneficence: wisdom, wealth, riches, and honor.

58. The Chronicler had prepared his readers for this in 1 Chr 16:39–40; 21:29. In the passage under consideration he again says no less than four times that these ritual objects were to be found in Gibeon (vv. 3, 5, 6, 13a). The hypothesis raised by Welch (*Chronicler*, 31–32), that the passages mentioning the Tent of Meeting/the Tabernacle are late additions by a later editor of Chronicles, is groundless; cf. Williamson, *Chronicles*, 130.

Solomon's going to sacrifice there met the requirements of the Torah
and did not clash with them.[59]

Because of the Chronicler's understanding that Solomon and all of Israel were only permitted to offer incense or sacrifice on the altar in front
of the Tent of Meeting in Gibeon, he also omitted the testimony in the
book of Kings to the existence of a ritual custom followed by Solomon
and the people in sacrificing at the high places (1 Kgs 3:2–3). This is
why he omits information concerning burnt-offerings and peace-offerings that Solomon offered up in Jerusalem immediately after his return
from Gibeon (1 Kgs 3:15b). Instead he stresses a fourth time that the
Tent of Meeting stood alongside the high place in Gibeon (2 Chr 1:13a):

1 Kgs 3:15b	*2 Chr 1:13a*
ויבוא (שלמה) ירושלם	ויבא שלמה לבמה[60]
ויעמד לפני ארון ברית ה׳	אשר בגבעון ירושלם
ויעל עלות ויעש שלמים	מלפני אהל־מועד
And he came to Jerusalem	So Solomon came to the high
and stood before the Ark	place that was in Gibeon,
of the Covenant of the Lord,	to Jerusalem
and offered up burnt offerings	from the Tent of Meeting.
and made peace offerings	

Generally speaking, according to the Chronicler's understanding, the
Tent of Meeting instituted by Moses and the altar built by Bezalel
served Israel until the establishment of the Temple by King Solomon.
The Temple was a permanent replacement for the Tent of Meeting / the
Tabernacle, which was the mobile Temple, enveloped in holiness ever
since the days of the wandering in the wilderness. However, the Chronicler's words concerning the Tent of Meeting / the Tabernacle of the
Lord and the brazen altar in Gibeon stem from his intention to create
harmony between 1 Kings 3 and Lev 17:8–9. He tried to portray Solomon to his potential readers (who were familiar with all five books of the

---

59. Abramsky believes that in 2 Chr 1:3–6 the Chronicler acts to solve the problem of why "Solomon did not sacrifice near the Ark of God, for which David pitched a
tent in Jerusalem" ("King Solomon," 5). However, if this had been the difficulty the
Chronicler was facing, why would he omit the section of the text in 1 Kgs 3:15b: ויבוא
(שלמה) ירושלם ויעמד לפני ארון ברית ה׳ ויעל עלות ויעש שלמים 'and he [= Solomon] came to Jerusalem and stood before the Ark of the Covenant of the Lord and offered up burnt
offerings and peace offerings'? Abramsky's explanation of this (p. 12 n. 15), "that the
silence in Chronicles regarding the offering up of sacrifices in Jerusalem is intended
to blunt to some degree the wonder at the narrative of Solomon going to Gibeon," is
not convincing.

60. An error derived from מהבמה 'from the high place'; for this, see example 14.6
n. 20 (p. 305).

Pentateuch) as a personality without blemish. In other words, the founder of the Temple in no way exceeded the Torah's mandate regarding ritual matters; on the contrary, he behaved precisely in accordance with its instructions. For this reason, one should not regard 1 Chr 16:39–40; 21:29; 2 Chr 1:3, 5, 6, 13a as reliable historical traditions.[61]

This conclusion becomes doubly authoritative by virtue of the following points.

(a) According to the books of the Former Prophets, the Tent of Meeting / the Tabernacle of the Lord was at Shiloh from the days of the conquest of the land to the days of Eli the priest and Samuel, who was still a child.[62] These books show no sign that the Tabernacle—the Tent of Meeting—was transferred from Shiloh to Gibeon or to any other place. In fact, toward the end of the First Temple period, Jeremiah the prophet draws the attention of the frequenters of the Temple to the Tabernacle of desolate Shiloh: "Go now to my place that was in Shiloh, where I had my name dwell at first, and see what I did to it because of the wickedness of my people Israel" (Jer 7:12; and 7:14; 26:6). Similarly, in Ps 78:60: "And he abandoned the Tabernacle at Shiloh, the Tent where he resided among men." It is likely that the Tabernacle was destroyed by the Philistines along with the town of Shiloh toward the end of the era of the Judges (approximately mid–eleventh century B.C.E.), after their victory in the battle of Ebenezer (1 Samuel 4). The archaeological findings at Tell Shiloh (Khirbet Seilun) also testify to its being destroyed at that time.[63]

---

61. Contrary to Auerbach (*Wüste und Gelobtes Land*, 1.103, 158) and Grintz ("High Priesthood," 137–38 = *Biblical Ethnology*, 273–74), who regard these verses in Chronicles as reliable testimony and even draw historical conclusions from them. Similarly, see also Hertzberg, "Mizpa," 176–77; on p. 177, Hertzberg wrote "Es ist aber eine sehr klare Sache, wenn ursprunglich das Heiligtum von Gibeon selbst, das alte zeltheiligtum mit dem Altar Jahwes, gemeint ist." See also Eichrodt, *Theologie*, 62 n. 57 (= ET, *Theology*, 1.111 n. 3); Schunk, *Benjamin*, 134 n. 126, 135 n. 130; and Schley, *Shiloh*, 26, 161, 198, 235 n. 46.

62. See, for example, Josh 18:1: "And the whole congregation of the children of Israel assembled at Shiloh and set up the Tent of Meeting there" and similarly vv. 8–10; 21:2; 22:11–12; Judg 21:19; 1 Samuel 1–4.

63. See Finkelstein, *Archaeology*, 225–26, 232. For the state of research into the question of the substance of the Shiloh tabernacle, the identification of the town Shiloh, the date of its destruction and the relationship of the archaeological finds at Ḥirbet Silon to the biblical narrative—see Schley, *Shiloh*, 11–99. The word באדם in Ps 78:60 means "among human beings," and compare "and so shall he do *for the Tent* of Meeting *that dwells with them* in the midst of their impurity" (Lev 16:16), and similarly "But will God in truth dwell with men on the earth?" (2 Chr 6:18). Goitein's hypothesis ("City of Adam," 86–88) that this word is intended for the town of Adam (Tell ed-Damiah), located near the Jabbok's outlet to the Jordan, "and that during one of the disasters which were visited on Shiloh (such as the great landslide in the days of

(b) In none of the early books is there any sign that the Tabernacle / the Tent of Meeting was in Gibeon. It is difficult to assume that the same Deuteronomistic historiographer who knew how to trace the detailed history of the Ark of the Lord from the time it fell into the hands of the Philistines up to the time it was brought to Jerusalem, to the Temple that had been erected for it (1 Samuel 4–6; 2 Samuel 6; 1 Kings 8), had no idea or deliberately ignored the fact that the Tabernacle of the Lord and the bronze altar were in Gibeon the whole time. The words "in the mountain before the Lord," mentioned in the narrative about the execution of Saul's sons by the Gibeonites in 2 Sam 21:9, as well as 21:6, "in Gibeah of Saul, the chosen of the Lord" (which is merely a distortion of "in Gibeon, in the mountain of the Lord")[64] indicate the sanctified place where "the great high place in Gibeon" was located (1 Kgs 3:4).

The "Tent of Meeting" mentioned with the Ark in 1 Kgs 8:4 may refer to the tent that David pitched for the Ark in Jerusalem (2 Sam 6:17 // 1 Chr 16:1; 2 Chr 1:4; and in 1 Chr 6:17 this tent is called משכן אהל־מועד); it may also be a later gloss.[65]

(c) According to the Chronicler, David brought the Ark up to Jerusalem but left the Tabernacle of the Lord and the bronze altar / the burnt-offering altar in Gibeon. He even went as far as appointing groups of priests to officiate in each place. However, in Liver's words: "It is unimaginable for the Tent of Meeting and the altar of the Lord to be in one place and the Ark of God to be elsewhere."[66] If David brought only the Ark of the Lord to Jerusalem, it would be reasonable to assume that it was all that remained—that the Tent of Meeting was no longer in existence.[67]

In light of all the above, it is easy to understand why, in 1 Chr 21:27–30, the Chronicler introduced an "addition" to the text that he adduced from 2 Samuel 24 (with certain emendations) regarding the selection of the threshing floor of Araunah, the Jebusite, as the site for Solomon's

---

Eli and his sons) the Tent was transferred" to the town of Adam is not supported by any other source. Moreover, there is little likelihood that, in the heat of the Philistine conquest and destruction of the city of Shiloh, the defeated Israelites succeeded in saving the Shiloh Tabernacle and carrying it to an insignificant and distant town under the Philistines' watchful eyes.

64. See the LXX, ad loc.; cf. Driver, *Samuel*, 351–52.

65. Cf. Wellhausen, *Prolegomena*, 43–44 (= ET, 43–44); Gray, *Kings*, 209; Haran, *Temple*, 141 n. 11. In any case, the words אהל מועד and so on in 2 Chr 5:5, adduced from Kings, refer here to the Tent of Meeting, the Tabernacle that Moses made in the wilderness and that had been brought from Gibeon to the new Temple in Jerusalem.

66. Liver, *Priests and Levites*, 81–82 n. 102 (= "Gibeonites," 72–73).

67. Against Friedman ("Tabernacle," 242–48), who believes that the Tabernacle, the Tent of Meeting, was stored in Solomon's Temple until the Temple's destruction in 587/6 B.C.E.!

Temple. The Chronicler was compelled to compose an "addition" here, despite the fact that from a literary standpoint it creates an anticlimax and even generates some degree of tension with the previous narrative.[68] In order to explain why David offered up sacrifices on an altar on the threshing floor of Araunah, the Jebusite, rather than "in the Tabernacle of the Lord that Moses made in the wilderness and the altar of burnt offering" (which, according to the Chronicler, "were at that time in the high place at Gibeon") he wrote, "but David could not go before it to inquire of God, for he was terrified of the sword of the angel of the Lord" (v. 30). The fact that the altar to the Lord was set up on Araunah's threshing floor *according to the Lord's commandment*, delivered by Gad the prophet (2 Sam 24:18–19 // 1 Chr 21:18–19), did not satisfy the Chronicler.

7.19 1 Kgs 8:65–66 relates that Solomon and all of Israel observed "the festival"[69] seven days—that is, from the 15th to the 21st day of the seventh month, as the Deuteronomistic law makes clear (Deut 16:13–15).[70] 'And on the eighth day' (ו)ביום השמיני,[71] that is, *on the 22d day of the seventh month*, all of the celebrants went home. In other words, Solomon and all of Israel were not familiar with, or at least did not celebrate, העצרת 'the Azeret' (which the sages later called שמיני עצרת), in accordance with the priestly law (Lev 23:33–36; see Num 29:35–36):

בחמשה עשר יום לחדש השביעי הזה חג הסכות שבעת ימים . . . (ו)ביום השמיני
מקרא קודש יהיה לכם, והקרבתם אשה לה', עצרת הוא כל מלאכת עבדה לא תעשו
On the fifteenth day of this seventh month there shall be the Feast of Tabernacles for seven days . . . (and) on the eighth day there shall be

---

68. No conclusion should be drawn to the effect that this "addition" is post-Chronistic, as has been argued, for example, by Kittel, *Chronik*, 81; Rothstein-Hänel, *Chronik*, 392–93; and see Japhet, *Ideology*, 141.

69. The word החג either with the definite article or without in the Bible refers to the Feast of Tabernacles, as can be seen from 1 Kgs 12:32–33, which speaks of Jeroboam, who ordained חג בחדש השמיני בחמשה עשר יום לחדש כחג אשר ביהודה . . . בחדש אשר בדא מלבו 'a feast in the eighth month, on the fifteenth day of the month, like the feast that is in Judah, . . . in the month that he had devised of his own heart"; and similarly in Ezek 45:25: "In the seventh [month], on the fifteenth day of the month, at the feast, he shall make the same provision for the seven days." In the list of sacrifices for the days of the year in Numbers 28–29, the Feast of Tabernacles is not mentioned by name; all that is said (29:12) is as follows: ובחמשה עשר יום לחדש השביעי . . . וחגתם חג לה' שבעת ימים 'And on the fifteenth day of the seventh month . . . and you shall keep a feast unto the Lord seven days"; and see also Neh 8:14, 18, and 2 Chr 7:9.

70. And no wonder, for the book of Kings is known to have been edited by a Deuteronomistic school.

71. This is the reading in the LXX and in the parallel text in 2 Chr 7:10—וביום—which seems preferable to the MT reading—ביום.

a holy convocation; and you shall bring the fire offering to the Lord; it is a day of solemn assembly; you shall not do any servile work.

The Chronicler harmonized the narrative in Kings and the requirements of the Priestly law and wrote (2 Chr 7:8–10):

ויעשו ביום השמיני עצרת . . . וביום עשרים ושלשה לחדש השביעי שלח
את העם לאהליהם שמחים וטובי לב

And on the eighth day they held a solemn assembly . . . and on the twenty-third day of the seventh month he sent the people away to their tents, joyful and glad of heart.

In other words, Solomon and all Israel celebrated the Azeret on the 22d day of the 7th month according to the commandment of the books of Leviticus and Numbers, and it was only on the next day, the 23d of the month, that they scattered to their homes:

1 Kgs 8:65–66	*2 Chr 7:8–10*
So Solomon held the feast at that time, and all Israel with him, . . . seven days and seven days, even fourteen days.[72] *(And) on the eighth day* he sent the people away, . . . and they went to their tents.	So Solomon held the feast at that time seven days, and all Israel with him. . . . *And on the eighth day they held a solemn assembly. . . . And on the twenty-third day of the seventh month,* he sent the people to their tents.

It appears, however, that the above "harmonization" contains an anachronism: the Chronicler attributes to Solomon and his contempo-

---

72. The words ושבעת ימים ארבעה עשר יום 'and seven days, even fourteen days' do not appear in the LXX, in either the Vaticanus or Lucianic versions. According to these two versions, the celebrations lasted ἑπτὰ ἡμέρας 'seven days'. And thus the continuation of the verse *ביום השמיני* (ו) . . . את העם . . . וילכו לאהליהם '(and) on the eighth day* he sent the people away . . . and they went to their tents' clearly indicates that the celebration of the dedication of the Temple coincided with that of החג 'Tabernacles', lasting seven days; for it does not say "and on the fifteenth day he sent the people away" but "on the eighth day he sent the people away." The words ושבעת ימים ארבעה עשר יום are thus a later gloss, apparently on the basis of the verse in the parallel text in 2 Chr 7:9; cf. Thenius, *Könige*, 142; Burney, *Kings*, 129; Stade, *Kings*, 109; Ehrlich, *Mikrâ ki-Pheschutô*, 284; Elmslie, *Chronicles* (1916), 196. The words ושבעת ימים may also have resulted from dittography, after which a final interpolation was added, ארבעה עשר יום. This is against Hurowitz (*Temple Building*, 245), who claims that "Solomon celebrated the dedication of the Temple (8:65) seven days and seven days, even fourteen days," and against Naor ("Solomon and Hiram," 100), who combines the narratives in Kings and Chronicles.

raries a "solemn-assembly" celebration, something that was a custom in the Chronicler's day (the Second Temple period) but seems not to have been a custom in the early days of the First Temple. Indeed, in the earliest sources of the Torah (J, E, D), and in the historiographic, prophetic, and lyrical literature of the First Temple period and the period of the Babylonian Exile, no mention whatever is made of a festival "of solemn assembly." Except for the Priestly sources (P) mentioned above, this festival is mentioned only once in the historiography of the Second Temple period—in Neh 8:18: ויעשו חג שבעת ימים וביום השמיני עצרת כמשפט 'and they celebrated the festival for seven days, and on the eighth day a solemn assembly as was decreed'.

7.20 In the description of the Temple dedication in Kings, the text concerning the Ark reads as follows (1 Kgs 8:3): ויבאו כל זקני ישראל וישאו הכהנים את הארון 'And all the elders of Israel came, and the priests took up the Ark'. However, the bearing of the Ark by the priests contradicts the verse in Deut 10:8: בעת ההיא הבדיל ה' את שבט הלוי לשאת את ארון ברית ה' לעמד לפני ה' לשרתו 'At that time the Lord set apart the tribe of Levi to bear the Ark of the Covenant of the Lord, to stand before the Lord to minister to him' (and see Deut 31:9, 25—D). This verse makes it clear that other members of the tribe of Levi, even if they are not sons of Aaron the priest, are also allowed to bear the Ark. That the Ark was borne by the Levites is also clear from the narrative regarding the sons of Kohath, the Levites who bore the holy vessels that were in the Tent of Meeting, including the Ark, which was carried by rods on the shoulders (Num 4:1–15; also 1:50; 3:31; 7:9; 10:17; Exod 25:14–P). The Chronicler created harmony between the narrative in the dedication of Solomon's Temple and the requirements of the Torah. He replaced the word הכהנים 'the priests' in the early text with the word הלוים 'the Levites', writing (2 Chr 5:4): ויבאו כל זקני ישראל וישאו *הלוים* את הארון 'And all the elders of Israel came, and the *Levites* took up the ark'. There is a similar feature further along in the description. Instead of (1 Kgs 8:4), ויעלו את ארון ה' ואת אהל־מועד ואת כל כלי הקדש אשר באהל ויעלו אתם *הכהנים והלוים* 'and they brought up the Ark of the Lord and the Tent of Meeting and all the holy vessels that were in the Tent, and *the priests and the Levites* brought them up',[73] he wrote (2 Chr 5:5), ויעלו את הארון ואת אהל־מועד . . . העלו אתם *הכהנים הלוים* 'and they brought up the Ark and the Tent of Meeting . . . *the Priests the Levites* brought them up'.[74] In light of this discussion, it

---

73. See above, example 7.18, paragraph c (p. 146).

74. For the term הכהנים הלוים 'the Priests the Levites', see Deut 17:9, 18; 18:1; 24:8; 27:9; and see Noy, "Levites' Part," 63–78. In his opinion, the term was invented by the Levites and was added to the original text of the book of Deuteronomy, originally meaning that all of the Levites were priests. Noy does not discuss 2 Chr 5:5.

is possible to clarify certain emendations that the Chronicler made to the narrative of the bringing of the Ark from the home of Obed-edom, the Gittite, to the City of David. In 2 Sam 6:13–14 no mention is made of the tribal origin of נשאי ארון ה׳ 'the bearers of the Ark of the Lord'. It is thus reasonable to assume that they were "Israelites." In any case, in 1 Chr 15:26–27 the Chronicler left no room for doubt; he stressed again and again that the Ark-bearers were Levites:

ויהי בעזר האלהים [75]

את *הלוים* נשאי ארון ברית ה׳ . . .

ודויד מכרבל במעיל בוץ

וכל *הלוים* הנשאים את הארון . . .

And it came to pass, when God helped
the Levites who bore the Ark of the Covenant of the Lord. . . .
And David was wrapped in a robe of fine linen,
and all *the Levites* who bore the ark . . .

Furthermore, as an explanation of the failure of the first attempt to bring the Ark up (2 Sam 6:1–11 // 2 Chr 13:1–14), the Chronicler has David say: כי למבראשונה לא אתם פרץ ה׳ אלהינו בנו כי לא דרשנהו כמשפט 'For since it was not you at first, the Lord our God made a breach within us, for we sought Him not according to the rule' (1 Chr 15:13, "addition"). This verse hints at the narrative in 1 Chr 13:11 // 2 Sam 6:7, ויחר לדויד כי פרץ ה׳ בעוזא 'and David was displeased because the Lord had burst out against Uzza';[76] and a study of 1 Chronicles 15 reveals that the words לא דרשנהו כמשפט refer (a) to the tribal origin of the bearers of the Ark; and (b) to the way they bore the Ark—the first time.

(a) In the first Ark-bearing episode, the Ark was handled by *Uzza and his brothers, sons of Abinadab* (2 Sam 6:3 // 1 Chr 13:7). This time David commanded (1 Chr 15:2, "addition") לא לשאת את ארון האלהים כי אם הלוים כי בם בחר ה׳ לשאת את ארון ה׳ ולשרתו עד עולם 'that no one should bear the Ark of God except the Levites, for the Lord had chosen them to bear the Ark of the Lord and to minister to him forever'. Then David gave the relevant instruction (1 Chr 15:11–12),

---

75. The Chronicler may have altered the text here from ויהי כי צעדו to ויהי בעזר האלהים in order to emphasize the assistance of God in the success of the move (Curtis-Madsen, *Chronicles*, 218). Weiss ("Textual Notes," 57–58) thinks "that the Chronicler had before him the wording of Samuel with apparently just a minor change: ויהי כצעד instead of ויהי כי צעדו . . . , and that the Chronicler read or heard בסעד from מן סעד—a matter of assistance. And then he replaced this rare verb in the Bible with a synonymous one—עזר."

76. This wording is reminiscent of פן יפרץ בהם ה׳ 'lest the Lord break out against them' (Exod 19:22) with inverted word order: בהם ה׳ / ה׳ בנו.

ויקרא דויד לצדוק ולאביתר הכהנים וללוים לאוריאל לאוריאל, עשיה . . . ויאמר להם אתם
ראשי האבות ללוים התקדשו אתם ואחיכם והעליתם את ארון ה' אלהי ישראל אל
הכינותי לו

And David summoned Zadok and Abiathar the priests and the
Levites Uriel, Asaiah . . . and said to them: "You are the heads of the
chiefs of the Levites; sanctify yourselves, you and your kindred, and
bring up the Ark of the Lord God of Israel to the place I have
prepared for it."

And so indeed it was done (1 Chr 15:14–15):

ויתקדשו הכהנים והלוים להעלות את ארון ה' . . . וישאו בני הלוים את ארון
האלהים כאשר צוה משה כדבר ה'

And the priests and the Levites sanctified themselves to bring up
the ark of the Lord . . . , and the sons of the Levites bore the Ark of
God as Moses had commanded according to the word of the Lord.

(b) In the first episode of attempting to bring the Ark to Jerusalem,
the Ark was borne *on a wagon* (2 Sam 6:3 // 1 Chr 13:7), but this time
(1 Chr 15:15, "addition") וישאו בני הלוים את ארון האלהים כאשר צוה משה כדבר ה'
בכתפים ובמטות עליהם 'the sons of the Levites bore the Ark of God on their
shoulders with rods as Moses had commanded according to the word of
the Lord'. The Chronicler stresses that the bearing of the Ark by the Levites, on their shoulders with rods was כאשר צוה משה כדבר ה' 'as Moses
had commanded according to the word of the Lord'. In actual fact, David's wording of the reasoning, לא לשאת את ארון ה' האלהים כי אם הלוים כי בם
בחר ה' לשאת את ארון ה' ולשרתו עד עולם[77] 'that no one should bear the Ark of
God except the Levites, for the Lord has chosen them to bear the Ark of
the Lord and to minister unto Him forever', is based on the verse in
Deut 10:8: בעת ההיא הבדיל ה' את שבט לוי לשאת את ארון ברית ה' לעמד לפני ה'
לשרתו 'At that time the Lord set aside the tribe of Levi to bear the Ark
of the Covenant of the Lord, to stand before the Lord to minister to
him. . . '. And all of this was merely to demonstrate that this time David
conducted himself precisely according to the requirements of the Torah.

7.21 The book of 1 Samuel relates that the prophet Samuel "used to
minister to the Lord in the presence of Eli the priest" in the sanctuary at
Shiloh, while he was "wearing a linen ephod" (that is, dressed in a gar-
ment designed for those who ministered in the sanctuary: 1 Sam 2:11,
18; see also 3:3, 15). Samuel's familial-tribal origins are clear from the
description of his father, Elkanah, who was an אפרתי 'Ephrathite' from

---

77. So, too, are the words of Hezekiah, king of Judah, to the Levites in 2 Chr 29:11:
בני, עתה אל תשלו כי בכם בחר ה' לעמד לפניו לשרתו ולהיות לו משרתים ומקטירים 'My sons, now be
not negligent, for the Lord has chosen you to stand before him to minister to him and
to be his ministers and to make offerings to him'.

the town of Ramathaim Zuphim in the hill country of Ephraim (1:1).
Whether one interprets the term אפרתי as the title of a person belonging
to the tribe of Ephraim (see Judg 12:5; 1 Kgs 11:26)[78] or views it as the
title of a person from the town of Bethlehem in Judah (see 1 Sam 17:12;
Ruth 1:2), which the Bible also calls Ephrath or Ephrathah (see Gen
35:16, 19; 48:7; Mic 5:1; Ruth 4:11; and other texts)—that is, of the tribe
of Judah[79]—it is evident that Samuel was not a descendant of Levi.

Since Samuel was not a Levite, his service in the sanctuary was diametrically opposed to the texts in the Pentateuch according to which
only Levites were permitted to minister in the sanctuary, to stand
"before Aaron the priest and minister with him" (Num 1:50–51; 3:5–9;
18:2–4, 22–23 [P]); and זר [anyone not of the tribe of Levi] לא יקרב אליכם
'no stranger shall approach you' (18:4), and והזר הקרב יומת 'any stranger
approaching shall be put to death' (Num 1:50).[80] Moreover, according to
these verses, Samuel the prophet was in fact subject to the death pen-
alty for having served in the sanctuary of the Lord in Shiloh though he
was not a Levite.

The Chronicler attempted to resolve this contradiction between the
narrative in Samuel and the verses of the Torah. In the two genealogical
lists that he created, he listed Samuel as a Levite (1 Chr 6:7–13, 18–23).
In other words, the Chronicler preferred to build artificial construc-
tions[81] to transform Samuel into a Levite, even though they contradict
the explicit statements in the book of Samuel that show that he was an
אפרתי. His artificial construction created harmony between verses in the
book of Samuel that speak of Samuel's ministering to the Lord before
Eli the priest in the sanctuary of Shiloh and verses in the Torah that
rule that ministering before the Lord and his priests was the inheritance of the Levites alone.[82]

---

78. This is the opinion of, for example, Ehrlich, *Mikrâ ki-Pheschutô*, 435; Segal,
Samuel, 3; McCarter, *I Samuel*, 58; and so it seems to me as well.

79. According to this view, Elkanah, Samuel's father, was called אפרתי after the
city of his (or of his ancestors') origin, while he lived in Ramathaim Zuphim, in the
hill country of Ephraim; see Haran, "Festivals."

80. Similarly also Ehrlich, *Mikrâ ki-Pheschutô*, 435 (the clause והזר הקרב יומת in
Num 3:10 that he quotes is not appropo, for the verse is speaking of אהרן ובניו 'Aaron
and his sons', the word הזר in this context referring to anyone not descended from
Aaron, including Levites); Segal, *Samuel*, 3; McCarter, *I Samuel*, 58. Williamson ex-
presses a different view. In his opinion, Samuel was a *Levite* who resided in Ephraim
(Williamson, *Chronicles*, 72). But if this was indeed the case, why did the author of
Samuel not make an explicit note of it?

81. Thus, for example, the first list (1 Chr 6:7–13) comprises Exod 6:24 (cf. Num
3:19); 1 Sam 1:1; 8:2; several names that do not appear in any list of the sons of Ke-
hath or Zuph; and names that are repeated a number of times (e.g., Elkanah four
times; Assir twice).

82. Another view is expressed by Albright (*Archaeology*, 205 n. 44). He claims
that including Samuel in the list of Levites stems from the erroneous identification of

Ascribing Samuel to the tribe of Levi had the additional effect of glorifying this tribe, a favorite of the Chronicler[83]—saying, in effect, "See what a lofty person the tribe of Levi has produced!"

7.22 In 2 Sam 8:16–18 a list of important functionaries in David's kingdom appears. The list ends with the words (18b): ובני דוד כהנים היו 'and David's sons were priests'. The Masoretic reading כהנים is authentic and is not erroneous, as Mettinger[84] believes. The word כהנים does not mean "administrators of royal property," as Wenham has proposed;[85] neither does it mean "military advisors to the king," as Oren[86] would have it. There seems to be no reason whatever to explain the term כהנים differently here from the way we define it elsewhere in the Bible—in fact, the way it is used in the immediately preceding verse. At any rate, it seems that the Chronicler understood the term precisely thus. Since David was of the tribe of Judah (1 Chr 2:4–15; Ruth 4:18–22), 2 Sam 8:18 contradicts the verses in the Torah according to which the priesthood had been bestowed only on the sons of Aaron the high priest (see, for example, Num 17:1–5, 16–28; 18:1–7; 25:13; Lev 7:35–36; chap. 8—P). In 1 Chr 18:17 the Chronicler created harmony among these contradictory sources and wrote: [87] ובני דויד ראשונים ליד המלך 'And the sons of

Samuel's father, *Elkanah* (1 Sam 1:1), with *Elkanah*, son of Korah and descendant of Kohath, the son of Levi, who is mentioned in Exod 6:24. However, the Elkanah mentioned in Exodus was a participant in the Exodus from Egypt, whereas Elkanah, the father of Samuel, lived in the land of Israel during the days of Eli the priest, at the very close of the period of Judges (1 Samuel 1–2); it does not seem reasonable to attribute to the Chronicler so blatant an error or the inability to perceive the vast generation gap separating the two men, even though they bear the identical name. For one thing, it is evident in 1 Chr 6:8–12 that the Chronicler distinguished between Elkanah, the father of Samuel, and the Elkanah mentioned in Exod 6:24 (though, in contrast to Exod 6:24, he lists him as the son of Assir, son of Korah, son of Amminidab, son of Kohath and father of Abiasaph, rather than as the brother of Assir and Abiasaph as related in Exodus).

83. For the Chronicler's support of the Levites, see, for example, 2 Chr 34:30, ויעל המלך בית ה', וכל איש יהודה וישבי ירושלם והכהנים והלוים וכל העם compared with 2 Kgs 23:2, which speaks about הכהנים והנביאים וכל העם. For this topic, see de Vaux, *Ancient Israel*, 390–94; Gunneweg, *Leviten und Priester*, 204–15; also Kalimi, *Bibliography*, pp. 97–100, items 636–73.

84. Mettinger, *State Officials*, 6–7.

85. Wenham, "David's Sons," 79–82.

86. Oren, "Ira the Yairite," 233–34.

87. Cf. Curtis-Madsen, *Chronicles*, 237; Segal, *Samuel*, 291; McCarter, *II Samuel*, 255; against Willi, *Chronik*, 127; Williamson, *Chronicles*, 140. A harmonizing approach similar to the Chronicler's was adopted in the early translations of Samuel: the LXX αὐλάρχαι 'chiefs of the court'; *Targum Jonathan*: רברבין 'great men'; and the Peshiṭta. See also Josephus, *Ant.* 7.110; and R. David Kimḥi, ad loc. In the Greek translation of Chronicles καὶ υἱοὶ Δαυὶδ οἱ πρῶτοι διάδοχοι τοῦ βασιλέως 'and the sons of David were the chief heirs of the king', the influence of the title διάδοχος 'heir' is

David were the chief officials in the service of the king'. It seems that a similar reason, among several possibilities, led the Chronicler to omit 2 Sam 20:26, וגם עירא היארי היה כהן לדוד 'And Ira, the Yairite, was also a priest to David', which concludes a list of functionaries. Ira was a descendant of the Yair family from the northern part of the eastern bank of the Jordan (Num 32:41; Deut 3:14; Judg 10:3–5; 1 Kgs 4:13; 1 Chr 2:22–23) and not a descendant of Aaron, the high priest.[88]

7.23 After the installation of David as king over all Israel, the Philistines waged war against him but were roundly defeated. The narrative of the war, 2 Sam 5:17–21, ends with the words: ויעזבו שם את עצביהם וישאם דוד ואנשיו 'And they left their images there, and David and his men bore them away'. In other words, David and his men took the Philistines' idols abandoned on the battlefield as booty when the Philistines fled in panic.[89]

The taking of the idols by David (and his men) clearly contradicts Deut 7:25, which commands, when the Lord delivers the Gentiles into the hands of the children of Israel, פסילי אלהיהם תשרפון באש לא תחמד כסף וזהב עליהם ולקחת לך 'Burn the graven images of their gods with fire; do not covet the silver and gold that is on them or take it for yourself' (see also Deut 7:5; 12:3). Similarly, it portrays David either as one who did not

---

apparent; this title was used in the court of the Ptolemian kings of Egypt in the second century B.C.E.; see Gerleman, *Septuagint*, 17–18, and 14–21 for additional examples of such influence.

88. Against Oren ("Ira the Yairite," 233–34), who assumes that "David should not be viewed as deviating from Jewish tradition" (p. 233), and concludes: "Ira the Yairite-Jethrite was apparently a mighty man of Gentile origin who served as כהן לדוד—a military advisor of David's" (p. 234). For earlier harmonistic attempts at clarifying the verse in 2 Sam 20:26, see *Targum Jonathan*: "Ira the Yairite who was of Tekoa—was a great man in the eyes of David"; *Tosfot* to ʿ*Erub.* 63a: "perhaps his father came from Aaron while his mother was of Manasseh"!

89. The word וישאם is 3d-person singular with the 3d-person plural object suffix, derived from the root נשא, meaning 'picked up', 'took', and so on; and compare: אהליהם וצאנם יקחו / יריעותיהם וכל כליהם וגמליהם ישאו להם 'Their tents and their flocks shall they take / they shall bear away for themselves their curtains and all their vessels and their camels' (Jer 49:29); see also Lev 10:5; Num 16:15; Cant 5:7; 1 Chr 21:24; et al. Reminiscent of 2 Sam 5:21b, the verb נשא appears also in Jeremiah in a context of taking booty, and see also Ezek 29:19 and 1 Chr 18:11. The verse was already really understood in this fashion by the Greek translator in the LXX of 2 Sam 5:21: καὶ καταλιμπάνουσιν ἐκεῖ τοὺς θεοὺς αὐτῶν, καὶ ἐλάβοσαν αὐτοὺς Δαυὶδ καὶ οἱ ἄνδρες οἱ μετ' αὐτοῦ 'And they leave there their gods, and David and his men with him took them', and also by the Jewish sages in *b.* ʿ*Abod. Zar.* 44a: "Behold, he says, 'and they were burned with fire', yet since it does not say: 'and they burned them but rather 'and they bore them' we must conclude that they really bore them away"; and Rashi, ibid.: "They really bore them away—he took them with him and made use of them"; and see also *y.* ʿ*Abod. Zar.* 3.3 (42d); *t.* ʿ*Abod. Zar.* 3.19.

know of the command in Deuteronomy or as preferring to ignore it because of his greed for booty.

In an attempt to solve this problem, the Chronicler emended the final words of the narrative, writing (1 Chr 14:12), ויעזבו שם את אלהיהם, ויאמר דויד וישרפו באש 'and they left their gods there; and David gave an order, and they were burned with fire'. He thus harmonized the narrative in Samuel and the verses in the Torah, as other scholars have already observed.[90] It seems, however, that the verse in Chronicles should be read more carefully. The Chronicler did not say ויאמר דויד וישברם 'and David gave an order, and they shattered them'. For instance, he might have said something similar to what he said about Josiah: והאשרים והפסלים והמסכות שבר 'and he shattered the Asherim and the carved images and the cast images' (2 Chr 34:4, "addition"). Nor did the Chronicler use the verb כתת 'beat', as in his words ואת האשרים והפסלים כתת 'and he beat the Asherim and the carved images' (34:7, "addition") or "destroyed their gods," as Josephus wrote (Ant. 7.77), and so on. Instead, he preferred the language and style of the commandment in Deuteronomy until an analogy between the two was formed:

Deut 7:25: פסילי אלהיהם תשרפון באש 'the carved images of their gods you shall burn with fire'

---

90. Cf. Curtis-Madsen, Chronicles, 209; Galling, Chronik, 49; Rudolph, Chronik, 115; Segal, Samuel, 267; McCarter, II Samuel, 155; Seeligmann, "Beginnings of Midrash," 18–19. In a number of manuscripts of the Lucianic (L) recension of the LXX of Samuel there appears an integration of the MT of 2 Sam 5:21 with the MT of 1 Chr 14:12: καὶ κατακειποῦσιν ἐκεῖ οἱ ἀλλόφυλοι τοὺς θεοὺς αὐτῶν καὶ λαμβανοῦσιν αὐτοὺς Δαυεὶδ καὶ οἱ ἄνδρες αὐτοῦ καὶ λέγει Δαυεὶδ κατακαύσατε (e₂: -σετε) αὐτοὺς ἐν πυρὶ 'And they [the Philistines] leave there their gods, and David and his men with him took them. And David ordered: "burn them in fire!"' Evidently, no claim can be made on the basis of this late integrated text (as Lemke, "Synoptic Problem," 352, and McKenzie, Chronicler, 62, have claimed) that the Chronicler adduced part of his Vorlage here, a text that read וישרפו באש. Furthermore, it seems that Targum Jonathan on 2 Sam 5:21, ואוקידינון דוד וגברוהי 'and David and his men burned it' (and Rashi, R. David Kimḥi, and Rabbi Yeshayahu of Trani in the wake of the Targum), was influenced by the parallel text in Chronicles for reasons resembling the Chronicler's reasons. Grintz ("Life of David," 74 = Early Biblical Ethnology, 350) believes that the Chronicler understood the word וישאם in the early text as derived from 'burning'. Such a meaning is indeed familiar in Mishnaic Hebrew; for example: משיאין משואות 'lighting torches' (m. Roš Haš. 2:2–4; for discussion and additional references, see Lieberman, Tosefta Ki-Fshutah, part 5, 1028–29). However, because of the frequency of the harmonization phenomenon in the book of Chronicles, it seems more likely that the Chronicler was aware of the intended meaning of the text and emended it for the reasons listed above; cf. Seeligmann, "Beginnings of Midrash," 19 n. 15.

1 Chr 14:12: ויעזבו שם את אלהיהם[91] ויאמר דויד *וישרפו באש* 'and they left *their gods* there; and David commanded: let them *be burned with fire*'.

Thus, it is clear: not only did David not desire the Philistine gods or take them for himself or even simply destroy them, he got up and gave his men an order to deal with them precisely according to the wording of the Torah's precept.

7.24 In reply to the messengers sent by Josiah, king of Judah, who came to inquire of the Lord regarding "the words of the book" found in the House of the Lord, Hulda the prophetess says (2 Kgs 22:16): כה אמר ה' הנני מביא רעה אל המקום הזה ועל ישביו את כל דברי הספר אשר קרא מלך יהודה 'Thus says the Lord: "Behold, I am bringing evil upon this place and upon its inhabitants—all the words of the book that the king of Judah read"'. The prophetess's words, "that *the king of Judah* read," contradict the narrative of v. 10: ויקראהו שפן לפני המלך 'And *Shaphan* read it to the king'. To create harmony between these contradictory verses in the earlier narrative, the Chronicler altered the words of the prophetess as given in 2 Kgs and wrote, אשר קראו *לפני* מלך יהודה 'which they read *in front of* the king of Judah' (2 Chr 34:24), similar to the previous narrative, ויקרא בו שפן *לפני* המלך 'And Shaphan read in it *in front of* the king' (v. 18).

7.25 According to the book of Exodus, the Passover sacrifice should be taken only from a *flock* (Exod 12:3, 5, 21, and other verses) whereas, according to the parallel ordinance in Deuteronomy, it may be taken from a *flock* and from a *herd* (Deut 16:2). In 2 Chronicles 35, the Chronicler described Josiah's Passover while trying to deal with the disharmony between the Torah ordinances. In his words, Josiah and his princes contributed צאן ובקר '*flocks* and *herds*' (vv. 7–9) for the people but, while the *flocks* were intended as פסחים 'Passover sacrifices', the *herds* were intended as קדשים 'sacred offerings'. This distinction between the two is made not only in describing the preparation of the flesh

---

91. In the parallel text in Samuel: עצביהם 'their images'. This emendation, too, may have been executed by the Chronicler in order to broaden the base of the analogy between the text being considered and the text in Deuteronomy; in another case, he uses the text in Samuel word for word: לבשר את בית עצביהם 'to bring the news to the house of their (the Philistines') images' (1 Chr 10:9 // 1 Sam 31:9). Nevertheless, one must not rule out completely the possibility that the book of Chronicles preserved the original version at this point and that the word עצביהם 'their images' in the parallel text in the book of Samuel is a correction made by scribes trying to avoid calling the Philistine gods אלהים 'God' (though the term אלהים does serve throughout the Bible, generally speaking, to denote both the God of Israel [e.g., Gen 35:5; 41:38; Exod 18:21] and also the idols of the nations [e.g., Exod 20:3; Deut 5:7; 6:14; 7:4]).

of the two kinds of sacrifice in the Temple (v. 13) but also earlier, where
Josiah and his princes set them aside (vv. 7–9). Regarding the setting
aside of Josiah's sacrifices, the Chronicler wrote (2 Chr 35:7; see also
vv. 8–9):

וירם יאשיהו לבני העם צאן כבשים ובני עזים

הכל לפסחים לכל הנמצא למספר שלשים אלף

ובקר שלשת אלפים‎92

And Josiah contributed *flocks, lambs and kids*, for the people, as
Passover sacrifices for everyone present, for a total of thirty thousand, and three thousand *bulls*.

Concerning the preparation of two kinds of sacrifice he wrote (35:13):

ויבשלו הפסח באש כמשפט‎93

והקדשים בשלו בסירות ובדודים ובצלחות ויריצו לכל בני העם‎94

And they roasted the Passover lamb over a fire according to the
ordinance,
and the holy offerings they boiled in pots and in cauldrons and in
pans and carried them quickly to all of the people.

This harmonistic interpretation is expressed more explicitly in a *Midrash halacha* on Deut 16:2: "צאן ובקר‎—since the Passover is taken only
from the sheep or the goats, why does the Torah say צאן ובקר here? צאן
for the Passover sacrifice and בקר for the festive offering."‎95

7.26 The Chronicler was not satisfied with the general injunction regarding Josiah's Passover that occurs in the Deuteronomistic historiography (2 Kgs 23:21): עשו פסח לה׳ אלהיכם ככתוב על ספר הברית הזה 'Keep the
Passover unto the Lord your God, as it is written in this book of the
covenant'. He used various laws in detail that he found written "in the
book of the covenant" concerning Passover, including the way to prepare
the meat of the Passover sacrifice for eating. Since he understood that

---

92. A similar phenomenon is found in 2 Chr 30:24 as well, where Hezekiah and his
princes contributed *flocks and cattle* to the people for the needs of the "seven days of
rejoicing" that were added after his Passover.

93. For this clause, see in detail the next example.

94. Welch (*Chronicler*, 146) claims that the Chronicler followed the law in Deuteronomy, according to which the Passover sacrifice was taken from the flock (sheep) and
from the herd (cattle). A later editor, who opposed the law permitting the taking of
the Passover sacrifice from the "herd," adhering only to the law of Exodus 12, was the
one who distinguished here between "the Passover" (sacrifices that were brought
from the flock) and "the holy offerings" (brought from the herd). This claim, however,
is unsupported.

95. *Sifre, Re'eh*, 16.2 (ed. Finkelstein, §129, p. 187).

"this book of the covenant" referred to the entire five books of the Torah
and not just to Deuteronomy, he found in the Torah two mutually contradictory requirements concerning the preparation of the meat of the
Passover sacrifice for eating: the one demanded צלי אש . . . ואכלו את הבשר
'And they shall eat the flesh . . . roasted with fire' (Exod 12:8, P). This
passage reiterates the requirement, stressing it in negative terms: אל
תאכלו ממנו נא ובשל מבשל במים כי אם צלי אש 'Do not eat it raw or boiled in water but roasted over the fire' (12:9). The other requirement demanded
the exact opposite: ובשלת ואכלת 'and you shall *cook* it and eat it' (Deut
16:7, D). The Chronicler harmonized these mutually contradictory requirements while upholding both and placing them next to each other
(2 Chr 35:13): ויבשלו הפסח באש כמשפט 'They *cooked* the Passover *over the
fire* according to the ordinance'.[96]

Attempts similar to this one by the Chronicler were also made in the
Septuagint of Deut 16:7: καὶ ἑψήσεις καὶ ὀπτήσεις 'and you shall cook and
roast'; in *Jub.* 49:13: "And it is not fitting that they should boil it in water. And they shall not eat it raw but roasted in the fire, cooked with
care"; and later, in a *Midrash halacha*:[97]

ובשל'—אין בשל אלא צלי, שנאמר 'ובשלת ואכלת' ואומר 'ויבשלו את הפסח
באש כמשפט'. מכאן היה ר' יאשיה אומר: הנודר מן המבושל אסור בצלי
ובשל—the word בשל only means 'roast', as it is written ובשלת ואכלת
[Deut 16:7], and it has also been said, ויבשלו את הפסח באש כמשפט
[2 Chr 35:13]. Hence, R. Yoshajah said, "one who vows to abstain
from cooked meat may not eat roast meat either."

There is a similar reference in *y. Ned.* 6.1 (19b):

וקרייא שהצלוי קרוי מבושל, 'ויבשלו את הפסח' וגו' אין תימר שלא כהלכה,
רבי יונה בוצרייא אמר 'כמשפט'
It is said that roast is called cooked, "and they cooked the passover,
and so on" (2 Chr 36:13)—if you say that this was against the law,
R. Jonah Buzriya said, "according to the ordinance."[98]

---

96. Cf. Rudolph, *Chronik*, 327; Seeligmann, "Beginnings of Midrash," 31–32;
Williamson, *Chronicles*, 407. Welch's assumption (*Chronicler*, 146), that the words
באש כמשפט are an addition of a later editor of Chronicles, lacks a firm basis and
seems to derive from his tendency to ascribe to the Chronicler the decisive influence
of the book of Deuteronomy.

97. *Mekilta de Rabbi Ishmael*, Masechta de Pesaḥ, §6 (ed. Horovitz-Rabin, 21).

98. The Akkadian verb *bašālu* also appears in the sense of 'to roast' at times (see
CAD B 135). Yet it seems that the Chronicler was not thinking of this meaning here.

3. Harmonizing Divine Word and Divine Action

It was common for the Deuteronomistic historian to create an explicit link between the divine word and historical events. For him, the divine word is a motivating force in history to such an extent that the word generates history. The divine word does not return empty-handed—it does not return until it has achieved its entire aim, just as was foreseen by the prophet. In biblical terms (2 Kgs 10:10; see also 1 Kgs 8:24, 56; Josh 21:45; 23:14–16): כי לא יפל מדבר ה׳ ארצה אשר דבר ה׳ על . . . וה׳ עשה את אשר דבר ביד עבדו 'there shall fall to the earth nothing of the word of the Lord that the Lord spoke concerning . . . , for the Lord has done that which he spoke by his servant.' This functioning of the divine word, dictating the path of history until its fulfillment, is demonstrated in a number of places in the Former Prophets; for example, 1 Kgs 13:1–32 tells of the prophecy of the man of God from Judah concerning the altar erected by Jeroboam at Bethel and concerning the tale involving the prophet from Bethel. 2 Kgs 23:15–20 gives the fulfillment of the prophecy: ויטמאהו כדבר ה׳ אשר קרא איש האלהים אשר קרא את הדברים האלה 'and defiled it, *according to the word of the Lord* that the man of God proclaimed, who predicted these things' (2 Kgs 23:16b).

Another example: 1 Kgs 14:6–16 speaks of the prophecy of Ahijah the Shilonite concerning the dynasty of Jeroboam, son of Nebat. The text in 1 Kgs 15:29 reads as follows: ויהי כמלכו (בעשא) הכה את כל בית ירבעם, לא השאיר כל נשמה לירבעם עד השמידו *כדבר ה׳* אשר דבר ביד עבדו, אחיה השילני 'And it came to pass that, as soon as he was king, [Baasha] killed all the House of Jeroboam; he left not to Jeroboam any that breathed until he had destroyed him; *according to the saying of the Lord* that he spoke by the hand of his servant Ahijah the Shilonite'.[99] This theological pattern serves also as a literary technique that the Deuteronomistic historian used in attempting to portray the various sources uniformly that he integrated into his work and to link them together.[100]

In Chronistic historiography, the Chronicler sometimes transferred the divine word and its fulfillment from the earlier text into his own work almost in their present form. For example, הוא יבנה לי בית וכננתי את כסאו עד עולם 'he shall build me a house, and I will establish his throne forever' is adduced in 1 Chr 17:12 (// 2 Sam 7:13). In 2 Chr 6:10 (// 1 Kgs 8:20), we read about the realization of the divine word: ויקם ה׳ את דברו אשר דבר, ואקום תחת דויד אבי ואשב על כסא ישראל כאשר דבר ה׳, ואבנה הבית לשם ה׳ אלהי ישראל 'And the Lord has fulfilled his promise that he made; for I have

---

99. See also 1 Kgs 16:1–4; cf. 16:11–12; 2 Kgs 1:6; cf. 1:17; 2 Kgs 21:10–16; cf. 24:2–3; Josh 6:26; cf. 1 Kgs 16:34.

100. Cf. von Rad, "Deuteronomistische Geschichtstheologie," 189–204 (= ET, "Deuteronomistic Theology," 74–91).

succeeded David my father, and I have sat on the throne of Israel, as the Lord promised, and I have built the House for the name of the Lord, the God of Israel'.

At times, the Chronicler used only the fulfillment of the divine word from the earlier text, under the assumption that the reader would recognize the divine word from the context or remember it as it was narrated in the book of Kings.[101] For example, in 2 Chr 10:15 (// 1 Kgs 12:15) the realization of the promise of God is recorded: ולא שמע המלך אל העם כי היתה נסבה מעם האלהים למען הקים ה' את דברו אשר דבר ביד אחיהו השלוני אל ירבעם בן־נבט 'So the king did not listen to the people; for it was brought about by God, that the Lord might fulfill his word, which he spoke by the hand of Ahijah, the Shilonite, to Jeroboam, the son of Nebat'. At the same time, the divine word itself—the prophecy of Ahijah the Shilonite to Jeroboam, presented in 1 Kgs 11:29–30—is omitted from the book of Chronicles.[102] Furthermore, the Chronicler sometimes adds to the earlier text the story of the fulfillment of an early prophecy. For example:

(a) 2 Sam 5:1–2 says that the elders of Israel came to Hebron: וימשחו את דוד למלך על ישראל 'And they anointed David king over Israel'. In 1 Chr 11:1–3, the Chronicler presents the narrative from the earlier text, while noting that, thus, כדבר ה' ביד שמואל 'as the word of the Lord by the hand of Samuel' was realized, alluding to the narrative in 1 Sam 16:1–13, which he had omitted from his work.[103]

(b) In 2 Chronicles 36, after the Chronicler lists the circumstances that had led to the destruction of Jerusalem and to the Babylonian Exile, he notes that this happened in order (2 Chr 36:21) *למלאות דבר ה' בפי ירמיהו עד רצתה הארץ את שבתותיה . . . למלאות שבעים שנה* 'to fulfill the word of the Lord by the mouth of Jeremiah, until the land had served is Sabbaths . . . to complete seventy years', and thus alluded to the existence of Jeremiah's prophecies concerning the destruction of Jerusalem and the

---

101. The Chronicler assumes that the reader recognizes the divine word from the narrative in the books of the Former Prophets; see the introduction to chap. 10, pp. 194–195.

102. Japhet (*Ideology*, 162 n. 478) considers "2 Chr 10:15 an inconsistent holdover from 1 Kgs 12:15"—in light of the fact that, according to the book of Chronicles, every person and every generation is responsible for its own actions and its own fate, and there is place neither for privilege by "ancestral merit" nor for "sins of the fathers." However, 2 Chr 11:4 (// 1 Kgs 12:24)—כה אמר ה' לא תעלו ולא תלחמו עם אחיכם שובו איש לביתו כי מאתי נהיה הדבר הזה וישמעו את דברי ה' וישבו מלכת אל ירבעם 'Thus says the Lord: "You shall not go up or fight against your kindred; return every one to his house, for this thing is of me." So they hearkened to the word of the Lord and returned from going against Jeroboam'—repeatedly alludes to 2 Chr 10:15 // 1 Kgs 12:15!

103. And see further on as well, in 1 Chr 11:10: להמליכו כדבר ה' על ישראל 'to make him king, according to the word of the Lord concerning Israel'; and also 12:24: באו על דויד חברונה להסב מלכות שאול אליו כפי ה' '. . . came to David to Hebron, to turn the kingdom of Saul over to him, according to the word of the Lord'.

length of the Babylonian Exile and also to the existence of a divine word as expressed in the Torah (see Jer 25:11–12; 27:7; Lev 26:34–35).[104]

On occasion, however, the Chronicler tried to demonstrate the existence of the divine word in history not by explicit addition to the earlier text but by means of renewed literary structuring.

7.27 In 2 Chr 32:21b, the Chronicler emended the text of 2 Kgs 19:36–37 (= Isa 37:37–38), which tells of the withdrawal of Sennacherib from Judah and his assassination in Assyria, in order to harmonize it with Isaiah's prophecy of the same events in v. 7 (Isa 37:7):

2 Kgs 19:7	*2 Kgs 19:36–37*	*2 Chr 32:21b*
הנני נתן בו רוח	ויסע וילך	
ושמע שמועה *ושב*	וישב סנחריב מלך אשור	*וישב בבשת פנים*
לארצו	וישב בנינוה . . .	*לארצו* . . .
והפלתיו בחרב בארצו	בניו הכהו בחרב	ומיציאי מעיו שם
		הפילהו בחרב
Behold, I will put	He left	
a spirit in him,	and returned home	So he *returned* in
and he shall hear	and resided at	disgrace
a rumor *and return*	Nineveh . . .	to *his own land* . . .
to his own land,		some of his own
and I will fell	his sons killed him	sons *struck him down*
him by the sword	with the sword.	*there with a sword.*
in his own land.		

This textual harmonization places special stress on the fulfillment of the Divine word through Isaiah: Isaiah's prophecy relating to Sennacherib's withdrawal and assassination was precisely and fully realized, as the prophet had predicted it.[105]

7.28 In Nathan's prophecy, the Lord promises David (2 Sam 7:11): והניחתי לך מכל איביך 'and I will give you to rest from all your enemies'.[106]

---

104. For the literary structure of this passage in Chronicles, see chaps. 11 and 14.

105. Here the author of Kings (and, following him, the Chronicler as well) linked two historical events between which a period of some 20 years intervened: Sennacherib's retreat from Judah took place in the year 701 B.C.E., whereas he was assassinated in 681 B.C.E. For more on this, see also example 1.10 (pp. 32–33). This linkage was intended to demonstrate the fulfilling of Isaiah's prophecy (2 Kgs 19:7 = Isa 37:7), and the Chronicler made an even more obvious association.

106. Some read here: "and I will give him (= Israel) to rest from all his enemies." So, e.g., Driver, *Samuel*, 275; Budde, *Samuel*, 235; cf. McCarter, *II Samuel*, 193 (see there for additional literature). This reading lacks textual support and is unnecessary. The writer has gone back to speak to David, as in vv. 8–9; and cf. Segal, *Samuel*, 279.

In 1 Chr 17:10 the Chronicler made changes and wrote: והכנעתי את כל
אויביך 'and I will subdue all your enemies'. The roots נוח 'give rest' and
כנע 'subdue' appear frequently in Chronicles. As Japhet put it: "כנ״ע—of
the 36 times it appears in the Bible, 18 are in Chronicles. נו״ח in the
sense 'give rest' appears in Chronicles seven times, all in unparalleled
texts."[107] Thus, one cannot claim that the Chronicler preferred a common root over a rare one in 1 Chr 17:10. Japhet feels that the interchange resulted from the Chronicler's desire "to describe more authen-
tically the Lord's actions on behalf of David."[108] It is more reasonable,
however, to assume that the Chronicler wanted to harmonize the
Lord's promise to David (known in the jargon of literary research as
"the report member") with the actualization of the promise, as expressed in David's victory over the Philistines: ויך דויד את פלשתים ויכניעם
'David struck the Philistines and subdued them' ("the execution member," 1 Chr 18:1a // 2 Sam 8:1a). The harmonization emphasizes the
precision and completeness of the relationship between "the report
member" and "the execution member"—that is, the Lord fulfilled precisely what he had promised.

7.29 In his description of David's war against the Philistines at Baal-
perazim, the Chronicler introduced a number of changes into the earlier
text. These emendations created harmony between David's inquiry of
the Lord and the Lord's reply ("report members") and the realization of
the request in actual fact ("execution member"):

		2 Sam 5:19–20	1 Chr 14:10–11
Report Members {	David's inquiry of the Lord	האעלה אל פלשתים	האעלה על פלשתים
		התתנם בידי	ונתתם בידי
		Shall I go up to the Philistines? Will you give them *into my hands*?	*Shall I go up* against the Philistines and will you give them *into my hands*?
	The Lord's reply to David	עלה	עלה
		כי נתן אתן . . . בידך	ונתתים בידך
		Go up! for I shall surely give . . . *into your hands!*	*Go up!* for I will give them *into your hands.*

---

107. Japhet, "Interchanges," 36 n. 98.
108. Ibid., 36.

| *Execution Member* | Realization of the request | ויבא דוד בבעל פרצים
ויכם שם דוד ויאמר
פרץ ה׳ את איבי
לפני כפרץ מים
And David *came* to Baal-perazim. And David defeated them there, saying: "The Lord has burst forth against my enemies *before me* like a bursting of waters." | ויעל(ו) 109 בבעל פרצים
ויכם שם דויד ויאמר דויד
פרץ האלהים את אויבי
בידי כפרץ מים
And *they went up* to Baal-perazim. And David defeated them there, saying: "God has burst forth against my enemies *in my hand* like a bursting of waters." |

In the "execution member," the Chronicler made use of the root עלה 'go up' (ויעלו) in place of ויבא 'come') and of the noun ידים 'hands' (בידי) instead of לפני 'before me'), the words that appear in the "report members" (האעלה, עלה; בידי, בידך). Furthermore, he used the root נתן 'give' that appears in the early text, though he changed its grammatical form in order to create verbal harmony between the form appearing in David's question—ונתתם (in place of התתנם in Samuel)—and the form used in the Lord's reply—ונתתים (in place of נתן אתן in Samuel).

Generally speaking, the Chronicler created verbal harmony between the "report members" and the "execution member." This harmonization gives the reader the impression that the Lord was able to fulfill David's request both in its spirit and in its content.

The Chronicler ignored the root פרץ in the "execution member" and did not harmonize it with the root נתן in the "execution member" because this root expresses a stronger level of divine power and also because it integrates well with David's picturesque simile . . . *פרץ* האלהים *כפרץ* מים 'God *burst* forth . . . like a *bursting* of waters' and with the popular etymology of the place-name Baal-perazim.

---

109. The MT reading is ויעלו, plural (replacing ויבא דוד in the parallel verse in Samuel), the reference undoubtedly being to David and his men; and compare ויכו (v. 16) instead of ויך in the parallel verse in Samuel. Japhet ("Interchanges," 45–46) feels that ויעלו refers to the Philistines: "The style of the text in Samuel is somewhat awkward, with it repetition of the subject, 'David': . . . ויבא דוד ויכם שם דוד. While in Chronicles, the mention of David is dictated by the change of subject: ויעלו—Philistines—ויכם דויד." In a number of MT manuscripts, the LXX, the Vulgate, and the Peshiṭta, the form reflected is ויעל, singular (like ויבא, singular, in the parallel verse in Samuel), and this reading seems to be preferable; cf. Rudolph, *Chronik*, 114; Myers, *I Chronicles*, 104. At any rate, the singular form ויעל is a better match for the form האעלה in David's question and for עלה in the Lord's reply to David.

7.30 An example similar to the previous one can be found in the description of David's second war against the Philistines:

		2 Sam 5:24b, 25	1 Chr 14:15b, 16
Report Member	The Lord's word to David	כי אז יצא ה׳ לפניך להכות *במחנה* פלשתים For then the Lord will go out before you to strike *the* Philistine *camp.*	כי יצא האלהים לפניך להכות *את מחנה* פלשתים For God will go out before you to strike *down the* Philistine camp.
Execution Member	Fulfilling the Lord's word by David	ויעש דוד כן כאשר צוהו ה׳ ויך את פלשתים And David did so, as the Lord commanded him, and he struck *down* the Philistines.	ויעש דויד כאשר צוהו האלהים ויכו *את מחנה* פלשתים And David did as God commanded him, and they struck *down the* camp of the Philistines.

With regard to the general content, there is no significant difference between the text in Samuel and the text in Chronicles. From a literary viewpoint, the emendations introduced by the Chronicler in the earlier text harmonize the Lord's word to David ("report member") and the fulfillment of the Lord's word by David, in actual practice ("execution member"); that is, the word of the Lord came about in the manner that the Lord intended. This literary shaping stresses the ability of the Lord to have his word fulfilled in history.

7.31 1 Kgs 22:17 gives the prophecy of Micaiah, son of Imlah, about the king of Israel: ויאמר ה׳ לא אדנים לאלה ישובו איש לביתו בשלום 'and the Lord said: "These have no master; let them return every *man* to his house in peace".' Further along, the text relates the death of the king of Israel (v. 35), who had led the war against Aram and had persuaded Jehoshaphat, king of Judah, to support him, and notes (1 Kgs 22:36): ויעבר הרנה במחנה כבא השמש לאמר איש אל עירו ואיש אל ארצו 'And a cry went through the camp at sunset: "Every man to his city, and every man to his country"'. That is, except for the king of Israel, the men returned in peace, each man to his place.

In 2 Chronicles 18, the Chronicler presented the fatal prophecy regarding the king of Israel (v. 16) and also noted his death in battle (v. 34), paralleling the narrative in Kings. However, he omitted the passage in 1 Kgs 22:36 related to the return of the other men—"every man to his city, and every man to his country"—and, instead, told about Je-

hoshaphat immediately after the death of the king of Israel. His wording was identical to the wording of the prophecy of Micaiah, son of Imlah
(2 Chr 19:1): וישב יהושפט מלך יהודה אל ביתו בשלום לירושלם 'And Jehoshaphat, king of Judah, returned to his home in peace, to Jerusalem'.[110] By
means of his repetition of the prophetic words, the Chronicler apparently tried to demonstrate the fulfillment of the divine word,[111] precisely as Micaiah, son of Imlah, had expressed it. He did this while
avoiding explicit statements, such as כדבר ה׳ ביד מיכיהו בן־ימלא / כפי ה׳ /
כדבר ה׳ ביד עבדו מיכיהו, and so on.

It is noteworthy that, in all of the cases that are mentioned above, the
Chronicler avoided making any emendations in God's words or in His
words that had been expressed by prophet(s). For him, these phrases
are *ipsissima verba* 'the same words precisely'. He made changes in the
actions of mortals only in order to harmonize them with the Lord's
words stated previously.

---

110. For the contrast between the fate of the righteous king of Judah and the fate
of the wicked king of Israel, see example 15.10 (pp. 336–337).

111. Cf. Williamson, *Chronicles*, 286.

Chapter 8
Character Creation

A few of the ways that an author-creator (whether "narrator" or "historiographer") can express his attitude toward characters in his work are: the way he chooses to name them; the way he mentions them in various contexts; and the frequency with which he has them appear in a given episode. These decisions directly or indirectly influence the creation of the characters in an episode and the way that readers or hearers perceive them.

The Chronicler is not to be excluded from this category of author-creators. In several episodes, he has altered the form of the names of characters encountered in the books of Samuel–Kings, as well as the way the characters appear and the frequency of their occurrence. He has done so in order to render them (or some aspect of them) more or less prominent, in accordance with his personal attitude toward them, whether favorable or unfavorable. In other words, the Chronicler's preference for the personal name of a certain character rather than the general title that appears in an earlier text (or, conversely, his preference for the general title rather than the personal name) has the literary-rhetorical effect of rendering the character more or less prominent in the episode and clarifies the Chronicler's own attitude toward this character. These results are also influenced considerably by the Chronicler's choice regarding how often and in which contexts he mentions the characters—by their personal names or by their general titles (§§1–2).

Sometimes the Chronicler has chosen to denote a character in a particular way in order to give the reader a sense of the comfortable, informal (or the unbending, formal) atmosphere that prevailed on a certain occasion (for example, in a dialogue between two individuals on different hierarchical levels) or to create a certain literary effect or to impress characters on the reader's mind (see §3 below, pp. 180ff.). In certain cases the Chronicler creates a hierarchical balance in the meeting of representatives of different authorities (§4 below, pp. 182ff.).

1. Rendering Characters More Significant

A. David in the Census Narrative

David is without doubt the central figure in the narrative of the census in 2 Samuel 24, for the main thread of the tale involves his words

and deeds. Moreover, he is mentioned in the narrative (either by his personal name or by his title) frequently: 29 times in a chapter with only 25
verses(!), as well as not a few allusions. As if this were not enough, in
the parallel text in 1 Chr 21:1–22:1, the Chronicler tried to render the
figure he most admired even more significant.

I. Reshaping of David's Figure in the Census Narrative

The Chronicler eliminated the delicate balance that existed in the
narrative in Samuel between the use of the personal name דוד 'David'
(15 times) and the general title (ה)מלך '(the) king' (14 times),[1] preferring
to use the personal name דויד (23 times; this also expresses his personal,
unofficial attitude toward the hero) rather than the general (hierarchical, official) title, המלך (only 4 times!).[2] To achieve this literary effect, the
Chronicler used various literary and stylistic techniques.

(1) Using a Personal Name in Place of a General Title

1. 2 Sam 24:2   ויאמר המלך אל יואב   And *the king* said to Joab . . .
    1 Chr 21:2   ויאמר דויד אל יואב   And *David* said to Joab . . .

2. 2 Sam 24:9   ויתן יואב . . . אל המלך   And Joab gave . . . *the king*
    1 Chr 21:5   ויתן יואב . . . אל דויד   And Joab gave . . . *David*

3. 2 Sam 24:20   וישקף ארונה וירא את   When Arauna looked he saw
                  המלך   *the king*.
    1 Chr 21:21   ויבט ארנן וירא את   And Ornan looked and saw
                  דויד   *David*.

4. 2 Sam 24:20   וישתחו למלך אפיו   And he bowed down *to the*
                  ארצה   *king* with his face to the
                        ground.
    1 Chr 21:21   וישתחו לדויד אפים   And he bowed down *to David*,
                  ארצה   face to the ground.

---

1. The name דוד appears in 2 Sam 24:1, 10 (2×), 11 (2×), 12, 13, 14, 17, 18, 19, 21,
22, 24, 25; whereas the title (ה)מלך occurs in vv. 2, 3 (3×), 4 (2×), 9, 20 (2×), 21, 23, 23
(2×), 24.

2. The name דויד appears in 1 Chr 21:1, 2, 5, 8, 9, 10, 11, 13, 16 (2×), 17, 18 (2×), 19,
21 (3×), 22, 23, 25, 26, 28, 30; 22:1; whereas the title (ה)מלך occurs in vv. 3, 4, 6, 23;
and the phrase המלך דויד appears once, in 21:24. It should be noted that, despite the
Chronicler's omissions from and additions to the earlier text of Samuel, he main-
tained the total number of uses of the personal name, "David," plus uses of the general title, "the king": 29.

(2) Adding a Personal Name to a General Title

2 Sam 24:24	אל	ויאמר המלך	And the king said to
		ארונה ...	Arauna . . .
1 Chr 21:24		ויאמר המלך דויד	And King *David* said to
		לארנן ...	Ornan . . .

(3) Changing Direct Speech to Indirect Speech,
Thus Requiring the Use of a Name

2 Sam 24:18	ויבא גד אל דוד ...	And Gad came to David . . .
	ויאמר לו *עלה הקם* לה׳	and said *to him*: "*Rise and*
	מזבח	*erect* an altar to the Lord."
1 Chr 21:18	ומלאך ה׳ אמר אל גד	And an angel of the Lord told
	לאמר לדויד כי *יעלה*	Gad to say *to David* that
	דויד להקים מזבח לה׳ [3]	*David* should *rise and erect*
		an altar to the Lord.

(4) Omitting the General Title המלך 'the King'

1.	2 Sam 24:3	ויאמר יואב אל *המלך*	And Joab said to *the king*:
		ויוסף ה׳ אלהיך אל העם כהם	"May the Lord your God add
		וכהם מאה פעמים ועיני אדני	to the number of the people a
		המלך ראות ואדני *המלך*	hundredfold, and may the
		למה חפץ בדבר הזה	eyes of my lord the king see it,
			but why does my lord *the king*
			want this thing?"
	1 Chr 21:3	ויאמר יואב	And Joab said:
		יוסף ה׳ על עמו כהם מאה	"May the Lord add to the
		פעמים הלא אדני המלך	number of his people a
		כלם לאדני לעבדים למה	hundredfold—my lord the
		יבקש זאת אדני	king, are they not all my
			lord's servants!? but why

---

3. It is also possible that this variant is not just a matter of style but that it even has a theological function. That is, Gad the prophet, David's seer, does not command David to set up an altar on the threshing floor of Arauna on his own authority. He serves as a messenger to convey the words of (an angel of) the Lord to David. Indeed, this particular point is made by the Chronicler immediately: ויעל דויד בדבר גד אשר דבר בשם ה׳ 'And David went up under the instructions of Gad, who spoke in the name of the Lord' (1 Chr 21:19; in parallel to ויעל דוד כדבר גד כאשר צוה ה׳ 'And David went up under the instructions of Gad, as the Lord commanded'; 2 Sam 24:19; see also 1 Chr 21:9–10 // 2 Sam 24:11–12). The Chronicler's way of presenting things stresses once again that the authority for choosing the threshing floor of Arauna, the Jebusite, for the erection of the altar was divine and not merely mortal. For further discussion of this point, see Kalimi, "Land/Mount Moriah," 16–20.

| | | does my lord   request this?" |

2.   2 Sam 24:4

	ויצא יואב ושרי החיל	And Joab and the generals of
	לפני *המלך* לפקד	the army went out from
	את העם את ישראל	before *the king* to number the people, Israel.

1 Chr 21:4

| | ויצא יואב   ויתהלך | And Joab departed   and |
| | בכל ישראל | went throughout all Israel. |

These omissions contribute to the reduction in the total number of times the general title המלך is mentioned, and to the corresponding additional prominence gained by the personal name דויד.

(5) Using the Personal Name דויד *in "Additions"*

In his own "additions" to the early text, the Chronicler specifically chose to use the personal name דויד, rather than the general title המלך. For example:

1 Chr 21:16

	וישא דויד את עיניו,	And *David* looked up and saw
	וירא את . . . ויפל דויד	. . . and *David* and the elders,
	והזקנים מכסים בשקים	covered in sackcloth, fell on
	על פניהם[4]	their faces.

21:17   ויאמר דויד אל האלהים   And *David* said to God . . .

. . .

21:21   ויבא דויד עד ארנן   And *David* came to Ornan.

| 21:28 | בעת ההיא בראות דויד | At that time, when *David* saw |
| | כי ענהו ה׳ . . . | that the Lord had answered him . . . |

| 21:30 | ולא יכל דויד ללכת | And *David* could not go to |
| | לדרש אלהים. | inquire of God. |

| 22:1 | ויאמר דויד: זה הוא בית | And *David* said: "This is the |
| | ה׳ האלהים . . . | house of the Lord God." |

---

4. This verse, nonexistent in the MT and in the LXX of Samuel, appears also (with certain alterations discussed below, chap. 12) in 4QSam[a]: וישא [דויד את עיניו וירא את מלאך ה׳ עומד בין] הארץ ובין [הש]מ[י]ם וחר[ב]ו שלופה בידו [נטויה על ירושלים ויפלו דויד והזקנים בשקים [על פנ] יהם מתכ]סים] 'And [David] lifted up [his eyes and saw an angel of the Lord positioned between] the earth and [the he]avens, with his sword drawn in his hand [extended over Jerusalem; and David and the elders fell on] their [face], cove[red] in sackcloth'. Cross and, later, McKenzie believe that the Chronicler and the writer of the Qumran scroll copied what they had found in a third, independent source, and that the absence of the verse in the book of Samuel is the result of homoioarcton; see Cross, *Ancient Library*, 188 n. 40a; McKenzie, *Chronicler*, 55–56. If this is indeed the case, then this verse is not one of the Chronicler's "additions."

II. Transforming General Formulations into Personal Ones

In order to render the figure of David more prominent in the narrative, the Chronicler transformed the general formulations in the earlier text into more personal ones; for example:

1.   2 Sam 24:2   פקדו את העם *וידעתי*   Number the people *that I may*
     את מספר העם   *know* the number of the
     people.

     1 Chr 21:2   לכו ספרו את ישראל . . .   Go and count Israel . . . and
     והביאו אלי ואדעה את   bring (it) *to me* that *I may*
     מספרם   *know* their number.

2.   2 Sam 24:21   ויאמר דוד *לקנות*   And David said: "To *purchase*
     מעמך את הגרן *לבנות*   the threshing floor from you
     מזבח לה׳ ותעצר המגפה   *to build* an altar to the Lord,
     so that the plague may be
     stopped."

     1 Chr 21:22   ויאמר דויד . . . *תנה לי*   And David said ". . . Give *me*
     מקום הגרן *ואבנה* בו   the site of the threshing floor
     מזבח לה׳, בכסף מלא   *that I may build* an altar
     תנהו לי ותעצר המגפה   there to the Lord; give it *to*
     me for its full price, so that
     the plague may be stopped."

3.   2 Sam 24:25   ויעל עלות ושלמים   And he offered up burnt-
     ויעתר ה׳ לארץ   offerings and peace-offerings,
     and *the Lord responded* for
     the land.

     1 Chr 21:26   ויעל עלות ושלמים   And he offered up burnt-
     ויקרא אל ה׳ ויענהו   offerings and peace-offerings
     באש מן השמים   and *called* upon the Lord, *and
     he answered him* with fire
     from heaven.

The numerous examples of almost every point mentioned and their placement in concentrated fashion alongside one another in the census narrative show the Chronicler's efforts to achieve the literary effect described at the onset of this discussion.

B. "Israel" (People and Land) in the Census Narrative

Instead of the general nouns העם and הארץ used in the census narrative in 2 Samuel 24, the Chronicler, in 1 Chronicles 21, used ישראל in reference to both the people and the land of Israel, apparently in order to render them more prominent:

1.	2 Sam 24:2	שוטו נא . . . ופקדו את העם	Go throughout . . . and number *the people.*
	1 Chr 21:2	לכו ספרו את ישראל	Go now and count *Israel.*
2.	2 Sam 24:15	וימת מן העם	And there died *of the people*
	1 Chr 21:14	ויפל מישראל ⁵	And there fell *of Israel*
3.	2 Sam 24:8	וישטו בכל הארץ	And they went throughout all *the land.*
	1 Chr 21:4	ויתהלך בכל ישראל	And he went throughout all *Israel.*

In general, it seems that in the narrative of the census and the selection of the site of the altar by the Lord in the book of Chronicles, the Chronicler attempted to render David and Israel (the people and the land) more prominent because of his great feeling for them.

C. *Jehoiada the Priest*

The Chronicler's warm regard for Jehoiada the priest first becomes apparent from the positive words of appreciation with which he concluded the description of his lifetime (2 Chr 24:16b, "addition"): כי עשה טובה בישראל ועם האלהים וביתו 'For he had done good in Israel, and for God and his house'. Indeed, Jehoiada had preserved the Davidic dynasty: he saved Joash from the sword of Athaliah, brought him up, had him crowned king of Judah, and even helped marry him to women (2 Chr 23:10–21 // 2 Kings 11; 2 Chr 24:3, "addition"). During his term in the Temple, "they offered burnt-offerings in the House of the Lord continually all the days of Jehoiada" (2 Chr 24:14b, "addition"). In return for his welcome activity, Jehoiada enjoyed longevity—"And Jehoiada grew old and was full of days; he was one hundred thirty years old at his death" (v. 15, "addition"), and despite his not having been a king, they buried him "in the City of David, with the kings" (v. 16b, "addition"). All of this was in contrast to the fate of Joash: because of his evil deeds (vv. 18, 20–22, "addition") his days were shortened, "and they did not bury him in the burial places of the kings" (v. 25, contrary to 2 Kgs 12:22).[6]

The Chronicler made much of Jehoiada's positive character, especially in light of the ingratitude shown to him by Joash: Joash had Zechariah, Jehoiada's son, put to death "in the courtyard of the House of the Lord" (2 Chr 24:21),[7] "and Joash the king did not remember the

---

5. For the changes המלך ואנשיו / דויד וכל ישראל (2 Sam 5:6 // 1 Chr 11:4) and וילך דוד וכל העם אשר אתו / ויעל דויד וכל ישראל (2 Sam 6:2 // 1 Chr 13:6), see example 1.2 (p. 19).

6. For this, see in detail chaps. 9 and 15.

7. Jehoiada did not behave this way even with עתליה המרשעת 'wicked Athalia': כי אמר הכהן לא תמיתוה בית ה׳ 'For the priest said: "Do not put her to death in the *House of the Lord*"' (2 Chr 23:14 // 2 Kgs 11:15).

favor shown him by Jehoiada, Zechariah's father, *but killed his son*"
(v. 22). In contrast, Jehoiada and his wife Jehoshabeath (according to
the Chronicler) had saved Joash "out of the sons of the king who were
put to death," had hid him at great personal risk, had raised him, and
had seen to his needs (22:10–12; 24:3).[8]

The Chronicler's positive attitude toward Jehoiada is also clearly
shown by the hierarchical balance that he creates in his references to
him alongside the king and the king's *secretary*, while describing the repairs made to the Temple.[9]

In order to render Jehoiada's image even more prominent and, furthermore, to demonstrate his positive attitude to him, the Chronicler
mentions his name frequently. In 2 Kings 12, Jehoiada was mentioned
only *three times*: twice in the form "Jehoiada the priest" (vv. 8, 10), that
is, his personal name and general title; and once using his title only—
הכהן הגדול 'the high priest' (v. 11). In contrast, in the parallel text in
2 Chronicles 24, he is mentioned *ten times*: seven times by his personal
name—יהוידע (vv. 3, 12, 14 twice, 15, 17, 22); twice by his personal name
and his title—"Jehoiada the priest" (vv. 2, 25); and once as יהוידע הראש
'Jehoiada the chief' (v. 6).[10] However, he is not ever mentioned by his
general title only—הכהן 'the priest' or כהן הראש/הגדול 'chief/high priest'.[11]
This stands in contrast to Joash's being referred to by his general title
only—המלך 'the king'—time after time (8×) in 2 Chronicles 24,[12] occasionally alongside Jehoiada.

1. 2 Kgs 12:8   ויקרא המלך יהואש   And *King Jehoash* called
                       ליהוידע הכהן   to *Jehoiada the priest.*
    2 Chr 24:6   ויקרא המלך   And *the king* called *to*
                       ליהוידע הראש   *Jehoiada the chief.*

2. 2 Kgs 12:12   ונתנו * את הכסף המתכן   And *they gave* the money
                       על־ידי עשי המלאכה   that had been weighed out
                  הפקדים (*Qere*): המפקדים) into the hands of the workers
                       בית ה'   who were in charge of the
                                             House of the Lord.
         *referring to the king's secretary and the high priest in v. 11

---

8. 2 Chr 24:3, which is one of the Chronicler's "additions," appears detached from
any context: it is anchored neither in the schematic introduction (vv. 1–2) nor in the
description of the restoration of the House of the Lord (vv. 4–14).

9. For this, see below, §4, "Creating Hierarchical Balance" (pp. 182ff.).

10. Moreover, mention should be made of פקיד כהן הראש 'officer of *the chief priest*'
(v. 11) and זכריה בן יהוידע הכהן 'Zechariah, son of *Jehoiada the priest*' (v. 20).

11. Besides the case of פקיד כהן הראש (v. 11), which renders mention of the personal
name superfluous.

12. For this, see below, §2A, in the discussion of "Joash/Jehoash, King of Judah"
(pp. 174–177).

2 Chr 24:12	ויתנהו המלך ויהוידע אל עושה מלאכת עבודה בית ה׳	And *the king and Jehoiada* gave it to the ones in charge of the work in the House of the Lord.
3. 2 Chr 24:14	וככלותם הביאו לפני המלך ויהוידע את שאר הכסף	And when they were finished they brought the rest of the money to *the king and Jehoiada*.
4. 2 Chr 24:17	ואחרי מות יהוידע באו שרי יהודה וישתחו למלך, אז שמע המלך אליהם	After the death of *Jehoiada*, the princes of Judah came and bowed down to *the king*; then *the king* listened to them.

The image of Jehoiada is also rendered more prominent in the Chronicler's description of Joash's coronation (2 Chr 23:10–21 // 2 Kings 11). The Chronicler uses his name, Jehoiada, and/or his title wherever the earlier text does and also makes the following changes:

(1) Using a Personal Name in Place of a General Title

2 Kgs 11:18	וישם הכהן פקדת על בית ה׳	And *the priest* appointed officers over the House of the Lord.
2 Chr 23:18	וישם יהוידע פקדת בית ה׳	And *Jehoiada* appointed officers over the House of the Lord.

(2) Adding a Personal Name alongside a Title in the Text

2 Kgs 11:10	ויתן הכהן לשרי המאיות (Qere: המאות) את החנית	And *the priest* gave the officers over hundreds the spears.
2 Chr 23:9	ויתן יהוידע הכהן לשרי המאות את החניתים	And *Jehoiada the priest* gave the officers over hundreds the spears.[13]

---

13. "We have before us a fact worthy of our attention: in our sources, the personal name precedes the title כהן 'the priest' and the title נביא 'the prophet', such as אהרן הכהן 'Aaron the Priest', גד הנביא 'Gad the prophet'. In the Bible we find couplets of a personal name and the term הכהן, such as 'Aaron the Priest', 135 times and never in the opposite order" (Peretz, "Proper Noun and Title," 131).

(3) Adding a Personal Name Wherever He Saw Fit

2 Kgs 11:12	וימלכו אתו וימשחהו	And they installed him as
	ויכו כף ויאמרו	king and anointed him
	יחי המלך	and clapped their
		hands and said:
		"Long live the king!"
2 Chr 23:11	וימלכו אתו וימשחהו	And they installed him as
	יהוידע ובניו ויאמרו	king, and *Jehoiada and his*
	יחי המלך	*sons* anointed him and said:
		"Long live the king!"

Moreover, the name occurs also in the phrase אשת יהוידע הכהן 'the wife of Jehoiada the priest' in 2 Chr 23:11 ("addition").

2. Rendering Characters Less Significant

A. Joash/Jehoash, King of Judah

The picture of Joash, king of Judah, is different in the book of Chronicles from the description given in the book of Kings (2 Chronicles 24 // 2 Kings 12). According to Kings, Joash did "what was upright in the eyes of the Lord *all his days*" (2 Kgs 12:3). In Chronicles, Joash's reign is broken up into two mutually contradictory periods with regard to Joash's religious behavior: the first period is כל ימי יהוידע הכהן 'the entire *lifetime of Jehoiada the priest*', when Joash did what was upright in the eyes of the Lord (2 Chr 24:2); the second period is אחרי מות יהוידע '*after the death of Jehoiada*', when Joash abandoned the Lord and his Temple, worshiped "the Asherim and the images," and even treated his benefactor Jehoiada ungratefully by killing his son Zechariah in the Temple courtyard (vv. 17–22).[14] Ascribing these "sins" to Joash is a result of the Chronicler's fastidious system of retaliation and consequent desire to provide justification for Joash's defeat at the hands of Aram and his assassination by his servants.[15]

In addition to these explicit reflections on the second period of Joash's reign (reflections unknown from any source earlier than the book of Chronicles), the Chronicler adopted various other literary techniques, apparently to show his cool attitude toward Joash, to render him less prominent, and to damage his reputation.

---

14. For this division of Joash's reign into two periods, see Rudolph, *Chronik*, 273.

15. Cf. Japhet, *Ideology*, 167 n. 486, 173–75. Japhet notes (p. 174): "The change in outlook also affects the external aspect of the description: in the book of Kings there is no quantitative proportion between the two parts of Joash's reign (the first part is dealt with in seventeen verses, while the second—in five)." The Chronicler doubles the second part, thereby creating a balanced description.

(1) Increased Use of the General Title הַמֶּלֶךְ *'the King'*

In 2 Kings 12, Jehoash, king of Judah, is mentioned by his personal name, יְהוֹאָשׁ, six times (vv. 1, 2, 3, 5, 20, 21); by his personal name together with his title הַמֶּלֶךְ יְהוֹאָשׁ once (v. 8) and יְהוֹאָשׁ מֶלֶךְ יְהוּדָה once (v. 19),[16] but never by the general title הַמֶּלֶךְ alone. The Chronicler, on the other hand, makes use of the general title הַמֶּלֶךְ time and again, eight times in all, in 2 Chronicles 24,

(a) once, by omitting the personal name in the text but retaining the general title:

2 Kgs 12:8	וַיִּקְרָא הַמֶּלֶךְ יְהוֹאָשׁ	and *King Jehoash* called to
	לִיהוֹיָדָע הַכֹּהֵן	Jehoiada the priest
2 Chr 24:6	וַיִּקְרָא הַמֶּלֶךְ	and *the king* called to
	לִיהוֹיָדָע הָרֹאשׁ	Jehoiada the chief

(b) four times in alterations of 2 Kings 12 (2 Chr 24:8, 11, 12, 14);

(c) and three times in "additions" (24:17 [2×], 21).

The use of the general title הַמֶּלֶךְ 'the king' for Jehoash also stands out because the Chronicler uses the personal name Jehoiada (10×)[17] throughout his description and does not use any of Jehoiada's general titles, "the priest" or "the high priest"/"the chief priest," by itself; sometimes he even uses the name Jehoiada together with Jehoash's general title, "the king." In addition to the example adduced above (2 Chr 24:6), one can see this technique in 2 Chr 24:12 (compared with 2 Kgs 12:12) and 24:14, 17.[18]

The name Joash is mentioned only at the beginning of the chapter, in the introduction presenting the new king, whose reign is about to be described: twice in 2 Chr 24:1, 2 // 2 Kgs 12:1, 3, and once in the "addition" preceding the narrative concerning the repairs to the Temple, 24:4; and toward the end of the narrative, in vv. 22, 24 ("additions"), which will be treated below.

(2) Mentioning a Personal Name in Uncomfortable Situations

Toward the end of the narrative, where the Chronicler decides to denote the sin of the ruler of Judah and his punishment, he decides to mention the ruler's personal name (especially here).

---

16. 2 Kgs 12:7: the chronological note בִּשְׁנַת עֶשְׂרִים וְשָׁלֹשׁ שָׁנָה לַמֶּלֶךְ יְהוֹאָשׁ 'in the 23d year *of Jehoash's reign'* is not to be included here.

17. 2 Chr 24:3, 12, 14 (2x), 15, 17, 22–יְהוֹיָדָע; 2, 25–יְהוֹיָדָע הַכֹּהֵן; 6–יְהוֹיָדָע הָרֹאשׁ; and see also v. 20.

18. For details of this, see above, p. 171, in the discussion regarding Jehoiada the priest.

(a) After the narrative of the stoning to death of Zechariah, son of Jehoiada, "at the command of the king in the courtyard of the house of the Lord" (2 Chr 24:21), the Chronicler wrote (24:22): ולא זכר *יואש* המלך החסד אשר עשה יהוידע אביו עמו ויהרג את בנו 'and *Joash* the king was not mindful of the kindness that Jehoiada, Zechariah's father, had shown him, but killed his son'. It is as if he wanted to say, "the king" at whose command Zechariah was stoned was none other than "*Joash the king*," the ungrateful one.

(b) In describing the punishment, he wrote (2 Chr 24:23–24): עלה עליו חיל ארם ויבאו ויבאו אל יהודה וירושלם וישחיתו . . . . ואת *יואש* עשו שפטים 'the army of Aram came up against him; they came to Judah and Jerusalem and destroyed . . . and executed judgment against *Joash*'. Thus, the Chronicler chose to mention "the king's" private name in uncomfortable situations, which not only did not induce respect for him but also incited ascribing responsibility to him personally for various catastrophes.

(3) Omitting the Name "Joash" from the Text and
Then Alluding to It

The three verses concluding the description of the reign of Joash, king of Judah, in Chronicles merely refer to him in third-person singular (14 consecutive times!), omitting his personal name, "Joash," which occurs twice in the parallel text in Kings:

2 Kgs 12:21, 22, 20		*2 Chr 24:25–27*	
	.21	ובלכתם *ממנו*	.25
		כי עזבו *אתו* במחליים רבים	
ויקמו *עבדיו* ויקשרו־קשר		התקשרו עליו *עבדיו*	
		בדמי יהוידע הכהן	
ויכו את יואש בית מלא		ויהרגהו על *מטתו* וימת	
הירד סלא		ויקברהו בעיר דויד	
ויוזכר (*Qere*: ויוזבד) . . .	.22a	ולא *קברהו* בקברות המלכים	
ויהוזבד . . . *עבדיו הכהו*		ואלה המתקשרים עליו	.26
וימת ויקברו *אתו* עם *אבותיו*		זבד . . . ויהוזבד	
בעיר דוד			
ויתר דברי *יואש* וכל אשר *עשה*	.20	*ובניו ורב* (*Qere*: ירב) *משא*	.27
		עליו ויסוד בית האלהים	
הלוא הם כתובים על . . .		הנם כתובים על . . .	
וימלך אמציה *בנו תחתיו*	.22b	וימלך אמציה *בנו תחתיו*	

21.	And *his servants* arose and	25.	And when they had departed
	made a conspiracy *and*		*from him*, for they had left
	struck *Joash down* in the		*him* with many wounds, *his*
	house of Millo, on the way		*servants* conspired *against him*
22a.	down to Silla. For Jozacar		because of the blood of the son of
	. . . and Jehozabad . . . *his*		Jehoiada the priest, and they

servants struck him, and he
died; and they buried him
with his fathers in the City
of David.

20. Now the rest of the acts of
Joash and all that he did,
are they not written in . . .

22b. And Amaziah his son
reigned in his stead.

killed him on his bed; so he
died; and they buried him in the
City of David, but they did not
bury him in the sepulchres of
the kings.

26. And these are those who
conspired against him: Zabad
. . . and Jehozabad. . . .

27. As for his sons and the multitude
of oracles against him and the
rebuilding of the House of God—
they are written in . . . and Amaziah his son reigned in his stead.

Though the third-person singular form is found in 2 Kgs 12:20–22, it is
used far less often than in 2 Chr 24:25–27 (9 times, as opposed to 14),
while in 2 Kgs 12:20–22 the personal name "Joash" is mentioned twice.

B. Necho, King of Egypt

Josiah was killed near Megiddo (609 B.C.E.), while attempting to delay Pharaoh Necho II, who was hurrying to assist Assyria in its struggle
against Babylon and the Medes. After his return from the campaign,
Necho deposed Jehoahaz (Shallum), Josiah's son, whom "the people of
the land" had installed as king in his father's stead in Judah, and exiled
him to Egypt. Moreover, Necho imposed a heavy tribute on Judah and
installed the pro-Egyptian Jehoiakim, whose tyranny became infamous
(2 Kgs 23:29–24:7; 2 Chr 35:20–36:4; Jeremiah 22, etc.), as king over
the country.

It seems that this Egyptian ruler, who killed the righteous king
Josiah, exiled his son Jehoahaz, and severely violated the honor of the
Davidic dynasty and the sovereignty of the kingdom of Judah, was consequently treated rather coolly in the book of Chronicles. The Chronicler made a considerable effort to reduce his importance and to destroy
his reputation by omitting his traditional exalted title, Pharaoh; by
choosing other ways to refer to him; by reducing the number of times he
is mentioned in the text; and by rendering him significant in a difficult
situation; and so on.

(1) Omitting the Title "Pharaoh"

The word פרעה 'Pharaoh', the ancient traditional title, glorious and
sanctified, of the rulers of Egypt[19] appears, in one way or another, six

---

19. In Egyptian, "Pharaoh" is written: Pr-ꜥꜣ and means '(the) Great House'. After
the days of Thutmose III (1504–1451 B.C.E.), the term applied to Egyptian rulers by
metonymy. See Ellenbogen, Foreign Words, 139; Redford, "Pharaoh," 288–89.

times in the ancient text (2 Kgs 23:29, 33, 34, 35 [3×]). The Chronicler omitted it systematically from his descriptions, not mentioning it even once. For example:

2 Kgs 23:29	עלה *פרעה* נכה מלך מצרים[20]	*Pharaoh* Necho, king of Egypt, came up.
2 Chr 35:20	עלה נכו מלך מצרים	Necho, king of Egypt, came up.

Notice, too, the omission of this title from the early texts in the examples listed below.

(2) Referring to an Egyptian Ruler by His General Title Only

The Chronicler omitted the Egyptian ruler's personal name from the earlier text, referring to him only by his general title, "king of Egypt":

1. | 2 Kgs 23:33 | ויאסרהו פרעה נכה
ברבלה | And *Pharaoh* <u>Necho</u> confined
him in Riblah. |
    |---|---|---|
    | 2 Chr 36:3 | ויסירהו *מלך*
מצרים | And *the king of Egypt* deposed
him. |

2. | 2 Kgs 23:34 | וימלך פרעה נכה את
אליקים | And *Pharaoh* <u>Necho</u> installed
Eliakim as king. |
    |---|---|---|
    | 2 Chr 36:4 | וימלך *מלך מצרים* את
אליקים | And *the king of Egypt*
installed Eliakim *as king*. |

(3) Mentioning "Necho" with No Title Whatever

Twice the Chronicler mentioned the Egyptian ruler by his personal name only—"Necho" (2 Chr 35:22, "addition"; 2 Chr 36:4, an interpolation of 2 Kgs 23:34; see also below). Mentioning the personal name of an Egyptian ruler without denoting either his title "Pharaoh" or his general title "king of Egypt" is a phenomenon unique in the book of Chronicles; there is nothing like it in the Deuteronomistic History or in the other kinds of biblical literature, either.[21] It thus seems to be yet another literary effort on the part of the Chronicler to tarnish the image of the foreign ruler who treated the Davidic dynasty and the kingdom of Judah badly, both of which the Chronicler valued highly.

---

20. Compare this form with על חיל *פרעה* נכו מלך מצרים 'against the force of *Pharaoh* <u>Necho</u>, *king of Egypt*' (Jer 46:2); *פרעה* חפרע מלך מצרים '*Pharaoh* <u>Hophra</u>, *king of Egypt*' (Jer 44:30). For the various forms for mentioning Egyptian rulers in the Bible, see Kalimi, "Pharaoh," 782.

21. This feature is found in 2 Chr 12:5, 7 ("additions") as well, where Shishak robbed the Temple treasures.

(4) Limiting the Number of Times an Egyptian Ruler Is Mentioned

From a statistical point of view, the Chronicler reduced—in one way or another—the number of times the Egyptian ruler was mentioned by nearly half the number of times he was mentioned in the parallel text in the book of Kings: five times instead of eight.[22]

(5) Denoting a Personal Name in Difficult Situations

The Chronicler denoted the name of the Egyptian ruler explicitly in an extremely difficult situation: in the narrative of the killing of Josiah (2 Chr 35:20 // 2 Kgs 23:29, and in v. 22, an "addition"). Thus, he noted his name in a place where it was only alluded to in the earlier text, without any linguistic or stylistic reason.

2 Kgs 23:34	וימלך פרעה נכה את	And *Pharaoh Necho* installed
	אליקים ... ואת יהואחז	Eliakim as king . . . and took
	ויבא מצרים לקח	Jehoahaz and came to Egypt.
2 Chr 36:4	וימלך מלך מצרים	And the *king of Egypt*
	את אליקים ... ואת	installed Eliakim as king . . . ,
	יואחז לקח נכו ויביאהו	and *Necho* took Joahaz and
	מצרימה	brought him to Egypt.

The Chronicler thus mentioned the personal name of the Egyptian ruler in the specific context of the exiling of Jehoahaz, king of Judah; in other words, in a situation likely to stir up the Hebrew reader against the foreign tyrant who exiles Josiah's son whom "the people of the land" have accepted as king over them. The harsh impression this exile made on that generation must not be forgotten either; Jeremiah the prophet expressed this impression extremely well: "Weep not for the dead; neither bemoan him; weep especially hard for him who goes away, for he shall return no more to see his homeland" (Jer 22:10). This was the only time in the history of the kingdom of Judah that its king was exiled to Egypt, never to return, and the event was considered a terrible curse (cf. Deut 28:68).[23]

Generally speaking, the combination of all of these points indicates the Chronicler's efforts at achieving the desired literary effect with regard to Necho, king of Egypt.

---

22. In 2 Chr 35:20; 36:3, 4 (paralleling the early text); in 35:22 ("addition"); and in 36:4 (interpolation of the early text). On the other hand, it appears in 2 Kgs 23:29, 33, 34, 35 (3×); 24:7 (2×).

23. Indeed, according to 2 Chr 33:11–13, Manasseh, too, was led into exile—to Babylon—but he was restored to his throne sometime later (traces of this story have not been found in any other source).

3. Excursus: Nathan before David

In the scene preceding Nathan's prophecy (2 Sam 7:1–3 // 1 Chr 17:1–2), the Chronicler replaces the title המלך 'the king' with the personal name *David* three times, one following another:

2 Sam 7:1–3		1 Chr 17:1–2	
ויהי כי ישב *המלך* בביתו	.1	ויהי כאשר ישב דויד בביתו	.1a
וה׳ הניח לו מסביב מכל איביו			
ויאמר *המלך* אל נתן הנביא	.2	ויאמר דויד אל נתן הנביא	.1b
ראה נא אנכי יושב בבית ארזים		הנה אנכי יושב בבית הארזים	
וארון האלהים ישב בתוך היריעה		וארון ברית ה׳ תחת יריעות	
ויאמר נתן אל *המלך*	.3	ויאמר נתן אל דויד	.2
כל אשר בלבבך לך עשה כי ה׳ עמך		כל אשר בלבבך עשה כי האלהים עמך	

1. And it came about, when *the king* was residing in his house, and the Lord had given him rest from all his enemies around him,

1a. And it came about, when *David* resided in his house,

2. that *the king* said to Nathan the prophet: "Look here, I dwell in a house of cedars while the Ark of God stays in a tent."

1b. that *David* said to Nathan the prophet: "Look, I live in a house of cedars, while the Ark of the Covenant of the Lord is under a tent."

3. Then Nathan said to the *king*: "Whatever is in your heart, go and do, for the Lord is with you."

2. Then Nathan said to *David*: "Everything that is in your heart, do, for God is with you."

In 2 Sam 7:1–3, the use of the official title המלך fits its general context, for v. 1 tells of the end of the king's wars against the enemies of his kingdom (וה׳ הניח לו מסביב מכל איביו 'and the Lord had given him rest from all his enemies around him') and of his presence in his palace (not in his military headquarters, in a "fortress," or on the battlefield). These two circumstances serve as an appropriate background for his ambition to erect a Temple.[24] Furthermore, vv. 2–3 speak of a conference between the ruler of the kingdom and his court prophet.[25]

---

24. Compare with Solomon's words: —ועתה הניח ה׳ אלהי לי מסביב: אין שטן ואין פגע רע והנני אמר לבנות בית לשם ה׳ אלהי 'And now that the Lord my God has given me rest all around—there is neither adversary nor evil influence—I intend to build a House to the name of the Lord my God ' (1 Kgs 5:18–19[4–5]); and with the words of Deut 12:10–11: והניח לכם מכל אויביכם מסביב 'And when he has given you rest from your enemies all around'; and so on. See also above, example 2.1 (pp. 38–39).

25. Nathan's activity as "court prophet" becomes clear first from the narrative of his dramatic installation of Solomon as king in 1 Kings 1: Nathan takes an active part in the court intrigues as though he were one of the king's officials; and he even

In contrast, in the parallel text in the book of Chronicles, the use of the personal name David in v. 1a should be considered in light of the shortened text (the Chronicler omits the clause וה׳ הניח לו מסביב מכל איביו).[26] Here we have a description of the man David settled in his house—without reference to the state of the kingdom's security. However, the continued use of the term *David* in the second half of this verse and the next one (vv. 1b–2) has yet to be explained.

The average reader usually links a personal name with the *person* himself—the person whose name is being referred to; on the other hand, a person's title is linked mainly with his or her *outward status*. When a "king" is involved, this status includes his sovereign authority, his power, and his threatening capability. It is thus not impossible for the Chronicler to have chosen the personal name David here in order to give the reader the feeling that a meeting and conversation are being held between two human beings—"David" facing "Nathan"—rather than "*the king*," the highest official representative of the kingdom, on the one hand, facing "Nathan," the court prophet, the servant-subject who is obliged to obey his master's instructions and fulfill his requests absolutely, on the other hand. It seems that this change by the Chronicler might have indicated to the reader what the desired attitude toward Nathan's advice was. That is, the words כל אשר בלבבך עשה כי האלהים עמך 'everything that is in your heart, do, for God is with you' (v. 2b // 2 Sam 7:3b) were spoken by the prophet frankly and spontaneously and were not the words of a "servant," a court prophet who was obliged to serve his master and wished to fulfill his king/master's expectations and requests.

Directing the reader to this "desired" understanding of the words of Nathan the prophet, without leaving room for contemplation, is required especially here. On the one hand, the wording of David's statement is phrased to stress the opposition between his own situation ("Look, I dwell in a house of cedars") and that of the Ark ("while the Ark of the Covenant of the Lord is under a tent"). This opposition includes an indication of the "advice" desired from the prophet. However, God

---

bows down to the king "with his face to the ground" (v. 23, a feature not appearing in the context of any other prophet throughout the Bible), calls David אדנינו דוד 'David, our lord' (v. 11, and cf. v. 33), and says of himself, ולי אני עבדך 'And as for me, I *am your servant*' (v. 25, and cf. v. 27). The view that the king is required to receive the agreement of the Lord to erect the Temple is widespread in Mesopotamian temple construction documents as well. According to these inscriptions, the king is not allowed to build a temple without the unambiguous agreement of the gods; see Hurowitz, *Temple Building*, 135–39. The negative response David received also has its parallels in Mesopotamian construction documents; see ibid., 139ff.

26. For the reasons for this omission, see the discussion above in example 2.1 (pp. 38–39).

immediately intervenes, "the very night" after the meeting, unambiguously commanding: "Go tell David my servant: 'You are not the one who will build me a house to live in'" (v. 4 // 2 Sam 7:5), rejecting the words of the prophet.

4. Creating Hierarchical Balance

In the narrative about Jehoiada's conspiracy, Joash's coronation, and the Temple repairs (2 Kings 11–12 // 2 Chronicles 23–24), Jehoiada is mentioned by name (2 Kgs 11:4 // 2 Chr 23:1, 18; 24:3); by title—הכהן 'the priest' (2 Kgs 11:4, 18 // 2 Chr 23:15); and by name plus title—יהוידע הכהן 'Jehoiada, the priest' (2 Kgs 11:9 [2×], 14 // 2 Chr 23:6 [2×], 15; 2 Kgs 12:4 // 2 Chr 24:2). The title הכהן by which Jehoiada is known indicates the social stratum in which he originated but not his own hierarchical status in it. As long as this title served Jehoiada in a narrative that concerned him only, the Chronicler did not denote his status in the priestly hierarchy. However, when he described a meeting between Jehoiada and a representative of the State, he created hierarchical balance between the two:

1. 2 Kgs 12:8 says that "Jehoash *the king*" called "on Jehoiada *the priest*" and asked him: "Why are you not repairing the house?" The title "the king" indicates Jehoash's status at the very peak of his hierarchy, something that the title "priest" alone cannot do, as we have seen. Accordingly, the Chronicler apparently replaced the title "the priest" in the early text with the title הראש 'the chief' (an abbreviation for כהן הראש 'the chief [or, high] priest'[27]), thus creating hierarchical balance between the two individuals who were meeting. In other words: יהואש המלך 'Jehoash the king', standing at the peak of the state hierarchy, met with יהוידע הראש 'Jehoiada the high priest', standing at the peak of the priestly hierarchy:

2 Kgs 12:8	*2 Chr 24:6*
ויקרא המלך יהואש	ויקרא המלך
ליהוידע הכהן	ליהוידע הראש
ולכהנים ויאמר אלהם	ויאמר לו
מדוע אינכם מחזקים	מדוע לא דרשת על הלוים
את בדק הבית	להביא מיהודה ומירושלם
	את משאת משה עבד ה'

And *King* Jehoash called   And *the king* called
Jehoiada *the priest*   Jehoiada *the chief*

---

27. Compare with verse 11 and also with 1 Chr 27:5; 2 Chr 19:11; 26:20; 31:10; 2 Kgs 25:18 // Jer 52:24. The words כהן הראש in Ezra 7:5 seem to mean הכהן הראשון 'the first priest', not a title. See Batten, *Ezra–Nehemiah*, 304.

and the other priests and said to them: "Why are you not repairing the Temple?	and said to him: "Why have you not demanded of the Levites to bring in from Judah and from Jerusalem the tax levied by Moses, the servant of the Lord?"

2. The Chronicler acted similarly further on in the narrative as well. According to 2 Kgs 12:11, "the high priest," Jehoiada, who stood at the peak of the priestly hierarchy, accompanied the official of the state, "the king's scribe," in order to count the money found in the House of the Lord. Portraying "the high priest" as accompanying a state official going up to the House of the Lord to count money was viewed by the Chronicler as an insult to Jehoiada. As a result, he amended the earlier text and created hierarchical balance between the ranks of the representatives of the two agencies: alongside סופר המלך 'the king's scribe' he placed פקיד כהן הראש 'the high priest's official' (2 Chr 24:11).[28] In other words, it was not Jehoiada the high priest himself who accompanied the king's scribe to count the money but an official representative of his—like the official representative sent by Jehoash the king.

2 Kgs 12:11	2 Chr 24:11
ויעל סופר המלך	ובא סופר המלך
והכהן הגדול	ופקיד כהן הראש
And *the king's scribe* *and the high priest* went up	And *the king's scribe* and *the high priest's official* came

Montgomery[29] claims that the title הכהן הגדול 'the high priest' in 2 Kgs 12:11 was added during the Second Temple period and that the text originally read הכהן 'the priest'. In his opinion, כהן הראש is an earlier title. However, it seems clear that the Chronicler encountered the title הכהן הגדול and that he was the one who replaced it with כהן הראש. As a matter of fact, the latter phrase generally occurs in late texts (see the references from the book of Chronicles adduced above, no. 1, with n. 27 (p. 182), and a text written during the Babylonian Exile describing the destruction of the Temple and the Exile—2 Kgs 25:18 // Jer 52:24) and seems to be later than the phrase הכהן הגדול, which occurs in texts that may be early (such as Num 35:25, 28—twice; Josh 20:6; 2 Kgs 22:4, 8,

---

28. Cf. Wellhausen, *Prolegomena*, 195 (= ET, p. 200); Curtis-Madsen, *Chronicles*, 435–36; Williamson, *Chronicles*, 322.

29. See Montgomery, *Kings*, 429.

10, 12, 14; 23:4, 24; and in the chapter under consideration, 2 Kgs 12:11) as well as in later texts (such as Hag 1:1, 12, 14; 2:2, 4; Zech 3:1, 8; 6:11).

The Chronicler's special sensitivity to the status of the high priest stems not only from his awareness of the high position enjoyed by Jehoiada the high priest in the kingdom of Judah during the reign of Joash and from his sympathy for Jehoiada in contrast to his antipathy for Joash but also—and perhaps mainly—from the high religious and political status of the high priest in his own days (about 400–375 B.C.E.). The high status of the high priest can be deduced from the appeal made by the Jews of Elephantine to יהוחנן כהנא רבא וכנותה כהניא זי בירושלם 'Jehohanan the high priest and his colleagues, the priests who are in Jerusalem', parallel to their appeal to Bagohi, the governor of Judah, and the free men of Judah, asking for help in getting permission to restore the ruined temple of the Lord in Elephantine.[30] This is related in a letter of 407 B.C.E., because they had received no reply to their letter of 410.

The book of Judith, which was apparently written after the time of the book of Chronicles,[31] indicates that Joiakim the high priest acted as the supreme religious and political authority of the province of Yehud, whether independently (4:6; 11:14) or together with the Council of Elders—the *gerusia* (15:8). The high religious and secular rank of the high priest is also reflected in sources preceding Chronicles. Thus, for example, Haggai the prophet appeals *"to Zerubbabel, son of Shealtiel, the governor of Judah,* and *to Joshua, son of Jehozadak, the high priest"* (1:1; 2:2) as equally-ranking leaders of the nation (see also Ezra 5:2). In Neh 3:1, Eliashib the high priest appears at the head of the list of the builders of the wall of Jerusalem.[32] From the period after the Chronicler, one may note the silver coin of יוחנן [ן]הכוהן 'Johana[n], the priest', which, except for its inscription, closely resembles the type of coin of "Hezekiah, the governor," and both seem to date approximately to the middle of the fourth century B.C.E. As Barag puts it, "this shows that Johanan the priest enjoyed a very respectable status, equal to that of the governor. There is thus no doubt that he was the high priest."[33] In 332 B.C.E., the high priest headed the delegation that met with the new

---

30. See Cowley, *Aramaic Papyri,* no. 30, lines 18–19 (p. 112) // no. 31, lines 17–18 (p. 120).

31. For the date of the book of Judith, see Moore, "Judith, Book of," 1117–25, esp. 1123; Zenger, "Judith/Judithbuch," 406–7. For another opinion, see Grintz, *Judith,* 15–17.

32. For additional evidence of this, see Tcherikover, "History of Jerusalem," 230.

33. Barag, "Silver Coin," 4–21, esp. 20–21. The minting of coins by the high priest in Judea (that is, not by the state agency authorized by the king of Persia), indicates the weakening or even the collapse of Persian rule in Judea; see Ephʿal, "Syria–Palestine," 152. For a detailed review and discussion on the coins of *Yehud Medinta,* see Machinist, "First Coins of Judah," 365–80.

ruler of Palestine, Alexander the Great (Josephus *Ant.* 11.325–39;
b. Yoma 69a). Hecataeus of Abdera (ca. 300 B.C.E.) relates that the Jews
had no king, but that their supreme authority was vested in a man
whom they termed "high priest," and that they believed that he was act-
ing as a messenger handing down divine instructions.[34]

---

34. Diodorus Siculus, in: *Aegyptiaca Bibliotheca Historica*, 40.3. See Stern, *Greek
and Latin Authors*, 1.26–28. On this subject, see also Tcherikover, "History of Jerusalem," 221–51; Mantel, "High Priesthood," 192–93; idem, "Oral Law," 28–29 and references to earlier literature on the subject there (especially p. 215 nn. 14, 15).

Chapter 9
"Measure for Measure"

There are instances in which the Chronicler redesigned the text of Samuel–Kings in accordance with the "measure for measure" principle.[1] From a literary point of view, this principle is characterized by the repetition of a word or a phrase in both the description of a (good or bad) deed and the description of the retribution for the deed (reward or punishment). This repetition links the two parts of the episode (or the two episodes) and stresses the relationship between them.

By means of this "measure for measure" designing, the writer strives, first and foremost, to render absolute divine justice more tangible. In other words, the degree of retribution is meted out according to the measure of the "deed." Moreover, he tries to introduce into the consciousness of the reader the idea that the success of the righteous man or the failure of the evil man is not a mere chance occurrence but stems from the guiding hand of the Lord. This principle is particularly effective when it is put in the mouth of a prophet who is warning of punishment, using the device of repeated words from time to time during the episode.

Most of the episodes in Chronicles that have been redesigned using this literary technique deal with sin and its punishment. A minority involve a good deed (or goodness that the Lord reckoned as a deed)[2] for which a reward was promised or given.

The designing of episodes according to the "measure for measure" principle is not unique to Chronistic historiography. It is also found in early biblical historiography. For example, in Judg 1:6–7 Adoni-bezek

---

1. This expression was coined in Talmudic literature; see, for example, b. Sanh. 90a; Šabb. 105b; Ned. 32a; Gen. Rab. 9:7. This is also true of its expanded form: במדה שאדם מודד, בה מודדין לו 'A man is measured with the same yardstick with which he measures (others)' (m. Soṭa 1:7; cf. t. Soṭa 4.1; Gen. Rab. 9:11); see also Matt 7:2: "the measure you give is the measure you will get." It may also be compared with the Latin formulas: quid pro quo and qualis culpa talis poena ('the punishment resembles the sin in quality'). The biblical formula was apparently כאשר עשה כן יעשה לו 'As he did it, so shall it be done to him' (Lev 24:19b); compare: ויאמרו: לאסור את שמשון עלינו, לעשות לו כאשר עשה לנו . . . ויאמר להם (שמשון): כאשר עשו לי, כן עשיתי להם 'And they said: "We have come up to bind Samson, to do unto him as he did unto us." . . . And he [Samson] said to them: "As they did to me, so I have done to them"' (Judg 15:10–11); כאשר עשיתי כן שלם לי אלהים 'As I did, so God has repaid me' (Judg 1:7); כאשר שכלה נשים חרבך, כן תשכל מנשים אמך 'As your sword left women bereft, so shall your mother be bereft among women' (1 Sam 15:33).

2. For this, see below, example 9.5 (pp. 191–192).

says to the men of Judah who had just cut off his thumbs and big toes, "Seventy kings with their thumbs and big toes cut off collected scraps under my table. As I did, so God has repaid me."[3] The wording of several casuistic laws in the Pentateuch evidence the retribution principle—for example, "He who spills human blood—his own blood shall be spilled by men" (Gen 9:6; compare Exod 21:12); "an eye for an eye," and so on (Exod 21:23–25; Lev 24:17–22; Deut 19:16–21).[4] Examples also appear in the various types of wisdom literature, such as, "He who blocks his ears to the cry of the poor shall himself call but not be answered" (Prov 21:13 and cf. 26:27);[5] and in Second Temple literary genres as well, such as in the historical novel of Esther and the book of Tobit.[6]

It is worth mentioning that this phenomenon occurs in Assyrian royal inscriptions as well. Thus, for instance, a text from the so-called annals of Ashurbanipal states: "I tore out of the mouths (v. tongues) of those whose slanderous mouth had uttered blasphemies against my god Ashur and had plotted against me, his god-fearing prince. . . . The others I smashed alive with the very same statues of protective deities with which they had smashed my own grandfather Sennacherib. . . ."[7]

9.1 According to the book of Chronicles, after the death of Jehoiada the priest, Joash, king of Judah, listened to the advice of his officials:

2 Chr 24:18   ויעזבו את־בית יהוה אלהי   *and they abandoned* (the
אבותיהם ויעבדו   House of)[8] *the Lord the God*
את־האשרים ואת־העצבים   *of their fathers* and worshiped
the asherim and the images.

The warning voiced by Zechariah, the son of Jehoiada,

---

3. See also 1 Sam 15:33; 2 Sam 12:10ff.; 1 Kgs 21:19.

4. See Loewenstamm, "Measure for Measure," 840–46.

5. See also Ps 9:16; Qoh 10:8; Job 31:9–10, 21–22.

6. For example, Haman was hanged on the gallows that he had prepared for Mordechai (Esth 5:14; 7:9–10); "Do not hide your face from every poor man, so that the face of God shall not be hidden from before you" (Tob 4:7).

7. See Luckenbill, *ARAB*, vol. 2, §795; Pritchard, *ANET*, 288b.

8. The word "House" in this description of their sin seems secondary: it does not appear in the parallel expressions further on in the passage—that is, in the warning pronounced by Zechariah the prophet, "because you have abandoned the Lord" (v. 20), and in justifying the punishment: "for they have abandoned the Lord God of their fathers" (v. 24). The word also does not appear in the LXX of this verse. This is also true of the reading ברית 'covenant' rather than בית 'house', a reading that appears in a solitary manuscript of the MT and that is preferred by Rudolph, *Chronik*, 276. Neither does the word בית (or ברית) fit in well in the "measure for measure" literary structure with which the entire episode is designed.

2 Chr 24:20b ‫כי־עזבתם את־יהוה ויעזב‬ because *you abandoned the*
‫אתכם‬ *Lord, he has abandoned* you,

phrased according to the principle of "measure for measure" retribution,[9] fell on deaf ears. Consequently, "at that same time the next year" the prophet's warning was realized. For this reason, the Chronicler reworked the narrative of the campaign of Hazael, king of Aram, to the land of Israel, which appears in 2 Kgs 12:18–19. According to the narrative in 2 Kings, Hazael captured Gath and prepared "to advance upon Jerusalem" (v. 18). Only after Joash paid him tribute did he withdraw from Jerusalem (v. 19). The Chronicler omitted the capture of Gath[10] and the tribute paid by Joash, as well as the fact that, as soon as the tribute was paid, the king of Aram moved out of Judah. He transformed the Aramean threat to Judah into an actual invasion, during which all of the sinful elements in the kingdom were punished[11] "measure for measure," as the prophet had prophesied regarding them. He is speaking about both the people and the officials when he says that (2 Chr 24:24a), ‫כי במצער אנשים באו חיל ארם ויהוה נתן בידם חיל לרב מאד כי עזבו את־יהוה‬
‫אלהי אבותיהם‬ 'although the army of Aram came with but few men, the Lord delivered into their hands a large force, for *they had abandoned the Lord, the God of their fathers*'. As for Joash, the Aramean (as it were, the 'scourge of the wrath of the Lord') executed judgment on him (v. 24b): ‫ובלכתם ממנו כי עזבו אתו במחליים רבים‬ 'and when they withdrew, *they abandoned him* (= Joash) with multiple wounds' (v. 25a). The Aramean judged Joash in the same way that he had acted toward the Lord: ‫ויעזבו‬
‫את בית יהוה אלהי אבותיהם‬ '*they abandoned the* (House of the) *Lord, the God of their fathers*'.

9.2 2 Kgs 12:21 says of the assassination of Joash, king of Judah: ‫ויקמו עבדיו ויקשרו־קשר ויכו את־יואש‬ 'His servants rose up, made a conspiracy, and struck Joash', noting neither the background about the assassination nor the motives of the assassins.[12] The author of Chronicles, on the other hand, viewed the assassination of Joash as a "punishment," and, in accordance with his theology, supplied the "sin." According to the Chronicler, Joash's "sin" provided the background for his assassination: "His servants conspired against him *because of the blood*

---

9. And see "*You abandoned me*, and so *I have abandoned you* into the hands of Shishak" (2 Chr 12:5); see also below, examples 9.4 (pp. 190–191); 9.6–8 (pp. 192–193).

10. For this omission, see the discussion in example 4.6 (p. 89).

11. For the punishment of the sinful elements in Judah, each person for his or her own sins, see Curtis-Madsen, *Chronicles*, 438; Japhet, *Ideology*, 174–75. These scholars, however, make no reference to the proposed literary formulation of the text under consideration.

12. For a detailed discussion of this topic, see example 1.9 (pp. 29–32).

of the son[13] *of Jehoiada the priest* and killed him" (2 Chr 24:25b).[14] Furthermore, he altered a number of the words of the passage in the book of Kings: instead of ויקשרו־קשר 'they made a conspiracy', he wrote התקשרו עליו 'they conspired against him'; in place of ויכו את יואש 'and they struck Joash', he used ויהרגהו 'and they killed him'.[15] His reason for preferring these particular words seems to have been to contrast the fate of Joash with the fate of Zechariah, son of Jehoiada, the priest (vv. 21–22), and to formulate a "sin" and "punishment" in accordance with the "measure for measure" principle, for Zechariah was murdered at the command of King Joash:

2 Chr 24:21–22	ויקשרו עליו וירגמהו	*And they conspired against him*
	אבן במצות המלך בחצר	and stoned him *at the king's*
	בית יהוה ולא־זכר יואש	*command*[16] in the court of the
	המלך החסד אשר עשה	House of the Lord; and Joash
	יהוידע אביו עמו ויהרג	the king did not remember the
	את־בנו	kindness that Jehoiada, his
		father, had shown him,
		but killed his son.

Indeed, the same standard was then used in measuring out retribution to Joash: התקשרו עליו עבדיו בדמי בני יהוידע הכהן ויהרגהו 'His servants *conspired against him* because of the blood of the son of Jehoiada, the priest, *and killed him*'. The Chronicler thus linked the story of Joash's assassination with the murder of Zechariah, both overtly ("because of the blood of the son of Jehoiada, the priest") and covertly (by repetitive use of the same verbal roots in both passages).

9.3 In this light, it is easier to understand the Chronicler's decision to use the word ויהרג instead of the word ויך that appears in the earlier text when he described the way that Amaziah, king of Judah, punished

---

13. In the LXX of this verse, the singular form appears: υἱοῦ Ἰωδὲ *'the son* of Jehoiada', and similarly in the Vulgate. That only one son was involved seems clear from vv. 20–24, which mention the murder of Zechariah, son of Jehoiada the priest, alone. The MT seems to evidence a case of dittography of the letter י from the next word: יהוידע 'Jehoiada'; cf. Rudolph, *Chronik*, 276; idem, *BHS*, 1550.

14. For the implementation of the retribution system regarding Joash, see Japhet, *Ideology*, 167 n. 486, 175.

15. For the change על מטתו / בית מלא הירד סלא further along in the text, see example 2.14 (p. 49).

16. The phrase "and they stoned him *at the king's command*" (v. 21) appears here in light of the reproof voiced by Zechariah: "Why do you transgress *against the Lord's command*" (v. 20). That is, the people of Judah were transgressing against "the Lord's command" while upholding "the king's command"—and stoning a priest and a prophet in the court of the House of the Lord!

the assassins of his father, Joash (2 Chr 25:3 // 2 Kgs 14:5). In other words, the *killers* of Joash *were killed* by his son Amaziah. Joash, who *killed* Zechariah, son of Jehoiada the priest, *was killed* by his servants, who *were killed* by Amaziah, son of Joash.[17] In contrast to all of these, Jehoiada, who saved Joash from the sword of Athaliah, enjoyed a long life: ויזקן יהוידע וישבע ימים וימת בן־מאה ושלשים שנה במותו 'Jehoiada grew old, full of days, and was one hundred thirty years old at his death' (2 Chr 24:15, an "addition").[18] Malamat[19] notes correctly that Jehoiada's prolonged lifespan according to this passage, 130 years, is surprising, considering our knowledge of life expectancy in the Bible and in the ancient Near East. The literary analysis of the texts presented here clarifies the background for attributing such a long life to Jehoiada, giving us yet another reason to question the Chronicler's historical reliability.

9.4 In 1 Kgs 14:22–24, the Deuteronomistic historian lists the sins of Judah one by one; immediately afterward (vv. 25–28), he describes Shishak's campaign against Judah. The Chronicler links these two passages, shaping them in accordance with the "measure for measure" principle. He shortens the 1 Kgs 14:22–24 passage to a single verse, adding that King Rehoboam sinned as well:[20] "And it came to pass when Rehoboam's kingdom was established and when he had become strong, he *abandoned the Law of the Lord*,[21] and all of Israel with him" (2 Chr 12:1). Further on, the Chronicler speaks of the reason for Shishak's campaign against Judah: because "they were unfaithful to the Lord" (vv. 2–4). He adds the words of Shemaiah, the prophet, to Rehoboam and his princes, who had gathered together in Jerusalem for fear of Shi-

---

17. The description in the book of Kings also includes the covert use of the principle of "measure for measure." The writer used the very same word to describe the assassination of Joash ("the sin") that he used to describe the killing of the assassins ("the punishment"): ויכו את יואש 'they struck Joash"; ויך את עבדיו המכים את המלך אביו 'he struck his servants, who had struck the king, his father' (2 Kgs 12:20; 13:5–6). However, in contrast to the book of Chronicles, Kings provided no information about the murder of Zechariah. The Chronicler thus emended the texts in the book of Kings, integrating them with his narrative of the murder of Zechariah.

18. With the expression "and he grew old . . . full of days, and died," compare "and Isaac perished and died . . . old and full of days" (Gen 35:29); "and Job died, old and full of days" (Job 42:17).

19. Malamat, "Longevity," 217–18.

20. In the introduction to Rehoboam's reign (1 Kgs 14:21), no mention is made of his having done what was evil in the eyes of the Lord; this is true, too, of the summation of his reign (vv. 29–30). The sins of this king are alluded to in the introduction to the reign of Abijam, his son, in 1 Kgs 15:3: "And [Abijam] committed all of the sins of his father [Rehoboam], which he had committed before his time."

21. According to 2 Chr 11:13–17, in his first three years on the throne, Rehoboam walked "in the way of David and Solomon."

shak: "This is what the Lord has spoken: 'You *have abandoned me*, so I too *have abandoned you* into the hand of Shishak'" (v. 5):

1 Kgs 14:22–28	*2 Chr 12:1–12*
	1. And it came to pass when Rehoboam's kingdom was established and when he had become strong, that he עזב את־תורת יהוה *abandoned* the Law of the Lord, and all of Israel with him.
22–24. ויעש יהודה הרע בעיני יהוה *And Judah did evil in the eyes of the Lord* . . . they did almost all the abominations of the Gentiles that the Lord had expelled in favor of the Israelites.	
25. And it came to pass in the fifth year of King Rehoboam that Shishak, king of Egypt, came up against Jerusalem	2. And it was in the fifth year of King Rehoboam that Shishak, king of Egypt, came up against Jerusalem כי מעלו ביהוה *for they had been unfaithful to the Lord* . . .
	5. And Shemaiah, the prophet, came to King Rehoboam and the princes of Judah who had gathered together in Jerusalem for fear of Shishak and said to them: 'This is what the Lord has spoken: אתם עזבתם אתי ואף־אני עזבתי אתכם 'You *have abandoned me*, so I too *have abandoned you* into the hand of Shishak.'"

9.5 The Chronicler transformed the rhetorical question in 2 Sam 7:5: האתה תבנה־לי בית לשבתי 'Will you (be the one to) build me a house for My dwelling?' (to which the reply is negative) into a decisive declaration: לא אתה תבנה־לי הבית לשבת 'You will not (be the one to) build me the house to dwell in!' (1 Chr 17:4). He also adds, in place of בית יעשה־לך יהוה 'the Lord will *make*[22] you a house' (2 Sam 7:11), ובית יבנה־לך יהוה 'and the Lord will *build* you a house' (1 Chr 17:10).

---

22. The root עשה together with בית is found also in Exod 1:21: ויעש להם בתים 'and he made *houses for them*'. In the commentary on the prophecy of Nathan from Cave 4 at

These alterations, which create a kind of parallel structure between the rejection of David's proposal and the Lord's promise to him, seem to be intended to render more prominent the measure that the Lord meted out to David as a reward for his good intentions: David wanted *to build a house for the Lord*—that is, to erect a Temple, "a House of the Lord." The Lord postponed this until the next generation, yet on the spot he promised to reward David in the same way: *to build him a house*. The word בית here means a dynasty, "the house of David," as the continuation of the passage makes amply clear: "And it will come to pass, when your days will have been fulfilled to go to be with your ancestors, that I shall establish your offspring after you, one of your sons, and I shall establish his kingdom" (1 Chr 17:11 // 2 Sam 7:12). This also derives from Psalm 89, which is based on the prophecy of Nathan: "For all eternity I shall establish your offspring / and I shall build your throne for all generations" (Ps 89:5). A "house," a dwelling-place, David already had, as related at the onset of our chapter: "And it came to pass, when David was settled *in his house*" (1 Chr 17:1 // 2 Sam 7:1, and see also 1 Chr 14:1 // 2 Sam 5:11).

9.6 In 2 Chr 30:6b (an "addition"), the Chronicler formulated the words spoken by Hezekiah, king of Judah, to the Northern tribes, inviting them to come and celebrate the Passover in Jerusalem, according to the "measure for measure" principle:

2 Chr 30:6	וילכו הרצים באגרות מיד	And the messengers went off
	המלך . . . לאמר בני ישראל	with letters written by the king
	שובו אל־יהוה אלהי	. . . saying: "People of Israel,
	אברהם יצחק וישראל	*return to the Lord*, God of
	וישב אל־הפליטה הנשארת	Abraham, Isaac, and Israel
	לכם מכף מלכי אשור	so that *He may return* to the remnant left of you who have escaped from the hand of the kings of Assyria."

Similarly in v. 9:

2 Chr 30:9	כי בשובכם על־יהוה	For when you *return to the*
	אחיכם ובניכם לרחמים לפני	*Lord*, your kindred and
	שוביהם	children will find mercy before
	ולשוב לארץ הזאת	their captors to *return to this land.*

Qumran (4QFlorilegium), this appears: ו[ה]גיד לכה כיא בית יבנה לכה 'and he told you *that he would build* a house for you'. See Allegro, "Qumran Literature," 176; and also the LXX, ad loc.: ὅτι οἶκον οἰκοδομήσεις αὐτῷ. The wording of these passages seems to have been influenced by the text in Chronicles.

9.7 According to 2 Chronicles 15, the divine spirit rested on Azariah, son of Oded, who went forth before Asa and said (v. 2):

2 Chr 15:2	שמעוני אסא וכל־יהודה	Hear me, Asa, and all Judah
	ובנימן	and Benjamin!
	יהוה עמכם *בהיותכם עמו*	The Lord is with you *when you are with him,*
	ואם־תדרשהו *ימצא לכם*	and, if you seek him, *he will be present for you,*
	ואם־תעזבהו *יעזב אתכם*	but, if you forsake him, *he will abandon you.*

Furthermore, v. 4 reads: וישב בצר־לו על־יהוה אלהי ישראל ויבקשהו *וימצא להם* 'Then (Israel), when in dire straits, *returned to the Lord*, God of Israel and *sought him*, and *he was present for them*'. The rest of the text describes Asa's religious and ritual innovations, the sacrifices that the people offered up, and the vow that they took. The Chronicler concludes (vv. 14–15):

2 Chr 15:14–15	וישבעו ליהוה בקול	Then they took a vow to the
	גדול . . . וישמחו כל־יהודה	Lord in a great voice . . . and
	על־השבועה כי בכל ־לבבם	all Judah rejoiced in this vow
	נשבעו ובכל ־רצונם בקשהו	for *they had taken the vow*
	וימצא להם וינח יהוה להם	*with all their heart*, and *with*
	מסביב	*all their desire they sought him*, and *he was present for them, and the Lord gave them rest all around.*[23]

9.8 According to 1 Chr 28:9 (an "addition"), David phrased his words to Solomon, his son, in "measure for measure" fashion:

1 Chr 28:9	אם־תדרשנו *ימצא לך*	If you seek him, *he will be present for you,*
	ואם־תעזבנו *יזניחך לעד*	but if you forsake him, *he will abandon you forever.*

This principle, discernible in these three speeches in "additions" in the book of Chronicles, casts serious doubts on their authenticity.

---

23. See also 2 Chr 14:5–6 in this regard. In this formulation, the Chronicler combined two expressions that he used separately in other places: וימצא להם 'And he will be present for them' (2 Chr 15:4; cf. there v. 2: ימצא לכם 'He will be present for you (pl.)'; 1 Chr 28:9: ימצא לך 'He will be present for you (sing.)'; מסביב (ה') וינח לנו 'And he gave us rest all around' (2 Chr 14:6; cf. there v. 5: כי הניח ה' לו 'And the Lord gave him rest'; 20:30: וינח לו אלהיו מסביב 'And his God gave him rest all around'; outside of Chronicles, see, e.g., 2 Sam 7:1; 1 Kgs 5:18).

Chapter 10
Allusion

Allusion, in the sense that I mean it, is intertextual structuring—directing the reader from one text to a second text by borrowing a word, phrase, or linguistic-literary device from the first text and inserting it into the second text.

Allusion provides a text with a dimension that is above and beyond the context and range of the literary unit in which it is embedded. "Realization of an allusion is a function of [the reader's] awareness, knowledge, and skill."[1] A text whose message is conveyed partly by means of literary allusion requires the reader to be familiar with the text being alluded to. Such a text demands that the interpreter be aware: aware of the importance of allusion in building meaning; aware that maximal meaning derives from the correlation of both texts; and aware that the above-mentioned elements may appear in the text being alluded to but not in the text being interpreted.[2]

A linguistic unit is repeated in order to make a connection in the reader's mind between the text currently being read and a specific text elsewhere and to maximize the potential power of the text. Locating a literary allusion in a text and defining it are the most important components of interpretation. Ignoring literary allusion, erroneously identifying a text being alluded to, or ignoring the elements activated by the realization of an allusion may cause a mistake in interpretation.[3]

On occasion in the book of Chronicles, the Chronicler alluded to episodes or topics mentioned in detail in an earlier text or to a narrative elsewhere in his own work (in the "additions") by repeating a linguistic unit that already appeared in the episode alluded to. The Chronicler seems to have assumed that potential readers would be familiar with episodes that appeared in earlier books and that an allusion would suffice to jog their memories. At any rate, a reader would be unable to understand many passages in the book of Chronicles without prior knowledge of the contents of Samuel–Kings.[4] It thus seems likely that the Chronicler attempted, on principle, to base his work on the narra-

---

1. See Ben-Porat, "Literary Allusions," 2.

2. Cf. ibid., 2.

3. Cf. ibid., 2, 12.

4. For this subject, see Willi, *Chronik*, 56–66; and see also Curtis-Madsen, *Chronicles*, 180; Rudolph, *Chronik*, 93, regarding 1 Chronicles 10; ibid., 113; Williamson, *Chronicles*, 115, regarding 1 Chr 13:5b; Rudolph, *Chronik*, 227, regarding Solomon, etc.

tives in the earlier books, rather than to undermine them or replace them, as several scholars have claimed.[5] Literary allusions are found throughout the book of Chronicles: in texts that are parallel to passages in the books of Samuel and Kings, in "additions," in passages that appear only in Chronicles, and in comments embedded in genealogical lists.

This literary phenomenon is common in other biblical works as well. For instance, Gen 24:7, "The Lord, God of the heavens, who took me *out of my father's house and* from the land of my birth and who spoke to me and swore to me saying: 'To your seed I shall give this land,'" alludes to Gen 12:1, "And the Lord said to Abram: '*Go forth* out of your land and away from the place of your birth *and from your father's house* to the land that I shall show you." It also contains an allusion to the Lord's promise to Abram, "To your seed I shall give this land" (12:7). Isa 28:21 apparently alludes to the stories of David's wars against the Philistines in 2 Sam 5:17–25 (// 1 Chr 14:8–16).[6] Ps 105:8–15 (// 1 Chr 16:15–22) alludes to the stories of the patriarchs in the book of Genesis. Verses 8–11 (// 1 Chr 16:15–18) allude to the land promised to the patriarchs in Gen 12:7; 15:17; 22:15–18; 26:2–5; 27:13–15; 35:9–13. Verses 12–15 (// 1 Chr 16:19–22) allude to the wanderings of the patriarchs and their contacts with various kingdoms, as related in Gen 12:10–20; 20:1–18; 26:7–11; 31:24, 29.[7]

1. Integrating Allusions into an Earlier Text

A. In Concluding Formulas

Occasionally, the Chronicler alluded to one of his own "additions" when he borrowed one of the concluding formulas from the books of Kings that appear at the ends of the narratives about the kings of Judah. He may have been attempting to draw the reader's attention again to the passages that appear only in his book. For example:

10.1 In the concluding formula at the end of the passage about the reign of Jotham, king of Judah, 2 Kgs 15:36 reads,

ויתר דברי יותם אשר עשה
הלא הם כתובים על ספר דברי הימים למלכי יהודה

---

5. For example, Steuernagel, *Einleitung*, 389; von Rad, *Geschichtsbild*, 133.

6. For this, see example 7.13 (pp. 134–136).

7. For additional examples of historical allusions in genealogical lists and in prophetic and other biblical writings, see Tur-Sinai, "Historical References," 74–79; Yellin, "Allusion," 210–13; for allusions in prophetic literature, see also Watson, *Hebrew Poetry*, 300.

As for the rest of the acts of Jotham and all that he did,
, are they not written in the Book of the Annals of the
Kings of Judah?

In 2 Chr 27:7, the Chronicler deviates from his usual formula, "as for the
rest of the acts of . . . , *the early ones and the later ones*."[8] He expands
the Kings text and alludes to things that he recounted about Jotham in
his own description of Jotham's reign:

ויתר דברי יותם וכל מלחמתיו ודרכיו

הנם כתובים על ספר מלכי ישראל ויהודה

As for the rest of the acts of Jotham *and all his wars and his ways*
behold, they are written in the Book of the Kings of Israel and
Judah!

"*And all his wars*" alludes to v. 5 (an "addition"): "And *he fought* against
the king of the children of Ammon."[9] "*And his ways*" alludes to v. 6 (an
"addition"): "And Jotham became mighty because he established *his
ways* before the Lord his God."

10.2 The concluding formula referring to the short reign of Abi-
jam/Abijah, king of Judah, in 1 Kgs 15:7 reads: "And the rest of the acts
of Abijam *and all that he did*, are they not written in the Book of the Annals of the Kings of Judah?"

In 2 Chr 13:22, the Chronicler omitted the words "*and all that he
did*," and in their stead he wrote, "and his ways and his sayings," alluding to the sayings of Abijah related in 13:3–20 (an "addition"): "And the
rest of the acts of Abijah *and his ways and his sayings* are written in the
commentary of the prophet Iddo. "*And his sayings*" alludes to Abijah's
speech on Mount Zemaraim (13:4–12).[10] "*And his ways*" alludes, apparently, to his religious behavior as expressed in 13:10–11: "But as for us,
the Lord is our God and we have not forsaken him. . . . [The priests] offer burnt-offerings to the Lord . . . for we keep the charge of the Lord our
God, while you have forsaken him"[11] (see also 13:18b).

---

8. See, e.g., 2 Chr 26:22 in contrast to 2 Kgs 15:6 (Uzziah); 2 Chr 12:15 in contrast
to 1 Kgs 14:29 (Rehoboam); 2 Chr 9:29 in contrast to 1 Kgs 11:41 (Solomon); also
1 Chr 29:29 (David) as compared with 1 Kgs 2:11–12.

9. True, this speaks of a "war," not of "his wars," plural. And perhaps in v. 7 the
reading of the Greek translation καὶ ὁ πόλεμος 'and the war' is to be preferred.

10. For this speech, see Throntveit, *Speech and Royal Prayer*, 36–38, 107–9, 115,
116; Dillard, *2 Chronicles*, 107, 109; Deboys, "Portrayal of Abijah," 55–59.

11. For an instance in which "his ways" refers to the religious conduct of a king,
see, for instance, 2 Chr 27:6–7.

10.3 The concluding formula relating to the reign of Manasseh, king of Judah, in 2 Kgs 21:17 is quite general:

> The rest of the acts of Manasseh, *and all that he did,*
> *and the sin that he committed*
> are they not written in the Book of the Annals of the Kings of
> Judah?

In 2 Chr 33:18–19, the Chronicler adds allusions to things that he had related earlier in detail:

18. The rest of the acts of Manasseh
 • *his prayer to his God,*
    and the words of the seers who spoke to him in the name of the
      Lord, the God of Israel,
    behold they are written in the Acts of the Kings of Israel.
19. *His prayer and how [God] was entreated of him,*
    all his sin and his transgression, and the places where he built
    high places and set up the Asherim and the images—*before he*
    humbled himself—
    behold, they are written in the records of My seers.[12]

The expressions *"his prayer to his God"* (v. 18) and *"his prayer and how [God] was entreated of him"* (v. 19) allude to what is related in 33:12–13 ("addition"): "And when he was in distress *he sought the Lord his God . . . and prayed to Him, and He received his entreaty* and heard his supplication." The words *"and the words of the seers that spoke to him in the name of the Lord, the God of Israel"* (v. 19) apparently allude to v. 10, "And the Lord spoke to Manasseh and to his people," especially to the parallel text in 2 Kgs 21:10, "And the Lord spoke *by means of His servants the prophets,* saying. . . ."

The excerpt "all his sin and his transgression, *and the places* where *he built high places"* alludes to v. 3: "And he re*built the high places . . .* and set up altars to the Baals"; similarly (vv. 4–5), *"And he built* altars in the House of the Lord . . . *and he built* altars for all the host of heaven in the two courts of the House of the Lord." The phrase "and set up *the Asherim"* alludes to v. 3, "and he made *Asheroth"*; "and *the images"* alludes to v. 7, "and he placed *the image* of the idol"; "*before he humbled himself"* alludes to v. 12, "And [Manasseh] *humbled himself* greatly before the God of his fathers."

---

12. In the LXX: "the seers." Kittel's proposal (*BH*, 1427), "his seers," seems likely. The ‪ו‬ that concludes the word ‪חוזיו‬ was erroneously omitted because of the ‪ו‬ that opens the following word, ‪וישכב‬ (v. 20)—haplography; cf. Ehrlich, *Mikrâ ki-Pheschutô*, 468.

10.4 Two of the things that the concluding formula in 2 Kgs 8:24 relates about Joram, king of Judah, are the king's death and his son's
coronation: "And his son, Ahaziah, reigned   in his stead."

In 2 Chr 22:1 the Chronicler adds to the earlier text the information
that Joram's son was "Ahaziah, his *youngest* son," and "*the band that
came with the Arabians*[13] *to the camp had killed all the older sons.*"
These additions allude to 2 Chr 21:16–17 (an "addition"): "And the Lord
stirred up against Jehoram the anger of the Philistines and the Arabians[14] who are near the Ethiopians. They came up against Judah and invaded it.[15] Then they carried away all the property found in the king's
house, as well as his sons and his wives, so that no son was left to him
besides Jehoahaz,[16] *the youngest* of his sons."

10.5 The concluding formula regarding Joash, king of Judah, in
2 Kgs 12:20 reads as follows:

> Now the rest of the acts of Joash and all that he did,
> are they not related in the Book of the Annals of the Kings of
> Judah?

In 2 Chr 24:27, the Chronicler omitted the words "now the rest of the
acts of Joash and all that he did" from the earlier text and instead alluded to things he had previously related concerning Joash:

> Now *as for his sons, the multitude of burdens* (משא) *against him,*
> *and the rebuilding of the House of God,*
> behold, they are written in the Commentary on the Book of the
> Kings.

"*As for his sons*" alludes to 24:3 (an "addition"): "And Jehoiada married
two wives, and he fathered *sons and daughters.*"[17]

---

13. For the meaning of the phrase הבא בערבים, see example 13.5, and n. 20 in particular (p. 281).

14. For the phrase (. . .)ו (. . .) את רוח . . . ה' ויער, see 1 Chr 5:26: "And the God of
Israel stirred up the spirit (of Pul, king of Assyria) and (the spirit of Tilgath-pilneser,
king of Assyria)."

15. For the phrase ויעלו ביהודה ויבקעוה, see Isa 7:5: "Let us go up against Judah . . .
and conquer it."

16. "*Jeho*ahaz," in contrast to the other order of the components of the name in
22:1, "Ahaz*iahu*" (similarly in the parallel text in the book of Kings). In the Greek,
Syriac, and Aramaic translations at this point, "Ahaz*iahu*" appears, as in 22:1.

17. Contrary to Yeivin, who believes "that the word 'בניו(ו)' is to be applied up until
v. 26, i.e., that those conspiring against him were his sons, the sons of foreign women"
("The Divided Kingdom," 105). In light of the discussion here, and especially in light
of 2 Kgs 12:22, which states that those who attacked him were "*his servants*" (cf. also
2 Kgs 14:5 // 2 Chr 25:3), there is no room for Yeivin's idea.

"*And the multitude*[18] *of burdens against him*" may allude to "*the tax of* (מַשָּׂאת) Moses, servant of the Lord,*" that the people brought freely in response to the request by Joash (vv. 6, 9), as in this passage: "And when they saw that the money was *a great amount* . . . and they gathered *a great amount* of money" (v. 11).[19]

"*And the rebuilding of the House of God*" alludes to "*the restoration of the House of the Lord . . . to repair the House of the Lord*" (v. 12, and see "to repair *the House of your God*"), the story that appears in vv. 5–14.[20]

B. In Other Texts

10.6 According to 2 Kgs 22:10–13, when Shaphan, the scribe, read the book that had been found in the Temple to Josiah, king of Judah, the king tore his garments and commanded his servants, "Go and inquire of the Lord for me, *for the people, and for all of Judah*[21] concerning the words of this book that has been found. For the wrath of the Lord is great" (v. 13).

In 2 Chr 34:21, the Chronicler adduced this passage. However, in place of the words "for the people, and for all of Judah," he wrote "*and*

---

18. Such are the *Kethiv*, Latin, Syriac, and Ethiopic readings, but the *Qere* is ירב (an interchange of ו/י, which are similar graphically).

19. Some scholars believe that the expression מַשְׂאַת משה עבד ה' 'the tax of Moses, servant of the Lord' (v. 6)/מַשְׂאַת משה עבד האלהים 'the tax of Moses, servant of God' (v. 9) refers to the donation of the half-shekel mentioned in Exod 30:12: "When you take a census of all the children of Israel"; see, for example, the commentary of R. David Kimḥi; the commentary attributed to Rashi; Curtis-Madsen, *Chronicles*, 435; Rudolph, *Chronik*, 275. Liver proposed interpreting the word מַשָּׂא here as 'donation, tax' ("Episode of the Half-Shekel," 114; cf. Ezek 20:40). Accordingly, the meaning of the phrase under consideration in Chronicles is "the donation that Moses assessed the people of Israel in the desert for the purpose of setting up the Tent of Meeting." The problematic phrase ורב המשא עליו may thus be translated as 'the sizable donation that they brought to him'. Others claim that the word מַשָּׂא is used here in the sense of 'prophecy'; see מַשָּׂא בבל אשר חזה ישעיהו 'the prophecy of Babylon that Isaiah foresaw', Isa 13:1; also 15:1; 17:1; 19:1; 21:1, 11, 13, etc. If it means 'prophecy', then the Chronicler was alluding to v. 19 (an "addition"): "And he sent *prophets* to bring them back to the Lord, and they testified to them, but they would not listen"; see Kimḥi; Curtis-Madsen, *Chronicles*, 439; Elmslie, *Chronicles* (1916), 279; Coggins, *Chronicles*, 242; and cf. Williamson, *Chronicles*, 326. This interpretation, however, seems less likely.

20. The infinitive form וְיֵסוּד appears here in the sense of 'to repair, to strengthen'; see also *BDB*, 413b. And, in fact, the repairing of the Temple in the book of Chronicles is carried out against the background of the narrative concerning Athaliah and her sons, who "broke down the House of God" (v. 7).

21. The phrases "for the people" and "for all of Judah" are examples of hendiadys. "And for all of Judah" is not a superfluous sequence of words that should be omitted, as has been proposed by Jepsen, *BHS*, 665; and Montgomery, *Kings*, 527, for example. At any rate, there is no textual support for the opinion that one of these phrases was added to the text at a later date.

for the remnant in Israel and in Judah."²² The term הנשאר בישראל 'the remnant in Israel' is apparently identical to שארית ישראל 'the remnant of Israel', which the Chronicler also added to an earlier verse, v. 9:

2 Kgs 22:4	2 Chr 34:9
Go up to Hilkiah, the high priest, that he may count up the money brought to the House of the Lord, which the gatekeepers collected *from the people*	And they came to Hilkiah, the high priest, and delivered²³ the money that had been brought to the House of God, which the Levites, the gatekeepers, collected *from the hand of Manasseh and Ephraim and from all the remnant of Israel and from all Judah and Benjamin, and they returned to Jerusalem.*

Similarly, the term is identical to ישראל הנמצא in 2 Chr 35:18, which was added by the Chronicler to the text adduced from 2 Kgs 23:23. The terms הנשאר בישראל, שארית וישראל, and ישראל הנמצא apparently allude to הפליטה הנשארת ... מכף מלכי אשור 'the remnant ... escaped from the hand of the kings of Assyria' (2 Chr 30:6), whom Hezekiah invited to cele-

---

22. "The remnant in Israel and in Judah": for "the remnant in Israel," see below; "the remnant in Judah" apparently refers to the people who remained in the kingdom of Judah after Sennacherib's campaign of 701 B.C.E., for according to the Sennacherib prism, the Assyrian king exiled some 200,150 people from Judah, in addition to those who died or who were displaced as a result of the destruction and ruin that he left behind in the land of Judah. According to the Chronicler, however, Sennacherib's campaign was destined to fail dismally (see 2 Chronicles 32, especially, vv. 1, 21–22; it should be noted that, according to the author of the book of Kings as well, no forced exile took place in Judah in Sennacherib's time); it is thus more reasonable to assume that the writer anachronistically inserted the situation from his own day (the period after the Babylonian Exile and the Restoration) into the text about Josiah; cf. Rudolph, *Chronik*, 324. Another explanation was offered by Japhet (*Ideology*, 333 n. 243): "In the course of time, נשאר came to have a broader meaning, along the lines of נמצא"; and see 2 Chr 35:18; 1 Chr 13:2; Neh 1:3. Accordingly, "the remnant in Judah" actually meant the people living in Judah.
23. It may reasonably be assumed that the reading ויתנו 'and they gave' is the original one and that the word ויתם 'that he may sum up' in the parallel text in the book of Kings is an error for ויתנו. In other words, the letter ם is the integrated form of נו. See 2 Kgs 22:5, ויתנה, a resumptive repetition of the very same verb in v. 4. Compare Weiss, "On Ligatures in the Bible," 4–5, where there is also an earlier review of commentaries on the topic. Yet there is also the possibility that the word ויתם in the book of Kings is an error for ויתך / ויתיכו. See also further on in the text: את הכסף התיכו עבדיך 'Your servants *melted down* the silver' (2 Kgs 22:9 // 2 Chr 34:17). Compare Ehrlich, *Mikrâ ki-Pheschutô*, 385 (for the מ / כ interchange, see Weiss, "On Ligatures in the Bible," 5 n. 18). Rudolph corrected the word ויתנו in 2 Chr 34:9 to ויתכו, accordingly (*Chronik*, 320).

brate the Passover in Jerusalem (30:1–7) and in whose cities ritual reforms were carried out by Hezekiah (31:1) and Josiah (34:6–7).[24] These terms refer to the residents of the area that in the past had been the kingdom of Israel—the residents who had not been exiled by the Assyrian kings in the second half of the eighth century B.C.E.—and the terms allude to the destruction of the kingdom of Israel and to the Assyrian Exile, as narrated in 2 Kings 17 (see also 15:29). The passages under consideration, 2 Kgs 15:29 and chapter 17, were omitted from the book of Chronicles.

10.7 In 1 Chr 11:3, the Chronicler copied 2 Sam 5:3, "and they anointed David king over Israel," and followed it immediately with כדבר ה׳ ביד שמואל 'in accordance with the word of the Lord by Samuel' (see also 1 Chr 11:10 and 12:24).[25] This addition alludes to 1 Sam 15:28; 16:1–13, regarding the choosing of David from among the sons of Jesse and anointing him king over Israel instead of Saul, in accordance with what the Lord said by Samuel. These narratives, which were omitted from the earlier account in the book of Chronicles, are alluded to in the Chronicler's words in 1 Chr 28:4 (an "addition") as well: *"Then the Lord God of Israel chose me out of all my father's house to be king over Israel forever; for He chose Judah as prince and, from the house of Judah, my father's house, and, from among the sons of my father, He wished to install me as king over all Israel."*[26]

10.8 In 2 Chr 2:16a, the Chronicler adds to the parallel text in 1 Kgs 5:29–30:

And Solomon counted all the *foreign people who were in the land of Israel,*
after the census in which David, his father, had counted them,
and they were found to be one hundred fifty-three thousand six hundred.

The phrase *"after the census in which David, his father, had counted them"* alludes to 1 Chr 22:2ff. (an "addition"): "Then David gave orders to assemble *the foreigners who were in the land of Israel"* (in the retaking

---

24. The historical reliability of these passages in the book of Chronicles is debatable. Some regard them positively; for example, Cross, "Samaria and Jerusalem," 82–83; others regard them negatively; for example, Oded, "II Kings 17," 37–50.

25. For a discussion of this passage from a different point of view, see chap. 7, §3: "Harmonizing Divine Word and Divine Action" (pp. 159–165).

26. For the selection of David to reign over Israel, see also 2 Chr 6:5–6 // 1 Kgs 8:16 (homoioteleuton occurred in Kings: שם שמי . . . שם שמי); 1 Chr 17:7 // 2 Sam 7:8. See in detail Kalimi, "Jerusalem: The Divine City," 191–94.

of the census in 1 Chr 21:1–22:1 // 2 Samuel 24, nothing is said about
having counted the foreigners).

10.9 In 2 Chr 3:1, the Chronicler adds the precise location of the site
of Solomon's Temple to the earlier text of 1 Kgs 6:1, while alluding to
the episode of *the binding of Isaac* (Gen 22:1–14, especially v. 2b) and to
the episode of *the census* (1 Chr 21:1–22:1 // 2 Samuel 24):[27]

> Then Solomon began to build the House of the Lord in Jerusalem
> *on Mount Moriah,*[28] *where [the Lord] appeared to David, his*
> *father—on the site that David had prepared—on the threshing floor*
> *of Ornan the Jebusite.*[29]

10.10 2 Kgs 24:19 (// Jer 52:2) says of Zedekiah, king of Judah: "He
did what was evil in the eyes of the Lord, *just as Jehoiakim had done.*"
In 2 Chr 36:12, the Chronicler omitted the words "just as Jehoiakim had
done" and wrote instead: "He did what was evil in the eyes of the Lord
his God; *he did not humble himself before Jeremiah the prophet [who*
spoke] from the mouth of God."[30] By means of this emendation, the
Chronicler apparently attempted to allude to Jer 37:2: "And (Zedekiah)
. . . *did not listen to the words of the Lord that He spoke through Jere-*
miah the prophet" (see also 38:15, 20–21).

10.11 2 Kgs 24:20 reads as follows: "Then Zedekiah rebelled against
the king of Babylon." In 2 Chr 36:13 the Chronicler wrote: "And he
rebelled against Nebuchadnezzar the king, *who had made him swear*
by God." The words "*who had made him swear by God*" allude to Ezek
17:11–21, concerning the pact made by the king of Babylon with the
king of Judah and how Zedekiah violated it and how he was punished:
"Then he [the king of Babylon] took one of the royal offspring and made
a pact with him, *putting him under oath. . . . But he rebelled against*
him. . . . Thus says the Lord God, 'As I live, *is it not My oath that he has*
scorned and My covenant that he has violated? I shall put it on his
head'" (17:13–15, 19).

---

27. For the literary structure of this addition, its possible aims, and the significance of the failure of the episode of the construction (in 1 Kgs 5:16–9:9) to mark the
site of the Temple, see Kalimi, "Land/Mount Moriah," 25–32.

28. For the relationship between "Mount Moriah" here and the term "the land of
Moriah" in Gen 22:2b, see ibid., 9–32.

29. For this version of the written text, see chap. 3, §4: "Addition of the Site of
Events," and example 3.22 and notes thereto (pp. 82–83).

30. For the expression "did not humble himself before . . . ," see 2 Chr 33:23: "Neither did he humble himself before the Lord."

10.12 1 Kings 22 speaks of a meeting between the king of Israel and Jehoshaphat, king of Judah. In 2 Chronicles 18, the Chronicler preceded the narrative of the meeting with the sentence: ויהי ליהושפט עשר וכבוד לרב ויתחתן לאחאב 'Jehoshaphat had an abundance of riches and honor, *and he allied himself with Ahab by marriage*' (18:1). The words ויתחתן לאחאב allude to the marriage of Jehoram, king of Judah, Jehoshaphat's son, to "the daughter of Ahab" (2 Chr 21:6 // 2 Kgs 8:18).[31]

10.13 In 2 Chronicles 22, the Chronicler speaks about Ahaziah, king of Judah, who went with Jehoram, king of Israel, to wage war against Hazael, king of Aram, in Ramoth-gilead. He also relates that Jehoram was wounded in the fighting and that Ahaziah went down to Jezreel to visit him (22:2–6 // 2 Kgs 8:26–29). At this point, the Chronicler inserts an "addition" (22:7–8), alluding to the anointing of Jehu, son of Nimshi, and to the massacre that he perpetrated in both royal houses. These episodes are related in 2 Kgs 9:1–26, but the Chronicler omits the account of Jehu from his book, except for this allusion in the middle of the story about Ahaziah:

> And the defeat of Ahaziah was ordained by God through his going to visit Joram. *When he arrived there, he went out with Jehoram to meet Jehu, son of Nimshi*, whom the Lord had anointed to cut down the House of Ahab. And it came to pass that, when Jehu was executing judgment on the house of Ahab, . . . (2 Chr 22:7)

The words "when he arrived there, he went out with Jehoram to meet Jehu, son of Nimshi," allude to 2 Kgs 9:21, "*And Jehoram, king of Israel, went out with Ahaziah, king of Judah, each in his own chariot, and they went out to meet Jehu and found him.*" The words "*whom the Lord had anointed to cut down the house of Ahab*" allude to 2 Kgs 9:1–10, especially vv. 6b–8, "Thus said the Lord, God of Israel: '*I have anointed you as king* over the nation of the Lord, over Israel, *and you shall strike down the House of Ahab . . . and I shall cut Ahab down.*'"

10.14 In describing the conspiracy of Jehoiada, the priest, against Athaliah, 2 Kgs 11:10 relates that Jehoiada gave "to the captains of hundreds the spears and *the shields* that had belonged to King David, which were in the House of the Lord."[32] Some scholars think that this

---

31. But see 2 Chr 22:2 // 2 Kgs 8:26, 27c; 2 Chr 22:10 // 1 Kgs 11:1—texts noting that the mother of Ahaziah, son of Jehoram, was "Athaliah, daughter of Omri." For this, see example 20.1 (p. 381–382).

32. For the placing of weapons in temples, see depositing the sword of Goliath the Philistine in the chief sanctuary of the Lord at Nob (1 Sam 21:10); depositing Saul's weapons in the temple of Astarte (1 Sam 31:10 // 1 Chr 10:10; see also 1 Kgs 10:17 //

verse (2 Kgs 11:10) is a late gloss based on the parallel text of 2 Chr 23:9
because it contradicts 2 Kgs 11:8, which speaks of a guard that was already armed.[33] However, it seems to me that 11:10 was an integral part
of the book and that the weapons listed in it served mainly ceremonial
needs. There is thus no substantial contradiction between 11:10 and
11:8.[34] The clause *"the shields* that had belonged to King David" apparently alludes to 2 Sam 8:7 (// 1 Chr 18:7): "And David took the golden
shields that had belonged to the servants of Hadadezer and brought
them to Jerusalem." The succeeding verses show that David apparently
sanctified these shields to the Lord from the rest of the booty that he
took from Israel's neighbors (2 Sam 8:11–12 // 1 Chr 18:10–11).

In 2 Chr 23:9, the Chronicler adduced the 2 Kgs 11:10 text but added
the words ואת המגנות 'and the bucklers',[35] apparently alluding to *the
bronze bucklers* that Rehoboam, king of Judah, had made and left "with
the captains of the guard protecting the entrance to the king's house" ("all
the golden bucklers that Solomon had made" were stolen by Shishak,
king of Egypt, 2 Chr 12:9–11 // 1 Kgs 14:26–28):

2 Kgs 11:10	*2 Chr 23:9*
Then the priest gave to the	Then Jehoiada, the priest, gave to the
captains of hundreds the spears	captains of hundreds the spears
and the shields[36]	*and the bucklers and the shields*
that had belonged to King David	that had belonged to King David
and that were in the House of	and that were in the House of
the Lord.	God.

It seems that the Chronicler believed that only the שלטים 'the shields'
had belonged to King David, according to 2 Sam 8:7 // 1 Chr 18:7, not

---

2 Chr 9:16). In "a letter to the god of Ashur," Sargon II relates that on his eighth campaign (714 B.C.E.) he defeated Urzana, the king, captured his city, Muṣaṣir, and removed many weapons from the temple to the god Haldia; see Luckenbill, *ARAB*,
vol. 2, §173. This custom continued into the Hellenistic period. Thus, 1 Macc 6:1–2 relates that Alexander, son of Philip of Macedon, left "golden shields, breastplates, and
weapons" in the temple of an Elymais city in Persia.

33. Thus, e.g., Curtis-Madsen, *Chronicles*, 428; Montgomery, *Kings*, 420; Gray,
Kings, 573; Snaith, *Kings*, 247.

34. Cf. Williamson, *Chronicles*, 316.

35. The plural form מגנות is unique, as is חניתים. More generally accepted are the
forms מגנים, חניתות (see, e.g., Isa 2:4 // Mic 4:3). In place of the collective noun חנית, the
Chronicler (and the translators of the LXX, Peshiṭta, and Vulgate of 2 Kings) used
החניתים (plural) to create clear numerical harmony between this form and שרי המאות
'the captains of hundreds'.

36. For the meaning of the term שלט, see Borger, *Waffentrager*, 385–98. According
to Borger, שלט (*šalṭu* in Akkadian, and also the word in Aramaic) meant 'a quiver (for
arrows)'.

"the spears" or "the bucklers." In other words, the relative phrase
אשר למלך דויד refers only to the last item in the list of armaments—
השלטים 'the shields' (unlike the sages who added the musical notations
to the biblical text, who placed a *zaqep* over the word השלטים in both parallel texts). For a similar phenomenon, see Gen 18:8a: "And [Abraham]
took butter and milk and the calf [that] he had prepared and placed
[them] before them," where the relative clause אשר עשה '[that] he had
prepared' refers only to "the calf," not to the "butter and milk."

2. Adducing an Entire Narrative in an Allusion to an Earlier Text

There are instances in which the Chronicler presents an entire narrative from an earlier text by means of a simple allusion, assuming that
a reader can find the details of the narrative in the earlier text.

10.15   According to 2 Kgs 19:14ff. (// Isa 37:14ff.), during the Assyrian
crisis Hezekiah prayed to the Lord his God. His prayer is presented in
vv. 15–19 (// Isa 37:15–20). In the parallel text in 2 Chronicles 32, the
Chronicler has omitted this prayer from the narrative, though he alludes to it:

2 Kgs 19:15–19	2 Chr 32:20
Then Hezekiah prayed	*Then Hezekiah*, the king, and the prophet Isaiah, son of Amoz, *prayed* because of this and shouted to heaven.
before the Lord and said, "O Lord, God of Israel, seated among the cherubs, You are God. . . ."	

10.16   In 2 Chr 32:24, the Chronicler alluded to 2 Kgs 20:1–11 (// Isa
38:1–8, 21–22), concerning Hezekiah's illness, his prayer, what Isaiah
said to him, and the sign that was given to him that he would recover:

2 Kgs 20:1–11	2 Chr 32:24
1. In those days Hezekiah fell ill to death; Isaiah, the prophet, came to him and said to him, "This is what the Lord said, 'Command your household, for you are dying and you shall not live.'"	In those days Hezekiah fell ill to the point of death
2. He turned his face around to the wall *and prayed to the Lord,*	*and prayed to the Lord,*

saying,
3. "Please, O Lord, remember that
   . . .

4. And it came to pass, when Isaiah
   had not yet left the middle court,
   the word of the Lord came to him
   saying,

5. *"Return and say to Hezekiah . . .*   *and He said to him*
   'Behold, I am healing you;
   on the third day you shall go up
   to the House of the Lord.

6. I shall add fifteen years to your
   life and save you and this city
   from the hand of the king of
   Assyria. . . .' "

8. Then Hezekiah said to Isaiah,
   "What is a *sign* (אות) that the Lord
   will heal me and that I shall go
   up to the House of the Lord on
   the third day?"

9. Isaiah said, *"This is a sign* (אות)   *and gave him a sign* (מופת).
   for you from the Lord. . . ."

The phrase "and prayed to the Lord" alludes to Hezekiah's prayer in
2 Kgs 20:3 // Isa 38:3. The phrase "and gave him a sign (מופת)" almost
certainly alludes to the narrative of the moving of the shadow on the
dial of Ahaz in 2 Kgs 20:8–11 // Isa 38:7–8,[37] which served as a sign to
Hezekiah that he would be healed by the Lord and that he would go up
to the House of the Lord on the third day (2 Kgs 20:8 // Isa 38:22). "The
sign" (מופת) is also mentioned further on, in 2 Chr 32:31. Here the
Chronicler uses a synonym of the word אות 'sign' that appears in the earlier text.[38] The fragmentary phrase ויאמר לו 'and He said to him' (32:24)
apparently means "and he [Isaiah] spoke to him [to Hezekiah]."[39] The
phrase may be referring to 2 Kgs 20:5–6 (// Isa 38:5–6): "Return[, Isaiah,] *and say to Hezekiah,* . . . 'This is what the Lord has spoken, . . . "Behold I am healing you . . . I shall add fifteen years to your life and save
you from the hand of the king of Assyria." ' "

---

37. For the dial of Ahaz, see Yadin, "Dial of Ahaz."
38. For the synonymity of מופת/אות see, for example, Ps 78:43; 105:27; and compare with Deut 13:2–3; *Sifre Numbers*, Naso, 23.21: "אות means מופת, מופת means אות;
but the Torah used two words."
39. The Greek translation at this point, καὶ ἐπήκουσεν ('and he heard, and he was
answered'), seems secondary.

The Chronicler may have elected merely to allude to the narrative in 2 Kgs 20:1–11 because the words spoken by Hezekiah, "What is a *sign* that the Lord will heal me and that I shall go up on the third day to the House of the Lord?" (2 Kgs 20:8), show a lack of faith in the promise made by the prophet, "This is what the Lord has spoken, . . . 'Behold, I am healing you; on the third day you shall go up to the House of the Lord'" (20:5). Furthermore, in his prayer to the Lord that He heal him, Hezekiah relied on his own righteousness: "Please, O Lord, remember that *I have walked* before you in truth and with a whole heart and *I have performed* what is good in Your eyes" (20:3); whereas, in the Lord's reply it seems that, while He did indeed see Hezekiah's tears and hear his prayer, his cure (the addition of fifteen years to his lifespan and saving him from Assyria) was not (or not only) because of Hezekiah but *"for My sake and for the sake of David, My servant"* (20:5–6).[40] This hubris overshadowed Hezekiah's righteousness and did not suit the image painted in 2 Chronicles 29–32 (especially 29:1; 31:20; 32:1, 20).

10.17 2 Kgs 20:12–19 (// Isa 39:1–8) describes the delegation sent by Merodach-baladan, king of Babylon,[41] to Hezekiah, king of Judah, at the time of his illness (the delegation visited Jerusalem, apparently, in the fourteenth year of the reign of King Hezekiah—714/13 B.C.E.), Hezekiah's friendly attitude toward the delegation, and the prophet's reaction to this.[42] The Chronicler did not use this narrative in his work, although he alluded to it in 2 Chr 32:31: "Also regarding the intermediaries of the princes of Babylon who sent [them] to him[43] to inquire of the miracle that had transpired in the land." In the book of Kings the goal of the visit is כי שמע כי חלה חזקיהו 'he had heard that Hezekiah had taken ill' (2 Kgs 20:12, and similarly in Isa 39:1), describing an event in

---

40. The words spoken by the Lord do not fit the Chronicler's concept of retribution either. According to this conception, one is rewarded for one's own deeds and not for those of one's forefathers. For this topic in the book of Chronicles, see Japhet, *Ideology*, 162–63.

41. For Merodach-baladan and the periods during which he reigned in Babylon, see Tadmor-Cogan, "Hezekiah's Fourteenth Year," 200 n. 14, 201 n. 19.

42. For the literary structure of this story, its location in the anthology of the story of Isaiah the prophet, and the period of its redaction, see ibid., 198–201.

43. The word מליץ means 'translator' (cf. Gen 42:23) or 'intermediary' (Job 33:23; Isa 43:27). Delitzsch (*Schreibfehler*, 122, §134d) suggests the reading שׂר־בבל מליצי 'the intermediaries of *the prince of* Babylon'. He claims that the *maqqep* was distorted into a *yod*. In this case, "the prince of Babylon" here means Merodach-baladan (cf. Rudolph, *Chronik*, 312). The LXX, Vulgate, and Aramaic read הַמְשַׁלָּחִים 'the dispatchers' here, and this reading seems preferable (and cf. Curtis-Madsen, *Chronicles*, 494; Ehrlich, *Mikrâ ki-Pheschutô*, 467; Rudolph, *Chronik*, 312). Ehrlich (*Randglossen*, 381) suggests reading הֵם שְׁלָחִים, and this possibility cannot be ruled out completely.

ancient international affairs that prompted state visits between friendly kingdoms.[44] The Chronicler, however, writes that the goal of the visit was "to inquire of the *miracle* (מוֹפֵת) that had transpired in the land," thus informing the reader just how renowned the miracle was that the Lord had performed on behalf of Hezekiah. The Chronicler seems to have linked the story of the miracle with the story of the delegation from Babylon because of the literary proximity already existing between the two in the book of Kings (2 Kgs 20:1–11, 12–19). The expression בָּעֵת הַהִיא 'at that time' (20:12a) serves merely as a transition from one narrative to the other.[45] The "miracle" (מוֹפֵת) in 2 Chr 32:31 is the same as "the sign" (מוֹפֵת) in 32:24, referring to the story of the moving of the shadow on the dial of Ahaz.

3. Integrating Allusions into "Additions"

A. In Genealogical Lists

10.18 The story of Achan's embezzlement of forbidden booty and the flight of the Israelites from the troops of Ai that resulted from this embezzlement in Joshua 7 does not appear in the book of Chronicles. The Chronicler, however, saw fit to allude to it in a comment that he introduced into the genealogy of the tribe of Judah, in 1 Chr 2:7: "And the children of Carmi: Achar, a source of filth in Israel, who embezzled forbidden booty."[46]

10.19 In 1 Chr 2:3–4, "the sons of Judah were Er, Onan, and Shelah; these three were born to him of Bath-shua the Canaanitess. Now Er, Judah's firstborn, was evil in the eyes of the Lord, so He put him to death. And Tamar, his daughter-in-law, bore him Perez and Zerah," the Chronicler alludes to the narrative concerning Judah and Tamar in Genesis 38.[47]

10.20 In 1 Chr 5:1–2, the Chronicler apparently alludes to a number of passages in the book of Genesis:

---

44. For this custom, see the detailed discussion of David's delegation to Nahash, king of the Ammonites, in example 15.20 (pp. 346–349). The true purpose of the delegation was apparently the creation of an anti-Assyrian coalition (against Sargon II).

45. The Babylonian delegation's visit to Judah was perceived by the Chronicler as the Lord's testing of Hezekiah; for this, see Japhet, *Ideology*, 193.

46. This story seems to have been alluded to in Hos 2:17 as well: "And I shall give her *her vineyard* from there and *the valley of Achor* as a doorway of hope" (cf. Josh 7:24, 26), and in Isa 65:10.

47. On this issue, see also below, example 20.4 (p. 383).

And the sons of Reuben, the firstborn of Israel (for he was the first-born but, because he defiled his father's couch, his birthright was given to the sons of Joseph, son of Israel, so he is not reckoned as firstborn in the genealogy; for, although Judah was prominent among his brothers and a ruler is descended from him, the birth-right was Joseph's).

The words "*Reuben, the firstborn of Israel* (for he was the firstborn *but, because he defiled his father's couch*)" allude to Jacob's blessing in Gen 49:3–4: "*Reuben, you are my firstborn* / my strength and the beginning of my power. . . . For you mounted your father's bed / then *you defiled my couch*, going up on it." See also the narrative in Gen 35:22: "Then Reuben went and lay with Bilhah, his father's concubine."

The phrase "*his birthright was given to the sons of Joseph*, son of Is-rael, so he is not reckoned as firstborn in the genealogy; . . . the birth-right was Joseph's" apparently alludes to Gen 48:5: "As for your two sons who have been born to you in the land of Egypt . . . they are mine; Ephraim and Manasseh are to me as Reuben and Simeon" (see also 48:22). In other words, Joseph, who received twice as large an inheri-tance (one inheritance for Ephraim and one for Manasseh), was consid-ered the firstborn (see Deut 21:17) instead of Reuben.

"For, although Judah was prominent among his brothers and a ruler is descended from him" alludes to Jacob's blessing in Gen 49:8: "Judah, your brethren will accept you. . . . The sons of your father will bow down to you."

B. In Other Additions

10.21 The Chronicler concluded his description of Saul's defeat on Mount Gilboa (1 Chr 10:1–12 // 1 Sam 31:1–13) this way: "And Saul died for his betrayal; he betrayed the Lord by not carrying out (אשר לא שמר) His word and also by inquiring of a ghost and seeking its guidance (לשאל באוב לדרש)" (1 Chr 10:13). The phrase "he betrayed the Lord" al-ludes to Saul's embezzlement of the forbidden Amalekite booty, as re-counted in 1 Samuel 15; the words "by not carrying out (אשר לא שמר)" allude not only to 1 Samuel 15 (and see also 1 Sam 28:18, "since you did not obey the voice of the Lord and carry out His wrath upon Amalek") but also, and mainly, to 1 Sam 13:13–14: "Then Samuel said to Saul, 'You have acted foolishly; *you have not carried out* (לא שמרת) the com-mandment of the Lord your God . . . *you have not carried out* (לא שמרת) that which the Lord your God commanded you.'" The phrase "to inquire *of a ghost and seek its guidance*" alludes to the narrative concerning Saul and the witch at Endor in 1 Samuel 28 (see 28:7, "Search out for me a woman with a *ghost* (בעלת אוב), so that I may go to her *and seek guid-ance* from her (ואדרשה בה)," and v. 17, "And Samuel said, 'Why do you ask (תשאלני‎), since the Lord has departed from you'"). 1 Samuel 13, 15, and 28 are not adduced in the book of Chronicles.[48]

10.22 1 Chr 12:1 reads, "And these are those who came to David at Ziklag, while he was still confined because of Saul, son of Kish." This verse alludes to 1 Sam 27:1–7, about the escape of David to Achish, king of Gath, a narrative that is not found in the book of Chronicles.

10.23 1 Chr 12:20–22 reads: "Also some of Manasseh deserted to David when he came with the Philistines to wage war against Saul. However, he did not assist them, for the captains of the Philistines sent him away advisedly, saying, 'He will desert to his master Saul—to [the jeopardy of] our heads.' As he went to Ziklag, these deserted to him from Manasseh: . . . ."[49] Here the Chronicler is alluding to 1 Sam 28:1–2 and 29:1–11 in considerable detail. Especially instructive is the analogy between 1 Chr 12:21, בראשנו יפול אל אדניו‎ 'he will desert to his master Saul—to [the jeopardy of] our heads', and 1 Sam 29:4, ובמה יתרצה זה אל‎ האנשים ההם אדניו הלוא בראשי‎ 'By what means will this man be accepted by his master? Is it not by means of the heads of those people?'[50]

The Philistine captains are here speaking of themselves in the third person, "the heads of *those people*," just as a person cursing himself and ascribing the curse to others would do (see Exod 1:10: "*they* [will] join our enemies and fight against us and *withdraw* from the land";[51] Num 16:14: "Will you put out the eyes of *those men*?"). The Chronicler was not mindful of this and adduced their statements in first-person plural: בראשנו יפול אל אדניו‎ 'to [the jeopardy of] *our heads*'.[52]

---

48. Cf. Willi, *Chronik*, 56; against Mosis, *Untersuchungen*, 41. And see example 15.2a (pp. 327–329).

49. For the chiastic structure and the "repetitive introduction" that the Chronicler created in this excerpt, see below, examples 11.8 (p. 221) and 13.17 (pp. 293–294), which deal with these verses.

50. Here the Chronicler has quoted 1 Sam 29:4 in word order that is chiastically parallel to 1 Samuel. For this device, see example 12.40 (p. 247).

51. On this verse, see *b. Soṭa* 11a.

52. For this phenomenon, see also Zech 2:12: "For he who touches you touches the apple of *his eye*," instead of "the apple of *My* eye." See also 1 Sam 25:22, "May God do so *to the enemies of David* and more also," in contrast to the LXX: τάδε ποιήσαι ὁ θεὸς τῷ Δαυὶδ ('May God do so *to David*'); 2 Sam 12:14, "However, by this deed you have utterly scorned the enemies of the Lord"; Yaron adduced a parallel text from Egyptian literature for this one ("Coptus Decree," 89–91). For the opposite phenomenon, see Num 11:15: "If this is what you will do to me, please put me to death at once . . . lest I view *my* evil end," and Rashi explains: "It should have written '*their* evil end', but the Scripture modifies the expression. And this is one of the scribal corrections in the Torah." See also the list of verses expounded in *Mekilta de-Rabbi Ishmael, Beshalach, Masechta deShira*, §6 (ed. Horovitz-Rabin, 135). This phenomenon is well known from the Aggadic Midrashim, too; see, for instance, *b. Ber.* 7a.

10.24 1 Chr 26:26–27 reads: "He, Shelomoth, and his brothers were over all the treasuries of the holy objects *dedicated by David the king . . . from the wars and from the booty* that he dedicated for the maintenance of the House of the Lord." These verses seem to allude to 2 Sam 8:10–12 (// 2 Chr 18:10–11): "These also *King David dedicated to the Lord*, together with the silver and the gold that he dedicated *from all of the nations that he vanquished*, from Aram,[53] Moab, the Ammonites, the Philistines, Amalek, and from the *booty* of Hadadezer, son of Rehob, king of Zobah."

10.25 In 1 Chr 27:23–24 the Chronicler alludes to the narrative concerning the census in 1 Chr 21:1–22:1 // 2 Samuel 24: "And David did not count those twenty years old and under,[54] for the Lord had promised to make Israel as numerous as the stars in the sky.[55] *Joab, son of Zeruiah, began to count them but did not finish;*[56] *yet, for this, wrath came upon Israel*, and the number was not included in the account of the Annals of King David."

10.26 2 Chr 13:6 (an "addition") states, *"then Jeroboam, son of Nebat, servant of Solomon*, the son of David, rose up *and rebelled against his lord*," alluding to 1 Kgs 11:26–28, which does not appear in the book of Chronicles: *"Then Jeroboam, son of Nebat . . . , servant of Solomon, raised his hand against the king*, and this is reason that he raised his hand against the king. . . ."

10.27 The stories about the ritual enterprises of Jeroboam, son of Nebat, king of Israel, in 1 Kgs 12:26–33 and 13:33 are not presented in the book of Chronicles. These stories are not directly linked to the history of the kingdom of Judah, which is central to the Chronicler's work. Nonetheless, he did find room to allude to them. 2 Chr 11:13–15 (an "addition") says, "The priests and Levites throughout Israel presented themselves to him from their territories. For the Levites had left their plots and their inheritances[57] and had gone to Judah and Jerusalem, because *Jeroboam and his sons had prevented them from serving as*

---

53. In a number of manuscripts of the MT, LXX, and Peshitta, it is מאדם 'from Edom'.

54. According to Num 1:3, everyone "from twenty years old and *upward*" is to be counted.

55. See Gen 15:7; 22:17.

56. See 1 Chr 21:6. The text does not say that Joab *intended to complete* the census but was unsuccessful, as Williamson thinks (*Chronicles*, 177). There is thus no contradiction between this passage and 1 Chr 21:6, which says that Joab did not count Levi and Benjamin, *"for [he] despised the word of the king."*

57. For the Levites' plots and inheritances, see 1 Chr 6:39–66 [6:54–81]; Lev 25:32–34; Num 35:1–5; Josh 21:5–42.

*priests for the Lord and had set up his own priests for the high places
and* שעירים[58] *and the calves that he had prepared.*" Similar references
are found in Abijah's speech on Mount Zemaraim (2 Chr 13:8b–9, an
"addition"): "And you have the *golden calves* that Jeroboam *made for
you as gods.* Have you not driven out the priests of the Lord, the sons of
Aaron, and the Levites and *made priests* for yourselves in the manner of
the peoples of the lands? *All who come to consecrate themselves* with a
bull or seven rams[59] become priests of what are no gods." These verses
allude to 1 Kgs 12:28, 31, 32; and 13:33: "Then the king took counsel <u>and</u>
<u>made</u> two <u>calves of gold</u> and said to them, 'You have gone up long enough
to Jerusalem; *behold your gods, O Israel. . . .*' And he made *cult places
and appointed priests from among all the people, who were not of the
sons of Levi. . . .* So he did in Bethel, sacrificing <u>*to the calves that he had*</u>
<u>*made*</u>, and he placed *the priests of the high places that he had made* in
Bethel.*"* "*Jeroboam . . . made priests for the high places from among all
the people; he consecrated any who wanted to be priests for the high
places.*"

10.28 In the prayer of Jehoshaphat, king of Judah (2 Chr 20:10–11),
the Chronicler wrote: "And now, behold, the descendants of Ammon,
Moab, and Mount Seir, whom You did not let Israel invade when they
came out of the land of Egypt, and whom they avoided and did not destroy; behold, they are rewarding us by coming to drive us out of Your
possession that You have given us to inherit." This passage is an allusion to Deut 2:2–8, about *"the descendants of Esau* who live *in Seir"*—
that is, "do not provoke them, for I shall not give you any of their land,
even as much a footstep, since I have given *Mount Seir to Esau* for an
inheritance." There is more in this chapter regarding <u>Moab</u> (verse 9)
and <u>the descendants of Ammon</u> (vv. 18–19);[60] see also Num 20:14–21;
Judg 11:15–26. This allusion also demonstrates that, despite the Chronicler's minimal reference to the Exodus from Egypt, the wanderings in
the desert, and the conquest of the land, he did not deny them.[61]

---

58. שעירים are not mentioned in connection with Jeroboam in the book of Kings,
and the Chronicler may have wanted this addition to blacken Jeroboam's image even
further. For the prohibition of the worship of שעירים, see Lev 17:7; and for the meaning
of the term, see Snaith, "Meaning of שעירים," 115–18.

59. For this, see Exod 29:1; Dillard, *2 Chronicles*, 109.

60. The Chronicler noted the names of the peoples living on the eastern bank
of the Jordan in chiastic order to the order of the parallel text in the book of Deuteronomy.

61. See also 1 Chr 17:21 // 2 Sam 7:23; 2 Chr 5:10 // 1 Kgs 8:9; 2 Chr 6:5 // 1 Kgs
8:16; 2 Chr 7:22 // 1 Kgs 9:9; cf. von Rad, *Geschichtsbild*, 77–78; Williamson, *Chronicles*, 296–97; against Japhet, *Ideology*, 378; idem, "Conquest," 216 n. 58.

10.29 In his speech to the priests and the Levites, Hezekiah, king of Judah, reviewed the condition of the Temple and of the nation and urged his audience to take decisive action (2 Chr 29:4–11). In this review there are a number of allusions to the narration concerning the period of Ahaz, Hezekiah's father, in 2 Chronicles 28.

The words "for our ancestors *transgressed* and did what is evil *in* the eyes of *the Lord*, and they abandoned Him" (29:6) seem to be alluding to 2 Chr 28:19, "for [Ahaz] caused a disturbance in Judah and *transgressed against the Lord*," and to the text further on, 28:22, "And at the time of his distress, he continued *to transgress against the Lord*—he, Ahaz the king" (see also 28:6: "when they abandoned the Lord, the God of their ancestors").

The words "they also *shut the doors* of the porch" (29:7a) allude to what the Chronicler said concerning Ahaz in 28:24: "*And he shut the doors* of the House of the Lord." True enough, unlike Ahaz his father, Hezekiah in his great righteousness, "in the first year of his reign, in the first month,[62] *opened the doors* of the House of the Lord and repaired them" (2 Chr 29:3).

In 29:8–9, "and it came to pass that the wrath of the Lord came upon Judah and Jerusalem, and He made them an object of horror, desolation, and hissing . . . and behold, our fathers fell by the sword, *and our sons and our daughters* and our wives *are in captivity* for this reason," the Chronicler seems to be alluding to what he said about Ahaz in 28:5–8: "Then the Lord delivered him into the hand of the king of Aram, who defeated him *and took captive a great number of his people* and brought them to Damascus; and he was also delivered into the hand of the king of Israel, who defeated him with great slaughter; and Pekah, son of Remaliah, killed one hundred twenty thousand in Judah in a single day . . . , and the people of Israel *captured* two hundred thousand of their kin—women, *sons, and daughters*."[63] It is also possible that these

---

62. The date "in the first year of his reign, during the first month" is a "pseudo-date." The Chronicler used this phrase to say that "Hezekiah the righteous king took care of the affairs of the Temple from his very first day as king" (see Cogan, "Chronology," 201–3). It should be noted that this was stressed even more further on, in v. 17: "[The priests] began *on the first of the very first month* to sanctify [the house]." Thus, on the very day that Hezekiah ascended to his father's throne, he hurried to open the doors of the House of the Lord and even gathered the priests and the Levites together in the eastern square, spoke to them, and urged them to purify the House of the Lord (vv. 3–11). Furthermore, they consecrated themselves on that very day and began to sanctify the House of the Lord (vv. 12–27). These dates also are a kind of "pseudo-date": "And they began *on the first day of the first month* to consecrate. *On the eighth day* of the month they reached the porch of the Lord and consecrated the House of the Lord for eight days. *On the sixteenth day of the first month* they finished."

63. In 2 Chr 29:9 the Chronicler recorded the list of captives in an order that is chiastic with the list in 2 Chr 28:8.

verses contain an allusion to the words of the prophet Oded in 2 Chr 28:9: "Behold, *in the wrath of the Lord, God* of your fathers, *at Judah,* He delivered them into your hand and you have killed them in a rage."

2 Chr 29:8–9 also apparently alludes to 28:17, "Furthermore the Edomites came and defeated Judah and *carried away captives.* And the Philistines also raided the cities of the Judean lowlands and desert" (v. 18).

Chapter 11
Chiasmus

Chiasmus is a term that refers to a bisectional structure (at least) in which the units of the one section repeat in inverse order those of the other section (thus, the *chi-*, or X-shaped, structure of two double-sections). In other words, what heads a series of units in the first section now closes the list in the second, while the item that closes the series here now heads it there.

Chiasmus[1] was a common early literary device used in the literatures of the ancient world. It appears in Sumero-Akkadian literature, Ugaritic literature, the Bible, apocryphal books, New Testament, rabbinic literature, and in classical literature as well.[2] In recent years, all of its forms and degrees have been studied from all points of view, from the framework of single expressions and sentences to the framework of broader literary units.[3] Paradoxically enough, the more that its widespread, variegated use in ancient Near Eastern literature becomes apparent, the more we can narrow our questions concerning the thematic and conceptual literary effects that are embedded in the technical, external structure of chiasmus (especially in limited frameworks): Are these aesthetic-artistic devices aimed at varying the style of a text, thus beautifying it? Or are there deeper meanings hidden in chiastic structures? Many answers to these questions have been proposed: they are mnemonic devices to assist memory; they focus a reader's attention on the topics or concepts at the heart of the chiastic structures; they are a kind of

> framework through which the author may compare, contrast, juxtapose, complement, or complete each of the flanking elements in the chiastic system. In addition, a marked degree of intensification can be introduced throughout the system both by building to a

---

1. For alternate names for this literary device, less common in scholarly literature, see p. 10 in the introduction by Welch (ed.), *Chiasmus in Antiquity.*

2. See the articles and bibliography in ibid. For chiasmus in the New Testament, see also Thomson, *Chiasmus.* On pp. 14–18, Thomson also briefly surveys chiasmus in Semitic and Classical literature. For the biblical literature, see also the secondary sources listed in the footnotes below.

3. For the history of the study of this feature, see ibid., 9.

climax at the center as well as by strengthening each element individually upon its chiastic repetition.[4]

Some even claim that chiastic repetition was the way that people thought and wrote in antiquity. This cannot be true about broad, complex literary units, however, in which chiastic structures had to have been planned deliberately by master authors and poets.

This plethora of answers shows that an overall explanation of the phenomenon has not yet been found. Explanations for individual cases are dependent on the literary senses, deliberations, and understanding of individual scholars. However, even the very identification of a chiastic structure embedded in a text is useful both for literary-structural analysis and for textual, exegetical, and ideological analysis.[5]

1. Chiasmus in the Hebrew Bible and in the Book of Chronicles: The State of the Research

Many studies have been devoted to the phenomenon of chiasmus in the Hebrew Bible, which was identified in various verses as far back as Rabbi Abraham ibn Ezra.[6] Chiastic structures that have been found in the Bible (and in other ancient literatures) have been amassed in a catalog appended to *Chiasmus in Antiquity*, edited by J. W. Welch.[7] A perusal of this catalog reveals that examples of chiasmus have been noted mainly in poetry and biblical prose but rarely in works of history.[8] Thus, while 183 chiastic patterns have been distinguished in Genesis, 273 in Isaiah, and 441 in Psalms, only 33 have been identified in Samuel, 11 in Kings, 10 in Chronicles, and 3 in the books of Ezra and Nehemiah.

---

4. Ibid., 10–15, especially p. 10; D. N. Freedman, in his introduction, ibid., 7; see also various articles on chiasmus that appear there; see the additional literature listed in the following footnotes.

5. For examples of this, see Radday, "Chiasm in Biblical Narrative," 48–72; Kogut, "Chiasm," 196–204; Paran, *Priestly Style*, 163–74.

6. For instance, in ibn Ezra's commentary on Joel 3:3: "'I shall place signs in the heavens / and on the earth—blood and fire and pillars of smoke'—it is the custom of writers in the holy language, when mentioning two things, to begin to relate the words of the second first, and afterwards to go back to the first at the end"; see also his commentary on Exod 17:7, Josh 24:4, and the examples collected by Melammed, *Bible Commentators*, 2.575–76. In addition to the works listed in n. 5 above, the following should be noted: Lund, "Chiasmus in the OT," 104–26; idem, "Chiasmus in the Psalms," 281–312; Loewenstamm, "Chiastic Structures," 1–5; Weiss, "On Chiasmus" (Weiss made no distinction between chiasmus and chiastic parallelism, dealing with them as a single feature); Sappan, "Chiasmus in Biblical Poetry," 534–39; Di Marco, "Der Chiasmus in der Bibel," 36:21–97; 37:49–68; Radday, "Chiasmus," 50–117; Watson, "Chiastic Patterns," 118–68.

7. See Welch (ed.), *Chiasmus in Antiquity*, 287–352.

8. Ibid., 297–338, and see also in detail Radday, "Chiasmus," 50–117; Watson, "Chiastic Patterns," 118–68; and above, n. 6.

A careful examination of the 10 Chronicles references listed in Welch's catalog[9] leaves only 7 of them intact: 1 Chr 9:44; 16:22; 22:14; 24:7; 2 Chr 17:3–4; 17:8a; 32:7–8.[10] There is no sign of a chiastic structure in the other 3 references: 1 Chr 21:8a; 21:8b; 2 Chr 21:10b.[11] Moreover, one of the 7 chiastic structures, 1 Chr 16:22, is not the work of the Chronicler; it is a quotation from Ps 105:15. The remaining 6 examples are found in the "additions" to the books of Samuel–Kings that the Chronicler worked into his Chronicles.

There were 2 other examples of chiastic structure in the "additions" in Chronicles that scholars had already noted, but for some reason they were not mentioned by Welch. One appears in the genealogical lists of Judah in 1 Chr 2:10–4:23;[12] the other is the chiasmus between 1 Chr 23:2, "And [David] gathered together all of the **leaders of Israel** and the priests *and the Levites*," and the continuation, which provides the details: "the courses *of Levites* (23:3–32), the courses *of priests* (chap. 24), and the twelve **leaders** for each month of the year" (chap. 27).[13] After the publication of the book edited by Welch, 3 more examples of chiasmus in the book of Chronicles were published.[14] But out of all of the examples of chiastic structure in the book of Chronicles already considered by scholars, only *one* is the sort that the Chronicler created by changes introduced into the earlier text.[15]

---

9. Ibid., 338.

10. König, *Biblische Literatur*, 145–46, 171–72, dealt with the chiastic structures in 1 Chr 9:44; 22:14; 24:7; 2 Chr 17:8a, which were adduced also by Di Marco, "Der Chiasmus in der Bibel," *LB* 37, 64; F. R. Smith (mentioned in Welch [ed.], *Chiasmus in Antiquity*, 338) pointed to the structure in 1 Chr 16:22; Weiss, "On Chiasmus," 51 considered the structures in 2 Chr 17:3–4; 32:7–8.

11. These three places were first indicated by König and thereafter by Di Marco (see the previous footnote).

12. See Curtis-Madsen, *Chronicles*, 82; Johnson, *Genealogies*, 70; Myers, *I Chronicles*, 159; Williamson, "Genealogy of Judah," 358.

13. Cf. Curtis-Madsen, *Chronicles*, 261; Myers, *I Chronicles*, 159.

14. See Williamson, "We Are Yours," 164–76, especially pp. 168–70; Hill, "1 Chronicles XVI," 97–101, especially p. 100; Dillard, "Solomon Narrative," 85–93, especially pp. 86–90; see also his *2 Chronicles*, 5–7. For the chiastic structures pointed out by Dillard and Williamson, see below, §2. Hill has noted that the Chronicler in 1 Chronicles 16 arranged the psalms he had brought into his work in a chiastic structure:

1 Chr 16:8:	Give thanks unto the Lord	(= Ps 105:1)
16:9:	Sing unto the Lord	(= Ps 105:2)
16:23:	Sing unto the Lord	(= Ps 96:1)
16:34:	Give thanks unto the Lord	(= Ps 107:1)

See also below, example 13.2, n. 14 (p. 280).

15. See Dillard, "Solomon Narrative," 86–90; and also below, example 11.23 (pp. 223–224).

The small number of chiastic structures in Chronicles has been explained by Radday this way: "When they[16] were written, chiasm was no longer en vogue."[17] This explanation, however, is now discredited in light of the chiastic structures found in my research and in light of their frequent use in the rest of the late biblical books[18] and in other literary works from the Second Temple period.[19]

Examples below of chiastic structures created by the Chronicler in changes that he made in the narratives that he borrowed from the books of Samuel–Kings are taken (A) from limited literary units and (B) from larger literary units. Added to these are a number of examples of chiastic structure in the "additions" of the book of Chronicles that have not yet been detected by other scholars.

2. Chiastic Structures

A. Chiastic Structures in Limited Literary Units

11.1 In 1 Chr 2:13, the Chronicler presents the list of the sons of Jesse. The first three names in the list are transmitted in accordance with 1 Sam 17:13 but in reverse word order. This inversion of word order not only creates chiastic parallelism between Chronicles and Samuel, it also creates chiasmus in the book of Chronicles itself:

1 Sam 17:13	*1 Chr 2:13*
And the name of his [Jesse's] three sons . . .	And Jesse[20] became the father of
Eliab the firstborn	his firstborn, *Eliab*,
and his second, *Abinadab*	and *Abinadab*, the second,
and the third, *Shammah*.	and *Shimea*, the third.

1 Chr 2:13
And Jesse became the father of his firstborn, *Eliab*,
and *Abinadab*,   the second.

---

16. Radday is referring to the books of Chronicles, Ezra, and Nehemiah. Here he is following in the footsteps of scholars who view these books as a single composition.

17. Radday, "Chiasmus," 52.

18. For instance, in the books of Haggai, Zechariah, Malachi, Esther, Jonah, and Qohelet. A list of chiastic structures in these books appears in Welch (ed.), *Chiasmus in Antiquity*, 321–23, 337.

19. See Wright, "Structure of the Book of Wisdom," 165–84; the list of references to this literature in the catalog prepared by Welch (ed.), *Chiasmus in Antiquity*, 338–40, and the bibliography adduced there.

20. The name אישׁי appears in the previous verse without א: ישׁי (so also in the parallel text of Ruth 4:22). Compare the biblical name 'Jezebel' איזבל, which has been found inscribed on a seal in the form of יזבל; and see Avigad, "Seal of Jezebel," 274–76, pl. 56.

For a similar rearrangement of an ordinal number and a proper noun so as to create a chiastic structure, compare:

a. 1 Chr 24:7:   And the first lot fell   *to Jehoiarib*;
                 to Jedaiah   the second.
b. 1 Chr 25:9:   And the first lot fell   *for Asaph to Joseph*;
                 to Gedaliahu   the second.

11.2 In 1 Chr 3:4b, the Chronicler gave the sum of the years of David's reign in Hebron and in Jerusalem in reverse order from the order in Samuel,[21] thus creating a chiastic structure in Chronicles:

2 Sam 5:5	*1 Chr 3:4b*
a. *In Hebron*	b. And he reigned
b. he reigned	a. *there* [*in Hebron*][22]
c. . . . seven years and six months.	c. seven years and six months.
a. *In Jerusalem*	c. **Thirty-three years**
b. he reigned	b. he reigned
c. **thirty-three years.**	a. *in Jerusalem.*

1 Chr 3:4b

And he reigned there	seven years and six months.
Thirty-three years	*he reigned in Jerusalem.*

While the parts of the structure are indeed different in literal content, they are identical in general intent.

11.3 In 2 Chr 1:11 the Chronicler adduced the Lord's words to Solomon found in 1 Kgs 3:11 but changed the word order, thus creating chiastic parallelism between the two texts, on the one hand, and a set of chiastic structures within his own composition, on the other hand:

1 Kgs 3:11	*2 Chr 1:11*
a. You did not ask for yourself	c. You did not ask for wealth,
	property and honor, or *the*
	lives of those who hate you.
b. **longevity,**	b. **Also longevity**

---

21. For this, see chap. 12, "Chiasmus between Parallel Texts," pp. 232ff.

22. The changed word order here may stem from the use of a different form of the verb מלך 'to reign' (inverted future, instead of simple past). However, the very decision taken by the Chronicler to use this verb form, which requires an inversion of the order of the words in the text, may well indicate his intention of creating a chiastic parallelism with the text in 2 Sam 5:5, as indeed he does immediately thereafter in 1 Chr 3:4b.

c. and you did not ask for   a. you did not ask for.
   yourself wealth. Nor did you
   ask for *the lives of your*
   enemies.

2 Chr 1:11

And you did not ask for   *wealth, property and honor, or the*
                                  lives of those who hate you.
Also longevity   you did not ask for.
But you did ask for
yourself   *wisdom and knowledge.*

The unit "you did not ask for" merely changes its position, not its meaning, whereas the other unit changes both its position and its literal content, though not its general intent.

11.4 The Chronicler reshaped the list of the descendants of Judah as listed in Genesis 38 in a chiastic structure in 1 Chr 2:3–4:

a. *Er and Onan and Shelah*—   c. **And Tamar, his daughter-in-law,**
b. these three were born to him   b. bore him
c. **of Bath-Shua the Canaanitess.** a. *Peretz and Zerah.*

Chiastic structures are found in the "additions" in the book of Chronicles, as well. For example:

11.5 In the genealogical list of Manasseh in 1 Chr 7:15–16:

And Machir took a wife for Huppim and for Shuppim.
The name of his sister was *Maacah*, and the name of the second
   one was Zelophehad.
And Zelophehad had daughters, while *Maacah*, wife of Machir,
   bore a son whom she named Peresh.

11.6 In his summary of Saul in 1 Chr 10:13–14, the Chronicler wrote:

a. And also to consult *a ghost*   b. to seek guidance,
b'. while not seeking guidance   a'. from *the Lord.*

11.7 In the words of Amasai to David, in 1 Chr 12:19:

To you, David, and with you, son of Jesse,   there is peace.
Peace be   *to you.*

11.8 In the list of David's assistants, in 1 Chr 12:20–21:

a. Some *of the Manassites*

b. deserted to David when he came with the Philistines . . .

b'. As he went to Ziklag, there deserted to him

a'. *of the Manassites* . . .

11.9 In the investiture of Solomon, David called for people to assist his son in building the Temple. The people willingly donated: "Then *rejoiced* **the people** (וישמחו העם) for these had given wholeheartedly, for with a whole heart they had offered freely to the Lord; **David the king** also *rejoiced* (וגם דויד המלך שמח) greatly" (1 Chr 29:9; cf. the building of the Tabernacle in Exod 35:4–29).[23]

11.10 In David's prayer in 1 Chr 29:14–16:

For *all things come from You*

and of Your hand have we given to You . . .

from Your hand it comes

and is all Your own.

11.11 In the prophecy of Shemaiah, the prophet, during Shishak's campaign, found in 2 Chr 12:5–6:

Then Shemaiah, the prophet, came to *Rehoboam*

and to the officials of Judah. . . .

Then the officials of Israel humbled themselves

and the king.

11.12 In the speech by Abijah, king of Judah, from the summit of Mount Zemaraim, in 2 Chr 13:8–11:

a. And now, *you* (אתם) intend to withstand the kingdom of the Lord in the hand of the sons of David, because *you* (אתם) are a great multitude and there are golden calves with you . . .

b. As for us (ואנחנו), the Lord is our God and we have not abandoned Him. . . .

b'. For we (ואנחנו) are keeping the charge of the Lord our God,

a'. but *you* (אתם) have abandoned Him.

Apparently, by this chiastic structure, the Chronicler was attempting to center attention on Judahites who were loyal to the Lord's cult.

---

23. Compare this verse in 1 Chronicles 29 with 2 Chr 15:12–15 and 24:10 and see the discussion of Muffs, *Love and Joy*, 183–86.

11.13 In the narrative of Sennacherib's campaign against Judah, in 2 Chr 32:17:

And he wrote letters defaming the Lord, the God of Israel, and saying of Him,

a. "Just as *the gods of the nations*   b. did not save their people from
   in other lands   my hand,

b'. so [He] will not save,   a'. *the God of Hezekiah*, his people
                               from my hand."

11.14 Relying on the books of Leviticus and Jeremiah about the cause and duration of the Babylonian Exile, the Chronicler wrote in 2 Chr 36:21:

a. *to fulfill* the word of the Lord   b. only when the land has made up
   by the mouth of Jeremiah: for its sabbaths;
   all the days that it lay desolate

b'. it kept sabbath,   a'. *to fulfill* seventy years.

11.15 In the narrative about Josiah's Passover in 2 Chr 35:7–8:

a. Then [he] *raised*,   b. Josiah, for the people a
                             contribution from the flock. . . .

b'. And his officials, as a
   contribution for the people,   a'. . . . [they] *raised*. . . .

11.16 Similarly, 2 Chr 35:13, in the description of the preparation for the Passover sacrifice and the holy offerings:

a. *And they cooked*   b. the passover in fire according
                             to the ordinance,

b'. and the holy offerings   a'. *they cooked* in pots and caldrons
                             and pans.

11.17 In the description of the reign of Jotham, king of Judah, in 2 Chr 27:3:

a. He *built*   b. the upper gate of the House of
                             the Lord,

b'. and on the wall of Ophel   a'. he *built* extensively.

11.18 In the description of the sins of Ahaz, king of Judah, in 2 Chr 28:24b–25:

a. *And he made altars for him*   b. in every corner in Jerusalem,
b'. and in every town of Judah   a'. *he made high places*

11.19 In the description of the destruction of Jerusalem by Nebuchadnezzar in 2 Chr 36:19, the Chronicler created a twofold chiastic structure:

a. Then *they burned*
    and tore down
b′. All of her palaces
    and all of her worthy vessels

b. the House of God
    the wall of Jerusalem.
a′. *they burned with fire,*
    they destroyed.

11.20 In the Lord's promise to Solomon, in 2 Chr 1:12:

a. *It was not like this* with the kings
b′. and after you

b. who were before you,
a′. *it will not be like this.*

11.21 In the description of the armies that took part in the war between Abijah, king of Judah, and Jeroboam, king of Israel, in 2 Chr 13:3:

a. *With an army of valiant warriors . . .*
b′. chosen men

b′. chosen men . . .
a′. *mighty, valiant warriors.*[24]

11.22 In the details of the annual tribute brought to Jotham, king of Judah, by the Ammonites, in 2 Chr 27:5:

a. *ten thousand measures*
b′. and of barley

b. of wheat,
a′. *ten thousand.*

B. Chiastic Structures in Larger Literary Units

Alongside the "simple" chiastic structures in limited literary units, the Chronicler also created chiastic structures in units of broader scope, an indication of his literary-artistic talents:

11.23 It seems that the narrative of Solomon's reign in 2 Chronicles 1–9 was formulated in accordance with a chiastic structure, as Dillard has shown (see outline, p. 224).[25] Thus, the dedication of the Temple and the appearance of the cloud of glory within it, the choice of Jerusalem, the promise to David, and the readiness to forgive are presented at the center of the structure. Is it not possible that, at the very center of this chiastic structure, the Chronicler desired to focus his readers' attention on just these matters, which were so significant to him?

---

24. The MT phrase גבור חיל 'man of war' in the Targum, Peshiṭta, and Vulgate is גבורי חיל 'men of war'.

25. See Dillard, "Solomon Narrative," 86–90.

A. Solomon's wealth and wisdom (1:1–17)
   B. Recognition by nations and dealings with Hiram (2:1–17)
      C. Temple construction / foreign labor (3:1–5:1)
         D. Dedication of the Temple (5:2–7:10)
            1. a. Summons ⎫
               b. Sacrifice ⎬ (5:2–14)
               c. Music
               d. Cloud of Glory ⎭
            2. Solomon speaks to the people (6:1–11)
               a. Exodus (6:5)
               b. Choice of Jerusalem (6:6–11)
            2′. Solomon speaks to God (6:12–42)
               a. Promises to David (6:16–17)
               b. Eyes open; hear and forgive (6:20–21)
            1′. d′. Cloud of Glory ⎫
                 c′. Music ⎬ (7:1–10)
                 b′. Sacrifice
                 a′. Dismissal ⎭
         D′. Divine response (7:11–22)
            2″. God speaks to Solomon (7:12–18)
               b. Eyes open; hear and forgive (7:13–16)
               a. Promises to David (7:17–18)
            2‴. God speaks to the people (7:19–22)
               b. Choice of Jerusalem (7:19–21)
               a. Exodus (7:22)
      C′. Other construction / foreign labor (8:1–16)
   B′. Recognition by nations and dealings with Hiram (8:17–9:12)
A′. Solomon's wealth and wisdom (9:13–28)

Additionally, it appears that the Chronicler created the following chiastic structures (though more limited in their scope) within his narrative of Solomon's reign:

11.24 The words that conclude 1 Kgs 8:10, 'והענן מלא את בית ה '*the cloud filled the House of the Lord*', are repeated at the end of the following verse as well, 'מפני הענן כי מלא כבוד ה' את בית ה '*because of the cloud, for the glory of the Lord filled the House of the Lord*'. The Chronicler copied these words into his book once in the order of chiastic parallelism (2 Chr 5:13b // 1 Kgs 8:10b) and once in the order in which they appear in the earlier text (2 Chr 5:14b // 1 Kgs 8:11b). Thus, these verses are

not an addition to the book of Chronicles by a later editor, as claimed
by Rudolph.[26]

1 Kgs 8:10–11	2 Chr 5:11a, 13b–14
10. And it came to pass, when the priests were leaving the holy place, *and the cloud* filled **the House of the Lord**.	11a. And it came to pass, when the priests were leaving the holy place . . . 13b. **The House** was filled *with the cloud* of the House of the Lord.[27]
11. And the priests could not stand to officiate because of *the cloud,* for the glory of the Lord filled **the House of the Lord**.[28]	14. And the priests could not stand to officiate because of *the cloud* for the glory of the Lord filled **the House of God**.[29]

It appears that the inverted word order here was intended not just to
create chiastic parallelism between 2 Chr 5:13b and 1 Kgs 8:10b (with
all that this entails)[30] but mainly to formulate a structure of chiasmus
(of three members) between the two texts that he copied into his book:

---

26. Rudolph, *Chronik*, 211; in this respect, see also, at length below, example 14.2 (pp. 299–300).

27. This repetition of the word "House" is misplaced, apparently stemming from a gloss based on the following v. 14b (as in the parallel text in 1 Kgs 8:11). Some suggest reading as in the LXX^{A, B, L} δόξης κύριον 'cloud of glory'; see, e.g., Begrich, *BH*, 1383; Rudolph, *Chronik*, 211.

28. Wevers ("Double Readings," 308) assumes that two occurrences of the term "the Lord" in the MT are the result of a double reading: in the one reading, the term "the Lord" comes after the word "glory," a reading that has survived in the LXX: ἐπλη-σεν δόξα κυρίου τὸν οἶκον 'and the glory of the Lord filled the House'; and in the other reading, the term "the Lord" comes after the word "House," a reading that has survived in K₃₀: "and glory filled the House of the Lord" (Wevers's general meaning is clear, but the wording of his aforesaid article seems to be erroneous. The wording here has been adduced after correcting the error). At any rate, the present wording of the text is reflected in 2 Chr 5:14 (with the interchange of "the Lord"/"God") and in 2 Chr 7:2 (an "addition"): "for the glory of the Lord filled the House of the Lord." That is, even if there is a "double reading" in the MT, it took place at a very early stage, reflected in the Chronicler's *Vorlage*.

29. Whatever the reason was for the interchange "the Lord"/"God," one must not ignore the fact that here it creates a variation in style by not repeating the term "the Lord" mentioned earlier in the expressions "glory of the Lord" (v. 14) and "the cloud (of the House) of the Lord" (v. 13). See also n. 30 (below) and example 15.19 (pp. 345–346).

30. In addition to the change in word order, the Chronicler attempted to vary the style of the earlier text by making use of parallel terms as well: "the House" instead

A. *And the House*
  B. *was filled*
    C. *with the cloud (of the House) of the Lord.*
      D. **And the priests could not stand to officiate**
    C'. because of *the cloud,*
  B'. for the glory of the Lord *filled*
A'. *the House of God.*

By means of this chiastic structure, the Chronicler apparently tried to focus his readers' attention on the words positioned in the center of the structure: "the priests could not stand to officiate." The central position of these words becomes clearer in light of the analogy between this verse and the verse in which Moses completed erecting the Tabernacle: "**Moses could not come into the Tent of Meeting**, for *the cloud* rested on it, and the glory of the Lord *filled the Tabernacle*" (Exod 40:35). 2 Chr 5:13 thus shows that the sanctity of the new Temple was no less than the sanctity of the Tabernacle that Moses constructed in the desert. The holiness was so intense that it was not possible to worship the Lord in the place designated for worship, the Tabernacle/Temple. This intensity is expressed in the following example as well.

11.25 In 2 Chr 7:1–2 (an "addition"), the Chronicler repeated the above text, concluding it with Solomon's prayer, and making certain stylistic emendations and variations (these will be discussed elsewhere).[31] Here also the Chronicler adduced the text once in chiasmus in parallel order and once as it was, apparently with the purpose of creating a chiastic structure in his work that had the inability of the priests to enter the House of the Lord at its center:

1 Kgs 8:11 // 2 Chr 5:14	*2 Chr 7:1*	*2 Chr 7:2*
And the priests could not stand to officiate because of the cloud,		And the priests could not enter the House of the Lord,
for it filled,	and the <u>glory of the Lord</u>	*for it filled,*
<u>the glory of the Lord</u>,	*filled*	<u>the glory of the Lord</u>,
the House of the Lord/God.	the House.	the House of the Lord.

---

of "the House of the Lord"; "the cloud (of the House) of the Lord" instead of "the cloud" (v. 13); "the House of God" instead of "the House of the Lord" (v. 14).

31. By this repetition the Chronicler creates an *inclusio* for Solomon's prayer. On this issue, see in detail below, example 14.2 (pp. 299–300).

2 Chr 7:1–2
  A. *And the glory of the Lord*
    B. *filled* <u>the House</u>.
      C. **And the priests could not enter the House of the Lord**,
    B'. for it *filled*,
  A'. *the glory of the Lord*, <u>the House of the Lord</u>.

11.26 1 Kgs 10:14–15 speaks of the gold that Solomon received from various governors and tradesmen in his kingdom. The Chronicler copied this text into his book (2 Chr 9:13–14), adding "bringing gold and silver to Solomon" at the end (14b):

1 Kgs 10:14–15	*2 Chr 9:13–14*
The weight of the gold that came to Solomon	*The weight of the gold that came to Solomon*
in a single year was	in a single year was
six hundred sixty-six talents of	six hundred sixty-six talents of
gold, besides what came from	gold, besides what came from
the merchants and the traders	the merchants and the traders
and all the kings of Arabia and	bringing [goods] and all the kings of
the governors of the land	Arabia and the governors of the land
	coming with gold and silver
	to Solomon.

Because the noun "gold" and the verb root בו״א ('come') had already been mentioned at the opening of the text (2 Chr 9:13a = 1 Kgs 10:14a), mentioning them again in the expression under consideration in inverted order created a chiastic structure in the Chronicler's book:

  A. The weight of the *gold*
    B. that <u>came</u> to Solomon
      C. in a single year was six hundred sixty-six talents of gold,
        besides what came from the merchants and the traders
        bringing [goods] and all the kings of Arabia and the
        governors of the land
    B'. <u>coming with</u>[32]
  A'. *gold* and silver to Solomon.

The similarity of the concluding words to the opening words of the passage serves to frame the text between them.[33] Using the root בוא (in its plural form) and the noun "gold" in chiastic order in the

---

32. The subject of "coming with" is "all the kings of Arabia and the governors of the land," while the subject of "comes" is "gold."
33. For this, see example 14.9 (pp. 307–308).

two sections of the frame apparently served to attract the attention of the reader to the material between them—"see the vast amount of gold that reached Solomon *in a single year!*"—highlighting the king's great wealth and magnificence, which was what the Lord had promised to Solomon.

11.27 The narrative about David's installation as king in 1 Chronicles 11–12, which partially parallels verses in 2 Samuel 5 and 23, is formulated in a chiastic structure:[34]

A. 1 Chr 11:1–9 (// 2 Sam 5:1–10) David's coronation at Hebron
      (and the capture of Jerusalem)
   B. 1 Chr 11:10–47 (// 2 Sam 23:8–39) Support for David at Hebron
      C. 1 Chr 12:1–8 ("addition") Support for David at Ziklag
         D. 1 Chr 12:9–16 ("addition") Support for David at the
            stronghold
         D′. 1 Chr 12:17–19 ("addition") Support for David at the
            stronghold
      C′. 1 Chr 12:20–23 ("addition") Support for David at Ziklag
   B′. 1 Chr 12:24–38 ("addition") Support for David at Hebron
A′. 1 Chr 12:39–41 ("addition") David's coronation at Hebron

Support from mighty warriors at the stronghold is what is stressed at the center of the structure.

11.28 At the opening of the genealogy of the tribe of Reuben in 1 Chr 5:1–3a the Chronicler wrote (according to the narrative in the book of Genesis):

A. *The children of Reuben, the firstborn of Israel,* for he was the
      firstborn,
   B. but, because he desecrated his father's couch, his birthright was
         given to the sons of Joseph, son of Israel, so that he is not
         related in the genealogy to the birthright.
      C. **For Judah became prominent among his brothers and
         a candidate for leadership came from him,**
   B′. but the birthright was Joseph's.
A′. *The children of Reuben, the firstborn of Israel. . . .*

Scholars have already noticed this chiastic structure in 1 Chr 5:1–3a.[35] The only point that remains to be noted here is that each of the sections of the structure (A–B; B′–A′) is itself designed chiastically,

---

34. See Williamson, "We Are Yours," 168–70.
35. See Shinan-Zakovitch, *Reuben and Bilhah*, 14.

in addition to the chiastic structuring of the entire unit, which placed *Judah* at its center.

Section A–B: 1 Chr 5:1

a. *The children of Reuben,*   b. the firstborn of Israel . . .
b'. his birthright was given   a'. *to the sons of Joseph.*

Section B'–A': 1 Chr 5:2–3

b. but the birthright   a. *was Joseph's.*
a'. *The children of Reuben,*   b'. the firstborn of Israel. . . .

This feature is also found in the "additions" in the book of Chronicles. For example:

11.29 The text in 2 Chr 17:1–5 reads as follows concerning Jehoshaphat, king of Judah:

> And Jehoshaphat his son reigned in his stead and strengthened himself against Israel.

A. *He placed* forces *in all* the fortified cities of *Judah* and *appointed* viceroys in the land of *Judah.* . . .
  B. The Lord was with Jehoshaphat,
    C. for he walked
      D. in the former ways of David his father;
        E. nor did he *inquire* of the Baals,
        E'. but of the God of his fathers he *inquired,*
      D'. and in His commandments
    C'. he walked. . . .
  B'. Therefore, the Lord established the kingdom in his hand,
A'. and *all Judah placed* tribute before Jehoshaphat.[36]

The Chronicler may have been trying to direct the reader to his main statement about Jehoshaphat by means of this chiastic structure: "nor did he inquire of the Baals, but of the God of his fathers he inquired." In fact, this sentence is emphatic, not only by virtue of its position at the very center of the chiastic structure but also by its statement of opposition ("nor . . . but . . .")[37] and internal chiastic

---

36. Weiss noted the chiasmus between the verbs הלך 'walk' and דרש 'inquire' in vv. 3–4 but overlooked the complex chiastic structure of the entire unit ("On Chiasmus," 51).

37. Compare this antithetical statement with a similar structure that the Chronicler created with regard to Saul in 1 Chr 10:13–14 (see above, example 11.6, p. 220). However, from the standpoint of content, Jehoshaphat's words are diametrically opposed to Saul's, and he may have tried to create an contrastive analogy between the two royal figures; for this, see example 15.13 (p. 339).

design. Precisely at the turning point of the complex chiastic construction of the larger unit, the Chronicler also created a "simple"
chiastic pattern in order once again to attract the attention of the
reader to the most significant point of the entire unit.

From a literary-technical standpoint, the Chronicler may have been
trying to say that, from this point on, the members are adduced in inverted order.

11.30 The speech delivered by Jahaziel, son of Zechariah, in 2 Chr
20:14–18:

> Then the spirit of the Lord settled on Jahaziel, son of Zechariah,
> . . . in the middle of the assembly, and he said:
>
> A. "Listen, *all Judah and inhabitants of Jerusalem*
>   B. and King *Jehoshaphat,* . . .
>   C. *You—be not afraid and do not fear* . . . ,
>   D. *for the battle is not yours but God's; tomorrow go down*
>   against them. . . .
>   D'. *It is not for you to fight* this battle; take your position,
>   stand still, and see *the Lord's salvation* on your behalf.
>   C'. *Do not be afraid, do not fear.* . . ."
>   B'. Then *Jehoshaphat* bowed, his face to the ground,
> A'. *and all Judah and the inhabitants of Jerusalem* fell down before the
>   Lord to worship the Lord.[38]

The Chronicler was apparently trying to make the view expressed at
the center of the unit more prominent: *"the battle is . . . God's."* In
fact, this view is found in other places in the book of Chronicles as
well—for example, in connection with the battle of the Reubenites,
Gadites, and half-tribe of Manasseh against the Hagrites, Jetur, Na-
phish, and Nodab: "When they received help against them, the Hagrites were delivered into their hand together with all that were with
them, for they had cried out to God in the battle and He had turned
to them because they trusted in Him. . . . There were many casualties, *because the battle was of God*" (1 Chr 5:18–22).[39]

---

38. In his expanded article, Weiss ("Chiasm in the Bible," 270) notes the chiastic
parallelism between vv. 15 and 17:

> v. 15: Be not afraid and do not fear . . . *for the war is not for you* . . .
> v. 17: *It is not for you* . . . do not be afraid and do not fear.

Weiss, however, did not discern the complex chiastic structure of the entire unit, as
presented above.

39. For the connection between 1 Chr 5:18–22 and 1 Chr 5:10, see Japhet, *Ideology*, 192 n. 566.

It should be noted that occasionally the Chronicler also copied chiastic structures that he found in the earlier texts, such as 1 Chr 6:40–41[55–56] // Josh 21:11–13:

> *They gave them* <u>Hebron</u>. . . .

> <u>But the fields of the city and its villages</u> *they gave to Caleb, son of Jephunneh.*

> *To the sons of Aaron they gave* <u>the cities of refuge and Hebron</u>. . . .

See also 1 Chr 16:22 // Ps 105:15. These duplications of existing chiastic structures of course increase the total number of chiastic structures found in Chronicles.

Chapter 12
Chiasmus between Parallel Texts

Chiasmus between parallel texts, in the sense that I am using this phrase in this book, is the presentation of textual components in an order that is the inverse of the order in which they appear in another literary framework, so that placing the two texts opposite one another gives rise to a chiastic structure.

The exploitation of this technique apparently stems primarily from an author-copyist's natural need to vary a text without altering its contents. Furthermore, adducing a text in chiastic order renders the copyist's active intervention in the text he is copying more prominent. Seidel assumed that biblical authors made use of this technique whenever they wanted to quote a verse from another book: "A prophet who uses the airy wording of a verse hovering before his very eyes, uses it in inverted order, writes the latter phrase in that verse first, and the former phrase subsequently."[1] Weiss explained it in picturesque language: "Just as a person ties the end of one string to the beginning of the next, so the poet, wishing to consider something that has been said, does it by referring first to the latter part and then to the earlier part."[2]

The Chronicler copied words and phrases into his book in inverse order from their order of appearance in the books of Samuel–Kings, creating "chiastic parallelism" between his text and the earlier text. It should be stressed that, despite his prolific, varied use of this technique, the actual number of earlier texts presented chiastically in the book of Chronicles is small relative to the total number of texts copied in the order in which they appear in the books of Samuel–Kings.

The reasons listed above for the creation of "chiasmus between parallel texts" apply to the Chronicler as well as to other biblical authors. Moreover, occasionally the Chronicler inverted the word order of the earlier text in order to introduce variety of meaning—that is, to stress a word, name, or phrase that appeared in the earlier text or to render it more prominent.[3] Sometimes, the presentation of a text in the order of chiasmus between parallel texts had a direct effect on its contents: whether by clarifying it (for example, כל הרצין העם // כל העם הרצים, 2 Kgs

---

1. Seidel, "Parallels," 2.
2. Weiss, *Bible from Within*, 94–95.
3. For examples of this, see chap. 8, "Character Creation."

11:13 // 2 Chr 23:12)[4] or by a deliberate diversion in order to neutralize a difficulty (for example, inverting the order of events in the narrative on Jehoshaphat's stumbling attempt to set sail for Ophir, 2 Chr 20:35–37 // 1 Kgs 22:49–50).[5] Occasionally, the adducing of the early text in the order of "chiasmus between parallel texts" was mainly intended to create a structure of "chiasmus between parallel texts" within the framework of a literary unit (or between two literary units) in the book of Chronicles itself[6] and/or to create a chiastic structure in the book.[7]

Familiarity with the feature can also refute conclusions about history, textual and otherwise, that various scholars have sought to draw from changes in the word order in a text.

This literary-structural phenomenon is not unique to the Chronicler but is also known from parallel texts in other books of the Hebrew Bible. In the past, the study of this feature in the Hebrew Bible has focused to a large extent on parallel texts found in the various kinds of poetic literature, such as parallels between prophetic texts and psalms (for instance, between Isaiah/Jeremiah and the Psalms) or between the prophecies of various prophets (for example, between Jeremiah and Obadiah, Isaiah, Amos, or Habakkuk). Similarly, the phenomenon has been observed between prophecy and proverbs (such as between Isaiah and Proverbs) or between psalms or prophecy and the Pentateuch (such as between the Psalms and the Torah or between Micah and the Torah).[8] The phenomenon also appears between parallel laws in the Pentateuch (for instance, between Exod 23:8, וְשֹׁחַד לֹא תִקָּח 'and a bribe *you shall not take*', and Deut 16:19, וְלֹא תִקַּח שֹׁחַד 'and *you shall not take* a bribe'), and between 2 Kings 25 and Jeremiah 52 (for instance, 2 Kgs 25:7, וְאֶת בְּנֵי צִדְקִיָּהוּ שָׁחֲטוּ לְעֵינָיו 'the sons of Zedekiah *they slew* before his eyes', and Jer

---

4. For the relevant discussion, see example 6.5 (p. 114).

5. See example 6.7 (pp. 115–119).

6. See the examples below, in §4 (pp. 256ff.).

7. See the examples above, in chap. 11 (pp. 215ff.).

8. For instance, Seidel found 110 examples of "chiasmus between parallel texts" in parallels between the book of Isaiah and the book of Psalms (Seidel, "Parallels," 1–97). He also pointed them out in parallels between the book of Isaiah and the book of Proverbs (idem, "Phraseology," 98–108); and between Micah and the Pentateuch (idem, "Micah, Chapter 6," 142–56; see also his *Studies in Bible*, 4–6 n. 4). Weiss dealt with this phenomenon in parallels between Psalms and the Pentateuch (*Bible from Within*, 95, 97) and between phrases repeated in the selfsame literary sector (ibid., 113–16; for this, see also Seidel, "Inner Parallels," 109–21). Structures of "chiasmus between parallel texts" also exist in parallel passages between Jeremiah and Psalms. For examples, see Brin-Hoffman, "Chiasmus in the Bible," 283, 289; Garsiel, "Parallels between Jeremiah and Psalms," 44. Similarly between Jeremiah and the books of Deuteronomy, Amos, Isaiah, Habakkuk, and Obadiah; see Brin and Hoffman, "Chiasmus in the Bible," 285–89.

52:10, ‎וישחט מלך בבל את בני צדקיהו לעיניו 'the king of Babylon *slew* the sons of Zedekiah before his eyes'). Nevertheless, the examples below show for the first time the existence, scope, and variety of this phenomenon in the parallel historiographical texts. Contrary to most of the examples found in other studies, where it is difficult to determine which writer used the other's text with "chiasmus between parallel texts," in our examples it is self-evident that the Chronicler made use of the earlier text because of the relatively precise dating of the parallel texts.

In these examples, I have discerned "chiasmus between parallel texts" (1) in structures created when the same words and phrases found in the text of Samuel–Kings were copied and (2) in structures in which synonymous words or phrases (or those of similar meaning) replace the words of the earlier text. I also show a number of instances in which (3) the Chronicler borrowed from other biblical books but reordered the material to create chiasmus and, similarly, in which he repeated certain elements in "additions," creating chiasmus between parallel texts. Finally, I present cases (4) in which the words of the text from Samuel–Kings were borrowed in inverted order in order to create a structure of chiasmus between parallel texts within the framework of the book of Chronicles itself.

1. Chiasmus between Parallel Texts: Using the Words of the Earlier Text

Two-Member Structures

12.1 2 Sam 7:20 ‎ומה יוסיף **דוד** עוד לדבר אליך
And what can **David** say *more* to you?

  1 Chr 17:18 ‎מה יוסיף עוד **דויד** אליך
And what *more* can **David** add?

12.2 2 Sam 10:19 ‎ויראו ארם להושיע **עוד** *את בני־עמון*
So the Arameans were afraid **anymore** to help *the Ammonites*.

  1 Chr 19:19 ‎ולא אבה ארם להושיע *את בני־עמון* **עוד**
So the Arameans were not willing to help *the Ammonites* **anymore**.[9]

---

9. Compare Isa 62:8 MT: ‎אם אתן את דגנך **עוד** מאכל לאיביך 'I shall not give **your grain** *any more* to be food for your enemies'.

1QIsa[b]: ‎אם אתן **עוד** את דגנך מאכל לאיביך 'I shall not give *any more* **your grain** as food for your enemies'.

See below, n. 10, and pp. 245–246 n. 31.

12.3   1 Kgs 10:5   ולא היה **בה** עוד רוח

                 And there was not **in her** spirit *any longer*.

          2 Chr 9:4   ולא היה עוד **בה** רוח

                 And there was *no longer* any spirit **in her**.

The following example may also be useful here:

          2 Sam 5:13   ויולדו **עוד** לדוד בנים ובנות

                 And there were **more** born *to David*, sons

                 and daughters.

          1 Chr 14:3   ויולד דויד **עוד** בנים ובנות

                 And *David* had **more** sons and daughters.

However, it is also possible that this change occurred due to the shift from the passive *Niphal* in Samuel (ויולדו) to the active *Hiphil* in Chronicles (ויולד).[10]

12.4   2 Sam 24:4   **ויחזק** דבר המלך אל יואב

                 And there **prevailed** against Joab *the word*

                 of the king.

          1 Chr 21:4   ודבר המלך **חזק** על יואב

                 And *the word of the king* **prevailed** against

                 Joab.

The only point distinguishing ויחזק ("imperfect" *waw*-consecutive) and חזק (simple past) is the shift from the consecutive tenses that were

---

10. This feature, one text copied from another but in chiastic order, can also be discerned in comparing the MT of the Torah with the Samaritan. A number of examples are similar to the examples considered here:

(a) Gen 8:21   MT: לא אסף **לקלל עוד** את האדמה 'I will not *curse* the earth **ever again**'.

            Sam.:   לא אסף עוד **לקלל** את האדמה 'I will **never again** *curse* the earth'

(b) Gen 35:10   MT: לא יקרא **שמך עוד** יעקב '**Your name** will not be Jacob *any longer*'.

            Sam.:   לא יקרא עוד **שמך** יעקב '*No longer* will **your name** be Jacob'.

(c) Deut 34:10   MT: ולא קם **נביא עוד** בישראל כמשה 'No **prophet** has *since* arisen in Israel like Moses'.

            Sam.:   ולא קם עוד **נביא** בישראל כמשה 'Never *since* has there arisen **a prophet** in Israel like Moses'.

(d) Lev 18:23   MT: לא תתן שכבתך **לטמאה בה** '. . . **to be defiled** *with it*'

            Sam.:   לא תתן שכבתך **בה לטמאה** '. . . *with it* **to be defiled**'

For additional examples, see Sperber, "Parallel Transmission," 240–42 §121; Talmon, "Textual Study," 156.

characteristic of the language of the classic biblical books to the tenses more common to the later books of the Hebrew Bible.

12.5 1 Kgs 8:65   ויעש שלמה **בעת ההיא** *את החג* וכל ישראל עמו קהל גדול
So Solomon held **at that time** *the feast*, and all Israel with him, a great assembly. . . .

    2 Chr 7:8   ויעש שלמה *את החג* **בעת ההיא** וכל ישראל עמו קהל גדול מאד
So Solomon held *the feast* **at that time**, and all Israel with him, a very great assembly. . . .

12.6 1 Kgs 10:3   לא היה **דבר** *נעלם* מן המלך
There was **nothing** *hidden* from the king.

    2 Chr 9:2   ולא *נעלם* **דבר** משלמה
There was *hidden* **nothing** from Solomon.

12.7 2 Sam 24:18   עלה הקם **לה׳** *מזבח*
Ascend, set up **to the Lord** *an altar*.

    1 Chr 21:18   כי יעלה דויד להקים *מזבח* **לה׳**
David will ascend to set up *an altar* **to the Lord**.

12.8 1 Kgs 15:13   וגם את מעכה . . . אשר עשתה **מפלצת** *לאשרה*
And also Maacah . . . who made **an abomination** *for Asherah*.

    2 Chr 15:16   וגם מעכה . . . אשר עשתה *לאשרה* **מפלצת**[11]
And also Maacah . . . who made *for Asherah* **an abomination**.

12.9 2 Sam 5:11   וישלח חירם . . . אל דוד ועצי ארזים **וחרשי עץ** *וחרשי אבן קיר*
Hiram sent . . . David cedar trees and **carpenters** and *stone*[12] *masons*.

    1 Chr 14:1   וישלח חירם . . . אל דויד ועצי ארזים *וחרשי קיר* **וחרשי עצים**
Hiram sent . . . David cedar logs and *stone masons* and **carpenters**.

---

11. Compare the last two examples with the chiastic structure in 1 Chr 29:21: ויזבחו לה׳ *זבחים* ויעלו עלות **לה׳** 'Then they sacrificed **to the Lord** *sacrifices* and offered *burnt-offerings* **to the Lord**.

12. The word אבן 'stone', which does not appear in Chronicles, also does not appear in 4QSamª, קיר [וח]רשי עץ וחרשי '[and car]penters and masons' (see Cross, "Biblical Text," 293), or in the Lucianic recension: καὶ τέκτονας ξύλων καὶ τέκτονας τοίχου ('and carpenters and masons'). In Codex Vaticanus, the word קיר 'wall' is missing: καὶ τέκτονας ξύλων καὶ τέκτονας λίθων ('and carpenters and stone masons'). As Talmon

12.10 2 Kgs 22:6   לחרשים ולבנים ולגדרים ולקנות **עצים ואבני מחצב**
to the carpenters and to the builders and to the
masons for buying **timber** and *quarried stone.*

2 Chr 34:11   ויתנו לחרשים ובנים לקנות **אבני מחצב ועצים**
they gave it to the carpenters and the builders
to buy *quarried stone* and **timber.** [13]

12.11 1 Sam 31:13   ויקחו את עצמתיהם **ויקברו**
Then they took **their bones** *and buried them.*

1 Chr 10:12   **ויקברו** את עצמותיהם
Then *they buried* **their bones.** [14]

12.12 2 Sam 10:9   וירא יואב כי היתה **אליו** *פני המלחמה*
Joab saw that **against him** was *set the battle.*

1 Chr 19:10   וירא יואב כי היתה *פני המלחמה* **אליו**
And Joab saw that *the battle* was *set* **against
him.**

("Textual Study," 155 n. 211) suggests, the word אבן may be either a reading synonymous with the word קיר or a later gloss of this word; see his discussion of these verses
in his writings: Talmon, *Double Readings,* 20; idem, "Massoretic Text," 167; idem,
"Textual Transmission," 121. The plural form of the word עצים, instead of עץ in the
earlier text, is common in later Hebrew; compare with אנשי שמות 'men of fame' (pl.
'fame') (1 Chr 5:24; 13:20) in contrast to אנשי שם 'men of fame' (sing. 'fame') (in Gen
6:4). For additional examples, see Weiss, "The Language of Chronicles," 88–89.

13. Compare this example with 1 Chr 22:2, 4, in which the Chronicler describes
David's preparations for the building of the Temple this way: ויעמד חצבים לחצוב אבני גזית
לבנות בית האלהים . . . ועצי ארזים לאין מספר 'And he engaged stonecutters to quarry **hewn
stone** to build the House of God . . . and *cedar logs* without number.' Further along,
in vv. 14–15, David tells Solomon about his preparations: "With great pains I have
prepared for the House of the Lord . . . *and timber* **and stone** (ועצים ואבנים) I have prepared, and you may add to these. You have an abundance of workmen: hewers and
workers of **stone** *and timber* (אבן ועץ) and those skillful in any kind of work." For a
similar feature, see Jer 2:27: "Who say *to a log:* 'You are my father' and **to a stone:**
'You have begotten me'"; Jer 3:9: "and she committed adultery with **a stone** and *a
log.*" This is also true in regard to iron and bronze in 1 Chr 22:3, in the description of
David's preparations: "and **iron** in abundance . . . and *bronze* in abundance, *beyond
weighing*"; further on, when David tells Solomon of his preparations, he says: "*bronze*
and **iron** *beyond weighing,* for it was in such abundance" (v. 14; cf. also v. 16).

14. For a similar example, see: 1 Kgs 15:24: **וישכב** אסא . . . **ויקברו** 'Then Asa **lay
down** . . . *and they buried him*'; 2 Chr 15:14: **ויקברהו** בקברתיו **וישכיבהו** במשכב 'Then they
buried him in his burial place **and they laid him down** in his resting place', except
that, here, active (Chronicles) and passive (Kings) verb forms are used. From here on,
the examples are arranged according to order of appearance in the book of Chronicles.

12.13 2 Sam 10:11   ויאמר אם תחזק ארם *ממני*

He said, "If the **Arameans** are too strong *for me*."

1 Chr 19:12   ויאמר אם תחזק *ממני* ארם

He said, "If too strong *for me* are the **Arameans**."

12.14 2 Sam 10:12   וה' *יעשה* *הטוב בעיניו*

And the Lord **will do** *what seems good to Him*.

1 Chr 19:13   וה' *הטוב בעיניו* *יעשה*

And *what seems good to Him* the Lord **will do**.

12.15 2 Sam 10:13   ויגש יואב והעם אשר עמו *למלחמה* *בארם*

And Joab and the people who were with him went out **to war** *against the Arameans*.

1 Chr 19:14   ויגש יואב והעם אשר עמו לפני *ארם* *למלחמה*

And Joab and the people who were with him went out *against the Arameans* **to war**.

The change in preposition used—ב in Samuel, לפני in Chronicles—has nothing to do with the word order chosen by the Chronicler.

12.16 1 Kgs 3:13   וגם אשר לא שאלת *נתתי לך* גם *עשר* גם כבוד

And **I** also **give you** what you have not requested, both *riches* and *honor*.

2 Chr 1:11–12   יען אשר . . . ולא שאלת עשר נכסים וכבוד . . . *ועשר* ונכסים *וכבוד אתן לך*

Because . . . you did not request riches, property, and honor . . . , *riches*, property, *and honor* **I will** also **give you**.

12.17 1 Kgs 10:28b   ומקוה סחרי המלך *יקחו* *מקוה* במחיר

. . . from Kue, and the king's merchants **received** them *from Kue* at a price.

2 Chr 1:16b   ומקוא סחרי המלך *מקוא* *יקחו* במחיר

. . . from Kue, and the king's merchants *from Kue* **received** them at a price.

The inverted word order in 2 Chr 1:16b obviously cannot serve as a basis for the claim made by Schley[15] that the text contains the remnant of an early lyric fragment: מקוה סחרי המלך / מקוה יקחו במחיר. This inverted word order is the Chronicler's doing and not, as Schley imagines, the work

---

15. Schley, "1 Kings 10:26–29," 595–601, especially pp. 597–99.

of the redactor of the book of Kings in converting early poetry to prose. Schley's proposal is also invalidated by the very fact that the earlier text, 1 Kgs 10:26–29, was based on an official document of the realm, written in prose. Talmon[16] is of the opinion that the position of the word קוה/א in the text was not stable, so that, in each of the two parallel texts, "two separate readings were preserved":

ומקוה(א) סחרי המלך יקחו במחיר	(1 Kings and 2 Chronicles)
סחרי המלך יקחו מקוה במחיר	(1 Kings)
סחרי המלך מקוא יקחו במחיר	(2 Chronicles).

If this was indeed the case, the change before us is a change in wording, not in literary style.

12.18 1 Kgs 10:29   ותעלה ותצא מרכבה ממצרים
                       A chariot was imported *from Egypt.*

        2 Chr 1:17   ויעלו ויוציאו ממצרים מרכבה
                       They imported *from Egypt* **a chariot**.

12.19 1 Kgs 8:29   להיות עיניך פתחת אל הבית הזה לילה ויום
                       That Your eyes may be open toward this House
                       night *and day.*

        2 Chr 6:20   להיות עיניך פתחות אל הבית הזה יומם ולילה
                       That Your eyes may be open toward this House
                       day **and night**.[17]

The Septuagint (OG and Lucianic version) of Kings has ἡμέρας καὶ νυκτός ('day and night'). It is difficult to determine here whether the Chronicler was reflecting his *Vorlage*, which had the same word order as the Greek translations, or whether both he and the Greek translators copied the names from the earlier text, reordering the words to create "chiasmus between parallel texts."

Two parallel verses in Jeremiah and Psalms resemble this example:

        Jer 14:17   תרדנה עיני דמעה לילה ויומם
                       My eyes shed tears **night** *and day.*

        Ps 42:4   היתה לי דמעתי לחם יומם ולילה
                       My tears have been my food *day* **and night**.

---

16. Talmon, "Double Readings," 67.

17. The word יומם uses an archaic form that combines the noun יום and an enclitic מ; compare with אמנם (from אמן) = באמת; ריקם (from ריק); פתאום (from פתע); see Kautzsch (ed.), *Gesenius' Hebrew Grammar*, p. 295 (§3). This מ is especially common in Ugaritic: see Gordon, *Ugaritic Textbook*, 103–4; Hummel, "Enclitic Mem," 85–107. It is noteworthy that this archaic form appears in the later text—Chronicles.

However, whereas in the chiastic parallelism between 1 Kgs 8:29 and 2 Chr 6:20 one may reasonably state that it was the Chronicler who inverted the word order of the text in Kings, in the chiastic parallelism between Jer 14:17 and Ps 42:4 it is difficult to determine with any degree of certainty who made use of which text in inverting the word order because the precise dating of Psalm 42 cannot be determined with certainty.[18]

12.20 1 Kgs 8:39 כי אתה ידעת לבדך את לבב כל בני האדם
For **You know** *alone* every human heart.

2 Chr 6:30 כי אתה לבדך ידעת את לבב בני האדם
For **You** *alone* **know** the human heart.

12.21 1 Kgs 8:65 ויעש שלמה בעת ההיא את החג
Solomon celebrated **at that time** *the festival*.

2 Chr 7:8 ויעש שלמה את החג בעת ההיא
Solomon celebrated *the festival* **at that time**.

12.22 1 Kgs 9:6 ולא תשמרו מצותי חקתי
you did not keep **My commandments**, *My regulations*.

2 Chr 7:19 ועזבתם חקתי ומצותי
you abandon *My regulations* and **My commandments**.

12.23 1 Kgs 9:17–18 ויבן שלמה את גזר ואת בית חרן תחתון ואת בעלת
ואת תמר (Qere) תדמר) במדבר בארץ
Solomon built Gezer, **Lower Beth-horon, Baalath**, *and Tmr (Qere: Tadmor) in the wilderness*, within the land.

2 Chr 8:4–6 ויבן את תדמר במדבר . . . ויבן את בית חורון
העליון ואת בית חורון התחתון . . . ואת בעלת
[Solomon] built *Tadmor in the wilderness* . . . and he built Upper Beth-horon **and Lower Beth-horon** . . . **and Baalath**.

---

18. The phrase under consideration occurs in chiastic order further along in Solomon's prayer in the book of Kings:

1 Kgs 8:29 לילה ויום '**by night** and *by day*'
1 Kgs 8:59 יומם ולילה '*by day* and **by night**'.

Verse 59 does not appear in the book of Chronicles.

12.24 1 Kgs 9:20   כל העם הנותר מן האמרי *החתי*
All the people who were left of **the Amorites**,
the Hittites, . . .

  2 Chr 8:7   כל העם הנותר מן *החתי* **והאמרי**
All the people who were left of *the Hittites*,
the Amorites, . . .

The Septuagint (OG and Lucianic) of Kings has τοῦ Χετταίου καὶ τοῦ
Ἀμορραίου ('the Hittites, the Amorites'), matching the order of the
names in the parallel text in Chronicles. Here also it is difficult to determine whether the Chronicler was reflecting a *Vorlage* that contained
the same order of names as the Greek passages, or both the Chronicler
and the Greek translators reversed the word order to create chiasmus
between parallel texts when they copied their *Vorlagen*. Similar to this
example is the internal parallelism in the book of Ezekiel:

  Ezek 16:3   *אביך האמרי ואמך חתית*
your father was an Amorite *and your mother a
Hittite*.

  Ezek 16:45   *אמכן חתית ואביכן אמרי*
your mother was a Hittite **and your father an
Amorite**.

The literary framework of the book of Joshua also has similar examples:

  Josh 9:1   ויהי כשמע כל המלכים . . . **החתי** *והאמרי*
And it came to pass, when all the kings heard . . .
the Hittites *and the Amorites*.

  Josh 11:1–3   ויהי כשמע יבין מלך חצור . . . *והאמרי* **והחתי**
And it came to pass, when Jabin, king of Hazor,
heard . . . *and the Amorites* **and the Hittites**.

12.25 1 Kgs 9:24b–25a   אז . . . העלה שלמה **שלש פעמים בשנה** *עלות*
ושלמים על המזבח אשר בנה לה'
Then . . . Solomon offered **three times a
year** *burnt-offerings and peace-offerings to the
Lord on the altar that he had built*.

  2 Chr 8:12–13   *אז העלה שלמה עלות לה' על מזבח ה' אשר בנה*
לפני האולם . . . **שלוש פעמים בשנה**
Then Solomon offered *burnt-offerings to the
Lord on the altar of the Lord that he had built
in front of the porch* . . . **three times a year**.

12.26 1 Kgs 9:27–28a   וישלח חירם . . . ידעי הים **עם עבדי שלמה ויבאו** אופירה
Then Hiram sent . . . those familiar with the sea,
together with Solomon's servants,
and they went to Ophir.

2 Chr 8:18   וישלח לו חורם . . . יודעי ים **ויבאו עם עבדי שלמה** אופירה
Then Huram sent to him . . . those familiar with
the sea, *and they went* **with Solomon's
servants** to Ophir.

12.27 1 Kgs 12:15   כי היתה סבה מעם ה' למען הקים **את דברו אשר דבר ה'**
For it was a turn of affairs brought about by the
Lord in order to keep **His word that was
spoken** by *the Lord*.

2 Chr 10:15   כי היתה נסבה מעם האלהים למען הקים ה' **את דברו אשר דבר**
For it was a turn of affairs brought about by God
in order that *the Lord* might keep **His word
that He had spoken**.[19]

12.28 1 Kgs 12:16   **וירא** *כל ישראל* כי לא שמע המלך אליהם
So it was seen *by all Israel* that the king would
not listen to them.

2 Chr 10:16   *וכל ישראל* [**ראו**] כי לא שמע המלך להם
When all Israel [**saw**] that the king would not
listen to them.

The word ראו 'saw' does not appear in the Masoretic Text that we have,
yet, in light of its occurrence in a number of Hebrew manuscripts, the
Peshiṭta, Aramaic Targum, Vetus Latina, and the Vulgate, it is reasonable to assume that it appeared in the original text of Chronicles as it
does in the parallel text in Kings and that it was erroneously omitted
from the version we have today (haplography?).

12.29 1 Kgs 22:4   ויאמר . . . כמוני כמוך **כעמי כעמך**
He said . . . , "I am as you are; **my people** are
as your people."

2 Chr 18:3   ויאמר . . . כמוני כמוך *וכעמך* **עמי**
He said . . . , "I am as you are, *and your people* are
as my people."

12.30 1 Kgs 22:43   וילך בכל דרך **אסא** *אביו*
He walked in all the way of **Asa**, *his father*.

2 Chr 20:32   וילך בדרך *אביו* **אסא**
He walked in the way of *his father*, **Asa**.

---

19. Compare 1 Sam 1:23: אך יקם ה' **את דברו** 'May the Lord keep His word'.

12.31 2 Kgs 11:8   והיו את המלך **בצאתו ובבאו**
And they were with the king **in his goings**
and his comings.

2 Chr 23:7   והיו את המלך כבאו **ובצאתו**
And they were with the king *in his comings*
and his goings.

12.32 2 Kgs 11:17   ויכרת יהוידע את הברית בין ה' **ובין המלך** *ובין העם*
להיות לעם לה'
Then Jehoiada sealed the covenant between
the Lord **and the king** *and the people*, that
the people would be the Lord's.

2 Chr 23:16   ויכרת יהוידע ברית בינו *ובין כל העם ובין המלך*
להיות לעם לה'
Then Jehoiada sealed a covenant between him
and all the people **and the king**, that
the people would be the Lord's.

12.33 2 Kgs 16:3   וגם את **בנו העביר באש**
He even made **his son** *pass* through
the fire.

2 Chr 28:3   *ויבער את בניו באש*
and *burned* **his sons** with fire.

Geiger[20] claims that the reading ויבער in 2 Chr 28:3 is the original version, whereas the word העביר 'pass' is at best an emendation of the word הבעיר 'burned': "This change was first made in the Pentateuch, which became a book often read, and afterwards in the Prophets as well . . . , while it was only in the book of Chronicles, which is a late book seldom read, that the word הבעיר remained on one occasion." If this were the case, however, we would expect to find ויבער rather than העביר in reference to Manasseh as well (2 Chr 33:6). Furthermore, Geiger goes on to claim that the purpose of this emendation was "to reduce as far as possible the degree of influence of Moloch-worship in Israel." What good would this emendation do, however, if, as Geiger himself notes, "the burning and butchering of children is still discussed there in other terms which have not been emended"?

An error may have crept into the Masoretic Text of Chronicles: ויבער ~ העביר (inverted letter order). In fact, the Septuagint, Peshiṭta, and Aramaic Targum all have ויעבר, as does the parallel text in 2 Kgs 16:3. Furthermore, the usual biblical idiom is להעביר X באש 'to pass X through the fire' (Deut 18:10; 2 Kgs 21:6 // 2 Chr 33:6; 2 Kgs 23:10; see also Ezek

---

20. Geiger, *Urschrift und Übersetzungen*, 305.

20:26; as well as Rabbinic literature, for example *b. Sanh.* 64b).[21] It is also not impossible that the Chronicler was influenced by Jeremiah's and Ezekiel's prophecies regarding Moloch, in which the alternation העביר ~ הבעיר is found in conjunction with the words זבח and שחט.[22] It must further be noted that the proximity of this narrative involving Ahaz, who acted according to "the abominations of the heathen" (2 Kgs 16:3 // 2 Chr 28:3), to the ensuing narrative about the Sepharvites, who "burned their offspring with fire" (2 Kgs 17:31), may have influenced the Chronicler to emend his text in this manner.[23]

In 2 Chr 28:3 and in 33:6, the Chronicler wrote בניו 'his sons' instead of בנו 'his son', which appears in the earlier text.[24] This phrase, which is also used with regard to Manasseh, king of Judah, is however used in 33:6 with word order that is the same as the word order of 2 Kgs 21:6: "*And he passed* **his son** *through the fire*" // "*And he passed* **his sons** *through the fire.*"[25]

12.34 2 Kgs 18:22 (= Isa 36:7)   הלוא הוא אשר *הסיר חזקיהו* את במתיו ואת מזבחתיו
Is it not He whose high places and altars **were removed by** *Hezekiah*?

2 Chr 32:12   הלוא הוא *יחזקיהו* **הסיר**[26] את במותיו ואת מזבחתיו
Is it not He [whose] high places and altars *Hezekiah* **removed**?

There appears to be another example of this change in word order:

2 Sam 6:10a   ולא אבה דוד להסיר
But **David** did not want to *remove*.

1 Chr 13:13   ולא הסיר דויד
But were not *removed by* **David**.

However, since the Chronicler omitted the word אבה 'wanted' from the earlier text, the change in word order was obligatory. That is, ולא הסיר

---

21. Compare Ehrlich, *Mikrâ ki-Pheschutô*, 463–64; Japhet, "Interchanges," 44–45.

22. See Cogan, *Imperialism and Religion*, 78 n. 63.

23. For a discussion of the matter of burning children or passing them through fire in ancient Near Eastern rituals, see example 3.19 n. 55 (p. 78).

24. For this, see example 7.5 (pp. 128–129).

25. Contrast this example with this pair: 2 Kgs 25:7, "**And the sons of Zedekiah** *they slaughtered*"; Jer 39:6 (= 52:10), "*And he slaughtered . . .* **the sons of Zedekiah.**" This change may stem from the use of the imperfect + *waw*-consecutive verb form, however.

26. This is an example of an asyndetic relative clause, which is common in archaic language (usually in biblical poetry; see, e.g., Deut 32:11; Isa 61:10–11; Hab 2:14; Ps 42:2; 83:15–16; 123:2; Job 7:2–3). For this feature, see Blau, "Asyndetic Prepositional Clauses," 277–85.

דויד was then the only word order that was linguistically possible for the Chronicler to use.

12.35 2 Kgs 23:29   וילך המלך יאשיהו *לקראתו*
King **Josiah** went *toward him.*[27]

2 Chr 35:20   *לקראתו* ויצא יאשיהו
Went *toward him* **Josiah**.

12.36 The following two examples should be added here:

2 Sam 24:16		*1 Chr 21:16*
MT	4QSam*a*	
	[. . . ויפל דויד והזקנים	ויפל דויד והזקנים
_____	על פנ]יהם	מכסים בשקים
_____	מתכ]סים[בשקים 28	על פניהם
	[. . . David and the elders	David and the elders
_____	fell **on their**] **faces**	fell, *covered in*
_____	cov[ered] *in sackcloth.*	*sackcloth*, **on their faces**.

The text dealt with in 4QSam*a* and in 1 Chronicles may have been omitted from the Masoretic Text (and from the Septuagint) of the book of Samuel because of a technical error in copying (perhaps homoioarcton: וישא דויד . . . ויאמר דויד).[29] Since the phenomenon of copying in the order of chiasmus between parallel texts is also apparent in a comparison of the Masoretic Text of 2 Sam 5:8, ואת הפסחים ואת העורים שנאו נפש דוד 'the **blind** and the *lame*, the hated of David's soul' with 4QSam*a*, ואת העורים] 'the *lame* and the **blind**, the hated of David's[30] soul', as well as in a comparison of the Masoretic Text of Isaiah with 1QIsa*b* and 1QIsa*b*,[31] it is difficult to determine with any certainty who

---

27. Compare 2 Kgs 16:10: וילך אחז לקראת תגלת־פלאסר 'Ahaz went to meet Tiglath-pileser' (this verse has no parallel in Chronicles).

28. The Qumran fragment as quoted here is from McKenzie, *Chronicler*, 55. A somewhat different reconstruction of the fragment was published by Cross, "Biblical Text," 294.

29. See Cross, *Ancient Library*, 188–89 n. 40a; Ulrich, *Qumran Text*, 157; McKenzie, *Chronicler*, 55.

30. This Qumran fragment of Samuel was published by McKenzie, ibid., 43–44. This part of the Samuel text (2 Sam 5:8) was omitted by the Chronicler in 1 Chronicles 11.

31. See above, n. 9 (p. 234), as well as the examples in Kutscher, *Isaiah Scroll*, 563–64, under the heading "Different Word Order"; for instance:

(a) Isa 43:3, MT   נתתי כפרך מצרים
I have given **as your ransom** *Egypt*.

1QIsa*a*   נתתי *מצרים* כופרך
I have given *Egypt* **as your ransom**.

copied the text from the book of Samuel in the order of chiasmus between parallel texts: the Chronicler or the copyist of the scroll or each
of them from an independent *Vorlage*. At any rate, the change in the order of the phrases על פניהם / מתכסים בשקים cannot serve as an indication
that 4QSam[a] was independent of 1 Chr 21:16,[32] since both the Chronicler and the Qumran scribes frequently used the order of chiasmus between parallel texts in their work.

12.37 In 1 Chr 17:1b the Chronicler omitted the text concerning David that is present in 2 Sam 7:1b,[33] but in 1 Chr 22:9 ("addition") he
used the words, but applied them to Solomon instead, chiastically in
comparison with the order in 2 Samuel:

2 Sam 7:1b	וה׳ הניח לו [לדוד] **מסביב מכל איביו**
	and the Lord gave him [David] rest **round** **about** *from all his enemies.*
1 Chr 17:1b	. . . .
1 Chr 22:9	והנחותי לו [לשלמה] **מכל אויביו מסביב**
	And I have given him [Solomon] rest *from all his* *enemies* **round about**.

Three-Member Structures

12.38 1 Kgs 3:4	אלף *עלות* יעלה שלמה על המזבח[34]
	A thousand *burnt-offerings* **Solomon offered on the altar**
2 Chr 1:6	ויעל שלמה שם על מזבח . . . *עלות אלף*
	Solomon offered on the altar . . . *burnt-offerings* **a thousand**.

(b)   Isa 37:32, MT   כי מירושלם תצא שארית ופליטה מהר ציון
a remnant shall go forth **from Jerusalem** and escapees
from Mount Zion (= 2 Kgs 19:32).

1QIsa[a]   כיא מציון תצא שארית ופליטה מירושלים
a remnant shall go forth *from Zion* and escapees
from Jerusalem.

(c)   Isa 37:33, MT   ולא יורה שם חץ ולא יקדמנה מגן ולא ישפך עליה סללה
he shall not shoot an arrow there; neither shall he come
before it with a shield *or cast up a rampart against it.*

1QIsa[a]   ולוא ישפוך עליהא סוללה ולוא ירא שם חץ ולוא יקדמנה מגן
he shall not cast up a rampart against it; **neither shall he**
shoot an arrow there or come before it with a shield.

For different word order, compare the MT of Jeremiah 10 with the LXX and 4QJer[b].

32. Against Ulrich, *Qumran Text*, 157; McKenzie, *Chronicler*, 55.

33. For the reason for this omission, see example 2.1 (pp. 38–39).

34. From a syntactical viewpoint, the word order of 1 Kgs 3:4 matches the regular
Aramaic word order—that is, object-predicate-subject.

Embedded in this verse in Chronicles is a linguistic feature that usually appears in later Hebrew, a noun that precedes its modifying number.[35] However, when the Chronicler moved יעלה שלמה על המזבח out of its original position in the earlier text, he revealed that his primary purpose was forming a structure of chiasmus between parallel texts, for he could have written, for instance, עלות אלף יעלה/העלה שלמה שם על מזבח 'burnt-offerings a thousand Solomon offered up there on the altar'.

12.39   1 Kgs 6:1   . . . ויהי . . . *בשנה הרביעית בחדש זו הוא החדש השני*
ויבן הבית לה'

And it came to pass . . . **in the fourth year** . . .
in the month of Ziv, which is the second month
he built the House of the Lord

2 Chr 3:1–2   ויחל שלמה **לבנות את בית ה'** . . . *בחדש השני בשני*
בשנת ארבע למלכותו

Solomon began **to build the House of the Lord**
. . . *in the second month*, on the second day,
in the fourth year of his reign

2. Chiasmus between Parallel Texts: Using Alternate Words

The Chronicler occasionally created structures of chiasmus between parallel texts between the book of Chronicles and the books of Samuel and Kings by substituting synonymous or nearly synonymous words for the words used in the earlier text.[36] In these instances, the transcribed text not only displays inverted word order but also substitutes words with the same general meanings. Thus, the Chronicler twice varied the earlier texts without changing their content.

Two-Member Structures

12.40   1 Sam 29:4   *ובמה יתרצה זה את אדניו הלוא בראשי האנשים ההם*
**For how will this man be reconciled to his
lord?** *Will it not be with the heads of those men?*

1 Chr 12:20   **בראשנו יפול אל אדניו שאול**
at the cost of our heads **he will desert to his
lord, Saul**.

---

35. For this, see the appendix to this chapter: "Diachronic Chiasmus" (pp. 269–74).

36. This brings up a serious question in its own right: are the interchanges of synonyms in these texts a result of textual changes or are they literary-stylistic changes? Interchanges of synonymous nouns and verbs are common both in biblical literature and in manuscripts and versions (original or translated) of this literature. For a thorough discussion of this question, see Talmon, "Textual Study," 130–31. Without ruling conclusively on the matter, I think that most of the examples adduced below evidence

12.41 2 Sam 6:6 וישלח עזה אל ארון האלהים **ויאחז** בו

Uzza reached out [his hand] to **the ark of God**
and took hold of it.

1 Chr 13:9 וישלח עזא את ידו *לאחז* את **הארון**

Uzza reached out his hand *to take hold* of
the ark.

12.42 2 Sam 6:10b **אליו** *את ארון ה׳* על עיר דוד

into his care *the ark of the Lord* in
the City of David.

1 Chr 13:13b *את הארון* **אליו** אל עיר דויד

the ark **into his care** in the City of David.[37]

12.43 2 Sam 7:12–13 והקימתי את זרעך אחריך . . . והכינתי את ממלכתו
הוא יבנה **בית לשמי**

I will raise up your offspring after you . . . and
I will establish his kingdom; he will build
a House *for my name*.

1 Chr 17:11–12 והקימותי את זרעך אחריך . . . והכינותי את מלוכתו
הוא יבנה לי **בית**[38]

I will raise up your offspring after you . . . and
I will establish his kingdom; he will build
for me **a House**.

---

literary-stylistic interchanges or the like (such as the interchange of the proper nouns
אלהים / ה׳) rather than textual variants.

37. Compare this example with example 12.11 above (2 Sam 10:9 // 1 Chr 19:10;
p. 237). There is a similar interchange in the Pentateuchal Priestly source:

Lev 9:12 וימצאו בני אהרן **אליו** *את הדם*
The sons of Aaron brought **him** *the blood*.

Lev 9:18 וימצאו בני אהרן *את הדם* **אליו**
The sons of Aaron brought *the blood* **to him**.

And yet another one between the MT and the Samaritan Pentateuch:

Exod 3:2, MT וירא **מלאך ה׳** *אליו*
An angel of the Lord appeared *to him*.

Samaritan וירא *אליו* **מלאך ה׳**
There appeared *to him* **an angel of the Lord**.

38. The use of the noun מלכותו 'his kingdom' in the book of Chronicles instead of
the noun ממלכתו 'his kingdom' in the books of Samuel and Kings is apparently one
sign of Late Biblical Hebrew. See, for example:

2 Sam 5:12 וידע דוד כי הכינו ה׳ . . . וכי נשא **ממלכתו**
David perceived that the Lord had established him . . . and had
exalted his kingdom.

1 Chr 14:2 וידע דויד כי הכינו ה׳ . . . כי נשאת למעלה **מלכותו**
David perceived that the Lord had established him . . . and had
exalted his kingdom.

12.44 2 Sam 7:27   כי אתה ה' . . . גליתה את אזן עבדך לאמר **בית אבנה לך**
For You, O Lord, . . . have made this revelation to
Your servant, saying, "**A house** *I will build you.*"

         1 Chr 17:25   כי אתה אלהי גלית את אזן עבדך *לבנות לו* **בית**
For You, my God, have revealed to Your servant
that you will build him **a house.**

12.45 2 Sam 10:1–2   וישלח דוד **לנחמו** *ביד עבדיו*
And David sent **to console him** *by means
of his servants.*

         1 Chr 19:2   וישלח דויד *מלאכים* **לנחמו**
And David sent *messengers* **to console him.**

12.46 2 Sam 24:3   **ואדני המלך** *למה חפץ בדבר הזה*
And my lord the king, *why does he desire this?*

         1 Chr 21:3   *למה יבקש זאת* **אדני**
Why should [he] request this, **my lord?**

12.47 1 Kgs 3:9a   **ונתת לעבדך** *לב שמע*
Give Your servant *an understanding mind.*

         2 Chr 1:10a   *חכמה ומדע* **תן לי**
Wisdom and knowledge **give me.**

12.48 1 Kgs 3:9b   כי מי יוכל לשפט את עמך **הכבד** *הזה*
For who can govern **great** *this* people of Yours?

         2 Chr 1:10b   כי מי ישפט את עמך *הזה* **הגדול**
For who will rule *this* **large** people of Yours?

12.49 1 Kgs 12:18   וירגמו **כל ישראל** *בו* אבן וימת
all Israel stoned *him* to death.

         2 Chr 10:18   וירגמו *בו* **בני־ישראל** אבן וימת
they stoned *him*, **the children of Israel**,
to death.

---

    1 Kgs 9:5   והקמתי את כסא **ממלכתך**
         I shall establish the throne of your kingdom.
    2 Chr 7:18   והקימותי את כסא מלכותך
         I shall establish the throne of your kingdom.
Compare also:
    2 Kgs 11:1   כל זרע **הממלכה**
         all the royal family.
    2 Chr 12:25   כל זרע **המלוכה**
         all the royal family.
See also 1 Chr 22:10; 28:7 ("addition"); Hurvitz, *Transition Period*, 79–82.

12.50   1 Kgs 15:23b   **רק לעת זקנתו** *חלה* [*אסא*] **את רגליו**

in his old age [Asa] *was diseased* in his feet.

      2 Chr 16:12a   *ויחלא אסא* **בשנת שלושים ותשע למלכותו** ברגליו

Asa *was diseased* in the thirty-ninth year
of his reign in his feet.

12.51   2 Kgs 14:7   הוא הכה את אדום *בגי המלח* (Qere): מלח)

He **struck down Edom** *in the Salt Valley.*

      2 Chr 25:11   וילך *גיא המלח* ויך את בני־שעיר

He went *to the Salt Valley* **and struck down
the men of Seir.**[39]

12.52   2 Kgs 18:4   *הוא* **הסיר את הבמות** *ושבר את המצבת וכרת את האשרה*

He **removed the high places,** *broke the pillars,
and cut down the Asherah.*

      2 Chr 31:1   *. . . יצאו כל ישראל . . . וישברו המצבות ויגדעו האשרים*
וינתצו את הבמות *ואת המזבחת*

and all Israel went out . . . *and broke the pillars,
cut down the Asherim,* **and shattered the
high places** and the altars.

12.53   2 Kgs 21:20–21   ויעש [אמון] הרע בעיני ה' כאשר עשה מנשה אביו . . .
ויעבד את הגללים *אשר עבד אביו וישתחו להם*

[Amon] did what was evil in the sight of the Lord,
as Manasseh his father had done. . . .
He worshiped *the idols that his father had
worshiped and bowed down to them.*

      2 Chr 33:22   ויעש [אמון] הרע בעיני ה' כאשר עשה מנשה אביו
ולכל הפסילים אשר עשה מנשה אביו זבח אמון **ויעבדם**

[Amon] did what was evil in the sight of the Lord,
as Manasseh his father had done. *To all the
idols that Manasseh his father had made,
Amon sacrificed,* **and he worshiped them.**

12.54   2 Kgs 21:23   ויקשרו **עבדי אמון** עליו וימתו את המלך בביתו

Amon's servants conspired *against him,*
and they killed the king in his palace.

      2 Chr 33:24   ויקשרו עליו . . . **עבדיו** וימיתהו בביתו[40]

Against him **his servants** conspired,
and they killed him in his palace.

---

39. For this change in word order in Chronicles, see Kalimi, "Paronomasia," 27–
41, esp. 32.

40. Compare this example with example 12.49 immediately above (1 Kgs 12:18 //
2 Chr 10:18).

12.55 2 Kgs 22:7 כי באמונה הם עשים
honestly *they* acted.

2 Chr 34:12 והאנשים עשים באמונה
the men acted honestly.

12.56 2 Kgs 24:20 (= Jer 52:3) וימרד צדקיהו במלך בבל
Zedekiah rebelled *against the king of Babylon.*

2 Chr 36:13 במלך נבוכדנאצר מרד
Against King Nebuchadnezzar he rebelled.

12.57 2 Sam 6:17 ויעל דוד עלות לפני ה' ושלמים
Then David offered up burnt-offerings
to the Lord, *as well as peace-offerings.*

1 Chr 16:1 ויקריבו עלות ושלמים לפני האלהים[41]
They sacrificed burnt-offering
and peace-offerings to God.

12.58 1 Kgs 3:5 בגבעון נראה ה' אל שלמה בחלום הלילה
In Gibeon the Lord appeared to Solomon
in a dream *in the night.*

2 Chr 1:7 בלילה ההוא נראה אלהים לשלמה
That *night* God appeared to Solomon.[42]

12.59 1 Sam 28:6–7 relates that at first וישאל שאול בה' 'Saul ask[s] of
the Lord' but, when the Lord does not reply, he seeks out אשת בעלת
אוב ואלכה אליה ואדרשה בה 'a woman who divines by *a ghost,* that I may go
to her *and inquire of her.*' In 1 Chr 10:13–14, the Chronicler inverts the
order: לשאול באוב לדרוש ולא דרש בה 'he consulted *a ghost, inquiring
thereby,* and did not inquire of the Lord'.

A Three-Member Structure

2 Sam 10:3		1 Chr 19:3	
בעבור חקר		בעבור לחקור	
את העיר[43]	.a	ולהפך	.c
ולרגלה	.b	ולרגל	.b
ולהפכה	.c	הארץ	.a
שלח דוד את עבדיו אליך		באו עבדיו אליך	

---

41. This is a sample of the well-known simplified style typical of the later language (and even more so of Rabbinic Hebrew).

42. Compare this example with Jer 39:4, "and they went out **at night** *from the
town*," in contrast to 52:7, "and they went out *of the town* **at night**."

43. Four manuscripts of the MT read בארץ 'in the land' here (*BH*, 470). For the
בעיר ~ בארץ interchange, see a detailed description in example 15.20 (pp. 346–349),
esp. n. 69 (pp. 348–349).

<table>
<tr><td>in order to search</td><td>in order to search,</td></tr>
<tr><td>a. **the city**,</td><td>c. *to overthrow*,</td></tr>
<tr><td>b. *to spy it out*,</td><td>b. *and to spy out*</td></tr>
<tr><td>c. *and to overthrow it*</td><td>a. **the land**</td></tr>
<tr><td>David sent his servants to you.</td><td>his servants came to you.</td></tr>
</table>

3. Chiasmus between Parallel Texts from Other Biblical Books and Chronicles

The feature of chiasmus between parallel texts is found in the book of Chronicles in passages that the Chronicler borrowed from other books of the Bible and in "additions."

A. Texts from Other Biblical Books

Two-Member Structures

12.60 Gen 3:16   ואל האשה אמר הרבה ארבה עצבונך והרנך **בעצב** *תלדי* בנים
And to the woman He said, "I will greatly multiply your distress in childbearing; **in pain** *you shall bear* children."

1 Chr 4:9   ואמו קראה שמו יעבץ לאמר כי *ילדתי* **בעצב**
His mother named him Jabez, saying, "*I gave birth* **in pain**."

This is a word-play on the name יעבץ ('Jabez') ~ בעצב ('in pain') using the verse from Genesis.

12.61 The Chronicler placed the words spoken about Bezalel, son of Uri, son of Hur, in Exod 31:2–5 (compare 35:30–33) in the mouth of Huram, king of Tyre, and presented them in the order of chiasmus between parallel texts:

Exod 31:2–5   **ובכל** מלאכה **לחשב מחשבת** *לעשות בזהב ובכסף ובנחשת*
ובחרשת **אבן** *למלאת ובחרשת* **עץ** *לעשות בכל מלאכה*
   ... **and in all** kinds of workmanship; **to devise skillful designs**, *to work in gold, silver, and bronze*, and in cutting *stones* for setting, and in carving *wood* for work in every craft.

2 Chr 2:13   יודע *לעשות בזהב ובכסף ובנחשת* בברזל *באבנים ובעצים*
   ... **ולחשב כל מחשבת** אשר ינתן לו
   [a man] ..., trained *to work in gold, silver, bronze,*[44] iron, *stone, and wood* ... **and to devise any kind of skillful design** that may be assigned to him.

---

44. Compare with Solomon's request to Huram, king of Tyre, in v. 6.

12.62 Ps 132:10   בעבור דוד עבדך אל תשב פני משיחך
For the sake of **David Your servant**, *do not turn away the face of Your anointed one.*

2 Chr 6:42   אל תשב פני משיחך זכרה לחסדי דויד עבדך
Do not turn away the face of Your anointed one; remember your mercy toward **David Your servant.**

12.63 Zech 8:10   וליוצא ולבא אין שלום
Everyone who goes out or comes in *has no safety.*

2 Chr 15:5   אין שלום ליוצא ולבא
No safety **has anyone who goes out or comes in.**

12.64 Zech 4:10   עיני ה׳ המה משוטטים בכל הארץ
the eyes of *the Lord*, which range throughout the whole earth.

2 Chr 16:9   ה׳ עיניו משטטות בכל הארץ[45]
The Lord—**His eyes** range throughout the whole earth.

12.65 Mal 1:9   הישא מכם פנים
Will He show **to any of you** *favor?*

2 Chr 30:9   ולא יסיר פנים מכם
He will not turn away His *favor* **from any of you.**

12.66

Ps 96:10–11	1 Chr 16:30–31
a. אמרו בגוים ה׳ מלך	b. אף תכון תבל בל תמוט ישמחו השמים ותגל הארץ
b. אף תכון תבל בל תמוט . . . ישמחו השמים ותגל הארץ	a. ויאמרו בגוים ה׳ מלך
a. **Say among the nations: the Lord reigns!**	b. *The world also is established so that it cannot be moved. Let the heavens be glad, and let the earth rejoice,*
b. *The world also is established so that it cannot be moved. . . . Let the heavens be glad, and let the earth rejoice.*	a. **and let them say among the nations: the Lord reigns!**

45. Compare this verse with Prov 15:3: "And in every place **the eyes of** *the Lord* observe the evil and the good." This verse is cited in Aramaic in the mosaic inscription from the En-Gedi synagogue (line 13); see Kalimi, "History of Interpretation," 31–33, esp. p. 32; idem, *Jewish Tradition and Exegesis.*

Since adducing a passage with the word order inverted is a common literary feature of the book of Chronicles, Tur-Sinai's[46] explanation of the inverted word order in 1 Chr 16:30–31, "that portions of the rhymes were read from top to bottom instead of from right to left or conversely," seems groundless.

12.67 Josh 21:18   את ענתות ואת מגרשה ואת עלמון ואת מגרשה

Anathoth with its plots of land
and Almon with its plots of land.

1 Chr 6:45[60]   ואת עלמת ואת מגרשיה ואת ענתות ואת מגרשיה

Alemeth with its plots of land
and Anathoth with its plots of land.

A Three-Member Structure

Exod 14:13–14	2 Chr 20:15, 17
a. **אל תיראו**	c. ‏. . . כי לא לכם המלחמה כי לאלהים‏
	‏לא לכם להלחם בזאת‏
b. ‏התיצבו וראו את ישועת ה'‏	b. ‏התיצבו, עמדו וראו את ישועת ה'‏
‏אשר יעשה לכם . . .‏	‏עמכם . . .‏
c. ‏ה' ילחם לכם‏	a. ‏אל תיראו ואל תחתו‏

a. **Do not be afraid,**

b. *stand firm, and see the Lord's deliverance on your behalf. . . .*

c. ***The Lord will fight for you.***

c. ***For the battle is not yours but God's. . . . It is not for you to fight.***

b. *Stand firm, stand still, and see the deliverance that the Lord is preparing for you. . . .*

a. **Do not be afraid** and do not tremble.

Literary Units in the Order of Chiasmus between Parallel Texts

Genesis 25 lists the descendants of Abraham in the following order:

a. **the sons of Keturah** (vv. 1–4)
b. *the sons of Ishmael* (vv. 12–16).

In 1 Chronicles 1, the Chronicler copied these two lists in inverted order, creating a chiasmus with the parallel text in Genesis:

b. *the sons of Ishmael* (vv. 29–31)
a. **the sons of Keturah** (vv. 32–33).

---

46. See Tur-Sinai, "To the Chief Musician," 335–50, esp. p. 337.

Once again, because adducing a literary unit in inverted order is a frequent compositional feature in Chronicles, the inverted order of the lists of Keturah's and Ishmael's sons cannot be considered an argument in support of Williamson's claim that the list of Keturah's sons in Chronicles is a late addition.[47]

B. Chiasmus between Parallel Texts in "Additions"

12.68 1 Chr 5:22   כי מהאלהים *המלחמה*
God's was *the war.*

2 Chr 20:15   כי לא לכם *המלחמה* כי **לאלהים**
the war is not yours but **God's.**

12.69

2 Sam 5:3	*1 Chr 11:3*	*1 Chr 11:10*
וימשחו את דוד למלך	וימשחו את דויד למלך	המתחזקים עמו[48] במלכותו
		עם כל ישראל להמליכו
על ישראל	**על ישראל**	*כדבר ה׳*
	. . . כדבר ה׳	**על ישראל**
And they anointed	And they anointed	who gave him support in
David king	David king	his kingdom, with all
		Israel, to crown him
over Israel.	**over Israel**	*according to the word*
		of the Lord,
	according to the	**over Israel.**
	word of the Lord.	

12.70 1 Chr 22:8   דם לרב **שפכת** *ומלחמות* גדלות עשית
You have shed much **blood** and waged
great *wars.*

1 Chr 28:3   כי *איש מלחמות* אתה **ודמים שפכת**
For you are a *warrior* and **have shed blood.**

12.71 Solomon's letter to Huram reads as follows (2 Chr 2:6): ועתה
וכרמיל ותכלת[49] . . . ובארגון ... שלח לי איש חכם לעשות בזהב 'Now send me a skillful man to work in gold . . . , purple, **crimson**, and *blue*'. Huram's reply to Solomon (vv. 12–13) reads as follows: ועתה שלחתי איש חכם ... יודע **ובכרמיל** ובבוץ *בתכלת*, בארגמן . . . בזהב לעשות 'Now I have sent a skillful man

---

47. See Williamson, *Chronicles*, 43.

48. **המתחזקים עמו**, that is, 'those assisting him'; compare Dan 10:21: **מתחזק** אחד ואין; **עמי** על אלה 'no one is helping me against them'; see also 1 Chr 12:23: כי לעת יום ביום יבאו **לעזור** על דויד 'from day to day men came to David to help him'.

49. The word ארגון is a late form of the word ארגמן 'purple', which appears further on in v. 13 (as well as in 3:14 and in other books of the Bible); compare ארגונא in Biblical Aramaic: Dan 5:7, 16, 29. The Chronicler used the late form alongside the early one, apparently to achieve stylistic variety.

. . . who knows how to work in gold . . . , purple, *blue*, fine linen, and **crimson**'.

12.72 Furthermore, Solomon says to Huram (2 Chr 2:9): והנה לחטבים לכרתי העצים נתתי חטים . . . ושערים . . . ויין *ושמן* . . . 'Now I will provide for the hewers, those who cut the timber, . . . wheat, . . . barley, . . . **wine**, and . . . *oil*'. In Huram's reply to Solomon (2:14), on the other hand, we find: ועתה החטים והשערים *והשמן והיין* אשר אמר אדני ישלח לעבדיו 'Now, as for the wheat, barley, *oil*, and **wine** that my lord said he would send to his servants, . . .'

12.73 2 Chr 12:12   וגם ביהודה היה *דברים טובים*
Moreover, **in Judah there were**
good conditions [things].

    2 Chr 19:3   . . . (יהושפט) אבל *דברים טובים* נמצאו עמך
But *good things* **were found with you**
[in you, Jehoshaphat].

12.74 2 Chr 15:1	2 Chr 20:14	2 Chr 24:20
a. **ועזריהו בן עודד**	a. ויחזיאל בן זכריהו . . .	c. *ורוח אלהים*
b. *היתה עליו*	b. *היתה עליו*	b. *לבשה*
c. *רוח ה'*	c. *רוח ה'*	a. **את זכריה בן יהוידע הכהן**

a. **Azariah, son of Oded**	a. **Jahaziel, son of Zechariah . . .**	c. *And the spirit of God*
b. —*there enveloped him*	b. —*there enveloped him*	b. *enveloped*
c. *the spirit of the Lord.*	c. *the spirit of the Lord.*	a. **Zechariah, son of Jehoiada, the priest**.

12.75 2 Chr 21:14, in Elijah's letter to Jehoram, king of Judah, reads: הנה ה' נגף מגפה גדולה בעמך **ובבניך ובנשיך** ובכל רכושך 'Behold, the Lord will inflict a great plague on your people, **your children, your wives**, *and all your possessions*'. Further on (v. 17), the Chronicler relates that the Arabs and the Philistines who invaded Judah: וישבו את כל *הרכוש* *הנמצא לבית המלך* וגם **בניו ונשיו** 'captured *all the possessions that were in the house of the king*, **his children, and his wives**'.

4. Chiastic Parallelism with Samuel–Kings and Internal Chiasmus between Parallel Texts

Occasionally, using the words of a passage from Samuel–Kings in inverted order created a structure of chiasmus between parallel texts within the framework of a literary unit or between two different literary units in the book of Chronicles itself. In these cases, the Chronicler again used more than one style of alteration.

A. Inverted Word Order plus Original Word Order in the Parallel Texts

Sometimes the Chronicler used a phrase that appeared in two different contexts in the earlier text, once in the order of chiasmus between parallel texts and once in the order of its appearance in the original text. In this way the Chronicler varied the use of the phrase in his own work and created a structure of chiasmus between parallel texts in the book of Chronicles itself. For instance:

12.76 In 1 Chr 17:4, the Chronicler presented Nathan's prophecy found in 2 Sam 7:5 in the order of chiasmus between parallel texts:

2 Sam 7:5	לך ואמרת **אל עבדי** אל דוד : כה אמר ה' . . .
	Go, say **to My servant**, *to David*: "This is what the Lord said. . . ."
1 Chr 17:4	לך ואמרת אל דויד **עבדי**: כה אמר ה' . . .
	Go, say *to David*, **My servant**, "This is what the Lord said. . . ."

Three verses further on, in the prophecy of the eternal nature of the Davidic dynasty, he adduced the identical phrases in their original order:

2 Sam 7:8	כה תאמר **לעבדי** לדוד : כה אמר ה' . . .
	This is what you will say **to My servant**, *to David*, "This is what the Lord said. . . ."
1 Chr 17:7	כה תאמר **לעבדי** לדויד : כה אמר ה' . . .
	This is what you will say **to My servant**, *to David*, "This is what the Lord said. . . ."

In this way, therefore, he created a chiastic parallelism between the two passages in his book:

1 Chr 17:4	לך ואמרת אל דויד **עבדי**: כה אמר ה' . . .
1 Chr 17:7	כה תאמר **לעבדי** לדויד : כה אמר ה' . . .

12.77 The narrative of David's victory over Moab ends with the following words:

2 Sam 8:2　　　ותהי מואב **לדוד** *לעבדים* נשאי מנחה
The Moabites became **to David** *slaves*
and bearers of tribute.

1 Chr 18:2　　　ויהיו מואב *עבדים* **לדויד** נשאי מנחה
The Moabites became *slaves* **to David**
and bearers of tribute.

Farther along in the text, the narrative of David's victory over Aram
concludes with the identical words:

2 Sam 8:6　　　ותהי ארם **לדוד** *לעבדים* נושאי מנחה
The Arameans became **to David** *slaves*
and bearers of tribute.

1 Chr 18:6　　　ויהי ארם **לדויד** *עבדים* נשאי מנחה
The Arameans became **to David** *slaves*
and bearers of tribute.

In this way, a chiastic parallelism between the two texts used in
1 Chronicles was achieved:

1 Chr 18:2　　　The Moabites became *slaves* **to David** and
　　　　　　　　bearers of tribute.

1 Chr 18:6　　　The Arameans became **to David** *slaves* and
　　　　　　　　bearers of tribute.

12.78 The total number of years of David's reign in Hebron and in
Jerusalem is given twice in the book of Chronicles, once in 1 Chr 3:4, in
chiasmus between parallel texts with 2 Sam 5:5,

2 Sam 5:5		2 Chr 3:4b	
בחברון	a.	וימלך	b.
מלך ...	b.	שם (בחברון)[50]	a.
שבע שנים וששה חדשים		שבע שנים וששה חדשים	
ובירושלם	a.	*ושלשים ושלוש שנה*	c.
מלך	b.	מלך	b.
שלשים ושלוש שנים	c.	**ובירושלם**[51]	a.

a. In Hebron　　　　　　　b. *And he reigned*
b. *he reigned . . .*　　　　　a. there [in Hebron]
　　seven years and six months,　　　seven years and six months,

---

50. The changed word order בחברון מלך וימלך / וימלך שם stems from the use of the *waw*-
consecutive with imperfect verbal form (וימלך).

51. Adducing 2 Sam 5:5 in the order of chiasmus between parallel texts also created a chiastic structure in 1 Chr 3:4. For this, see example 11.2 (p. 219).

a. **and in Jerusalem**   c. *and thirty-three years*
b. he reigned   b. he reigned
c. *thirty-three years*   a. **in Jerusalem**

and once in 1 Chr 29:26–27, as it appears in 1 Kgs 2:11:

1 Kgs 2:11	*1 Chr 29:26–27*
	ודויד בן ישי מלך על כל ישראל
הימים אשר מלך דוד על ישראל	והימים אשר מלך על ישראל
ארבעים שנה	ארבעים שנה
בחברון מלך שבע שנים	*בחברון מלך שבע שנים*
ובירושלם מלך שלשים ושלש שנים	**ובירושלם מלך שלשים ושלוש**

	And David, son of Jesse, reigned over all Israel.
The time that David reigned over Israel	The time that he reigned over Israel
was forty years;	was forty years;
in Hebron *he reigned seven years*,	**in Hebron** *he reigned seven years*,
and in Jerusalem he reigned thirty-three years.	**and in Jerusalem he reigned thirty-three.**

In this manner, a chiastic parallelism was created within the framework of the book of Chronicles—between 3:4b and 29:27:

1 Chr 3:4b	*1 Chr 29:27*
וימלך	*בחברון*
שם (בחברון)	*מלך*
שבע שנים וששה חדשים	שבע שנים
ושלשים ושלוש שנה	**ובירושלם**
מלך	*מלך*
בירושלם	שלשים ושלוש

12.79 In 2 Chr 9:28, the Chronicler borrowed a phrase from 1 Kgs 10:28 as a chiasmus between parallel texts:

1 Kgs 10:28   ומוצא הסוסים אשר **לשלמה** *ממצרים* ומקוה
               the import of the horses belonging **to Solomon**
               was from Egypt and from Kue
2 Chr 9:28   ומוציאים סוסים *ממצרים* **לשלמה** ומכל הארצות
               importing horses *from Egypt* **for Solomon**
               and from all the countries,

whereas in 2 Chr 1:16 he adduced the very same phrase, this time in its original order:

1 Kgs 10:28   ומוצא הסוסים אשר **לשלמה** *ממצרים* ומקוה

2 Chr 1:16   ומוצא הסוסים אשר **לשלמה** *ממצרים* ומקוא

and in this manner a chiastic parallelism was created between the two references in the book of Chronicles:

2 Chr 1:16   ומוצא הסוסים אשר **לשלמה** *ממצרים* ומקוא

2 Chr 9:28   .ומוציאים סוסים *ממצרים* **לשלמה** ומכל הארצות

B. Original Word Order plus Inverted Word Order in an "Addition"

The inverse of the above feature also appears. In this case, the Chronicler presents a text from Samuel–Kings in its original word order, but in an "addition" he cites the same text (or a very similar text) in inverted word order. Thus, he creates chiasmus between parallel texts, (a) between the words of the "addition" and the words in Samuel–Kings; and (b) between the two texts within the framework of the book of Chronicles:

Two-Member Structures

12.80 1 Kgs 7:40–45 recounts that Hiram made for King Solomon "the two **pillars** . . . and the *one sea* . . . and *all the vessels . . . made* of burnished bronze." The Chronicler inserts this text into 2 Chr 4:11–16, using the same word order for the equipment. However, in 1 Chr 18:8, which is an addition to 2 Sam 8:8, he mentions the equipment in reverse order: "wherewith Solomon made the *bronze sea* and the **pillars** and the vessels of bronze."

12.81

1 Kgs 8:65	*2 Chr 7:8*	*1 Chr 13:5*
ויעש שלמה בעת ההיא	ויעש שלמה את החג	ויקהל דויד את כל ישראל
את החג וכל ישראל	בעת ההיא . . . וכל ישראל	
עמו קהל גדול	עמו קהל גדול מאוד	
מלבוא חמת	**מלבוא חמה**	*מן שיחור* [52] *מצרים*
עד נחל מצרים	עד נחל מצרים	**ועד לבוא חמת**

52. For the term שיחור 'Shihor', see also Josh 13:3; Isa 23:3; Jer 2:18. This is an Egyptian term that means 'the water/pool of (the goddess) *Hor(us)*' and refers to the Nile or its arm/branch. The 'Brook of Egypt' is generally identified with Wadi el Arish in the Sinai, which is mentioned also in Num 34:5, 8 and Josh 15:4, 47 as the southwestern border of the Promised Land; see Curtis-Masden, *Chronicles*, 205, 349. Apparently, the Chronicler mistakenly equated the 'Shihor of Egypt' and the 'Brook of Egypt'. On some historical and geographical mistakes of the Chronicler, see below, chap. 20, §3 (pp. 392–403).

So Solomon held the feast at that time, and all Israel with him, a great assembly, from **the entrance of Hamath** to *the Brook of Egypt*	So Solomon held the feast at that time . . . and all Israel with him, a very great assembly, from **the entrance of Hamath** to *the Brook of Egypt*	So David assembled all Israel from *the Shihor of Egypt* to **the entrance of Hamath**

12.82 *1 Kgs 10:6, 9* | *2 Chr 9:5, 8* | *2 Chr 2:10–11*

ותאמר [מלכת־שבא] אל המלך . . . a. **יהי ה׳ אלהיך ברוך** אשר חפץ בך לתתך על כסא ישראל b. *באהבת ה׳ את ישראל לעלם* *וישימך למלך* . . .	ותאמר [מלכת־שבא] אל המלך . . . a. **יהי ה׳ אלהיך ברוך** אשר חפץ בך לתתך על כסאו למלך לה׳ אלהיך b. *באהבת אלהיך את ישראל להעמידו לעולם* *ויתנך עליהם למלך* . . .	ויאמר חורם מלך צר בכתב וישלח אל שלמה b. *באהבת ה׳ את עמו* *נתנך עליהם מלך* ויאמר חורם a. **ברוך ה׳ אלהי ישראל** 53 . . .

Then [the Queen of Sheba] said to the king, . . . a. "May **the Lord your God be blessed,** for He has delighted in you and placed you on the throne of Israel. b. *Because of the Lord's eternal love for Israel, He has made you king."*	Then [the Queen of Sheba] said to the king . . . a. "May **the Lord your God be blessed,** for He has delighted in you and placed you on His throne as king unto the Lord your God. b. *Because of your God's love for Israel,* to establish them forever, *He has placed you over them as king."*	Then Huram, king of Tyre, said in a document that he sent to Solomon, b. *"Because of the Lord's love for His people, He has made you king over them."* And Huram said, a. "May **the Lord God of Israel be blessed. . . ."**

Chiasmus between parallel texts also exists between words in the first line of 2 Chr 9:8 (// 1 Kgs 10:9) and the last line of 2 Chr 2:11:

2 Chr 9:8   יהי ה׳ אלהיך ברוך
May **the Lord your God** be *blessed*.

2 Chr 2:11   ברוך ה׳ אלהי ישראל
Blessed is **the Lord God of Israel**.

---

53. The Chronicler inserted into 2 Chr 2:10–11 (in the speech by Huram) a passage from 1 Kgs 10:9a (= 2 Chr 9:8) that is attributed to the Queen of Sheba!

12.83 *1 Sam 31:2*	*1 Chr 10:2*	*1 Chr 8:33 (= 9:39)*
וידבקו פלשתים	וידבקו פלשתים אחרי	ושאול הוליד
את שאול ואת בניו	שאול ואחרי בניו	
ויכו פלשתים	ויכו פלשתים	
את יהונתן	את יונתן	את יהונתן
ואת אבינדב	**ואת אבינדב**	*ואת מלכי־שוע*
ואת מלכי־שוע	*ואת מלכי־שוע*	**ואת אבינדב** [54]
The Philistines overtook	The Philistines overtook	Saul became the father of
Saul and his sons,	Saul and his sons,	
and the Philistines	and the Philistines	
killed Jonathan	killed Jonathan	Jonathan
and Abinadab	**and Abinadab**	*and Malchishua*
and Malchishua.	*and Malchishua.*	**and Abinadab**.

12.84 *1 Kgs 8:20*	*2 Chr 6:10*	*1 Chr 22:11*
ואקם תחת דוד אבי	ואקום תחת דויד אבי	עתה בני יהי ה' עמך
ואשב על כסא ישראל	ואשב על כסא ישראל	והצלחת
כאשר דבר ה'	**כאשר דבר ה'**	*ובנית בית ה' אלהיך*
ואבנה הבית לשם ה'	*ואבנה הבית לשם ה'*	**כאשר דבר עליך**
אלהי ישראל	*אלהי ישראל*	
And I rose up in place	And I rose up in place	Now, my son, may the
of David my father,	of David my father,	Lord be with you,
and I sat on the	and I sat on the	and may you succeed
throne of Israel	throne of Israel	
as the Lord	**as the Lord**	*in building the*
promised,	**promised,**	*House of the Lord*
		your God,
and I built the House	*and I built the House*	**as He promised**
for the name of the	*for the name of the*	**you**.
Lord, God of Israel.	*Lord, God of Israel.*	

12.85 *1 Kgs 5:30b[16b]*	*2 Chr 2:17*	*2 Chr 2:1*
שלשת אלפים ושלש מאות	**ושלשת אלפים ושש מאות**	*ומנצחים עליהם*
הרדים בעם העשים במלאכה	*מנצחים להעביד את העם*	**שלשת אלפים ושש מאות**
three thousand three	**three thousand six**	*and controlling*
hundred . . .	**hundred**	*them*
controlling the people	*controllers to make*	**three thousand six**
who did the work.	*the people work.*	**hundred**.

---

54. For chiasmus between parallel texts in the presentation of names, see, for example:

Isa 49:6, MT   להקים את שבטי **יעקב** ונצירי *ישראל* להשיב

    to establish the tribes of **Jacob** and to restore the offspring of *Israel*;

    1QIsaᵃ   להקים את שבטי *ישראל* ונצירי **יעקב** להשיב

    to establish the tribes of *Israel* and to restore the offspring of **Jacob**.

12.86 *1 Kgs 8:39*	*2 Chr 6:30*	*2 Chr 30:27*
ואתה תשמע	ואתה תשמע	וישמע בקולם
		ותבוא תפלתם
השמים	מן השמים	*למען קדשו*
מכון שבתך [55]	*מכון שבתך* [56]	**לשמים**[57]
May You then hear	May You then hear	Then He heard their voice and their prayer arrived
in heaven,	**from heaven,**	*at His holy place,*
Your dwelling-place.	*Your dwelling-place.*	**in heaven.**

12.87 *2 Kgs 22:13*	*2 Chr 34:21*	*1 Chr 10:13*
על אשר לא שמעו אבתינו	**על אשר לא שמרו אבותינו**	*על דבר ה׳*
על דברי הספר הזה	*את דבר ה׳ לעשות ככל*	**אשר לא שמר**
	הכתוב על הספר הזה	
because our fathers	**because** our fathers	*because of the*
did not hear	**did not observe**	*word of the Lord,*
the words of this book.	*the word of the Lord,*	**which he**
	to do everything	**did not observe.**
	written in this book.	

Here Benzinger, Begrich, and Curtis and Madsen[58] prefer the Septuagint and Peshiṭta, which are identical with the parallel 2 Kgs 22:13: על אשר לא שמעו אבתינו על דברי הספר הזה. However, the Chronicler seems to be explaining that the phrase לא שמעו 'did not hear' is the equivalent of לא שמרו 'did not observe', for, as far as he was concerned, the children of Israel "heard" the Torah from Moses at Mount Sinai. The fact that the expression על אשר לא שמרו . . . את דבר ה׳ / על דבר ה׳ אשר לא שמר appears in the book of Chronicles in these two places only and the fact that the link of "chiasmus between parallel texts" exists between them indicates that the Masoretic Text of 2 Chr 34:21 reflects the original

---

55. Compare vv. 23, 25, 30, 33, 35.

56. Compare vv. 32, 34, 39, 43, 45.

57. 2 Chr 30:27 may be used in comparison with the following text, which has a similar structure and also appears in Solomon's prayer:

1 Kgs 8:30   ואתה תשמע אל *מקום שבתך* אל **השמים** ושמעת וסלחת
May You then hear in *Your dwelling-place,* in **heaven**;
may You hear and forgive.

2 Chr 6:21   ואתה תשמע *ממקום שבתך* מן **השמים** ושמעת וסלחת
May You then hear from *Your dwelling-place,* from **heaven**;
may You hear and forgive.

Compare the wording of this verse also with Deut 26:15a השקיפה *ממעון קדשך מן השמים* וברך את עמך את ישראל . . . 'Look down from *Your holy habitation, from heaven,* and bless Your people, Israel . . .'.

58. Benzinger, *Chronik,* 131; Begrich, *BH,* 1429; Curtis-Madsen, *Chronicles,* 509–10.

version. The reading in the Septuagint and the Peshiṭta is merely the result of an editor's harmonizing of Chronicles and the earlier Kings, showing a preference for the latter.

Structures of Three or More Members

12.88

2 Sam 7:13–14a // 1 Chr 17:12–13a	1 Chr 22:10	1 Chr 28:6–7a
הוא יבנה בית	הוא יבנה לי בית	הוא יבנה בית	הוא יבנה ביתי
לשמי		לשמי	וחצרותי
וכננתי את כסא	וכננתי את כסאו	<u>והוא יהיה לי</u>	<u>כי בחרתי בו</u>
ממלכתו עד עולם	עד עולם	<u>לבן</u>	<u>לי לבן</u>
אני אהיה לו לאב	אני אהיה לו לאב	ואני לו לאב	ואני אהיה לו לאב
<u>והוא יהיה לי לבן</u>	<u>והוא יהיה לי לבן</u>	[59] והכינותי	והכינותי
		כסא מלכותו על	את מלכותו
		ישראל עד עולם	עד [60]לעולם

---

59. Here the Chronicler used the word והכינותי (compare 2 Sam 7:12c // 1 Chr 17:11c) instead of וכננתי (2 Sam 7:13 // 1 Chr 17:12). This change is merely one of stylistic variation and lacks any thematic significance.

60. In Ps 89:27–28, which is based on Nathan's prophecy, there is also a parallel to 2 Sam 7:14; see also Ps 2:7. The relationship of the future king (Solomon) to God is expressed here by means of a phrase that originally described an adoptive relationship in family law in the ancient Near East. "Viewing a king as the offspring of a god is a common motif in the literature and art of the ancient Near East. Despite rejecting the literal interpretation of the concept, Israel accepted it in a borrowed sense" (Paul, "Adoption Formulae," 31–32; see also the relevant literature cited there). An adoption formula serves in the biblical text not only to denote a personal relationship (a king to the Lord) but also to denote a national relationship (the people [or part of them] to the Lord). It is found in 2 Sam 7:24 // 1 Chr 17:22 and is quite widespread in the Pentateuch and in the Latter Prophets as well—also with a rearrangement of the components parts. For example:

Exod 6:7a	*Lev 26:12b*
ולקחתי אתכם לי לעם	והייתי לכם לאלהים
והייתי לכם לאלהים	ואתם תהיו לי לעם
And I shall take you to be My people,	**And I shall be your God,**
and I shall be your God.	*and you will be My people.*
Deut 29:12	*Deut 26:17–18*
למען הקים אתך היום לו לעם	את ה' האמרת היום להיות לך לאלהים . . .
והוא יהיה לך לאלהים	וה' האמירך היום להיות לו לעם סגלה
in order to establish you today	**You have elevated the Lord today**
as His people	**to be your God . . .**
and He will be your God.	*and the Lord has elevated you today to be His unique people.*

Compare also Exod 4:22; Deut 14:1; 32:6. The formula occurs five times in the book of Jeremiah, again with a rearrangement of its components parts (24:27; 30:22; 31:1, 33; 32:38 and compare also 31:8), as well as five times in the book of Ezekiel (37:23

He will build a House for My name,	He will build a House for Me,	He will build a House to My name,	He will build My House and courts,
and I will establish the throne of his kingdom forever;	**and I will establish his throne forever;**	*and he will be as a son to Me*;	*for I have chosen him as a son to Me,*
I will be as a father to him, **and he will be as a son to Me.**	*I will be as a father to him,* **and he will be as a son to Me.**	*and I—as a father to him,* **and I will establish the throne of his kingdom over Israel forever.**	*and I will be as a father to him,* **and I will establish his kingdom forever.**

12.89

2 Sam 8:16–18 [61] //	*1 Chr 18:15, 17*	*1 Chr 27:34*
‫ויואב בן צרויה‬ .a	‫ויואב בן צרויה‬ .a	**‫יהוידע בן‬** .c ‫בניהו‬ ... [62]
... ‫על הצבא‬ .b	... ‫על הצבא‬ .b	‫ושר הצבא למלך‬ .b
‫ובניהו בן יהוידע‬ .c ‫והכרתי והפלתי‬	‫ובניהו בן יהוידע‬ .c ‫על הכרתי והפלתי‬ [63]	‫יואב‬ .a
a. **Joab**, son of Zeruiah,	a. **Joab**, son of Zeruiah,	c. ***Jehoiada, son of Benaiah*** ...
b. *over the army* ...	b. *over the army* ...	b. *and the* king's *general,*
c. ***Benaiah, son of Jehoiada***, was over the Cherethites and the Pelethites.	c. ***Benaiah, son of Jehoiada***, over the Cherethites and the Pelethites.	a. **Joab**.

A similar feature can be seen in Exod 6:26–27: ‫הוא אהרן ומשה אשר אמר ה' להם‬ ‫הוציאו את בני־ישראל‬ ... ‫הם המדברים אל פרעה מלך מצרים להוציא את בני־ישראל ממצרים‬ ‫הוא משה ואהרן‬ 'It was **Aaron** and *Moses* to whom the Lord said: "Bring the Israelites out ... "; they were the ones who were speaking to Pharaoh, king of Egypt, to bring the Israelites out of Egypt—it was *Moses* and **Aaron**'. In light of these examples of changes in the order in which functionaries were listed in order to achieve stylistic variety, the conclusions

[= 11:20; 14:11; 36:28] and in inverse order in 37:27). In Hos 1:9 it is expressed in the negative: ‫אתם לא עמי ואנכי לא אהיה לכם‬ (apparently a mistake for ‫לא אלהיכם‬); compare Hos 2:25b; 11:1; Zech 8:8; also *Jub.* 2:19–20; 19:29. For a detailed discussion, see Smend, *Bundesformel*; Fensham, "Father and Son," 121–35.

61. This list is repeated in 2 Sam 20:23, which has no parallel in the book of Chronicles.

62. A name inversion took place here; compare with 1 Chr 27:5–6, as well as 1 Chr 11:22, 24 (= 2 Sam 23:20, 23); 18:17. Indeed, a number of manuscripts have: ‫בניהו בן‬ ‫יהוידע‬; see Rudolph, *BHS*, 1509.

63. The Peshiṭta, Targum, Vulgate, and a number of MT manuscripts have: ‫על הכרתי‬ ‫ועל הפלתי‬; compare with the parallel text in 2 Sam 20:23: ‫ועל הפלתי‬ ‫הכרתי‬ [*Qere*] ‫על הכרי‬. These translations and manuscripts seem to have preserved the original reading.

drawn by Mettinger[64] based on the order of the appearance of functionaries in the books of Samuel–Kings must be viewed with skepticism, along with his explanations of deviations from this "order."

12.90 In Solomon's prayer in 1 Kgs 8:37–39, Solomon lists natural disasters that were liable to occur in Israel and asks the Lord to hear the cries of his people and to heal them. In 2 Chr 6:28–30, the Chronicler lists these disasters in the order in which they appear in the earlier text. In 2 Chr 7:13, however, he inserts a short summary of this request into the Lord's response to Solomon (paraphrasing it) and lists two of the disasters in the order of chiasmus between parallel texts (a two-member structure). Elsewhere (2 Chr 20:5–13), in the prayer that he attributes to Jehoshaphat, he again uses the words of Solomon's request,[65] this time adducing the catastrophes in the order of chiasmus between parallel texts (a three-member structure):

1 Kgs 8:37–39	*2 Chr 6:28–30*	*2 Chr 7:13*	*2 Chr 20:9*
a. **רעב כי יהיה** באַרץ	a. **רעב כי יהיה** בארץ	a. **הן אעצר השמים ולא יהיה מטר**	c. אם תבוא עלינו רעה חרב [66]
b. **דבר כי יהיה**	b. **דבר כי יהיה**	c. **והן אצוה על חגב לאכול הארץ** [68]	c. **שפוט** [67]
c. **שדפון ירקון ארבה חסיל**	c. **שדפון וירקון ארבה וחסיל**	b. **ואם אשלח** דבר בעמי	b. **ודבר**
כי יהיה ... ופרש	כי יהיה ... ופרש	ויכנע עמי ...	a. **ורעב**
כפיו אל הבית הזה	כפיו אל הבית הזה	ואני אשמע מן השמים ואסלח	נעמדה לפני
ואתה תשמע	ואתה תשמע		הבית הזה
השמים מכון	מן השמים מכון		ולפניך כי
שבתך וסלחת ...	שבתך וסלחת ...		שמך בבית הזה
			ונזעק אליך
			מצרתנו ותשמע
			ותושיע [69]

---

64. See Mettinger, *State Officials*, 7–9.

65. For the relationship of Jehoshaphat's prayer to Solomon's, see the commentary attributed to Rashi on 2 Chr 20:9; Curtis-Madsen, *Chronicles*, 406–7; Rudolph, *Chronik*, 261; Japhet, *Ideology*, 68.

66. The word חרב is apparently referring to אם ינגף / בהנגף עמך ישראל לפני אויב 'If Your people, Israel, is defeated by an enemy', which appears in 2 Chr 6:24 // 1 Kgs 8:33.

67. The word שפוט may be used here as a general term for the misfortunes listed in 2 Chr 6:28 // 1 Kgs 8:37: "blight or mildew, locust or caterpillar," reminiscent of Ezek 14:21: "For thus says the Lord God: 'I have dispatched to Jerusalem My four deadly acts of judgment (שפטי הרעים)—sword, famine, fierce animals, and plague.'" (For the meaning of the word שפוט, see BDB, 1048a: "act of judgment"; cf. Ezek 23:10: שפוטים.) Elmslie views the phrase חרב שפוט as a construct form meaning חרב המשפט 'the sword of judgment' and compares this phrase with the one in Ezek 14:17 (Elmslie, *Chronicles* [1916], 251).

68. The Greek Lucianic recension reads: τὸ ξύλον 'the tree'; compare with Exod 10:15; Joel 1:6–7.

69. Compare this text with Jer 7:10, "then will you come and stand before this House, which is called by My name, and say, 'We have been saved'!"

a. If there is in the land a **famine**	a. If there is in the land a **famine,**	a. **If I shut up heaven and there is no rain**	If evil comes upon us, the sword,
b. if there is a *plague*	b. if there is a *plague*	c. **and if I order the locust to eat up the land**	c. *judgment,*
			b. *plague,*
c. if there is *blight, mildew, locust, or caterpillar* . . .	c. if there is *blight, mildew, locust, or caterpillar* . . .	b. and if I send *plague* on My people	a. **or famine,**
			we will stand in front of this House
any individual can spread forth his hands toward this House; then may You hear in Heaven, Your dwelling-place, and forgive.	any individual can spread forth his hands toward this House; then may You hear from Heaven, Your dwelling-place, and forgive.	and My people humble themselves . . . then I will hear from heaven, and I will forgive.	and in front of You, for Your name is on this House, and we will cry to You in our distress, and You will hear and save.

12.91 In the narrative of transferring the Ark from the house of Abi-nadab in Kiriat-jearim, in 1 Chr 13:8, the Chronicler listed the names of musical instruments in the order in which they appeared in the earlier text (2 Sam 6:5). In the description of the preparations for the transferring of the Ark from the house of Obed-Edom the Gittite, in 1 Chr 15:16 (an "addition"), however, he presented the identical instruments in reverse order:

2 Sam 6:5	1 Chr 13:8	1 Chr 15:16
ודוד וכל בית ישראל	ודויד וכל ישראל	ויאמר דויד לשרי הלוים
משחקים לפני ה׳ . . .	משחקים לפני האלהים . . .	להעמיד את אחיהם
		המשררים בכלי שיר
ובכנרות	**ובכנרות**	*נבלים*
ובנבלים ובתפים	*ובנבלים* ובתפים	**וכנרות**
ובמנענעים	ובמצלתים	ומצלתים משמיעים
ובצלצלים	ובחצצרות	להרים בקול לשמחה
Then David and all the house of Israel were playing before the Lord . . .	Then David and all Israel were playing before God . . .	Then David told the chiefs of the Levites to appoint their relatives to play on musical instruments,
on lyres, *harps,* tambourines, castanets, and cymbals.	**on lyres,** *harps,* tambourines, cymbals, and trumpets.	*on harps,* **lyres,** and cymbals to raise loud sounds of rejoicing.

Further along in the chapter (15:19–24), the Chronicler describes the execution of the plan given in v. 16, creating chiasmus between parallel texts in the listing of the musical instruments:

1 Chr 15:16	*1 Chr 15:19–21, 24*
Then David told the chiefs of the Levites to appoint their relatives to play on musical instruments: **harps, lyres,** *and cymbals,* to raise loud sounds of rejoicing.	Then the musicians Heman, Asaph, and Ethan played on bronze *cymbals to sound aloud* . . . **on harps** . . . **on lyres** . . . *playing on trumpets* before the Ark of God.

In v. 28, he describes the transfer of the Ark from the house of Obed-Edom to Jerusalem. Once again, in the list of musical instruments, he creates chiasmus between parallel texts with the order of instruments already presented in vv. 19–21, 24:

1 Chr 15:19–21, 24	*1 Chr 15:28*
a. **on** . . . **cymbals to sound aloud** . . . **on psalteries** . . . **on harps**	c. and all Israel brought up *the Ark of the Covenant of the Lord* . . .
b. . . . *playing on trumpets*	b. and *on trumpets*
c. before *the Ark of God*	a. **and on sounding cymbals, on lyres and harps**

12.92 In the narrative about transferring the Ark from the house of Obed-Edom to the City of David (1 Chr 15:28), the Chronicler uses the text of 2 Sam 6:15, adding the musical instruments present in the story of transferring the Ark from the house of Abinadab in Kiriat-jearim (1 Chr 13:8 // 2 Sam 6:5)—but in chiastic order:

2 Sam 6:5	//	*1 Chr 13:8*	*1 Chr 15:28*	//	*2 Sam 6:15*
Then David and all the house of Israel played before the Lord with instruments made of cypress-wood		Then David and all Israel played before God with all their might and with songs,	And all Israel brought up the Ark of the Covenant of the Lord with the sound of a shofar and the sound of a horn		Then David and all the house of Israel were transferring the Ark of the Lord with the sound of a shofar and the sound of a horn.

a. **and with lyres**,	a. **and with lyres**,	d. *and with trumpets*		
b. *harps, tambourines,* castanets, and cymbals.	b. *harps, tambourines,* c. cymbals, d. *and trumpets*.	c. and cymbals, b. *harps,* a. **and lyres**.		

Appendix:
Diachronic Chiasmus

Chiasmus between parallel texts is *a-chronic chiasmus*: a literary-stylistic feature devoid of any chronological significance. In the book of Chronicles, there are also a considerable number of words and phrases presented in inverted order that may be defined as *diachronic chiasmus*: a linguistic feature with chronological significance. This feature, again with word order inverse to the word order in the earlier text, stems in the main from a development that took place in the Hebrew language during the long period between the composition of the classical books (Samuel and Kings) and the composition of the book of Chronicles, one of the latest biblical books.

In Chronicles one may discern two groups of diachronic chiasmus: (1) one, a widespread group, is the inverse recording of a cardinal number and its noun; (2) the other is the inverse recording of certain word pairs compared with the order in which they were recorded in the earlier text.

A. The Inverse Recording of a Cardinal Number and Its Noun

In the Hebrew of the First Temple period, nouns were commonly written *after* cardinal numbers, whereas in the Hebrew used during the Second Temple period, the reverse order was generally preferred: the noun preceded the cardinal number.[70] Sometimes the Chronicler altered

---

70. Compare Kropat, *Syntax*, 51; Polzin, *Late Biblical Hebrew*, 58; and also GKC §134c/p. 432. According to GKC (ibid., n. 4):

From Herner's tables [Herner, *Syntax der Zahlwörter*, 55–66, 68] it appears . . . that in the documents J, E, D of the Pentateuch and in Jos 1–12, Judges, Samuel, Isaiah, Jeremiah, the Minor Prophets, Psalms, Megilloth, and Job, the numeral never, or very rarely, stands *after* its noun; in Kings and Ezekiel it stands several times *after*; in the Priestly Code nearly always *after*; in Chronicles, Ezra, Nehemiah, and Daniel, nearly as often *after* as *before* the noun.

These scholars stress that, in long lists dating from the First and Second Temple periods, nouns precede cardinal numbers. Some Hebrew inscriptions from the First Temple period use the formula noun + cardinal number—in other words, like the later structure. For instance, in Ostracon no. 2 from Tell Qasile: שׁ= זהב אפר לבית חרן 'Ophir gold for Bet Horon, *sh*[ekels **thirty**]' (see Maisler [= Mazar], "Tell Qasile," 67); and also in inscriptions from Arad: יין ב /// [= יין בתים שלושה] (see Aharoni, *Arad*, inscription 1, line 3). These cases show that the structure under consideration apparently served in similar contexts in the First Temple period as well (cf. Hurvitz, *Linguistic Study*, 168 n. 31). And compare these examples with 2 Sam 24:24: חמישים שׁקלים *'shekels* **fifty**'.

the ancient formula to the structure used in his time—the Second Temple period.[71] But not always. The following structures, for example, עומד על שני עשר בקר ... שני טורים 'two *rows of panels* ... standing on **twelve** *head of cattle*' (1 Kgs 7:24–25), אין בארון רק שני לחות 'there was nothing in the ark but **two** *tablets*' (1 Kgs 8:9), ותתן למלך מאה ועשרים ככר זהב 'she gave the king **one hundred twenty** talents of gold' (1 Kgs 10:10), were not inverted in the parallel texts in 2 Chr 4:3–4; 5:10; 9:9.

Occasionally, the Chronicler used the earlier structures; for example, 2 Chr 6:13 ("addition"): "its length was **five** *cubits* and its width **five** *cubits*." In general we may say that the Chronicler considered himself free to use both early and late structures in his book,[72] apparently for reasons of linguistic-stylistic variation and, sometimes, in order to create chiastic structures. Thus, for example:

> 2 Chr 30:24   Hezekiah, king of Judah, gave the people
> **a thousand** *bulls* and **seven thousand** *sheep*,
> and the princes gave the people *bulls*
> **a thousand** and *sheep* **ten thousand.**
> 1 Chr 22:14   gold, *talents* **a hundred thousand**;
> and silver, **a thousand thousand** *talents*.[73]

In this group of nouns plus cardinal numbers, there are two-member chiastic structures and three-member chiastic structures:

Two-Member Structures

12.93 1 Kgs 6:23   He made ... **two** *cherubs*.
       2 Chr 3:10   He made ... *cherubs* **two.**

---

71. The following Aramaic text was found on an ostracon from Tel el-Farʿa that has been dated paleographically to the end of the fifth century B.C.E.: "For sowing in the field, b(arley)—**k(urim)** *3* / in the estate (or in another), **k(urim)** *35*" (the reading is according to Naveh, "Two Aramaic Ostraca," 184–86). Similarly in the Arad inscriptions; for example, יין ב(תים) שלושה (inscription 1, line 3); also in insc. 4, line 3; insc. 6, line 4; insc. 8, line 5; insc. 9, line 3; insc. 10, line 2; see also Aharoni, *Arad*, 12, 20, 22, 24, 25, 26. These inscriptions were located in Stratum VI, which is dated to between 605 and 595 B.C.E. (pp. 8, 11).

72. The Chronicler preceded a noun with a cardinal numer 44 times and a cardinal number with a noun 76 times, which is 63.3% of the total. See Polzin, *Late Biblical Hebrew*, 59 and 81 n. 67; similar data emerge from Herner's tables (*Syntax*, 55–66, 68). It is also worthwhile to mention the usage of early structures alongside the later ones. See, just for an example, 2 Chr 6:13: "Solomon had made a bronze platform *five* **cubits** long, *five* **cubits** wide, and **cubits** *three* high."

73. See also 1 Chr 23:4–5; 29:7; 2 Chr 11:21. And compare this feature, for instance, with the description of the erection of the Tabernacle in Exod 36:17 (P): "And he made *loops* **fifty** on the edge of the outermost curtain in the first set, and he made **fifty** *loops* on the edge of the curtain in the second set."

12.94 1 Kgs 7:38   He made **ten** *basins*.
           2 Chr 4:6   He made *basins* **ten**.

12.95 1 Kgs 7:16   He made two capitals . . . **five** *cubits* the height
                          of the first capital and **five** *cubits* the height of
                          the second capital.
           2 Chr 3:15b   and the capital that was on the top of it—
                          cubits **five**.

12.96 1 Kgs 7:15   He formed the **two** *pillars* of bronze; **eighteen**
                          cubits was the height of the first column.
           2 Chr 3:15a   He made . . . *pillars* **two**,[74] *cubits*
                          thirty-five high.

12.97 1 Kgs 7:26   the flower of a lily, holding **two thousand** *baths*.
           2 Chr 4:5   like the flower of a lily, מחזיק [it held][75]
                          baths—**three thousand** it held.

12.98 Josh 21:33   **thirteen** *cities*.
           1 Chr 6:47   *cities* **thirteen**.[76]

Three-Member Structures

12.99   *1 Kgs 5:25[11]*   *2 Chr 2:9[10]*
   a. **twenty thousand**   c. of beaten ***wheat*** for your servants
   b. *measures*   b. *measures*
   c. ***of wheat***, food for his   a. **twenty thousand**
      household
   a. **twenty**   c. . . . and ***oil***
   b. *measures*   b. *baths*
   c. ***of crushed oil***   a. **twenty thousand**

12.100   *1 Kgs 6:2b*   *2 Chr 3:3b*
   a. **sixty**   c. ***the length*** . . .
   b. *cubits*   b. was *cubits*
   c. ***long***   a. **sixty**
   a. **and twenty**   c. ***and the width***

---

74. Compare this structure with 2 Chr 4:12 (// 1 Kgs 7:41): "He made . . . *columns*
two."

75. The word מחזיק 'it held' may have been added here in order to explain the word
יכיל 'holds' at the end of the verse. Indeed, the LXX reads only: χωροῦσαν (= יכיל), as in
Kings. Compare Ehrlich, *Mikrâ ki-Pheschutô*, 449; Curtis-Madsen, *Chronicles*, 332.

76. Additionally, compare 1 Chr 22:14, "Gold—*talents* **one hundred thousand**,"
with the formula in 1 Kgs 9:14: "**One hundred twenty** *talents* of gold."

b. _____ [77]   b. was *cubits*
c. *wide*   a. **twenty**

12.101   *1 Kgs 6:3*   *2 Chr 3:4*
a. **twenty**   c. *its length across the width
                                          of the house*
b. *cubits* was   b. was *cubits*
c. *its length across the width*   a. **twenty**
   of the house

12.102   *1 Kgs 6:20*   *2 Chr 3:8*
a. **and twenty**   c. **and its width**
b. *cubits*   b. *cubits*
c. *in width*   a. **twenty**

12.103   *1 Kgs 6:24*   *2 Chr 3:11*
a. **and five**   c. *the one wing*
b. *cubits*   b. *cubits* long
c. *the one wing of the cherub*   a. *five . . .*
a. **and five**   c. **and the other wing**
b. *cubits*   b. *cubits* long
c. *the other wing of the cherub*   a. five[78]

B. The Inverse Recording of Word Pairs

In his study, " 'Diachronic Chiasmus' in Biblical Hebrew," A. Hurvitz mentions three word pairs that were generally recorded in the Second Temple period in inverted order compared with the order current in the First Temple period.[79] The first two pairs that he mentions also appear

----

77. In the LXX, Peshiṭta, Vulgate, and a number of MT manuscripts, we find אמה 'cubits', as in the previous section of the text and in the parallel text in Chronicles.

78. Compare this verse and its structure with the continuation of the text in v. 12.

79. See Hurvitz, "Diachronic Chiasmus," 248–55. Avishur (*Word Pairs*, 253–60) disagrees with the conclusions in Hurvitz's study, claiming, "The change of order always has stylistic significance, never linguistic significance, both in general—as regards all word pairs—and in particular, concerning the three pairs Hurvitz deals with" (Avishur, pp. 253–54; see also his article: "Word Order," 340 n. 23). However, as Talshir has noted, Avishur did not take into account the distribution of these three pairs throughout the Bible (Talshir, "Septuagint," 309–10). For example, if the order "silver and gold" is found *mostly* in First Temple period literature, while the order "gold and silver" is found *mostly* in Second Temple period literature, it may reasonably be assumed that the difference in order stems from some linguistic development. Moreover, the late occurrence of the pair "gold and silver" is confirmed from the apocryphal book of Esdras and from extrabiblical sources (Hurvitz, "Diachronic Chiasmus," 248–53; Talshir, "Septuagint," 310–11). The late appearance of the pair "great and small" is also confirmed from extrabiblical sources.

inverted in the book of Chronicles, but the third one occurs in inverse order only in Chronicles:

12.104 2 Sam 8:10   Then Toi sent Joram . . . who brought vessels
                         of **silver**, *gold*, and bronze.

       1 Chr 18:10   Then he sent Hadoram . . . and all sorts of vessels
                     of *gold*, **silver**, and bronze.[80]

12.105 2 Kgs 23:2   and the priests, prophets, and all the people,
                         from the smallest to *the greatest*.

       2 Chr 34:30   the priests, Levites, and all the people,
                     from the greatest to **the smallest**.[81]

12.106 2 Sam 24:2   Please wander throughout the tribes of Israel,
                         from Dan to *Beer-sheba*.

       1 Chr 21:2   Go and tell Israel, *from Beer-sheba* to **Dan**.

This phrase occurs in precisely this form in 2 Chr 30:5 as well (an "addition"). For the expression עד מבאר־שבע 'from Beer-sheba to . . .', see also 2 Chr 19:4; Neh 11:30.[82]

The Chronicler was free to present these word pairs both in the earlier order and the later, apparently for purposes of linguistic-stylistic variation. The order "gold and silver" appears in the book of Chronicles 12 times (1 Chr 18:10; 22:14, 16; 29:2, 3, 5; 2 Chr 2:6, 13; 9:14, 21; 24:14; 25:24); the order "silver and gold" appears 9 times (1 Chr 18:11; 2 Chr 1:15; 5:1; 9:24; 15:18; 16:2, 3; 21:3; 32:27).[83] This finding seems to

---

80. See also Dan 5:2, מאני דהבא וכספא 'vessels of gold and silver', for another instance when the (construct form of the) word כלי is not repeated before the second item. This also may be a sign of a later period; and see Hurvitz, "Diachronic Chiasmus," 249 n. 4 and earlier relevant literature listed there.

81. The word והנביאים 'and the prophets' was apparently replaced by the word והלוים 'and the Levites' for ideological reasons; see Seeligmann, "Beginning of *Midrash*," 24–29.

82. Hurvitz ("Diachronic Chiasmus," 254 n. 26) surmises that this interchange was caused by "historical circumstances to be interpreted in light of the borders of the province of Yehud during the Restoration period; within these borders, which encompassed the land of Judah only, Beersheba was a concrete concept—as opposed to Dan which lay far to the north." However, as far as may be learned from the sources, during the lifetime of the Chronicler, Yehud-Medinta ('the province of Yehud') did not extend as far as Beer-sheba. For the borders and settlements of Yehud-Medinta, see Stern, "Geographic-Historical Background," 241–43.

83. However, as already mentioned, the extensive general distribution of the pattern "gold and silver" in late biblical literature (30 occurrences) in contrast to its relatively sparse distribution in early biblical literature (10 times); and, on the other hand, the frequent distribution of the pattern "silver and gold," particularly in the

strengthen the assumption that the Hebrew of the Second Temple period was actually in the transition stage between Classical Hebrew and
Mishnaic Hebrew.

Sometimes the Chronicler used both forms in order to create chiastic
structures; for example, in place of the phrase "vessels of **silver** and
vessels of *gold*" in 2 Sam 8:10, the Chronicler wrote in 1 Chr 18:10:
"vessels of *gold* and **silver**." However, immediately thereafter he copied
the linguistic pattern in the earlier original as it stood—1 Chr 18:11
(// 2 Sam 8:11): "These also King David dedicated to the Lord, with **the
silver** *and the gold* that he had carried off . . . ," thus creating a chiastic
structure in his book:

> 1 Chr 18:10   vessels of *gold* **and silver**
> 1 Chr 18:11   **the silver** *and the gold.*[84]

All in all, we may conclude that the phenomenon of diachronic chiasmus is not limited to a mere three-word pairs.[85] It also encompasses not
a few cases of the inverted recording of a cardinal number and its noun,
which can be seen by comparing late biblical historical passages with
their parallel earlier counterparts.

---

early books of the Bible, and its relatively infrequent distribution in the later books—
these are what determine the antiquity of the one pattern and the late vintage of the
other, and this conclusion is supported by extrabiblical testimony (against Avishur,
Word Pairs, 258 n. 13).

84. See also the similar 2 Chr 9:21, "*gold* **and silver**," and v. 25, "vessels of **silver**
and vessels of *gold*" (// 1 Kgs 10:22, 25).

85. Rofé ("David and Goliath") claims that an additional word pair of "diachronic
chiasmus" appears in 1 Sam 17:11: "And Saul and all Israel heard these words of the
Philistine, **and they trembled** and *feared* greatly (ויחתו וידא מאוד)." According to
him, "Classical Biblical Hebrew used to say אל תירא ואל תחת 'do not *fear* nor **tremble**'
(Deut 1:21, etc.). Only here in the entire Bible does the pair יר״א—חת״ת occur in an inverse order, which, insofar as one can explain it, is one of the signs of the later language." However, an examination of the pair יר״א—תח״ת shows that it appears in the
Hebrew Bible 12 times: 5 times in earlier books (Deut 1:21; 31:8; Josh 8:1; 10:25; Jer
23:4) and 7 times in later books (Ezek 2:6; 3:9; 1 Chr 22:13; 28:20; 2 Chr 20:15, 17;
32:7). Therefore, it was customary to say אל תירא ואל תחת, both in Classical Hebrew
and in the later language. The inverted phrase ויחתו וידא does not appear even once
in Late Hebrew. It thus seems difficult to draw conclusions regarding the date of its
formation from a single, unusual appearance in 1 Sam 17:11 (whatever the accepted
view of the date of the composition and final redaction of 1 Samuel 17 may be!).

Chapter 13
Repetitions

1. Resumptive Repetition

Resumptive repetition (*Wiederaufnahme*)[1] is the repetition of a word or phrase after an interval of a number of words or phrases, in order to renew the connection with the central descriptive theme of the text. The words or phrases constituting the interval are usually a late addition introduced into an earlier text. In these cases, the resumptive repetition served as a literary technique that a later writer used to signal the fact that he had introduced his own words into an earlier, already formulated text.

Resumptive repetition was noted as early as the medieval Jewish exegetes; for example, Exod 6:29–30 repeats the content of 6:10–12, because of the interval in the main theme of the narrative created by vv. 13–28 (the genealogy of Moses and Aaron). Rashi in his commentary on v. 30 writes: "'Then Moses said in the Lord's presence'—this is what he said above: הן בני־ישראל לא שמעו אלי (v. 12); the text here is repeated because the theme was interrupted. Such is the system, as if a person were saying, 'Let us return to the beginning.'"[2] This literary technique is used frequently in the books of the Bible.[3] It becomes especially prominent when one is comparing "parallel texts." In the case of Chronicles, we can clearly see that the Chronicler introduced his own words into passages from Samuel–Kings by means of resumptive repetition, as the examples below demonstrate.

There are a number of exceptions to the rule, however: sometimes the words that constitute the interval were not a "late addition" introduced into an earlier text at all but were part of the earlier text, the Chronicler having seen fit to formulate them into a resumptive repetition. Occasionally, the words constituting the interval were taken, at least partly,

---

1. This is the German term, which is often used in biblical study and was borrowed from the field of classical literary criticism.

2. For similar examples, see Rabbi Abraham ibn Ezra on Num 15:40 and on Ruth 1:22.

3. See also the examples provided in the following works: Kuhl, "Wiederaufnahme," 1–11 (especially the examples from the book of Jeremiah); Bar-Efrat, *Narrative Art*, 25–26 (examples from the Pentateuch and Former Prophets); Rofé, *Prophetical Stories*, 63 n. 13 (2 Kgs 6:17–18), 144 (1 Kgs 22:17–19); Schmoldt, "Zwei 'Wiederaufnahmen,'" 423–26. See also below for examples from the books of Exodus and Nehemiah (p. 291).

from an earlier text, which the Chronicler introduced into narrative that appears only in his book.

Finally, the Chronicler sometimes quoted the word or phrase making up the resumptive repetition exactly, and on other occasions he quoted it but introduced slight changes or even shortened it, apparently for purposes of literary variation.

The numerous examples of "resumptive repetition" from the book of Chronicles, as introduced in this chapter, contradict Seeligman's claim absolutely: "There are only a few occurrences of 'Resumptive Repetition' in the book of Chronicles. It seems that this technique was out of usage in this late stage of the Israelite historiography."[4]

13.1 In 2 Chr 6:13b, the Chronicler repeated a phrase from v. 12b (// 1 Kgs 8:22b), נגד כל קהל ישראל ויפרש כפיו 'in the presence of all the congregation of Israel and spread out his hands', because of an addition that he had introduced into the text (v. 13a: כי עשה שלמה . . . ויברך על ברכיו 'for Solomon had made . . . and kneeled on his knees').[5] This addition separated the text in v. 12 from that in v. 14. In other words, v. 13b serves as a resumptive repetition linking v. 12 (// 1 Kgs 8:22) to its continuation in v. 14 (// 1 Kgs 8:23):

1 Kgs 8:22–23	2 Chr 6:12–14
22a. ויעמד שלמה לפני מזבח ה׳	12a. ויעמד לפני מזבח ה׳
b. נגד כל קהל ישראל ויפרש כפיו	b. **נגד כל קהל ישראל ויפרש כפיו**
	13a. כי עשה שלמה כיור נחשת ויתנהו
	בתוך העזרה חמש אמת ארכו וחמש
	אמות רחבו ואמות שלוש קומתו,
	ויעמד עליו ויברך על ברכיו 6

4. Seeligmann, "Biblische Geschichtsschreibung," 54 n. 23.

5. For the purpose of the "addition," see Curtis-Madsen, *Chronicles*, 342. He believes that the Chronicler tried, by means of this "addition," to move Solomon away from before the altar, which was a sanctified place for priests. Similarly Wellhausen, *Prolegomena*, 181 (ET, 186); Ehrlich, *Mikrâ ki-Pheschutô*, 450; Montgomery, *Kings*, 196. Montgomery suggests another explanation of this "addition": by means of the words ויעמד עליו ויברך על ברכיו 'and he stood on it and knelt on his knees' (2 Chr 6:13a), the Chronicler wanted to resolve the contradiction between 1 Kgs 8:22 (which relates that Solomon *stood* "before the altar of the Lord") and v. 54b (which relates that, after concluding his prayer, Solomon "*arose* from before the altar of the Lord, from kneeling on his knees"). It is difficult, however, to attribute such an intention to the Chronicler. This contradiction does not exist at all in his book because he did not cite 1 Kgs 8:54bff.

6. Gray believes that "the parallel passage in II Chron. 6.13 significantly omits any mention of the altar and depicts Solomon as officiating on a bronze scaffold" (Gray, *Kings*, 219). He concludes, "This reflects the increased status and cultic monopoly of

.b נגד כל קהל ישראל ויפרש כפיו

השמים	השמימה
23. ויאמר ה׳ אלהי ישראל	14. ויאמר ה׳ אלהי ישראל
אין כמוך אלהים בשמים...	אין כמוך אלהים בשמים...

22a. Then Solomon stood before the altar of the Lord	12a. Then he stood before the altar of the Lord
b. **in the presence of all the congregation of Israel and spread out his hands**	b. **in the presence of all the congregation of Israel and spread out his hands—**
	13a. for Solomon had made a bronze basin and put it in the court, five cubits long, five cubits wide, and three cubits high, and he stood on it and knelt down on his knees
	b. **in the presence of all the congregation of Israel and spread out his hands**
to the heavens.	to the heavens.
23. And he said: "O Lord, God of Israel, there is no god like You in heaven. . . ."	14. And he said: "O Lord, God of Israel, there is no god like You in heaven. . . ."

At first glance, one might claim that 2 Chr 6:13 is not an "addition" made by the Chronicler but is a reflection of his *Vorlage*; the words were omitted from the book of Kings by homoioteleuton: a copyist's eyes skipped from the words נגד כל קהל ישראל ויפרש כפיו to the very same words appearing further along.[7] However, because of the frequency of the use of resumptive repetition in the book of Chronicles and because of the following signs of late language employed in 2 Chr 6:13, we must conclude that this passage is the Chronicler's own creation:

(a) The word עזרה 'court' appears in the Hebrew Bible 9 times: 3 times in Chronicles, in passages with no parallels (once in this verse and twice in 2 Chr 4:9), and 6 times in the book of Ezekiel (43:14 [3×]; 43:17, 20; and 45:19). On the other hand, the word is very common in

---

the priestly caste in the post-exilic period." Whatever the reason is for the Chronicler's "addition" regarding the erection of the "bronze scaffold" in the vestibule, it cannot be the fact that the altar is not mentioned in v. 12a, for the Chronicler had already mentioned it in the previous verse: ויעמד [שלמה] לפני מזבח ה׳.

7. Such is the belief, for example, of: Bertheau, *Chronik*, 263–64; Albright, *Archaeology*, 152; Rudolph, *Chronik*, 213; Lemke, "Synoptic Problem," 357–58.

Rabbinic Hebrew[8] and in the Aramaic Targumim.[9] Thus, we may reasonably assume that the word עזרה did not exist in early Hebrew but in the later language (and in the language of Ezekiel, during a transition stage between the two) and afterwards, in the Hebrew of the Mishnah and the Targumim. Furthermore, the phrase חצר הגדולה 'the great court', which appears in the description of the building of the Temple in 1 Kgs 7:12, was altered in the parallel text in 2 Chr 4:9 to העזרה הגדולה 'the great court', apparently in accordance with the linguistic custom in the Second Temple period—the Chronicler's period.[10]

(b) The syntactical form ואמות שלוש in our verse, that is, the noun preceding its cardinal number, is widespread in later Hebrew in general and in the Chronicler's language in particular. Thus, for example, compare: והארך . . . אמות ששים ורחב אמות עשרים 'the length . . . cubits sixty and the width cubits twenty' (2 Chr 3:3), ארכו . . . אמות עשרים ורחבו אמות עשרים 'its length . . . cubits twenty and its width cubits twenty' (2 Chr 3:8), כיורים עשרה 'basins ten' (2 Chr 4:6) with their parallel texts: ששים אמה ארכו ועשרים (אמה) רחבו 'sixty cubits in length and twenty (cubits) in width' (1 Kgs 6:2), עשרים אמה ארך ועשרים אמה רחב 'twenty cubits long and twenty cubits wide' (1 Kgs 6:19), עשרה כיורות 'ten basins' (1 Kgs 7:38).[11]

Rudolph,[12] who discerns homoioteleuton in the book of Kings, attributes the passage in 2 Chr 6:13 to the Chronicler's *Vorlage* and attempts to support this claim by means of the linguistic-stylistic character of the text. In his opinion, the use of the word קומה in the sense 'tall, high' is not part of the Chronicler's style but the style of the author of the book of Kings. Even if this is true, however, it does not prove an early date for v. 13, for the Chronicler felt free to use both early and late forms. Furthermore, what determines the date of a passage is its latest words and forms, not the opposite!

13.2 In 2 Chr 12:9a the Chronicler repeated what he had written before in v. 2b (// 1 Kgs 14:25b): ויעל שישק מלך מצרים על ירושלם 'Then Shishak, king of Egypt, came up against Jerusalem'. He did this after "adding" to the earlier text: כי מעלו בה '. . . ועבודת ממלכות הארצות 'for they had betrayed

---

8. See *m. Mid.* 5:1; *b. Yoma* 16b. For additional references, see Kosovsky, *A Thesaurus of Tannaitic Hebrew*, 4.1357; Kasowski, *A Thesaurus of Talmudic Hebrew*, 28.317–21.

9. See, for example, Isa 1:12: מי בקש זאת מידכם—רמס חצרי 'Who demanded of you—to trample *My courts*?' which is translated into Aramaic: מן תבע דא מידכון—למיתי ולאתדשא עזרתי; so, too, in Targum Jonathan on 1 Sam 3:3.

10. See Hurvitz, *Linguistic Study*, 78–81.

11. For this, see also Kropat, *Syntax*, 51; Polzin, *Late Biblical Hebrew*, 58–59, 81 n. 67. See also the discussion and examples adduced above in the appendix to chap. 12, "Chiasmus between Parallel Texts" (pp. 269–274).

12. Rudolph, *Chronik*, 213.

the Lord . . . and serving the kingdoms of other lands' (vv. 2c–8).[13] This "addition" intervenes between v. 2b and vv. 9bff., parallel with 1 Kgs 14:26ff. In other words, v. 9a is a resumptive repetition of v. 2b before the continuation of the passage in v. 9b:[14]

1 Kgs 14:25–26	2 Chr 12:2–9
25a. ויהי בשנה החמישית למלך רחבעם	2a. ויהי בשנה החמישית למלך רחבעם
b. עלה שושק (Qere) שישק) מלך מצרים על ירושלם	b. עלה שישק מלך מצרים על ירושלם
	c. כי מעלו בה׳ . . .
	3–8. Details of Shishak's armies, his Judean conquests, the speech delivered by Shemaiah, the prophet, and the surrender of the king and his officers.
	9a. ויעל שישק מלך מצרים על ירושלם
26. ויקח את אצרות בית ה׳ ואת אצרות בית המלך . . .	b. ויקח את אצרות בית ה׳ ואת אצרות בית המלך . . .
25a. In the fifth year of King Rehoboam,	2a. In the fifth year of King Rehoboam,
b. **Shishak, king of Egypt, went up against Jerusalem**	b. **Shishak, king of Egypt, went up against Jerusalem**
	c. for they had betrayed the Lord. . . .
	3–8. Details as above.
	9a. **And Shishak, king of Egypt, went up against Jerusalem**
26. and took away the treasures of the House of the Lord and the treasures of the house of the king.	b. and took away the treasures of the House of the Lord and the treasures of the house of the king.[15]

13.3 The cubit customary in the Chronicler's day was, apparently, a long cubit, equal to seven handbreadths, one more than the short

---

13. The statement that 2 Chr 12:2c–8 is an "addition" compares the verses with the book of Kings but takes no stand regarding the historical reliability of the details given. For the reliability of the details in these verses, see Mazar, "Shishak's Campaign," 141; for the opposite opinion, see, for example, Ehrlich, *Mikrâ ki-Pheschutô*, 453; Willi, *Chronik*, 175; and Naʾaman, "Pastoral Nomads," 271–72.

14. Compare with Seeligmann, "Biblische Geschichtsschreibung," 315.

15. It is worth noting that as a result of this "resumptive repetition" the literary unit in 2 Chr 12:1–12 came to be shaped chiastically (see Van Grol, "Servants We Are," 219–21).

cubit used when Solomon's Temple was built.[16] Consequently, when the
Chronicler quoted the dimensions of the Temple as described in the
book of Kings, he introduced a comment into the earlier text, stressing
that the cubit mentioned was that "of the former measure" (2 Chr
3:3b)—that is, equal to the short, earlier cubit—rather than the one customary in his time. Because of the interval that this comment created
between the word אמות 'cubits' and the number ששים 'sixty', denoting the
number of cubits, the Chronicler repeated the word אמות before the
number ששים:

1 Kgs 6:2	*2 Chr 3:3*
והבית אשר בנה המלך שלמה לה׳	הוסד שלמה לבנות את בית האלהים
ששים	הארך
אמה	**אמות** במדה הראשונה
ארכו	**אמות ששים** [17]
The House that King Solomon	Solomon's measurements for
built for the Lord was	building the House of God:
sixty	its length
cubits	in **cubits**—of the former standard—
long.	**cubits** sixty.

13.4 In 2 Chr 1:6, the Chronicler inserted the fact of the existence of
a "bronze altar before the Lord, which was at the Tent of Meeting" (compare with vv. 3, 5, 13a).[18] This led him to repeat the verb ויעל 'he offered'
that appears at the head of the verse, together with the modifier עליו 'on
it' that alludes to the phrase על מזבח הנחשת, in order to link the beginning with the rest of the verse after his own words:

1 Kgs 3:4c	*2 Chr 1:6*
אלף עלות	**ויעל** שלמה שם על *מזבח הנחשת*
	לפני ה׳ אשר לאהל מועד
יעלה שלמה על המזבח ההוא	**ויעל** *עליו* עלות אלף [19]

---

16. The long cubit is mentioned in the description of Ezekiel's Temple: וביד האיש
קנה המדה שש אמות באמה ואמה וטפח 'and in the man's hand was the measuring reed: six long
cubits, each being a cubit and a handbreadth in length' (Ezek 40:5; cf. 43:13). This
cubit was used in Mesopotamia as well; see also Scott, "The Hebrew Cubit," 205–
14; Stern, "Measures and Weights," 848–49; see also Kaufman, "Medium Cubit,"
120–32. The statement by Ehrlich, *Mikrâ ki-Pheschutô*, 449, "and the latter measure [used in the Chronicler's day] was smaller than the former [used in Solomon's
day]," is not accurate.

17. The Chronicler used the words from the book of Kings in the order of "chiasmus between parallel texts"; for this, see the appendix to chap. 12 (pp. 269–274).

18. For the reason for this introduction, see the detailed discussion in example
7.18 (pp. 142–147).

19. The Chronicler adduced the words of 1 Kgs 3:4c in the order of "chiasmus between parallel texts" in his own book; for this device, see example 12.38 (pp. 246–247).

| A thousand offerings | Solomon **offered** there *on the bronze altar* before the Lord, which was at the Tent of Meeting, |
| Solomon **offered** *on that altar.* | **and he offered** *on it* a thousand offerings. |

13.5 In 2 Chr 22:1a the Chronicler wrote וימליכו יושבי ירושלם את אחזיהו בנו הקטן תחתיו 'Then the inhabitants of Jerusalem *crowned* **Ahaziah, his** young **son, in his stead**', parallel to the text of 2 Kgs 8:24, וימלך אחזיהו בנו תחתיו 'Then **Ahaziahu, his son, reigned in his stead**'. Immediately thereafter (v. 1b), he notes: [20]כי כל הראשנים הרג הגדוד הבא בערבים במחנה 'for the band that came into the camp with the Arabs killed all the former ones', in accordance with his narrative in 21:16–17:

ויער ה׳ על יהורם את רוח הפלשתים והערבים . . . וישבו את כל הרכוש הנמצא
לבית המלך וגם בניו ונשיו, ולא נשאר לו בן כי אם יהואחז (LXX, Aramaic)
אחזיהו קטן בניו [21] (and Peshiṭta: אחזיהו)

Then the Lord aroused the anger of the Philistines and the Arabs
. . . and they carried away all the possessions belonging to the
house of the king, along with his sons and his wives, so that the
only son left to him was Jehoahaz [LXX, etc.: Ahaziah], his youngest son.

Because the comment intervenes between the words וימליכו . . . תחתיו and their continuation אחזיהו במלכו [22]בן ארבעים ושתים שנה 'Ahaziah was forty-two years old when he became king' (v. 2), the Chronicler repeated

---

20. The translation of הבא בערבים as 'which came with the Arabs' is used by Curtis-
Madsen, *Chronicles*, 419–20; Elmslie, *Chronicles* (1916) 264, in his translation of the
text; and Rudolph, *Chronik*, 268. Another reading is proposed by Ehrlich, *Mikrâ ki-
Pheschutô*, 461: 'of Arabs'—that is, a מ/ב interchange. Naʾaman ("Pastoral Nomads,"
272 n. 33) assumed that "perhaps the original source mentioned the time (הבא בערב
'who came in the evening', הבא [בין ה]ערבים 'who came [between the] two evenings', or
the like), which stressed the surprise element of the attack, but the Chronicler did not
understand the expression and interpreted it by mistake as an allusion to the ethnic
group of the Arabs." It is very difficult to suppose, however, that the Chronicler did
not understand a simple and common expression such as הבא [בין ה]ערבים. This expression occurs in the Hebrew Bible several times (e.g., Exod 16:12; 29:39, 41; Num 9:3,
5, 11). It appears in regard to the Passover sacrifice (Exod 12:6; Lev 23:5; Num 28:4,
8)—an actual commandment that the Chronicler and his community had to obey precisely. For the expression הבא הערב, compare שבה היא ובבוקר היא באה בערב 'she would go
in the evening and leave in the morning' (Esth 2:14); ואתה תצא בערב לעיניהם 'and go out
again in the evening in their sight' (Ezek 12:6).
21. For the historical and historiographical aspects of these texts, see Naʾaman,
"Pastoral Nomads," 272–73.
22. The LXX (Vaticanus and Alexandrinus) has בן עשרים שנה 'twenty years old',
while the Lucianic recension and Peshiṭta have בן עשרים ושתים שנה 'twenty-two years
old', like the parallel text in the book of Kings.

the words of v. 1c, וימלך אחזיהו בן יהורם מלך יהודה 'Ahaziah, son of Jehoram, king of Judah, reigned' in order to renew the link with it:

2 Kgs 8:24–26	2 Chr 21:20–22:2
24. וישכב יורם עם אבתיו	21:20b. וילך [יהורם] בלא חמדה
ויקבר עם אבתיו בעיר דוד	ויקברהו בעיר דויד
	ולא בקברות המלכים
וימלך אחזיהו בנו תחתיו	22:1a. **וימליכו יושבי ירושלם את**
	אחזיהו בנו הקטן תחתיו
25a. בשנת שתים עשרה שנה ליורם	b. כי כל הראשנים הרג הגדוד
בן אחאב מלך ישראל	הבא בערבים למחנה
b. מלך אחזיהו בן יהורם	c. **וימלך אחזיהו בן יהורם**
מלך יהודה	**מלך יהודה**
26. בן עשרים ושתים שנה	22:2. בן ארבעים ושתים שנה
אחזיהו במלכו	אחזיהו במלכו
ושנה אחת מלך בירושלם	ושנה אחת מלך בירושלם

24.	Then Joram slept with his fathers and was buried with his fathers in the City of David,	21:20b.	He [= Jehoram] departed to no one's regret, and they buried him in the City of David, but not in the tombs of the kings.
	and Ahaziah, his son, reigned in his stead.	22:1a.	**And the inhabitants of Jerusalem crowned Ahaziah, his youngest son, in his stead,**
25a.	In the twelfth year of Joram, son of Ahab, king of Israel,	b.	for all the older sons were killed by the band that came to the camp with the Arabs.
b.	Ahaziah, son of Jehoram, king of Judah, reigned.	c.	**Ahaziah, son of Jehoram, king of Judah, reigned.**
26.	Ahaziah was twenty-two years old when he reigned, and he reigned in Jerusalem one year.	2.	Ahaziah was forty-two years old when he reigned, and he reigned in Jerusalem one year.

In 22:1c, the Chronicler seems to have used the words of 2 Kgs 8:25b, replacing the word מלך with the word וימלך.[23]

13.6 1 Chr 11:1–3, 11:10–12:47 tells about the coronation of David by "all Israel" and about the widespread support that he received from all of the tribes, their leaders, and their warriors. The narrative of the con-

---

23. In 2 Kgs 8:25, the writer/redactor synchronized the kings of Israel and the kings of Judah. The Chronicler usually omitted the synchronizations that he encountered in the book of Kings, just as he did here.

quest of Jerusalem (11:4–9 // 2 Sam 5:6–10) intervenes between the narrative of the arrival of **"all Israel"** in Hebron to anoint *"David king over Israel, according to the word of the Lord* through Samuel" (11:1–3 // 2 Sam 5:1–3) and the list of the tribal warriors and leaders who supported David's coronation (11:10–12:47 // 2 Sam 23:8–39). In order to link the two, the Chronicler repeated the phrase with which he had concluded his narrative of David's coronation in Hebron, using it also as an introduction to the list of mighty men and tribal leaders: "And these are the leaders of David's warriors who supported him in his reign with **all Israel** *to crown him, according to the word of the Lord, over Israel"* (1 Chr 11:10).[24]

The link between the two sections was strengthened by arranging the new introduction (v. 10b) in chiastic order compared with the previous conclusion (v. 3b):

1 Chr 11:3b	וימשחו את דוד למלך **על ישראל** *כדבר ה׳*
	they anointed David king **over Israel**
	in accordance with the word of the Lord.
1 Chr 11:10b	המתחזקים עמו . . . להמליכו *כדבר ה׳* **על ישראל**
	those who supported him . . . to make him king—
	in accordance with the word of the Lord—
	over Israel.

13.7 The words ותקרע את בגדיך ותבך לפני 'you tore your clothes and wept before Me' (2 Chr 34:27b // 2 Kgs 22:19) describe a tangible enactment of what was said previously about the humility of Josiah: יען רך לבבך ותכנע מלפני אלהים 'since your heart was soft and you were humble before God' (34:27a). However, since the cause of this humility, בשמעך את דבריו[25] על המקום הזה ועל ישביו 'upon hearing His words regarding this place and its inhabitants' (34:27b), separates the two, the Chronicler repeated the words ותכנע לפני[26] 'and you humbled yourself before Me' in order to link the humility with its tangible expression:

---

24. The phrases כדבר ה׳ ביד שמואל 'according to the word of the Lord by the hand of Samuel' (v. 3b) and המתחזקים עמו במלכותו עם כל ישראל להמליכו כדבר ה׳ על ישראל 'those who gave him strong support in his reign, together with all of Israel, to crown him king, according to the word of the Lord, over Israel' (1 Chr 11:10b) are "additions" introduced by the Chronicler into the passages borrowed from Samuel. For these "additions," see also chap. 7, §3 (p. 160).

25. The LXX has τοὺς λόγους μου 'My words'—probably the correct reading; see Curtis-Madsen, *Chronicles*, 511.

26. The word לפני here refers to the speaker ('before me'), whereas previously it referred to a "third person"—מלפני אלהים 'before God'.

2 Kgs 22:19	2 Chr 34:27
יען רך לבבך **ותכנע מפני** ה׳	יען רך לבבך **ותכנע מלפני** אלהים
בשמעך אשר דברתי על המקום הזה	בשמעך את דבריו על המקום הזה
ועל ישביו להיות לשמה ולקללה	ועל ישביו[27]
ותקרע את	**ותכנע לפני** ותקרע את
בגדיך ותבכה לפני	בגדיך ותבך לפני

Since your heart was soft and	Since your heart was soft and
you humbled yourself before	**you humbled yourself before**
the Lord when you heard what	God when you heard His words
I spoke against this place	against this place
and its inhabitants, that they	and its inhabitants,
would become desolate and	
cursed	**you humbled yourself before Me**
and you tore your clothing and	and tore your clothing and you wept
wept before Me, . . .	before Me, . . .

The repetitive phrase ותכנע לפני in Chronicles is thus a literary technique,
"resumptive repetition," not a textual error ("dittography"), as surmised
by Delitzsch;[28] or an expression designed "to moderate the transition from
third to first person," as Rudolph believed;[29] or a first attempt to draw
special attention to the idea of humility before the Lord, as Williamson
claimed.[30]

It should be noted that in this case, which is different from the previous examples, the words composing the interval are not a "late addition"
introduced into the earlier text but a part of it.

13.8 The Deuteronomistic historian relates that, after Solomon's
prayer at the dedication of the Temple, the Lord appeared to Solomon,
saying: "I have heard your prayer . . . I have consecrated this House . . .
and put My name there" (1 Kgs 9:3). In 2 Chr 7:12b, the Chronicler
quoted 1 Kgs 9:3a and added ובחרתי במקום הזה לי לבית זבח 'and I have
chosen this place as a House of sacrifice for Me' (v. 12c), as well as a
short summary of Solomon's prayer (vv. 13–15).[31] When he decided to

---

27. The Chronicler may have omitted the words להיות לשמה ולקללה because he considered them a curse against Jerusalem, the holy city. A similar explanation was proposed by Montgomery to clarify the omission of the word ולקללה in the LXX (Lucian)
of Kings (Montgomery, *Kings*, 528).

28. See Delitzsch, *Schreibfehler*, 83 (§85b).

29. Rudolph, *Chronik*, 324.

30. Williamson, *Chronicles*, 402. Though retrospectively this repetition emphasizes the idea that humility before the Lord cancels out evil decrees (and cf. 2 Chr
7:14; 12:12) since, subsequent to Josiah's humility, the execution of the decree was
postponed for another generation.

31. See 2 Chr 6:26–28, 40; see also chap. 12, "Chiasmus between Parallel Texts."

continue the passage from Kings (v. 3b), he repeated the word בחרתי
(16a) in order to link up the continuation with the words he had previously written:

1 Kgs 9:2–3		2 Chr 7:12–16	
.2	וירא ה׳ אל שלמה . . .	וירא ה׳ אל שלמה . . .	.12a
.3a	ויאמר ה׳ אליו: שמעתי את תפלתך . . .	ויאמר לו: שמעתי את תפלתך	.b
		ובחרתי במקום הזה לי לבית	.c
		זבח 32	
		הן אעצר השמים . . . ואזני	.13–15
		קשבות לתפלת המקום הזה	
		33(summary of Solomon's prayer)	
.3b	הקדשתי את	ועתה בחרתי והקדשתי את	.16a
	הבית הזה . . .	הבית הזה . . .	

2.	Then the Lord appeared to Solomon. . . .	12a.	Then the Lord appeared to Solomon . . .
3a.	And the Lord said to him, "I have heard your prayer . . .	b.	and said to him, "I have heard your prayer,
		c.	and **I have chosen** this place as a House of sacrifice for Myself.
		13–15.	If I block the heavens . . . my ears will be attuned to the prayer made in this place [summary of Solomon's prayer],
3b.	I have consecrated **this House**."	16a.	for now **I have chosen** and consecrated **this House**."

If this is indeed a resumptive repetition, then Japhet's claim—that the repetition of the word בחרתי means that "the intended sacrificial function of the chosen house is stressed, and by means of the standard formula, the focus is shifted from the chosenness of Jerusalem to the chosenness of the Temple"[34]—is doubtful.

13.9 The verses concluding David's reign in 1 Chr 29:26–30 (partly parallel to 1 Kgs 2:11–12) intervene between Solomon's coronation (1 Chr 29:20–24) and his trip to Gibeon to sacrifice to the Lord (2 Chr 1:2–13a // 1 Kgs 3:4–15a)—his first act as king in the book of Chronicles.

---

32. Compare with 2 Chr 2:3: הנה אני בונה בית לשם ה׳ אלהי להקדיש לו, להקטיר לפניו קטרת סמים ומערכת תמיד ועלות 'I am building a House to the name of the Lord my God and dedicate it to Him for offering Him fragrant incense, for the regular offering, and for burnt-offerings'; similarly v. 6.

33. See 2 Chr 6:26–28, 40.

34. Japhet, *Ideology*, 90.

The Chronicler linked these two narratives in his introduction to the story of Solomon's going to Gibeon (2 Chr 1:1) by repeating the words that concluded the coronation narrative (1 Chr 29:25):

1 Chr 29:20–24 The narrative about Solomon's coronation

25 . . . **ויגדל ה׳ את שלמה** למעלה לעיני כל ישראל ויתן עליו הוד מלכות

Then the Lord exalted Solomon *highly in the eyes of all Israel and invested him with royal majesty.*

26–30 The conclusion of David's reign (vv. 26–28 // 1 Kgs 2:11–12)

2 Chr 1:1 ויתחזק שלמה בן דויד על מלכותו³⁶ וה׳ אלהיו עמו³⁵ **ויגדלהו למעלה.**

Then Solomon, son of David, established himelf over his kingdom, the Lord his God being with him and **exalting him** *highly.*

2–13a (// 1 Kgs 3:4–15a) Solomon's trip to Gibeon

The repetition was varied by means of certain stylistic changes. The link between the narratives was also shown by the fact that this general report, **ויצלח**[שלמה] וישמעו אליו כל ישראל וכל השרים והגברים 'he was successful, and all Israel listened to him, and all the officials and the mighty men . . .', in the coronation narrative (1 Chr 29:23–24) is demonstrated in actuality by his trip to Gibeon: ויאמר שלמה לכל ישראל, לשרי האלפים והמאות ולשפטים ולכל נשיא לכל ישראל ראשי האבות, וילכו שלמה וכל הקהל עמו לבמה אשר בגבעון 'And Solomon summoned all of Israel, the captains of thousands and of hundreds, the judges, all of the leaders of Israel, and the tribal leaders, and Solomon went with the entire entourage to the high place that is in Gibeon' (2 Chr 1:2–3a).³⁷

---

35. The phrase **וה׳ אלהיו עמו** 'the Lord his God being with him' appears to be the realization of David's blessing of Solomon: "Now, my son, may the Lord be with you and may you succeed and *build the House of the Lord* your God" (1 Chr 22:11; cf. v. 16: ויהי ה׳ עמך 'and may the Lord be with you'; 28:20). In 1 Chr 29:23 the Chronicler stresses the fulfillment of the second part of the blessing: וישב שלמה על כסא ה׳ תחת אביו *ויצלח* 'And Solomon sat on the throne of the Lord in his father's stead, *and he was successful*'; compare also כל הבא על לב שלמה לעשות בבית ה׳ ובביתו *הצליח* 'everything that entered Solomon's heart to do in the *House of the Lord* and in his own house *succeeded*' (2 Chr 7:11, instead of: כל חשק שלמה אשר חפץ לעשות _____ 'everything that Solomon desired to do _____' in 1 Kgs 9:1). Both David's blessing and the last passage are adduced in connection with the building of the House of the Lord.

36. For the phrase ויתחזק . . . על מלכותו, compare 2 Chr 12:13; 13:21; 17:1; and 21:4; also 1 Chr 11:10.

37. This verse is abbreviated from "he told them to go with him to the high place in Gibeon, and they went with him." Compare 1 Chr 21:27: ויאמר ה׳ למלאך וישב חרבו אל נדנה 'Then the Lord commanded the angel, and he returned his sword to its scabbard'; Gen 4:8: . . . ויאמר קין אל הבל אחיו ויהי בהיותם בשדה 'Cain said to Abel, his brother, when they were in the field . . .'; for the subject of abbreviated passages, see chap. 20, §1C "Inconsistency in the Completion of Elliptical Verses" (pp. 384–385).

In the previous examples, the "repetition" linked passages that dealt with the same event and, in general, the intervening words were introduced into the earlier text of Samuel–Kings by the Chronicler. In this case, the repetition occurs in order to link up two different narratives, the central figure of each being Solomon. The intervening words here (1 Chr 29:26–28) originate from the earlier text (1 Kgs 2:11–12), whereas the narrative in 1 Chr 29:20–25 has no parallel in that text.

13.10 In 2 Chr 20:35–36, the words הוא הרשיע לעשות 'he acted wickedly' intervene between the beginning of the narrative, ואחרי כן אתחבר יהושפט מלך יהודה עם אחזיה מלך ישראל 'Afterward Jehoshaphat, king of Judah, **joined with** Ahaziah, king of Israel', and its continuation, לעשות אניות ללכת תרשיש 'to build boats to sail to Tarshish'. In order to link these two passages, the Chronicler used the phrase ויחברהו עמו 'and he joined him' before presenting (with certain changes) the rest of the passage from the book of Kings:

1 Kgs 22:49–50	2 Chr 20:35–36
יהושפט	אחרי כן אתחבר יהושפט מלך יהודה
	עם אחזיה מלך ישראל,
	הוא הרשיע לעשות,
	ויחברהו עמו [38]
עשר (Qere: עשה) אניות תרשיש . . .	לעשות אניות ללכת תרשיש . . .
Jehoshaphat	Afterward Jehoshaphat, king of
	Judah, **joined with** Ahaziah, king of
	Israel, who acted wickedly.
	He **joined him**
built ships of the Tarshish type.	to build ships to sail to Tarshish.

---

38. The words כ/בהתחברך, ויחברהו, אתחבר (in vv. 35–37) derive from the root חב"ר. R. David Kimḥi was the first to comment on these: "אתחבר is like התחבר, the אל"ף replacing the ה"א—similar to וכל מלבושי אגאלתי (Isa 63:3), as in "הגאלתי" (and cf. his commentary to 1 Kgs 11:17; 2 Kgs 13:20; Jer 4:20; 50:11). Actually it is the prefixed -ת (of *Hithpael*) that was replaced by -את, apparently under western Aramaic influence; see GKC §54a/p. 149; also Curtis-Madsen, *Chronicles*, 413. The root חב"ר, used by the Chronicler in defining the nature of the partnership in the shipping business and sea trade between Judah and Israel in the ninth century B.C.E., appears also in the Wen-Amon scroll (the first quarter of the eleventh century B.C.E.). It has *ḫubûr*, in the very same context and with the same meaning: a partnership in sea trade and shipping business between Egypt and Byblos (Gebal), on the one hand, and between Sidon and (apparently) a Philistine city, on the other hand. The noun חברים appears in Job 40:30, parallel to the noun כנענים 'tradesmen' (cf. Isa 23:8; Prov 31:24; and see the Aramaic Targum on the verse: תגריא). This word (*ḫubûr*/חבר) thus served as a technical term in Phoenician and in Hebrew in the context of international shipping relations and trade; see also Mazar, "Philistines, Israel, and Tyre," 65–66; Goedicke, *Report of Wenamon*, 66–69, 152; Katzenstein, "The Phoenician Term Ḥubur," 599–602.

This repetition is an abbreviated, not an exact, quotation, as other examples are, apparently for purposes of literary variation.

13.11 Resumptive repetition is also found in the "additions" in the
book of Chronicles. For instance, in 1 Chronicles 22 David orders Solomon, his son, to build a House for the name of the Lord (v. 11), telling
him of the numerous preparations he has already made and giving details in a list of building materials. At the end of the list he repeats the
word הכינותי 'I have provided' and continues instructing his son, ועליהם
תוסיף 'and to these you must add more' (vv. 14–15):

1 Chr 22:14–15

והנה בעניי **הכינותי** לבית ה׳	With great pains **I have provided** for the House of the Lord
זהב ככרים . . . וכסף . . . ככרים	gold talents . . . and silver . . . talents.
ולנחשת ולברזל אין משקל . . .	And as for bronze and iron—beyond weighing.
ועצים ואבנים	Also wood and stone
הכינותי ועליהם תוסיף 39	**I have provided**, and to these you must add more.
ועמך לרב עשי מלאכה חצבים . . .	You have an abundance of workmen: stonecutters, . . .

13.12 In 2 Chr 15:8–15, the Chronicler describes Asa's religious and
ritual reforms. According to him, the king of Judah got rid of the abom-
inable idols from the land, restored the altar of the Lord, and gathered
into Jerusalem not only "all of Judah and Benjamin" but also "those
from Ephraim, Manasseh, and of Simeon who were living with them."
Regarding the last point, the Chronicler wished to add a few words of
clarification: "for they deserted to him from Israel in great numbers
when they saw that the Lord, his God, was with him" (v. 9). Since this
clarification interrupted the sequence of his main narrative, he repeated the root קב״ץ in the beginning of v. 10 in order to link the continuation of the narrative with what had preceded:

וכשמע אסא הדברים האלה . . .	Now, when Asa heard these things . . .
התחזק ויעבר השקוצים . . .	he courageously put away the abominable idols . . .
ויחדש את מזבח ה׳ . . .	and restored the altar of the Lord

---

39. And compare with 1 Chr 22:5: ויאמר דויד: שלמה בני נער ורך, והבית לבנות לה׳ להגדיל
למעלה . . . **אכינה** נא לו, **ויכן** דויד לרב לפני מותו 'Then David said, "My son, Solomon, is but a
young lad, and the House to be built for the Lord is to be magnificent. . . . I will prepare for the building"'.

ויקבץ את כל יהודה ובנימן	and **gathered together** all of Judah and Benjamin
והגרים עמהם מאפרים ומנשה	and those from Ephraim,
ומשמעון	Manasseh, and Simeon who were living with them,
כי נפלו עליו מישראל לרב	for they deserted to him from Israel in great numbers
בראתם כי ה' אלהיו עמו	when they saw that the Lord, his God, was with him.
ויקבצו ירושלם בחדש השלישי	They **gathered together** in Jerusalem
לשנת . . .	in the third month of the year . . .
. . . ויזבחו לה' ביום ההוא	and sacrificed to the Lord on that day.

2. Repetitive Introductions

A *repetitive introduction* is essentially no different from a resumptive repetition except for its position in the sequence of a passage. It is generally found at the beginning of a new passage rather than the middle, as is a resumptive repetition.

13.13 In 2 Chr 3:1, the Chronicler began his description of the building of the Temple with the words: *ויחל שלמה לבנות את בית ה'* 'Then Solomon **began to build** the *House of the Lord*', parallel to 1 Kgs 6:1b: *ויבן הבית לה'* 'he **built** the *House for the Lord*'. Then he added the precise location of the Temple and the circumstances of its designation (v. 1b).[40] When he went back to complete the rest of the text, he reintroduced *ויחל לבנות* 'and he began to build' (v. 2a):

1 Kgs 6:1	*2 Chr 3:1–2*
1a. ויהי בשמונים שנה וארבע מאות	1a. **ויחל** שלמה **לבנות** את בית ה'
שנה . . . בשנה הרביעית בחדש זו	
הוא החדש השני למלך שלמה	b. בירושלם
על ישראל	
	בהר המוריה אשר נראה [ה]/[41]
	לדויד אביהו
	אשר הכין במקום דויד[42]
	בגרן ארנן היבוסי

---

40. For this addition, its structure, and possible aims, see in detail Kalimi, "Land/Mount Moriah," 25–31.

41. The context here requires the word ה'; see example 3.22 n. 76 (p. 83).

42. This verse should be interpreted as if written במקום אשר הכין דויד; see example 3.22 (pp. 82–83) n. 77.

b.   ויבן הבית לה׳   ויחל לבנות .2a

                               b.   בחדש השני בשני בשנת ארבע

                                        למלכותו [43]

1a. In the four hundred
eightieth year after . . . in
the fourth year—in the
month of Ziv, the second
month—of Solomon's
reign over Israel

b. *he built* the House of the
Lord.

1a. Solomon **began to build**
the House of the Lord

b. In Jerusalem
on Mount Moriah,
where [the Lord] appeared to
David, his father,
where David had designated,
on the threshing floor of Ornan,
the Jebusite.

2a. He **began to build**

b. in the second month, on the
second day,
in the fourth year of his reign.

13.14 In 2 Chr 2:10–15, the Chronicler presented the reaction of
Huram, king of Tyre, and his reply to Solomon's request for help, parallel to 1 Kgs 5:21–23. Immediately after this opening, ויאמר חורם מלך צר
בכתב וישלח אל שלמה 'Huram, king of Tyre, **said** in a letter that he sent to
Solomon', he put the following words in Huram's mouth: באהבת ה׳ את עמו
נתנך עליהם מלך 'out of the Lord's love for His people, He has appointed you
king over them'. This is the statement that was made by the Queen of
Sheba to Solomon (2 Chr 9:8 // 1 Kgs 10:9). Then, when the Chronicler
was ready to cite the rest of the text from 1 Kgs 5:21, he repeated his
opening one more time in these words: ויאמר חורם (v. 11):

1 Kgs 5:21	2 Chr 2:10–11
ויהי כשמע **חירם** את דברי שלמה	**ויאמר חורם** מלך צר בכתב וישלח
וישמח מאד **ויאמר**	אל שלמה
	באהבת ה׳ את עמו נתנך עליהם מלך
ברוך ה׳ היום	**ויאמר חורם** ברוך ה׳ אלהי ישראל
	אשר עשה את השמים ואת הארץ
אשר נתן לדוד בן חכם	אשר נתן לדויד המלך בן חכם

Now when **Hiram** heard
Solomon's words, he rejoiced
greatly and **said**,

Then **Huram**, king of Tyre, **said** in a
letter that he sent to Solomon,

"Out of the Lord's love for His people,
He has appointed you king over
them!"

---

43. The Chronicler adduced the passage from 1 Kgs 6:1 as a "chiasmus between
parallel texts"; see also example 12.39 (p. 247).

"Blessed is the Lord
today, Who has given David
a wise son."

Also **Huram said**: "Blessed is the
Lord God of Israel, Maker of heaven
and earth, Who has given King David
a wise son."

There is a parallel to this example in Exod 1:15–16, Lev 16:1–2, and
Neh 8:9–10:

Exod 1:15–16

ויאמר מלך מצרים למילדת העברית   **Then the king of Egypt said**
אשר שם האחת שפרה   to the Hebrew midwives—
ושם השנית פועה,   of whom one's name was Shiphrah
and the other Puah—

ויאמר בילדכן את העבריות,   **then he said**: "When you assist the
Hebrew women to give birth,
וראיתן על האבנים אם בן הוא . . .   and see them on the birthstool, if it is
a son. . . ."

Lev 16:1–2

וידבר ה' אל משה   **The Lord spoke to Moses**
אחרי מות שני בני אהרן   after the death of the two sons of
בקרבתם לפני ה' וימתו   Aaron who died when they
encroached upon the presence of
the Lord.

ויאמר ה' אל משה   **The Lord said to Moses:**
דבר אל אהרן אחיך   Tell your brother Aaron
ואל יבא בכל עת אל הקדש . . .   that he is not to come whenever he
chooses into the sanctuary. . . .

Neh 8:9–10

ויאמר נחמיה הוא התרשתא . . .   **And Nehemiah**, who was the
לכל העם   governor . . . **said to all the people,**
היום קדש הוא לה' אלהיכם   "This day is holy to the Lord your God,
אל תתאבלו ואל תבכו   do not mourn or weep."
כי בוכים כל העם כשמעם את דברי   For all the people wept when they
התורה   heard the words of the Torah.
ויאמר להם לכו אכלו משמנים ושתו   **Then he said to them**, "Go your way,
ממתקים ושלחו מנות לאין נכון לו   eat the fat and drink sweet wine and
כי קדוש היום לאדנינו ואל תעצבו . . .   send portions to him for whom nothing
is prepared; for this day is holy to our
Lord; and do not be grieved. . . ."

Apparently, these examples had been used as a literary model by the
Chronicler in his reshaping of the earlier texts from the Torah and the
Former Prophets.

13.15 In 1 Chr 11:10ff., the Chronicler listed the leaders of David's mighty men, parallel to the list in 2 Sam 23:8ff. The introduction to this list in 1 Chr 11:10a, ‏ואלה ראשי הגבורים אשר לדויד‎ 'These are the leaders of **David's mighty men**', on the whole resembles the introduction in 2 Sam 23:8a: ‏אלה שמות הגברים אשר לדוד‎ 'These are the names of **David's mighty men**'. However, because of the "addition" in 1 Chr 11:10b,[44] which intervenes between the introduction to the list and the list itself, the Chronicler repeated himself and reintroduced the list, [45](‏מספר‎)‏ואלה‎ ‏הגברים אשר לדויד‎ 'These are (the number of) **David's mighty men**' (v. 11a):

<table>
<tr><td align="center">2 Sam 23:8</td><td align="center">1 Chr 11:10–11</td></tr>
<tr><td align="right">‏אלה שמות הגברים אשר לדוד‎ 8a.</td><td align="right">‏ואלה ראשי הגבורים אשר לדויד‎ 10a.</td></tr>
<tr><td></td><td align="right">‏המתחזקים עמו במלכותו עם כל‎ b.
‏ישראל להמליכו כדבר ה׳ על‎
‏ישראל‎</td></tr>
<tr><td></td><td align="right">‏ואלה (מספר) הגברים אשר לדויד‎ 11a.</td></tr>
<tr><td align="right">b. ‏ישב בשבת תחכמני ראש השלשי‎</td><td align="right">‏ישבעם בן חכמוני ראש השלושים‎ b.</td></tr>
<tr><td>8a. These are the names of David's mighty men:</td><td>10a. These are the leaders of David's mighty men,</td></tr>
<tr><td></td><td>b. who gave him strong support in his kingdom, together with all Israel, to make him king, according to the word of the Lord about Israel.</td></tr>
<tr><td></td><td>11a. These are (the number of) David's mighty men:</td></tr>
<tr><td>b. Josheb-basshebeth a Tahchemonite; he was leader of the Three.</td><td>b. Jashobeam, the Hachmonite, was leader of the Three.</td></tr>
</table>

13.16 In the list of Reubenites in 1 Chronicles 5, v. 3a repeats v. 1a, ‏(ו)בני ראובן בכור ישראל‎ '(and) the children of Reuben, the firstborn of Israel', because of an explanatory "addition" that the Chronicler introduced immediately after he began the list (vv. 1b–2: ‏כי הוא ... והבכורה‎ ‏ליוסף‎ 'for he . . . and the birthright was Joseph's')—an "addition" that

---

44. Compare this "addition" with 1 Chr 11:3b.

45. The word ‏מספר‎ may have entered the text from a gloss that originally referred to the word ‏השלושים‎ in the second part of the verse (11b; with Rudolph, *Chronik*, 96; and, earlier, Rothstein-Hänel, *Chronik*). It is also not impossible that we have here an "abbreviated verse" that actually means ‏ואלה הגברים במספר שמותם‎ 'and these are the mighty men, numbered by name'.

intervenes between the introduction in v. 1a and its continuation in v. 3b:[46]

<table>
<tr><td align="center">Gen 46:9[47]</td><td align="center">1 Chr 5:1–3</td></tr>
<tr><td align="right">ובני ראובן</td><td align="right">1a. ‏ובני ראובן בכור ישראל‎[48]</td></tr>
<tr><td></td><td align="right">b. ‏כי הוא הבכור ובחללו יצועי אביו‎</td></tr>
<tr><td></td><td align="right">‏נתנה בכרתו לבני יוסף בן ישראל‎</td></tr>
<tr><td></td><td align="right">‏ולא להתיחש לבכרה‎</td></tr>
<tr><td></td><td align="right">2. ‏כי יהודה גבר באחיו ולנגיד ממנו‎</td></tr>
<tr><td></td><td align="right">‏והבכרה ליוסף‎</td></tr>
<tr><td></td><td align="right">3a. ‏בני ראובן בכור ישראל‎</td></tr>
<tr><td align="right">‏חנוך ופלוא וחצרן וכרמי . . .‎</td><td align="right">b. ‏חנוך ופלוא חצרון וכרמי . . .‎</td></tr>
</table>

And the children of Reuben,   1a.   **And the children of Reuben, the firstborn of Israel,**

      b.   for he was the firstborn; but when he polluted his father's bed, his birthright was given to the sons of Joseph, son of Israel, so that he is not enrolled in the genealogy according to the birthright;

      2.   though Judah became strong among his brothers and a leader was from him, yet the birthright belonged to Joseph.

      3a.   **The children of Reuben, the firstborn of Israel,**

Hanoch, Pallu, Hezron, and Carmi. . . .   b.   Hanoch, Pallu, Hezron, and Carmi. . . .

13.17 In 1 Chr 12:20–23, the Chronicler wanted to list the names of the warriors who joined David from the tribe of Manasseh: ‏וממנשה נפלו על‎ ‏דויד‎ 'from Manasseh there deserted to David . . .' (20a).[49] But since he

---

46. See R. David Kimḥi to 1 Chr 5:3: "the children of Reuben—because he had interrupted the matter, he repeated for a second time 'the children of Reuben'"; similarly, Curtis-Madsen, *Chronicles*, 119.

47. Compare with Num 26:5–7.

48. Compare with Num 26:5: *"Reuben, the firstborn of Israel. The descendants of Reuben. . . ."*

49. Compare this style with the continuation of the text: ‏יפול אל אדניו שאול‎ 'he will desert to his master, Saul'; similarly 2 Chr 15:9: ‏כי נפלו עליו מישראל לרב‎ 'they deserted to him from Israel in great numbers'; Jer 21:9: ‏יחיה‎ . . . ‏והיוצא ונפל על הכשדים‎ 'and he who goes out and surrenders to the Chaldeans . . . shall live'; Jer 37:13, 14; 52:15; see also Jer 39:9: "deserted to him," that is, joined him.

had interrupted the narrative by dating the episode, . . . בבאו עם פלשתים
בלכתו אל צקלג 'when he came with Philistines . . . as he went to Ziklag'
(20b–21a), he reintroduced the list, though in inverted word order, נפלו
עליו ממנשה 'there deserted to him from Manasseh' (21b):[50]

1 Chr 12:20–23[19–22]

וממנשה נפלו על דויד	.20a	**From Manasseh there deserted to David—**
בבאו עם פלשתים על שאול למלחמה ולא עזרם כי בעצה שלחהו סרני פלשתים לאמר בראשינו יפול אל אדניו שאול[51]	.b	when he came with Philistines for the battle against Saul, but he did not help them, for the Philistine rulers had sent him away advisedly, saying: "He will desert to his master Saul at the cost of our heads"—
בלכתו אל ציקלג	.21a	as he went to Ziklag,
נפלו עליו ממנשה	.b	**there deserted to him from**
עדנח ויוזבד וידיעאל ומיכאל . . .	.c	**Manasseh** Adnah, Jozabad, Jediael, Michael, . . .

---

50. For this, see example 12.40 (p. 247).

51. The statement by Mosis (*Untersuchungen,* 19 n. 9) to the effect that the text in 1 Chr 12:20 is secondary is groundless.

Chapter 14
Inclusio

An *inclusio* is a word, phrase, or group of phrases that is used at the opening of a literary unit of any scope and then is repeated at the end of it. The aim of this literary technique may have been to define the limits of a literary unit,[1] to tighten its various component parts into a single unit (for example, items in a list; literary expressions that have been borrowed from various books and integrated into one unit; or, as in our case, material written by the Chronicler that has been added to a passage from Samuel–Kings), and to give a unit the appearance of continuity and uniformity.

Similar to resumptive repetition, an inclusio signals the borders of a literary unit. In contrast to it, however, the words repeated at the conclusion do not serve as a technical device to return the reader to a previous line of thought but adhere to the unit itself as an integral part of it. Furthermore, the words repeated in this way are not necessarily a sign of a late addition to an earlier text.

The technique of literary inclusio has been discerned in research mainly in biblical poetry[2] and, to a lesser extent, in early prose and historical narrative,[3] but in the history of the book of Chronicles almost no

---

1. An inclusio functions similarly to our parentheses, which enclose a word, phrase, or short passage, in modern prose. This is also nicely expressed by the English term *cyclic composition* or the German *Ringkomposition*, that is, the Greek term κύκλος.

2. See the examples in Jeremiah and Zephaniah, listed by König, *Biblische Literatur*, 350; in Amos and Job, listed by Segal, *Introduction to the Bible*, 1.73–74; in Psalms, listed by Dahood, *Psalms*, 5, 14, 27, 29, 41, 43, etc.; in Isaiah and Ezekiel, listed by Talmon, "Textual Study," 149–52. See also Ps 8:2a (2b–9) 10; 103:1b (1c–22b) 22c; cf. Psalm 104.

3. See the examples in Judges, listed by Segal, *Introduction to the Bible*, 1.73–74; in Samuel and Esther, listed by Talmon, "Textual Study," 149–52; and in Samuel and Kings, listed by Bar-Efrat, *Narrative Art*, 216; and from the Priestly source in the Pentateuch, listed by Paran, *Priestly Style*, 150–62; see also Gen 6:7–9 (10–12) 13–15a; 9:1 (2–6) 7; Exod 6:13 (14–25) 26–27; and also 2 Kgs 8:20a (20b–21) 22 = 2 Chr 21:8a (8b–9) 10a; 1 Kgs 6:1b (2–36) 37 [numbers in parentheses indicate the locations of the main text that is formed by an inclusio]. The closing words about the kingdom of Joash/Jehoash, king of Israel, in 2 Kgs 14:15–16 are repeated from 2 Kgs 13:12–13 and create an inclusio. In between these verses, the Deuteronomistic historian tells about the king's visit to a dying Elisha, his war with Aram, and the war with Amaziah, king of Judah (13:14–14:14). Thus, the exclusion of 2 Kgs 13:12–13 by the Lucianic recension of the LXX stems from misunderstanding the literary device created

sign of it at all has been seen. The examples adduced below clearly demonstrate the considerable use that the Chronicler made of this literary technique in giving a renewed literary appearance to the passages that he took from the books of Samuel–Kings. It turns out to have been one of the most prominent writing devices of the Chronicler. Formulating the earlier passages into inclusios was done in various ways: (1) by adding a word, phrase, or group of phrases at the beginning of a passage in accordance with the wording of the conclusion; at the conclusion of a passage in accordance with the wording of the beginning; at the beginning and conclusion of a passage; or (2) by sharpening and stressing the already existing beginning and concluding words of an earlier passage. Occasionally the Chronicler would repeat word-for-word in one unit (introduction or conclusion) what was written in the other; on other occasions, he would introduce various unimportant changes (apparently for reasons of stylistic variety), in which case the concluding/opening phrases resemble the opening/concluding phrases—that is, they are similar to them in form and substance but not identical. Similarly, sometimes the Chronicler uses the word order of one unit in the formation of the other unit; at other times he uses the same words in reverse order, thereby creating a chiastic structure. In these cases, the chiasmus seems not to have been created for its own sake but primarily for the sake of forming an optimal inclusio in which the concluding/opening phrase is identical with the opening/concluding phrase.

In the book of Chronicles one discovers inclusios not only in narrative passages but also in lists. The Chronicler sometimes compiled name lists from various contexts in the Pentateuch and Former Prophets and framed them with an inclusio. Occasionally he attached a numerical inclusio to a list, as well. This was apparently done to prevent additions to or deletions from the list, either deliberately or because of erroneous interpretation. For instance, the number תשעה 'nine' that closes the list of David's sons born in Jerusalem (1 Chr 3:5) indicates that the repetition of the names אלישמע and אליפלט is not an error and that the names are not to be omitted.[4] The number ששה 'six' at the opening of the list of Azel's sons (1 Chr 8:38 // 9:44) may have been put there to prevent erroneously reading בְּכֹרוֹ as 'his firstborn' instead of בֹּכְרוּ 'Bochru', the name of Azel's second son.[5]

---

here. For the same reason, Driver's conclusion (*Introduction*, 186) is baseless: "The repetition of the closing formula in the case of Jehoash in 2 Kgs 13:12–13 and 14:15–16 is no doubt the result of some error; its position in 13:12–13, immediately after the opening formula (vv. 10–11), is contrary to analogy." Similarly, too, the hypothesis of Cogan and Tadmor (*II Kings*, 145) is unacceptable (they follow Burney and Skinner).

4. Cf. Keel, *2 Chronicles*, 25 (appendixes).

5. See Keel, *1 Chronicles*, ccxxv; see also Loewenstamm ("Bochru," 129), who believes "that this is a name meaning 'firstborn', with an *-u* suffix." Such a name,

The examples in §1 below are inclusios that appear in narrative texts, and the examples in §2 are inclusios that appear in lists.

1. Inclusios in Narrative Texts

A. Comprehensive Literary Units

14.1 The narrative of Solomon's reign in Chronicles begins with a description of his dream in Gibeon (2 Chr 1:1–13a // 1 Kgs 3:4–15). It ends with the words שלמה] על ישראל [שלמה [וימלך 'and [Solomon] reigned over Israel' (2 Chr 1:13b // 1 Kgs 4:1). The rest of the narrative from 1:14 to the formula that sums up the period of Solomon's reign in 2 Chr 9:29–31 (// 1 Kgs 5:16–10:29; 11:41–43) is framed by a literary inclusio containing a description of the king's economic and military wealth. In other words, the Chronicler used words already found at the end of the description of Solomon's reign (1 Kgs 10:26–28 // 2 Chr 9:25–28) at the beginning of his description as well (2 Chr 1:14–16), immediately after 1:13b, וימלך [שלמה] על ישראל.

1 Kings	*2 Chronicles*
	1:14a–16. Then Solomon gathered together chariots and horsemen. He had one thousand four hundred chariots and twelve thousand horsemen. He placed them in chariot towns and with the king in Jerusalem. And the king made silver and gold common[6] and made cedar as plentiful as eucalyptus trees on the plains. The origin of the horses that **Solomon had** was *Egypt* **and Kue**.

however, has no parallel in all of biblical and epigraphical personal names. Moreover, in the LXX and Peshiṭta, the reading is "firstborn." It is thus possible that one of the names was indeed omitted from the list, as occurred in 1 Chr 3:22 (but see the possibility raised by Curtis-Madsen, *Chronicles*, 102) and in 1 Chr 6:42 (where two names were omitted). In order to reach the number "six," the Masoretes read "Bochru" in place of בְּכֹרוֹ 'his firstborn'. The translator of the Peshiṭta took a different line: he divided the name עזריקם into two—עזרי and קם—and counted each of them as an individual name. It seems that the use of the numerical inclusio was intended to prevent such ingenious machinations, as well.

6. The phrase ואת הזהב appears in the LXX of 1 Kgs 10:27 as well. In contrast to Williamson (*Chronicles*, 196), I find it difficult to determine positively whether this word appeared in the Chronicler's *Vorlage* or whether he added it here in order to glorify Solomon's wealth (and thus he is followed by the LXX of 1 Kgs 10:27).

5:16–10:25. A description of Solomon's reign.	1:17–9:24. A description of Solomon's reign.

5:16–10:25. A description of
Solomon's reign.

10:26–28.   Then Solomon
gathered together chariots
and horsemen. He had
one thousand four hundred
chariots and twelve thousand
horsemen that he stationed
in chariot towns and with
the king in Jerusalem.
And the king made silver
in Jerusalem as common as
stones, and cedars he made
as plentiful as eucalyptus
on the plains.
The origin of **Solomon's**
horses was *Egypt* **and Kue**.

1:17–9:24. A description of
Solomon's reign.

9:25–28.   And Solomon had four
thousand אריות סוסים[7] and
chariots, and twelve thousand
horsemen that he stationed in
chariot towns and with the
king in Jerusalem. . . .

And the king made silver
in Jerusalem as common as
stones, and cedars he made
as plentiful as eucalyptus
on the plains.
They imported horses *from*
Egypt **for Solomon and**
from every land.

The Chronicler used the phrase ממצרים לשלמה 'from Egypt for Solomon'
at the end of the concluding remarks (2 Chr 9:28) as a chiasmus between parallel texts relative to the phrase in the book of Kings; and in
chiastic order relative to the very same phrase at the end of the introduction to his own description of the Solomonic era (2 Chr 1:16):

2 Chr 1:16   לשלמה ממצרים
2 Chr 9:28   ממצרים לשלמה

By means of this structure, the Chronicler strengthened the link between the introduction and the conclusion, as well as strengthening the
relationship among the passages that were juxtaposed within the fram-
ing introduction and conclusion.

Unlike Yeivin, then, I would not deduce from the position of 2 Chr
1:14–16 (at the onset of the description of Solomon's reign) that it
should be attributed "to an early period in the days of Solomon's reign."
His position is that, at the beginning of Solomon's reign, he had 1,400
chariots, "and as time went by and the state became stronger and
wealthier, its chariot fleet became stronger and more numerous as well,
until, shortly before the end of the Solomonic period, it numbered some
4,000 chariots,"[8] as related in 2 Chr 9:25 (at the end of the description
of Solomon's reign).

---

7. The phrase אריות סוסים may be a distortion of ארות סוסים in 1 Kgs 5:6: ויהי לשלמה
ארבעים אלף ארות סוסים למרכבו ושנים עשר אלף פרשים 'Solomon had 40,000 horse stables
for his chariots and twelve thousand horsemen'.

8. Yeivin, "Marginal Glosses," 395–96.

14.2 The author of the book of Kings noted that, prior to Solomon's prayer (1 Kgs 8:12–53), "the cloud filled the House of the Lord to such an extent that the priests were unable to stand and serve because of the cloud" (8:10b–11). For his part, the Chronicler presented Solomon's prayer (2 Chr 6:1–40), added Ps 132:8–10 (// 2 Chr 6:41–42), and mentioned the matter of the cloud that filled the House of the Lord, and so on. He described this, not only before Solomon's prayer (2 Chr 5:13b–14 // 1 Kgs 8:10b–11), but also after it (2 Chr 7:1b–2). Similarly, he split the text of 1 Kgs 8:10 into two, inserting an "addition" of his own into it (2 Chr 5:11b–13b). The addition comprised words of song and thanksgiving uttered by the priests, Levites, and singers, who made "themselves heard in unison to praise and give thanks to the Lord . . . and to praise the Lord, for He is good, for His lovingkindness endures forever." The Chronicler ascribed the same words of thanksgiving in 7:3b to "all the children of Israel," in the continuation of the repeated כבוד ה' מלא את הבית וגו' 'the glory of the Lord filled the House', and so on, in 7:1b–2.

These emendations and additions create a literary inclusio that strengthens the ties among the passages from Kings and Psalms that make up Solomon's prayer in Chronicles. Moreover, the repetitions themselves stress the glory of the Lord in the new Temple and the rejoicing of all strata of the populace at the event (priests, Levites, singers, and all Israel):

	1 Kgs 8:10–53		*2 Chr 5:11–7:3*
8:10a.	Now when the priests left the holy place,	5:11a.	Now when the priests left the holy place. . . .
		11b–13a.	A description of the priests, Levites, and singers who sang in "unison in praise **and thanksgiving to the Lord** . . . and in praise to the Lord, **for He is good; for His lovingkindness endures forever.**"
10b.	**a cloud filled the House of the Lord.**	13b.	**And the House was filled with the cloud of the House of the Lord.**
11.	**The priests were unable to stand and serve because of the cloud, for the glory of the Lord filled the House of the Lord.**	14a.	**The priests were unable to stand and serve because of the cloud, for the**
		b.	**glory of the Lord filled the House of God.**
12–53.	Solomon's prayer.	6:1–40.	(// 1 Kgs 8:12–53) ⎱ Solomon's
		41–42.	(// Ps 132:8–10) ⎰ prayer.
		7:1b.	**And the glory of the Lord filled the House.**

2a. **The priests were unable to
enter the House of the Lord,**
 b. **for the glory of the Lord
filled the House of the Lord**
3b. . . . and [all the Israelites]
bowed down **and gave thanks
to the Lord, for He is good;
for His lovingkindness
endures forever**.

The component parts of the conclusion of the inclusio (7:1b–2b and 7:3b)
were presented chiastically in relation to the same phrases in the introduction (5:13a–14b):

2 Chr 5:13a–14b (Introduction)	*2 Chr 7:1b–2b, 3b (Conclusion)*
a. . . . . להלל ולהדות לה׳ . . . ובהלל לה׳	b. וכבוד ה׳ מלא את הבית
כי טוב כי לעולם חסדו	ולא יכלו הכהנים לבוא אל בית ה׳
	כי מלא כבוד ה׳ את בית ה׳
b. והבית מלא ענן בית ה׳	a. וישתחוו [כל בני ישראל] והודות
ולא יכלו הכהנים לעמוד לשרת מפני הענן	לה׳ כי טוב כי לעולם חסדו
כי מלא כבוד ה׳ את בית האלהים	

Furthermore, the Chronicler created chiastic structures within the introduction of the inclusio (between 5:13b and 5:14b) and within the conclusion (between 7:1b and 7:2b)—on the one hand; and, on the other
hand, he presented the phrase that opens the conclusion to Solomon's
prayer (7:1b) in chiastic relation to the same phrase in the close of the
introduction to Solomon's prayer (5:14b):

Introduction:	2 Chr 5:13b	*מלא ענן בית ה׳*	*והבית*
	14b	*את בית האלהים*	*כי מלא כבוד ה׳*
Conclusion:	2 Chr 7:1b	*מלא*	*וכבוד ה׳*
	2b	*כבוד ה׳*	*כי מלא*

All of these chiastic structures bind together and strengthen the components of the introduction and the conclusion themselves, as well as
binding both tightly together, thus contributing to binding the original
texts and the inclusio into one literary unit.

Consequently, the hypothesis of Rudolph, that 2 Chr 5:11a and 13b–
14 were added to the book of Chronicles by a later editor under the influence of the parallel text in 1 Kgs 8:10–11, must be rejected.[9] The
Chronicler himself had already used these verses elsewhere (in 2 Chr
7:1–3). Furthermore, the verses are foundational to the literary structure that he was creating.

---

9. Rudolph, *Chronik*, 211.

14.3 In 1 Kgs 5:16–36, the Deuteronomistic historian describes Solomon's preparations regarding building materials and manpower for the construction of the Temple: his negotiations with Hiram, king of Tyre, regarding the supply of Lebanese cedar and his conscription of a work force from all of Israel to do the woodworking, stonecutting, and so on.

In 2 Chr 2:1–17, the Chronicler borrows the description from 1 Kings 5 (while making various additions and omissions) and creates a literary inclusio for it. He lists the workmen (porters, hewers, and supervisors) not only at the end of the description, as it is in the book of Kings, but also at the onset. Similarly, he formulates the phrase that refers to the supervisors at the opening of the description (v. 1d) in chiastic order relative to the very same phrase at the conclusion of the description (v. 17c). Thus, a chiastic structure is created between line d and lines b–c in v. 1:

<table>
<tr><td align="center">1 Kgs 5:16–32[2–12]</td><td align="center">2 Chr 2:1–17</td></tr>
<tr><td></td><td>1a. Then Solomon counted</td></tr>
<tr><td></td><td>b. seventy thousand porters,</td></tr>
<tr><td></td><td>c. eighty thousand hewers
in the mountains,</td></tr>
<tr><td></td><td>d. and supervisors
three thousand six hundred.</td></tr>
<tr><td>16–26[2–12]. And Solomon
wrote to Hiram,
saying, . . . [the letter to
Hiram, his reply, and the
Israel-Tyre treaty].[10]</td><td>2–15. And Solomon
sent to Huram, king of Tyre,
saying, . . . [the letter to
Huram and his reply].</td></tr>
<tr><td>27–28[13–14]. Raising a
thirty-thousand-men work
force from all Israel and
organizing it into three labor
groups, each of which took
turns working one month in
Lebanon.</td><td></td></tr>
<tr><td>29–30[15–16]. Solomon had
seventy thousand laborers
and eighty thousand hewers
in the mountains . . .</td><td>16. Then Solomon counted all the
aliens in the land of Israel . . .
of them he assigned</td></tr>
<tr><td></td><td>17a. seventy thousand as laborers,</td></tr>
<tr><td></td><td>b. eighty thousand as hewers
in the mountains,</td></tr>
</table>

10. This unit actually begins with v. 15, which tells about the diplomatic delegation sent by Hiram to Solomon to congratulate him on his accession to the throne. This verse was omitted in Chronicles, apparently to show that King Solomon was the initiator of the diplomacy with Hiram, king of Tyre.

and three thousand three hundred **men supervising those doing the work.** 31–32[17–18]. Unfolding the literary unit concerning the woodworking and stonecutting.

c. *and three thousand six*[11] *hundred* **as supervisors to keep the people at work.**

2 Chr 2:1 is thus part of a literary inclusio into which the Chronicler fit the passage that he took from the book of Kings, not "a secondary text," as a number of scholars believe.[12] The identification of this literary construction does not even allow room for conjecturing a "duplication," as Bertheau and Curtis-Madsen do.[13] In their opinion, the duplication stems from the fact that the Chronicler sometimes presented an event as he recalled it at the moment, but then, when he came to it in the book of Kings, he presented it again. The second time, he reported it in full, because he had not completed the telling of the event the first time. The claim that the Chronicler cited passages from memory seems unlikely in itself, because the "duplications" that we have are identical in content and style. Furthermore, these scholars do not explain the Chronicler's motivation for presenting passages from memory before he encountered them in the text of the book of Kings.

Because the formulation of texts within a literary inclusio is a feature of the Chronicler's literary-historiographical writing device, it also seems improper to conclude with Abramsky that in 2 Chr 2:1 the Chronicler was trying to extol Solomon's name—that is, that "Solomon already had a similar number of workmen, even before he made contact with Hiram."[14]

14.4 In 2 Chr 27:8 (an "addition"), the Chronicler repeats the introduction to Jotham's reign that is found in 27:1a (// 2 Kgs 15:33a). Thus, he creates a literary inclusio around the material that he borrowed from 2 Kgs 15:33b–35, 36 (// 2 Chr 27:1b–4, 7) plus the narrative of Jotham's war against the Ammonites, which is found only in his book (27:5–6):

---

11. The parallel text in the book of Kings has the word שלש 'three'. The letter ש sometimes served as an abbreviation for the numbers שנים, שלוש, שש, שבע, שמונה 'two', 'three', 'six', 'seven', 'eight', and so on (see Driver, "Abbreviations," 125). It is thus possible that what was written at first was the abbreviation ש' מאות, and the MT scribe of Kings read this as שלש, while the LXX–Lucianic scribe of Kings read שבע and the LXX–Vaticanus scribe of Kings and the scribe of Chronicles read שש. It is also possible that either שש or שלש is a corruption of the other, because they are phonetically and graphically similar to each other.

12. See, e.g., Rudolph, *Chronik*, 201; Williamson, *Chronicles*, 198.

13. See Bertheau, *Chronik*, 232–33; Curtis-Madsen, *Chronicles*, 320.

14. See Abramsky, "King Solomon," 7.

2 Kgs 15:33–38	*2 Chr 27:1–9*
33a. **He was twenty-five years old when he ascended to the throne, and he reigned in Jerusalem sixteen years.**	1a. **Jotham was twenty-five years old when he ascended to the throne and reigned in Jerusalem sixteen years.**
33b–35a. [Jotham's mother's name and an evaluation of Jotham's religious conduct.]	1b–2. [Jotham's mother's name and an evaluation of Jotham's religious conduct.]
35b. Jotham's construction project.	3–4. Jotham's construction projects.
	5–6. Jotham's war with the Ammonites.
36. And the rest of Jotham's deeds. . . .	7. And the rest of Jotham's deeds. . . .
	8. **He was twenty-five years old when he ascended the throne, and he reigned in Jerusalem for sixteen years.**
37. At that time the Lord began to send. . . .	
38. Then Jotham slept with his fathers and was buried.	9. Then Jotham slept with his fathers, and they buried him.

2 Chr 27:8 is therefore not a superfluous repetition made by some scribe or copyist, as believed by some scholars,[15] or a late marginal comment erroneously included in the text,[16] but a deliberate repetition used by the Chronicler to fit the description of Jotham's reign into an inclusio.

14.5 The narrative of the reign of Jehoram, king of Judah, in the book of Chronicles resembles our previous example. In 2 Chr 21:20a, the Chronicler repeated the introduction to Jehoram's reign that had already been presented in 21:5 // 2 Kgs 8:17, thus creating a literary inclusio around (a) the text that he adduced from 2 Kgs 8:18–22 (// 2 Chr 21:6–10) and (b) Elijah's letter to Jehoram and the fulfillment of Elijah's prophecy and so on (2 Chr 21:11–19), which are found in his book only:

2 Kgs 8:16–24	*2 Chr 21:1–20*
	1–4. The narrative of Jehoram's succession and his assassination of his brothers.

15. So, e.g., Curtis-Madsen, *Chronicles*, 455; Williamson, *Chronicles*, 343.
16. So, e.g., Rudolph, *Chronik*, 286.

16. Synchronism between Joram,
    son of Ahab, and Jehoram,
    son of Jehoshaphat.

17. **He was thirty-two**   5.   **Jehoram was thirty-two**
    years old when he became   **years old**
    king, and he reigned eight   **and reigned eight**
    years in Jerusalem.   **years in Jerusalem.**

18–19. An evaluation of Joram's   6–7. An evaluation of Jehoram's
    religious image.   religious image.

20–22. The rebellion of Edom   8–10. The rebellion of Edom
    and Libnah.   and Libnah.

                                   11. The construction of high places in
                                        the Judean Hills.

                                   12–15. Elijah's letter to Jehoram.

                                   16–19. The fulfillment of the
                                        prophecy in the letter.

                                   20a. **He was thirty-two years old**
                                        when he became king, and he
                                        reigned eight years in
                                        Jerusalem.

23. Conclusion to Joram's period.

24. Joram's burial place.   b.   Jehoram's burial place.

14.6 1 Kgs 3:4–15 describes Solomon trip to Gibeon. The narrative
opens with the words "the king went [from Jerusalem] to Gibeon" (v. 4a)
and closes with the words "he came back to Jerusalem" (v. 15b).[17] Two
stories that took place in Gibeon were then bound up together here: one
tells about the great sacrifice offered by Solomon on the high place in
Gibeon (v. 4), and the other tells about the prophetic dream that Solomon had while he was in Gibeon (vv. 5–15a).

A special literary frame was also devoted to the story about the
dream in Gibeon: "The Lord appeared to Solomon in Gibeon *in a dream.*
. . . *Solomon awoke, and behold! it was a dream*" (vv. 5a, 15a).[18]

The Chronicler broke up this frame by omitting the words בחלום and
ויקץ שלמה והנה חלום 'in a dream' and 'Solomon awoke, and behold! it was
a dream' (2 Chr 1:7a, 13).[19] However, he expanded the introduction and

---

17. Compare with this construction, for example, *"He came* to Bethlehem . . . *and
he rose and went* to Rama" (1 Sam 16:4, 13); "He and two men with him went; *they
came* to the woman['s place] at night . . . *and they rose and went* that night" (1 Sam
28:8, 25). The conclusion of the narrative is clearly marked by the central figure's returning to his own place. This is to give the reader the feeling that the story has come
to an end.

18. Compare this construction with Gen 41:1, 7: "Pharaoh *dreamed* . . . *Pharaoh
awoke, and behold! it was a dream.*"

19. For the reason for this omission, see above, example 2.19 (pp. 53–54).

conclusion of the narrative about Solomon's trip to Gibeon: "*And Solomon* **and all the people with him** *went* [*from Jerusalem*] **to the high place that was** *in Gibeon*, **for God's Tent of Meeting was there**. . . . *Solomon came from* **the high place**[20] *that was in Gibeon*, **from the Tent of Meeting**, *to Jerusalem*" (vv. 3, 13a).[21] Furthermore, the Chronicler put the entire narrative into an external literary inclusio that opened and closed with mention of Solomon's reign over Israel: "**Then Solomon, son of David, reigned firmly over his kingdom**. . . . **He reigned over Israel**" (vv. 1a, 13b):

1 Kgs 3:4–15	*2 Chr 1:1–13*
	1a. **Then Solomon, son of David, reigned firmly over his kingdom**. . . .
4a. *And the king went* [*from Jerusalem*] *to Gibeon*.	3. *And Solomon* **and all the people with him** *went* [*from Jerusalem*] **to the high place that was in Gibeon, for God's Tent of Meeting was there**. . . .
4b. The narrative of the great sacrifice at Gibeon.	4–6. The narrative of the great sacrifice at Gibeon.
5a. The Lord appeared to Solomon in Gibeon in a night-**dream**.	7a. That night God appeared to Solomon. . . .
5b–14. The narrative of the prophetic dream.	7b–12. The narrative of God's revelation to Solomon.
15a. **Solomon awoke, and behold! it was a dream.**	
b. *and he came back* **to Jerusalem**	13a. *And Solomon came from* **the high place that was in**

---

20. Read מהבמה 'from the high place' with the LXX, Vetus Latina, and Vulgate. Haplography seems to have taken place in the MT: שלמה מהבמה, with the letter ל having been added later, as in v. 3; cf. Curtis-Madsen, *Chronicles*, 317; Rudolph, *Chronik*, 196; idem, *BHS*, 1514; and against Abramsky (*Saul and David*, 383 n. 4), who thinks that the translations found in the versions are "commentary, a way of straightening out the language."

21. The words לבמה אשר בגבעון וגו' 'to the high place that is in Gibeon, etc.', in 2 Chr 1:13a, may be a late gloss introduced into the text, in which case they should be omitted; thus, e.g., Curtis-Madsen, *Chronicles*, 317 (with W. E. Barnes, cited there); Elmslie, *Chronicles* (1916), 171: "This clause yields no sense in the Hebrew and is probably a misplaced gloss"; and also in his other commentary on *Chronicles* (1954) 444: "from before the tabernacle of the congregation—is a revisional addition." However, the similarity of the conclusion and introduction indicates a deliberate act by the Chronicler rather than a late gloss. It is also unclear why such a gloss would be introduced here at all.

> Gibeon, from the Tent of
> Meeting, to Jerusalem,
> b. *and he reigned over Israel.*

14.7 The description of the preparations for the arrival of the Ark and the account of its being brought from the home of Obed-Edom to Jerusalem appear in 1 Chr 15:1–16:1 in an inclusio:

2 Sam 6:14–17	*1 Chr 15:1–16:1*
	15:1. Then he built houses in the City of David **and prepared a place for the Ark of God and set up a tent for it.**
	2. Then David said **that the Ark of God was to be borne only by the Levites,** for the Lord had chosen them to bear the Ark of the Lord. . . .
	3. Then **David** gathered together **all of Israel** to Jerusalem **to bring up the Ark of the Lord to the place** that he had prepared for it. . . .
	4–16. The preparations in Jerusalem; lists of the Levites;
	17–24. the stationing of the singers;
12b–17. The bringing up of the ark.	25ff. the bringing up of the ark.
14. David was prancing fiercely before the Lord. . . .	27. David was wrapped in a robe of fine linen, **as also were the Levites bearing the Ark.** . . .
15. **David and all the house of Israel brought up the Ark of the Lord.** . . .	28. **All Israel brought up the Ark of the Covenant of the Lord.** . . .
16. As the Ark of the Lord entered the City of David. . . .	29. As the Ark of the Covenant of the Lord entered the City of David. . . .
17. **They brought the Ark of the Lord and placed it in the place within the Tent that David had set up for it**, and David offered up burnt-offerings before the Lord and peace-offerings.	16:1. **They brought the Ark of God and placed it within the Tent that David had set up for it**, and they sacrificed burnt-offerings and peace-offerings before God.

The individual parts that conclude the literary inclusio are presented in chiastic order relative to the same parts in the introduction: setting up the Tent, the Levites bearing the Ark, and the accompaniment by David and all Israel. Thus, 1 Chr 15:1, 3 take their content from 1 Chr 15:18, 16:1, which parallel 2 Sam 6:15, 17.

B. Limited Literary Units

14.8 In 1 Kgs 6:24–25, 27b, the author of Kings described the wings of the cherubs, including their dimensions. The Chronicler placed this description in an inclusio that opens וכנפי הכרובים ארכם אמות עשרים 'the wings of the cherubs—twenty cubits' (2 Chr 3:11a) and concludes: וכנפי הכרובים האלה פרשים[22] אמות עשרים 'the wings of these cherubs extended twenty cubits' (v. 13a).[23] He used their 'length' in the introduction (v. 11) instead of the verb 'extend' in the conclusion to achieve literary variety.

This inclusio compresses the details about the cherubs' wings and the way they were positioned in the inner sanctum. Similarly, it creates a construction that moves "from general to specific and back to general," as will be shown in detail below.[24]

14.9 1 Kgs 10:14–15 refers to the amount of "gold that was brought to Solomon" in a single year. The Chronicler repeats these words at the end of the paragraph, creating a literary inclusio:

1 Kgs 10:14–15	*2 Chr 9:13–14*
The weight of **the gold** that **came to Solomon** in a single year was six hundred sixty-six talents of gold, besides the peddlers and the trade of the tradesmen (מסחר הרכלים)	The weight of **the gold** that **came to Solomon** in a single year was six hundred sixty-six talents of gold, besides the peddlers and the merchants (והסחרים) who brought[25]

---

22. In the MT, פְּרֹשִׂים 'extended', although some read פְּרֶשִׂים 'spreading', as in the LXX, Vulgate, and Aramaic Targum; see, e.g., Rudolph, *Chronik*, 204; idem, *BHS*, 1517; Begrich, *BH*, 1380.

23. For the "chiasmus between parallel texts" structure between 2 Chr 3:11 and 1 Kgs 6:24, see example 12.103 (p. 272).

24. See below, example 19.19 (pp. 378–379).

25. The Chronicler may have replaced the phrase מסחר הרכלים 'the trade of the tradesmen' in Kings with the word הסחרים 'the merchants' because of the change that had taken place in the meaning of the word רוכל in later Hebrew: according to Neh 13:20 and also in Mishnaic Hebrew (see, e.g., *m. Maʿaś.* 2:3; *b. Giṭ.* 67a), רוכל is a (wandering) tradesman dealing in small trade; this is also the meaning of the word רוכלא in Aramaic (see, e.g., *b. Giṭ.* 33a; *b. B. Qam.* 36b). This later meaning, to which the later reader was accustomed, does not suit the specific context of the earlier text, which is concerned with international trade. The word מביאים seems to have been copied erroneously from the end of the verse.

and all the kings of Arabia and the governors of the land	it, and all the kings of Arabia and governors of the land **who came with gold** and silver to **Solomon**.

The Chronicler presented the concluding words that he added at the end of the paragraph in chiastic relation to the words of the introduction:

הזהב . . . בא לשלמה	The **gold** . . . that *came* to Solomon
מביאים זהב . . . לשלמה	*came* with **gold** . . . to Solomon

This contributed to the esthetic charm of the literary inclusio created by the Chronicler, as well as to the compression of its individual parts.

14.10 The Chronicler introduced the description of Josiah's ritual reform in Judah and Jerusalem in a literary inclusio, which opens and closes with the same words: ירושלם (את)ו יהודה את טהר 'he cleansed Judah and Jerusalem' (2 Chr 34:3b; 5b). This literary inclusio binds together the actions and items that were partially taken from 2 Kgs 23:6, 16 and partially "added" by the Chronicler:

2 Kgs 23:6, 16	*2 Chr 34:3b–5*
	3b. In the twelfth year, he began **to cleanse Judah and Jerusalem** of [26] the high
6. He took the *Asherah* out of the House of the Lord, out of Jerusalem, to the Kidron Valley, and burned it in the Kidron Valley,	places and the *Asherahs* and the images and the cast idols.
	4. And in his presence they tore down the altars of the Baals. They demolished the sun-images that were above them and broke down the Asherahs and the images and the cast idols;[27]
ground it to dust, *and scattered* its dust on the graves of the common people.	*he made dust of them and scattered it over the graves of those who had sacrificed to them.*
16. When he saw *the graves* . . . he took *the bones* from *the graves and burned*	5a. *He also burned the bones of the priests on their altars.*

---

26. The cleansing of Jerusalem also includes the cleansing of the House of the Lord; compare "to cleanse the land *and the House*" (v. 8).

27. For the nature of the ritual objects listed here, see the modern commentaries on this verse. For the חמנים 'sun-images', see Kalimi, *Bibliography*, 175–76, entries 1710–24. Haran ("The 'Incense Altars'," 322–24) is of the opinion that חמן was a wooden ritual instrument that used to be placed on an altar.

them on the altar and
defiled it.

b. **He cleansed Judah and
Jerusalem.**

It should be noted that while according to the book of Kings one of the
purposes of burning the bones on the altar was to *defile* the altar, according to the book of Chronicles the very same act was intended *to
cleanse* Judah and Jerusalem. According to the Chronicler, the altars
themselves could never enjoy any sanctity whatever. They were already
impure and would always remain impure, regardless of the effect of the
sacrifice offered on them.

14.11 1 Sam 31:6 sums up the casualties of the defeat on Mount Gilboa in the order of their relationship to the monarchy: "*Saul, his three
sons, his armor-bearer,* and *all his men* died."[28] In 1 Chr 10:6, the
Chronicler omitted "his armor-bearer" and "all his men," stating instead, "all his house."[29] Similarly, he used the root מות again at the end
of the list, creating a literary inclusio that began and ended with the
same root, מתו . . . וימת, enclosing only the references to members of the
royal family.

This inclusio links the component parts of the list in Chronicles and
compresses them together. It also places greater stress on the most important consequence of the defeat as far as the Chronicler was concerned—the death of all the members of the royal family and the
subsequent vacuum in the central administration of Israel.[30] In this

---

28. In contrast, in 1 Sam 31:1–5, the list of casualties is apparently presented according to the chronological development of events: the flight of "the men of Israel"
(i.e., the army) and their fall on Mt. Gilboa (v. 1); the fall of Saul's three sons (v. 2);
the suicide of Saul and his armor-bearer (vv. 4–5). The components of the concluding
list in v. 6 are adduced in chiastic order relative to those in vv. 1–5:

vv. 2, 4: **the death of Saul's three sons**	*the death of Saul*
v. 6a: *So Saul died*	**and his three sons**
vv. 1, 4: **the fall of the men of Israel**	*the death of Saul's armor-bearer*
v. 6b: *the death of Saul's armor-bearer*	**the death of all his men**

29. The word ביתו 'his house' here refers to "his family" (cf., e.g., Gen 7:1: "Come,
you and all *your house*, into the ark") or "his dynasty" (cf. 1 Chr 17:10 // 2 Sam 7:11).
At any rate, this is a metonymic use of the word; the Chronicler used the name of a
dwelling place to mean the people living in it.

30. The deaths of both "his armor-bearer" and "all his men" seem to have been
omitted in order to stress the deaths of "Saul, his three sons, and all his family," the
main aspect of this narrative as far as the Chronicler was concerned. The separation
of Saul from his armor-bearer was also expressed by omitting the word עמו 'with him',
the word with which the description of the death of Saul's armor-bearer concludes in
1 Sam 31:5.

way, he could present David as reigning over *"all Israel"* immediately after the defeat on Gilboa (1 Chr 10:14; 11–12), omitting the narrative of Eshbaal's reign over the Northern tribes (2 Sam 2:8–4:12):[31]

1 Sam 31:6	1 Chr 10:6
וימת	וימת
שאול	שאול
ושלשת בניו	ושלשת בניו
ונשא כליו	
גם כל אנשיו ביום ההוא	וכל ביתו
יחדו	יחדו
	מתו

Then	Then
Saul	Saul
and his three sons	and his three sons
and his armor-bearer	
and **all his men**	and **all his House**
died together on that day.	died together.[32]

14.12 There is similar case of literary manipulation further along in the chapter as well, in 1 Chr 10:13a–14a, in the Chronicler's summarizing "addition" to the story in 1 Samuel 31. This "addition" also opens and concludes with the root מות: *וימת* . . . *וימת שאול* 'So Saul **died**. . . . So He [God] *put him* [Saul] *to death*':

> So Saul **died**
> for his betrayal. He betrayed the Lord
> because he did not observe the command of the Lord.
> He also enquired of a witch
> and did not enquire of the Lord.
> So He **put him to death**.

Unlike the narrative of Saul's death in vv. 4, 6, these verses (13a–14a) stress the fact that Saul's death was not just a death by chance in war but a deliberate death at the hands of the Lord because of his sins.[33] The reader is led from וימת שאול through the details of his sins to וימיתהו 'so

---

31. For this subject in detail, see example 1.1 (pp. 18–19).

32. For the contradiction between 1 Chr 10:6 and 1 Chr 8:39–40 // 9:39–44; 1 Chr 15:29 // 2 Sam 6:16, see example 20.7 (pp. 389–390).

33. Compare 1 Sam 28:18–19. 1 Chr 10:13–14 is thus a realization of the words spoken by the prophet Samuel to Saul in 1 Sam 28:16–19. The death of Saul and his sons and the defeat of Israel in the battle of Gilboa are explained there as they are here: "As you did not heed the voice of the Lord, neither did you carry out His wrath against Amalek—therefore the Lord has done this thing to you this day" (1 Sam 28:18).

[the Lord] put [Saul] to death'. The literary inclusio renders the relationship of וימת to וימיתהו more prominent, with the sins that brought this about listed between the two related words.[34]

14.13 In the narrative about the acquisition of the threshing floor, David says to Arauna/Ornan, the Jebusite, that the reason for his visit is "to purchase the threshing floor from you" in order "to build an altar to the Lord" (2 Sam 24:21). The Chronicler placed these words spoken by David in an inclusio that opens and closes with the words תנה(ו) לי 'give (it) to me' (1 Chr 21:22):

2 Sam 24:21b	1 Chr 21:22
David said, "**To purchase** the threshing floor **from you**, to build an altar to the Lord."	David said to Ornan, "**Give me** the place of the threshing floor[35] so that I can build an altar to the Lord there; for the full price **give it to me**."[36]

Further along, we are told that Arauna/Ornan was prepared to give David not only the site of the threshing floor to build the altar but also the materials that he had available for the offering of sacrifices: הבקר לעלה והמרגים וכלי הבקר לעצים 'the cattle for burnt-offerings, the threshing boards, and the yokes of the cattle for wood' (2 Sam 24:22).[37] The Chronicler next presented this list, adding the phrase "and wheat for the

---

34. The formulation of the "sins" in itself contributes further to the compression of the various parts of the passage—one sin being expressed in synonymous parallelism and the other in antithetical parallelism, with the parts presented in chiastic order:

> Then Saul died
> **for his betrayal. He betrayed**   *the Lord*
> *because the command of the Lord*   **he did not observe.**
> He also **of a witch**   *enquired*
> *and did not enquire*   **of the Lord.**
> So He put him to death.

For the antithetical parallelism, cf. 2 Chr 17:3c–4a; see also the details in example 15.12 (pp. 337–339).

35. The Chronicler emphasizes that David was interested in the *site* of the threshing floor in order to build an altar to the Lord, since he had no need for the threshing floor itself.

36. Here the Chronicler emulates Abraham's words to the Hittites, especially to Ephron, son of Zohar, in Gen 23:9: "Let him give it to me *for the full price*." See also further along, in 1 Chr 21:24: "No, I will buy it *for the full price*" (instead of: "No, I will buy it from you *for a price*," in 2 Sam 24:24); cf. Zakovitch, "Assimilation," 181.

37. Compare this with the use of the wagon and cows by the people of Beth-shemesh, after the Ark of the Lord arrived from the land of the Philistines: "They split the wood of the wagon and offered up the cows as a burnt-offering to the Lord" (1 Sam 6:14).

meal-offering,"[38] and fitting it into another literary inclusio. Matching the structure תנהו לי . . . תנה לי 'give *me* . . . **give it *to me*** that already existed in David's request, he changed Arauna's reply from "may take" (in 2 Samuel) to "**take (it) for yourself**"and constructed the wheat addition into yet another literary inclusio, הכל נתתי . . . ראה נתתי 'behold **I have given** . . . **I give** all of it':

2 Sam 24:22–23a	1 Chr 21:23
Then Arauna said to David,	Then Ornan said to David,
"My lord the king *may take*	*"Take for yourself*, and may my
and offer whatever he	lord the king do whatever he
wishes.	wishes.
Behold	**Behold, I have given**
the cattle for burnt-offerings,	the cattle for burnt-offerings,
the threshing boards, and the	the threshing boards for wood,
yokes of the cattle for wood."	
	and wheat for a meal-offering.
Arauna, the king,[39]	**I give all of it.**[40]
gave everything to the king.	

14.14 With the words ולא שאלת 'because you did not request', the author of the book of Kings introduces the three requests that Solomon did not make for himself. The Chronicler put all three of these requests into an inclusio that opens and closes with the same words, (ו)לא שאלת:

1 Kgs 3:11	2 Chr 1:11
Because you did not request	**Because you did not request**
for yourself longevity,	
you did not request for yourself	

---

38. This addition was apparently made under the influence of Exod 29:38–41 and Num 15:8–9; 28:12–13 (P), which require a meal-offering to be presented with a burnt-offering (cf. Curtis-Madsen, *Chronicles*, 252; against Williamson, *Chronicles*, 149–50). This was also the custom in the Chronicler's day, the Second Temple era. He introduced the wheat in v. 20 in preparation "for the burnt-offering" (wheat is not mentioned in this story in the book of Samuel either). This addition is similar, in principle, to the word לחם, which was added to 1 Sam 1:24 in connection with Hannah's sacrifice at Shiloh in 4QSamᵃ and in the LXX. In the words of Segal, 'bread' was added "because they understood that the cow was a thanksgiving sacrifice, with which bread is offered (Lev 7:13)" (Segal, *Samuel*, 13–14).

39. The word המלך 'the king' does not appear in the early translations. If it is authentic in the MT, it may be that the narrator was indicating Arauna's status prior to the conquest of Jerusalem; for other opinions on this, see McCarter, *II Samuel*, 508.

40. While the words "Arauna, the king, gave everything to the king" in 2 Sam 24:23a are, apparently, those of the redactor of the book of Samuel, in 1 Chr 21:23 the Chronicler has turned them into a continuation of Arauna's words to David: "*I give everything.*"

wealth,
and you did not request
the lives of your enemies, . . .

wealth, property or honor,
the lives of those who hate you—
not even longevity
did you request, . . .

The Chronicler also rearranged the words of the earlier passage into a chiastic structure, which further strengthened the links between the requests that Solomon did not make.[41]

Further along, we find a similar feature concerning the Lord's promise to Solomon:

<table>
<tr><td align="center">1 Kgs 3:13</td><td align="center">2 Chr 1:12</td></tr>
<tr><td align="center" dir="rtl">‏. . . לֹא הָיָה כָמוֹךָ
אִישׁ בַּמְּלָכִים כָּל יָמֶיךָ</td><td align="center" dir="rtl">‏לֹא הָיָה כֵן
לַמְּלָכִים אֲשֶׁר לְפָנֶיךָ
וְאַחֲרֶיךָ
לֹא יִהְיֶה כֵן</td></tr>
<tr><td align="center">no king has ever had
like you.</td><td align="center">such as none of the kings
has had before you,
nor shall any after you have.</td></tr>
</table>

Here also the words in Chronicles are arranged in chiastic order.[42]

C. Perfecting an Existing Inclusio

14.15 Occasionally the Chronicler perfected a literary inclusio structure that he found in the earlier text. For example, the description of the peace-offering at the Temple dedication ceremony appears in 1 Kgs 8:62–63 in an inclusio that has two *similar* phrases: ‏וְהַמֶּלֶךְ וְכָל יִשְׂרָאֵל עִמּוֹ‎ ‏הַמֶּלֶךְ וְכָל בְּנֵי־יִשְׂרָאֵל‎ . . . . 'Then the king and all Israel with him . . . the king and all the descendants of Israel'. The Chronicler omitted the word ‏עִמּוֹ‎ 'with him', replaced the proper nouns ‏יִשְׂרָאֵל‎ and ‏בְּנֵי־יִשְׂרָאֵל‎ with the common noun ‏הָעָם‎ 'the people'. This omission and these stylistic emendations created a new situation, in which the literary inclusio contained two *identical* phrases, ‏(וְ)הַמֶּלֶךְ וְכָל הָעָם‎ '(Then) the king and all the people' (2 Chr 7:4a, 5b), thus perfecting the literary structure:

<table>
<tr><td align="center">1 Kgs 8:62–63</td><td align="center">2 Chr 7:4–5</td></tr>
<tr><td>62. Then the king and all
Israel with him</td><td>4. Then the king and all the
people</td></tr>
</table>

---

41. For this, see example 11.3 (pp. 219–220). This passage in Chronicles is arranged in chiastic order relative to its order in the parallel passage in Kings; for this, see example 12.16 (p. 238).

42. For this, see example 11.3 (pp. 219–220).

made a sacrifice to the Lord.	made a sacrifice to the Lord.[43]
63. Solomon made as peace-offering sacrifices to the Lord:	5. King Solomon made the sacrifice:
cattle twenty-two thousand; sheep one hundred twenty thousand. They also dedicated the House of the Lord— **the king and all the descendants of Israel**.	cattle twenty-two thousand; sheep one hundred twenty thousand. They also dedicated the House of God— **the king and all the people**.

For another example of perfecting an inclusio in the earlier text, see example 14.19 below (the lists of David's offspring).

D. Literary Inclusios in "Additions"

Literary inclusios can also be found in the "additions" of the book of Chronicles.

14.16 In 2 Chr 36:21, the Chronicler introduced various phrases taken from Lev 26:34 and Jer 29:10 and surrounded them with a literary inclusio that contains the word למלאות 'to complete, to fulfill':

למלאות דבר ה׳ בפי ירמיהו	**to fulfill** the word of the Lord by the mouth of Jeremiah:
עד רצתה הארץ את שבתותיה	only when the land has made up for its sabbaths;
כל ימי השמה שבתה	all the days that it lay desolate it kept sabbath,
למלאות שבעים שנה[44]	**to fulfill** seventy years.

The formulation of the phrases into a chiastic structure reinforced the links among them even further.[45]

14.17 In 2 Chr 27:5, the Chronicler has framed the list of yearly tribute paid by the Ammonites to Jotham, king of Judah, with an inclusio:

The Ammonites gave him that year
one hundred talents of silver,

---

43. Compare this verse with 2 Chr 5:6: "Then King Solomon and all the congregation of Israel who had assembled with him before the Ark, were sacrificing sheep and cattle without number" (// 1 Kgs 8:5).

44. Ehrlich notes here: "This is done to glorify and exalt the remission of lands. This was apparently needed in the days of this writer" (*Mikrâ ki-Pheschutô*, 470).

45. For the chiastic structure, see example 11.14 (p. 222).

ten thousand measures of wheat,
and of barley ten thousand.
This same amount
the Ammonites returned to him
in the second and third years.

Some of the components of this list are also arranged in chiastic order.[46]

14.18 For additional examples of literary inclusio in "additions," see:
1 Chr 26:26–28: הוא שלמות ואחיו . . . שלמית ואחיו 'This Shelomoth and his
brothers . . . Shelomoth and his brothers'; 2 Chr 30:13: ויאספו ירושלם עם רב
קהל לרב מאד . . . 'Many people gathered together in Jerusalem . . . a
crowd in great abundance'.

2. Literary and/or Numerical Inclusios in Lists or Collections of Lists

A. The List of David's Offspring

14.19 In 1 Chr 3:1–9, the Chronicler presents a list of David's offspring borrowed from a collection of lists and names found in various
contexts in the book of Samuel: 2 Sam 3:2–5 (the list of David's sons
born in Hebron); 2 Sam 5:14–16 (the list of David's sons born in Jerusalem); 2 Sam 15:16 (information on David's concubines, by whom the
Chronicler concluded that David fathered sons); and 2 Sam 13:1 (Tamar, David's daughter). First, he compiled the list of David's sons by *his
wives* from the two passages in the book of Samuel: 2 Sam 3:2–5 and
5:14–16. Then, the total number of years that David reigned in Hebron
and Jerusalem was given as a link between the two. Third, the Chronicler separated the list of David's wives' sons (1 Chr 3:1b–8) from the information concerning "the sons of the concubines; and Tamar, their
sister" (1 Chr 3:9b) with the conclusion of the literary inclusio that he
placed around the list of wives' sons. The inclusio contains the opening
words "these are the sons of David" (3:1a) and the closing words "all
these were sons of David" (3:9a):

3:1a.	**"These are the sons of David. . . ."**
1b–4a.	The list of David's sons born in Hebron (according to 2 Sam 3:2–5).
4b.	The years of David's reign in Hebron. ⎫ (according to The years of David's reign in Jerusalem. ⎬ 2 Sam 5:5)
5–8.	The list of David's sons born in Jerusalem (according to 2 Sam 5:14–16).
9a.	**"All these were sons of David."**

46. For this chiastic structure, see example 11.22 (p. 223).

This literary inclusio also serves to bind tightly together the collection of lists and names adduced within it and gives it uniformity and sequentiality. Moreover, the Chronicler makes use of additional literary devices to achieve an even tighter bond among the texts within the literary inclusio:

1. Perfecting the literary inclusio that appears in 2 Sam 3:2a–5b, the list of David's sons born in Hebron:

	2 Sam 3:2a, 5b	*1 Chr 3:1b, 4a*
	וילדו (Qere) וַיִּוָּלְדוּ) לדוד בנים בחברון	אשר נולד לו בחברון
	. . .	. . .
	אשר ילדו לדוד בחברון	ששה נולד לו בחברון
	Sons were born to David in Hebron	which were born to him in Hebron
	. . .	. . .
	which were born to David in Hebron.	*six* were born to him in Hebron.

2. Forming a numerical inclusio around the list of David's sons born in Hebron (ששה 'six') and the list of those born in Jerusalem (ארבעה לבת־שוע 'four' to Bath-shua' and תשעה מיתר נשיו 'nine from the rest of his wives'; 1 Chr 3:4a, 5c, 8).
3. Placing a transition—2 Sam 5:5 (the summary of the years of David's reign in Hebron and Jerusalem)—between the list of David's sons born in Hebron and the list of sons born in Jerusalem, as already noted. The Chronicler did not copy 2 Sam 5:5 mechanically, however, but altered the word order to create a chiastic structure in his own work, thus strengthening already-existing bonds.[47]
4. Strengthening the bond between the list in 2 Sam 3:2–5 and 2 Sam 5:5 by substituting the adverbial שם 'there' (referring to Hebron) for the word חברון in 5:5:

	2 Samuel		*1 Chronicles*
3:5	. . . These were born to David **in Hebron**.	3:4a	. . . were born to him **in Hebron**.
5:5	**In Hebron** he reigned . . . seven years.	b	And he reigned **there** seven years.

To sum up, the Chronicler attempted to provide the collection of lists and names that he borrowed from various places in the book of Samuel

---

47. For this chiastic structure, see below and example 11.2 (p. 219).

with a sequential and uniform appearance. He did this by means of several literary techniques: the creation of a literary inclusio at the beginning and end of his compilation of all the texts; the perfection of an existing literary inclusio in the earlier text; the addition of numerical inclusios; the use of a third text as a transition between two different texts, while inverting the order of its component parts; and the use of an adverbial particle instead of a place-name in the earlier text:

2 Samuel 3 and 5	*1 Chronicles 3:1–9*
	These are the sons of David
3:2a Sons **were born to David in Hebron** [the names of David's sons who were born in Hebron].	who **were born to him in Hebron** [the names of David's sons who were born in Hebron].
3:5b These **were born to David** *in Hebron.*	*Six* **were born to him** *in Hebron.*
5:5 ***In Hebron*** he reigned . . . *seven years and six months* **In Jerusalem he reigned** *thirty-three years.*	**He reigned** *there seven years and six months, and thirty-three years* **he reigned in Jerusalem.**
5:14–16 These are the names of those born to him in Jerusalem: Shammua, Shobab, Nathan, Solomon,	These were born to him in Jerusalem:[48] Shima, Shobab, Nathan, and Solomon— **four by Bath-shua, daughter of Ammiel;**
Ibhar, Elishua, Nepheg, Japhia, Elishama, Eliada, and Eliphelet.	and Ibhar, Elishama, Eliphelet, Nogah, Nepheg, Japhia, Elishama, Eliada, and Eliphelet—*nine.*[49]
	All these were sons of David,
15:16 David's concubines.	besides the sons of the concubines;
13:1 Tamar, David's daughter.	and their sister was Tamar.

---

48. The word ירושלים is spelled plene (that is, with a second *yod*), as in 2 Chr 25:1; 32:9; Esth 2:6; and Jer 26:18, in contrast to ירושלם (without a second *yod*), as it is spelled everywhere else in the Bible (662 times). Compare the spelling דויד (with a *yod*) in Chronicles, in contrast to דוד (without a *yod*) everywhere else in the Bible.

49. The list of David's sons born in Jerusalem is given with certain changes and with no numerical inclusio in 1 Chr 14:4–7 as well.

B. The List of Zerah's Sons

14.20 In 1 Chr 2:6, the Chronicler formulated a genealogical list for the descendants of Zerah by combining the list of ancient sages in 1 Kgs 5:11[4:31] with the list of Zerah's descendants in Josh 7:1 (see also 7:18), lists that are not connected genealogically or in any other way. In order to provide this list with a uniform appearance and to bind its component parts together, he placed it inside both a literary inclusio and a numerical inclusio: "**The sons of Zerah** . . . *all in all*, five" (כלם 'all in all' being an abbreviated form of כל בני זרח 'all the sons of Zerah').

Josh 7:1	1 Kgs 5:11[4:31]	1 Chr 2:6
. . . son of Zabdi		**The sons of Zerah**:
son of Zerah . . .		Zimri,[50]
	Ethan the Ezrahite,	Ethan,
	Heman,	Heman,
	Calcol,	Calcol,
	and Darda	and Dara[51]
	—sons of Mahol.	—**all in all**, five.

It appears that the combination of the list of sages with the list of the sons of Zerah is to be explained in light of the phonetic resemblance of the name Zerah and the adjective "the Ezrahite," which modifies Ethan: the Chronicler derived האזרחי from זרח,[52] thus linking the two lists.[53] The fact that the list of sages ends with the phrase "the sons of Mahol" seems not to have bothered him at all in his derivation.

C. The List of Judah's Sons

14.21 In 1 Chr 2:3–4, the Chronicler borrowed the list of the names of Judah's sons from the book of Genesis, placing it within a literary inclusio ("the sons of Judah . . . all the sons of Judah") and a numerical inclusio ("five"):

---

50. The name Zimri is probably an error for the name Zabdi in Josh 7:1: the labial consonant מ replaced the labial consonant ב because of their phonetic similarity; and the consonant ר replaced the consonant ד because of their graphic similarity. For examples of ב/מ and ר/ד interchanges in the Bible, see Sperber, "Parallel Transmission," 164, 167 (this example is not adduced in Sperber's list, however).

51. In the Vulgate, Aramaic Targum, and Peshitta, as well as in a number of manuscripts of the Greek translation, דרדע (Darda) appears, as in 1 Kgs 5:11[4:31].

52. And, in the Chronicler's wake, *Tg. Jonathan* on 1 Kgs 5:11 has איתן בר זרח 'Ethan, son of Zerah'.

53. The term אזרחי may be derived from the noun אזרח—that is, native-born, son of a pre-Israelite family in the land of Canaan (Num 9:14); cf. Albright, *Archaeology*, 127, 205 n. 44, 210 n. 95.

Gen 38:2–30	*Gen 46:12*[54]	*1 Chr 2:3–4*
2–5. Judah saw there the *daughter* of a *Canaanite* man *named Shua* . . . She conceived and bore a son, and he named him *Er.*	**Judah's sons:**	***Judah's sons:***
	Er,	*Er,*
She conceived again and bore a son and named him *Onan.*	**Onan,**	*Onan,*
Then she bore yet another son and named him *Shelah.*	**Shelah,**	*and Shelah—* *three* were born to him by **Bath-shua, the Canaanitess.**
7. *Now, Er, Judah's firstborn, was evil in the sight of the Lord, and the Lord put him to death.*		*Now, Er, Judah's firstborn, was evil in the sight of the Lord, and He put him to death.*
10. . . . *What* [*Onan*] *did was evil in the eyes of the Lord, and He put him to death as well.*		_____ [55]
24. Judah was told: *Tamar, your daughter-in-law,* has played the whore.		Tamar, his *daughter-in-law,* bore him
29. Behold, his brother emerged . . . and he was named *Perez;* afterward, his brother emerged . . . and he named him *Zerah.*	**Perez,**	*Perez*
	and Zarah.	and *Zarah.* ***Judah's sons—*** *five* in all.
	Then Er and Onan died.	

---

54. Gen 46:12 (P), which lists the sons of Jacob who went to Egypt, follows the narrative in Gen 38:2–5, 29–30; see also Num 26:19–20.

55. For some unknown reason, the Chronicler refrained from noting the death of Onan, as related in Gen 38:10; 46:12; and Num 26:19.

Once again the Chronicler shaped the portions of the text into a chiastic pattern within the literary inclusio and added a numerical inclusio— not only to the entire list but also to the first part of the list:

> **Judah's sons**:
> Er, Onan, and Shelah—
> *three* were born to him
> by Bath-shua, the Canaanitess. . . .
> Tamar, his daughter-in-law, bore him
> Perez and Zerah.
> **Judah's sons**—*five* in all.

D. The List of the Inhabitants of Jerusalem

14.22 A list of the inhabitants of Jerusalem appears in 1 Chr 9:2–17 and in Neh 11:3–19. The list in the book of Nehemiah seems to be the original one, and the Chronicler copied his list from there, with several emendations:[56]

1. The list in Neh 11:3–19 fits in well with Neh 7:4–5, which reads, "The city was extensive and large, but there were very few people in it," and with Nehemiah's own efforts to expand the number of inhabitants of Jerusalem. That is to say, 7:4–5 is the natural continuation of 11:1–2, which reads, "The leaders of the people lived in Jerusalem, while the rest of the people drew lots to enable one out of ten to settle in Jerusalem. . . . Then the people wished those well who volunteered to live in Jerusalem."
2. A comparison of the list in 1 Chronicles 9 with the list in Nehemiah 11 reveals that the list in 1 Chronicles 9 contains several changes that fit in well with the book of Chronicles:

   a. In 1 Chr 9:3, the phrase ומן בני אפרים ומנשה 'and of the descendants of Ephraim and Manasseh' appears, a phrase not found in the parallel, Neh 11:4. Indeed, the rest of the list only mentions members of the tribes of Judah and Benjamin; there is no trace of "descendants of Ephraim and Manasseh." Reference to "the descendants of Ephraim and Manasseh" appears again in connection with Jerusalem in 2 Chr 15:9–10; 36:1, 10–11, 18 (an "addition"; the phrase is also found in 2 Chr 31:1; 34:6). This fits in well with the Chronicler's intent to show that representatives of "all Israel" had settled in Jerusalem.[57]

---

56. See in detail Kalimi, "Ethnographical Introduction," 559–61.

57. Cf. Japhet, *Ideology*, 300. Against Benzinger (*Chronik*, 36), Kittel (*Chronik*, 52), and Rudolph (*Chronik*, 85), who think that the phrase under consideration is historical and was found in the Chronicler's *Vorlage*.

b. In 1 Chr 9:9 this phrase is found: כל אלה אנשים ראשי אבות לבית אבות אבתיהם 'all these men were heads of clans, by their clans'. This phrase, which does not appear in the parallel text in the book of Nehemiah, can be found in a number of additional places in the book of Chronicles; for example, 1 Chr 5:24; 2 Chr 23:24; see also 1 Chr 7:7, 9, 40 (an "addition").

c. Neh 11:3 contains the phrase "and the sons of the servants of Solomon." This expression, which is also present in Neh 7:57, 60 (// Ezra 2:55, 58), appears nowhere in the book of Chronicles, and the Chronicler seems to have omitted it from this list.[58]

The Chronicler presented the list from the book of Nehemiah and added the list of gatekeepers (1 Chr 9:17–34a). The list opens with the words ובירושלם ישבו 'In Jerusalem there lived' (9:3a // Neh 11:4a) and concludes with the very same words in inverse order, "These lived in Jerusalem" (9:34b // 8:28b, an "addition"):

Neh 11:3–19	1 Chr 9:3–34
4a. **In Jerusalem there lived**	3a. **In Jerusalem** there lived. . . .
4b–19. List of Jerusalem residents.	3b–17. List of Jerusalem residents.
	17–34a. List of gatekeepers.
	34b. **These lived in Jerusalem**.

The words "in Jerusalem there lived . . . these lived in Jerusalem" create a literary inclusio for the list of the residents of Jerusalem in the book of Chronicles, an inclusio that tightens up the component parts of the expanded list—the list borrowed from the book of Nehemiah plus the list added by the Chronicler. In this way, the impression is given that it was one long, complete list. Presenting the concluding words in the inverse order of the introduction stresses this literary structure and binds the component parts of the list together with even more strength.

E. The List of Issachar's Children

14.23 The Chronicler added a numerical "inclusio" to the list of the children of Issachar in the Pentateuch:

---

58. Segal refers to these and other data but does not draw the appropriate conclusion from them ("Books of Ezra and Nehemiah," 87–88). His assumption that the authors of the books of Chronicles and Nehemiah "made use of various versions of a single source" remains unproved (so already Graf, *Geschichtlichen Bücher*, 230; Benzinger, *Chronik*, 35).

Gen 46:13	*Num 26:23–24*	*1 Chr 7:1*
The children of	The descendants of	For the sons[59] of
Issachar:	Issachar by families:	Issachar:
Tola, Puvah,	of Tola . . . of Puvah,	Tola, Puah,
Iob, and Shimron	of Jashub . . . of	Jashub,[60] and
	Shimron.	Shimron—*four*.

F. Genealogical Lists That Have No Parallel

Literary and/or numerical inclusios are also used to shape genealogical lists that have no parallel in other biblical books.

14.24 1 Chr 2:25–33

> **The sons of Jerahmeel**
> the firstborn of Hezron **were**:
> his firstborn—Ram,
> and Bunah, Oren, Ozem,
> and Ahijah. . . . The sons of Jonathan:
> Peleth and Zaza;
> **these were the sons of Jerahmeel**.

14.25 1 Chr 8:38 (// 9:44)

> **Azel had** *six* **sons and these are their names**:
> Azrikam,
> Bocheru,
> Ishmael,
> Sheariah
> Obadiah,
> and Hanan;
> all **these were the sons of Azel**.

The Chronicler strengthened the link between the concluding and introductory words by arranging them in chiastic order in 9:44:

> **Azel** had six *sons and these* are their names. . . .
> All *these were the sons of* **Azel**.

The list was also provided with a numerical "inclusio"—"six"—which this time appeared in the introduction.

14.26 Note other examples:

---

59. In Codex Alexandrinus of the LXX, the Vulgate, and the Peshiṭta, we find וּבְנֵי 'and the sons', without a *lamed* ('for').

60. The *Qere*, LXX, and Vulgate all have יָשׁוּב (Yashub), as in the book of Numbers.

1 Chr 7:8: The sons of Becher . . . all these were the sons of Becher.
1 Chr 7:10–11: The sons of Jediael . . . all these were the sons of
Jediael.
1 Chr 4:5–6: Naarah bore him . . . these were the sons of Naarah.

14.27 In 1 Chr 2:1b–8, the Chronicler placed all of the genealogical lists of the tribes of Israel within a literary inclusio:

1 Chr 2:1a	**"These are the children of Israel."**[61]
1b–2	A detailed list of the tribes.
2:3–4:43	The tribe of Judah, the House of David, the tribe of Simeon.
5:1–26	The tribes of the east bank of the Jordan: Reuben, Gad, and half the tribe of Manasseh.
5:27–6:66	The tribe of Levi, the cities of the priests and the Levites.
7:1–5	The descendants of Issachar.
6–12	The descendants of Benjamin.
13	The descendants of Naphtali.
14–19	The descendants of Manasseh.
20–29	The descendants of Ephraim.
30–40	The descendants of Asher.
8:1–40	The descendants of Benjamin by dwelling place and the house of Saul.
9:1a	**"So all Israel** was enrolled by families. And behold, they are inscribed in the Book of the Kings of Israel and Judah."[62]

1 Chr 9:1a thus serves as a "conclusion" to the genealogical lists that precede it in chaps. 2–8 rather than as an "introduction," composed by some later interpolator, to the list of the residents of Jerusalem that follows it in 9:2ff. (// Neh 11:3ff.), as a number of scholars believe.[63] This verse (9:1a) is part of the literary inclusio construction within which the Chronicler placed the genealogical lists of 2:1b–8:40.[64]

---

61. Compare this opening with Gen 46:8; also Gen 25:13, 36:10; Exod 1:1.

62. The rest of the verse, 1 Chr 9:1b, "were exiled to Babylon for their unfaithfulness," is apparently a late gloss influenced by the exile of the tribes of the east bank of the Jordan, in 1 Chr 5:25–26; cf. Liver, "So All Israel Was Enrolled," 237.

63. See, e.g., Öttli, *Chronik*, 37; Bertheau, *Chronik*, 91–92; Benzinger, *Chronik*, 35; Curtis-Madsen, *Chronicles*, 168–69. For the difficulties in this assumption, see also Rothstein-Hänel, *I Chronik*, 163–73; Rudolph, *Chronik*, 83; and, with them, Liver, "So All Israel Was Enrolled," 235.

64. Liver believes, based on a material analysis of 1 Chr 9:1, that 9:1a is the *conclusion* of the lists in 1 Chronicles 2–8 (Liver, ibid., 234–40, 248).

14.28 Occasionally, the Chronicler added only a numerical inclusio to a list. For example:

> The son of Shecaniah: Shemaiah. The sons of Shemaiah:[65] Hattush, Igal, Bariah, Neariah, and Shaphat—**six**. The sons of Neariah: Elioenai, Hizkiah, and Azrikam—**three**. The sons of Elioenai: Hodaviah, Eliashib, Pelaiah, Akkub, Johanan, Delaiah, and Anani—**seven**. (1 Chr 3:22–24)

> Their kindred by their clans: Michael, Meshullam, Sheba, Jorai, Jacan, Zia, and Eber—**seven**. (1 Chr 5:13)

---

65. The words "and the sons of Shemaiah" were apparently not in the original passage but were added by dittography; without these words, the number of names would not come to *six*. Cf. Rudolph, *Chronik*, 31; idem, *BHS*, 1464.

Chapter 15
Antithesis

Antithesis is a literary device used to draw lines of contrast between the deeds or fate (or other details) of two characters. There are instances in which changes made by the Chronicler created a contrast between the actions, way of life, fate, or power of gods, kings, leaders, and various ethnic groups in such a way that one of them served as a kind of "antitype" to another. In this way, the Chronicler rendered the unique characteristics of characters more prominent, one in light of another.

Occasionally he even succeeded in getting certain *ideas* across to his readers by using antithesis in his descriptions of ancient images. For example: consulting the Lord in contrast to consulting idols; loyalty to the Lord in contrast to betraying him; humbling oneself before the Lord rather than rebelling against him; the end of an evil king/leader versus the end of a God-fearing king/leader; relying on the Lord contrasted to relying on flesh and blood. Antithesis also served as a didactic device to instruct the reader about "theological pragmatism"—that is, how worthwhile it is to rely on the Lord and walk in his paths rather than rebel against him and/or rely on idols or human beings.

Occasionally, the Chronicler created antithesis between characters in the same narrative, while on other occasions he generated it between figures in different narratives and places. Sometimes the antithesis is expressed overtly and explicitly, while at other times he left its discovery to the literary sensitivities of the reader as he created antithetical analogies to link the antithetical characters. At times, the Chronicler did not rely on these methods. Instead, he expressed an unambiguous viewpoint but formulated it in "antithetic parallelism," either in a short summary that he added to the earlier text or in a speech that he ascribed to a prophet.

The two examples closing this chapter show that the Chronicler also sharpened existing antitheses that he found in the earlier texts and rendered them even more prominent by introducing a number of changes. This literary device is known from other biblical works, as well as from classical literature.[1] With regard to the reworking of an early text by a later writer, one should note, for instance, the "antithetical characters"

---

1. See Fraenkel, "Antithesis," 129–46 and the earlier bibliography there; also Krašovec, *Antithetic Structure*.

created by Josephus for Rebecca at the well—a feature not found in the biblical narrative in Gen 24:12–22:

> [Eliezer] approached the well and asked the maidens to give him drink. *But they declined*, saying that they wanted water to carry home and not for serving him, for it was no easy matter to draw it. One only of them all rebuked the rest for their churlishness to the stranger, saying . . . *and with that she graciously offered him some.* (*Ant.* 1.246; see also the end of 1.245)

1. Contrasting the Deeds of Persons and Groups

15.1 The Chronicler contrasted what the Philistines did to Saul's head to what the men of Jabesh-gilead did to his body. In both descriptions, he used the same root נשא (in the sense of 'take', 'remove')[2] in place of the roots that were used in the earlier text—כרת and לקח:

1 Chr 10:9: [של שאול] את ראשו [הפלשתים] וישאו 'they [the Philistines] *removed* his [Saul's] head', instead of ויכרתו את ראשו 'they *cut off* his head' (1 Sam 31:9).

1 Chr 10:12: את גופת שאול [אנשי יבש־גלעד] וישאו 'they [the men of Jabesh-gilead] *removed* Saul's body', instead of ויקחו את גוית שאול 'they *took* Saul's body' (1 Sam 31:12).

The difference between the two uses of נשא is profound: the Philistines went off with Saul's head in triumph: "They sent it throughout the land of the Philistines to inform their idols and the people" (1 Chr 10:9 // 1 Sam 31:9) and impaled his skull in the temple of Dagon (1 Chr 10:10), whereas the men of Jabesh-gilead bore away Saul's body (and the bodies of his sons) with sadness and mourning, brought him to bury in their city, and respectfully adopted severe mourning customs: ויצומו שבעת ימים 'they fasted for seven days' (1 Chr 10:12 // 1 Sam 31:13).[3]

---

2. In this sense, both verses were translated into Greek: ἔλαβον 'took'. For this meaning of the root נשא, see, e.g., Gen 21:18; 2 Kgs 4:36; the writer of the book of Ezra also replaced the root לקח in the book of Deuteronomy with נשא, much in the way that the Chronicler used the root נשא in place of לקח (1 Chr 10:12 // 1 Sam 31:12):

Deut 7:4   You shall not give your daughter to his son or *take* (לקח) his daughter for your son.

Ezra 9:12   You shall not give your daughters to their sons or *acquire* [נשא 'take'] their daughters for your sons.

3. The phrase שבעת ימים 'seven days' creates an analogy with 1 Sam 11:3 concerning the delay of שבעת ימים that was granted the men of Jabesh-gilead, during which Saul saved them from Nahash, the Ammonite (cf. R. David Kimḥi on 1 Sam 31:13 and the commentary ascribed to Rashi on 1 Chr 10:12). This analogy renders the special regard of the men of Jabesh-gilead for Saul and his sons more prominent: taking their

15.2 The Chronicler contrasted Saul's final battle with the Philistines to David's battles with the Philistines.

15.2a Before he set out to wage war against the Philistines, David *inquired of the Lord* and received his blessing. Consequently, he overcame the Philistines, enjoying unusual success: ויכם שם דויד ויאמר דויד: פרץ האלהים את אויבי בידי כפרץ מים 'David defeated them there and said: "God has burst out against my enemies by my hand like a bursting flood"' (1 Chr 14:10–11 // 2 Sam 5:19–20). He conducted his next battle in the same way. He inquired of the Lord, executed his instructions, and overcame the Philistines (1 Chr 14:13–16 // 2 Sam 5:22–25).

Saul did not act in this fashion. According to the Chronicler, Saul לא דרש בה' 'did not inquire of the Lord' before he went to battle with the Philistines. Instead, he consulted a medium. This statement in Chronicles is diametrically opposed to 1 Sam 28:6: *וישאל שאול בה'* גם בחלמות גם באורים גם בנביאים ולא ענהו ה' 'Saul inquired of the Lord, but the Lord did not reply to him—not by dreams, Urim, or prophets,' after which he turned to the witch of Endor (see also 1 Sam 28:15). Ehrlich sums up the difference in the two historiographers' presentations this way: "Hence you see just how this writer [the Chronicler] revels in condemning Saul."[4]

Perhaps I may suggest another solution to the seeming contradiction between the two books. According to the outlook of the Chronicler, if someone inquires of the Lord, he replies; but if someone deserts him, then he or she is abandoned:

> If you inquire of him he will be there for you, but if you forsake him he will ignore you forever. (1 Chr 28:9)

> The Lord is with you when you are with him. If you inquire of him he will be there for you, but if you abandon him he will abandon you. (2 Chr 15:2)

---

bodies from the wall of Beth-shean and burying them honorably in Jabesh-gilead, an act involving great effort and self-jeopardy, followed by a fast that lasted all seven of the days of mourning (it was customary to fast just one day—on the first day of the mourning period; see 2 Sam 1:12; 3:35; Ps 35:13–14).

A similar antithesis may be detected in the tales about Joseph in the book of Genesis, though the narrator used different senses of the root נשא in Genesis 40, thus creating a kind of antithetic parallelism between the words of Joseph to the chief butler—בעוד שלשת ימים *ישא* פרעה את ראשך והשיבך על כנך 'In another three days Pharaoh will remember you (*ישא* . . . את ראשך = 'he will lift up your head', or 'remember you'); cf. further on in v. 20; Exod 30:12; Num 1:2; 2 Kgs 25:27) and restore you to your position'—and his words to the chief baker—בעוד שלשת ימים *ישא* פרעה את ראשך מעליך ותלה אותך על עץ 'In another three days Pharaoh will remove (*ישא* . . . את ראשך = 'he will remove your head') your head and will hang you on a tree' (Gen 40:13, 19).

4. Ehrlich, *Mikrâ ki-Pheschutô*, 438.

Then all of Judah rejoiced over the oath; *for with all their hearts*
they took the oath and with all their might they sought him, and he
was there for them, and the Lord gave them rest all around. (2 Chr
15:15)

Since the Chronicler could not resolve this theological understanding
with 1 Sam 28:6, which says, "Saul inquired of the Lord, but the Lord
did not reply to him" (also 28:15), he altered the Samuel narrative to
adjust it to his own understanding: וגם לשאול באוב לדרוש ולא דרש בה׳ 'furthermore, he consulted a ghost, seeking guidance, *and did not seek*
guidance from the Lord' (1 Chr 10:13–14). For the Chronicler, the Lord's
not replying to Saul could only stem from Saul's not asking/inquiring of
the Lord with all his heart and might. If Saul had done so, the Lord
would certainly have replied to him.[5]

Furthermore, according to 1 Sam 28:15, Samuel was angry at Saul
for having disturbed his tranquility, not for having inquired of a medium. Consulting a medium is not listed in 28:18–19 as one of the sins
that led to Saul's downfall at Gilboa. The Chronicler, on the other hand,
did consider conjuring a serious sin, because of the statute in Lev 19:31;
20:6, 27; Deut 18:11.[6] In fact, this was one of the reasons given for the
Philistines' overcoming Saul and for his death. His was no hero's death,
chosen to avoid being taken alive by the enemy (1 Sam 31:3–4 // 1 Chr
10:3–4); it was death by the hand of the Lord, וימיתהו [ה׳] '[the Lord] put
him to death' (1 Chr 10:13), such as befitted a person who consulted a
medium (see Lev 20:6, 27).

The principle is that human-national history is controlled by the Lord.
This is stressed by the repeated use of the root מות 'die' throughout the
narrative: כי מת שאול . . . וימת שאול . . . כי מתו מתו . . . יחדו מתו . . . וימת שאול . . .
וימיתהו . . . (vv. 5, 6, 7, 13, 14, and see also further along). The Chronicler
might also have viewed the deaths of Saul and his sons as the fulfillment
of Samuel's prophecy: ויתן ה׳ גם את ישראל עמך ביד פלשתים ומחר אתה ובניך
עמי,[7] גם את מחנה ישראל יתן ה׳ ביד פלשתים 'The Lord will also deliver Israel

---

5. Compare Ps 145:18: "The Lord is near to all who call on him / *to all who call on*
him in truth." Against Mosis (*Untersuchungen*, 39–41), who believes that what the
Chronicler said of Saul ("furthermore, he consulted a ghost, seeking guidance, and
did not seek guidance from the Lord") does not refer to a specific instance in the context of war against the Philistines on Mt. Gilboa but was a general practice—that is,
Saul was accustomed to consulting witches instead of the Lord. Mosis bases his opinion on the contradiction between 1 Chr 10:13–14 and 1 Sam 28:6, 15.

6. See also Isa 8:19; 19:3b; 2 Kgs 21:6; 23:24. Interestingly enough, the Chronicler
did not list the killing of the priests of Nob (1 Sam 22:6–23) and of the Gibeonites, in
violation of the Israelites' vow to them (2 Sam 21:2–3), in the list of Saul's sins; unlike, for example, Josephus (*Ant.* 6.378) and the postbiblical Jewish sages (*Lev. Rab.*
26:7), who do list the killing of the priests of Nob as a sin.

7. In LXX Luc., this is μετὰ σου 'with you'.

your people into the hands of the Philistines, and tomorrow you and
your sons will be with me. The Lord will also deliver the camp of Israel
into the hands of the Philistines' (1 Sam 28:19).

15.2b 1 Sam 31:7 relates: ויראו אנשי ישראל אשר בעבר העמק ואשר בעבר
הירדן, *כי נסו אנשי ישראל* וכי מתו שאול ובניו, ויעזבו את הערים וינסו 'When the men
of Israel who were on the other side of the plain and on the other side of
the Jordan saw that *the men of Israel fled* and that Saul and his sons
were dead, they abandoned their towns and fled'. In 1 Chr 10:7, however, the Chronicler omitted the second phrase אנשי ישראל 'men of Israel'
and wrote: ויראו כל איש ישראל אשר בעמק כי נסו _____ _____ *וכי מתו שאול ובניו,*
ויעזבו עריהם וינסו 'When all the men of Israel who were in the valley saw
that *Saul and his sons had fled* and had died, they abandoned their
towns and fled'. That is, according to Chronicles, it was Saul and his
sons who fled the battlefield, not "the men of Israel," as would seem to
be the case from the earlier text. Thus, it was Saul and his sons who
caused the defeat that led to the Israelites' abandoning their towns.[8]
This is despite the beginning of the narrative, *וינסו אנשי ישראל מפני פלשתים*
'the men of Israel fled* from the Philistines' (1 Sam 31:1), which the
Chronicler included with only minor alterations in 1 Chr 10:1.

In another instance, the Philistines were pursuing David. According
to the Chronicler, וישמע דויד ויצא *לפניהם* 'when David heard this, *he went
out against them*' (1 Chr 14:8). This is in contrast to 2 Sam 5:17, however, which says, וישמע דוד וירד *אל המצודה* 'when David heard this, *he
went down to the stronghold*'. We may conclude from this verse that at
first David fled from the Philistine advance and hid in a "stronghold."

These changes create a clear contrast between David's heroism—going out fearlessly against the Philistines, fighting them, and winning
glorious victories—and Saul—who was afraid of the Philistines (ויחל
[שאול] מן היורים '[Saul] *feared* the archers', 1 Chr 10:3 // 1 Sam 31:3),[9] fled
them, put an end to his life, and brought on a great Israelite defeat. Furthermore, the two cases were of the Lord. The Lord was the one who put
Saul to death—Saul, who had sought the mediation of a witch rather

---

8. Of course, כי נסו שאול ובניו וכי מתו would be a more suitable, less ambiguous wording, whereas the Chronicler made his omission without changing the word-order of
the sentence. However, the text seems to indicate clearly the suggested interpretation
that it was Saul and his sons who fled the battlefield.

9. See also 1 Sam 28:5: וירא שאול את מחנה פלשתים וירא ויחרד לבו מאד 'When Saul saw
the Philistine encampment, *he was afraid and very worried*', and also 28:20: וימהר
שאול ויפל מלא קומתו ארצה וירא מאד מדברי שמואל 'Then Saul hurriedly fell full length on the
ground, for *he was very afraid* of Samuel's words'. It seems that ירא 'fear, afraid, awe'
is used as a motif in the description of Saul's life in the book of Samuel. See as well
1 Sam 15:24: כי ידאתי את העם ואשמע בקולם 'for *I feared* the people and so I listened to
their voice'; 18:29: ויאסף לֵרֹא מפני דוד עוד 'So he was even more *afraid* of David'.

than "inquiring of the Lord" (1 Chr 10:14, an "addition"). The Lord was the one who went out before David—David, who had inquired of the Lord (1 Chr 14:10, 14 // 2 Sam 5:19, 23), who gave him glorious victories, even "bringing the *fear of him* on all nations," including the Philistines (1 Chr 14:17b, an "addition").

15.2c At the battle of Gilboa, Saul was defeated by the Philistines, and his body and weapons were abandoned on the battlefield as a result of the hurried flight of אנשי ישראל 'the men of Israel' (according to the Chronicler, Saul and his sons were among those fleeing), where they fell into the hands of the Philistines as booty. The Philistines deposited Saul's weapons in the "temple of their gods" (1 Chr 10:10; according to 1 Sam 31:10, בית עשתרות 'the temple of Astarte'). In contrast, in the battle against David, it was the Philistines who were defeated, and in their flight they abandoned אלהיהם 'their gods' (1 Chr 14:12; in 2 Sam 5:21, עצביהם 'their images') on the battlefield. These gods were then captured as booty by David and his soldiers.

Rudolph, in his commentary on 1 Chr 10:10a, argues that the Chronicler used the word אלהיהם in place of עשתרות because he did not dare utter the name Astarte.[10] This hypothesis seems doubtful in light of the antithesis demonstrated here between Saul's defeat at the hands of the Philistines and David's victory over them.

15.2d After Saul's defeat on Gilboa, the Philistines cut off his head, took his armor as booty, "and sent them throughout the land of the Philistines to inform their idols and the people" (1 Chr 10:9 // 1 Sam 31:9). In contrast, after David's victories, "David's fame went throughout all the lands" according to the Chronicler (1 Chr 14:17a, an "addition").

15.3 The list of David's sons born in Jerusalem is adduced twice in the book of Chronicles: once in 1 Chr 3:5–8, in the genealogical lists of the Davidic dynasty, and again in 1 Chr 14:4–7, parallel to 2 Sam 5:14–16. A number of scholars are of the opinion that the presence of a second list is due only to the need to parallel the earlier text.[11] It would be more reasonable, however, to assume that the second list was presented in order to achieve some aim of the Chronicler. Otherwise he would have omitted it, just as he omitted other parallel passages.[12]

It seems that the placement of the lists of David's sons born in Jerusalem, including Solomon, right after David's victories over the Philistines (1 Chr 14:8–17 // 2 Sam 5:17–25) was intended to make a contrast.

---

10. Rudolph, *Chronik*, 95.
11. So, e.g., Rothstein-Hänel, *Chronik*, 265; Rudolph, *Chronik*, 113.
12. Cf. Mosis, *Untersuchungen*, 77; Williamson, *Chronicles*, 117.

The contrast is between what happened to David after he inquired of the Lord and went out to battle the Philistines and what happened to Saul after he inquired by conjuration and went out to battle the Philistines. The horrible results of the Gilboa battle were that "Saul took the sword and fell on it . . . , and Saul, his three sons, *and all his house* died," 1 Chr 10:6. These words replaced the words of 1 Sam 31:6, "Saul took his sword and fell on it . . . , and Saul, his three sons, *his armorbearer, and all his men* died."[13] David, on the other hand, enlarged his family circle, wed additional wives, and fathered more sons, including Solomon, to continue ביתו 'his dynasty'.[14] From a chronological standpoint, the conquest of Jerusalem and the birth of David's sons in the city took place after the Philistines' wars against David—wars that broke out in reaction to David's being anointed king over the Northern tribes (1 Chr 14:8 // 2 Sam 5:17). The writer of the book of Samuel and subsequently the writer of the book of Chronicles altered the order of events in order to portray the conquest of Jerusalem as David's first act after being anointed.[15]

Moreover, David built *a house* in Jerusalem with the aid of workmen and materials sent by Hiram, "for the Lord had established him as king over Israel, and his kingdom was highly exalted" (1 Chr 14:1–2 // 2 Sam 5:11–12, "exalted his kingdom"). This event also took place after David's Philistine battles, though the books of Samuel and Chronicles have placed it before their descriptions of the battles.

The second appearance of the list of David's sons stresses his ascent and growing strength,[16] both on the family level and on the international scene, as opposed to the downfall and loss of both the dynasty and the kingdom of Saul (1 Chr 10:13–14, an "addition").

15.4 Amaziah, king of Judah, does not heed the advice of Joash, king of Israel, and antagonizes him "out of evil" (2 Chr 25:17–19 // 2 Kgs 14:8–10), and the Chronicler explains: ולא שמע אמציהו כי מהאלהים היא למען תתם ביד כי דרשו את אלהי אדום 'Amaziah did not listen, *because it was God's doing, in order to deliver them over* [*to the enemy*], **for they had inquired of the gods of Edom**' (2 Chr 25:20, instead of just ולא שמע אמציהו 'Amaziah did not listen', in 2 Kgs 14:11). Indeed, further on we read of the fall of Amaziah into the hands of Joash, "who brought him to Jerusalem *and broke down the wall of Jerusalem*" (2 Chr 25:23 // 2 Kgs 14:13).

---

13. The word ביתו appears here in the sense of 'his family' or 'his dynasty'; see above, chap. 14 n. 29 (p. 309).

14. Cf. Mosis, *Untersuchungen*, 79; Williamson, *Chronicles*, 117.

15. For a detailed discussion of this, see example 1.2 (pp. 19–22).

16. That the begetting of sons was an indication of growing strength, see, for example, 2 Sam 3:1–5; 2 Chr 11:17–23.

The Chronicler contrasted these actions of Amaziah to the actions
of his son, Uzziah: "as long as **[Uzziah] inquired of the Lord**, *God
granted him success*" (2 Chr 26:5, an "addition"). Uzziah did fight
against the Philistines, *"breaking down the wall of Gath, the wall of
Jabneh, and the wall of Ashdod . . .* , and **God helped him** against the
Philistines, the Arabs living in Gur-baal, and the Meunites. The Ammonites[17] paid tribute to Uzziah, and his reputation spread to the borders
of Egypt, for he became very strong" (26:6–8, an "addition"). To summa-
rize the matter: Amaziah inquired of the Edomite gods, and for this reason the Lord delivered him into the hands of Joash, king of Israel, who
broke down the walls of Jerusalem. In contrast, Uzziah inquired of the
Lord. Consequently, the Lord helped him and made him successful. He
broke down the walls of the Philistine cities.

This literary formulation renders the question of the historical reliability of 2 Chr 26:5–8 more pointed.[18] In any case, it is difficult to accept the statement by Elat that this passage in Chronicles "was taken
from a royal inscription from the time of Uzziah, or was influenced by it
in its style, and lists Uzziah's exploits and achievements."[19]

15.5 In his evaluation of Jotham, king of Judah, the Deuteronomistic
historian writes in 2 Kgs 15:34: ויעש הישר בעיני ה' ככל אשר עשה עזיהו אביו
עשה[20] 'He did what was right in the sight of the Lord, just as Uzziah, his
father, had done'. In 2 Chr 27:2, the Chronicler quotes this evaluation
but adds a reservation: ויעש הישר בעיני ה' ככל אשר עשה עזיהו אביו רק לא בא
אל היכל ה' 'He did what was right in the sight of the Lord, just as Uzziah,
his father, had done—*except that he refrained from invading the Temple
of the Lord*'. This addition draws a clear contrast between the behavior
of Jotham and the behavior of Uzziah, his father, of whom it is said:
וימעל בה' אלהיו ויבא אל היכל ה' 'He betrayed the Lord his God *by invading
the Temple of the Lord*' (2 Chr 26:16).[21]

---

17. The LXX has Μιναῖοι (= Meunites), as does 2 Chr 20:1. The MT reading seems
to have suffered a letter interchange, for the Ammonites are generally known in the
Bible as בני־עמון 'the children of Ammon'. Thus, Reviv is not accurate in saying: "for
the Ammonites brought tribute to Uzziah (2 Chr 26:8)" (Reviv, *From Clan to Monarchy*, 207).

18. Against Yeivin, "'Uzziah," 127–28; and also in his article "The Divided Kingdom," 165–67, referring to the text in 2 Chr 26:5–8 as if it were historical information, and even building hypotheses on it; similarly: Oded, "Israel and Judah," 151; Reviv,
From Clan to Monarchy, 207; Williamson, *Chronicles*, 334 (and see additional references there).

19. Elat, *Economic Relations*, 188.

20. The words ויעש . . . עשה create a literary inclusio in the book of Kings. The
omission of the word עשה in 2 Chr 27:2 shatters this inclusio.

21. The Deuteronomistic historian relates that the Lord afflicted Uzziah with leprosy (2 Kgs 15:5) but does not say why the Lord afflicted the righteous king, who was

The Chronicler sharpened the contrast between the behavior of the two kings in other verses: Uzziah החזיק עד למעלה 'became very strong'[22] (2 Chr 26:8, an "addition") and הפליא להעזר (which means 'to strengthen oneself,[23] to overcome one's enemies') עד כי חזק 'until he became a strong' king. But, וכחזקתו 'when he became strong' in his kingdom, גבה לבו עד להשחית וימעל בה' אלהיו ויבא אל היכל ה' להקטיר על מזבח הקטרת 'his heart grew destructively proud. *He betrayed the Lord his God* in entering the Temple of the Lord to sacrifice on the altar of incense' (26:15–16, an "addition"). Jotham, on the other hand, נלחם עם מלך בני־עמון ויחזק עליהם ויתנו לו בני־עמון בשנה ההיא מאה ככר כסף ועשרת אלפים כרים חטים 'fought with the king of the children of Ammon and *overcame* them. The children of Ammon gave him one hundred talents of silver and ten thousand cors of wheat that year' (2 Chr 27:5, an "addition"). In spite of this, his heart did not become proud; neither did he betray the Lord or "come into the Temple of the Lord." Another form of the word ויחזק 'overcame' is used this time—ויתחזק: יותם כי הכין דרכיו לפני ה' אלהיו 'Jotham *strengthened himself*[24] because *he ordered his ways before the Lord his God*' (27:6, an "addition").

15.6 Ahaz and his grandson Manasseh are described in the books of Kings and Chronicles as great sinners among the kings of Judah: they each passed their sons through fire and performed abominations like those of the nations that the Lord had expelled/destroyed "before the Israelites" (compare 2 Chr 28:3 // 2 Kgs 16:3 with 2 Chr 33:6, 9 // 2 Kgs 21:6, 9). However, although King Ahaz, ובעת הצר לו ויוסף למעול בה' **'when [he was] in distress** *continued to betray the Lord*' (2 Chr 28:22, an "addition"), Manasseh, וכהצר לו חלה את פני ה' אלהיו[25] ויכנע מאד מלפני אלהי אבתיו **'when [he was] in distress** *sought out the Lord his God and humbled himself greatly before the God of his fathers*' (2 Chr 33:12, an "addition").

According to the book of Kings, Ahaz sinned, but Manasseh was more evil than Ahaz, becoming the greatest sinner of all of the kings of the

---

one of the few kings of Judah to do "what was right in the sight of the Lord." True to his retribution system, the Chronicler did not leave a "punitive" situation without some "sin" preceding it. Thus, before his description of Uzziah's leprosy, he quoted these words: וכחזקתו גבה לבו עד להשחית וימעל בה' אלהיו ויבא אל היכל ה' להקטיר על מזבח הקטרת 'But when he became strong, his heart grew destructively proud. He betrayed the Lord his God in entering the Temple of the Lord to sacrifice on the altar of incense' (2 Chr 26:16).

22. Cf. Curtis-Madsen, *Chronicles*, 32, no. 87; 35, no. 127.

23. Compare with Isa 41:6: איש את רעהו יעזרו / ולאחיו יאמר חזק 'Each *will strengthen* the other / and will tell his brother: *be strong*."

24. Cf. Ezra 7:28; see Curtis-Madsen, *Chronicles*, 29, no. 38.

25. Compare this passage with Exod 32:11: "Then Moses sought out the Lord his God."

Davidic dynasty. However, according to the book of Chronicles, Ahaz remained evil all the days of his life, while Manasseh repented of his sins.[26]

15.7 The writer of the book of Kings compared the religious rituals adopted by Amon, king of Judah, with those of Manasseh, his father (2 Kgs 21:20–21):

> He did what was evil in the sight of the Lord, as Manasseh, his father, had done.

> He walked in all the way in which his father walked.

> He worshiped the idols that his father had worshiped and bowed down to them.

In 2 Chr 33:22, the Chronicler applied this comparison:

> He did what was evil in the sight of the Lord, as Manasseh, his father, had done.

> Amon sacrificed to all the images that Manasseh, his father, had made and worshiped them.

However, since according to the Chronicler Manasseh repented and corrected his ways (2 Chr 33:12–16, an "addition"), a step that Amon, his son, did not take, the Chronicler created a distinct, explicit contrast between the two men. Instead of saying, ולא הלך [אמון] בדרך ה' '[Amon] did not walk in the way of the Lord' (2 Kgs 21:22b), the Chronicler wrote, ולא נכנע [אמון] מלפני ה' כהכנע מנשה אביו '[Amon] did not humble himself before the Lord, as Manasseh, his father, had humbled himself' (2 Chr 33:23). This contrast is quite noticeable in light of the Chronicler's previous statement concerning Manasseh: וכהצר לו, חלה את פני ה' אלהיו, ויכנע מאד מלפני אלהי אבתיו 'when in distress, he sought out the Lord his God *and humbled himself greatly before the God of his fathers*' (v. 12).

15.8 The Chronicler contrasts the destiny of Ahaz and his kingdom with Abijah and the kingdom of Judah in their war with the kingdom of Israel and other neighbors. Abijah, king of Judah, states that, "for us, the Lord is our God, and we have not neglected him" (2 Chr 13:10, an "addition"). Therefore, God gave Israel into his hand: "The men of Israel fled before Judah, and *God gave them into their hand.* Abijah and his people defeated them in a great defeat" (13:16–17). The Chronicler also stresses that "the men of Israel were subdued at that time," while "the men of Judah prevailed, *because they relied on the Lord, the*

---

26. For the portrait of Manasseh in Kings and Chronicles, see Smelik, "King Manasseh," 129–89.

God of their fathers" (13:18). Furthermore, Abijah, king of Judah, pursued Jeroboam, king of Israel, and took some southern towns from his kingdom (13:19).

In contrast, Ahaz, king of Judah, "did not do what was right in the sight of the Lord" (2 Chr 28:1 // 2 Kgs 16:2). Therefore, *"the Lord his God gave him into the hand of the king of Aram. . . . He was also given into the hand of the king of Israel*, who defeated him in a great defeat" (2 Chr 28:5, an "addition"). Likewise, the Edomites invaded Judah and took away captives, and the Philistines "had made raids on the towns in the Shephelah and the Negeb" and had taken several towns, "for the Lord brought Judah low because of Ahaz, for he had behaved wantonly in Judah and *had been faithless to the Lord"* (28:17–19, an "addition").

15.9   This literary feature can also be found in texts that have no parallel in other biblical books. For example, in 2 Chr 28:5–15 the Chronicler describes the invasion of the kingdom of Judah by the kings of Aram and Israel. He relates that these kings caused a great slaughter in Judah and took many captives. The king of Aram took *שביה גדולה ויביאו דרמשק* 'many captives and brought them to Damascus' (28:5), while the Israelites captured *מאתים אלף נשים בנים ובנות וגם שלל רב בזזו מהם, ויביאו את השלל לשמרון* 'two hundred thousand women, boys, and girls and took much booty from them and *brought* the plunder *to Samaria'* (28:8). The Israelites, encouraged by the prophet Oded, took their "captives and clothed their nakedness with the booty. They dressed them, gave them sandals, gave them food and drink, anointed them, carried all the faltering ones on donkeys, and brought them to Jericho, the city of palms, near their kindred [that is, the people of Judah]" (28:15).[27] However, the Arameans seem to have enslaved their Judean captives (at any rate, nowhere is it said that they released them).[28]

The attitude of the Israelites toward the Judean captives is emphasized by the words *אחיהם* 'their kindred' (vv. 8, 15) and *אחיכם* 'your kindred' (v. 11) and by the fact that captors and captives alike believed in the same God (see the emphasis on *לה׳ אלהיכם, ה׳ אלהי אבותכם* in vv. 9, 10). Taking "kindred" into captivity was considered a sin that might arouse the wrath of the Lord. Returning the captives according to the exhortation of the prophet was a step taken to atone for this sin.

---

27. According to this verse, Jericho was in the territory of Judah, a statement that contradicts 1 Kgs 16:34; 2 Kgs 2:1–5, 15–22, which indicate that Jericho was in the territory of Israel. This seems to be due to the Chronicler's lack of understanding of the boundary-line separating the two kingdoms and his anachronistic projection of the situation in his own day, when Jericho was included in the territory of Yehud (Neh 3:2; 7:36).

28. For this custom with captives, see de Vaux, *Ancient Israel*, 256–57.

In light of this discussion, it is unlikely that the return of the captives to Judah was an actual historical event intended to strengthen Judah or to express the opposition of the Ephraimites to the policy of the Gilead party that was dominant in Samaria.[29]

2. Contrasting the Fate of Kings and Leaders

15.10 In response to the prophecies of Micaiah, son of Imlah, the king of Israel ordered: שימו את זה בית הכלא והאכילהו לחם לחץ ומים לחץ עד באי בשלום 'Put this man in prison and feed him scant amounts of bread and scant amounts of water until my *safe arrival*' (1 Kgs 22:27). In place of the word באי 'my arrival', the Chronicler wrote שובי 'my return' in 2 Chr 18:26, thus creating textual harmony with the rest of the verse: ויאמר מיכיהו אם שוב תשוב בשלום לא דבר ה' בי 'Micaiah said: "If you **return** *safely*, it is not the word of the Lord that is in me"' (2 Chr 18:27 // 1 Kgs 22:28). Some think that the wording of 2 Chr 18:26, עד שובי בשלום 'until my safe *return*', reflects the original wording and that it was an interchange of parallel roots שוב / בוא that took place in the book of Kings.[30] However, the reason for the difference is the Chronicler's desire to rectify the lack of literal harmony between the text and the words of the prophet, בשלום אם שוב תשוב, together with his desire to create a clear contrast between the words of the king, עד באי בשלום 'until my *safe* arrival', and what actually happened to him: וימת המלך ויבוא שמרון 'So the king *died* coming to Samaria' (1 Kgs 22:9, 27, 37). The high frequency of occurrences of textual harmonization in the book of Chronicles and the integration of the root שוב with the addition made by the Chronicler to the earlier text of 2 Chr 19:1[31] (below) strengthen the assumption that the original version is the one preserved in Kings.[32] The change also emphasizes the contrast that the Chronicler created between the fate of the wicked king of Israel, who did not return home safely but was wounded in the battle of Ramoth-gilead, וימת לעת בוא השמש 'and *died* as the sun set' (2 Chr 18:32–34 // 1 Kgs 22:34–35), and the fate of the righteous king of Judah, who returned home safely. This the Chronicler stated explicitly in 2 Chr 19:1 (an "addition"): וישב יהושפט מלך יהודה אל ביתו בשלום לירושלים 'Jehoshaphat, king of Judah, **returned** home *safely* to Jerusalem'. The change under consideration also emphasizes the contrast between the words of the king of Israel, עד שובי בשלום 'until *I return safely*' (2 Chr 18:26), and those of the Lord, לא אדנים לאלה ישובו איש לביתו בשלום 'These [the Israel-

---

29. For this opinion, see Reviv, "Historical Background," 11–16; idem, *The Elders*, 132–34.

30. So Japhet, "Interchanges," 33.

31. This root is repeated four times in 2 Chr 18–19:1 and serves as a key word.

32. The LXX and the Vulgate of Kings have "my return," but this does not in any way indicate what was present in the earlier text; see Japhet, "Interchanges," 33 n. 87.

ites] have no master; let each *return safely* to his home' (2 Chr 18:16 // 1 Kgs 22:17), and his prophet: ויאמר מיכיהו אם שוב תשוב בשלום וגו׳ 'Micaiah said, "*If you return safely*, the Lord has not spoken by me"' (2 Chr 18:27 // 1 Kgs 22:28). In the end, it was the words of the Lord by his prophet that were fulfilled.[33]

15.11 In his concluding remarks on the reign of Joash, king of Judah, the Deuteronomistic historian describes the king's assassination by his servants and his interment: ויקברו אתו עם אבתיו בעיר דוד 'They buried him with his fathers in the City of David' (2 Kgs 12:21). The Chronicler, on the other hand, spoke of the assassination of Joash by his servants but altered the passage that referred to his burial. According to him, Joash was indeed buried in the City of David, but לא קברהו בקברות המלכים 'they did not bury him in the tombs of the kings' (2 Chr 24:25). The reason for this change seems to have been to contrast the fate of Joash with the fate of Jehoiada, the high priest: the life of Joash—who, in the period of his reign subsequent to Jehoiada's death, deserted the Lord and his Temple, worshiped the Asherim and images, and was responsible for the assassination of Zechariah, son of Jehoiada (2 Chr 24:18, 21)—was shortened as a result of his assassination by his servants. Despite his being a king, "*they did not bury him in the tombs of the kings*" (v. 25).

The life of Jehoiada the priest, on the other hand—who had saved Joash from the sword of Athaliah, had him crowned king of Judah, and served the Lord and his House faithfully—was lengthened to "a hundred and thirty years." Furthermore, though he was not a king, "*they buried him* in the City of David *with the kings*, for he had done good in Israel and for God and his House" (2 Chr 24:14b–16, an "addition").

The main purpose for the change in Chronicles was to adapt the earlier story to the Chronicler's philosophy of retribution, which is summed up in the principle "deal kindly with good people, according to their work, and harshly with evil people, according to their wickedness." The antithesis between Joash and Jehoiada emphasizes this.

15.12 The Chronicler created a contrast between what happened to Hezekiah and what happened to Sennacherib after his campaign in the land of Judah:

15.12a Sennacherib returned to his country בבשת פנים 'shamefacedly' (2 Chr 32:21, an "addition" to 2 Kgs 19:36 = Isa 37:37)[34] and

---

33. For this, see above, example 7.31 (pp. 164–165).

34. For the lot of the wicked (the foes of the Lord) being בשת פנים, see for example, Ps 31:17–18; 83:17–18: "Fill their faces with shame ... may they be shamed and alarmed forever; may they be embarrassed and perish"; 97:7.

was assassinated by the people closest to him, sons "who had sprung from his loins."[35] Regarding Hezekiah, in contrast, רבים מביאים מנחה לה׳ ליהוה ומגדנות ליחזקיהו מלך יהודה 'many were bringing offerings to the Lord in Jerusalem **and valuables to Hezekiah, king of Judah**' (2 Chr 32:23a, an "addition").[36]

15.12b 'There [in his land] *they struck* [*Sennacherib*] *down* with the sword' שם הפילהו בחרב (2 Chr 32:21, which replaced הכהו בחרב 'they *killed* him with a sword' in 2 Kgs 19:37 // Isa 37:38).[37] In contrast, Hezekiah gained prestige: וינשא לעיני כל הגוים מאחרי כן 'He *was exalted* in the sight of *all* nations after this' (2 Chr 32:23b, an "addition").

15.12c While Sennacherib was assassinated in "*the house of his god*" (2 Chr 32:21b; in the parallel text, "in the house of Nisroch, his god," 2 Kgs 19:37 = Isa 37:38), without his god's being able to protect him or to save him from the hands of his assassins, Hezekiah was saved by his God not only from the hands of Sennacherib, king of Assyria, but also from the hands of all his enemies: ויושע ה׳ את חזקיהו ואת ישבי ירושלם מיד סנחריב ומיד כל וינהלם[38] מסביב 'The Lord saved Hezekiah and the inhabitants of Jerusalem from the hand of Sennacherib and from the hand of all his enemies and drove them off from round about' (2 Chr 32:22, an "addition"). This salvation by the Lord also contrasts with Sennacherib's haughty pronouncements: אלהיכם לא יציל אתכם מידי 'your God will not save you from my hand'; לא יציל אלהי יחזקיהו עמו מידי 'Hezekiah's God will not save his people from my hand' (2 Chr 32:15, 17). The rescue of Hezekiah was his reward for right eousness and confidence in the Lord,

---

35. The *Qere* is מיציא מעיו; the *Kethiv*, מיציאו, seems to be a scribal error (a ו/י interchange). Compare 2 Kgs 17:13: נביאו, *Kethiv*; נביאי, *Qere*. Isa 60:21: מטעו, *Kethiv*; מטעי, *Qere*.

36. We find similar statements with regard to David (1 Chr 14:17, an "addition"), Jehoshaphat (2 Chr 17:10–11; 20:29), and Uzziah (2 Chr 26:8); see also 2 Chr 9:9, 23ff., with regard to Solomon.

37. For this change, see above, example 7.27 (p. 161).

38. In the LXX and Vulgate, we find וינח להם 'and he let them rest'. Some scholars prefer this reading to the MT: for example, Rudolph, *Chronik*, 310; Williamson, *Chronicles*, 385. It seems difficult to me to decide which reading is preferable: on the one hand, the Greek translator (or the scribe of his *Vorlage*) may erroneously have substituted the letter ה for the letter ח, which it resembles both in its graphic form and its pronunciation, and interpreted the לם as meaning להם '(to) them', in which case the MT is the original reading (and compare: על מי מנוחות ינהלני 'he leads me beside restful waters', Ps 23:2). On the other hand, the opposite process may have taken place, in which case the original reading was וינח להם מסביב 'he gave them rest round about', like other passages in the book of Chronicles. For example: והנחותי לו מכל אויביו מסביב 'I will give [Solomon] rest from all his enemies round about' (1 Chr 22:9); וינח לנו מסביב 'he gave us rest round about' (2 Chr 14:6; see also 15:15; 20:30). At any rate, from a semantic standpoint, there is no great difference between the two readings.

his God: ועמנו ה' אלהינו לעזרנו ולהלחם מלחמתינו 'The Lord, our God, is with us, to help us and to fight our wars' (2 Chr 32:8a).

15.13 In the conclusion of the reign of Saul that the Chronicler added to the text he took from 1 Samuel 31, he noted the king's negative behavior, which led to the liquidation of his kingdom and to his own death. In doing so, he used the literary device of antithesis (1 Chr 10:13–14):

13a. וימת שאול במעלו אשר מעל בה' . . .
13b. וגם לשאול **באוב לדרוש**
14a. **ולא דרש בה'** וימיתהו
ויסב את המלוכה לדויד בן ישי [39]

13a.   Saul died because of his unfaithfulness; he was unfaithful to the Lord . . .
13b.   and even consulted **a medium**, *seeking guidance,*
14a.   *and did not seek guidance* **from the Lord**. So he put him to death and turned the kingdom over to David, son of Jesse.

This literary structure of antithesis shows clearly that the passage under consideration is the deliberate result of the Chronicler's work and that v. 13b is not a "gloss—an exegetical comment made by a later writer," as claimed by Ackroyd.[40]

Ackroyd's argument also is voided in light of the existence of a similar example in 2 Chr 17:3–5 (an "addition"), which makes use of almost identical words in the context of Jehoshaphat, king of Judah, but this time from a positive standpoint:

ויהי ה' עם יהושפט כי הלך בדרכי דויד אביו הראשנים
ולא דרש לבעלים
כי **לאלהי אביו** דרש ובמצותיו הלך ולא כמעשה ישראל
ויכן ה' את הממלכה בידו

The Lord was with Jehoshaphat, because he walked in the earlier ways of David, his father.
He did not inquire of **the Baals**
but *inquired of* **the God of his fathers** and walked in his commandments, and not according to the deeds of Israel.
Thus, *the Lord established the kingdom in his hand.*

Along with his use of antithesis to shape these verses, the Chronicler also used a chiastic structure. These are the forms the Chronicler used to emphasize strongly the nature of the deeds of these kings.

---

39. For discussions of this passage from other points of view, see example 7.17 (pp. 139–140); example 11.6 (p. 220); example 12.87 (p. 263); and example 14.12 (pp. 310–311).

40. Ackroyd, "Chronicler as Exegete," 8.

15.14 In 2 Chr 13:20–21 (an "addition"), the Chronicler contrasted the fates of Jeroboam, king of Israel, and Abijah, king of Judah, after the war between them (13:2b–19). Jeroboam, the son of Nebat, who had forsaken "the commandment of the Lord" and was defeated in the war,[41] עצר כח לא 'did not recover his power'. He died an unnatural death (ויגפהו ה' וימת 'the Lord struck him down, and he died')[42] during Abijah's lifetime (v. 20). Abijah, on the other hand, who had kept "the Lord's commandment" and relied on him, won the battle, grew stronger, wed many women, and fathered many sons and daughters (v. 21):

ולא עצר כח ירבעם עוד בימי אביהו ויגפהו ה' וימת

ויתחזק אביהו   וישא לו נשים ארבע עשרה

ויולד עשרים ושנים בנים ושש עשרה בנות

Jeroboam did not recover his power in the days of Abijah: *the Lord struck him down, and he died.*
But Abijah grew stronger, *took fourteen wives, and fathered twenty-two sons and sixteen daughters.*

In creating this antithesis, the Chronicler ignored the following details that appear in the book of Kings:

(1) According to 1 Kgs 14:20; 15:1, 9, Jeroboam died *a normal death* a year or two *after* Abijah's demise.[43]

(2) All in all, Abijah could not have reigned more than three years (1 Kgs 15:2a // 2 Chr 13:2a), and it is difficult to imagine that, during his short reign after the battle with Jeroboam, he managed to wed 14 women and father 38 children. Note that, after his death, Abijah was succeeded by Asa, who was apparently his brother (see 1 Kgs 15:2, 10, 13), not his son. It is thus very possible that Abijah had no sons at all, at any rate none suitable to inherit the throne.[44]

The attribution of many sons and daughters to Abijah seems to serve as a motif for the divine blessing bestowed on the righteous king of Judah. This also seems to have been the case, for example, with Obed-edom, to whom the Chronicler ascribed 8 sons, noting: כי ברכו אלהים 'for God blessed him' (1 Chr 26:5, an "addition").[45]

---

41. See below, example 15.18 (pp. 343–344).

42. Compare 2 Chr 21:18; 1 Sam 25:38: ויגף ה' את נבל וימת 'The Lord struck Nabal down and he died'.

43. The Sages, who strived to maintain the narrative in the book of Chronicles as well as the information in Kings, were forced to interpret the expression ויגפהו ה' וימת as referring to Abijah, king of Judah! See *y. Yebam.* 16.3 (82b); *Gen. Rab.* 65:16; *Lev. Rab.* 33:5. R. David Kimhi, the commentary ascribed to Rashi, and R. Levi ben Gershon view this phrase as referring to Jeroboam but suggest various unlikely explanations to harmonize the narrative in Chronicles with the details in the book of Kings.

44. Cf. Wellhausen, *Prolegomena*, 205 [ET: 209–10].

45. Compare this passage with 1 Chr 13:14 // 2 Sam 6:11; and see further, for example, 2 Chr 11:17–23 (an "addition").

Thus, our conclusion must be that the literary construction of antithesis in 2 Chr 13:20–21 includes a number of literary-theological effects, but it seems to lack any realistic historical basis.[46]

15.15 The Chronicler seems to have contrasted the fate of Josiah, king of Judah, and the fate of Hezekiah, king of Judah, as well.[47]

3. Relying on the Lord Contrasted with Relying on Flesh and Blood

15.16 In 1 Chr 21:12 the Chronicler expanded the description of the punitive measures proposed by Gad, the prophet, to David. Instead of והוא רדפך _____ _____ אם שלשה חדשים נסך לפני צריך 'Will you *flee* for three months before your foes _____ _____ while they pursue you?' (2 Sam 24:13c), he wrote, למשגת[48] ואם שלשה חדשים נספה מפני צריך *וחרב איבך* 'either three months of *being killed* by your foes, with *the sword of your enemies* overtaking you . . .' (1 Chr 21:12c). And instead of ואם היות שלשת ימים דבר בארצך _____ _____ 'Do you prefer three days _____ _____ of pestilence in your land?' (2 Sam 24:13d), he wrote: ואם שלשת ימים *חרב ה'* ודבר בארץ **ומלאך ה' משחית בכל גבול ישראל** 'Do you prefer three days of *the sword of the Lord* and pestilence in the land, **with the angel of the Lord destroying throughout the territory of Israel**?' (1 Chr 21:12d). These expansions contrast the nature of the proposed punishments: *חרב איבך* 'the sword of your enemies' and *חרב ה'* 'the sword of the Lord'. This antithesis renders David's response to the prophet's proposal even more prominent:

ויאמר דויד אל גד
צר לי מאד
אפלה נא ביד ה' כי רבים רחמיו מאד
וביד אדם **אל אפל**[49]

Then David said to Gad,
"I am in great distress;
let me fall into the *hand of the Lord,* for His mercies are great;
but into *human hands* **let me not fall**."

---

46. Against Graf, *Geschichtlichen Bücher*, 137; Rudolph, *Chronik*, 239; Japhet, *Ideology*, 172, all of whom attribute historical reliability to this passage in Chronicles.

47. For details, see above, example 1.3 (pp. 22–23).

48. The form למשגת should be compared with the phrase further on, *לא למגפה* (1 Chr 21:17), and also *עזרו איש ברעהו למשחית* (2 Chr 20:23). A similar form is found in the Aramaic inscription on the tombstone of King Uzziah, dated to Second Temple days: לכה התית / טמי עוזיה / מלך יהודה / *ולא למפתח* 'Hither have been brought / the bones of Uzziah, / king of Judah. / *Do not open*'. See also above, example 5.9 (pp. 105–106).

49. Cf. Curtis-Madsen, *Chronicles*, 250.

David chooses a punishment at the hand of the Lord on principle (without naming a specific one—famine or pestilence), "for His mercies are great," rather than a punishment by humans (a military defeat). In this way, the Lord's many mercies are contrasted with the mercies of man—which are not many. Thus, the image of the believing David is also emphasized.

15.17 The literary feature of antithesis is also reflected in the "additions" found in the book of Chronicles. For instance, Asa, king of Judah, sent a bribe to Ben-hadad, king of Aram, to persuade him to violate his treaty with Baasha, king of Israel. Baasha had built a high stone and wood barricade "to prevent Asa from going out or coming in." Ben-hadad violated his treaty with Baasha and invaded the kingdom of Israel, thus causing the construction of the barricade to be stopped (1 Kgs 15:17–22 // 2 Chr 16:1–6).

The Chronicler was opposed to the idea of relying on human help.[50] He contrasted Asa's reliance on the king of Aram and its consequences with Asa's reliance on the Lord and its consequences, in the battle against Zerah, the Kushite (2 Chr 14:7–14), by means of words that he ascribed to Hanani, the Seer (2 Chr 16:7b–8):

בהשענך על מלך ארם ולא נשענת על ה' אלהיך, על כן נמלט חיל מלך
ארם [51] מידך. הלא הכושים והלובים היו לחיל לרב לרכב ולפרשים
להרבה מאד ובהשענך על ה' נתנם בידך

Because you relied on the king of Aram and did not rely on the Lord your God, *the troops of the king of Aram have escaped you.* Were not the Kushites and the Lybians a huge force with an abundant number of chariots and cavalry? **But because you relied on the Lord**, *he delivered them into your hand.*

Indeed, in the narrative of the battle against Zerah, the Kushite, the Chronicler made sure to stress that Asa relied on the Lord, even though he had built fortified cities in Judah and had well-equipped soldiers (2 Chr 14:5–7). He ascribed a prayer to Asa: ויקרא אסא אל ה' אלהיו, ויאמר עזרנו ה' אלהינו כי עליך נשענו ובשמך באנו על ההמון הזה . . . 'Then Asa called on the Lord his God, saying, ". . . Help us, O Lord our God, for *we rely on you*, and it is in your name that we have come against this multitude"'

---

50. That reliance on a king "of flesh and blood" is sinful can be found, for example, in Isa 7:7–9.

51. Luc. reads ישראל here, instead of ארם, and other commentators agree with Luc.; for example, Rudolph, *Chronik*, 248; idem, *BHS*, 1536. It is possible, however, that the Chronicler meant to say that, had Asa relied on the Lord, not only would he have defeated the king of Israel but also his ally, the king of Aram; see also Ehrlich, *Mikrâ ki-Pheschutô*, 456; Curtis-Madsen, *Chronicles*, 389; Williamson, *Chronicles*, 274.

(2 Chr 14:10). His reliance on the king of Aram is also emphasized by noting his nonreliance on the Lord:

בהשענך על מלך ארם ולא נשענת על ה׳ אלהיך

Because **you relied** on *the king of Aram* **and did not** rely on the *Lord your God.* . . . (2 Chr 16:7b)

The Chronicler created yet another contrast, a contrast between the period after Asa's reliance on the king of Aram, נסכלת על זאת, כי מעתה יש *עמך מלחמות* 'you have been foolish in this; *from now on you will have wars*' (16:9), and the period at the beginning of Asa's reign, כי שקטה הארץ *ואין עמו מלחמה* בשנים האלה כי הניח ה׳ לו 'for the land was tranquil *and he had no war*, for the Lord had given him rest' (14:5).[52] All of this happened because of these words that the Chronicler ascribed to Asa: "for we inquired of the Lord our God; we inquired of him, and he has given us rest round about" (14:6).[53]

15.18 In the speech made by Abijah, king of Judah, at Mt. Zemaraim, the Chronicler contrasts Abijah and the kingdom of Judah with Jeroboam and the kingdom of Israel. He describes Jeroboam and the kingdom of Israel thus (2 Chr 13:8–9):

ואתם המון רב ועמכם עגלי זהב אשר עשה לכם ירבעם לאלהים
הלא הדחתם את כהני ה׳ את בני אהרן והלוים
ותעשו לכם כהנים כעמי הארצות

You are a great multitude, and **you have the golden calves that Jeroboam made as gods for you.**
For *you overthrew the priests of the Lord, the descendants of Aaron, and the Levites,*
and you appointed priests for yourselves like the peoples of other lands.

However, he describes Abijah and the kingdom of Judah thus (13:10–11a):

ואנחנו ה׳ אלהינו ולא עזבנהו
וכהנים משרתים לה׳ בני אהרן והלוים במלאכת ומקטרים לה׳

But as for us—we have not abandoned the Lord our God.
We have priests serving the Lord who are descendants of Aaron, and the Levites are at their work, sacrificing to the Lord. . . .

---

52. Cf. Japhet, *Ideology*, 191 n. 565.
53. Cf. also 2 Chr 13:23[14:1]: וימלך אסא בו תחתיו—*בימיו שקטה הארץ עשר שנים* 'Asa his son reigned in his stead; *in his days the land was tranquil for ten years*' (an "addition" to 1 Kgs 15:8).

He goes on to note this in the clearest fashion:

כי שמרים אנחנו את משמרת ה' אלהינו
ואתם עזבתם אתו

> For **we** *keep the charge of the Lord our God,*
> **but you** *have abandoned him.*

Thus, despite the fact that Jeroboam waged war "with eight hundred thousand chosen men" (13:3b) and Abijah with only "four hundred thousand chosen men," that is, only about half of Jeroboam's force (v. 3a),[54] and despite Jeroboam's having set an ambush for the soldiers of Judah so that they had to face the battle "from in front and from behind" (v. 14), "God defeated Jeroboam and all Israel before Abijah and Judah. The Israelites fled before Judah, and God delivered them into their hands. Abijah and his men defeated them with great slaughter. Five hundred thousand chosen men of Israel fell dead." In other words, the number of Israelite dead was greater by one hundred thousand than the number of soldiers from Judah (vv. 15–17). And, indeed, "the men of Israel *were humbled* at that time," whereas the men of Judah *"prevailed,* for they had relied on the Lord God of their fathers" (v. 18).

Portraying Abijah, king of Judah, in a positive light—in complete contrast to the negative evaluation of the Deuteronomistic historian in 1 Kgs 15:3, "And [Abijam] repeated all the sins that his father had committed before him. Neither was his heart entirely with the Lord his God, as was the heart of David his ancestor"—was perhaps not only because of the Chronicler's concept of retribution[55] but also because of his desire to create literary antithesis, as described above. By means of this construction the Chronicler emphasized the superiority of the kingdom of Judah under the leadership of the Davidic dynasty ("the kingdom of the Lord in the hands of the descendants of David")[56] and the inferiority of the kingdom of Israel under the leadership of Jeroboam, thus solidly anchoring an important aspect of his theopolitics.

---

54. Compare with 2 Chr 14:7–8. The number of Israelites here is identical to their number in the narrative of the census in 2 Sam 24:9, "eight hundred thousand military men able to draw a sword," and the number of Judean men (four hundred thousand in 2 Chronicles 13) is close to the number in 2 Samuel 24: "five hundred thousand men." Did the Chronicler deliberately use the book of Samuel for his purposes here?

55. For this, see Japhet, *Ideology*, 172–73.

56. 2 Chr 13:8; see also 9:8 in comparison with 1 Kgs 10:9; 1 Chr 28:5; 29:23.

4. Perfecting an Existing "Antithesis"
in the Earlier Text

15.19 The narratives about David's battles with the Philistines (2 Sam 5:17–25 // 1 Chr 14:8–16) speak of the Lord's intervention on David's behalf. In the first war, the Lord promised him: נתן אתן את הפלשתים בידך 'I will surely deliver the Philistines into your hand' (2 Sam 5:19 // 1 Chr 14:10). Indeed, after his victory David said: פרץ ה׳ את איבי כפרץ מים 'the Lord has burst out against my enemies like a bursting flood' (2 Sam 5:20 // 1 Chr 14:11). In the second battle, David received instructions from the Lord concerning the timing of his assault on the Philistines that stated: כי אז יצא ה׳ לפניך להכות במחנה פלשתים 'then the Lord will go before you to strike down the Philistine army'. He obeyed these instructions and defeated the Philistines (2 Sam 5:22–25 // 1 Chr 14:13–16).

The gods of the Philistines went out with them to war as well, as can be seen from the verse concluding the first battle narrative: ויעזבו [הפלשתים] שם את אלהיהם[57] '[The Philistines] abandoned their gods there'. While the God of David went out before him and granted him victory after victory, the "gods" of the Philistines not only did not grant them victory or prevent their defeat by David and his God but were powerless even to see to their own escape. They were abandoned on the battlefield, where they fell into the hands of David and his men as booty (2 Sam 5:21b). In these narratives, then, the narrator contrasts the power and strength of the Lord God of David with the power and strength of the "gods" of the Philistines.

In 1 Chr 14:8–16, the Chronicler presented these narratives, while sharpening the contrast by introducing changes:

(1) He replaced the name YHWH ('the Lord') with the name (Ha-) Elohim ('[the] God'):[58]

2 Sam 5:19–25	1 Chr 14:10–16
19. וישאל דוד בה׳	10. וישאל דויד **באלהים**
20. ויאמר [דוד] פרץ ה׳	11. ויאמר דויד פרץ **האלהים**
23. וישאל דוד בה׳	14. וישאל עוד דויד **באלהים**
ויאמר לא תעלה . . .	ויאמר לו **האלהים**: לא תעלה . . .
24. . . . כי אז יצא ה׳ לפניך	15. כי יצא **האלהים** לפניך
25. ויעש דוד כן כאשר צוה ה׳	16. ויעש דויד כאשר צוהו **האלהים**

---

57. This is the reading in 1 Chr 14:12a and in the LXX of 2 Sam 5:21a and seems to be the original reading. The MT reading in Samuel, עצביהם, must be a later scribal emendation.

58. The change occurs throughout the entire text, except for 1 Chr 14:10b // 2 Sam 5:19b, perhaps because of the Chronicler's inconsistency (a fact known from other changes to the earlier text; see also chap. 20 of this book).

Using the name אלהים(ה) in these particular narratives highlights the
antithesis between the power and strength of אלהים(ה) '(the) God of David' and the power and strength of אלהיהם 'their gods' (the Philistines')
even more. That is, he who goes before David is called אלהים and those
whom the Philistines brought with them to the battlefield are called
אלהים; he is a single God, and these are multiple gods, but how vast the
difference is between their abilities!

The name YHWH in the earlier texts has been replaced by the name
Elohim 32 times in Chronicles.[59] Various explanations have been proposed for this phenomenon, the vast majority of which do not stand up
to criticism.[60] However, whatever the explanation for this interchange
in Chronicles may be, the very use of the name אלהים in this context
in Chronicles does emphasize the contrast with the Philistine "gods."
Japhet[61] states that "the transition in Chronicles" is "the result of the
process of manuscript transmission and not the work of the actual author of the book." However, in all of the textual witnesses of 2 Sam 5:17–
25 the name YHWH appears, whereas in the textual witnesses of 1 Chr
14:8–16 it is the name Elohim that appears. Why then should we not assume that the change was carried out by the Chronicler?

(2) According to the writer of the book of Samuel, when the "gods" of
the Philistines were found abandoned on the battlefield, they were
taken as booty by David and his men: וישאם דוד ואנשיו 'David and his men
carried them off' (2 Sam 5:20b). The Chronicler altered this passage and
wrote: ויאמר דויד וישרפו באש 'David gave the order and they were burned
by fire' (1 Chr 14:12b). The main reason for this change was to harmonize the book of Samuel with the book of Deuteronomy (7:25 et al.),[62] but
at the same time the nature of the Philistine "gods" (wood for a bonfire)
is stressed, and their impotence in the presence of the God of David
(אלה[ה]ים, who went out before him)[63] stands out sharply.

15.20 David treated Hanun, son of Nahash, king of the Ammonites,
according to the principle of "measure for measure" (1 Chr 19:2a //
2 Sam 10:2a):

---

59. For additional references, see Segal, "The Names YHWH and Elohim," 140;
Japhet, *Ideology*, 31 n. 64.
60. For a review, a discussion, and additional literature on this topic, see Japhet,
ibid., 30–37.
61. Ibid., 37.
62. For a detailed discussion of this topic, see above, example 7.23 (pp. 154–156).
63. And see, for example, the words of Deutero-Isaiah, a prophet during the Second Temple period: Isa 41:7; 44:9–20; 46:5–7, and also Ps 115:2–11 // 135:15–20 (see
also vv. 5–14).

ויאמר דויד: **אעשה חסד** עם חנון בן נחש
כי **עשה אביו** עמי **חסד** [64]

David said, "**I will deal** *loyally* with Hanun, son of Nahash,
because **his father dealt** *loyally* with me."

However, in return for the honor[65] that the delegation of David's men
wanted to grant Hanun, David's men received insults and embarrass-
ment (1 Chr 19:4–5 // 2 Sam 10:4–5). There is a clear contrast being
made between the intentions of David's servants in the land of the Ammonites and the treatment they received at the hands of "the officials of
the Ammonites." The latter suspect David's servants of unfriendly intentions and espionage, whereas the real purpose of the envoy was to
comfort mourners, a gesture aimed at encouraging friendly relations between the two kingdoms.[66] Indeed, the consoling of a mourning ally or
his successor was customary among friendly kingdoms in the ancient
Near East, and the step that David took here was an accepted one. Thus,
for example, after the death of David, Hiram, king of Tyre, sent "his
servants to Solomon, for he had heard that they had anointed him king
in place of his father" (1 Kgs 5:15a[1a]). The verse notes: כי אהב היה
חירם לדוד כל הימים 'for Hiram had been friendly to David at all times'
(5:15b[1b], the word אהב in this context referring to a "treaty").[67] The
delegation from Tyre apparently wanted to console Solomon on the occasion of his father's death and at the same time wanted to renew with
him the friendly relations and the treaty that characterized the relations between the two kingdoms in David's time (see also 2 Sam 5:11).
Indeed, the text goes on to speak of the trade relations between Israel
and Tyre and of their treaty (1 Kgs 5:16–26[2–12]).[68]

---

64. Some think that these words refer to the economic aid granted by Shobi, son of
Nahash, of Rabbat of the Ammonites, to David in Mahanaim during Absalom's revolt
(2 Sam 17:27). But this would mean that Absalom's revolt preceded the events in
1 Chronicles 19 // 2 Samuel 10, which is a problem. It is more reasonable to assume
that Nahash himself was David's ally against their common foe, Saul (for the enmity
between Nahash and Saul, see 1 Sam 11:1–11).

65. Note: המכבד דויד, 1 Chr 19:3 // 2 Sam 10:3.

66. If the term חסד in the given context meant "treaty," David, in sending a delegation to Hanun, may have wanted to continue the "treaty" and friendship with the new
king as well.

67. See Moran, "Love of God," 80–81.

68. In a similar situation, Burnaburis II, king of Babylon, wrote to Amenhotep IV,
king of Egypt: "Just as before you and my father treated one another well, so now you
and I together—may no other matter come between us." Further on in the letter, he
proposes to Pharaoh that trade relations between the two kingdoms be established;
see Knudtzon, *El-Amarna Tafeln*, vol. 1, document no. 6, lines 8–16.

The Chronicler tried to make the contrast found in 2 Sam 10:1–3 even greater by making changes and adding a few words:

2 Sam 10:2b–3	1 Chr 19:2b–3
וישלח דוד לנחמו ביד עבדיו אל אביו	וישלח דויד מלאכים לנחמו על אביו
ויבאו עבדי דוד ארץ בני עמון	**ויבאו עבדי דויד אל ארץ בני עמון**
	אל חנון לנחמו
ויאמרו שרי בני־עמון אל חנון אדניהם	ויאמרו שרי בני־עמון לחנון
המכבד דוד את אביך בעיניך כי שלח	המכבד דויד את אביך בעיניך כי שלח
לך מנחמים?	לך מנחמים?
הלוא בעבור **חקור** את **העיר ולרגלה**	הלא בעבור **לחקר ולהפך ולרגל הארץ**
ולהפכה שלח דוד את עבדיו אליך	באו עבדיו אליך
Then David sent his servants to *comfort [Hanun]* on his father's death. When David's servants arrived in the land of the Ammonites the officials of the Ammonites said to Hanun, their master, "Do you really think David is just honoring your father by sending you comforters? **Has not David sent** his servants in order *to investigate* **the town**, *spy it out, and overthrow it?"*	Then David sent messengers to *comfort [Hanun]* on his father's death. When ***David's servants arrived*** in the land of the Ammonites **to Hanun** *to comfort him,* the officials of the Ammonites said to Hanun, "Do you really think David is just honoring your father by sending you comforters? **Have not *his servants* come** in order *to investigate, overthrow, and spy out the land?"*

The "addition" "to Hanun to comfort him" reiterates and emphasizes the clear aim and intention of David's servants in coming "to the land of the Ammonites."

The rest of the "addition" and the changes that the Chronicler has introduced into the earlier text create an analogy between the part of the statement made by the servants of Hanun and the part of the text that reveals the aim of the coming of David's servants to the land of the Ammonites:

(1) The Chronicler writes "the land" (referring to ארץ בני עמון 'the land of the Ammonites', mentioned in the text, revealing the aim of the coming of David's servants) instead of העיר 'the town' in the earlier text.[69]

---

69. The LXX of 1 Chr 19:3 integrates the two parallel texts, so that the word "the land" appears alongside the word "the town," which appears in 2 Sam 10:3, as well: οὐχὶ ὅπως ἐξεραυνήσωσι τὴν πόλιν, καὶ τοῦ κατασκοπῆσαι τὴν γῆν 'Have not his servants come to you that they might search the city and spy out the land?' Similarly, a number of manuscripts and printed editions of *Targum Jonathan* (representing the Tiberian tradition) on 2 Sam 10:3 have ית קרתא (as in the MT and LXX—τὴν πόλιν 'the city').

(2) כאו עבדיו 'have not his servants *come*' (which links up nicely with ויבאו עבדי דויד 'When David's servants *arrived*'), instead of שלח דוד את עבדיו 'has not *David sent* his servants' in the earlier text.

(3) The word אליך 'to you' (also in the earlier text) links up nicely with the "addition" אל חנון 'to Hanun' in the previous verse.

This analogy sharpens the contrast between the aim of David's servants—"to comfort him" (which the Chronicler takes care to state two times, compared with the one statement in the earlier text)—and the words of Hanun's servants—"to investigate, overthrow, and spy out." In order to accent the matter, the Chronicler accumulated the verbs and presented them one after another, without any intervening material. In contrast, in 2 Samuel the object את העיר 'the town' intervenes between the verb חקר 'investigate' and the verbs לרגלה ולהפכה 'spy it out and overthrow it'.[70]

Other manuscripts have ית ארעא (as in four MSS of the MT; see Kittel, *BH*, 470 and 1 Chr 19:3), but this reading seems to be secondary. According to Talmon, the interchange הארץ/העיר in the parallel texts that we have, as well as the integration that the Greek translator made of them in 1 Chr 19:3, show that in certain cases the biblical authors (and their translators too) interpreted these words as a synonymous noun pair, each of which was able to replace the other (Talmon, "Textual Study," 345–46). At any rate, it seems that, even if the nouns העיר/הארץ replace one another in certain cases, as Talmon would have it, the very fact that the Chronicler chose to use the word הארץ (a choice not made to create any substantial content change) reinforces my claim that the change was intended to assist in the creation of literary antithesis.

70. For another example of this feature, see 2 Chr 28:15 (an "addition"):

ויחזיקו בשביה . . . וילבשום וינעלום ויאכלום וישקום ויסכום וינהלום בחמרים לכל כושל
ויבאום יריחו

they took the captives . . . , *clothed them, gave them sandals, gave them food and drink, anointed them, carried* all the faltering ones on donkeys, *and brought them* to Jericho.

The factor common to the two examples is the use of the same form a number of times in sequence; in 1 Chronicles 19, infinitive forms with a ל (לפעול—three times); in 2 Chronicles 28, conjugated verb forms in the ויקטול form + an enclitic 3d-person plural object suffix (ויפעלום—six times). For this feature in the Bible, see also, for example, Gen 25:34; Exod 1:7; 1 Sam 19:12; 2 Sam 1:12; and see Bar-Efrat, *Narrative Art*, 216–17.

Chapter 16
Simile

Simile is a comparison of two essentially unlike entities. This is done in order to clarify or concretize a characteristic, situation, relationship, or some other thing that the different entities share. In general, the comparison is carried out in Hebrew by means of the comparative prefix -כ 'like' or 'as' or a comparative particle: כמות, כמו, כעין, כך, כן.[1] Sometimes, however, the comparison is performed without either the comparative -כ or any comparative particle.

This literary device is especially common in biblical poetry, but it is also found in biblical historical writings and narratives.[2] It is common also in ancient Near Eastern literature, including royal inscriptions. Thus, for example: (1) Sennacherib says that he made Hezekiah, king of Judah, a prisoner in Jerusalem *"like a bird in a cage"*; (2) Esarhaddon describes himself: *"I became as mad as a lion. . . . I spread my wings like the (swift-)flying storm (bird). . . . Like lambs they gamboled* and (recognized) me as their lord by praying (to me)"; (3) in the Cyrus Cylinder, the numerous men of the Persian army are compared to water: "His [Cyrus's] vast army, *whose number like the waters of a river cannot be determined.*"[3]

In the book of Chronicles, the Chronicler occasionally introduced change(s) in order to create a simile. Literary similes are also found in the "additions" in Chronicles. Furthermore, the Chronicler adduced a considerable number of similes that he found in Samuel–Kings,[4] which increased the number of similes in his own book.

---

1. See Ornan, "Allusion's Structures," 40–47; Watson, *Hebrew Poetry*, 254–55.

2. See ibid., 257–62, as well as the examples Watson cites from Ugaritic and Akkadian literature and the references to additional bibliography. For examples found in the Pentateuch and the Former Prophets, see Bar-Efrat, *Narrative Art*, 209–10; Yellin ("Simile," 223–40) includes examples from throughout the Bible.

3. See Pritchard, *ANET* 288a (see also the citation from the Sennacherib inscription below, pp. 388–389 and n. 24), 289a, 315a, and see also above, example 13.17 (pp. 293–294).

4. For example, ועץ חניתו כמנור ארגים 'the staff of his spear was *like a weaver's beam*' (1 Chr 20:5 = 2 Sam 21:19); ויעש הרע בעיני ה׳ כתועבות הגוים אשר הוריש ה׳ מפני בני־ישראל 'he did what was evil in the sight of the Lord, according to the *abominations* of the nations that the Lord drove out before the children of Israel' (2 Chr 33:2 = 2 Kgs 21:2; also in 2 Chr 28:3 // 2 Kgs 16:3); אלה הצאן מה עשו 'but these *sheep*—what have they done?' (1 Chr 21:17 = 2 Sam 24:17); ראיתי את כל ישראל נפוצים כצאן אשר אין להם רעה 'I saw all of Israel scattered *like sheep* that have no shepherd' (2 Chr 18:16 = 1 Kgs 22:17);

There are also many instances of this literary device in the extra-biblical literature. One example can be found in Josephus's addition to the story of Gen 6:1–6. He says, "for many angels of God now consorted with women and begat sons who were overbearing and disdainful . . . in fact the deeds that tradition ascribes to them resemble the audacious exploits told by the Greeks of the giants" (*Ant.* 1.73).

16.1 2 Sam 23:21 describes the mighty Egyptian who was killed by Benaiah, son of Jehoiada, as follows:

אשר (*Qere*) איש: מראה	. . . a handsome man.
וביד המצרי חנית	The Egyptian had a spear in his hand.

In 1 Chr 11:23, the Egyptian's spear is compared with "a weaver's beam":

איש מדה . . .	an enormous man. . . .
ביד המצרי חנית *כמנור ארגים*	In the Egyptian's hand was a spear *like a weaver's beam*.

The simile "like a weaver's beam" seems to be referring to the shape and nature of the spear, not specifically to its size.[5] It appears in connection with the mighty Philistine in 1 Sam 17:7; 2 Sam 21:19 = 1 Chr 20:5.[6] But, while in those verses the comparison is between *"the staff of the spear"* and "a weaver's beam," here in 1 Chr 11:23, the Chronicler compares the *"spear"* with "a weaver's beam."[7]

16.2 The Deuteronomistic historian described the number of Israelites in the days of Solomon with the words: עם רב אשר לא ימנה*ולא* יספר מרב 'so many people that they **could not be numbered** or *counted* because of their multitude' (1 Kgs 3:8). With the very same words (though in inverse order) he also described the large number of cattle sacrificed during the dedication of the Temple: ולא ימנו מרב והמלך שלמה וכל עדת ישראל

ויתן המלך את הכסף בירושלם *כאבנים* ואת הארזים נתן *כשקמים* אשר בשפלה לרב 'the king made silver as common in Jerusalem *as stones*, and cedars he made as common *as sycamores* in the lowlands' (2 Chr 9:27 = 1 Kgs 10:27). These words also appear in 2 Chr 1:15; for this, see example 14.1 (pp. 297–298).

5. For this, and for the phrase מנור ארגים 'a weaver's beam', see Yadin, "Goliath's Javelin," 68–73.

6. For the connection between 1 Chr 11:23 and the verses under consideration from the book of Samuel, see above, example 3.1 (pp. 59–60); see also Willi, *Chronik*, 151.

7. The LXX of 2 Sam 23:21 reads: ἐν δὲ τῇ χειρὶ τοῦ Αἰγυπτίου δόρυ ὡς ξύλον διαβάθρας 'in the Egyptian's hand there was a spear like the wood of a ladder'. It seems that the translator was influenced by the wording of the parallel text, 1 Chr 11:23, and by 1 Sam 17:7 and 2 Sam 21:19.

מזבחים צאן ובקר אשר לא יסּפר . . . 'King Solomon and the entire assembly of
Israel . . . were sacrificing so many sheep and cattle that they *could not
be counted* or **numbered**' (1 Kgs 8:5).

The Chronicler may have thought it inappropriate to use the same
phrase to describe Israelites that was used to describe sacrificial sheep
and cattle. Consequently, he used the phrase צאן ובקר אשר לא יסּפרו ולא ימנו
מרב (1 Kgs 8:5) as it appears in 2 Chr 5:6, but in place of the words עם רב
עם רב כעפר הארץ (1 Kgs 3:8) he used the simile אשר לא ימנה ולא יסּפר מרב 'as
many people *as the dust of the earth*' (2 Chr 1:9).

Japhet holds that "the Chronicler adopts a more common phrasing
by substituting 'as many as the dust of the earth' for 'that cannot be
numbered or counted for multitude,'"[8] and in her wake Zalewski writes:
"the substitution may not be significant, but merely stem from the linguistic usage common in the Chronicler's lifetime."[9] Yet just how do
these scholars know that the phrase עם רב כעפר הארץ was more common
in the days of the Chronicler? And if this was so, it is surprising that the
Chronicler used the identical phrase from 1 Kgs 8:5 in 2 Chr 5:6, אשר לא
יסּפרו ולא ימנו מרב, with no change or substitution of some other linguistic
pattern. Furthermore, the phrase כעפר הארץ, which denotes a large number of human beings, appears only two other times in the Hebrew Bible
apart from 2 Chr 1:9 (Gen 12:16; 28:14). This is also true of לא ימנה ולא
יסּפר מרב, which is used twice to denote a large number of people (1 Kgs
3:8; Gen 15:10—partially) and once to denote a large number of sheep
and cattle (1 Kgs 8:5 // 2 Chr 5:6). From the available data, there is no
way of concluding that one of these phrases was any more common than
the other.

It appears that this simile, which is somewhat exaggerated,[10] renders the large number of Israelites in the Solomonic era tangible and
impressive. It also creates an analogy with other biblical texts that compare the number of Israelites with "the dust of the earth," such as the
Lord's promise to Abram, ושמתי את זרעך כעפר הארץ אשר אם יוכל איש למנות את
עפר הארץ גם זרעך ימנה 'I will make your offspring *like the dust of the earth*,
so that if it is possible to count the dust of the earth your offspring also

---

8. Japhet, *Ideology*, 93–94.

9. Zalewski, *Solomon*, 367.

10. The phrases עפר / עפר הארץ 'dust of the earth/dust'; חול ימים / חול אשר על שפת
הים 'sea sand / sand that is on the seashore'; and כוכבי השמים 'stars of the skies' are
all used as similes for very large numbers; see also Gen 22:17; Num 23:10a (read:
את רבע ישראל [following the Samaritan and LXX] וּמִי סָפַר / מִי מנה עפר יעקב. The word רבע
here means אבק 'dust'; compare Akkadian *tarbuʾ(t)u(m)*, *turbuʾ/ttu*, *tartūtu* [see von
Soden, *Akkadisches Handwörterbuch*, 3.1328; for the parallel words עפר/אבק, cf. Deut
28:24); 1 Kgs 4:20; Ps 78:27; Job 27:16.

can be counted' (Gen 13:16); and to Jacob, וְהָיָה זַרְעֲךָ כַּעֲפַר הָאָרֶץ 'and your offspring shall be *like the dust of the earth*' (Gen 28:14). This means that the Chronicler may have wanted to show that the promise given by the Lord to the Hebrew patriarchs regarding the large number of their descendants was fulfilled precisely during the days of King Solomon.

Moreover, it seems to me that the change further along in the text regarding the number of Israelites, from עַמְּךָ הַכָּבֵד הַזֶּה 'this *large* people of yours' (1 Kgs 3:9) to עַמְּךָ הַזֶּה הַגָּדוֹל 'this *great* people of yours' (2 Chr 1:10),[11] was mainly intended to direct the reader to the concept proposed above, because the use of the phrase עַמְּךָ ... הַגָּדוֹל '*great* **people**' alongside the simile עַם רַב כַּעֲפַר הָאָרֶץ 'as many people *as the dust of the earth*' reinforces the analogy with the Lord's promise to the patriarchs: וְאֶעֶשְׂךָ **לְגוֹי גָּדוֹל** (Abraham, Gen 12:2; 18:18); וְאַבְרָהָם הָיוֹ יִהְיֶה **לְגוֹי גָּדוֹל** וְעָצוּם, כִּי **לְגוֹי גָּדוֹל** אֲשִׂימְךָ שָׁם (Jacob, Gen 46:3).[12]

Purely from the aspect of style, the use of two different phrases to express a large number of things made for more variegation in the book of Chronicles.

16.3 In 2 Chr 32:17, the Chronicler summarized 2 Kgs 19:16–18 (see also vv. 22, 23 // Isa 37:17–24) by forming a simile: כְּ . . . כֵּן 'like/as . . . so', apparently in order to emphasize the absurdity of the comparison made by Sennacherib, king of Assyria, between the God of Hezekiah and the gods of the foreign nations:

2 Kgs 19:16–18	2 Chr 32:17
הַטֵּה ה' אָזְנְךָ וּשְׁמָע	
. . . אֵת דִּבְרֵי סַנְחֵרִיב	
אֲשֶׁר שָׁלַח לְחָרֵף אֱלֹהִים חָי	וּסְפָרִים כָּתַב לְחָרֵף לֵה' אֱלֹהֵי יִשְׂרָאֵל
אָמְנָם ה' הֶחֱרִיבוּ מַלְכֵי אַשּׁוּר	וְלֵאמֹר עָלָיו לֵאמֹר
אֶת הַגּוֹיִם וְאֶת אַרְצָם וְנָתְנוּ	כֵּאלֹהֵי גּוֹיֵ הָאֲרָצוֹת אֲשֶׁר לֹא הִצִּילוּ
אֶת אֱלֹהֵיהֶם בָּאֵשׁ כִּי לֹא אֱלֹהִים הֵמָּה	עַמָּם מִיָּדִי כֵּן לֹא יַצִּיל אֱלֹהֵי חִזְקִיָּהוּ
כִּי אִם מַעֲשֵׂה יְדֵי אָדָם עֵץ וָאָבֶן	עַמּוֹ מִיָּדִי
Incline your ear, O Lord, and hear	
. . . the words of Sennacherib,	
which he has sent to mock the	He wrote letters showing contempt
living God!	for the Lord, God of Israel,

11. For the inverted word order in 2 Chr 1:10b in comparison with 1 Kgs 3:9b, see example 12.48 (p. 249).

12. Williamson has another opinion in *Israel*, 64; idem, *Chronicles*, 196; he thinks that the Chronicler was influenced in this case by Gen 28:14 (referring to Jacob), which demonstrates how important Jacob was to the Chronicler. However, the identical words appear earlier *twice*—regarding Abraham; what, then, is Jacob's advantage over Abraham?

Indeed, O Lord, the kings of Assyria have destroyed the nations and their lands, and have put their gods into the fire, for they are not God, but made by human hands—wood and stone!	and to speak against him, saying: "Just *as* the gods of the nations in other lands did not save their people from my hands, *so* the God of Hezekiah will not save his people from my hands!"

Similarly, further along, in 32:18–19: "They called out loudly in the language of Judah. . . . They spoke of the God of Jerusalem as if he were *like* the gods of the peoples of the land, which are made by human hands."

The literary device of simile is used in the "additions" in the book of Chronicles as well; for example:

16.4 In the list of David's assistants, who joined him while he was still in Ziklag, 1 Chr 12:9 relates:

ומן הגדי נבדלו אל דויד למצד מדברה
גברי החיל, אנשי צבא למלחמה, ערכי צנה ורמח
ופני אריה פניהם וכצבאים על ההרים למהר

From the Gadites there went over to David at the fortress in the desert mighty, experienced warriors, expert shield- and spear-bearers, *whose faces were like the faces of lions. They moved as swiftly as deer on the mountains.*

In the simile כצבאים על ההרים למהר 'they moved as swiftly as deer on the mountains',[13] the comparison is formed by using a comparative -כ, whereas in the previous simile, ופני אריה פניהם 'whose faces were [like] the faces of lions', there is no comparative -כ or any other comparative particle, although the comparison between the component parts is quite clear.

16.5 Further along in chap. 12, there is still another simile (1 Chr 12:23): כי לעת יום ביום יבאו על דויד לעזרו עד למחנה גדול כמחנה אלהים 'For from day to day men kept coming to David to help him, *until there was a great army, like an army of God*'.[14]

16.6 The speech delivered by Abijah, king of Judah, in 2 Chr 13:5 reads: הלא לכם לדעת כי ה׳ אלהי ישראל נתן ממלכה לדויד על ישראל לעולם לו ולבניו

---

13. Compare this with its parallel in 2 Sam 2:18: כאחד הצבאים אשר בשדה 'as a deer in the field'. For the synonymity of הר/שדה, see Cant 2:8–9; 8:14; see also Talmon, "Emendation of Biblical Texts," 121–24.

14. For the phrase מחנה אלהים, see Gen 32:3.

ברית מלח 'You must surely be aware that the Lord God of Israel gave the kingship over Israel forever to David and his sons—*a covenant of salt*'. The phrase ברית מלח 'a covenant of salt' serves as a simile without a comparative -כ or any other comparative particle. The simile emphasizes the eternality of the promise given to the Davidic dynasty, similar to salt, which does not decay over time.[15]

16.7 In the letters that Hezekiah, king of Judah, sent to the Northern tribes, he requested: עתה אל תקשו ערפכם כאבותיכם—תנו יד לה' ובאו למקדשו 'Now do not be as stubborn *as your ancestors were*—give a hand to the Lord and come to his Temple' (2 Chr 30:8).[16]

---

15. See Rudolph, *Chronik*, 237; Japhet, *Ideology*, 454–55. The phrase should be interpreted the same way in Num 18:19 (the Priestly source; for the relationship between the two passages, see Japhet, pp. 454–56). And compare this phrase with Lev 2:13: מלח ברית אלהיך 'the salt of the covenant of your God'. A parallel expression expressing a similar set of relations is found in Akkadian; for example, *ša ṭabtu ša mār* ᵐ*Iakini ilḫimu* '[and whoever] tasted the salt of the sons of Jachin'; see also Harper, *ABL*, vol. 7, nos. 4–10, 747; Oppenheim, "Beer and Brewing Techniques," 43–44 n. 39. This idiom is apparently also where the punitive measure of "strewing salt" on the violators of a covenant comes from; see, for example, Deut 29:22. See also Kalimi, "He Sowed It with Salt," 10.

16. Compare this simile with what is said about the Northern tribes in 2 Kgs 17:14: ויקשו את ערפם כערף אבותם 'they hardened their necks [= were stubborn] as the their ancestors had done'. For the phrase תנו יד לה' 'give the Lord a hand', see Myers, *II Chronicles*, 175.

Chapter 17
Key Words

Martin Buber defined a key word (*Leitwort*) as follows:

> a linguistic word or root repeated significantly within a text or a
> sequence of texts or an anthology of texts. The significance of these
> repetitions is the single meaning of the texts which becomes clear.
> The repetition does not have to be of the very same word; on the
> contrary, it can be the root of the word which is repeated, and dif-
> ferent words can themselves often reinforce the overall dynamic
> effect of the repetition.[1]

By means of a key word, a narrator can link different stories impercep-
tibly, without interrupting the progress of the narrative, since inter-
ruption might damage the construction of the narrative. The author
attempts to convey a specific message to the reader, which he introduces
by repeating words or phrases.

The "key word" feature in the book of Chronicles evolved in a number
of ways: occasionally the Chronicler added a word or linguistic root, altering or replacing a word that he found in the earlier text; on other occasions, he used a word or root that already existed in the earlier text
and repeated it in the text(s) that he added.[2] This literary feature is
found in a number of places in the Hebrew Bible, as other scholars have
noted,[3] and is not unique to Chronicles.

17.1 1 Kings 22 recounts that Jehoshaphat, king of Judah, went to
visit Ahab, king of Israel. Ahab proposed that he and Jehoshaphat wage
war jointly on the king of Aram in order to win back Ramoth-gilead for
Israel.[4] Apparently, this summit meeting was held to consider a political and military alliance. Ahab's inquiries to his servants, הידעתם כי לנו
רמת גלעד ואנחנו מחשים מקחת אתה מיד מלך ארם 'Do you know that Ramoth-

---

1. Buber, "Keyword," 284.

2. See examples 17.3 and 17.4 below (p. 361).

3. See the various examples from narratives in the Pentateuch as cited by Buber,
"Keyword," 286–307; and also Rosenzweig, "Biblical Story," 12–16; Bar-Efrat, *Narrative Art*, 212–15, 281–82 (examples from the books of Genesis, Exodus, Samuel,
Job, and the stories of Elijah); for examples from poetry, see Watson, *Hebrew Poetry*,
287–95.

4. The reason for the confrontation apparently was that the king of Aram did not
meet his obligation to repatriate the towns his father had captured from Israel (1 Kgs
20:34)—specifically, Ramoth-gilead.

gilead belongs to us, yet we are doing nothing to take it out of the hand of the king of Aram?' (v. 3), provided the purpose and the justification for the war.

In 2 Chronicles 18 the Chronicler omitted Ahab's question to his servants. He presented Jehoshaphat's visit to the king of Israel as a normal "family visit":

> Jehoshaphat had wealth and honor in abundance.[5] He married into Ahab's family and after a few years went down to Ahab in Samaria. (vv. 1 ["addition"], 2a)

During this visit, the king of Israel bestowed great honor on Jehoshaphat and his men and also persuaded Jehoshaphat to take part in a battle, though the justification and aims of the battle are left unstated:

> Ahab sacrificed *an abundance* of sheep and cattle *in his honor* and in honor of the men who were with him, *and persuaded him* to go up against Ramoth-gilead. (v. 2b, an "addition")

The king of Israel proved persuasive: Jehoshaphat went up against Ramoth-gilead, despite the prophecy by Micaiah, son of Imlah, that the campaign would fail (2 Chr 18:18–27 // 1 Kgs 22:19–28). However, Jehoshaphat, the righteous king in whom "good things" were found (2 Chr 17:6; 19:3 "addition"; 21:32 // 1 Kgs 22:43), was helped by the LORD. This was despite the fact that he went out to war in his usual clothing and did not disguise himself (in other words, he did not camouflage his appearance or his true identity by appearing as an ordinary soldier).[6] Despite the assault on him by the Aramean chariot captains, "God *persuaded them* [to turn away from] him" (2 Chr 18:31). In the end, he returned "safely to his home in Jerusalem" (2 Chr 19:1, "addition").

On the other hand, the evil[7] king of Israel (1 Kgs 16:30–34; chap. 21), who had persuaded Jehoshaphat to enter the war, was struck by an arrow that had not specifically been aimed at him. This happened despite

---

5. Compare this phrase with 2 Chr 17:5b: "And all Judah brought tribute to Jehoshaphat, *and he had wealth and honor in abundance.*"

6. According to 1 Kgs 22:30 // 2 Chr 18:29, the king of Israel turned to Jehoshaphat and suggested: "Disguise yourself and enter the battle, but you dress in your usual attire." However, further along we are informed that only the king of Israel disguised himself and entered the battle. The assault of the chariot captains on Jehoshaphat indicates that he did not disguise himself and entered the battle dressed in his normal, royal attire. The word התחפש seems to refer to camouflaging one's appearance or true identity. Another opinion is voiced by Malamat, "Historical Background," 241 n. 39. He believes that להתחפש means "to take up one's instruments of warfare."

7. The Chronicler identifies the "king of Israel" as Ahab, and see 2 Chr 18:2, 3 in comparison with 1 Kgs 22:1–3. For a summary of the question of the identity of the "king of Israel" in 1 Kings 20 and 22, see Pitard, *Ancient Damascus*, 115–25.

the fact that he disguised himself before entering battle (2 Chr 18:29 //
1 Kgs 22:30) and despite the "armor" that he wore. "An archer pulled his
bow *unknowingly* and struck the king of Israel."[8] And note where: "between the armor and the breastplate" (2 Chr 18:33 // 1 Kgs 22:34)! Furthermore, he did not return home safely but died, as Micaiah, son of
Imlah, had prophesied (2 Chr 18:34 // 1 Kgs 22:35).

Note, then, that the root סות 'persuade' serves in 2 Chronicles 18 as a
key word: in imitation of the "persuading" done by the king of Israel
(ויסיתהו 'persuaded him', singular suffixed object), the Chronicler inserted the word ויסיתם 'persuading them' (plural suffixed object), the persuading being accomplished by the Lord this time. The king of Israel's
persuading put Jehoshaphat's life in danger, while the Lord's persuading of the Aramean chariot captains saved Jehoshaphat's life and returned him home safely. Furthermore, the Lord, who persuaded the
chariot captains to leave Jehoshaphat in order to save his life, is the one
who sent the spirit to "seduce Ahab"—that is, to persuade, urge, or drive
him[9] to go off to war in order to lose his life (2 Chr 18:19–22 // 1 Kgs
22:20–23).

1 Kings 22		*2 Chronicles 18*	
		ויהי ליהושפט עשר וכבוד לרב	1.
		ויתחתן לאחאב	
ויהי בשנה השלישית	2.	וירד לקץ שנים	2.
וירד יהושפט מלך יהודה			
אל מלך ישראל		אל אחאב לשמרון	
ויאמר מלך ישראל אל עבדיו	3.	*ויזבח לו אחאב צאן ובקר*	
הידעתם כי לנו רמת גלעד		*לרב ולעם אשר עמו*	
ואנחנו מחשים מקחת אתה		*ויסיתהו לעלות אל רמות גלעד*	
מיד מלך ארם			
ויאמר אל יהושפט	4.	ויאמר אחאב מלך ישראל	3.
		אל יהושפט מלך יהודה	
התלך אתי למלחמה רמת גלעד ...		התלך עמי רמת גלעד ...	
ויהי כראות שרי הרכב	32.	ויהי כראות שרי הרכב	31.
את יהושפט		את יהושפט	
והמה אמרו אך מלך ישראל הוא		והמה אמרו מלך ישראל הוא	
ויסרו עליו להלחם ויזעק יהושפט		ויסבו עליו להלחם ויזעק יהושפט	
		וה' עזרו ויסיתם אלהים ממנו	
ויהי כראות שרי הרכב	33.	ויהי כראות שרי הרכב	32.
כי לא מלך ישראל הוא		כי לא היה מלך ישראל	
וישבו מאחריו ...		וישבו מאחריו ...	

---

8. Perhaps the ו of לתמו בקשת משך ואיש 'an archer pulled his bow unknowingly'
should be identified as an oppositive *waw*, unlike the ו in ממנו אלהים ויסיתם עזרו וה'.

9. The verb פתה has a similar meaning to the verb סות; see also BDB 834b.

	1. Jehoshaphat had wealth and honor in abundance, and he married into Ahab's family.
2. In the third year Jehoshaphat, king of Judah, went down to the king of Israel.	2. After some years, he went down to Ahab in Samaria,
3. *The king of Israel said to his officials: "Do you know that Ramoth-gilead belongs to us, yet we are doing nothing to take it out of the hand of the king of Aram?"*	*and Ahab slaughtered an abundance of sheep and cattle in his honor and in honor of the men who were with him,* **and persuaded him** *to go up against Ramoth-gilead.*
4. And he said to Jehoshaphat,	3. Ahab, king of Israel, said to Jehoshaphat, king of Judah,
"Will you go with me to war at Ramoth-gilead?" . . .	"Will you go with me to Ramot Gilead?" . . .
32. When the chariot captains saw Jehoshaphat, they said, "Surely he is the king of Israel," and they turned to fight against him. Jehoshaphat cried out.	31. When the chariot captains saw Jehoshaphat, they said, "He is the king of Israel," and turned to fight him.
	Jehoshaphat cried out, *and the Lord helped him,* **persuading them** *to turn away from him.*
33. When the chariot captains saw that he was not the king of Israel, they turned back from pursuing him.	32. When the chariot captains saw he was not the king of Israel, they turned back from pursuing him.

17.2 2 Kgs 14:8 relates: מלך . . . אז שלח אמציה מלאכים אל יהואש בן יהואחז ישראל לאמר לכה נתראה פנים 'Then Amaziah sent messengers to Jehoash, son of Jehoahaz . . . , king of Israel, to say: "Let us confront each other (in battle)"'. In 2 Chr 25:17, the Chronicler altered the earlier text, writing: מלך ישראל לאמר לך נתראה . . . ויעץ אמציהו מלך יהודה וישלח אל יואש בן יהואחז פנים 'Then Amaziah, king of Judah, *held a consultation* and sent to Joash, son of Jehoahaz . . . , king of Israel, to say: "Let us confront each other (in battle)"'. Now, this "consultation" motif is found in other places in Chronicles as well, an integral part of the "democratization" feature so common in the book.[10] However, the purpose of the "addition" of ויעץ 'held a consultation' in the above text appears clearer in light of vv. 14–16 (also an "addition"), which the Chronicler inserted before his account of the battle between Amaziah and Jehoash. According to these verses, after his victory over Edom, Amaziah took the gods of

---

10. For this trend in the book of Chronicles, see Japhet, *Ideology*, 416–23.

the Seirites, "set them up as his idols, bowed down to them, and offered sacrifices to them" (v. 14).[11] Amaziah was not immediately punished for this, although a prophet of the Lord was sent to admonish him. He paid no attention to this reproof by the prophet: "Why have you sought a people's idols who could not save their own people from your hands?" (v. 15).[12] In fact, the king replied to the prophet with scorn mixed with a threat: הליועץ למלך נתנוך חדל לך למה יכוך 'Have you been appointed *a consultant* to the king? Stop it! Why should you be beaten?' The prophet stopped but concluded: ידעתי כי *יעץ* אלהים להשחיתך כי עשית זאת ולא שמעת *לעצתי* 'I know that God *has advised* destroying you because you have done this and have not listened *to my advice*' (2 Chr 25:16). In other words, Amaziah, who did not listen *to the advice* of the prophet but scorned and threatened him ("have you been appointed *a consultant* to the king?"), was "*advised*" by his servants in the consultation and suffered a defeat because "God had *advised* [determined] destroying him" (v. 16a).

The repeated use of the root יעץ in Chronicles turns it into a key word with a twofold purpose: *to emphasize and to link*: (1) *to emphasize* the stupidity of Amaziah, who sought the idols of Edom that could not save Edom's people from his own hand, rejected the advice of the Lord via the prophet who attempted to save him from being punished, and listened to the advice of his own servants, a procedure that brought disaster on him; (2) *to link* Amaziah's defeat to punishment for sins that the Chronicler added in vv. 14–16, in accordance with the system of retribution characteristic of his historiography.[13] The description of the sin (vv. 14–16) is further linked to the description of the punishment (vv. 17–24) by repeating the phrase דרש את אלהי העם/אדום:

25:15 למה דרשת *את אלהי העם* אשר לא הצילו את עמם מידך
Why *have you sought a people's idols* who could not save their own people from your hands?

25:20 ולא שמע אמציהו כי מהאלהים היא למען תתם ביד כי *דרשו את אלהי אדום*
But Amaziah did not listen, for this was God's doing, in order to deliver them into the hand [of their enemies], for *they had sought the gods of Edom*.

---

11. For the phenomenon of adopting god(s) of defeated people, compare for instance the adoption of the chief god of the Aramean pantheon, Adad, by Shalmaneser III, king of Assyria. In the Monolith Inscription, Shalmaneser relates: "I received silver and gold as their tribute and offered sacrifices before the Adad of Aleppo." See Luckenbill, *ARAB*, vol. 1, §610; Pritchard, *ANET*, 278b. Another explanation is suggested by Yeivin ("The Divided Kingdom," 159); he thinks that Amaziah brought the Seirite images to the Temple "in order to exhibit them before the Lord as a symbol of degradation," as Mesha, king of Moab, did to the vessels of the Lord that he took from Nebo and displayed before Kemosh (the Mesha Stele, lines 17–18).

12. For the theological aspect of this verse, see Japhet, *Ideology*, 50.

13. Cf. Curtis-Madsen, *Chronicles*, 444; Japhet, *Ideology*, 314.

Furthermore, v. 20 (an "addition" to 2 Kgs 14:11a, ולא שמע אמציה 'But
Amaziah did not listen'), כי מהאלהים היא למען תתם ביד כי דרשו את אלהי אדום
'for this was God's doing, in order to deliver them into the hand [of their
enemies], for they had sought the gods of Edom', which appears in the
description of the punishment, is merely the fulfillment of the words of
the prophet in the description of the sin: כי יעץ אלהים להשחיתך כי עשית זאת
ולא שמעת לעצתי 'God has advised destroying you because you have done
this and have not listened to my advice (v. 16, "addition").[14]

17.3 2 Kgs 16:7 reads: וישלח אחז מלאכים אל תגלת פלסר מלך אשור לאמר
עבדך ובנך אני עלה והושעני מכף מלך ארם ומכף מלך ישראל הקומים עלי 'Then Ahaz
sent messengers to Tiglath-pileser, king of Assyria, saying: "I am your
servant and your son! Come and save me from the hands of the king of
Aram and the king of Israel, who are attacking me"'. In the parallel
text, 2 Chr 28:16, the Chronicler wrote: בעת ההיא שלח המלך אחז על מלכי
אשור לעזר לו 'At that time King Ahaz sent for the kings of Assyria to help
him.' The root עזר (לעזר לו) 'to help' was used instead of the root ישע
(עלה והושעני) 'to save', apparently for the purpose of creating a "key
word" in the narrative of Ahaz's reign in the book of Chronicles. In
vv. 20–21, the Chronicler says that Tiglath-pileser, king of Assyria, did
indeed come but, despite the large sum of money with which Ahaz
bribed him, "he [Tiglath-pileser] caused him [Ahaz] trouble and did not
strengthen him . . . and was not a help to him (ולא לעזרה לו)."[15]

The root עזר 'help' also appears further along in the narrative in
Chronicles (28:22–23). According to this passage, after his failure with
the king of Assyria, Ahaz did not give up: he sacrificed to the gods of
Damascus "and said that, because the gods of the kings of Aram helped
(מעזרים)[16] them, I will sacrifice to them so that they may help me
(ויעזרוני)." But, as before, instead of receiving help, the king of Judah
achieved the exact opposite—failure: והם היו לו להכשילו ולכל ישראל 'they
served to ruin him and all Israel'.

17.4 The root עזר serves as a key word in 1 Chronicles 11–12 (11:16,
28; 12:1, 3, 7, 10, 18, 19, 20, 22, 23, 34, 39 [in the last two places it is the
Aramaic form, עדר, that appears]); and the root פרץ serves the same
function in 1 Chronicles 13–15 (13:2, 11; 14:11; 15:13), as other scholars
have noted.[17]

---

14. For clearer examples of this feature in the book of Chronicles, see chap. 7, §3
(pp. 159–165).

15. Contrary to 2 Kgs 16:9: "Then the king of Assyria listened to him. The king of
Assyria came to Damascus, captured it, exiled it[s inhabitants] to Kir, and put Rezin
to death."

16. A *Hiphil* participal form; compare לעזיר in 2 Sam 18:3.

17. For a detailed discussion of this, see Allen, "Kerygmatic Units," 26–28, and the
references to earlier literature there.

Chapter 18
Numerical Patterns

Numerical patterns are whole numbers used in a literary unit to structure a "pattern in which the number of component parts is X + 1, with the final component being the decisive one."[1] These whole numbers not only shape what is being said in the unit but also constitute a means of emphasizing the item that matters most. Sometimes the number is mentioned explicitly in the literary unit, but on other occasions the reader must discover it by reading the unit carefully. This literary feature is common in almost all genres of the Bible as well as in postbiblical literature.[2]

1. Shaping a Text in a "Three-Four" Numerical Pattern

18.1 2 Sam 5:14–16 lists the sons of David who were born in Jerusalem. In 1 Chr 3:5–8, the Chronicler adduced this list[3] and added the phrase ארבעה לבת־שוע בת עמיאל 'four by Bath-shua, daughter of Ammiel' (v. 5c)[4] after the first four names in the list:

2 Sam 5:14–16	1 Chr 3:5–8
14. ואלה שמות הילדים לו בירושלם	5a. ואלה נולדו לו בירושלים
שמוע ושובב ונתן ושלמה	b. שמעא[5] ושובב ונתן ושלמה
	c. *ארבעה לבת־שוע בת עמיאל*
15. ויבחר ואלישוע . . .	6. ויבחר ואלישמע . . .
14. These are the names of those who were born to him in Jerusalem:	5a. These were born to him in Jerusalem:

---

1. See Zakovitch, *Three-Four*, 2; also pp. 1, 3.

2. See Weiss, "Because Three . . . and Because Four," 307–18 (= idem, *Bible from Within*, 13–26); Zakovitch, *Three-Four*, 1, 2, 3, and earlier literature given there.

3. The list is repeated in 1 Chr 14:3–7, parallel to 2 Sam 5:14–16; for this, see example 15.3 (pp. 330–331).

4. "Bath-shua, daughter of Ammiel" is simply "Bathsheba, daughter of Eliam" (2 Sam 11:3). This phrase does not appear in the Syriac translation of this verse, which, in the opinion of Zakovitch, may well be because of an attempt at "harmonization with the two parallel lists and an escape from the difficulty in presenting Solomon as the fourth son" (Zakovitch, *Three-Four*, 61).

5. In the list in 1 Chr 14:4 the name is read as in Samuel: שמוע. In the LXX of 1 Chr 3:5 and 14:4, the form of the name is Σαμαα.

362

	Shammua, Shobab,	b.	Shimea, Shobab,
	Nathan, Solomon,		Nathan, and Solomon—
		c.	*four by Bath-shua,*
			daughter of Ammiel—
15.	Ibhar, Elishua, . . .		and Ibhar, Elishama, . . .

By adding this phrase, the Chronicler reformulated the structure and content of the list: he split the list into two parts, distinguishing between David's sons by Bath-shua (v. 5b) and his sons by his other, anonymous wives (vv. 6–8). Furthermore, he listed Solomon not only as the fourth son of David in the list of all his sons born to him in Jerusalem but also as the fourth and last son of Bath-shua, David's wife.[6] This "addition" in Chronicles contradicts the data provided in Samuel–Kings, according to which Bath-sheba bore David only *two sons*: the one died shortly after his birth (2 Sam 11:27; 12:15–19), and the other was Solomon (12:24–25), who in time inherited the throne (1 Kings 1). The narrative of the succession (2 Samuel 9–20; 1 Kings 1–2)[7] acknowledges no son by Bath-sheba other than Solomon. According to 2 Sam 12:15, 24–25, Solomon was Bath-sheba's *first* son to survive after the death of "the child," not her *fourth and last* son.[8]

Positioning Solomon in the fourth slot in the list of Bath-shua's sons apparently indicates his significance. In other words, though Solomon was the youngest of Bath-shua's sons, he was selected to succeed his father, David, on the throne, while his three older brothers were not worthy of the kingdom.[9]

Preferring a younger son over older brothers is a common motif both in biblical literature and in the literature of other nations.[10] This motif was thus formulated intentionally, here in a "three-four" numerical pattern. In light of this discussion, the following conclusions can be drawn:

1. Contrary to Mosis's theory,[11] the phrase ארבעה לבת־שוע בת עמיאל in 1 Chr 3:5c is not a late interpolation made by the redactor of the book of Chronicles. It was written by the author of the list because

---

6. On this issue, see also Kalimi, "Ethnographical Introduction," 556–58.

7. For the uniformity of the narrative in 2 Samuel 9–20 and 1 Kings 1–2, see, for example, Wellhausen, *Composition des Hexateuchs*, 225ff.; Rost, *Thronnachfolge Davids*; Whybray, *Succession Narrative*, 8.

8. Cf. Rudolph, *Chronik*, 26.

9. Cf. Zakovitch, *Three-Four*, 60–61.

10. In biblical literature, see, for example, Genesis 21 (Ishmael and Isaac); 25–27 (Esau and Jacob); Exod 4:10–17 (Aaron and Moses); 1 Sam 16:1–13 (David and his brothers). In general literature, see Thompson, *Motif Index*, R 15512, H 1242, M 312.2.

11. Mosis, *Untersuchungen*, 77–78 n. 86.

he wanted to stress the significance of Solomon, who had been chosen to succeed David on the throne, despite being the youngest of
Bath-sheba's sons. This "youngest-son-rises-to-power" literary motif, a common motif in ancient Near Eastern literature, was then formulated in a "three-four" numerical literary pattern here.

2. Discovering the revised literary formulation of the earlier text neces-
sitates a depreciation of our opinion of the historical veracity of
1 Chr 3:5. It is unlikely that alongside an ancient tradition that was
aware of only two sons born to Bath-sheba and David there was
another ancient tradition of four sons born to Bath-sheba and
David—a tradition that reached the Chronicler.[12] Moreover, it is
impossible to draw historical, chronological conclusions on the basis
of 1 Chr 3:5, as Yeivin did when he said, "According to 1 Chr 3:5,
[Solomon] was her fourth son, that is, he was born in the twenty-first
year of David's reign, at the very earliest."[13]

This feature is repeated both in the continuation of the list in Chronicles (v. 15) about the sons of Josiah and also in the list of the sons of
Saul (1 Chr 8:33 = 9:39):

18.2 1 Chr 3:15 reads: ובני יאשיהו הבכור יוחנן, השני יהויקים, השלשי צדקיהו,
הרביעי שלום 'The sons of Josiah: the firstborn was Johanan, the second
Jehoiakim, the third Zedekiah, and *the fourth Shallum'*. Shallum (= Jehoahaz)[14] was born after Jehoiakim and before Zedekiah. Placing him
in the fourth slot, after Zedekiah, stems from wanting to formulate the
list according to the "three-four" pattern; that is, Shallum, who succeeded his father on the throne and reigned before his brothers
Jehoiakim and Zedekiah (2 Kgs 23:30–24:17 // 2 Chr 36:1–10), is presented here in fourth place.[15]

18.3 The list of Saul's sons in 1 Chr 8:33 (= 9:39) reads: ושאול הוליד את
יהונתן ואת מלכי־שוע ואת אבינדב ואת אשבעל 'Saul begat Jonathan, Malchi-
shua, Abinadab, and Esh-baal'. Esh-baal (= Ish-bosheth = Ishui), who
succeeded his father, is here listed in fourth place for the sake of the
"three-four" pattern, in contrast to second place, where he appears in
1 Sam 14:49.[16] It is worthwhile mentioning that the Chronicler formed
the list under discussion according to a "three-four" pattern, though he
did not include the story of Esh-baal's kingdom in his writing.

---

12. Against Rudolph, *Chronik*, 26; Yeivin, "Bath-Sheba," 379; and Ahituv,
"Shima," 132, who treat the text in 1 Chr 3:5 as a reliable historical source.

13. See Yeivin, "David," 634.

14. For more details, see example 5.8 (p. 105).

15. Cf. Zakovitch, *Three-Four*, 62–63.

16. Ibid., 64–65.

18.4 An example similar to example 18.1 is found in 1 Chronicles 28 (an "addition"). This passage presents Solomon as the Lord's choice for the kingship[17] and does it in the "three-four" numerical-literary pattern (vv. 4b–5).[18]

1. כי <i>ביהודה</i> בחר לנגיד
2. ובבית יהודה <i>בית אבי</i>
3. ובבני אבי בי רצה להמליך על כל ישראל
4. ומכל בני כי רבים בנים נתן לי ה׳
ויבחר <i>בשלמה</i> בני לשבת על כסא מלכות ה׳ על ישראל [19]

1. For he selected *Judah* as monarch,
2. and in the house of Judah, *my ancestral house,*
3. from my father's sons, he wanted to install *me* as king over all Israel.
4. And of all my sons—for the Lord has given me many sons—he selected my son *Solomon* to sit on the throne of the kingdom of the Lord over Israel.

2. Creating an Alternate Tradition and Formulating It in a "Six-Seven" Numerical Pattern

18.5 In 1 Samuel 16–17, two traditions have survived concerning the number of Jesse's sons: according to one, the earlier tradition, Jesse had *four* sons: Eliab, Abinadab, Shammah, and David (see 16:6–9 and 11ff.; 17:13–14 and 17–18, 28). According to the other tradition (the later of

---

17. For the election of Solomon, see also 1 Chr 29:1. The subject is unique in its treatment by the Chronicler; cf. Japhet, *Ideology*, 92; Knoppers, "Genealogy of Judah," 15–19.

18. Some believe that vv. 4–5 are a later elaboration of the concept of election in vv. 6, 10, for these verses interrupt the sequence of the Lord's words in vv. 3, 6ff., while they deal with the election of Solomon as king rather than with Solomon, the builder of the Temple, which appears further along in the speech; see Braun, "Temple Builder," 582 n. 4; idem, *1 Chronicles*, 268–69. It seems that this "elaboration" should not be dated to a late period, thus not attributing it to the Chronicler. Linguistically and stylistically the text suits the Chronicler, while the concepts embedded in it do not contradict those of the Chronicler. On the contrary, "in Chronicles, Solomon's election is associated with the construction of the Temple and directly linked to Nathan's prophecy that the Temple will be built by one of David's sons (1 Chr 28:5–16)" (Japhet, *Ideology*, 450).

19. Cf. Zakovitch, *Three-Four*, 140. On pp. 49–60, Zakovitch elaborates on the succession narrative in the book of Samuel, noting that there too "Solomon is presented on the fourth rung, on the top rung, of the pattern" (after Amnon, Absalom, and Adonijah). In one tradition in 1 Samuel, the choice of David himself is formulated in a "three-four" pattern; for this, see below, example 18.5.

the two), Jesse had double that number of sons, *eight:* the above-mentioned four, whose names appear in the text, and four whom the text leaves nameless (see 16:10–11; 17:12). Each of these traditions is formulated according to a different numerical pattern. One pattern uses the graduated numerical *"three-four"* pattern. That is, the *three* oldest sons—Eliab, Abinadab, and Shammah—were not qualified for the throne (16:6–9) and did not have the strength to fight the Philistine giant Goliath (17:11, 24–25). The *fourth* and youngest son, David, was discriminated against by his father and his brothers,[20] but he was the one anointed king over Israel (16:11–13; and he was the one who killed Goliath, 17:49–51). The other tradition has a graduated numerical *"seven-eight"* pattern. The *seven* oldest sons were not qualified for the throne (16:6–10), while the *eighth* and youngest son, David, was anointed king (and killed Goliath).[21]

The Chronicler, however, did not use either of these traditions concerning the sons of Jesse. He created an alternate list, in which he set the number of Jesse's sons at *seven* (1 Chr 2:13–15): ואישי הוליד את בכרו את אליאב ואבינדב השני ושמעא השלישי, נתנאל הרביעי, רדי החמישי, אצם הששי, דויד השבעי[22] 'Jesse became the father of Eliab his firstborn, Abinadab the second, Shimea the third, Nethanel the fourth, Raddai the fifth, Ozem the sixth, and David the seventh'. Zakovitch[23] believes that the transition from the graduated "seven-eight" pattern in 1 Samuel 16–17 to the graduated "six-seven" pattern in 1 Chr 2:13–15 stems from the Chronicler's misunderstanding of the text: he apparently erred in comprehending the verse ויעבר ישי שבעת בניו לפני שמואל 'then Jesse made his seven sons pass by before Samuel', in 1 Sam 16:10, thinking that David was included amongst them. The verses in Samuel concerning this tradition are so clear, however, that it is difficult to assume that the Chronicler could have erred in interpreting them, for immediately after "then Jesse made *his seven sons* pass before Samuel" the text continues: ויאמר שמואל אל ישי: לא בחר ה' באלה. ויאמר שמואל אל ישי: התמו הנערים? ויאמר: עוד שאר הקטן, והנה רעה בצאן 'Then Samuel said to Jesse, "The Lord has not selected these." Then Samuel asked Jesse, "Are these all your sons?" He replied, "The youngest is still left, but he is shepherding the flock"' (1 Sam

---

20. David was neither invited to the sacrificial feast with Samuel, the prophet, nor found fit to go out with his brothers to battle. When he appeared at the battlefield, Eliab, his oldest brother, scolded him (1 Sam 16:7, 11; 17:13–14, 28).

21. For a detailed analysis of both traditions and the relationship between them, as well as a discussion of the MT and LXX[B] of 1 Samuel 17, see Zakovitch, *Three-Four*, 42–27. For the narrative of David and Goliath according to the MT and LXX, see Barthélemy, Gooding, Lust, and Tov, *David and Goliath*.

22. The Chronicler took the names of the first three from 1 Sam 16:6–9 and invented the other three names; see example 3.17 (pp. 75–76).

23. Zakovitch, *Three-Four*, 49.

16:10–11). Furthermore, 1 Sam 17:12 states explicitly: ‏ודוד בן איש אפרתי‎ ‏הזה מבית לחם יהודה, ושמו ישי, ולו שמנה בנים‎ 'David was the son of an Eph-rathite from Bethlehem in Judah, named Jesse, who had *eight sons*'.

It thus seems that listing Jesse's sons as seven in number and orga-nizing them according to the numerical pattern "six-seven"—that is, the *six* oldest sons of Jesse were disqualified for the kingship, while the *sev-enth* son, David, was elected to succeed Saul[24]—was not done by chance. Apparently, the Chronicler determined the number of Jesse's sons as *seven* and listed David in the *seventh* slot because he attributed special significance to the mystical whole number *seven*. This number has a unique aura and denotes an unusual event with greater power than the numbers "four" or "eight," both in biblical and in general literature.[25] In fact, who could be worthier than David, the founder of the royal Israelite dynasty and one of the most important and prominent figures in the Chronistic history, to be included within the framework of the sanctified number "*seven*" and to be positioned in the seventh place? The postbib-lical Jewish sages and artists were already sensitive to this (*Lev. Rab.* 29:9; Midrash Psalms *Shocher-Tov* 9:11): "All sevenths are always fa-vored . . . the seventh son is favored, and it is said: 'David—the seventh' (1 Chr 2:15)."[26]

That the number "seven" is deliberately involved in the formulation of the list of Jesse's sons is also supported to some degree by the intro-ductory list in 1 Chr 2:10–12, which presents *seven* generations from

---

24. For additional examples of the "six-seven" numerical pattern in the Bible, see ibid., 38–39 and 47–49. See there also a review of the attempts in Jewish exegesis, from Josephus through the Peshiṭta and postbiblical sages and including the medi-eval commentators, to deal with the contradiction between the tradition in Samuel, with Jesse's *eight* sons, and in Chronicles, which lists only *seven*. In the KRT epic, col. II, lines 23–24 say that King KRT's bride will bring him *seven* sons / or even *eight*, and that the last of them will inherit the throne. Gordon, in his criticism of Pritchard (Gordon, *"ANET,"* 160–61) and also in his criticism of Cassuto (Gordon, *"Anath,"* 180–81), says that a similar trope of seven/eight sons of Jesse was the basis for the story of David's ascension to the throne; the part referring to Jesse's *seven* sons was preserved in Chronicles, while the part referring to *eight* survived in the prose of Samuel. Recently, McCarter (*I Samuel*, 276) cited Gordon's opinion as a possible so-lution to the problem. It seems, however, that Gordon's opinion is completely ground-less, as correctly noted by Zakovitch, *Three-Four*, 49. It should also be noted that there is no basis whatever for viewing the narratives of David's ascension in the Bible as an epos.

25. For the significance and unique nature of the number "seven" in the Bible, see Segal, "Numerals," 19; in general literature, see Noy, *Form and Content*, 266–70; cf. Sarfati, "Number," 182–83.

26. On the number of Jesse's sons in the biblical writings, Judeo-Hellenistic arts, rabbinic literature, and Medieval Christian art, see in detail Kalimi, "Transmission of Tradition," 1–9. In 1 Chr 3:24, Anani, the last descendant of David, also appears in the seventh place; see Kalimi, "Ethnographical Introduction," 556 n. 2.

Ram to Jesse: Ram, Amminadab, Nahshon, Salma, Boaz, Obed, and Jesse.[27] In other words, there were *seven* forefathers before David, and Jesse had *seven* sons, David being the *seventh*.

In summation, in place of the traditions regarding the number of Jesse's sons in the book of Samuel, based on the literary numerical patterns of "three-four" and "seven-eight," the Chronicler created an alternate "tradition," formulating it in a "six-seven" numerical pattern. There is thus no reason to prefer the list of Jesse's sons in Chronicles to the list in the book of Samuel.[28]

---

27. The list appears in Ruth 4:20–22 as well. Noth (*ÜS*, 119–20 n. 5; ET: *Chronicler's History*, 151 n. 27) and Rudolph (*Chronik*, 16), as well as those scholars who consider Ruth to have been composed in the Second Temple period believe that the list in Ruth was taken from Chronicles. As they put it, the list in Chronicles is fuller than the one in Ruth and includes the names of David's brothers! But the names Nethanel, Raddai, and Ozem in the list of David's brothers seem to be of late vintage (for this, see above, example 3.17, pp. 75–76). At any rate, because of the lack of data, it is difficult to determine who took the list from whom, and it is no less problematic to claim "that these two sources are taken from an early genealogical document," as claimed by Malamat ("King Lists," 41) and, in other words, by Myers (*I Chronicles*, 13–14): "Both lists may go back to an original temple source."

28. Against Noth, *ÜS*, 119–20 n. 5, 132–33 (ET: *Chronicler's History*, 52, 151 n. 27); Rudolph, *Chronik*, 16–17; Myers, *I Chronicles*, 13–14; Williamson, *Chronicles*, 51.

Chapter 19
Generalization and Specification

Occasionally, the Chronicler reshaped passages from Samuel–Kings, as well as passages that appear only in his own work, with a structure that moves

1. from general to specific or
2. from specific to general or
3. from general to specific and back to general.

These kinds of structures already existed in earlier biblical literature, including works by the Deuteronomistic historian. For examples of "general to specific" structures, see Gen 9:5; 27:3; Exod 7:19 (and see R. Abraham ibn Ezra's commentary on this verse); Lev 1:2; 1 Kgs 9:10; 2 Sam 8:11–12 // 1 Chr 18:11. For structures that move "from specific to general," see Exod 34:18–24; 2 Kgs 19:37 // Isa 37:38. For an example of movement "from general to specific and back to general," see Deut 14:26.

These literary structures were observed by postbiblical Jewish sages, who first described the phenomena in guidelines, or "rules," for interpreting the Bible. In Tannaitic literature, the fourth of the thirteen rules with which R. Ishmael interpreted the Torah relates to lines of thought that progress "from general to specific," and similarly, in Hillel's seven rules (*Sifra de-bei Rav* [also known as *Torat Kohanim*] 1, chap. 3). *Aboth de Rabbi Nathan*, Version A, chap. 37, which is parallel to the last source, reads: "from general to specific," "and from specific to general" (compare *t. Sanh.* 7.11). "From general to specific and back to general" is R. Ishmael's sixth rule, out of thirteen.

1. From General to Specific

19.1 In 2 Chr 2:16–17[17–18] the Chronicler's narrative moves "from general to specific." First he recorded the total number of laborers who took part in the construction of the Temple (v. 16[17]), and then he detailed the number of the various professionals, one after another (v. 17[18]), parallel to the earlier passage in 1 Kings 5:

369

1 Kgs 5:29–30[15–16]	2 Chr 2:16–17[17–18]

29. ויהי לשלמה   16. ויספר שלמה כל האנשים הגירים

אשר בארץ ישראל אחרי הספר אשר

ספרם דויד אביו וימצאו

מאה וחמשים אלף ושלשת אלפים

ושש מאות

שבעים אלף נשא סבל   17. ויעש מהם

ושמנים אלף חצב בהר ...   שבעים אלף סבל

30. שלשת אלפים ושלש מאות   ושמנים אלף חצב בהר

הרדים בעם העשים במלאכה   ושלשת אלפים ושש מאות[1]

מנצחים להעביד את העם

29. Solomon had	16. Then Solomon counted all the aliens in the land of Israel after the census that David, his father, had taken. And there were found to be *one hundred fifty-three thousand six hundred.*
seventy thousand laborers and eighty thousand hewers in the mountains ...	17. He assigned them seventy thousand as laborers, eighty thousand as hewers in the mountains,
30. three thousand three hundred men supervising those doing the work.	and three thousand six hundred supervisers to keep the people at work.

19.2 2 Kgs 22:9 relates that Shaphan the scribe reported to King Josiah about the execution of his instructions concerning repairs being made to the Temple (vv. 3–5). In 2 Chr 34:16b, the Chronicler first inserted *a general report*. Only then did he follow it up with *the details* from the earlier text, thus creating a "general to specific" structure:

2 Kgs 22:9	2 Chr 34:16–17

ויבא שפן הספר אל המלך   ויבא שפן את הספר אל המלך[2]

וישב את המלך דבר ויאמר   וישב עוד את המלך דבר לאמר

---

1. On the difference between the numbers "three thousand three hundred" (1 Kings 5) and "three thousand six hundred" (2 Chronicles 2), see example 14.3 n. 11 (p. 302).

2. The reference to bringing the book to the king does not match the narrative further along, in v. 18: "Then Shaphan, the scribe, told the king, 'Hilkiah gave me a book.'" The Chronicler (or a later copyist-scribe) mistakenly read ויבא שפן את הַסֵּפֶר 'then Shaphan brought the book' in place of ויבא שפן הַסֹּפֵר 'then Shaphan, the scribe, came', because of the similar consonants (vowel-signs not having been added yet). See Curtis-Madsen, *Chronicles*, 508–9; Benzinger, *Chronik*, 131.

כל אשר נתן ביד עבדיך הם עשים

התיכו עבדיך את הכסף הנמצא בבית
ויתנהו על ⁻יד עשי המלאכה
המפקדים בית ה׳

ויתיכו את הכסף הנמצא בבית ה׳
ויתנדהו על יד המפקדים ועל יד
עשי המלאכה ³

Then Shaphan the scribe came to
the king, and reported to the
king,

Then Shaphan brought the book to
the king and further reported to the
king,

**"Everything you have given your
servants they are doing:**

"Your servants have melted down   *they have melted down*
the silver in the House   *the silver in the House of the Lord,*
and have given it to the workmen   *and have given it to those in*
in charge of the House of the   *charge and to the workmen."*
Lord."

In both of these examples, the Chronicler placed a "general" section before the "specific" information that he cited from the book of Kings. However, in the next three examples below, "specific" information appears in
the book of Chronicles before the "general" material quoted from Kings,
perhaps in order to minimize the content of the earlier text in favor of
the "the specific" information cited.

19.3 1 Kgs 9:25 says that King Solomon offered sacrifices "three
times a year" on the altar that he erected to the Lord. In 2 Chr 8:12–13
the Chronicler lists the names of the festivals in detail, בחג המצות ובחג
השבעות ובחג הסכות 'on the Festival of Unleavened Bread and on the Festival of Weeks and on the Festival of Tabernacles', alongside the general
expression שלוש פעמים בשנה 'three times a year'.[4] In this way, the Chronicles narrative is constructed "from general to specific."

19.4 According to 1 Kgs 5:21[7], Hiram applied a general description
to Solomon, calling him "a wise son." In 2 Chr 2:11[12], however, the
Chronicler added detail to the general expression: יודע שכל ובינה וכו׳ 'en-
dowed with intelligence and understanding', and so on:

1 Kgs 5:21[7]	*2 Chr 2:11[12]*	
ויאמר [חירם]	ויאמר חורם	
ברוך ה׳ היום	ברוך ה׳ אלהי ישראל . . .	
אשר נתן לדוד	אשר נתן לדויד המלך	
בן חכם	**בן חכם**	general

---

3. The Chronicler may have separated עשי המלאכה 'the workmen' from המפקדים
'those in charge' because he thought the latter were Levites (see v. 12); cf. Curtis-
Madsen, *Chronicles*, 509.

4. For further discussion of these verses, see example 3.4 (pp. 63–64) and example
12.25 (p. 241).

	יודע שכל ובינה specific
על העם הרב הזה	אשר יבנה בית לה' ובית למלכותו
Then [Hiram] said,	Then Hiram said,
"Blessed be the Lord today,	"Blessed be the Lord, God of Israel, . . .
who has given David	who has given King David
a wise son	**a wise son**
	endowed with intelligence and understanding to build a House to the Lord and a palace for his kingdom."
over this great people."	

In these "additions" inserted by the Chronicler, he not only glorifies the image of Solomon but also apparently tries to say that David's blessing to his son Solomon came true: והצלחת ובנית בית ה' אלהיך . . . אך יתן לך ה' שכל ובינה ויצוך על ישראל 'that *you may succeed in building the House of the Lord* your God . . . may the Lord *give you intelligence and understanding*, so that when he gives you charge over Israel . . .' (1 Chr 22:11–12, "an addition").[5]

19.5 1 Kgs 15:7b relates: ומלחמה היתה בין אבים ובין ירבעם 'There was war between Abijam and Jeroboam'. In 2 Chr 13:2b, the Chronicler presented this passage, which is "general," and added a "specific" description of the war between Abijah/Abijam and Jeroboam: ויאסר אביה את המלחמה בחיל גבורי מלחמה . . . וירבעם ערך עמו מלחמה 'Then Abijah waged war with an army of warriors . . . and Jeroboam waged war against him' (13:3 [13:3–20 is an "addition"]).[6]

19.6 The author of the book of Kings did not note the precise location of Solomon's Temple. In 2 Chr 3:1, the Chronicler added the location of the Temple in great detail. This description was formed in a tricyclical pattern, moving *from the general to the specific*. First, the name of the city in which the Temple was erected is given—בירושלם; then comes the name of the hill in Jerusalem—בהר המוריה; and finally, the special area on the hill—[7]במקום אשר הכין דויד בגרן ארנן היבוסי 'in the place that David had prepared, on the threshing floor of Ornan, the Jebusite':

5. Compare with 1 Kgs 5:9[4:29]: ויתן אלהים חכמה לשלמה ותבונה הרבה מאד ורחב לב כחול אשר על שפת הים 'God gave Solomon great wisdom as well as much insight, and breadth of understanding as vast as the sand on the seashore'. On this feature in the Chronistic history, see above, chap. 7, §3 (pp. 159–165).

6. Cf. Rudolph, *Chronik*, 235.

7. This verse must be rearranged to be comprehensible: from MT אשר הכין במקום במקום אשר הכין דויד בגרן ארנן היבוסי to דויד בגרן ארנן היבוסי; and in fact this is the wording in the LXX, Vulgate, and Peshiṭta. On this issue, see in detail above, example 3.22 (pp. 82–83).

1 Kgs 6:1

2 Chr 3:1–2

ויחל שלמה לבנות את בית ה׳
בירושלם
בהר המוריה
אשר נראה [ה׳] לדויד אביהו
אשר הכין במקום דויד
בגרן ארנן היבוסי

ויהי בשמונים שנה וארבע מאות
שנה לצאת בני ישראל מארץ מצרים
בשנה הרביעית בחדש זו הוא החדש
השני למלך שלמה על ישראל
ויבן הבית לה׳

ויחל לבנות
בחדש השני בשני בשנת ארבע
למלכותו ⁸

Then Solomon began to build the
House of the Lord *in Jerusalem*
on Mt. Moriah,
where [the Lord] appeared to David,
his father,
at the place that David had prepared,
on the threshing floor of Ornan,
the Jebusite.

In the four hundred eightieth
year after the Israelites' exodus
from the land of Egypt, in the
fourth year of Solomon's reign
over Israel, in the month of Ziv,
which is the second month,
he began to build the
House of the Lord.

Then he began to build in the
second month, on the second day,
in the fourth year of his reign.

19.7 In the "addition" to 1 Kgs 22:32 that the Chronicler placed in 2 Chr 18:31b, describing the rescue of Jehoshaphat, king of Judah, from the Aramean chariot captains in the battle at Ramoth-gilead, he structured his presentation "from general to specific":

---

8. The omission of the dating with respect to the exodus from Egypt apparently stems not only from literary considerations (i.e., that the Chronicler tried to avoid a doubled notation of the date of the founding of the Temple—one stemming from the date of the exodus from Egypt and immediately afterward another stemming from the number of years of Solomon's reign) but also from ideological considerations: he may have tried to cut off all links between the exodus from Egypt and the building of the Temple; for this, see Japhet, *Ideology*, 381; Amit, "Exodus Tradition," 143–44; Hoffman, *Doctrine of the Exodus*, 187–88.

1 Kgs 22:32	*2 Chr 18:31*
ויהי כראות שרי הרכב את יהושפט	ויהי כראות שרי הרכב את יהושפט
והמה אמרו: אך מלך ישראל הוא,	והמה אמרו: מלך ישראל הוא,
ויסרו עליו להלחם ויזעק יהושפט	ויסבו עליו להלחם ויזעק יהושפט
	וה׳ עזרו
	ויסיתם אלהים ממנו
Now when the chariot captains saw Jehoshaphat, they said, "Surely he is the king of Israel," and they moved toward him to fight, and Jehoshaphat shouted out.	Now when the chariot captains saw Jehoshaphat, they said, "He is the king of Israel," and they surrounded him to fight. Jehoshaphat shouted out, **and the Lord helped him.** *God diverted them away from him.*

The general description is **וה׳ עזרו**; the specific follows, *ויסיתם אלהים ממנו*, describing how the Lord helped Jehoshaphat and saved him from the chariot captains.

19.8 According to 2 Chronicles 13 (an "addition"), during a speech delivered by Abijah, king of Judah, from the summit of Mt. Zemaraim, Jeroboam, king of Israel, ambushed him from behind: ויהיו לפני יהודה והמארב מאחריהם 'they were in front of Judah, and the ambush was behind them' (v. 13). Thus, the Judeans had to fight on two fronts at once. The Judeans and the priests prayed and shouted out to the Lord, who sent them salvation. The structure of the account of the Lord's salvation of Judah moves "from general to specific" (vv. 15–20):

ויהי בהריע איש יהודה		
והאלהים נגף את ירבעם וכל ישראל לפני אביה ויהודה	general	(a)
וינוסו בני־ישראל מפני יהודה,	specific	
ויתנם אלהים בידם		
ויכו בהם אביה ועמו מכה רבה		
ויפלו חללים מישראל חמש מאות אלף איש בחור		
ויכנעו בני־ישראל בעת ההיא . . .		
וירדף אביה אחרי ירבעם		
וילכד ממנו ערים	general	(b)
את בית־אל ואת בנותיה	specific	
ואת ישנה ואת בנותיה		
ואת עפרון ובנתיה		

Now when the men of Judah shouted,

   (a) general   **God defeated Jeroboam and all Israel before Abijah and Judah.**

         specific   *The Israelites fled before Judah,*
                 and God delivered them into their hands.
                 Abijah and his army defeated them roundly.

Five hundred thousand chosen men of Israel fell dead,
and the Israelites surrendered at that time. . . .

(b) general **Then [Abijah] captured towns from him:**
  specific *Bethel and its villages,*
  Jeshanah and its villages,
  and Ephron and its villages.

19.9 Similar to the previous example and using almost the same language, style, and structure is the Chronicler's description of the defeat of Zerah the Kushite by Asa, king of Judah in 2 Chr 14:11–14a ("addition"). At first he wrote in a general fashion: ויגף ה' את הכושים לפני אסא ולפני יהודה 'Then the Lord defeated the Kushites before Asa and before Judah'. Immediately afterward, he described the Kushite defeat in great detail:

וינסו הכושים
וירדפם אסא והעם אשר עמו עד לגרר
ויפל מכושים לאין להם מחיה כי נשברו לפני ה' ולפני מחנהו
וישאו שלל הרבה מאד
ויכו את כל הערים סביבות גרר כי היה פחד ה' עליהם . . .
ויבזו את כל הערים כי בזה רבה היתה בהם
וגם אהלי מקנה הכו
וישבו צאן לרב וגמלים

The Kushites fled.
Asa and the army that was with him pursued them to Gerar,
and the Kushites fell until none remained alive, for they were
  shattered before the Lord and his army.
And they carried off a great deal of booty.
They defeated all the towns around Gerar, for the fear of the Lord
  was on them. . . .
They plundered all the towns, for there was much spoil in them.
They also attacked the tents of those who had cattle
and carried off sheep in abundance and camels.

19.10 In 1 Chr 15:16 (an "addition"), the Chronicler relates: ויאמר דויד לשרי הלוים להעמיד את אחיהם המשררים 'Then David ordered the Levite officers to appoint their kindred as musicians',

  general בכלי שיר
    with musical instruments—
  specific נבלים וכנרות ומצלתים משמיעים
    להרים בקול לשמחה
    harps, lyres, and sounding cymbals—
    to play loudly for joy.

19.11 We read in 1 Chr 28:1 (an "addition"):

וַיַּקְהֵל דָּוִיד

general   **אֶת כָּל שָׂרֵי יִשְׂרָאֵל**

specific   *שָׂרֵי הַשְּׁבָטִים וְשָׂרֵי הַמַּחְלְקוֹת הַמְשָׁרְתִים אֶת הַמֶּלֶךְ וְשָׂרֵי הָאֲלָפִים*

וְשָׂרֵי הַמֵּאוֹת וְשָׂרֵי כָל רְכוּשׁ וּמִקְנֶה לַמֶּלֶךְ וּלְבָנָיו, עִם הַסָּרִיסִים וְהַגִּבּוֹרִים

וּלְכָל גִּבּוֹר חַיִל

אֶל יְרוּשָׁלָם

Then David assembled
all the officers of Israel:
the officers of the tribes, the officials of the divisions serving the king, the captains of thousands, the captains of hundreds, the stewards of all the property and cattle belonging to the king and his sons, with the eunuchs, the mighty warriors, and all the warriors to Jerusalem.

19.12 According to the book of Chronicles, after the death of Jehoiada, the priest, Joash, king of Judah, abandoned the Lord and his Temple to worship "the Asherim and the images" (2 Chr 24:17–18, an "addition"). Before Joash and his people were punished for these sins, they were admonished by prophets. The prophets' admonition is presented in a "general to specific" structure (vv. 19–20, an "addition"):

general   **וַיִּשְׁלַח בָּהֶם נְבִאִים** לַהֲשִׁיבָם אֶל ה' וַיָּעִידוּ בָם וְלֹא הֶאֱזִינוּ

Then **He sent them prophets** to bring them back to the Lord, and they testified against them, but they would not listen. (v. 19)

specific   *וְרוּחַ אֱלֹהִים לָבְשָׁה אֶת זְכַרְיָה בֶּן יְהוֹיָדָע הַכֹּהֵן*

וַיַּעֲמֹד מֵעַל לָעָם וַיֹּאמֶר לָהֶם: כֹּה אָמַר הָאֱלֹהִים... [9]

The spirit of God took possession of *Zechariah, son of Jehoiada the priest,* who stood up above the people and said to them: "This is what God has said. . . ." (v. 20)

19.13 2 Chr 35:7 (an "addition"), the narrative about Josiah's Passover, relates:

	וַיָּרֶם יֹאשִׁיָּהוּ לִבְנֵי הָעָם	Josiah contributed to the people
general	**צֹאן**	**a flock,**
specific	*כְּבָשִׂים וּבְנֵי עִזִּים*[10]	*lambs and kids . . .*
	הַכֹּל לַפְּסָחִים לְכָל הַנִּמְצָא	for the Passover sacrifices for everyone present.

---

9. Cf. Japhet, *Ideology*, 174.

10. Cf. Exod 12:5: מִן הַכְּבָשִׂים וּמִן הָעִזִּים תִּקָּחוּ 'you may take it from the sheep or from the goats'.

19.14–15 For additional examples, see 1 Chr 10:13a (G), 13b (S);[11] 2 Chr 28:5 (G), 28:6–7, and perhaps also 28:8 (S).[12]

2. From Specific to General

19.16 1 Kgs 5:20[6] says that Solomon addressed Hiram: ועתה צוה ויכרתו לי ארזים מן הלבנון[13] 'Now, order [your men] to cut me down *cedars* from Lebanon'. In reply to Solomon, Hiram said: שמעתי את אשר שלחת אלי אני אעשה כל חפצך בעצי ארזים ובעצי ברושים 'I have heard the message that you sent me; I will do whatever you desire with *cedar* and *cypress* trees' (v. 22).

The Chronicler, however, provided details of other kinds of trees in Solomon's appeal to Hiram (2 Chr 2:7), and in Hiram's reply to Solomon he used the general word, עצים (2:15):

2:7	specific	ושלח לי עצי ארזים ברושים ואלגומים[14] מהלבנון
		and send me *cedar, cypress, and sandalwood trees* from Lebanon
2:15	general	ואנחנו נכרת **עצים מן הלבנון** ככל צרכך
		and we will cut down **trees from Lebanon**, according to all your needs

These changes created a "specific to general" structure in the narrative about the exchange of letters between Solomon and Hiram in 2 Chronicles 2.

19.17 2 Sam 10:6 relates that the Ammonites hired את ארם בית רחוב ואת ארם צובא . . . ואת מלך מעכה . . . ואיש טוב 'Arameans from Beth-rehob and

---

11. Cf. Rudolph, *Chronik*, 97.

12. Cf. Japhet, *Ideology*, 315 n. 182.

13. Instead of the word ארזים, the LXX has: ξύλα 'trees'. This seems to be an emendation in light of the content of v. 22, according to which Hiram tells Solomon that he will provide him not only with ארזים but also with ברושים 'cypresses'. In fact, as Burney says, ארזים were mentioned specifically because they were the most important trees (*Kings*, 54). The LXX emendation may also have been influenced by the rest of this verse: כי אתה ידעת כי אין בנו איש יודע לכרת עצים כצדנים 'for you know that we have no one who knows how to cut *trees* down like the Sidonians'. Benzinger, Stade, and Šanda, however, prefer the LXX version.

14. Sandalwood (אלגומים) trees are not mentioned in the exchange of letters between Solomon and Hiram in the book of Kings. This word seems to have been added by the Chronicler to the list of trees from Lebanon. For the question of the identity of this tree with the *elammakku*-tree in Akkadian sources, for the possibility of growing this tree in northern Syria in ancient times, and for the question of its botanical identity today, see Greenfield-Mayerhofer, "ʾAlgummim/ʾAlmuggim," 83–89, especially 86–87. For the form אלגומים, see also 2 Chr 9:10, 11 as compared with 1 Kgs 10:11, 12—אלמגים (inverse letter order?).

Arameans from Zoba ... and the king of Maacah ... and the men of
Tob'. Further on, we read that David dispatched Joab and all the warriors and that the Ammonites came out and waged "war at the entrance
to the gate," while "the Arameans from Zoba and Rehob and the men
of Tob and Maacah were by themselves out in the field" (v. 8).[15] The
Chronicler listed in detail the kingdoms from which the Ammonites
hired mercenaries: מן ארם נהרים ומן ארם מעכה ומצובה רכב ופרשים ... ואת מלך
מעכה ואת עמו 'from Aram-naharaim, Aram-maacah, and Zoba—chariots
and cavalry ... and the king of Maacah and his army' (1 Chr 19:6–7).
However, further along he listed them in general terms: ויצאו בני־עמון
ויערכו מלחמה פתח העיר והמלכים אשר באו לבדם בשדה 'Then the Ammonites
went out and waged war at the entrance to the city, **while the kings
who had come** remained by themselves out in the field' (v. 9). This
change created a progression "from specific to general" in Chronicles.

19.18 In 1 Chr 16:42 (an "addition"), the Chronicler formulated his
words in a "specific to general" structure:

	ועמהם הימן וידותון	Heman and Jeduthu had with them
specific	חצצרות ומצלתים למשמיעים	*trumpets and cymbals for music*
general	וכלי שיר האלהים [16]	**and musical instruments for sacred song.**

3. From General to Specific and Back to General

19.19 The Chronicler shaped his description of the dimensions of the
wings of the cherubs in 1 Kgs 6:24–25 and 27b, among others, "from
general to specific and back to general." He lists the overall length of the
four cherubic wings at the beginning and at the end of his description,
while in the middle he lists the length of each wing in detail:

1 Kgs 6:24–25, 27b	*2 Chr 3:11–13*
	וכנפי הכרובים ארכם
	אמות עשרים
וחמש אמות כנף הכרוב האחת	כנף האחד לאמות חמש ...
וחמש אמות כנף הכרוב השנית	והכנף האחרת אמות חמש ...

---

15. The list of names in this verse is presented chiastically to the list of names in
v. 6:

v. 6:   ארם בית רחוב ואת ארם צובא ואת מלך מעכה ... ואיש טוב
v. 8:   ארם צובא ורחוב ואיש טוב ומעכה

16. This verse is presented chiastically parallel to 1 Chr 15:16.

עשר אמות מקצות כנפיו ועד קצות
כנפיו ועשר באמה הכרוב השני . . .
ויפרשו את כנפי הכרבים

וכנף הכרוב האחד *אמות חמש* . . .
והכנף האחרת *אמות חמש* . . .
כנפי הכרובים האלה פרשים
אמות עשרים . . .

The cherubs' wings extended
twenty cubits;
the one wing—*five cubits* . . .

Five cubits was the length of
one wing of the cherub,
and *five cubits* the length of
the other wing of the cherub;
it was ten cubits from the tip of
one wing to the tip of the other.
The second cherub also measured
ten cubits. . . . They spread the
wings of the cherubs.

and the other wing—*five cubits* . . .

and the one cherub's wing—
five cubits . . .
and the other wing—*five cubits*. . . .
The wings of these cherubs
when spread was
twenty cubits . . .

19.20 In 2 Kgs 12:12–15 the author says that the silver donated for repairing the Temple was used only for this purpose and was not used to make vessels. In contrast to this, 2 Chr 24:12–14a states that, after the House of the Lord had been completely restored, vessels for Temple service were made from the leftover silver:

2 Kgs 12:14–15

2 Chr 24:14a
וככלותם הביאו לפני המלך
ויהוידע את שאר הכסף
ויעשהו כלים לבית ה׳
כלי שרת והעלות וכפות
וכלי זהב וכסף

אך לא יעשה . . . בית ה׳ ספות כסף
מזמרות מזרקות חצצרות
כל כלי זהב וכלי כסף
מן הכסף המובא בית ה׳ כי לעשי
המלאכה יתנהו וחזקו בו את בית ה׳

After finishing, they brought the rest
of the money to the king and
Jehoiada, and with it they made
vessels for the House of the Lord,
vessels for service and ladles, pans,
and vessels of gold and silver.

However, there was not made
. . . for the House of the Lord
silver cups, snuffers, basins,
trumpets, or any gold or silver
vessels from the money brought
to the House of the Lord. It was
given to the workmen to repair
the House of the Lord with it.

The harmonistic solution for the contradiction proposed by the Sages in
b. *Ketub.* 106b: כאן שגבו ולא הותירו, כאן שגבו והותירו 'In Chronicles they had

enough and had some left over; in Kings they had enough but none left over' is unacceptable. Also, the explanation provided by Elmslie, that the Chronicler apparently did not know of or understand 2 Kgs 12:13–14, is unacceptable.[17]

The change in Chronicles should be understood in light of the earlier words of the Chronicler: כי עתליהו המרשעת בניה פרצו את בית האלהים וגם כל קדשי בית ה' עשו לבעלים 'the sons of the wicked Athaliah broke into the House of God *and even used all the holy vessels in the House of the Lord to serve the Baals*' (v. 7, an "addition"). At any rate, the earlier passage from Kings was restructured "from general to specific and back to general" in 2 Chr 24:14b:

general	ויעשהו כלים לבית ה'	and with it they made **vessels for the House of the Lord,**
specific	*כלי שרת והעלות וכפות*	*vessels for service and ladles, pans,*
general	וכלי זהב וכסף	**and vessels of gold and silver**

---

17. Elmslie, *Chronicles* (1916), 276.

Chapter 20
Inconsistency, Disharmony, and Historical Mistakes

Three other aspects of the Chronicler's work complete the general picture of his literary-historiographical activity:

1. Inconsistency in the reworking of earlier passages for inclusion in the book of Chronicles.
2. Alterations made to the passages that the Chronciler drew on, the alterations resulting in disharmony with other parts of Chronicles or with other biblical texts. This is in contrast to occasions on which the Chronicler put considerable effort into "content harmonization."[1]
3. Some historical alterations, apparently stemming from gaps in his knowledge of the history, geography, linguistics, and cultural background of the Israelite region during the period of the Monarchy.

The evidence presented in the first two sections below in regard to the Chronicler's reformulation of earlier sources in accord with his literary, historical, and historiographical criteria, in addition to changes to agree with his theological concepts[2] shows that inconsistencies and exceptions in the widespread reworking of earlier sources are not always evidence of additions and editing carried out by later writers. It may even be possible for other scholars who read this book to be able (to some degree) to use the data presented below in analyzing the work of other biblical writers, instead of subjecting them to the usual Greek-Western criteria of consistency and absolute conformity.

1. Inconsistency in Adapting an Earlier Text

A. Inconsistency in the "Revision" of Early History

20.1 2 Kgs 8:18 states that Athaliah was *"the daughter of Ahab,"* whereas 8:26 states that she was *"the daughter of Omri,"*[3] king of Israel"—that is, Ahab's sister. The Chronicler used these contradictory

---

1. See chap. 7, §2, pp. 140–158.

2. See the examples presented by Japhet, *Ideology*, 221, 227–28, 254; and in this study, above, example 10.16 n. 40 (p. 207).

3. Lucian's "Ahab" is secondary. The translator is harmonizing the contradictory data in 2 Kgs 8:18 and 8:26.

passages in his book as they were (2 Chr 21:6; 22:2; see also 2 Kgs 11:1 //
2 Chr 22:10), without omitting either or attempting to harmonize one
with the other. Even the translator of the Peshiṭta emended 2 Chr 21:6,
replacing the words "the daughter of Ahab" with "the sister of Ahab,"
the former being the wording that appears in all of the other textual
witnesses. In this way, the Peshiṭta translator adjusted the passage to
match 2 Chr 22:2, which has "the daughter of Omri." A similar harmonization was attempted in modern times in the Revised Standard Version, though in this case, the RSV committee altered 2 Chr 22:2 to read
"the granddaughter of Omri" in an effort to harmonize this text with
21:6, "the daughter of Ahab."[4]

20.2 1 Sam 7:1–2 states that the Ark of the Lord remained in the
home of Abinadab on the hill for twenty years and that Abinadab dedicated his son "to protect the Ark of the Lord." 1 Chr 13:7 // 2 Sam 6:3
tells how David brought the Ark of the Lord up from the home of Abinadab. In the similar case of Obed-edom, the Gittite (1 Chronicles 15),[5]
the Chronicler traced Obed-edom's genealogy to the tribe of Levi because only Levites were permitted to carry the Ark; in the case of Abinadab, in chap. 13, the Chronicler did not do this.

The Chronicler's task was performed many generations later by Josephus, who apparently followed the same line of thinking. Josephus
introduced into his tale, which parallels 1 Sam 7:1, the idea that Abinadab was a Levite: "since there lived there a man *of the stock of Levi*,
Aminadab,[6] reputed for *his righteousness* and piety, they brought the
ark into his house, as to a place beseeming God, being the abode of a
righteous man" (*Ant.* 6.18).[7]

20.3 In the Deuteronomistic history, the sum of David's reign appears once in 2 Sam 5:5: "*At Hebron he reigned* over Judah *seven years
and six months*, and at Jerusalem he reigned over all Israel and Judah
thirty-three years"; and once in 1 Kgs 2:11: "*he reigned seven years in
Hebron*, and thirty-three years in Jerusalem." The Chronicler presented

---

4. It may reasonably be concluded that Athaliah was Omri's daughter and Ahab's
sister; cf. Katzenstein, "Parents of Athaliah," 194–97; idem, "Athaliah," 430; Williamson, *Chronicles*, 305; Thiel, "Athaliah," 511. "Daughter of Ahab" probably means
"member of the household of Ahab."

5. See example 2.22 (pp. 56–57).

6. As in the LXX: Ἀμιναδάβ ('Aminadab'), while in the MT it is אבינדב (a labial consonant substitution מ/ב); compare the MT of 1 Kgs 4:11: בן אבינדב; the LXX and *Ant.*
have: υἱοῦ Ἀμιναδάβ ('son of Aminadab').

7. Compare his description in *Ant.* 7.83: "*A righteous man* named [Obed-Edom], *a
Levite by descent*." Some exaggerate, as did Josephus, and say that Abinadab was a
priest, identifying the hill (Heb., "Gibeat") in Kiriath-jearim with Geba, the city of
priests mentioned in Josh 21:17; see, e.g., Klein, "Priests' and Levites' Cities," 86–87.

these totals twice in his book as well (1 Chr 3:4; 29:27), but without any attempt at harmonizing the two.

B. Inconsistency in Harmonizing the Contents

The Chronicler also was inconsistent in his harmonizations. Thus, for example:

20.4 In the genealogy of Judah in 1 Chr 2:4, the Chronicler hints at Judah and Tamar's affair that is recounted in Genesis 38: "Tamar, his daughter-in-law, bore him Perez and Zerah." This hint is surprising, as noted in the commentary attributed to Rashi: "How does he bring himself to mention the shameful act of David's ancestress?" It is especially surprising, because the affair was in violation of the Torah injunction "Do not uncover the nakedness of your daughter-in-law" (Lev 18:15), transgression of which was punishable by death ("If a man lies with his daughter-in-law, both of them shall be put to death, for they have committed an abomination—their blood is upon them," Lev 20:12; see also Ezek 22:11). The Chronicler for some reason let this disharmony stand. He could have, for example, adduced this list without including the (single Hebrew) word "his daughter-in-law" or without mentioning Tamar's name or attaching a "punishment" to Judah (though he sinned unintentionally).

20.5 According to 1 Kgs 14:21, the mother of Rehoboam, king of Judah, was Naamah, an *Ammonitess*. That is, Solomon married an Ammonite woman. The Chronicler presents this information in his work (2 Chr 12:13) though it contradicts the Pentateuch's law that forbids marriages with Ammonites and Moabites (Deut 23:4–5)—that is, he did not attempt to harmonize history with the law.[8]

20.6 In 2 Chr 34:28 (// 1 Kgs 22:22) the Chronicler presented the prophecy of Huldah, the prophetess, regarding Josiah: "I will gather you to your ancestors and you shall be gathered to your grave *in peace*, so that your eyes do not see all the disaster that I am bringing on this place and its inhabitants." True, Josiah was not witness to all the disaster that the Lord brought on the people and the land. However, the story of Josiah's death in the war against Necho, king of Egypt, in the Valley of Megiddo contradicts Huldah's prophecy "you shall be gathered to your grave *in peace*," demonstrating clearly that the prophecy was not fulfilled in its entirety.[9] The Chronicler did not touch this problem.

---

8. For additional discussion of this issue, see Kalimi, *An Ancient Israelite Historian*, 54 n. 81.

9. Hence it may be concluded that the prophecy was not *post eventum* but preceded Josiah's death; cf. Curtis-Madsen, *Chronicles*, 510; Elmslie, *Chronicles* (1916), 336; Montgomery, *Kings*, 526.

C. Inconsistency in the Completion of "Elliptical Verses"

The Chronicler did not always complete "elliptical phrases" that he found in earlier books.[10] For example, he used the words of 1 Kgs 8:9 in his book (2 Chr 5:10) just as they were: "where the Lord drew up with the Israelites" (meaning, "where the Lord drew up *a covenant* with the Israelites"). The same thing occurs in the Chronicler's version of 1 Kgs 9:5, "as I spoke of David, your father." In 2 Chr 7:18 the Chronicler altered the text but did not complete it, stating, "as I drew up with David, your father" instead of "as I drew up *a covenant* with David, your father."[11] He may have refrained from completing these phrases because their intent was clear to the average reader. Nevertheless, these examples do show that the Chronicler was not consistent in his reworking of elliptical phrases found in the earlier texts.

Furthermore, the Chronicler himself occasionally wrote elliptically. Thus, for example, in 2 Chr 13:10 (an "addition") he wrote, "but we are _____ the Lord our God's, and we have not abandoned him," instead of "but we are *with* the Lord our God, and we have not abandoned him." Several examples of this have to do with the Hebrew idiom "to find strength." For instance, in 2 Chr 20:37 (an "addition") he wrote, "they did not find _____ to travel to Tarshish" instead of "they did not find *strength* to travel to Tarshish [= were not able to travel to Tarshish]."[12] In 2 Chr 14:10[11] (an "addition") he wrote, "in your name we have come against this multitude; O Lord, you are our God; let no mortal find _____ against you" instead of "Let no mortal find *strength* against you [prevail against you]," just as in 2 Chr 13:20 ("an addition"), "Jeroboam did not recover his *strength*"; and in 2 Chr 22:9 ("an addition"), "the House of Ahaziah did not find *strength* to reign [had no one able to rule the kingdom]."

2 Chr 1:2–3 ("an addition") is elliptical: "Then Solomon said to all Israel, to the captains of the thousands . . . to the heads of families _____.[13] Then Solomon, and all the crowd with him, went to the high place that was at Gibeon." In other words, he told them to go with him to the high place at Gibeon, and then they went with him. Similarly, 2 Chr 2:2[3], "Then Solomon sent word to Hiram, king of Tyre, 'As you did with David my father and sent him cedar to build himself a house to

---

10. For the Chronicler's completing of "elliptical verses," see chap. 3, §2 (pp. 68–74).

11. For this verse, see Kalimi, "Paranomasia," 27–41. See also 1 Sam 20:16: "Jonathan drew up with the House of David" in place of "Jonathan drew up *a covenant* with the House of David."

12. See R. David Kimḥi's commentary, ad loc.

13. Compare Gen 4:8: "Cain said to Abel, his brother, _____ . And when they were in the field, Cain rose up against his brother Abel and killed him." The LXX filled in the gap: Διέλθωμεν εἰς τὸ πεδίον ('let us go out into the plain').

live in _____,'" is apparently an elliptical verse that should be completed with "so do with me."[14]

In this category also falls the lack of syntactical connection in 1 Chr 29:3 ("an addition"), "in addition to everything I have prepared for the sacred House" instead of "in addition to everything *that* (אשר) I have prepared for the sacred House"; and in 2 Chr 32:31 ("an addition"), "to test him to know everything in his heart" instead of "to test him to know everything *that* was in his heart," as we find written in Deut 8:2: "to test you to know *that* which was in your heart."[15]

Perhaps the best way to view the elliptical sentences appearing in the "additions" is that they were a kind of high style that was an attempt to imitate earlier language in order to provide the "addition" (or an emendation by the Chronicler himself) with literary character that would be thought to be "early."

2. Changes in the Earlier Text
Leading to Disharmony

A. Changes Leading to Disharmony
Elsewhere in the Bible

Occasionally, a change introduced by the Chronicler created disharmony with a verse in the Pentateuch or elsewhere in the Bible, or even with a verse in his own book.

20.7 The rephrasing of the date of the Temple's dedication in the book of Chronicles creates disharmony with the injunction concerning the Day of Atonement in the Pentateuch. According to the book of Kings, after the Temple was erected, Solomon gathered together in Jerusalem "all the men of Israel in the month of Ethanim, *at the Festival*, which is the seventh month. . . . So they dedicated the House of the Lord" (1 Kgs 7:51[8:1]–8:2[3], 63). Further on we are told: "*Solomon celebrated the Festival at that time, and all of Israel with him . . . for seven days* and seven days—fourteen days. *On the eighth day he dismissed the people*, who blessed the king and returned to their tents" (8:65–66). The words "and seven days—fourteen days" are a late gloss, apparently

---

14. Cf. Curtis-Madsen, *Chronicles*, 320. There may be other examples in 1 Chr 11:11a and 2 Chr 25:20: "give them into the hand _____"; see also example 15.4 (pp. 331–332).

15. For the lack of the conjunction אשר in these writings, see, for example, Sir 44:20: "who observed the commandments and entered into a covenant with him"—בא 'and entered' instead of ואשר בא '*and who* entered'; 47:13: "who established a House for His Name and set up a holy place to stand forever"—"and set up," in place of ואשר הציב 'and who set up'.

based on the parallel text, 2 Chr 7:9.[16] In fact, the continuation of the verse, *"On the eighth day* he dismissed the people, who . . . returned to their tents,"* shows clearly that the celebration of the Temple dedication coincided with the celebration of the "Festival" and lasted only seven days.[17]

The Chronicler was apparently of the opinion that "one joyous event is not to be celebrated together with another joyous event," a dictate that was made explicit later, in rabbinic literature.[18] To the Chronicler, the dedication of the Temple was an event in the history of Israel so sublime that it was worthy of being commemorated separately, of having all labor stopped in its honor, and of not being celebrated at the same time as the Festival of Tabernacles. The Festival was itself a period of rejoicing that every Israelite was obliged to observe by virtue of a Torah injunction (Lev 23:33–36; Num 29:12–34; Deut 16:13–15). For this reason, in 2 Chr 7:8–10 he separated the celebration of the Temple dedication from "the Festival" celebration and wrote:

> At that time Solomon observed the Festival for seven days, and all of Israel with him. . . . On the eighth day they held a convocation, for they observed **the dedication of the altar for seven days**[19] *and the Festival for seven days.* **On the twenty-third day of the seventh month he dismissed the people** to their tents, rejoicing and in good spirits.

The Chronicler did not notice, however, that the reworking of the date of the dedication of the Temple in his book created disharmony with Lev 23:26–32 and Num 29:7–11 concerning the Day of Atonement, which falls on the tenth day of the seventh month—a day of self-denial. His words would indicate that Solomon, together with all the men of Israel, celebrated the dedication of the altar/Temple for seven days, from

---

16. See the detailed discussion in example 7.19 (pp. 147–149).

17. According to Exod 29:37, the dedication of the altar in the Tabernacle lasted *seven days* as well; compare 29:30; Lev 8:33 (but according to Num 7:10–88, it lasted twelve days). A Mesopotamian example that provides a parallel to the length of the temple dedication may be found in the cylinder inscription of Gudea, king of Lagash: the dedication of the temple named [lu]É-ninnu to the god Ningirsu lasted *seven days*; see Falkenstein and von Soden, *Hymnen und Gebete*, 180.

18. *Y. Moʿed Qaṭ.* 1.7 (6a); *b. Moʿed Qaṭ.* 9a; and see also *Yal.* 2.193 on 1 Kgs 8:65.

19. The phrase חנכת המזבח 'the dedication of the altar' appears in the Hebrew Bible only in 2 Chr 7:9 and in connection with the altar in the Tabernacle (Num 7:10, 11, 84, 88, source P). As noted above, according to Exod 29:37 (P) the dedication of the altar in the Tabernacle lasted "seven days" as well. Thus the Chronicler's wording may have been influenced by the Priestly literature, though in 2 Chr 7:5 (// 1 Kgs 8:63) he writes, "they dedicated the House of God," perhaps in order to state that the dedication of the altar was the most important part of the dedication of the Temple and its vessels.

the eighth to the fourteenth of the seventh month; from the fifteenth to
the twenty-first of that month they observed the Festival of Tabernacles; on the twenty-second day of the month they celebrated "the
eighth day of convocation"; "and on the twenty-third day of the seventh
month he dismissed the people to their tents." Hence Solomon and all
Israel were unaware of—or at least did not observe—the requirement of
self-denial on the Day of Atonement in the year in which the Temple
was dedicated. As R. David Kimḥi writes in his commentary on 2 Chr
7:9: "The dedication was a joyous occasion with peace-offerings, with
food and with drink." The talmudic sages were well aware of this, explaining it as follows:

> Rabbi Levi said: "It is written 'that the dedication of the altar they
> celebrated for seven days and the Festival—for seven days' (2 Chr
> 7:9), but there are not seven days before the Festival that do not
> include the Sabbath and the Day of Atonement. During those
> seven days Israel ate and drank and rejoiced and lit candles. After-
> wards they repented and were sorry for this, saying: 'We must be
> guilty for having desecrated the Sabbath and for not having denied
> ourselves on the Day of Atonement!' In order to persuade them
> that the Holy One desired their actions, an echo was heard to say,
> 'You all have places in the World to Come!' "[20]

20.8 2 Kgs 18:19 (= Isa 36:4) says that Rabshakeh addressed Hezekiah's officials: "The Rabshakeh said to them, 'Please tell Hezekiah:
thus says the great king, the king of Assyria,[21] *What is the basis of your
trust?*'" Instead of the words "What is the basis of your trust," the
Chronicler wrote in 2 Chr 32:10: "Thus says Sennacherib, king of Assyria, *In what are you trusting that you sit under siege in Jerusalem?*"
Further along in Chronicles, the severe consequences of undergoing
siege are emphasized: "Is not Hezekiah misleading you, so as to allow
you to die of hunger and thirst?" (v. 11).

---

20. *Gen. Rab.* 35:3; similarly in *b. Moʿed Qaṭ.* 9a: "R. Farnakh said, quoting R. Yohanan: 'That year Israel did not observe the Day of Atonement and were worried lest
they had become deserving of annihilation. An echo was heard to say: You are all invited to partake of the life of the World to Come'"; see also *Yal.* 2.193 (on 1 Kgs 8:65)
and R. David Kimḥi on 2 Chr 7:9.

21. In the parallel text in 2 Chr 32:10, the Chronicler wrote: "Thus says *Sennacherib, the king of Assyria. . . .*" Yet the title "the great king, the king of Assyria," which
appears only once more in Rabshakeh's speech (2 Kgs 18:28 // Isa 36:13), seems to be
one of the authentic titles borne by the kings of Assyria: *šarru rabbu . . . šar Aššur*
('the great king . . . the king of Assyria'); see Cohen, "Speech of Rab-Šāqê," 38–39, and
see references there to additional bibliographical information.

Undergoing "siege in Jerusalem" and its consequences[22] were diametrically opposed to Isaiah's prophecy in 2 Kgs 19:32–33 (// Isa 37:33–34):

> Thus says the Lord concerning the king of Assyria, "He shall not enter this city, shoot an arrow there, move a shield before it, or put up a siege ramp against it; by the route that he comes up, he shall go back, and this city he shall not enter."[23] The Lord has spoken.[24]

The description of Jerusalem as a city under Assyrian siege in the book of Chronicles was presented first and foremost for the purpose of glorifying the great miracle that the righteous Hezekiah experienced. That is, Jerusalem, its king, and its people were saved despite the Assyrian siege to which they were subjected. Chronicles also emphasizes the enormity of Sennacherib's failure: he was unsuccessful in capturing the city, despite besieging it.

At first glance, the Assyrian siege of Jerusalem is supported by the tale of the Assyrian King Sennacherib's third campaign (701 B.C.E.), described in his "annals": šāšu kīma iṣṣūr quppi qereb ᵘʳᵘUrsalimmu āl šarrūtīšu ēsiršu, ᵘʳᵘbīrāti elīšu urakkišma āṣê abul ālīšu utirra ikkibuš 'and him [Hezekiah] I imprisoned like a bird in a cage within Jerusalem, his capital city. I barricaded him with outposts, and the exit from

---

22. In 2 Chr 32:2–5 ("an addition"), the Chronicler describes the preparations for the siege made by Hezekiah. In this description, the Chronicler relied on 2 Kgs 20:20 and especially on Isa 22:8–11: "On that day you looked to the armor in the houses of the forest and you saw that there were many breaches in the City of David. You collected the waters of the lower pool, counted the houses of Jerusalem, broke down the houses to fortify the wall, and made a reservoir between the two walls for the waters of the old pool." But, while Isaiah expresses dissatisfaction at these acts and views them as a symptom of lack of faith in the Lord ("you did not look to him who did it or have regard for him who planned it long ago"), the Chronicler does not protest against Hezekiah. He says that he trusted in the Lord and encouraged the people to act likewise (2 Chr 32:6–8, "an addition"), contrary to Isaiah.

23. "This city he *shall not enter*" is a chiastic repetition of "he *shall not enter* this city," which are the opening words of the prophet. From a literary point of view, these phrases create a literary "inclusio" for the paragraph.

24. Williamson (*Chronicles*, 383) believes that the Chronicler omitted these words, found in 2 Kgs 18:17b, ". . . with a great army to Jerusalem. They went up and came to Jerusalem," thereby stressing the fact that "he [Sennacherib] was at Lachish with all his forces" (2 Chr 32:9), in order to remove the disharmony between 2 Kgs 18:17b and the words of Isaiah in 2 Kgs 19:32 (// Isa 37:33). However, the Chronicler's own description of the Assyrian siege of Jerusalem (2 Chr 32:10–11) contradicts Isaiah's description, already mentioned. Furthermore, emending the words "sitting under siege" to read "sitting in the fortress" (as Myers, *II Chronicles*, 186, does) is not supported by any textual witness; this change is intended merely to adapt the biblical text to the proposed explanation.

the gate of his city I made taboo for him'.[25] In truth, however, this is propaganda intended to obscure the fact that Jerusalem, the capital city, was not taken and that Hezekiah, the rebellious king of Judah, was not deposed.[26] "One may reasonably assume," as Tadmor puts it, "that Jerusalem was not really put under siege, but rather merely under blockade, without the usual artifacts of siege,"[27] and apparently for only a very short period of time.

20.9 In 1 Chr 15:29 (// 2 Sam 6:16), the Chronicler mentions the existence of Michal, Saul's daughter, whereas in 1 Chr 8:33 // 9:39 he mentions Eshbaal, Saul's son, whose name did not appear in the list of Saul's sons who fell on Mt. Gilboa (1 Chr 10:2 // 1 Sam 31:2); and in 1 Chr 8:34–40 // 9:40–44 he lists twelve generations in a list of the descendants of Saul's son, Jonathan.[28] In other words, 1 Chr 10:6b, "all his [Saul's] house died together," instead of the words of 1 Sam 31:6, "Saul, his three sons, his armor-bearer, and all his men died together on that day," contradicts 1 Chr 15:29 and the genealogical list in 1 Chronicles 8–9 (not to mention 2 Samuel 2–4; 9; 21).

There seems to be no justification, however, for immediately concluding that the genealogical lists in 1 Chronicles 8–9 are from a later date than the Chronicler himself.[29] Neither can we claim that noting the death of "all the house" of Saul in 1 Chr 10:6 is "nothing more than a careless statement by the Chronicler."[30] It would be more reasonable to conclude that this contradiction is yet another example of the occasional inconsistencies in the Chronicler's reworking and editing of the earlier material. That is, on the one hand, the Chronicler wanted to show that David was true to his oath to Jonathan never to stop being loyal to his descendants (1 Sam 20:15) and to the oath that Saul asked him to make: "'Swear to me by the Lord that you will spare my progeny, so that my name and my family's name will not be erased,' and David promised" (24:22–23). On the other hand, the Chronicler refused to

---

25. The citation is according to the Sennacherib inscription (which is located in the Oriental Institute of the University of Chicago), col. III, lines 27–30. See also Luckenbill, *Annals of Sennacherib*, 33; Pritchard, *ANET*, 288a.

26. For this, see in detail Tadmor, "Sennacherib's Campaign," 65–80, especially pp. 74–75.

27. Ibid., 75, and see also p. 78.

28. The list in its present form goes back to the period of the Babylonian exile; cf. Demsky, "Genealogy," 18–20, 23.

29. This, for example, is the contention of Rudolph, *Chronik*, 95. Noth denies the Chronicler's authorship of Saul's genealogy but does so for completely different reasons (*ÜS*, 122; ET: *Chronicler's History*, 41–42).

30. Curtis-Madsen, *Chronicles*, 181.

concede his view that David's ascent to the throne took place immediately after the death of Saul and was made possible by the death of all members of the royal family on Mt. Gilboa.[31] Nonetheless, it cannot be said that the lists in 1 Chronicles 8–9 provide a "suitable introduction" to the 1 Chronicles 10 narrative about Saul's death.[32]

20.10 In 2 Chr 3:10–13, the Chronicler presented the description of the cherubs and their position in the Holy of Holies found in 1 Kgs 6:23–28. He also noted that there was a drape with cherubs embroidered on it (v. 14, "an addition"). The word פרכת "drape" appears in the Bible 25 times: 24 times in the Priestly source (P) in the Pentateuch, in connection with the Tent of Meeting/Tabernacle; and once in 2 Chr 3:14 in a verse that has no parallel in the book of Kings. The passage in Chronicles is almost identical to the passage concerning the Tabernacle in Exod 26:31–35 and 36:35–36 about the drape that separated the Holy Place from the Holy of Holies. Furthermore, there is no other reference to a drape in Solomon's Temple anywhere in the Bible (not even in the description of the Temple in the book of Ezekiel).[33] These facts give rise to the possibility that the matter of the drape was added here by the Chronicler under the influence of the description of the Tabernacle:

Exod 26:31; 36:35		2 Chr 3:14
26:31 ועשית פרכת תכלת וארגמן		ויעש את הפרכת תכלת וארגמן
ותולעת שני ושש משזר		וכרמיל ובוץ
מעשה חשב יעשה אתה כרבים . . .		ויעל עליו כרובים
36:35 ויעש את הפרכת תכלת וארגמן		
ותולעת שני ושש משזר		
מעשה חשב עשה אתה כרבים		
26:31 *You shall make a drape of blue, purple,* and scarlet yarn and of fine twisted linen. Make it with *cherubs* skillfully worked into it. . . .		*He made the drape of blue, purple,* and crimson yarn and fine linen and worked *cherubs* into it.

---

31. Another example of several diverse trends interwoven into the book of Chronicles; see 1 Chr 21:1–27, 22:1 in contrast to 21:28–30. See also Japhet, *Ideology*, 142.

32. Against Elmslie, *Chronicles* (1916), 62; Myers, *I Chronicles*, 73; Demsky, "Genealogy," 17.

33. Cf. Curtis-Madsen, *Chronicles*, 327; Myers, *II Chronicles*, 18; Mosis, *Untersuchungen*, 143–44; Williamson, *Chronicles*, 209. Against Rudolph, who claims (with Thenius, Šanda, and others) that the "drape" was mentioned in 1 Kgs 6:21b, between the words ויעבר and ברתיקות, but erroneously omitted by a later scribe because of its similarity to the word ברתיקות (*Chronik*, 204–5). This claim is unsupported by the early witnesses to the text of the book of Kings. Moreover, mentioning the פרכת in 1 Kgs 6:21b would contradict vv. 31–32 in the same chapter as well as 7:50, as will be shown below.

36:35 *He made the drape of blue,*
       purple, and scarlet yarn and
       fine twisted linen,
       with *cherubs* skillfully
       worked into it.

According to 1 Macc 1:22, one of the things that Antiochus took as booty from the Temple was a drape. And when Judas Maccabeus purified the Temple, "they put the bread on the table and *hung up the drapes*" (4:51). According to Josephus (*J.W.* 5.5.5–6), there was a drape in Herod's Temple that separated the Holy Place from the Holy of Holies. The existence of a drape in the Second Temple was witnessed in the Mishnah (*m. Yoma* 5:1) and in early Christian sources (Matt 27:51 // Luke 23:45) as well. It is thus feasible that a drape was hanging in the Second Temple during the days of the Chronicler. Perhaps he concluded, anachronistically, that it was present in Solomon's Temple as well and used the description of the drape found in the story of the erection of the Tabernacle in Exodus. It is as though he wanted to say that, just as the drape existed earlier in the Tabernacle erected by Moses and later in Zerubbabel's Temple,[34] so it existed in Solomon's Temple. This addition of the drape to his description of Solomon's Temple, using the description in Exodus, was apparently also intended to attribute to Solomon's Temple some of the appearance of the sanctified Tabernacle set up by Moses in the desert.[35] At any rate, the "addition" describing the drape that hung at the entrance to the sanctuary (the Holy of Holies) and separated it from the Holy Place contradicts the picture drawn in 2 Chr 4:22b // 1 Kgs 7:50b concerning the doors that were erected at the entrance to the Holy of Holies for the same purpose. It also contradicts 1 Kgs 6:31–32: "*For the entrance to the Holy of Holies he made doors* of olivewood . . . and in the two doors of olivewood *he carved cherubs.*"

In light of the frequent occurrence of the phenomenon under consideration in the book of Chronicles, the disharmony between 2 Chr 3:14 and 2 Chr 4:22b seems to be the result of inconsistency in the Chronicler's literary-historiographical reworking of the early texts. He added to 2 Chr 3:14 without reworking or omitting the words of 1 Kgs 7:50b, but he also used it later just as it was (2 Chr 4:22b). If this is indeed the case, the following are examples of conclusions that must not be drawn

---

34. Against Mosis, *Untersuchungen*, 144.

35. For the addition of details to the description of the erection of Solomon's Temple in accordance with the description of the erection of Moses' Tabernacle, compare further, for instance, the description of the skills attributed to Hiram of Tyre in 2 Chr 2:6, 13 with the description of the skills of Bezalel in Exod 35:32, 35.

hastily: 2 Chr 3:14 is a late addition made by "a second Chronicler";[36] and 2 Chr 4:22 is a late addition based on the verse in 1 Kings 7.[37]

20.11 In 1 Chr 18:1, the Chronicler altered the difficult passage in 2 Sam 8:1–2, "David took Metheg-ammah out of the hand of the Philistines" to read "[David] took Gath and its villages from the Philistines." This alteration contradicts 1 Kgs 2:39–41, which states that during Solomon's time two slaves "ran away to King Achish, son of Maacah, of Gath."[38]

B. Deviations and Contradictions between Chronicles and Torah Legislation

Occasionally, the Chronicler explained that a certain action was taken "as it was written" or "as Moses instructed," and so on, apparently in order to give the step constitutional-religious authority. A detailed examination shows, however, that sometimes there are deviations and contradictions between a passage in Chronicles and the laws of the Torah.[39] Several scholars have concluded from this that the Torah used by the Chronicler differed from the Torah in our hands.[40] However, that "Torah" undoubtedly would also have been attributed to Moses, and it is difficult to assume that two different, contradictory Torahs coexisted in the Chronicler's day, each attributed to Moses. Furthermore, it is likely that the Torah text had already been finalized by that time and probably had also been canonized (see Neh 8:1–3, 8–9, 13–14, 18). The difference between some passages in Chronicles and their counterparts in the Pentateuch, therefore, apparently stems from differences between the Chronicler and modern scholars in interpreting—in understanding—the Torah.[41]

3. Historical Mistakes

Several historical differences between the text of the early books and the book of Chronicles apparently stem from the Chronicler's lack of awareness of the use of certain technical idioms and unchanging linguistic structures and his lack of awareness of the real historical and

---

36. Thus Galling, *Chronik,* 83.

37. See, e.g., Benzinger, *Chronik,* 89; Rudolph, *Chronik,* 3, 205; Mosis, *Untersuchungen,* 137 n. 38.

38. For a detailed discussion of this, see example 6.3 (p. 112).

39. Compare Japhet, *Ideology,* 239, and see the examples on pp. 240–44 and the earlier literature on the subject given there.

40. See von Rad, *Geschichtsbild,* 63 and n. 106; Rudolph, *Chronik,* xv; Japhet, *Ideology,* 244 n. 149.

41. For a different opinion, see Shaver, *Torah and the Chronicler,* 128.

geographical facts of the period of the Monarchy. These are some of the signs of the time gap separating the later historian, who lived in the Persian period, and the early sources at his disposal in his book on the history of the First Temple period. In other words, despite the Chronicler's many literary and historiographical talents, his work is not free of errors and misunderstandings.

This phenomenon is also observable in other historiographical sources—for example, in the historiography of the Hasmonean revolt:

(a) In 1 Macc 1:29 we are told: "Two years later the king sent a minister of taxation (ἄρχοντα φρονολογίας) to the cities of Judah." This is apparently a reference to Appollonius, who was called "captain of the Mysians" in 2 Macc 5:24 because he was in command of the mercenary force from the land of Mysia (Μυσία), in northwest Asia Minor. The Greek translator of 1 Maccabees was apparently unfamiliar with this geographical term and with the military title derived from it, so he paraphrased it, explaining: מוסים 'Mysians' = מסים 'taxes'.[42]

(b) In 1 Macc 3:13, Seron is termed "commander of the army of Syria" (ἄρχων τῆς δυνάμεως Συρίας). However, it is clear from v. 14 that Seron was not the head of the Seleucid army: "He [Seron] said: 'I will make a name for myself and become a noble of the kingdom, for I will wage war against Judas and his companions, who ridicule the word of the king.'" Only the Seleucid king himself was the commander-in-chief of the army, and the commanding officers of the various expeditions were determined by him. Later, when Josephus made use of this source (*Ant.* 12.288), he paraphrased it erroneously, apparently using the term accepted in his day for "commander of the army of Syria" and describing Seron as "commander of the armies of Coele-Syria" (στρατηγός τῆς κοίλης Συρίας).[43]

The following are a number of examples of historical mistakes made in the book of Chronicles:

20.12 The phrase אני/אניות תרשיש 'fleet/ships of Tarshish' serves as a technical idiom in the Bible, with a fixed linguistic structure, to denote a type of ship having specific dimensions, shape, strength, and carrying capacity. These ships served in the merchant fleets of Tyre and Israel and sailed the Mediterranean and the Red Sea (1 Kgs 10:22; 22:49; Isa 2:16; 23:1, 14; Ezek 27:25; Ps 48:8).[44]

---

42. Cf. Goldstein, *I Maccabees*, 211–12; idem, *II Maccabees*, 265.

43. See Goldstein, *I Maccabees*, 246; Bar-Kochva, "Seron and Cestius Gallus," 15–16.

44. Cf. Elat, "Tarshish," 944. However, Elat was not aware that Don Isaac Abarbanel already felt this, as he notes in his commentary on 1 Kgs 10:22: "They were called 'ships of Tarshish' by virtue of their structure: they were built like the ships

1 Kgs 10:22, speaking of Solomon, relates "that the king had ships of Tarshish at sea. . . . Once every three years the ships of Tarshish would come, bearing gold and silver." Similarly, we are told that Jehoshaphat, king of Judah, built "ships of Tarshish to sail to Ophir for gold. But he did not sail, for the ships broke up at Ezion-geber" (1 Kgs 22:49).

These narratives are related in the parallel texts in Chronicles but with a change in the language: "fleet/ships of Tarshish" becomes "ships *sailing* to Tarshish":

2 Chr 9:21	כִּי אֳנִיּוֹת לַמֶּלֶךְ	For the king had **ships**
	הֹלְכוֹת תַּרְשִׁישׁ . . .	*sailing* to **Tarshish**.
2 Chr 20:36–37	וַיְחַבְּרֵהוּ עִמּוֹ	Then he joined him in
	לַעֲשׂוֹת **אֳנִיּוֹת** *לָלֶכֶת*	building **ships** *to sail to*
	תַּרְשִׁישׁ וַיַּעֲשׂוּ	**Tarshish** and made the
	. . . אֳנִיּוֹת בְּעֶצְיוֹן גָּבֶר	ships in Ezion-geber. . . .
	וַיִּשָּׁבְרוּ **אֳנִיּוֹת**	And the ships broke up, so
	וְלֹא עָצְרוּ	that they were not able to
	לָלֶכֶת אֶל תַּרְשִׁישׁ	*sail to* Tarshish.

Täckholm believes that here the Chronicler preserved an early, more accurate tradition. He claims that "Tarshish" is the name of a place in Africa on the coast of the Red Sea, where precious stones—"Tarshish" stones (Exod 28:20; 39:13)—were found. The name "Tarshish" was given to the ships because of their destination and their cargo (Tarshish stones and tropical goods).[45] However, there is no supporting evidence for the claim that Solomon and Hiram imported "Tarshish" in vessels of

made in Tarshish, and all ships constructed anywhere following the same pattern were called 'ships of Tarshish.'" Scholars have proposed various explanations for the term "Tarshish," its derivation, and the reason for its application to the noun "ships." For a review of these proposals, see Elat, ibid., pp. 944–45; idem, *Economic Relations*, 147–48, 181–82; idem, "Tarshish and Phoenician," 56–59; Hoenig, "Tarshish," 181–82; The Egyptian "ships of Byblos" (*kbn.t/kpn.t*) that sailed to Punt, in the vicinity of Ophir (for its location on the northern coast of Somali, see Malamat, "Kingdom of David and Solomon," 169–70; or "either in Sudan or, farther south, along the Eritrian-Somalian coast," as carefully expressed by Markoe, *Phoenicians*, 33), can serve as a typical example of the idiom "ships of Tarshish." In the first quarter of the fifteenth century B.C.E., "ships of Byblos" served Queen Hatshepsut by importing goods from Punt, goods identical to those that Solomon and Hiram imported from Ophir in "ships of Tarshish"; see Breasted, *Records of Egypt*, 2.109, §265; Naville, *Temple of Deir el-Bahari*, part 3, pls. 69–79; Kitchen, "Punt," 1198–1201. For the Egyptian term "ships of Byblos," see Horn, "Byblos," 53. Another example, taken from the Semitic world, is *anyt.miḫd* ('ships of Maḫid'), mentioned in Ugaritic documents; see Dietrich-Loretz-Sanmartín, *Texte aus Ugarit*, 202, §4.81. It is likely, as Alt says, that these were boats constructed the same way as boats were built in Maḫid (Ugarit's harbor) and for similar purposes; see Alt, "Ägyptisch-Ugaritisches," 69 n. 3.

45. See Täckholm, "Tarsis," 151 n. 6, 145, 151–53, 166; idem, "Tarsis-Tartessos-problem," 46ff.

Tarshish. See further below, especially in connection with the location
of Tarshish. There is also no justification for Elat's assumption that the
reading תרשיש in 2 Chr 9:21; 20:36–37 "is an error made by a scribe or a
copyist."[46] Elat does not explain just how this error came about, and
there is no support for his claim in the various witnesses to the text.
Furthermore, it is difficult to assume that one "scribe or copyist" made
the same mistake in two verses that are connected with the reigns of
two different kings.

It seems to me that this alteration was made deliberately by the
Chronicler in order to clarify the meaning of the phrase אני(ות) תרשיש. As
a late historian, he was no longer aware of the use of the technical idiom
"ships of Tarshish" to denote a type of boat. He altered the fixed linguistic construction and turned the name "Tarshish" into the name of a
place on the Red Sea coast. This was an early attempt to explain the
term אניות תרשיש, similar to the attempts made in later Jewish literature. For instance:

a. In the Septuagint of 1 Kgs 10:22, the translator wrote ναῦ ἐκ
Θαρσὶς 'ships *from* Tarshish' in place of the words "ships of Tarshish." That is, "ships of Tarshish" were merely "ships coming
from Tarshish."

b. In *Ant.* 8.181, Josephus wrote: "for the king [Solomon] had many
ships stationed in the *Sea of Tarshish* (Ταρσικὴ θάλασσα), as it
was called." In other words, "ships of Tarshish" were merely ships
that set sail in the Sea of Tarshish.

c. In *Tg. Jonathan* on Isa 2:16 (ועל כל אניות תרשיש), we find ועל כל נחתי
ספני ימא. The translator seems to have understood 'Tarshish' to be
related to θαλάσσης 'sea'; the Septuagint had already translated
the phrase πλοῖον θαλάσσης 'ships of the sea'.[47]

d. The Aramaic translation of 2 Chr 20:36 uses the name טורסוס (in
place of תרשיש) and alongside it gives the explanation לימא רבא 'to
the great sea'.

These translators apparently attempted to explain the word "Tarshish"
itself with reference to the most similar-sounding Greek word. Evidently, these explanations are far from being straightforward interpretations of the word.[48]

The inaccuracy of the explanation proposed in Chronicles stands out
prominently in light of the clear narrative of the earlier text: "Jehosha-

---

46. Elat, "Tarshish," 942.

47. And later also Jerome, in his commentary, ad loc.; see Ginzberg, "Hieronymus
zu Jesaja," 280–81.

48. Against Hoenig, who adopts the explanation that "Tarshish" = sea ("Tarshish," 181–82).

phat built ships of Tarshish to sail *to Ophir* for gold" (1 Kgs 22:49)—"to Ophir," not "to Tarshish"! Moreover, according to this text, the objective of the ships of Tarshish built by Jehoshaphat was to import *gold*. That gold was imported from Ophir is also clear from the narrative about the naval expeditions in the days of Solomon (1 Kgs 9:26–28 // 2 Chr 8:17–18; 1 Kgs 10:11 // 2 Chr 9:10).[49] On the other hand, from Tarshish, they used to import primarily silver but also iron, tin, and lead (Jer 10:9; Ezek 27:12).

The Chronicler's explanation does not fit the historical and geographical facts of the First Temple period either. The fact is that there was a port (or ports) named Tarshish in the Mediterranean basin, not on the Red Sea coast, where Ezion-geber was located (near modern Elat), from which Jehoshaphat wanted to set sail to Tarshish, according to the Chronicler. That Tarshish was on the Mediterranean coast is clear from the words of Esarhaddon, king of Assyria:

> *šarrāni*[meš] *ša qabal tamtim kalîšunu ultu māt Iadanana māt Iaman adi māt Tarsisi ana šēpeya iknušu*

> all the kings living on the sea, from Iadanan [= Cyprus] and Greece to Tarshish, surrendered at my feet.[50]

The narrative about the prophet Jonah, who fled from the Lord, also says, "Then he went down to Jaffa and found a boat sailing for Tarshish" (Jonah 1:3). The Table of Nations in Gen 10:4–5 (which the Chronicler copied into his work: 1 Chr 1:7!) lists Tarshish with the other descendants of Javan, who were Elishah (= Cyprus), Kittim, and Dodanim.[51]

20.13 2 Kgs 15:5 speaks of Jotham, bearer of the title על הבית 'over the house', who became ruler over Judah after his father, King Uzziah,[52] was afflicted with leprosy:

וינגע ה' את מלך	The Lord struck the king,
ויהי מצרע עד יום מתו	so that he remained leprous until the day

---

49. Hence the term "Ophir gold" in Isa 12:12; Ps 45:10; Job 28:16; 1 Chr 29:4 and also on an ostracon (no. 2) from Tel Qasile; see Maisler (= Mazar), "Tell Qasile," 67.

50. See Borger, *Asarhaddon*, p. 86 no. 57:10–11.

51. "Dodanim" in the MT; "Rodanim" in several ancient versions and in 1 Chr 1:7 (interchange of ד and ר; compare, among many other examples, Gen 36:26 חמדן with 1 Chr 1:41 חמרן; and see above, p. 16), followed by the RSV. Scholars differ regarding the precise location of biblical "Tarshish." For the various opinions on the subject, see Elat, *Economic Relations*, 148–53; idem, "Tarshish," 942–44; idem, "Tarshish and Phoenician," 55–69; Hoenig, "Tarshish," 181–82; Markoe, *Phoenicians*, 34, 211.

52. Uzziah seems to have officially kept the title "king." The title was given to Jotham only after his father's death; see 2 Kgs 15:7b // 2 Chr 26:23b; 2 Kgs 15:32 // 2 Chr 27:1.

of his death,

וישב בבית החפשית [53]

and he lived in Beth ha-ḥophshith.

[54]ויותם בן המלך על *הבית* שפט

Jotham, the king's son, was *over*

את עם הארץ [55]

the household, ruling the people of the land.

In 2 Chr 26:21, the Chronicler wrote: "Jotham, his son, [was] *over the house of the king*," instead of the title "over the household" in the early text.

Elsewhere in the Hebrew Bible, apart from this text, the title "over the household" appears in Solomon's list of officials in 1 Kgs 4:6: "Ahishar, over the household."[56] The common, full form of the title, אשר על הבית, appears in early biblical historical writing (1 Kgs 16:9; 18:3; 2 Kgs 18:18); in classical prophecy (Isa 22:15; compare with 36:3); in a burial inscription from the village of Shiloah: זאת [קברת] . . .]יהו אשר על הבית 'This is [the grave of . . .]iahu, who was over the household';[57] in the impression of a seal found at Lachish: [א]שר על הבי[ת] / לגדליהו 'To Gedaliahu / [w]ho was over the house[hold]' which, based on its orthography, dates to approximately 600 B.C.E.;[58] on a seal ל[י]דו אשר על הבית '[to] Ydw who is [ov]er the household', which Avigad dates to the seventh

---

53. For the phrase בית החפשית, see the detailed discussion in example 6.4 (pp. 112–114).

54. The title שפט is used here in the sense of "ruler" (rather than "judge"). Such a meaning of the title is found in verses in which it appears parallel to the title מלך 'king' (e.g., Isa 33:22; Hos 7:7; Ps 2:10) or שר 'prince, chief' (e.g., Amos 2:3; Mic 7:3; Prov 8:16; see also 1 Sam 8:5–6, 20; Mic 4:14; Dan 9:12). This sense of the title שופט can also be found in other Semitic languages, for example, *ṭpt* in Ugaritic, used parallel to מלך / זבל; and *šapāṭu* in Akkadian. See also Ehrlich, *Mikrâ ki-Pheschutô*, 366. Against Katzenstein, who interprets the verb לשפט here in the sense of לדון 'to judge' ("The Royal Steward," 152).

55. The phrase עם הארץ 'people of the land' seems to mean all of the subjects of the kingdom of Judah (cf. 2 Kgs 25:3 // Jer 52:6; Lev 4:27; 20:2, 4; Ezek 33:2; 39:13) and is not to be linked with the political-technical term in 2 Kgs 11:14–20; 21:24; 23:30, 35; 25:19 (against Cogan-Tadmor, *II Kings*, 167).

56. It is also possible that this is a mistaken separation of the letters into two words, the early version being ואחי שר על הבית 'Ahi is prince over the household'. In fact, the LXX[B] has καὶ Ἀχει ἦν οἰκονόμος 'Ahi is prince over the household', whereas the Lucianic (LXX[L]) version has καὶ Ἀχιήλ οἰκονόμος 'Ahiel is prince over the household'. It can also be read: ואחי[ ] [א]שר על הבית 'Aḥi[ ] [w]ho is over the household'. The name *Aḥi* may be a shortened form of Aḥijah, Aḥiel, Aḥimelek, and so on. The term οἰκονόμος served as the title of a district governor in Ptolemaic Egypt, and this may be a translator's archaic usage; see Mettinger, *State Officials*, 72–73.

57. See Donner-Röllig, *KAI*, 35, no. 191B, line 1; Avigad, "Royal Steward," 66–72; idem, *Early Ancient Monuments*, 9–17; Ussishkin, "Short Inscription," 297–303.

58. See Moscati, *L'epigrafia ebraica*, 62, no. 30. Some identify the "Gedaliahu" on this seal with Gedaliah ben Ahikam ben Shaphan (though the Bible does not say that Gedaliah bore the title "[who] is over the household"), who was appointed governor of Judah by Nebuchadnezzar II, king of Babylon, after the destruction of Jerusalem (2 Kgs 25:22; Jer 40:7); see, for example, de Vaux, *Ancient Israel*, 130.

century B.C.E. based on orthography and the form of the decorative pattern;[59] and in three other seal impressions: לאדניהו / אשר על הבית 'to
Adoniahu / who is over the household' (this prince used two different
seals) and אשר / [ע]ל בית לנתן 'to Nathan, who is / [ov]er [the] household'
(in this one, the definite article preceding the word בית was erroneously
omitted).[60]

The phrase (אשר) על הבית '(who is) over the household' was thus an administrative technical phrase, a title having a fixed linguistic pattern,
borne by someone in an administrative position who served in the royal
bureaucracy during the First Temple period. The function was not limited to matters of the royal palace alone. Rather, the person who was
'over the household' was the chief minister in the kingdom. His authority spread to all important matters of the kingdom. We can see this in
several biblical verses, especially in Isaiah, which refers to Eliakim ben-
Hilkiah, who was to take the title אשר על הבית from Shebna:

> I will give your government into his hand, and he will be a father to
> the inhabitants of Jerusalem and to the house of Judah. I will place
> the key of the house of David on his shoulder. He will open and
> none will shut, and he will shut and none will open. (Isa 22:21–22).

"Eliakim ben-Hilkiah, who was over the household," headed the list of
officials who went out to the Rabshakeh (Isa 36:3 // 2 Kgs 18:18). Elah,
king of Israel, drank too much in the home of "Arza, who was over the
household," in Tirza (1 Kgs 16:9). "Obadiah, who was over the household," was given the same task as King Ahab himself (to search the
parched countryside for water for the animals, 1 Kgs 18:3, 6). And the
very fact that the crown prince, Jotham, held this position even after he
began to rule in place of his father, who had been struck with leprosy
(2 Kgs 15:5), indicates the importance of the position.[61]

The change from the technical administrative term "over the household" that appears in the earlier text to "over the king's house" in
Chronicles apparently stems from the Chronicler's mistaken interpretation of the term. As a late historian, he was no longer aware of the

---

59. See Avigad, "Hebrew Seals," 123–24.

60. See idem, *Hebrew Bullae*, 21–23. According to Avigad, Adonijah and Nathan
could have served the kings of Judah from Josiah to Zedekiah (just like contempo-
raries of Baruch ben-Neriah, the scribe).

61. See de Vaux, *Ancient Israel*, 129–31; Katzenstein, "The Royal Steward," 150.
Against Mettinger (*State Officials*, 73–79), who limits the authority of "(who is) over
the household" to responsibility for the king's property, while comparing it with the
Egyptian title *mr pr wr* 'the supreme supervisor over the household (= the property)'.
From a typological perspective, אשר על הבית can apparently best be compared with a
parallel title from the Semitic world, the Akkadian title *ša pān ekalli* (see CAD E 62a)
as well as *ša eli bîtî / ša eli bîtanu/i*; see Ebeling-Meissner, "Beamter," 464–65.

phrase's original meaning and of its fixed linguistic structure as a royal title, so he paraphrased it[62] but by doing so limited the authority of the official to "the king's house" only.

20.14 The word בֶּדֶק appears in the Bible in the sense of "crack, fissure" in a structure or in a boat. This is the meaning of the word in closely-related Semitic languages as well; for example, *bdqt* in Ugaritic;[63] *batqu* in Akkadian;[64] and one sense of the Aramaic word בדקא.

In early Biblical Hebrew, repairing a fissure in a certain structure was expressed by a fixed idiom: X חזק בדק, literally, 'strengthen a crack in X'. It appears six times in the book of Kings, חזק (את) בדק הבית/בית ה', in connection with the restoration of the Temple in the days of Joash and Josiah, kings of Judah (2 Kgs 12:6–9, 13; 22:5). It is also found twice more in "transition-period" Hebrew, though with changed word order. These examples are found in Ezekiel's prophecy about Tyre, in connection with the repairing of a boat: מחזיקי בדקך (Ezek 27:9, 27). And there is a parallel expression in Akkadian: *batqu ša . . . ṣabātu*.[65]

The Chronicler, on the other hand, instead of using the fixed idiom לחזק בדק הבית 'repairing a crack in the Temple', which had been used in the narrative of the restoration of the Temple in 2 Kgs 22:5, wrote לבדוק ולחזק הבית 'examining and repairing the Temple' (2 Chr 34:10), a phrase unparalleled in the entire Bible. He may not have been aware of the meaning of the word בדק or of the fixed technical idiom חזק (את) בדק הבית / בית ה' and therefore confused the noun בדק ('crack, fissure') with the verb בָּדַק ('examine, search') derived from it.

This may also be why the Chronicler did not use the word or the technical phrase in the narrative of the restoration of the Temple in the days of Joash. A comparison of 2 Chronicles 24 with 2 Kings 12 shows that, instead of בָּדֶק והם יחזקו את בדק הבית לכל אשר ימצא שם 'they will *repair the*

---

62. On the other hand, the words בן המלך 'the son of the king' in this passage were understood by the Chronicler in a genealogical sense (he wrote בנו 'his son' in order to shorten the text; cf. 1 Chr 3:3, לעגלה אשתו 'by Eglah, *his wife*', instead of 'by Eglah, *the wife of David*', in 2 Sam 3:5). Even if we adopt the opinion that "the son of the king" was the title of a person holding a position in the royal bureaucracy in Israel (see Brin, "Son of the King," 5–20, 85–90, 240 and earlier literature given there), it is difficult to assume that Jotham also held the title "the son of the king" along with the more prominent position of "(who is) over the household." (Jotham apparently played a lesser role, policing and imprisoning [Jer 36:26; 38:6], or, in any case, was not one of the leading officals [in 1 Kgs 22:26 // 2 Chr 18:25, he is listed after "the governor of the city"]; see also Yeivin, "Son of the King," 160; idem, "Administration," 117.)

63. See Gordon, *Ugaritic Textbook*, 51:17–19, VII, *wypth bdqt ʿrpt* 'and opened a crack, a fissure, in the clouds'.

64. See CAD B 167b.

65. See Greenfield, "Lexicographical Notes," 221 n. 24; see the example given by Hurowitz, "Fiscal Practice," 293.

cracks in the Temple wherever one is found' (2 Kgs 12:6), the Chronicler wrote וקבצו מכל ישראל כסף *לחזק את בית אלהיכם* 'collect money from all Israel *to repair the Temple of your God*' (2 Chr 24:5a); and instead of לחזק את בדק בית ה' 'to repair the cracks in the House of the Lord' (2 Kgs 12:13), he wrote לחזק את בית ה' 'to repair the House of the Lord' (2 Chr 24:12). More changes of this sort can be found in a comparison of the following passages:

2 Kgs 12:7–9	2 Chr 24:5b–6
7. *לא חזקו* הכהנים את *בדק הבית* . . .	5b. ולא *מהרו* הלוים
8. מדוע אינכם *מחזקים את בדק הבית*	6. מדוע לא דרשת על הלוים
ועתה אל תקחו כסף מאת מכריכם	להביא מיהודה ומירושלם
כי *לבדק הבית* תתנהו	את משאת משה עבד ה' . . .
9. ויאתו הכהנים . . . ולבלתי חזק	
את *בדק הבית*	

7. the priests *had not repaired the cracks in the Temple.* . . .	5b. the Levites *did not act quickly.* . . .
8. "Why are you not *repairing the cracks in the Temple?*" Now therefore do not accept any more money from your donors but set it aside for *the cracks in the Temple.*"	6. "Why have you *not demanded* that *the Levites bring in* from Judah and Jerusalem the tax levied by Moses, the servant of the Lord?"
9. Then the priests agreed . . . not *to repair the cracks in the Temple.*	

It is also possible that the Chronicler was interpreting the word בדק in the sense of 'reinforce, repair'. A verb derived from this root is found in Ben Sira (ca. 200 B.C.E.): "In whose generation the Temple was *repaired* (נבדק) / and in whose days the Temple *was reinforced* (חזק)" (Sir 50:1);[66] in Rabbinic Hebrew: "of the fund for the repairing of the Temple" (*m. Šeqal.* 4:2); "the funds dedicated to the repairing of the Temple do not free other suitable funds dedicated to the altar sacrifices" (5:4); and "all the altar sacrifices are for the altar, and those dedicated to the repairing of the Temple are for the repairing of the Temple" (*m. Meʿil.* 9:2).[67] Based on these examples, the words לבדוק ולחזק in 2 Chr 34:10 were used as a hendiadys.

This is one general example of erroneous use of an expression/word or explanation based on a late interpretation.[68] Whatever the cause, it

---

66. See Segal, *Ben-Sira*, 342–43.

67. For additional examples, see Kasowski, *A Thesaurus of Talmudic Hebrew*, 7.34–36.

68. Against Willi, who believes that the substitution of לבדוק ולחזק הבית for לחזק בדק הבית was intended to create a stronger effect in Chronicles (*Chronik*, 89).

is clear that the verse has a meaning different from the sense intended by the earlier author.

20.15 According to 1 Kgs 9:26–28, Solomon built ships at Ezion-geber, near Elath[69] on the shore of the Red Sea, and Hiram, king of Tyre, sent "his servants, sailors who were familiar with the sea"[70] to Solomon. Hiram's servants sailed to Ophir with Solomon's servants to import gold.

In 2 Chr 8:17–18 the Chronicler apparently wanted to show that Solomon initiated this expedition. He wrote that Solomon went "to Ezion-geber and to Elath on the seacoast" (instead of "Ezion-geber, near Elath" in Kings!); and Hiram sent him not only Tyrian sailors but also ships: "Hiram sent him, with his servants, *ships and servants familiar with the sea.* They went to Ophir with Solomon's servants and imported gold . . . from there." This does not seem to be a textual error, as Rudolph claims. He emends the text to read, "And for the ships he sent him servants who know well the sea."[71] At any rate, there is no textual support for either the supposed error or for the proposed emendation. The Chronicler's citation is a paraphrase of the earlier text[72] that ignored the vast geographical and technological problems prohibiting the dispatch of ships from Tyre on the Phoenician coast to Ezion-geber on the Red Sea—either by land[73] or by sea. It is unreasonable to assume that Hiram's ships sailed from Tyre around the African continent to reach Ezion-geber. Neither is there any evidence of a canal linking the Nile and the Red Sea during the Solomonic era.[74] However, these possibilities existed in the Chronicler's day, as we read in Herodotus 2.158 and 4.42 and on steles set up by Darius I (522–486 B.C.E.) along the route of the canal between the Nile and the Red Sea. On one of the steles, Darius said, "I ordered this canal to be dug to link the river flowing throughout Egypt with the sea coming from Persia . . .

---

69. The LXX translates it Αἰλαθ (= Elath), as in 2 Kgs 14:22. This verse in 1 Kings contradicts the claim made by Glueck that Ezion-geber and Elath are two names for the same location ("Elath, Eloth," 268, 272). It is reasonable "to locate Ezion-geber on the coast of the Sinai Peninsula, opposite the island of Jezirat Farʿan, or on the island itself, but the name Elath must be connected with the later Elat (ʿAqaba)" (Aḥituv, "Ezion-geber," 332–33).

70. "Sailors" and "who were familiar with the sea" are an example of hendiadys.

71. Rudolph, *Chronik*, 220.

72. Cf. Curtis-Madsen, *Chronicles*, 355; Elmslie, *Chronicles* (1916), 202.

73. No reference is made here to transporting materials or parts to build ships in Ezion-geber but only to "ships" themselves.

74. See Butzer, "Kanal," 312–13.

and ships sail from Egypt along this canal to Persia."[75] But the sources
available to us do not indicate that this canal existed during the period
of the United Monarchy.

20.16 2 Sam 10:6 does not say where the Aramean and the other
armies that the Ammonites hired to help them camped. In 1 Chr 19:7
the Chronicler added the name of the location to the earlier text: "They
came *and camped before Medaba.*"[76] In contrast, in vv. 16–17, he omitted the place-name Helam, where the armies of Hadadezer assembled;
this name does appear in 2 Sam 10:16–17. The omission may have
stemmed from the fact that the Chronicler was not familiar with the
place. As a result, he may have read אלהם 'to them' instead of חלאמה
'Helam' in 2 Sam 10:17:[77]

2 Sam 10:16–17	1 Chr 19:16–17
וישלח הדדעזר ויצא את ארם	וישלחו מלאכים ויוציאו את ארם
אשר מעבר הנהר *ויבאו חילם* . . .	אשר מעבר הנהר . . . .
ויגד לדוד ויאסף את כל ישראל	ויגד לדויד ויאסף את כל ישראל
ויעבר את הירדן ויבא *חלאמה*	ויעבר הירדן ויבא *אלהם*
Hadadezer sent and brought the	They sent messengers to bring the
Arameans who were beyond the	Arameans who were beyond the
Euphrates, *and they came to*	Euphrates . . . .
Helam. . . . When they told	When David was told, he
David, he gathered together all	gathered together all Israel,
Israel, crossed the Jordan, and	crossed the Jordan, and
came *to Helam.*	came *to them.*

Indeed, the precise location of Helam is disputed to this day.[78]

20.17 This phenomenon of mistaken, late interpretations is even
more significant when we consider a comment made by the Chronicler
at the end of the genealogical list of the tribes on the east bank of the
Jordan River. 2 Kings 15 describes two Assyrian expeditions to the land
of Israel. One was during the days of Menahem ben-Gadi, king of Israel:

---

75. See Weissbach, *Keilinschriften*, 102–5, and especially §3 on pp. 104–5 (Gewicht-
Inschriften, Dar. Pond. 9); and also Tsafrir, "Suez Region," 94–95. For a comprehensive discussion of the four steles that were erected by Darius I, and on the Greek as
well as other sources, see Redmount, "Canals of the Pharaohs," 127–35.

76. For this, see example 3.24 (p. 84).

77. Against Curtis-Madsen, *Chronicles*, 241 and others, who emend here in accordance with the verse in 2 Samuel: ויבא חלאמה 'and he came to Helam'.

78. See Kallai, "Helam," 114; McCarter, *II Samuel*, 273.

Pul, king of Assyria, came against the land. Menahem gave Pul a thousand talents of silver to support him in maintaining his hold on the kingdom. (v. 19)

The other expedition was during the reign of Pekah, king of Israel:

Tiglath-pileser, king of Assyria, came and captured Ijon, Abel-beth-maacah, Janoah, Kedesh, Hazor, Gilead, Galilee, and all the land of Naphtali and exiled them to Assyria. (v. 29)[79]

These expeditions took place during the reigns of two kings of Israel, with a time interval between them. The expedition against Menahem apparently took place in 738 B.C.E.,[80] whereas the expedition against Pekah apparently occurred at the end of 733 or the beginning of 732 B.C.E. The two expeditions were undertaken by a single Assyrian king with two names: "Pul" (this is the Pūlu mentioned in Neo-Babylonian sources)[81] and "Tiglath-pileser" (this is the Tukultī-apil-Ešarra[82] who appears in Assyrian documents).

In 1 Chr 5:26 the Chronicler closed the genealogical lists of the Transjordanian tribes with a comment about the end of the tribes during the period of the Assyrian Empire. This comment indicates that he was not aware that the names "Pul" and "Tiglath-pileser/Tilgath-pilneser" mentioned in Kings were two different names for a single Assyrian king; as a result, he listed them as though they were two Assyrian kings:

The God of Israel stirred up *the spirit of Pul, king of Assyria, and the spirit of Tilgath-pilneser,*[83] *king of Assyria*, to exile Reuben, Gad, and the half-tribe of Manasseh and bring them to Halah, Habor, Hara,[84] and the river Gozan, to this day.[85]

---

79. Compare this verse with the Annals of Tiglath-pileser III; see Luckenbill, *ARAB*, vol. 1, §772, §§815–19; Pritchard, *ANET*, 283–84.

80. See Tadmor, "Azariahu in Assyrian Inscriptions," 180–87.

81. See idem, "Pul," 443; Cogan-Tadmor, *II Kings*, 171–72, and the earlier literature cited there.

82. For this name, see Tadmor, "Tiglat-Pileser," 415; Cogan-Tadmor, *II Kings*, 187.

83. In 1 Chr 5:6; 2 Chr 28:20: תלגת־פלנאסר. These are late forms of the name תגלת־פלאסר, apparently resulting from dissimilation.

84. The name *Hara* is not mentioned in 2 Kgs 17:6 and 18:11, on the basis of which the Chronicler compiled his list; nor does it appear anywhere else in the Bible or extrabiblical literature. It may be the result of dittography with the following word, ונהר. If this is indeed the case, the correct reading is וחבור נהר גוזן, that is, in the jurisdiction of Habor, which is the river in the Assyrian district of Gozan.

85. On this phenomenon, see also example 15.9 n. 27 (p. 335).

Conclusion

1. In General

The main focus of this study—the first, to the best of my knowledge, to treat these specific issues—is to expose and define systematically and comprehensively the Chronicler's writing methods and techniques and to explore certain methodological aspects of biblical historiography. As is true of other biblical authors, the Chronicler's historiographical methods and literary techniques are not handed down to us along with the text he produced. His methods and techniques are elusive; the scholar must ferret them out through close literary examination of the text. It is in this process that the parallel texts prove to be of great value. A careful comparison of the text of Chronicles with its sources, first and foremost the books of Samuel–Kings, points clearly to the forms and structures, literary devices and techniques, and the methods of historiographical editing and adaptation that the Chronicler applied to the earlier texts.

The uncovering of these historiographical methods and literary techniques is of paramount importance in understanding the content, ethos, and full meaning of the text of Chronicles. Far from being mere rhetorical embellishments or extraneous ornaments irrelevant to full comprehension of the text, these methods and techniques are an integral part of the content itself. In the words of Goethe, *Gehalt bringt die Form mit; Form ist nie ohne Gehalt* ('Content determines form; form never exists without content').[1] Without an awareness of the Chronicler's forms, structures, methods, and techniques, we cannot properly appreciate the full import, depth, and particular tone of what he wrote. It is impossible to separate the "what" from the "how," the content from the form, the "historical description" from "its literary formulation" and "its historiographical redaction," the picture of an event from the size and type of frame that surrounds it, the quantity and strength of the lines and colors that it comprises.

Meticulous identification of the Chronicler's literary and historiographical methods by thorough examination of even the smallest details enables us to determine the precise nature of the changes that the Chronicler made to the earlier texts—his additions, omissions, rearrangements, and editing—and hence the significance and degree of

---

1. Goethe, "Paralipomena," 541; see also Weiss, *Bible from Within*, 21–27, and additional references there.

historical credibility of the Chronicles text. These literary and historiographical methods are also of considerable importance in assessing the credibility of the "additions" of the book of Chronicles, disregarding temporarily the question whether the Chronicler had access to extrabiblical sources, since lost, or what the nature of those sources was before the Chronicler adapted them.

This study has thus provided new criteria for the evaluation of the picture of history portrayed by Chronicles—that is, the problem of the reliability of the book as a source for the history of Israel in the Monarchic period, a problem still to be solved by scholars of biblical history.[2]

Awareness of the Chronicler's methods of writing, copying, literary-historiographical editing, and reworking facilitates the study of other aspects of the book of Chronicles as well:

2. The Textual Aspect

We have reexamined the assumed corruptions, omissions, and "textual emendations" of various kinds posited by translators, commentators, and especially modern scholars. Our examination leaves no room for these hypotheses, omissions, and emendations and has even given rise to a new understanding of various verses as a result of our growing familiarity with the literary and historiographical techniques that determined their present form.[3] Thus, we have concluded that these differences between the parallel texts of Samuel–Kings and Chronicles mostly stem from the creative literary involvement of the Chronicler with the earlier texts rather than from his "carelessness" or the "carelessness" of later transmitters and copyists, or even intentional modifications by later scribes or theologians.[4]

Awareness of these methods also provides us with some inkling of the free use that the pre-Masoretic transmitters of the "biblical" text may have made of earlier texts; that is, during this period, those who copied "biblical" texts did not restrict themselves to preserving the existing

---

2. For a summary and review of the various opinions on this topic, see Welten, *Geschichte*, 1–6; Japhet ("Historical Reliability," 83–107), who concludes as follows: "As yet, the question of the Chronicler's historical reliability cannot be considered 'a closed case.' We are still looking forward to the broadening of our knowledge, a deepening of our understanding, a clarification of our terms and definitions, an improvement of our evaluation, all of which may enlighten our use of the book of Chronicles as a source for the history of Israel" (p. 99).

3. See also the examples in Kalimi, "Literary Study of Chronicles," 190–212.

4. This does not mean, however, that the Masoretic Text of the book of Chronicles is entirely free of such textual corruptions, as has been noted in several places in this study. See, for example, p. 71 nn. 37–38, p. 83 nn. 76–77, p. 187 n. 8, p. 207 n. 43, p. 225 n. 27, p. 318 n. 50, p. 324 n. 65.

texts but emended and modified them for reasons such as creating textual harmony or giving meaning to obscure passages—as did the Chronicler with the passages that he took from the books of Samuel–Kings.

3. The Ideological-Theological Aspect

We have referred regularly to the Chronicler's theology, which
greatly influenced his writing.[5] Nevertheless, we have found that many
of the changes that the Chronicler made in the early sources that he
used can be explained, not by a particular opinion or outlook that he
may have held, but by the literary technique that he decided to apply.
In other words, if a certain text in Chronicles can be dealt with according to a given literary device (if it clearly fits in with the methods and
literary techniques used by the Chronicler), it becomes difficult or even
impossible to attribute it to the writer's opinions or beliefs.

4. The Uniformity of Chronicles

Scholars disagree about the question of the uniformity of the book of
Chronicles. Is the book all of a piece, a historiographical composition to
be attributed to a single author, the Chronicler? Or is it a mosaic in
which the Chronicler's original work has been fused with other literary
strata—the additions and completions of later authors and redactors?
Even the scholars who support the "mosaic" theory disagree regarding
the identity and scope of these secondary strata. This question arises
largely with regard to the various lists in 1 Chronicles 1–9; 12:1–23;
chaps. 23–27; and parts of chaps. 15–16. Some view these chapters as
an integral part of the Chronicler's original work;[6] others see them
(entirely or partially) as a late addition resulting from the work of a
late redactor / "second Chronicler" or a number of redactors.[7] Between

---

5. See, for instance, example 2.16 (pp. 50–51); example 7.22 (pp. 153–154); chap. 9
(pp. 186–193); example 15.2 (pp. 327–330); example 15.4 (pp. 331–332); examples
15.16–18 (pp. 341–344).

6. See, e.g., Keil, *Chronicles*, 21–22; Curtis-Madsen, *Chronicles*, 6–8, 57, 260–61;
Mazar, "Chronicles," 597, 605–6; Japhet, *Ideology*, 229 n. 106, 278–85, 288–89,
352ff. With regard to chaps. 1–9, see also idem, "Biblical Historiography," 189–91;
idem, "Conquest," 218; Johnson, *Genealogies*, 47–55; Liver, *Priests and Levites*, 11
(with regard to chaps. 23–26, 27); Williamson, *Chronicles*, 14, 39 (with regard to
chaps. 1–9); 104–6 (with regard to 12:1–23); and for 12:1–23, see also idem, "We Are
Yours," 164–76.

7. So, for example, de Vaux (*Ancient Israel*, 390) and Newsome ("Understanding,"
215) deny that the Chronicler wrote chaps. 1–9 and 23–27. Welch (*Judaism*, 185–86;
idem, *Chronicler*, 1), Uffenheimer (*Visions of Zechariah*, 175), Myers (*I Chronicles*,
xxxi, xxxii), Freedman ("Purpose," 215), Cross ("Reconstruction," 11–18), and McKenzie (*Chronicler*, 25–26) deny that the Chronicler wrote chaps. 1–9. Mosis (*Untersuchungen*, 44 n. 2) denies the the Chronicler wrote chaps. 23–27.

these extremes, there is yet another approach, according to which the main body of the lists are indeed late additions by the hands of various redactors, the Chronicler himself, however, being the source for some of the lists.[8]

The existence of similar features (techniques and various literary and historiographical devices) in the parallel texts and in the "additions" of Chronicles (including the genealogical lists) *may* testify to the literary uniformity of the book and to its original scope. However, this is *not necessarily* certain, because a late author(s) and redactor(s) could have used or even imitated the same literary devices and historiographical features that the Chronicler adduced in his composition. In other words, the conclusions of this study may support scholars who hold that Chronicles is indeed the product of a single writer, the Chronicler (except, perhaps, for a number of phrases scattered throughout the book).

5. The Image of the Writer and of His Book

Recognition of the Chronicler's creativity, primarily his literary techniques and historiographical methods, also shows the author in a new light: no longer is he to be viewed as a passive scribe-copier but as an inspired artist with a variegated range of literary and historiographical talents—a skilled professional historian with sophisticated writing methods at his disposal.[9] He was a writer who not only selected material from the earlier books suitable to his aims but also rewrote, expressing the words in a fresh style and formulating them with a new literary mode.[10]

This may also be said of the parallel texts in Chronicles. They are neither a "pointless copy" nor a "boring repetition" of classical biblical history, a "review" that is "useless" to the reader. This attitude toward the parallel texts in Chronicles can be detected, for example, in the name given to the book by the translators-redactors of the Septuagint translations: παραλειπομένων—that is, "Omissions" (from Kings). In other

8. See, e.g., Eissfeldt, *Introduction*, 540 (= *Einleitung*, 668); Noth, *Chronicler's History*, 29–43, 149–52 (= *ÜS*, 152–73); Rudolph, "Problems of Chronicles," 402; idem, *Chronik*, 1–5, 93, 103, 149–50. Rudolph, for example, denies the Chronicler considerable sections of chaps. 1–9; 15–16; all of 12:1–23; and all of 23–27; as well as a few passages from chap. 28 and from 2 Chronicles. So, too, Willi, *Chronik*, 194–204; see also Ackroyd, *Israel under Babylon*, 295; idem, *Chronicles*, 20–21. Compare with Kalimi "Date of Chronicles," 350–51 n. 14.

9. For classification of the Chronicler as "historian" and his composition as "historical writing," see Kalimi "Characterization of the Chronicler," 29–39.

10. Yet it must be emphasized that there remains a certain lack of systemization in the literary and historiographical adaptation of the earlier texts for use in Chronicles, as shown in chap. 20 above. See also below, §8 below (pp. 410–411).

words, the significance of Chronicles was the additional material it provided, material not found in (or "omitted from," as it were) the book of
Kings, ἡ βίβλος βασιλειῶν (= Samuel–Kings in the Masoretic Text), from
which it was taken. The "parallel texts" were unimportant in themselves. The term *Paralipomenon* is found in the Vulgate as well and consequently also in a number of modern translations. A similar attitude
can be detected in the writings of commentators and philosophers from
various places and periods; for example, Don Isaac Abarbanel (1437–
1508) expressed his puzzlement in the introduction to his commentary
on Samuel:

> Why did Ezra the scribe repeat in Chronicles that which already
> appears here in Samuel? What was his purpose in reiterating
> these matters? That which is mentioned here need not have been
> written there, since they all already appear here.

A number of generations later, Baruch (Benedictus) de Spinoza (1632–
1677), one of the pioneers of modern critical biblical scholarship wrote
as follows:

> Concerning the two books of Chronicles. . . . As to the authorship
> of these books, their authority, utility, and doctrine, I come to no
> conclusion. I have always been astounded that they have been
> included in the Bible by those who excluded from the canon the
> book of Wisdom, the book of Tobit, and the other books that are
> called apocryphal.[11]

Actually, the appearance of Chronicles is not surprising. It is an impressive attempt, the first of its kind, to the best of our knowledge, to
describe the history of Israel under the leadership of the Davidic dynasty from its beginning until the destruction of the Solomonic Temple,
in a single comprehensive and systematic work. This work would have
been sorely needed by its generation, considering the religious, social,
linguistic, and literary norms that had developed since the composition
of Samuel and Kings. In other words, Chronicles illustrates the principle of "each generation with its own historiography." Its message was
different from that of the earlier historical works, from a different period, and aimed at a different audience. It was a message attuned to
contemporary local circumstances. Furthermore, that Samuel–Kings
was accepted into the canon is the surprising development, for Chronicles is far closer to the outlook of the canonizers than the earlier books,
as demonstrated by the examples given in chap. 7, §2 (pp. 140–158).

---

11. Spinoza, *Tractatus Theologico-Politicus*, chap. 10 (at the beginning). For the
English edition, cf. *The Chief Works of Benedict de Spinoza* (trans. from Latin with an
introduction by R. H. M. Elwes; New York, 1951) 146; B. Spinoza, *Tractatus Theologico-Politicus* (Gebhardt edition, 1925); trans. S. Shirley (Leiden, 1991), 186.

Nevertheless, this attitude toward Chronicles in general and toward its parallel texts in particular is apparently one of the reasons for its long neglect.[12] Even in modern biblical scholarship, the study of Chronicles has generally been undertaken to satisfy the needs of Pentateuch research, Chronicles itself remaining on the sidelines of scholarly interest until the last few decades. This study thus reveals an old-new literary-historical work that is gripping in its form and sophistication. Many of the Chronicler's alterations provide more than just minor linguistic emendations or even textual or theological modifications. They give the earlier texts a new literary aspect, with a form and meaning that are different from those of the parallel passages in Samuel–Kings.[13]

6. The Chronicler as Redactor and Author

As confirmed by McKenzie, the issue of the Chronicler as redactor "truly lies at the heart of Chronicles studies and continues to preoccupy nearly every treatment of this literature."[14] The numerous literary devices and stylistic techniques employed by the Chronicler, even in minor changes to the books of Samuel–Kings, reveal that redaction was part of his ingenious literary accomplishment; the process of redaction does not detract from the value of his work.[15] Thus, the Chronicler-as-redactor is, in fact, the Chronicler-as-author. This view of the Chronicler is similar to the perspective on the Deuteronomist posited by Martin Noth: "Dtr was not merely an 'editor'/'redactor,' but the author of a history work which brought together material from highly varied traditions and arranged it according to a carefully conceived plan."[16]

7. History and Historiography

A complete and thorough categorizing of the differences between Chronicles and its sources (i.e., the parallel texts) clearly shows the

---

12. For the treatment of Chronicles by Jewish scholars, see Kalimi "History of Interpretation," 5–41; idem, *Jewish Tradition and Exegesis*; see also p. 3 n. 9 above. For its neglect by the Christian world, see idem, "Chronicles in Christian Tradition."

13. See, in much more detail, Kalimi, "Characterization of the Chronicler," 33–38.

14. McKenzie, "Chronicler as Redactor," 87–88.

15. Thus, for instance, Steuernagel (*Einleitung*, 408), who described the Chronicler as "in the main only an editor" ("in der Hauptsache nur ein Redaktor"). See also Kalimi "Characterization of the Chronicler," 36.

16. Noth, *Deuteronomistic History*, 26 (= *ÜS*, 11: "Dtr war nicht nur 'Redaktor,' sondern der Autor eines Geschichtswerkes, das die überkommenen, überaus verschiedenartigen Überlieferungsstoffe zusammenfasste und nach einem durchdachten Plane aneinanderreihte"). Cf. McKenzie, "Chronicler as Redactor," 88–90.

literary and historiographical use that the Chronicler made of the earlier sources available to him. Thus, this is a unique, conspicuous example of a methodology that can shed light, though in a limited way, on the methods that other biblical redactors, authors, and historians used when they approached the ancient sources on which they drew (such as the author of Kings, who made use of various earlier sources in his work).

The present study highlights the many limitations of the biblical sources, primarily of Chronicles, for the modern scholar seeking to trace the course of early Israelite history; it strives to sharpen the historian's awareness of the complexities involved in drawing "historical conclusions" from these sources. The problem is especially serious, because for the moment these biblical sources are almost the only texts available for tracing the primary and continuous development of Israelite history during biblical times. The extrabiblical sources at our disposal at present generally serve to enrich our knowledge of numerous events mentioned in the Hebrew Bible or even to clarify various aspects of these events; in a number of cases we have even learned from these sources about events not mentioned in the Bible (for example, the participation of Ahab, king of Israel, in the battle of Qarqar in the year 853 B.C.E., was revealed in the monolithic inscription by Shalmaneser III, king of Assyria, which was discovered at Kurkh). On the basis of extrabiblical sources alone, however, it is impossible to detect even the central stream or the main lines of Israel's early history.

8. A "Critical" Aspect of Chronicles

The last chapter of this book presents another aspect, a "critical" or even "unfavorable" aspect, of the compositional achievement of the Chronicler. It completes a comprehensive analysis of the Chronicler's productive and complex literary and historiographical activity, demonstrating that there was some inconsistency in the literary and historical reshaping of the texts from the Torah, Samuel, and Kings in the book of Chronicles. Moreover, it illustrates that there were certain alterations introduced by the Chronicler when he cited earlier texts and that, when he did so, he caused disharmony with other passages in his own work or in other biblical writings (contrary to his usual effort to harmonize mutually contradictory passages, which I have shown in chap. 7, §2, pp. 140–158). Furthermore, a few historical modifications in Chronicles seem to originate from gaps in the Chronicler's own knowledge of the historical, geographical, lingusitic, and cultural background of the land and the people of Israel and others during the Monarchic period.

The first two sections of chap. 20, as well as the evidence of nonsystematic theological reshaping of some earlier texts,[17] demonstrate that inconsistency and lack of systematization in a wide-ranging biblical work are not necessarily evidence of late additions and redactions. Thus, we may draw an analogy, even if it is limited, between the Chronicler's work, which shows inconsistency in its methodologies, and the works of other biblical authors, which frequently are inappropriately criticized by scholars on the basis of Greek/Western criteria that demand completeness and consistency.

9. Research Model

This study also offers a model for the study of other parallel texts and their literary and historical variations. This is particularly true in the Bible[18] but also in ancient Near Eastern literature, such as Mesopotamian historical literature, because the nature of its compilation resembles that of the Hebrew Bible, in general. For example, the Neo-Assyrian royal inscriptions contain parallel episodes that were written at various intervals separated by relatively short periods of time. Most of these episodes are distinguished from one another by the order of their appearance in the entire complex relating to a particular king; by their length; by details of their content; by the objective(s) of their recounting; by their formulation, style, and literary form, as well as their development. Despite the fact that the length of time separating the parallel texts in Chronicles from those in Samuel–Kings is far greater than the length of time separating the parallel texts in the Neo-Assyrian royal inscriptions, and despite the lack of historical relationship between the literary adaptation of the parallel texts in Chronicles and that of the parallel episodes in the Neo-Assyrian inscriptions, there remain certain typological similarities between them, at least with regard to their writing and editing techniques.[19] Exploration of the literary and historiographical similarities between these historical sources may well contribute to an understanding of the methods and approaches of the ancient Near Eastern authors, as well as the literary

---

17. See, for instance, above, example 10.16 (pp. 205–207 n. 40), and the examples collected by Japhet, *Ideology*, 191–98, 215–16.

18. For a list of the parallel texts in the Bible, see Chapman, *Introduction*, 266; and those collected by Bendavid, *Parallels in the Bible*.

19. The study of parallel episodes in the Neo-Assyrian royal inscriptions has recently been intensified. See, e.g., Borger, *Einleitung*; Schramm, *Assyrischen Königsinschriften*; Spalinger, "Esarhaddon," 295–326; idem, "Assurbanipal," 316–28; Cogan, "Ashurbanipal Prism," 97–107; Tadmor, "History and Ideology," 13–33; Levin, "Inscriptions of Sennacherib," 58–75.

techniques that they employed in the adaptation of the historical sources to which they had access. Cogan's work[20] can serve as an example of this. Cogan demonstrates the deliberate use of pseudo-dating in this phrase: *šanat rēš šarrūti* 'the year of his reign'. It appears in eight of the editions of the "Babylonian Inscription" of Esarhaddon, king of Assyria, which were composed at different times, to express a historiosophic concept. He notes three examples of the deliberate use of similar chronological data in Chronicles (for example, 2 Chr 29:3: "in the first year of his [Hezekiah's] reign, in the first month").

*   *   *

All in all, this study, with its variety of literary and historiographical categories and hundreds of illustrative and comparative examples, shows the capacity of literary phenomena to explain even the minor variations between Chronicles and its biblical sources and to throw light on numerous passages. It establishes that the Chronicler was a prolific, industrious, and creative writer who should be considered an author as well as a redactor. It also demonstrates that the Chronicler worked from the full range of "biblical" sources—to mention some of them: the complete Torah, early historical writings, early and late prophetic sources, Psalms, and even Ezra–Nehemiah. This book argues that Chronicles, in the main, represents a unified composition.

It is my hope that the collective weight of the examples accumulated in this volume verifies my conclusions and will have an impact on several wider issues in Chronicles research and the study of biblical and ancient Near Eastern historical writing in general. These issues include, among others, the relationship between literary criticism and textual criticism, historical study and textual analysis, and an awareness of some inconsistencies in ancient oriental historians' treatment of sources. My desire is that this study will sharpen modern historians' awareness of the problematic nature of the biblical historical books, especially the book of Chronicles, and their limits in being used as historical sources. Furthermore, because the book of Chronicles is the only biblical composition for which we possess at least some actual sources, we may expect to extrapolate these conclusions and consider the types of technique and methods that probably were used by other biblical writers.

---

20. See Cogan, "Chronology," 197–209.

Bibliography

Abramsky, "King
Solomon"

Abramsky, *Saul and
David*

Ackroyd, "Chronicler as
Exegete"

Ackroyd, *Chronicles*

Ackroyd, "Concept of
Unity"

Ackroyd, *Israel under
Babylon*

Aharoni, *Arad*

Aharoni, *Land of the
Bible*

Aḥituv, *Ancient Hebrew
Inscriptions*

Aḥituv, "Ezion-Geber"

Aḥituv, "Shima"

Aḥituv, "Shipping"

Albright, *Archaeology*

Albright, "Chronicler"

Albright, "Votive Stele"

Allegro, "Qumran
Literature"

Allen, "Kerygmatic
Units"

Alt, "Ägyptisch-
Ugaritisches"

S. Abramsky. "The Chronicler's View of King Solomon."
Eretz-Israel 16 (H. M. Orlinsky Volume; 1982) 3–14.
[Hebrew]

S. Abramsky. *The Kingdom of Saul and David*. Jerusalem,
1977. [Hebrew]

P. R. Ackroyd. "The Chronicler as Exegete." *Journal for
the Study of the Old Testament* 2 (1977) 2–32.

P. R. Ackroyd. *I and II Chronicles, Ezra, Nehemiah:
Introduction and Commentary*. London, 1973.

P. R. Ackroyd. "Chronicles-Ezra-Nehemiah: The Concept
of Unity." *Zeitschrift für die alttestamentliche
Wissenschaft* 100 (1988) 189–201 (= idem, *The Chronicler
and His Age* [Journal for the Study of the Old Testament
Supplements 101; Sheffield, 1991] 344–59).

P. R. Ackroyd. *Israel under Babylon and Persia*. Oxford,
1979.

Y. Aharoni. *Arad Inscriptions*. Jerusalem, 1975. [Hebrew]

Y. Aharoni. *The Land of the Bible: A Historical Geography*.
2nd ed. Philadelphia, 1979.

S. Aḥituv. *Handbook of Ancient Hebrew Inscriptions*. The
Biblical Encyclopaedia Library 7. Jerusalem, 1992.
[Hebrew]

S. Aḥituv. "Ezion-Geber." Pp. 332–33 in vol. 6 of
Encyclopaedia Biblica. Jerusalem, 1971. [Hebrew]

S. Aḥituv. "Shima." P. 132 in vol. 8 of *Encyclopaedia
Biblica*. Jerusalem, 1971. [Hebrew]

S. Aḥituv. "Shipping." Pp. 1071–74 in vol. 5 of
Encyclopaedia Biblica. Jerusalem, 1971. [Hebrew]

W. F. Albright. *Archaeology and the Religion of Israel*.
Baltimore, 1942.

W. F. Albright. "The Date and Personality of the Chronicler." *Journal of Biblical Literature* 40 (1921) 104–24.

W. F. Albright. "A Votive Stele Erected by Ben-Hadad I of
Damascus to the God Melcarth." *Bulletin of the American
Schools of Oriental Research* 87 (1942) 23–29.

J. M. Allegro. "Further Messianic References in Qumran
Literature." *Journal of Biblical Literature* 75 (1956)
174–87.

L. C. Allen. "Kerygmatic Units in 1 and 2 Chronicles."
Journal for the Study of the Old Testament 41 (1988)
21–36.

A. Alt. "Ägyptisch-Ugaritisches." *Archiv für
Orientforschung* 15 (1945–51) 69–74.

Amit, "Exodus Tradition" — Y. Amit. "The Position of the Exodus Tradition in the Book of Chronicles." Pp. 139–55 in *Te'uda II: Bible Studies— Y. M. Grintz in Memoriam*, ed. B. Uffenheimer. Tel Aviv, 1982. [Hebrew]

Ashbel, "דמשק or דרמשק" — D. Ashbel. "Damešeq or Darmešq." *Beth Mikra* 12 (1967) 107–11. [Hebrew]

Auerbach, *Wüste und Gelobtes Land* — E. Auerbach. *Wüste und Gelobtes Land, Erster Band: Geschichte Israels von den Anfangen bis zum Tode Salomos*. Berlin, 1932.

Auld, *Kings without Privilege* — A. G. Auld. *Kings without Privilege: David and Moses in the Story of the Bible's Kings*. Edinburgh, 1994.

Avigad, *Ancient Monuments* — N. Avigad. *Ancient Monuments in the Kidron Valley*. Jerusalem, 1954. [Hebrew]

Avigad, *Hebrew Bullae* — N. Avigad. *Hebrew Bullae from the Time of Jeremiah*. Jerusalem, 1986. [Hebrew]

Avigad, "Hebrew Seals" — N. Avigad. "Several Hebrew Seals from the Collection of Dr. Hecht." Pp. 123–31 in *Festschrift Reuben Hecht*. Jerusalem, 1979. [Hebrew]

Avigad, "Royal Steward" — N. Avigad. "The Epitaph of a Royal Steward from Siloam Village." *Eretz-Israel* 3 (M.D.U. Cassuto Volume; 1954) 66–72. [Hebrew]

Avigad, "Seal of Jezebel" — N. Avigad. "The Seal of Jezebel." *Israel Exploration Journal* 14 (1964) 274–76.

Avishur, "Word Order" — Y. Avishur. "On Word Order in Biblical and Ugaritic Pairs." Pp. 335–51 in *Abraham Even-Shoshan Festschrift*, ed. B. Z. Luria. Jerusalem, 1985. [Hebrew]

Avishur, *Word Pairs* — Y. Avishur. *Word Pairs in the Bible and Their Parallels in the Semitic Ancient Near Eastern Literature*. Ph.D. dissertation. Hebrew University of Jerusalem. 1974.

Barag, "Silver Coin" — D. Barag. "A Silver Coin of Yohanan the High Priest and the Coinage of Judea in the Fourth Century B.C." *Israel Numismatic Journal* 9 (1986/87) 4–21.

Bar-Efrat, *Narrative Art* — S. Bar-Efrat. *Narrative Art in the Bible*. Journal for the Study of the Old Testament Supplements 70. Sheffield, 1989.

Bar-Kochva, "Seron and Cestius Gallus" — B. Bar-Kochva, "Seron and Cestius Gallus at Beith Horon." *Palestine Exploration Quarterly* 108 (1976) 13–21.

Barthélemy et al., *David and Goliath* — D. Barthélemy, D. W. Gooding, J. Lust, and E. Tov. *The Story of David and Goliath*. Göttingen, 1986.

Batten, *Ezra–Nehemiah* — L. W. Batten. *The Books of Ezra and Nehemiah*. International Critical Commentary. Edinburgh, 1913.

Baumgartner, *Lexikon zum AT* — W. Baumgartner. *Hebräisches und aramäisches Lexikon zum Alten Testament*. 3rd ed. Leiden, 1967.

Ben-Barak, "Coronation Ceremonies" — Z. Ben-Barak. "The Coronation Ceremonies of Joash and Nabopolassar in Comparison." *Studies in the History of the Jewish People and the Land of Israel* 5 (1980) 43–56. [Hebrew]

Bendavid, *Biblical Hebrew and Mishnaic Hebrew* — A. Bendavid. *Biblical Hebrew and Mishnaic Hebrew*. 2 vols. Tel Aviv, 1967–71. [Hebrew]

Bendavid, *Parallels in the Bible*	A. Bendavid. *Parallels in the Bible*. Jerusalem, 1972. [Hebrew]
Ben-Porat, "Literary Allusions"	Z. Ben-Porat. "Reader, Text and Literary Allusions: Aspects in the Actualization of Literary Allusions." *HaSifrut* 26 (1978) 1–25. [Hebrew]
Bentzen, *Introduction*	A. Bentzen. *Introduction to the Old Testament*. Vol. 2. Copenhagen, 1952.
Ben-Yashar, "Last Kings of Judah"	M. Ben-Yashar. "The Last Kings of Judah." Pp. 111–33 in *Studies in Bible and Exegesis*, ed. U. Simon. Ramat Gan, 1986. [Hebrew]
Benzinger, *Chronik*	I. Benzinger. *Die Bücher der Chronik*. Tübingen, 1901.
Benzinger, *Könige*	I. Benzinger. *Die Bücher der Könige*. Freiburg, 1899.
Bergman (= Biran), "Occupation"	A. Bergman (= Biran). "The Israelite Occupation of Eastern Palestine in the Light of Territorial History." *Journal of the American Oriental Society* 54 (1934) 163–77.
Bertheau, *Chronik*	E. Bertheau. *Die Bücher der Chronik*. Leipzig, 1854.
Bertholdt, *Einleitung*	D. L. Bertholdt. *Historisch-kritische Einleitung in die Schriften des alten und neuen Testaments*. Erlangen, 1813.
Bickerman, *Ezra*	E. Bickerman. *From Ezra to the Last of the Maccabees*. New York, 1966.
Biran-Naveh, "Aramaic Stele"	A. Biran and J. Naveh. "An Aramaic Stele Fragment from Tel Dan." *Israel Exploration Journal* 43 (1993) 81–98.
Biran-Naveh, "Tel Dan Inscription"	A. Biran and J. Naveh. "The Tel Dan Inscription: A New Fragment." *Israel Exploration Journal* 45 (1995) 1–18.
Blau, "Asyndetic Prepositional Clauses"	J. Blau. "Asyndetic Prepositional Clauses Opening with a Substantive in Biblical Hebrew." Pp. 277–85 in *Teʿuda II: Bible Studies—Y. M. Grintz in Memoriam*, ed. B. Uffenheimer. Tel Aviv, 1982. [Hebrew]
Blenkinsopp, *Ezra–Nehemiah*	J. Blenkinsopp. *Ezra–Nehemiah*. Old Testament Library. London, 1988.
Blenkinsopp, "Kiriath-Jearim"	J. Blenkinsopp. "Kiriath-Jearim and the Ark." *Journal of Biblical Literature* 88 (1969) 143–56.
Borger, *Asarhaddon*	R. Borger. *Die Inschriften Asarhaddon Königs von Assyrien*. Archiv für Orientforschung Beiheft 9. Graz, 1956.
Borger, *Einleitung*	R. Borger. *Einleitung in die assyrischen Königsinschriften, Erster Teil: Das zweite Jahrtausend v. Chr.* Leiden, 1961.
Borger, "Waffenträger"	R. Borger. "Die Waffenträger des Königs Darius." *Vetus Testamentum* 22 (1972) 385–98.
Braun, *1 Chronicles*	R. L. Braun. *1 Chronicles*. Word Biblical Commentary. Waco, Texas, 1986.
Braun, "Chronicles, Ezra and Nehemiah"	R. L. Braun. "Chronicles, Ezra and Nehemiah: Theology and Literary History." Pp. 52–64 in *Studies in the Historical Books of the Old Testament*. Vetus Testamentum Supplements 30. Leiden, 1979.
Braun, "Solomonic Apologetic"	R. L. Braun. "Solomonic Apologetic in Chronicles." *Journal of Biblical Literature* 92 (1973) 503–16.

Braun, "Temple Builder" R. [L.] Braun. "Solomon, the Chosen Temple Builder: The Significance of I Chronicles 22, 28 and 29 for the Theology of Chronicles." *Journal of Biblical Literature* 95 (1976) 581–90.

Breasted, *Records of Egypt* J. H. Breasted. *Ancient Records of Egypt.* Vol. 2. New York, 1906.

Breslavi, *Do You Know the Land?* J. Breslavi. *Do You Know the Land?* Vol. 4. Tel Aviv, 1956. [Hebrew]

Briggs and Briggs, *Psalms* C. A. Briggs and E. G. Briggs. *The Book of Psalms.* International Critical Commentary. 2 vols. Edinburgh, 1906–7.

Bright, *History* J. Bright. *A History of Israel.* 2nd ed. Philadelphia, 1972.

Brin, "The Roots עזר-עזז" G. Brin. "The Roots עזר-עזז in the Bible." *Lešonénu* 24 (1960) 8–14. [Hebrew]

Brin, "Son of the King" G. Brin, "On the Title בן המלך (= 'Son of the King')," *Lešonénu* 31 (1966) 5–20, 85–90, 240. [Hebrew]

Brin, "Working Methods" G. Brin. "Working Methods of Biblical Translators and Their Relevance in Establishing the Text." *Tarbiz* 57 (1988) 445–49. [Hebrew]

Brin-Hoffman, "Chiasmus in the Bible" G. Brin and Y. Hoffman. "On the Usage of Chiasmus in the Bible." Pp. 280–89 in *Festschrift M. Zeidel*, ed. A. Alinor, H. M. I. Gevaryahu, I. A. Zeidmann, B. Z. Luria, and P. Melzer. Jerusalem, 1962. [Hebrew]

Broshi, "Jaffa" M. Broshi. "Jaffa." Pp. 737–43 in vol. 3 of *Encyclopaedia Biblica*. Jerusalem, 1965. [Hebrew]

Brunet, "Chroniste" A. M. Brunet. "Le Chroniste et ses Sources." *Revue Biblique* 60 (1953) 481–508; *Revue Biblique* 61 (1954) 349–86.

Buber, "Keyword" M. M. Buber. "Keyword in the Pentateuchal Stories." Pp. 284–99 in *The Method of the Bible*. Jerusalem, 1978. [Hebrew]

Budde, *Samuel* K. Budde. *Die Bücher Samuel.* Tübingen, 1902.

Burney, *Kings* C. F. Burney. *Notes on the Hebrew Text of the Book of Kings.* Oxford, 1903.

Bury-Meiggs, *History of Greece* J. B. Bury and R. Meiggs. *A History of Greece to the Death of Alexander the Great.* 4th ed. London, 1975.

Butzer, "Kanal" K. W. Butzer. "Kanal, Nile—Rotes Meer." Pp. 312–13 in vol. 3 of *Lexikon der Ägyptologie*. Wiesbaden, 1980.

Cassuto, "Death of Baal" U. Cassuto. "The Death of Baal (Tablet I*AB of the Ras Shamra Texts)." Pp. 146–67 in vol. 2 of *Biblical and Oriental Studies*. Jerusalem, 1975.

Cassuto, *Goddess Anath* U. Cassuto. *The Goddess Anath.* Jerusalem, 1965.

Chapman, *Introduction* A. T. Chapman. *An Introduction to the Pentateuch.* Cambridge, 1911.

Childs, *Isaiah* B. S. Childs. *Isaiah and the Assyrian Crisis.* London, 1967.

Clements, *Isaiah* R. E. Clements. *Isaiah 1–39.* New Century Bible. London, 1982.

Cogan, "Ashurbanipal Prism" M. Cogan. "Ashurbanipal Prism F: Notes on Scribal Techniqes and Editorial Procedures." *Journal of Cuneiform Studies* 29 (1977) 97–107.

Cogan, "Chronology" M. Cogan. "The Chronicler's Use of Chronology as Illuminated by Neo-Assyrian Royal Inscriptions." Pp. 197–209 in *Empirical Models for Biblical Criticism*, ed. J. H. Tigay. Philadelphia, 1985.

Cogan, *Imperialism and Religion* M. Cogan. *Imperialism and Religion*. Missoula, Montana, 1974.

Cogan-Tadmor, "Ahaz and Tiglath-Pileser" M. Cogan and H. Tadmor. "Ahaz and Tiglath-Pileser in the Book of Kings: Historiographic Considerations." *Eretz-Israel* 14 (H. L. Ginsberg Volume; 1978) 55–61. [Hebrew]

Cogan-Tadmor, *II Kings* M. Cogan and H. Tadmor. *II Kings: A New Translation with Introduction and Commentary*. Anchor Bible 11. Garden City, New York, 1988.

Coggins, *Chronicles* R. J. Coggins. *The First and Second Books of the Chronicles*. The Cambridge Bible Commentary. Cambridge, 1976.

Cohen, "Speech of Rab-Šāqê" C. Cohen. "Neo-Assyrian Elements in the First Speech of the Biblical Rab-Šāqê." *Israel Oriental Studies* 9 (1979) 32–48.

Conder, "Temple of Joppa" C. R. Conder. "The Prayer of Ben Abdas on the Dedication of the Temple of Joppa." *Palestine Exploration Fund Quarterly Statement* (1892) 170–74.

Cook, "Uzziah" S. A. Cook. "Uzziah." Pp. 5240–44 in vol. 4 of *Encyclopaedia Biblica*, ed. T. K. Cheyne and J. S. Black. London, 1903.

Cowley, *Aramaic Papyri* A. Cowley. *Aramaic Papyri of the Fifth Century B.C.* Oxford, 1923.

Crenshaw, "Ecclesiastes" J. L. Crenshaw. "Ecclesiastes, Book of." Pp. 271–80 in vol. 2 of *Anchor Bible Dictionary*. New York, 1992.

Crockett, *Harmony* W. D. Crockett. *A Harmony of the Books of Samuel, Kings and Chronicles*. Grand Rapids, Michigan, 1951.

Cross, *Ancient Library* F. M. Cross. *The Ancient Library of Qumran and Modern Biblical Studies*. London, 1958.

Cross, "Biblical Text" F. M. Cross. "The History of the Biblical Text in the Light of Discoveries in the Judaean Desert." *Harvard Theological Review* 57 (1964) 292–97.

Cross, "Contribution" F. M. Cross. "The Contribution of the Qumran Discoveries to the Study of the Biblical Text." *Israel Exploration Journal* 16 (1966) 81–95.

Cross, "Oldest Manuscript" F. M. Cross. "The Oldest Manuscript from Qumran." *Journal of Biblical Literature* 74 (1955) 147–72.

Cross, "Qumran and Septuagint" F. M. Cross. "A New Qumran Biblical Fragment Related to the Original Hebrew Underlying the Septuagint." *Bulletin of the American Schools of Oriental Research* 132 (1953) 15–26.

Cross, "Reconstruction" F. M. Cross. "Reconstruction of the Judean Restoration." *Journal of Biblical Literature* 94 (1975) 4–18.

Cross, "Report" F. M. Cross. "A Report on the Biblical Fragments of Cave Four in Wâdi-Qumran." *Bulletin of the American Schools of Oriental Research* 141 (1956) 9–13.

Cross, "Samaria and Jerusalem" — F. M. Cross. "Samaria and Jerusalem." Pp. 81–94, 271–74 in Tadmor, *The Restoration—The Persian Period.*

Curtis-Madsen, *Chronicles* — E. L. Curtis and A. A. Madsen. *A Critical and Exegetical Commentary on the Books of Chronicles.* International Critical Commentary. Edinburgh, 1910.

Dahood, *Psalms* — M. Dahood. *Psalms 1–50: Introduction, Translation and Notes.* Anchor Bible 16. Garden City, New York, 1966.

Day, *Molech* — J. Day. *Molech: A God of Human Sacrifice in the Old Testament.* Cambridge, 1989.

Deboys, "Portrayal of Abijah" — D. G. Deboys. "History and Theology in the Chronicler's Portrayal of Abijah." *Biblica* 71 (1990) 48–62.

Delcor, "Jewish Literature" — M. Delcor. "Jewish Literature in Hebrew and Aramaic in Greek Era." Pp. 352–84 in W. D. Davies and L. Finkelstein (eds.), *The Hellenistic Age.* Vol. 2 of *The Cambridge History of Judaism.* Cambridge, 1989.

Delitzsch, *Schreibfehler* — F. Delitzsch. *Die Lese- und Schreibfehler im Alten Testament.* Berlin, 1920.

Demsky, "Geba" — A. Demsky. "Geba, Gibeah and Gibeon: An Historico-Geographic Riddle." *Bulletin of the American Schools of Oriental Research* 212 (1973) 26–31.

Demsky, "Genealogy" — A. Demsky. "The Genealogy of Gibeon (I Chronicles 9:35–44): Biblical and Epigraphic Consideration." *Bulletin of the American Schools of Oriental Research* 202 (1971) 16–23.

De Vries, *1 Kings* — S. J. De Vries. *1 Kings.* Word Biblical Commentary. Waco, Texas, 1985.

Dietrich-Loretz-Sanmartín, *Texte aus Ugarit* — M. Dietrich, O. Loretz, and J. Sanmartín. *Die Keilalphabetischen Texte aus Ugarit.* Alter Orient und Altes Testament 24/1. Neukirchen-Vluyn, 1976.

Dillard, *2 Chronicles* — R. B. Dillard. *2 Chronicles.* Word Biblical Commentary. Waco, Texas, 1987.

Dillard, "Solomon Narrative" — R. B. Dillard. "The Literary Structure of the Chronicler's Solomon Narrative." *Journal for the Study of the Old Testament* 30 (1984) 85–93.

Di Marco, "Der Chiasmus in der Bibel" — A. Di Marco. "Der Chiasmus in der Bibel." *Linguistica Biblica* 36 (1975) 21–97; *Linguistica Biblica* 37 (1976) 49–68.

Diringer, *Iscrizioni* — D. Diringer. *Le iscrizioni antico-ebraiche palestinesi.* Florence, 1934.

Dirksen, "David Disqualified" — P. B. Dirksen. "Why Was David Disqualified as Temple Builder? The Meaning of 1 Chronicles 22,8," *Journal for the Study of the Old Testament* 70 (1996) 51–56.

Donner-Röllig, *KAI* — H. Donner and W. Röllig. *Texte.* Vol. 1 of *Kanaanäische und Aramäische Inschriften.* Wiesbaden, 1966.

Dothan, "Cremation Burial" — M. Dothan. "A Cremation Burial at Azor: A Danite City." *Eretz-Israel* 20 (Y. Yadin Volume; 1989) 164–74.

Driver, "Abbreviations" — G. R. Driver. "Abbreviations in the Massoretic Text." *Textus* 1 (1960) 112–31.

Driver, "Burial Custom" — G. R. Driver. "A Hebrew Burial Custom." *Zeitschrift für die alttestamentliche Wissenschaft* 66 (1954) 314–15.

Driver, *Introduction* S. R. Driver. *An Introduction to the Literature of the Old Testament*. International Theological Library. 9th ed. Edinburgh, 1910.

Driver, *Samuel* S. R. Driver. *Notes on the Hebrew Text of the Books of Samuel*. Oxford, 1890.

Ebeling-Meissner, "Beamter" E. Ebeling and B. Meissner (eds.). "Beamter—d. Assyrische Zeit." Pp. 457–66 in vol. 1 of *Reallexikon der Assyriologie*. Berlin, 1928.

Ehrlich, *Mikrâ ki-Pheschutô* A. B. Ehrlich. *Divrê Soferim*. Vol. 2 of *Mikrâ ki-Pheschutô*. Berlin, 1900.

Ehrlich, *Randglossen* A. B. Ehrlich. Pp. 325–84 in vol. 7 of *Randglossen zur Hebräischen Bibel*. Leipzig, 1914.

Eichrodt, *Theologie* W. Eichrodt. *Theologie des Alten Testaments*. Stuttgart, 1962.

Eichrodt, *Theology* W. Eichrodt. *Theology of the Old Testament*. London, 1976.

Eichhorn, *Einleitung* J. G. Eichhorn. *Einleitung ins Alte Testament*. 2nd ed. Reutlingen, 1790.

Eissfeldt, *Einleitung* O. Eissfeldt. *Einleitung in das Alte Testament*. 2nd ed. Tübingen, 1956.

Eissfeldt, *Introduction* O. Eissfeldt. *The Old Testament: An Introduction*. Oxford, 1965.

Elat, *Economic Relations* M. Elat. *Economic Relations in the Lands of the Bible*. Jerusalem, 1977. [Hebrew]

Elat, "Tarshish" M. Elat. "Tarshish." Pp. 942–45 in vol. 8 of *Encyclopaedia Biblica*. Jerusalem, 1982. [Hebrew]

Elat, "Tarshish and Phoenician" M. Elat. "Tarshish and the Problem of Phoenician Colonisation in the Western Mediterranean." *Orientalia Lovaniensia Periodica* 13 (1982) 55–69.

Elat, "Trade" M. Elat. "Trade and Commerce." Pp. 173–86, 313–18 in vol. 2 of Malamat (ed.), *The Age of the Monarchies*.

Ellenbogen, *Foreign Words* M. Ellenbogen. *Foreign Words in the Old Testament: Their Origin and Etymology*. London, 1962.

Elliger, "Die dreissig Helden Davids" K. Elliger. "Die dreissig Helden Davids." *Palästina-Jahrbuch* 31 (1931) 29–75 (= pp. 72–118 in *Kleine Schriften zum Alten Testament*. Munich, 1966).

Elmslie, *Chronicles* (1916) W. A. L. Elmslie. *The Books of Chronicles*. The Cambridge Bible for Schools and Colleges. Cambridge, 1916.

Elmslie, *Chronicles* (1954) W. A. L. Elmslie. "The First and Second Books of Chronicles." Pp. 339–548 in vol. 3 of *The Interpreter's Bible*, ed. G. A. Buttrick. New York, 1954.

Endres-Millar-Burns, *Synoptic Parallels* J. C. Endres, W. R. Millar, and J. B. Burns (eds.). *Chronicles and Its Synoptic Parallels in Samuel, Kings, and in Related Biblical Texts*. Collegeville, Minnesota, 1998.

Eph'al, *Arabs* I. Eph'al. *The Ancient Arabs: Nomads on the Borders of the Fertile Crescent 9th–5th Centuries B.C.* Jerusalem, 1984.

Eph'al, "Assyrian Ramp" I. Eph'al. "The Assyrian Ramp at Lachish: Military and Lexical Aspects." *Zion* 49 (1984) 333–47. [Hebrew]

Eph'al, *Israel and Judah* I. Eph'al (ed.). *Israel and Judah in the Biblical Period*. Vol. 2 of *The History of Eretz-Israel*. Jerusalem, 1984. [Hebrew]

Eph⁽al, "Sennacherib"   I. Eph⁽al. "Sennacherib." Pp. 1063–69 in vol. 5 of
                            Encyclopaedia Biblica. Jerusalem, 1971. [Hebrew]
Eph⁽al, "Syria–   I. Eph⁽al. "Syria–Palestine under Achaemenid Rule."
    Palestine"   Pp. 139–64 in *Persia, Greece and the Western
                            Mediterranean c. 525 to 479 B.C.* Vol. 4 of *Cambridge
                            Ancient History.* 2nd ed. Cambridge, 1988.
Eph⁽al, "Tartan"   I. Eph⁽al. "Tartan." Pp. 946–48 in vol. 6 of *Encyclopaedia
                            Biblica.* Jerusalem, 1971. [Hebrew]
Evenari, "Cymbals"   H. Evenari. "Cymbals." *Tazlil* 3 (1966) 24–25. [Hebrew]
Falkenstein-von Soden,   A. Falkenstein and W. von Soden. *Sumerische und
    Hymnen und Gebete   akkadische Hymnen und Gebete.* Zurich, 1953.
Fallon, "Eupolemus"   F. Fallon. "Eupolemus." Pp. 861–72 in vol. 2 of *The Old
                            Testament Pseudepigrapha.* Anchor Bible Reference
                            Library. New York, 1985.
Feigin, "Transferring   S. I. Feigin. "Transferring the Ark from Kiryat Jearim to
    the Ark"   Jerusalem." Pp. 83–87 in *Missitrei Heavar: Biblical and
                            Historical Studies.* New York, 1943. [Hebrew]
Fensham, "Father and   F. C. Fensham. "Father and Son as Terminology for Treaty
    Son"   and Convenant." Pp. 121–35 in *Near Eastern Studies in
                            Honor of W. F. Albright,* ed. H. Goedicke. Baltimore, 1971.
Fensham, "Treaty   F. C. Fensham. "The Treaty between Solomon and Hiram
    between Solomon   and the Alalakh Tablets." *Journal of Biblical Literature* 79
    and Hiram"   (1960) 59–60.
Fenton, "Saris,   T. L. Fenton. "Saris, Rab-Saris." Pp. 1126–27 in vol. 5 of
    Rab-Saris"   *Encyclopaedia Biblica.* Jerusalem, 1971. [Hebrew]
Finkelstein, *Archaeology* I. Finkelstein. *The Archaeology of Israelite Settlement.*
                            Jerusalem, 1988.
Finkelstein, *Sifre on*   L. Finkelstein. *Sifre on Deuteronomy.* New York, 1993.
    Deuteronomy
Fohrer, *Introduction*   G. Fohrer. *Introduction to the Old Testament.* London,
                            1960.
Fox, "Ecclesiastes"   M. V. Fox. "Ecclesiastes." Pp. 70–83 in vol. 7 of
                            Encyclopaedia Biblica. Jerusalem, 1976. [Hebrew]
Fraenkel, "Antithesis"   L. Fraenkel. "Antithesis: A Literary Device." Pp. 129–46
                            in Uffenheimer, *Bible and Jewish History.*
Freedman, "Purpose"   D. N. Freedman. "The Chronicles' Purpose." *Catholic
                            Biblical Quarterly* 23 (1961) 436–42.
Friedman, "Tabernacle"   R. E. Friedman. "The Tabernacle in the Temple." *Biblical
                            Archaeologist* 43 (1980) 241–48.
Galling, *Chronik*   K. Galling. *Die Bücher der Chronik, Esra, Nehemia:
                            Übersetzt und erklärt.* Das Alte Testament Deutsch 12.
                            Göttingen, 1954.
Garsiel, *Kingdom of*   M. Garsiel. *The Kingdom of David.* Tel Aviv, 1975.
    David   [Hebrew]
Garsiel, *Parallels*   M. Garsiel. *Parallels between Jeremiah and Psalms.* Ph.D.
    between Jeremiah   dissertation. Tel Aviv University, 1973.
    and Psalms
Geiger, *Urschrift und*   A. Geiger. *Urschrift und Übersetzungen der Bibel in ihrer
    Übersetzungen   Abhängigkeit von der innern Entwickelung des
                            Judenthums.* 2nd ed. Frankfurt am Main, 1928.

Gelston, "End of
Chronicles"
A. Gelston. "The End of Chronicles." *Scandinavian
Journal of the Old Testament* 10 (1996) 53–60.

Gerleman, *Septuagint*
G. Gerleman. *Studies in the Septuagint: II Chronicles.*
Lund, 1946.

Gerleman, *Synoptic
Studies*
G. Gerleman. *Synoptic Studies in the Old Testament.*
Lund, 1948.

Gesenius-Kautzsch,
Hebrew Grammer
W. Gesenius. *Hebrew Grammer*, ed. E. Kautzsch, trans.
and rev. A. E. Cowley. 2nd English ed. Oxford, 1910.

Gibson, *Textbook*
J. C. L. Gibson. *Textbook of Syrian Semitic Inscriptions.*
Vol. 1: *Hebrew and Moabite Inscriptions*; vol. 2: *Aramaic
Inscriptions*; and vol. 3: *Phoenician Inscriptions.* Oxford,
1971–82.

Gilad, "Conquest of
Jerusalem"
H. Gilad. "The Conquest of Jerusalem by David." Pp. 99–
107 in *J. Gil Festschrift*, ed. Y. Hocherman, M. Lahav, and
Z. Zemarion. Jerusalem, 1979. [Hebrew]

Ginsberg, *Ugarit Texts*
H. L. Ginsberg. *The Ugarit Texts.* Jerusalem, 1936.

Ginzberg, "Hieronymus
zu Jesaja"
L. Ginzberg. "Die Haggada bei den Kirchenvätern: VI—
Hieronymus zu Jesaja." Pp. 279–314 in *Jewish Studies in
Memory of G. A. Kohut*, ed. S. W. Baron and A. Marx. New
York, 1935.

Glueck, "Elath, Eloth"
N. Glueck. "Elath, Eloth." Pp. 268–72 in vol. 1 of
Encyclopaedia Biblica. Jerusalem, 1965. [Hebrew]

Goedicke, *The Report of
Wenamon*
H. Goedicke. *The Report of Wenamon.* Baltimore, 1975.

Goethe, "Paralipomena"
J. W. von Goethe. "Paralipomena." Pp. 539–619 in vol. 5
of *Gedenkausgabe der Werke, Briefe und Gespräche*, ed.
E. Beutler. Zurich, 1949.

Goitein, "City of Adam"
S. D. Goitein. "The City of Adam in the Book of Psalms."
Bulletin of the Jewish Palestine Exploration Society 13
(1947) 86–88. [Hebrew]

Golan, *Hellenistic World*
D. Golan. *A History of the Hellenistic World.* Jerusalem,
1987.

Goldstein, *I–II
Maccabees*
J. A. Goldstein. *I–II Maccabees.* Anchor Bible 41–41A.
Garden City, New York, 1976–83.

Gordon, "Anath"
C. H. Gordon. "Review of U. Cassuto, *The Goddess Anath*."
Journal of the American Oriental Society 72 (1952) 180–
81.

Gordon, "ANET"
C. H. Gordon. "Review of J. B. Pritchard, *Ancient Near
Eastern Texts.*" *Journal of Biblical Literature* 70 (1951)
159–63.

Gordon, *Ugaritic
Textbook*
C. H. Gordon. *Ugaritic Textbook: Grammar, Texts in
Transliteration, Cuneiform Selections.* Rome, 1965.

Graf, *Geschichtlichen
Bücher*
K. H. Graf. Pp. 114–247 in *Die geschichtlichen Bücher des
Alten Testaments: Zwei historisch-kritische
Untersuchungen.* Leipzig, 1866.

Gramberg, *Chronik*
C. P. W. Gramberg. *Die Chronik nach ihrem
geschichtlichen Charakter und ihrer Glaubwürdigkeit neu
geprüft.* Halle, 1823.

Gray, *Kings*
J. Gray. *I and II Kings: A Commentary.* Old Testament
Library. 2nd ed. Philadelphia, 1970.

Gray, *Numbers*	G. B. Gray. *A Critical and Exegetical Commentary on Numbers*. International Critical Commentary. Edinburgh, 1903.
Grayson, *ABC*	A. K. Grayson. *Assyrian and Babylonian Chronicles*. Locust Valley, New York, 1975. Repr. Winona Lake, Indiana, 2000.
Greenfield, "Lexicographical Notes"	J. C. Greenfield. "Lexicographical Notes I." *Hebrew Union College Annual* 29 (1958) 203–28.
Greenfield-Mayrhofer, "ʾAlgummim/ ʾAlmuggim"	J. C. Greenfield and M. Mayrhofer. "The ʾAlgummim/ʾAlmuggim Problem Reexamined." Pp. 83–89 in *Hebräische Wortforschung: Festschrift W. Baumgartner*. Vetus Testamentum Supplements 16. Leiden, 1967.
Grintz, *Early Biblical Ethnology*	Y. M. Grintz. *Studies in Early Biblical Ethnology and History*. Jerusalem, 1969. [Hebrew]
Grintz, "High Priesthood"	Y. M. Grintz. "Aspects of the History of the High Priesthood." Pp. 258–77 in Grintz, *Early Biblical Ethnology* (= *Zion* 23/24 [1958–59] 124–40). [Hebrew]
Grintz, *Judith*	Y. M. Grintz. *The Book of Judith: A Reconstruction of the Original Hebrew Text with Introduction, Commentary, Appendices and Indices*. Jerusalem, 1986. [Hebrew]
Grintz, "Life of David"	Y. M. Grintz. "The Life of David according to the Book of Samuel and I Chronicles." *Beth Mikra* 1 (1956) 69–75 (= pp. 344–53 in Grintz, *Early Biblical Ethnology*).
Grintz, *Studies in the Bible*	Y. M. Grintz. *Studies in the Bible*. Jerusalem, 1979. [Hebrew]
Gunneweg, *Leviten und Priester*	A. H. J. Gunneweg. Pp. 204–15 in *Leviten und Priester: Hauptlinien der Traditionsbildung und Geschichte des israelitisch-jüdischen Kultpersonals*. Göttingen, 1965.
Halevy, "Notes géographiques"	J. Halevy. "Notes géographiques – דמשק." *Revue Semitique d'épigraphie et d'histoire ancienne* 2 (1984) 280–83.
Hanson, "Israelite Religion"	P. D. Hanson. "Israelite Religion in the Early Postexilic Period." Pp. 485–508 in *Ancient Israelite Religion: Essays in Honor of Frank Moore Cross*, ed. P. D. Miller Jr., P. D. Hanson, and S. D. McBride. Philadelphia, 1987.
Haran, "Catch-Lines"	M. Haran. "Catch-Lines in Ancient Palaeography and in the Biblical Canon." *Eretz-Israel* 18 (N. Avigad Volume; 1985) 124–29. [Hebrew]
Haran, "Festivals"	M. Haran. "Pilgrim-Feasts and Family Festivals." Pp. 289–316 in *Temples and Temple-Service*.
Haran, "Identical Lines"	M. Haran. "Explaining the Identical Lines at the End of Chronicles and the Beginning of Ezra." *Bible Review* 2 (1986) 18–20.
Haran, "Incense Altars"	M. Haran. "The 'Incense Altars' in the Archaeological Find and the Worship of the Host of Heaven in the Judaean Kingdom." *Tarbiz* 61 (1992) 321–32. [Hebrew]
Haran, "Priests and Levites"	M. Haran. "Priests and Levites." Pp. 137–200 in Haran, *Ages and Institutions in the Bible*. Tel Aviv, 1972. [Hebrew]

Haran, *Temples* M. Haran. *Temples and Temple-Service in Ancient Israel.* Oxford, 1978. Reprinted Winona Lake, Indiana, 1985.

Harper, *ABL* R. F. Harper. *Assyrian and Babylonian Letters.* Part 7: Chicago, 1902; part 11: Chicago, 1911.

Harrison, *Introduction* R. K. Harrison. *Introduction to the Old Testament.* Grand Rapids, Michigan, 1969.

Hauer, "Jerusalem" C. E. Hauer, Jr. "Jerusalem: The Stronghold and Raphaim." *Catholic Biblical Quarterly* 32 (1970) 571–78.

Haupt, "Midian und Sinai" P. Haupt. "Midian und Sinai." *Zeitschrift der deutschen morgenlandischen Gesellschaft* 63 (1909) 506–30.

Herner, *Syntax der Zahlwörter* S. Herner. *Syntax der Zahlwörter in AT.* Lund, 1893.

Hertzberg, "Mizpa" H. W. Hertzberg. "Mizpa." *Zeitschrift für die alttestamentliche Wissenschaft* 47 (1929) 161–96.

Hill, "1 Chronicles XVI" A. E. Hill. "Patchwork Poetry or Reasoned Verse? Connective Structure in 1 Chronicles XVI." *Vetus Testamentum* 33 (1983) 97–101.

Hobbs, *2 Kings* T. R. Hobbs. *2 Kings.* Word Biblical Commentary. Waco, Texas, 1985.

Hoenig, "Tarshish" S. B. Hoening. "Tarshish." *Jewish Quarterly Review* 69 (1979) 181–82.

Hoffman, *Decisive Evidence* M. Z. Hoffman. *Decisive Evidence against Wellhausen.* Jerusalem, 1918. [Hebrew]

Hoffman, *Doctrine of the Exodus* Y. Hoffman. *The Doctrine of the Exodus in the Bible.* Tel Aviv, 1983. [Hebrew]

Horn, "Byblos" S. H. Horn. "Byblos in Ancient Records." *Andrews University Seminary Studies* 1 (1963) 52–61.

Horovitz-Rabin, *Mechilta d'Rabbi Ismael* H. S. Horovitz and I. A. Rabin (eds.). *Mechilta d'Rabbi Ismael.* 2nd ed. Jerusalem, 1997. [Hebrew]

Hummel, "Enclitic Mem" H. Hummel. "Enclitic Mem in Early Northwest Semitic, Especially Hebrew." *Journal of Biblical Literature* 76 (1957) 85–107.

Hurowitz, "Fiscal Practice" V. (A.) Hurowitz. "Another Fiscal Practice in the Ancient Near East: 2 Kings 12:5–17 and a Letter to Esarhaddon (LAS 277)." *Journal of Near Eastern Studies* 45 (1986) 289–94.

Hurowitz, *Temple Building* V. (A.) Hurowitz. *I Have Built You an Exalted House: Temple Building in the Bible in the Light of Mesopotamian and Northwest Semitic Writings.* Journal for the Study of the Old Testament Supplements 115. Sheffield, 1992.

Hurvitz, "Diachronic Chiasmus" A. Hurvitz. "Diachronic Chiasmus in Biblical Hebrew." Pp. 248–55 in Uffenheimer, *Bible and Jewish History.*

Hurvitz, "Hebrew Language" A. Hurvitz. "The Hebrew Language in the Persian Period." Pp. 210–23, 306–9 in Tadmor, *The Restoration—The Persian Period.* [Hebrew]

Hurvitz, *Linguistic Study* A. Hurvitz. *A Linguistic Study of the Relationship between the Priestly Source and the Book of Ezekiel: A New Approach to an Old Problem.* Paris, 1982.

Hurvitz, *Transition Period* — A. Hurvitz. *Transition Period in Biblical Hebrew: A Study in Post-exilic Hebrew and Its Implications for Dating of Psalms*. Jerusalem, 1972. [Hebrew]

Ishida, "People of the Land" — T. Ishida. "The People of the Land and the Political Crises in Judah." *Annual of the Japanese Biblical Institute* 1 (1975) 23–38.

Japhet, "Authorship" — S. Japhet. "The Supposed Common Authorship of Chronicles and Ezra–Nehemiah Investigated Anew." *Vetus Testamentum* 18 (1968) 330–71.

Japhet, "Biblical Historiography" — S. Japhet. "The Biblical Historiography from the Persian Period." Pp. 176–202, 295–303 in Tadmor, *The Restoration—The Persian Period*.

Japhet, *Chronicles* — S. Japhet. *I & II Chronicles: A Commentary*. Old Testament Library. Louisville, 1993.

Japhet, "Conquest" — S. Japhet. "Conquest and Settlement in Chronicles." *Journal of Biblical Literature* 98 (1979) 205–18.

Japhet, "Historical Reliability" — S. Japhet. "The Historical Reliability of Chronicles: A History of the Problem and Its Place in Biblical Research." *Journal for the Study of the Old Testament* 33 (1985) 83–107.

Japhet, *Ideology* — S. Japhet. *The Ideology of the Book of Chronicles and Its Place in Biblical Thought*. Beiträge zur Erforschung des Alten Testaments und des antiken Judentum 9. Frankfurt am Main, 1989.

Japhet, "Interchanges" — S. Japhet. "Interchanges of Verbal Roots in Parallel Texts in Chronicles." *Hebrew Studies* 28 (1987) 9–50.

Jawitz, *History of Israel* — W. Jawitz. *The History of Israel*. Vol. 2. Warsaw, 1896.

Johnson, *Genealogies* — D. M. Johnson. *The Purpose of the Biblical Genealogies*. Cambridge, 1969.

Joines, "Bronze Serpent" — K. Joines. "The Bronze Serpent in the Israelite Cult." *Journal of Biblical Literature* 87 (1968) 245–56.

Jones, *Kings* — G. H. Jones. *1 and 2 Kings*. New Century Bible. Grand Rapids, Michigan, 1984.

Kaiser, *Introduction* — O. Kaiser. *Introduction to the Old Testament: A Presentation of Its Results and Problems*. Minneapolis, 1977.

Kalimi, "Abfassungszeit" — I. Kalimi. "Die Abfassungszeit der Chronik: Forschungsstand und Perspektiven." *Zeitschrift für die alttestamentliche Wissenschaft* 105 (1993) 223–33.

Kalimi, "Affiliation of Abraham" — I. Kalimi. "The Affiliation of Abraham and the *Aqedah* with Zion/Gerizim in Jewish and Samaritan Sources." Pp. 33–58 in Kalimi, *Early Jewish Exegesis and Theological Controversy*.

Kalimi, *An Ancient Israelite Historian* — I. Kalimi. *An Ancient Israelite Historian: Studies in the Chronicler, His Time, Place, and Writing*. Studia Semitica Neerlandica 46. Assen, 2005.

Kalimi, "Aramäische Grabinschrift" — I. Kalimi. "Könnte die aramäische Grabinschrift aus Ägypten als Indikation für die Datierung der Chronikbücher fungieren?" *Zeitschrift für die alttestamentliche Wissenschaft* 110 (1998) 79–81.

Bibliography 425

Kalimi, *Bibliography* I. Kalimi. *The Books of Chronicles: A Classified Bibliography.* Simor Bible Bibliographies 1. Jerusalem, 1990.

Kalimi, "Capture of Jerusalem" I. Kalimi. "The Capture of Jerusalem in the Chronistic History." *Vetus Testamentum* 52 (2002) 66–79.

Kalimi, "Characterization of the Chronicler" I. Kalimi. "The Characterization of the Chronicler and His Writing." Pp. 19–39 in Kalimi, *An Ancient Israelite Historian.*

Kalimi, "Chronicles in Christian Tradition" I. Kalimi. "History of Interpretation: I and II Chronicles in the Christian Tradition and Exegesis." [forthcoming]

Kalimi, "Date of Chronicles" I. Kalimi. "The Date of the Book of Chronicles." Pp. 347–71 in *Biblical Studies in Honor of Simon John De Vries.* Vol. 1: *God's Word for Our World*, ed. J. H. Ellens, D. L. Ellens, R. P. Knierim, and I. Kalimi. Journal for the Study of the Old Testament Supplements 388. London, 2004.

Kalimi, *Early Jewish Exegesis and Theological Controversy* I. Kalimi. *Early Jewish Exegesis and Theological Controversy: Sudies in Scriptures in the Shadow of Internal and External Controversies.* Jewish and Christian Heritage 2. Assen, 2002.

Kalimi, "Ethnographical Introduction" I. Kalimi. "The View of Jerusalem in the Ethnographical Introduction of Chronicles (1 Chr 1–9)." *Biblica* 83 (2002) 556–62.

Kalimi, "He Sowed It with Salt" I. Kalimi. "He Sowed It (= Shechem) with Salt (Judg. 9,45)." *EtMol: A Journal for the History of the Jewish People and the Land of Israel* 17 (1992) 10. [Hebrew]

Kalimi, "History of Interpretation" I. Kalimi. "History of Interpretation: The Book of Chronicles in Jewish Tradition—From Daniel to Spinoza." *Revue Biblique* 105 (1998) 5–41.

Kalimi, "Jerusalem—The Divine City" I. Kalimi. "Jerusalem—The Divine City: The Representation of Jerusalem in Chronicles Compared with Earlier and Later Jewish Compositions." Pp. 189–205 in *The Chronicler as Theologian: Essays in Honor of Ralph W. Klein*, ed. M. P. Graham, S. L. McKenzie, and G. N. Knoppers. Journal for the Study of the Old Testament Supplements 371. London, 2003.

Kalimi, *Jewish Tradition and Exegesis* I. Kalimi. *The Book of Chronicles in Jewish Tradition and Exegesis: Interpretation, Reception and Impact—History from the Earliest Times to the Beginning of Modern Biblical Scholarship.* Journal for the Study of the Old Testament Supplements 415. London, 2005.

Kalimi, "Land / Mount Moriah" I. Kalimi. "The Land / Mount Moriah, and the Site of the Jerusalem Temple in Biblical Historical Writing." Pp. 9–32 in Kalimi, *Early Jewish Exegesis and Theological Controversy.*

Kalimi, "Literary Study of Chronicles" I. Kalimi. "The Contribution of the Literary Study of Chronicles to the Solution of Its Textual Problems." *Biblical Interpretation* 3 (1995) 190–212.

Kalimi, "New Cart" I. Kalimi. "A New Cart and Brought It from the House of Abinadab (1 Sam 6,3)." P. 61 in *II Samuel*, ed. S. Abramsky and M. Garsiel. Tel Aviv, 1993. [Hebrew]

Kalimi, "Paronomasia"   I. Kalimi. "Paronomasia in the Book of Chronicles."
                          Journal for the Study of the Old Testament 67 (1995)
                          27–41.

Kalimi, "Pharaoh"   I. Kalimi. "Pharaoh." P. 782 in *Illustrated Dictionary and
                          Concordance of the Bible*, ed. S. M. Paul, E. Stern, and
                          G. Wigdor. New York, 1986.

Kalimi, "Shinar"   I. Kalimi. "Shinar." P. 1213 in *Eerdmans Dictionary of the
                          Bible*, ed. D. N. Freedman. Grand Rapids, Michigan, 2000.

Kalimi, "Transmission of I. Kalimi. "A Transmission of Tradition: The Number of
  Tradition"   Jesse's Sons—Biblical Writings, Judeo-Hellenistic Arts,
                          Rabbinic Literature and Medieval Christian Art."
                          Theologische Zeitschrift 57 (2001) 1–9.

Kallai, "Baal Perazim"   Z. Kallai. "Baal Perazim." Pp. 290–91 in vol. 2 of
                          Encyclopaedia Biblica. Jerusalem, 1965. [Hebrew]

Kallai, "Helam"   Z. Kallai. "Helam." P. 114 in vol. 3 of *Encyclopaedia
                          Biblica*. Jerusalem, 1965. [Hebrew]

Kaplan, *Archaeology*   J. Kaplan. *The Archaeology and History of Tel Aviv–Jaffa*.
                          Tel Aviv, 1958–59. [Hebrew]

Kaplan, "Excavations"   J. Kaplan. "The Excavations at the Ancient Jaffa." *Bulletin
                          of the Israel Exploration Society* 20 (1956) 192–94.
                          [Hebrew]

Karmon, "Geopolitical   Y. Karmon. "The Geopolitical Position of Eilat in
  Position"   Historical Perspective." *Studies in the Geography of Israel*
                          6 (1968) 53–80. [Hebrew]

Kasowski, *A Thesaurus*   C. J. Kasowski. *A Thesaurus of Talmudic Hebrew*. Vol. 7
  of Talmudic Hebrew   (Jerusalem, 1959); vol. 28 (Jerusalem, 1972). [Hebrew]

Kassis, "Gath"   H. E. Kassis. "Gath and the Struture of the 'Philistine'
                          Society." *Journal of Biblical Literature* 84 (1965) 259–71.

Katzenstein, "Athaliah" H. J. Katzenstein. "Athaliah." Pp. 430–31 in vol. 6 of
                          Encyclopaedia Biblica. Jerusalem, 1971. [Hebrew]

Katzenstein, "Parents of H. J. Katzenstein. "Who Were the Parents of Athaliah?"
  Athaliah"   *Israel Exploration Journal* 5 (1955) 194–97.

Katzenstein, "Phoenicia" H. J. Katzenstein. "Phoenicia." Pp. 464–77 in vol. 6 of
                          Encyclopaedia Biblica. Jerusalem, 1971. [Hebrew]

Katzenstein,   H. J. Katzenstein. "The Phoenician Term *Hubur* in the
  "Phoenician Term   Report of Wen-Amon." Pp. 599–602 in vol. 2 of *Atti del
  Hubur"   I Congresso Internazionale di Studi Penici e Punici*. Rome,
                          1983.

Katzenstein, "Royal   H. J. Katzenstein. "The Royal Steward (*Asher ʿal ha-
  Steward"   Bayith*)." *Israel Exploration Journal* 10 (1960) 149–54.

Katzenstein, *Tyre*   H. J. Katzenstein. *The History of Tyre*. Jerusalem, 1973.

Kaufman, "Medium   A. S. Kaufman. "Determining the Length of the Medium
  Cubit"   Cubit." *Palestine Exploration Quarterly* 116 (1984)
                          120–32.

Kaufmann, *Religion of*   Y. Kaufmann. *History of the Religion of Israel: From Its
  Israel   Beginnings to the Babylonian Exile*. 8 vols. Jerusalem,
                          1972. [Hebrew]

Keel, *1/2 Chronicles*   Y. Keel. *1/2 Chronicles*. Jerusalem, 1986. [Hebrew]

Kegler-Augustin, *Synopse*	J. Kegler and M. Augustin. *Synopse zum Chronistischen Geschichtswerk*. Beiträge zur Erforschung des Alten Testaments und des antiken Judentum 1. Frankfurt am Main, 1984.
Keil, *Apologetischer Versuch*	C. F. Keil. *Apologetischer Versuch über die Bücher der Chronik und über die Integrität des Buches Esra*. Berlin, 1833.
Keil, *Chronicles*	C. F. Keil. *The Books of Chronicles*. Edinburgh, 1872.
Keil, *Manual*	C. F. Keil. *Manual of Historico-Critical Introduction to the Canonical Scriptures of the Old Testament*. Vol. 2, trans. G. C. M. Douglas. Grand Rapids, Michigan, 1952.
Kelly, "David's Disqualification"	B. E. Kelly. "David's Disqualification in 1 Chronicles 22.8: A Response to Piet Dirksen." *Journal for the Study of the Old Testament* 80 (1998) 53–61.
Kelly, *Retribution*	B. E. Kelly. *Retribution and Eschatology in Chronicles*. Journal for the Study of the Old Testament Supplements 211. Sheffield, 1996.
Kitchen, "Punt"	K. A. Kitchen. "Punt." Pp. 1198–1201 in vol. 4 of *Lexikon der Ägyptologie*. Wiesbaden, 1982.
Kittel, *Chronik*	R. Kittel. *Die Bücher der Chronik*. Göttingen, 1902.
Klein, "David's Mighty Men"	S. Klein. "David's Mighty Men." *Bulletin* 7 (1940) 95–106 (= pp. 304–15 in *Bulletin of the Israel Exploration Society, Reader B*. Jerusalem, 1965). [Hebrew]
Klein, "Priests' and Levites' Cities"	S. Klein. "Priests', Levites' and Asyle Cities." Pp. 5–31 in vol. 3/4 of *The Eretz-Israel Studies*. Jerusalem, 1930. [Hebrew]
Klostermann, *Samuelis–Könige*	A. Klostermann. *Die Bücher Samuelis und der Könige*. 3rd ed. Nördlingen, 1887.
Knoppers, "Genealogy of Judah"	G. N. Knoppers. "Intermarriage, Social Complexity, and Ethnic Diversity in the Genealogy of Judah." *Journal of Biblical Literature* 120 (2001) 15–30.
Knudtszon, *El-Amarna Tafeln*	J. A. Knudtzon. *Die El-Amarna Tafeln*. Leipzig, 1915.
Koch, "Weltordnung und Reichsidee"	K. Koch. "Weltordnung und Reichsidee im alten Iran und ihre Auswirkungen auf die Provinz Jehud." Pp. 220–39 in *Reichsidee und Reichorganisation im Perserreich*, ed. P. Frei and K. Koch. Orbis Biblicus et Orientalis 55. Freiburg, 1996.
König, *Biblische Literatur*	E. König. *Stilistik, Rhetorik, Poetik in bezug auf die biblische Literatur*. Leipzig, 1900.
König, *Einleitung*	E. Könige. *Einleitung in das Alte Testament*. Bonn, 1893.
Kogut, "Chaism"	S. Kogut. "On Chaism and Its Role in Exegesis." *Shnaton* 2 (1977) 196–204. [Hebrew]
Kosovsky, *A Thesaurus of Tannaitic Hebrew*	B. Kosovsky. *A Thesaurus of Tannaitic Hebrew*. Vol. 4. Jerusalem, 1969. [Hebrew]
Kraeling, *Aram and Israel*	E. G. H. Kraeling. *Aram and Israel*. New York, 1918.
Krašovec, *Antithetic Structure*	J. Krašovec. *Antithetic Structure in Biblical Poetry*. Vetus Testamentum Supplements 35. Leiden, 1984.

Kropat, *Syntax*   A. Kropat. *Die Syntax des Autors der Chronik verglichen
                          mit der seiner Quellen.* Beiheft zur Zeitschrift für die
                          alttestamentliche Wissenschaft 16. Giessen, 1909.

Kuhl,   C. Kuhl. "Die 'Wiederaufnahme': Ein literarkritische
    "Wiederaufnahme"   Prinzip?" *Zeitschrift für die alttestamentliche Wissenschaft*
                          64 (1952) 1–11.

Kutscher, *Isaiah Scroll* E. Y. Kutscher. *The Language and Linguistic Background
                          of the Isaiah Scroll (1QIsaᵃ).* 2nd ed. Leiden, 1979.

Langdon, *Neu-*   S. Langdon. *Die neu-babylonischen Inschriften.* Leipzig,
    babylonischen   1912.
    Inschriften

Lemaire, "United   A. Lemaire. "The United Monarchy: Saul, David and
    Monarchy"   Solomon." Pp. 85–108 in *Ancient Israel*, ed. H. Shanks.
                          Washington, D.C., 1991.

Lemke, "Synoptic   W. E. Lemke. "The Synoptic Problem in the Chronicler's
    Problem"   History." *Harvard Theological Review* 58 (1965) 349–63.

Levin, "Inscriptions of   L. D. Levin. "Preliminary Remarks on the Historical
    Sennacherib"   Inscriptions of Sennacherib." Pp. 58–75 in *History,
                          Historiography and Interpretation*, ed. H. Tadmor and
                          M. Weinfeld. Jerusalem, 1983.

Levin, "Neo-Assyrian   L. D. Levin. "Manuscripts, Texts and the Study of the Neo-
    Royal Inscriptions"   Assyrian Royal Inscriptions." Pp. 49–70 in *Assyrian Royal
                          Inscriptions: New Horizons*, ed. F. M. Fales. Rome, 1981.

Licht, "Molech"   J. S. Licht. "Molech: The Devoting of Children to Molech."
                          Pp. 1113–18 in vol. 4 of *Encyclopaedia Biblica*. Jerusalem,
                          1962. [Hebrew]

Lieberman, *Hellenism*   S. Lieberman. *Hellenism in Jewish Palestine.* New York,
                          1950.

Lieberman, *Tosefta*   S. Lieberman. Part 5: Order Moʿed, of *Tosefta Ki-Fshutah:
    Ki-Fshutah   A Comprehensive Commentary on the Tosefta.* 2nd ed.
                          Jerusalem, 1992. [Hebrew]

Liver, "Episode of the   J. Liver. "Episode of the Half-Shekel in the Bible and Dead
    Half-Shekel"   Sea Scrolls." Pp. 109–30 in *Studies in Bible*.

Liver, "Hiram of Tyre"   J. Liver. "On the Chronological Problems of King Hiram of
                          Tyre." Pp. 189–97 in Liver, *Studies in Bible*.

Liver, "History and   J. Liver. "History and Historiography in Chronicles."
    Historiography"   Pp. 221–33 in Liver, *Studies in Bible*.

Liver, *House of David*   J. Liver. *The House of David from the Fall of the Kingdom
                          of Judah to the Fall of the Second Commenwealth and
                          After.* Jerusalem, 1959. [Hebrew]

Liver, "Israel and Edom" J. Liver. "The Wars of Israel and Edom." Pp. 190–205 in
                          Liver (ed.), *Military History*.

Liver, "King, Monarchy"   J. Liver. "King, Monarchy." Pp. 1080–1112 in vol. 4 of
                          Encyclopaedia Biblica. Jerusalem, 1962. [Hebrew]

Liver, *Military History* J. Liver (ed.). *The Military History of the Land of Israel in
                          Biblical Times.* Tel Aviv, 1970. [Hebrew]

Liver, *Priests and*   J. Liver. *Chapters in the History of the Priests and Levites:
    Levites   Studies in the Lists of Chronicles and Ezra and Nehemiah.*
                          Jerusalem, 1968. [Hebrew]

Liver, "So All Israel Was Enrolled"
J. Liver. "So All Israel Was Enrolled by Genealogies, and These Written in the Book of the Kings of Israel." Pp. 234–48 in Liver, *Studies in Bible.*

Liver, *Studies in Bible*
J. Liver. *Studies in Bible and the Judean Desert Scrolls.* Jerusalem, 1971. [Hebrew]

Lods, *Israel*
A. Lods. *Israel: From Its Beginnings to the Middle of the Eighth Century.* London, 1932.

Loewenstamm, "Bochru"
S. E. Loewenstamm. "Bochru." P. 129 in vol. 2 of *Encyclopaedia Biblica.* Jerusalem, 1965. [Hebrew]

Loewenstamm, "Chiastic Structures"
S. E. Loewenstamm. "Observations on Chiastic Structures in the Bible." Pp. 1–5 in *From Babylon to Canaan: Studies in the Bible and Its Oriental Background*, ed. A. Biram. Jerusalem, 1992.

Loewenstamm, "Expanded Limb"
S. E. Loewenstamm. "Expanded Limb in the Ugaritic and Biblical Poetry." *Lešonénu* 27–28 (1963–64) 111–26. [Hebrew]

Loewenstamm, "Hazael"
S. E. Loewenstamm. "Hazael." Pp. 87–88 in vol. 3 of *Encyclopaedia Biblica.* Jerusalem, 1965. [Hebrew]

Loewenstamm, "Measure for Measure"
S. E. Loewenstamm. "Measure for Measure." Pp. 840–46 in vol. 4 of *Encyclopaedia Biblica.* Jerusalem, 1965. [Hebrew]

Luckenbill, *Annals of Sennacherib*
D. D. Luckenbill. *Annals of Sennacherib.* Chicago, 1924.

Luckenbill, *ARAB*
D. D. Luckenbill. *Ancient Records of Assyria and Babylonia.* Vols. 1–2. Chicago, 1926–27.

Lund, "Chiasmus in the Old Testament"
N. W. Lund. "The Presence of Chiasmus in the Old Testament." *American Journal of Semitic Languages and Literature* 46 (1930) 104–26.

Lund, "Chiasmus in the Psalms"
N. W. Lund. "Chiasmus in the Psalms." *American Journal of Semitic Languages and Literature* 49 (1932–33) 281–312.

Luzzatto, *Isaiah*
S. D. Luzzatto. *Commentary to the Book of Isaiah,* ed. P. Schlesinger and M. Chovav. Tel Aviv, 1970. [Hebrew]

Machinist, "First Coins of Judah"
P. Machinist. "The First Coins of Judah and Samaria Numismatics and History in the Achaemenid and Early Hellenistic Periods. Pp. 365–80 in *Achaemenid—History VIII*, ed. H. Sancisi-Weerdenburg, A. Kuhrt, and M. C. Root. Proceedings of the Last Achaemenid History Workshop April 6–8, 1990, Ann Arbor, Michigan. Leiden, 1994.

Maisler (Mazar), "Tell Qasile"
B. Maisler (Mazar). "The Excavations at Tell Qasile." *Eretz-Israel* 1 (M. Schwabe Volume; 1951) 45–71. [Hebrew]

Malamat, *The Age of the Monarchies*
A. Malamat (ed.). *The History of the Jewish People: The Age of the Monarchies. Volume I: Political History*; *Volume II: Culture and Society.* Jerusalem, 1979. [Hebrew]

Malamat, "Foreign Policies"
A. Malamat. "Aspects of the Foreign Policies of David and Solomon." Pp. 195–222 in Malamat, *Israel in Biblical Times.*

Malamat, "Historical Background" — A. Malamat. "The Historical Background of Josiah's Bid for Armageddon." Pp. 223–41 in Malamat, *Israel in Biblical Times*.

Malamat, *Israel in Biblical Times* — A. Malamat. *Israel in Biblical Times: Historical Essays*. Jerusalem, 1983. [Hebrew]

Malamat, "Kingdom of David and Solomon" — A. Malamat. "Kingdom of David and Solomon and Its Relationship with Egypt." Pp. 167–94 in Malamat, *Israel in Biblical Times*.

Malamat, "King Lists" — A. Malamat. "King Lists of the Old Babylonian Period and Biblical Geneologies." Pp. 24–45 in Malamat, *Israel in Biblical Times* (= *Journal of the American Oriental Society* 88 [1968] 163–73).

Malamat, "Longevity" — A. Malamat. "Longevity: Biblical Concepts and Some Ancient Near Eastern Parallels." *Archiv für Orientforschung* 19 (1982) 215–24.

Mantel, "High Priesthood and Sanhedrin" — H. D. Mantel. "The High Priesthood and the Sanhedrin in the Time of the Second Temple." Pp. 264–81, 371–78 in *The History of the Jewish People: The Herodian Period*, ed. M. Avi-Yonah. Jerusalem, 1975.

Mantel, "Oral Law" — H. D. Mantel. "The Development of the Oral Law during the Second Temple Period." Pp. 41–64, 325–37 in *The History of the Jewish People: Society and Religion in the Second Temple Period*, ed. M. Avi-Yonah and Z. Baras. Jerusalem, 1977.

Markoe, *Phoenicians* — G. E. Markoe. *Phoenicians*. Berkeley, 2000.

Mazar, "Early Israelite Site" — A. Mazar. "An Early Israelite Site Near Jerusalem." *Qadmoniot* 13 (1980) 34–39. [Hebrew]

Mazar, "Chronicles" — B. Mazar. "Chronicles, the Book of." Pp. 596–606 in vol. 2 of *Encyclopaedia Biblica*. Jerusalem, 1965. [Hebrew]

Mazar, *Cities and Districts* — B. Mazar. *Cities and Districts in Eretz-Israel*. Jerusalem, 1976. [Hebrew]

Mazar, "David and Solomon" — B. Mazar. "The Era of David and Solomon." Pp. 76–100, 326 in vol. 1 of Malamat, *The Age of the Monarchies*.

Mazar, "David's Reign" — B. Mazar. "David's Reign in Hebron and the Conquest of Jerusalem." Pp. 235–44 in *In the Time of Harvest: Essays in Honor of A. H. Silver*, ed. D. J. Silver. New York, 1963 (= pp. 78–87 in *Biblical Israel: State and People*, ed. S. Aḥituv. Jerusalem, 1992).

Mazar, *Early Biblical Period* — B. Mazar. *The Early Biblical Period: Historical Studies*. Jerusalem, 1986.

Mazar, *Excavations and Discoveries* — B. Mazar. *Excavations and Discoveries: Essays in the Archaeology of Eretz-Israel*. Jerusalem, 1986. [Hebrew]

Mazar, "Gath and Gittites" — B. Mazar. "Gath and Gittites." Pp. 101–9 in Mazar, *Cities and Districts*.

Mazar, "Geba" — B. Mazar. "Geba." Pp. 411–12 in vol. 2 of *Encyclopaedia Biblica*. Jerusalem, 1965. [Hebrew]

Mazar, "Hill of God" — B. Mazar. "The Hill of God." Pp. 80–83 in Mazar, *Cities and Districts*.

Mazar, "Israelites Settlement" — B. Mazar. "The Israelites Settlement in the Mountain Area." Pp. 143–54 in Mazar, *Excavations and Discoveries*.

Mazar, "Jaffa and the Yarkon Area"
B. Mazar. "Jaffa and the Yarkon Area in Biblical Times." Pp. 155–66 in Mazar, *Excavations and Discoveries*.

Mazar, "Jerusalem in the Biblical Period"
B. Mazar. "Jerusalem in the Biblical Period." Pp. 11–44 in Mazar, *Cities and Districts*.

Mazar, "Military Elite"
B. Mazar. "The Military Élite of King David." Pp. 83–103 in Mazar, *Early Biblical Period*.

Mazar, "Philistines, Israel and Tyre"
B. Mazar. "Philistines and the Rise of Israel and Tyre." Pp. 63–82 in Mazar, *Early Biblical Period*.

Mazar, "Samaria Ostraca"
B. Mazar. "The Historical Background of the Samaria Ostraca." Pp. 173–88 in Mazar, *Early Biblical Period*.

Mazar, "Shishak's Campaign"
B. Mazar. "Pharaoh Shishak's Campaign to the Land of Israel." Pp. 139–50 in Mazar, *Early Biblical Period*.

McCarter, *I–II Samuel*
P. K. McCarter, Jr. *I–II Samuel: A New Translation with Introduction, Notes and Commentary*. Anchor Bible 8–9. Garden City, New York, 1984.

McKenzie, *Chronicler*
S. L. McKenzie. *The Chronicler's Use of the Deuteronomistic History*. Harvard Semitic Monographs 33. Atlanta, 1985.

McKenzie, "Chronicler as Redactor"
S. L. McKenzie. "The Chronicler as Redactor." Pp. 70–90 in *The Chronicler as Author: Studies in Text and Texture*, ed. M. P. Graham and S. L. McKenzie. Journal for the Study of the Old Testament Supplements 263. Sheffield, 1999.

Meek, "Uzziah"
T. J. Meek. "Uzziah." P. 1021 in *Dictionary of the Bible*, ed. J. Hastings, F. C. Grant, and H. H. Rowley. 2nd ed. Edinburgh, 1963.

Melammed, "Beraitha of Thirty-Two *Midot*"
E. Z. Melammed. "The Beraitha of Thirty-Two *Midot*." Pp. 1061–83 in vol. 2 of *Bible Commentators* (= pp. 34–56 in Melammed, *Essays in Talmudic Literature*. Jerusalem, 1986).

Melammed, *Bible Commentators*
E. Z. Melammed. *Bible Commentators*. 2nd ed. Jerusalem, 1978. [Hebrew]

Melammed, "Commentary of R. Isaiah"
E. Z. Melammed. "Concerning the Commentary of Rabbi Isaiah Teranni on Prophets and Hagiographa." Pp. 285–88 in *Biblical Studies in Texts, Translations and Commentators*. Jerusalem, 1984. [Hebrew]

Melam[m]ed, "Josephus and Maccabees I"
E. Z. Melam[m]ed. "Josephus and Maccabees I: A Comparison." *Eretz-Israel* 1 (M. Schwabe Volume; 1951) 122–30. [Hebrew]

Mettinger, *State Officials*
T. N. D. Mettinger. *Solomonic State Officials: A Study of the Civil Government Officials of the Israelite Monarchy*. Lund, 1971.

Michel, "Die Assur-Texte"
E. Michel. "Die Assur-Texte Salmanassers III (858–824)." *Die Welt des Orients* 1 (1947–52) 255–71.

Miller-Hayes, *History of Ancient Israel*
J. M. Miller and J. H. Hayes. *A History of Ancient Israel and Judah*. Philadelphia, 1986.

Montgomery, "Archival Data"
J. A. Montgomery. "Archival Data in the Book of Kings." *Journal of Biblical Literature* 53 (1934) 46–52.

Montgomery, *Kings*
J. A. Montgomery. *A Critical and Exegetical Commentary on the Books of Kings*, ed. H. S. Gehman. International Critical Commentary. Edinburgh, 1951.

Moore, "Judith, Book of" C. A. Moore. "Judith, Book of." Pp. 1117–25 in vol. 3 of *Anchor Bible Dictionary*. New York, 1992.

Moran, "Love of God" W. L. Moran. "The Ancient Near Eastern Background of the Love of God in Deuteronomy." *Catholic Biblical Quarterly* 25 (1963) 77–87.

Mortara, *Commentaries by RaLBaG* M. H. Mortara (ed.). *The Commentaries by RaLBaG on Ezra, Nehemiah and Chronicles*. Cracow, 1888. [Hebrew]

Mosca, *Child Sacrifice* P. G. Mosca. *Child Sacrifice in Canaanite and Israelite Religion: A Study in Mulk and מלך*. Ph.D. dissertation. Harvard University, 1975.

Moscati, *L'epigrafia ebraica* S. Moscati. *L'epigrafia ebraica, 1935–1950*. Rome, 1951.

Mosiman, *Zusammenstellung* S. K. Mosiman. *Eine Zusammenstellung und Vergleich der Paralleltexte der Chronik und der ältern Bücher des Alten Testaments*. Ph.D. dissertation. University of Halle. 1907.

Mosis, *Untersuchungen* R. Mosis. *Untersuchungen zur Theologie des chronistischen Geschichtswerkes*. Freiburger Theologische Studien. Freiburg im Breisgau, 1973.

Movers, *Kritische Untersuchung* F. C. Movers. *Kritische Untersuchung über die biblische Chronik: Ein Beitrag zur Einleitung in das AT*. Bonn, 1834.

Muffs, *Love and Joy* Y. Muffs. *Love and Joy: Law, Language and Religion in Ancient Israel*. New York, 1992.

Myers, *I–II Chronicles* J. M. Myers. *I–II Chronicles: Introduction, Translation and Notes*. Anchor Bible 12–13. Garden City, New York, 1965.

Na'aman, "Pastoral Nomads" N. Na'aman. "Pastoral Nomads in the Southwestern Periphery of the Kingdom of Judah in the 9th–8th Centuries B.C.E." *Zion* 52 (1987) 261–78. [Hebrew]

Naor, "Solomon and Hiram" M. Naor. "Solomon and Hiram and the Land of Cabul." Pp. 94–100 in *Western Galilee and the Coast of Galilee: The Nineteenth Archaeological Convention, 1963*. Jerusalem, 1965. [Hebrew]

Naveh, "Two Aramaic Ostraca" J. Naveh. "Two Aramaic Ostraca of the Persian Period." Pp. 184–90 in Uffenheimer, *Bible and Jewish History*.

Naville, *Temple of Deir el-Bahari* E. Naville. *Temple of Deir el-Bahari*. Part 3. London, 1898.

Newsome, "Understanding" J. D. Newsome, Jr. "Toward a New Understanding of the Chronicler and His Purposes." *Journal of Biblical Literature* 94 (1975) 201–17.

North, "Religious Aspects" C. R. North. "The Religious Aspects of Hebrew Kingship." *Zeitschrift für die alttestamentliche Wissenschaft* 50 (1932) 8–38.

Noth, *Chronicler's History* M. Noth. *Chronicler's History*. Journal for the Study of the Old Testament Supplements 50. Sheffield, 1987.

Noth, *Deuteronomistic History* M. Noth. *The Deuteronomistic History*. Journal for the Study of the Old Testament Supplements 15. 2nd ed. Sheffield, 2001.

Noth, *Geschichte Israels* M. Noth. *Geschichte Israels*. 2nd ed. Göttingen, 1954.

Noth, *History of Israel* M. Noth. *The History of Israel*. 2nd ed. London, 1958.

Noth, *Könige* M. Noth. *Könige*. Biblischer Kommentar, Altes Testament. Neukirchen-Vluyn, 1968.

Noth, *OT World* M. Noth. *The Old Testament World*. Philadelphia, 1966.

Noth, *ÜS* M. Noth. *Überlieferungsgeschichtliche Studien*. 2nd ed. Tübingen, 1957.

Noth, *Welt* M. Noth. *Die Welt des Alten Testaments*. 2nd ed. Berlin, 1953.

Noy, *Form and Content* D. Noy. *Form and Contents in Folktales*. Jerusalem, 1970. [Hebrew]

Noy, "Levites' Part" H. Noy. "The Levites' Part in the Composition of the Book of Deuteronomy." Pp. 63–78 in vol. 1 of *I. L. Seeligmann Festschrift*, ed. A. Rofé and Y. Zakovitch. Jerusalem, 1983. [Hebrew]

Oded, "Israel and Judah" B. Oded. "Israel and Judah." Pp. 101–201 in Eph'al (ed.), *Israel and Judah*.

Oded, "II Kings 17" B. Oded. "II Kings 17: Between History and Polemic." *Jewish History* 2 (1987) 37–50.

Öttli, *Chronik* S. Öttli. *Die Bücher der Chronik, Esra und Nehemia*. Nördlingen, 1889.

Olmstead, "Biblical Text" A. T. Olmstead, "Source Study and Biblical Text." *American Journal of Semitic Languages and Literature* 30 (1913) 1–35.

Oppenheim, "Beer and Brewing Techniques" A. L. Oppenheim. "On Beer and Brewing Techniques in Ancient Mesopotamia." Pp. 43–44 in Journal of the American Oriental Society Supplement 10. Baltimore, 1950.

Oren, "Ira the Yairite" A. Oren. "Ira the Yairite Also Was Chief Minister unto David (II Sam 20,26)." *Beth Mikra* 17 (1972) 233–34. [Hebrew]

Ornan, "Allusion's Structures" U. Ornan. "On the Analysis of Allusion's Structures in the Literary Compositions." *Lešonénu* 26 (1962) 40–47. [Hebrew]

Page, "Stela of Add-Nirari III" S. Page. "A Stela of Add-Nirari III and Nergal-Ereš from Tell al Rima." *Iraq* 30 (1968) 139–53.

Paran, *Priestly Style* M. Paran. *Forms of the Priestly Style in the Pentateuch: Patterns, Linguistic Usages, Syntactic Structures*. Jerusalem, 1989. [Hebrew]

Parpola, *Correspondence of Sargon* S. Parpola. *The Correspondence of Sargon II, Part I: Letters from Assyria and the West*. Helsinki, 1987.

Parpola, "Murderer of Sennacherib" S. Parpola. "The Murderer of Sennacherib." Pp. 171–82 in *Death in Mesopotamia*, ed. B. Alster. Mesopotamia 8. Copenhagen, 1980.

Paul, "Adoption Formulae" S. M. Paul. "Adoption Formulae." *Eretz-Israel* 14 (H. L. Ginsberg Volume; 1978) 31–36. [Hebrew]

Peretz, "Proper Noun and Title" Y. Peretz. "Juxtaposition of Proper Noun and Title." Pp. 129–33 in vol. 2 of *Proceedings of the Fourth World Congress of Jewish Studies*. Jerusalem, 1968. [Hebrew]

Petersen, *Late Israelite Prophecy*	D. L. Petersen. *Late Israelite Prophecy: Studies in Deutero-Prophetic Literature and in Chronicles*. Missoula, Montana, 1977.
Pfeiffer, *Introduction*	P. H. Pfeiffer. *Introduction to the Old Testament*. 3rd ed. New York, 1957.
Pisano, *Additions*	S. Pisano. *Additions or Omissions in the Books of Samuel*. Orbis Biblicus et Orientalis 57. Freiburg, 1984.
Pitard, *Ancient Damascus*	W. T. Pitard. *Ancient Damascus: A Historical Study of the Syrian City-State from Earliest Times until Its Fall to the Assyrians in 732 B.C.E.* Winona Lake, Indiana, 1987.
Polzin, *Late Biblical Hebrew*	R. Polzin. *Late Biblical Hebrew: Toward an Historical Typology of Biblical Hebrew Prose*. Missoula, Montana, 1976.
Porter, "Historiography"	J. R. Porter. "Old Testament Historiography." Pp. 125–62 in *Tradition and Interpretation*, ed. J. W. Anderson. Oxford, 1979.
Poulssen, *König und Tempel*	N. Poulssen. *König und Tempel im Glaubenzeugnis des Alten Testaments*. Stuttgart, 1967.
Pritchard, *ANET*	J. B. Pritchard (ed.). *Ancient Near Eastern Texts Relating to the Old Testament*. 3rd ed. Princeton, 1969.
Purvis, "Samaritan Pentateuch"	J. D. Purvis. "Samaritan Pentateuch." Pp. 408–17 in *Die Samaritaner*, ed. F. Dexinger and R. Pummer. Darmstadt, 1992 (= pp. 772–75 in *The Interpreter's Dictionary of the Bible: Supplementary Volume*. Nashville, 1976).
von Rad, "Deuteronomistic Theology"	G. von Rad. "The Deuteronomistic Theology of History in the Book of Kings." Pp. 74–91 in *Studies in Deuteronomy*. London, 1953.
von Rad, "Deuteronomistische Geschichtstheologie"	G. von Rad. "Die deuteronomistische Geschichtstheologie in den Königsbüchern." Pp. 189–204 in vol. 1 of *Gesammelte Studien zum Alten Testament*. Munich, 1971.
von Rad, *Geschichtsbild*	G. von Rad. *Das Geschichtsbild des Chronistischen Werkes*. Stuttgart, 1930.
Radday, "Chiasm in Biblical Narrative"	Y. T. Radday. "On Chiasm in the Biblical Narrative." *Beth Mikra* 9 (1964) 48–72. [Hebrew]
Radday, "Chiasmus"	Y. T. Radday. "Chiasmus in Hebrew Biblical Narrative." Pp. 50–117 in Welch (ed.), *Chiasmus in Antiquity*.
Rainey, "Eber-Hanahar"	A. F. Rainey. "Eber-Hanahar." Pp. 43–48 in vol. 6 of *Encyclopaedia Biblica*. Jerusalem, 1971. [Hebrew]
Rainey, "Philistine Gath"	A. F. Rainey. "The Identification of Philistine Gath: A Problem in Source Analysis for Historical Geography." *Eretz-Israel* 12 (N. Glueck Memorial Volume; 1975) 63*–86*.
Rainey, "Satrapy of 'Eber-Hanahar'"	A. F. Rainey. "Satrapy of 'Eber-Hanahar.'" Pp. 105–16, 277–80 in Tadmor (ed.), *The Restoration—The Persian Period*.
Rainey, "Shimʿôn/Shimrôn"	A. F. Rainey. "Toponymic Problems Shimʿôn/Shimrôn." *Tel Aviv* 3 (1976) 57–69; *Tel Aviv* 8 (1981) 146–51.
Rainey, "Shimron"	A. F. Rainey. "Shimron." Pp. 140–42 in vol. 8 of *Encyclopaedia Biblica*. Jerusalem, 1982. [Hebrew]

Redford, "Pharaoh"   D. B. Redford. "Pharaoh." Pp. 288–89 in vol. 5 of *The Anchor Bible Dictionary*. New York, 1992.

Redmount, "Canals of   C. A. Redmount. "The Wadi Tumilat and the 'Canals of the the Pharaohs"   Pharaohs.'" *Journal of Near Eastern Studies* 54 (1995) 127–35.

Rehm, *Könige*   M. Rehm. *Das erste Buch der Könige: Ein Kommentar.* Würzburg, 1979.

Rehm, *Untersuchungen*   M. Rehm. *Textkritische Untersuchungen zu den Parallelstellen der Samuel–Königsbücher und der Chronik.* Alttestamentliche Abhandlungen 13/3. Münster, 1937.

Rendtorff, *Einführung*   R. Rendtorff. *Das Alte Testament: Eine Einführung.* Neukirchen-Vluyn, 1983.

Rendtorff, *Introduction*   R. Rendtorff. *The Old Testament: An Introduction.* Philadelphia, 1991.

Reviv, *The Elders*   H. Reviv. *The Elders in Ancient Israel.* Jerusalem, 1989.

Reviv, *From Clan to Monarchy*   H. Reviv. *From Clan to Monarchy: Israel in the Biblical Period.* Jerusalem, 1981. [Hebrew]

Reviv, "Historical Background"   H. Reviv. "The Historical Background of 2 Chronicles 28,8–15." Pp. 11–16 in vol. 1 of *Nation and History: Studies in the History of the Jewish People*, ed. M. Stern. Jerusalem, 1983. [Hebrew]

Reviv, *Society*   H. Reviv. *Society in the Kingdoms of Israel and Judah.* Biblical Encyclopaedia Library 8. Jerusalem, 1993. [Hebrew]

Roberts, *Old Testament Text*   B. J. Roberts. *The Old Testament Text and Versions.* Cardiff, 1951.

Rofé, *Belief in Angels*   A. Rofé. *The Belief in Angels in the Bible and in Early Israel.* Ph.D. dissertation. Hebrew University of Jerusalem, 1969. [Hebrew]

Rofé, "David and Goliath"   A. Rofé. "The Battle of David and Goliath: Folklore, Theology, Eschatology." Pp. 117–51 in *Judaic Perspectives on Ancient Israel*, ed. J. Neusner, B. A. Levine, and E. S. Frerichs. Philadelphia, 1987.

Rofé, *Prophetical Stories*   A. Rofé. *The Prophetical Stories: The Narratives about the Prophets in the Hebrew Bible—Their Literary Types and History.* Jerusalem, 1988.

Rosenzweig, "Biblical Story"   F. Rosenzweig. "The Mystery of the Biblical Story." Pp. 12–16 in *Nahariym.* Jerusalem, 1978. [Hebrew]

Rost, *Thronnachfolge Davids*   L. Rost. *Die Überlieferung von der Thronnachfolge Davids.* Stuttgart, 1926.

Rothstein-Hänel, *Chronik*   J. W. Rothstein and J. Hänel. *Das erste Buch der Chronik übersetzt und erklärt.* Kommentar zum Alten Testament. Leipzig, 1927.

Rudolph, *Chronik*   W. Rudolph. *Chronikbücher.* Handbuch zum Alten Testament 21. Tübingen, 1955.

Rudolph, *Esra und Nehemia*   W. Rudolph. *Esra und Nehemia.* Handbuch zum Alten Testament 20. Tübingen, 1949.

Rudolph, "Haus der Freiheit"   W. Rudolf. "Ussias 'Haus der Freiheit.'" *Zeitschrift für die alttestamentliche Wissenschaft* 89 (1977) 418.

Rudolph, "Problems of Chronicles"
W. Rudolph. "Problems of the Book of Chronicles." *Vetus Testamentum* 4 (1954) 401–9.

Šanda, *Könige*
A. Šanda. *Die Bücher der Könige.* Münster, 1911.

Sappan, "Chiasm in Biblical Poetry"
R. Sappan. "Chiasm in Biblical Poetry." *Beth Mikra* 21 (1976) 534–39. [Hebrew]

Sarfati, "Number"
G. B. A. Sarfati. "Number." Pp. 170–85 in vol. 5 of *Encyclopaedia Biblica.* Jerusalem, 1971. [Hebrew]

Sarna, "Psalm 89"
N. M. Sarna. "Psalm 89: A Study in Inner Biblical Exegesis." Pp. 29–46 in *Biblical and Other Studies,* ed. A. Altman. Cambridge, Massachusetts, 1963 (= pp. 377–94 in Sarna, *Studies in Biblical Interpretation.* Philadelphia, 2000).

Schley, "1 Kings 10:26–29"
D. G. Schley. "1 Kings 10:26–29: A Reconsideration." *Journal of Biblical Literature* 106 (1987) 595–601.

Schley, *Shiloh*
D. G. Schley. *Shiloh: A Biblical City in Tradition and History.* Journal for the Study of the Old Testament Supplements 63. Sheffield, 1989.

Schmoldt, "Zwei 'Wiederaufnahmen'"
H. Schmoldt. "Zwei 'Wiederaufnahmen' in I Reg. 17." *Zeitschrift für die alttestamentliche Wissenschaft* 97 (1985) 423–26.

Schoors, "Isaiah"
A. Schoors. "Isaiah, the Minister of Royal Anointment?" *Oudtestamentische Studiën* 20 (1977) 85–107.

Schramm, *Assyrischen Königsinschriften*
W. Schramm. *Einleitung in die assyrischen Königsinschriften, Zweiter Teil: 934–722 v. Chr.* Leiden, 1973.

Schunk, *Benjamin*
K. D. Schunk. *Benjamin: Untersuchungen zur Entstehung und Geschichte eines israelitischen Stammes.* Beiheft zur Zeitschrift für die alttestamentliche Wissenschaft 86. Berlin, 1963.

Scott, "The Hebrew Cubit"
R. B. Y. Scott. "The Hebrew Cubit." *Journal of Biblical Literature* 77 (1958) 205–14.

Seeligmann, "Beginnings of Midrash"
I. L. Seeligmann. "The Beginnings of *Midrash* in the Books of Chronicles." *Tarbiz* 49 (1980) 14–32 (= pp. 454–74 in Seeligmann, *Studies in Biblical Literature.* Jerusalem, 1992). [Hebrew]

Seeligmann, "Biblische Geschichts-schreibung"
I. L. Seeligmann. "Hebräische Erzählung und biblische Geschichtsschreibung." *Theologische Zeitschrift* 18 (1961) 302–25.

Seeligmann, "Editorial Alteration"
I. L. Seeligmann. "Indications of Editorial Alteration and Adaptation in the Massoretic Text and the Septuagint." Pp. 279–95 in *Likkutei Tarbiz, Volume 1: A Biblical Studies Reader,* ed. M. Weinfeld. Jerusalem, 1979 (= pp. 319–38 in Seeligmann, *Studies in Biblical Literature.* Jerusalem, 1992). [Hebrew]

Seeligmann. "From Historic Reality"
I. L. Seeligmann. "From Historic Reality to Historiosophic Conception in the Bible." *P'raqim* 2 (ed. E. S. Rosenthal; 1969–74) 273–313 (= pp. 102–40 in Seeligmann, *Studies in Biblical Literature.* Jerusalem, 1992). [Hebrew]

Segal, "Numerals"
J. B. Segal. "Numerals in the Old Testament." *Journal of Semitic Studies* 10 (1965) 2–20.

Segal, *Ben-Sira*	M. Z. Segal. *The Book of Ben-Sira*. 2nd ed. Jerusalem, 1972. [Hebrew]
Segal, "Books of Ezra and Nehemiah"	M. Z. Segal. "The Books of Ezra and Nehemiah." *Tarbiz* 14 (1943) 81–103. [Hebrew]
Segal, "Ezra–Nehemiah"	M. Z. Segal. "Ezra–Nehemiah." Pp. 143–51 in vol. 6 of *Encyclopaedia Biblica*. Jerusalem, 1971. [Hebrew]
Segal, *Introduction to the Bible*	M. Z. Segal. *Introduction to the Bible*. 4 vols. Jerusalem, 1977. [Hebrew]
Segal, "The Names *YHWH* and *Elohim*"	M. Z. Segal. "The Names *YHWH* and *Elohim* in the Books of the Bible." *Tarbiz* 9 (1938) 123–62. [Hebrew]
Segal, "Nehemiah"	M. Z. Segal. "Nehemiah." Pp. 817–20 in vol. 5 of *Encyclopaedia Biblica*. Jerusalem, 1968. [Hebrew]
Segal, *Samuel*	M. Z. Segal. *The Books of Samuel*. Jerusalem, 1977. [Hebrew]
Seidel, "Inner-Parallels"	M. Seidel. "Inner-Parallels in the Book of Isaiah and in the Book of Jeremiah." Pp. 109–21 in Seidel, *Studies in Bible*.
Seidel, "Micah Chapter 6"	M. Seidel. "Micah Chapter 6." Pp. 142–56 in Seidel, *Studies in Bible*.
Seidel, "Parallels"	M. Seidel. "Parallels between the Book of Isaiah and the Book of Psalms." Pp. 1–97 in Seidel, *Studies in Bible*.
Seidel, "Phraseology"	M. Seidel. "Phraseology of the Book of Proverbs in Isaiah." Pp. 98–108 in Seidel, *Studies in Bible*.
Seidel, *Studies in Bible*	M. Seidel. *Studies in Bible*. Jerusalem, 1978. [Hebrew]
Shaver, *Torah and the Chronicler*	J. R. Shaver. *Torah and the Chronicler's History Work*. Atlanta, 1989.
Shenkel, "Synoptic Parallels"	J. D. Shenkel. "A Comparative Study of the Synoptic Parallels in I Paraleipomena and I–II Reigns." *Harvard Theological Review* 62 (1969) 63–85.
Shinan-Zakovitch, *Reuben and Bilhah*	A. Shinan and Y. Zakovitch. *The Story about Reuben and Bilhah*. Jerusalem, 1983. [Hebrew]
Smelik, "King Manasseh"	K. A. D. Smelik. "The Portrayal of King Manasseh: A Literary Analysis of II Kings xxi and II Chronicles xxiii." Pp. 129–89 in Smelik, *Converting the Past: Studies in Ancient Israelite and Moabite Historiography*. Oudtestamentische Studiën 28. Leiden, 1992.
Smend, *Bundesformel*	R. Smend. *Die Bundesformel*. Theologische Studien 68. Zurich, 1963.
Smend, *Entstehung*	R. Smend. *Die Entstehung des Alten Testaments*. Stuttgart, 1989.
Smith, *Samuel*	H. P. Smith. *A Critical and Exegetical Commentary on the Books of Samuel*. International Critical Commentary. Edinburgh, 1899.
Snaith, "Cult of Molech"	N. H. Snaith. "The Cult of Molech." *Vetus Testamentum* 16 (1966) 123–24.
Snaith, *Kings*	N. H. Snaith. "The First and Second Books of Kings." Pp. 1–338 in vol. 3 of *The Interpreter's Bible*, ed. G. A. Buttrick. Nashville, 1954.
Snaith, "Meaning of שעירים"	N. H. Snaith. "The Meaning of שעירים." *Vetus Testamentum* 25 (1975) 115–18.

von Soden, *Akkadisches Handwörterbuch* — W. von Soden, *Akkadisches Handwörterbuch*. 3 volumes. Wiesbaden, 1981.

Spalinger, "Assurbanipal" — A. Spalinger. "Assurbanipal and Egypt: A Source Study." *Journal of the American Oriental Society* 94 (1974) 316–28.

Spalinger, "Esarhaddon" — A. Spalinger. "Esarhaddon and Egypt: An Analysis of the First Invasion of Egypt." *Orientalia* 43 (1974) 295–326.

Sperber, "Parallel Transmission" — A. Sperber. "Hebrew Based upon Biblical Passages in Parallel Transmission." *Hebrew Union College Annual* 14 (1939) 153–251.

Sperber, *Targum Jonathan* — A. Sperber. *The Bible in Aramaic, Volume II: The Former Prophets according to Targum Jonathan*. Leiden. 1959.

Spinoza, *Theological-Political* — B. Spinoza. *Theological-Political Treatise and A Political Treatise*, trans. R. H. M. Elwes. New York, 1951; Gebhardt edition, 1925, trans. S. Shirley. Leiden, 1991.

Stade, "Anmerkungen" — B. Stade. "Miscellen: 16. Anmerkungen zu 2. Kö. 15–21." *Zeitschrift für die alttestamentliche Wissenschaft* 6 (1886) 156–59.

Stade, *Kings* — B. Stade. *The Books of Kings*. Leipzig, 1904.

Stade, "König Joram" — B. Stade. "König Joram von Juda und der Text von 2 Kön. 8,21–24." *Zeitschrift für die alttestamentliche Wissenschaft* 21 (1901) 337–40.

Stager, "Phoenician Carthage" — L. E. Stager. "Phoenician Carthage: The Commerical Harbour and the *Tophet*." *Qadmoniot* 17 (1984) 39–49. [Hebrew]

Stager, "Rite of Child Sacrifice" — L. E. Stager. "The Rite of Child Sacrifice at Carthage." Pp. 1–11 in *New Light on Ancient Carthage*, ed. J. G. Pedley. Ann Arbor, Michigan, 1980.

Stern, "Geographic-Historical Background" — E. Stern. "The Geographic-Historical Background of the Land of Israel in the Persian Period." Pp. 224–50 in Ephʿal (ed.), *Israel and Judah*.

Stern, "Many Masters of Dor" — E. Stern. "The Many Masters of Dor, Part 2: How Bad Was Ahab?" *Biblical Archaeology Review* 19/2 (1993) 18–29.

Stern, *Material Culture* — E. Stern. *The Material Culture of the Land of the Bible in the Persian Period (538–332 B.C.E.)*. Jerusalem, 1973. [Hebrew]

Stern, "Measures and Weights" — E. Stern. "Measures and Weights." Pp. 846–78 in vol. 4 of *Encyclopaedia Biblica*. Jerusalem, 1965. [Hebrew]

Stern, *Greek and Latin Authors* — M. Stern. *Greek and Latin Authors on Jews and Judaism*. Vols. 1–3. Jerusalem, 1974–84.

Steuernagel, *Einleitung* — C. Steuernagel. *Lehrbuch der Einleitung in das Alte Testament*. Sammlung Theologischer Lehrbücher. Tübingen, 1912.

Sukenik, "Epitaph of Uzziah" — E. L. Sukenik. "An Epitaph of Uzziah King of Judah." *Tarbiz* 2 (1931) 288–92. [Hebrew]

Sukenik (= Yadin), "Blind and Lame" — Y. Sukenik (= Yadin). "The Blind and Lame and the Capture of Jerusalem." Pp. 222–25 in vol. 1 of [*Proceedings of the*] *World Congress of Jewish Studies—Summer 1947*. Jerusalem, 1952. [Hebrew]

Tadmor, "Assyrian Campaigns" — H. Tadmor. "The Assyrian Campaigns." Pp. 261–85 in Liver (ed.), *Military History*.

Tadmor, "Azariah in Assyrian Inscriptions" — H. Tadmor. "Azariah of Judah in Assyrian Inscriptions." Pp. 158–93 in *The Kingdoms of Israel and Judah*, ed. A. Malamat. Jerusalem, 1961. [Hebrew]

Tadmor, "Chronology" — H. Tadmor. "Chronology." Pp. 245–310 in vol. 4 of *Encyclopaedia Biblica*. Jerusalem, 1962. [Hebrew]

Tadmor, "First Temple and Restoration" — H. Tadmor. "The First Temple and Restoration Ages." Pp. 93–173 in *History of The Jewish People, Volume I: Ancient Times*, ed. H. H. Ben-Sasson. Tel Aviv, 1969. [Hebrew]

Tadmor, "History and Ideology" — H. Tadmor. "History and Ideology in the Assyrian Royal Inscriptions." Pp. 13–33 in *Assyrian Royal Inscriptions: New Horizons*, ed. F. M. Fales. Rome, 1981.

Tadmor, "Jehu" — H. Tadmor. "Jehu." Pp. 473–78 in vol. 3 of *Encyclopaedia Biblica*. Jerusalem, 1965. [Hebrew]

Tadmor, "Pul" — H. Tadmor. "Pul." P. 443 in vol. 6 of *Encyclopaedia Biblica*. Jerusalem, 1971. [Hebrew]

Tadmor, "Rabshakeh" — H. Tadmor. "Rabshakeh." Pp. 323–25 in vol. 7 of *Encyclopaedia Biblica*. Jerusalem, 1976. [Hebrew]

Tadmor, *The Restoration—The Persian Period* — H. Tadmor (ed.). *The History of the Jewish People: The Restoration—The Persian Period*. Jerusalem, 1983. [Hebrew]

Tadmor, "Sennacherib's Campaign" — H. Tadmor. "Sennacherib's Campaign to Judah: Historical and Historiographical Considerations." *Zion* 50 (1985) 65–80. [Hebrew]

Tadmor, "Tiglath-Pileser" — H. Tadmor. "Tiglath-Pileser." Pp. 415–30 in vol. 8 of *Encyclopaedia Biblica*. Jerusalem, 1982. [Hebrew]

Tadmor-Cogan, "Hezekiah's Fourteenth Year" — H. Tadmor and M. Cogan. "Hezekiah's Fourteenth Year: The King's Illness and the Babylonian Embassy." *Eretz-Israel* 16 (H. M. Orlinsky Volume; 1982) 198–201. [Hebrew]

Täckholm, "Tarsis" — U. Täckholm. "Tarsis, Tartessos und die Säulen des Herakles." *Orientalia* 5 (1965) 143–200.

Täckholm, "Tarsis-Tartessosproblem" — U. Täckholm. "Neue Studien zum Tarsis-Tartessosproblem." *Orientalia* 10 (1974) 41–57.

Talmon, *Double Readings* — S. Talmon. *Double Readings: A Basic Phenomenon in the Transmission of the Old Testament Text*. Ph.D. dissertation. Hebrew University of Jerusalem, 1956.

Talmon, "Emendation of Biblical Texts" — S. Talmon. "On the Emendation of Biblical Texts on the Basis of Ugaritic Parallels." *Eretz-Israel* 14 (H. L. Ginsberg Volume; 1978) 117–24.

Talmon, "Judaean *Am Ha'aretz*" — S. Talmon. "The Judaean ʿAm Haʾaretz in Historical Perspective." Pp. 68–78 in *King, Cult and Calendar in Ancient Israel: Collected Studies*. Jerusalem, 1986.

Talmon, "Massoretic Text" — S. Talmon. "Double Readings in the Massoretic Text." *Textus* 1 (1960) 144–85.

Talmon, "Samaritan Pentateuch" — S. Talmon. "Outlines on the Textual Version of the Samaritan Pentateuch." *Tarbiz* 22 (1951) 124–28. [Hebrew]

Talmon, "Tanach, Text"   S. Talmon. "Tanach, Text." Pp. 621–41 in vol. 8 of
                          Encyclopaedia Biblica. Jerusalem, 1982. [Hebrew]
Talmon, "Textual Study"   S. Talmon. "The Textual Study of the Bible: A New
                          Outlook." *Shnaton* 2 (1977) 116–63. [Hebrew; English
                          version, pp. 321–400 in F. M. Cross and S. Talmon (eds.).
                          Qumran and the History of the Biblical Text. Cambridge,
                          Massachusetts, 1975]
Talmon, "Textual   S. Talmon. "Aspects of the Textual Transmission of the
    Transmission"   Bible in the Light of Qumran Manuscripts." *Textus* 4
                          (1964) 95–132. [Repr., pp. 71–116 in Talmon, *The World of
                          Qumran from Within: Collected Studies*. Jerusalem, 1989]
Talshir, "Septuagint"   Z. Talshir. "Linguistic Development and the Evaluation of
                          Translation Technique in the Septuagint." *Scripta
                          Hierosolymitana* 31 (1986) 301–20.
Thenius, *Könige*   O. Thenius. *Die Bücher der Könige*. Leipzig, 1849.
Thenius, *Samuel*   O. Thenius. *Die Bücher Samuels*. Leipzig, 1842.
Thiel, "Athaliah"   W. Thiel. "Athaliah." Pp. 511–12 in vol. 1 of *Anchor Bible
                          Dictionary*. New York, 1992.
Thompson, "Textual   J. A. Thompson. "Textual Criticism: Old Testament."
    Criticism"   Pp. 886–91 in *The Interpreter's Dictionary of the Bible:
                          Supplementary Volume*, ed. K. Crim et al. Nashville, 1976.
Thompson, *Motif Index*   S. Thompson. *Motif Index of Folk Literature*. Bloomington,
                          Indiana, 1955–58.
Thomson, *Chiasmus*   I. H. Thomson. *Chiasmus in the Pauline Letters*. Sheffield,
                          1995.
Throntveit, *Speech and   M. A. Throntveit. *When Kings Speak: Royal Speech and
    Royal Prayer*   Royal Prayer in Chronicles*. Society of Biblical Literature
                          Dissertation Series 93. Atlanta, 1987.
Torrey, *Ezra Studies*   C. C. Torrey. *Ezra Studies*. Chicago, 1910.
Tov, "Harmonizations"   E. Tov. "The Nature and Background of Harmonizations
                          in Biblical Manuscripts." *Journal for the Study of the Old
                          Testament* 31 (1985) 3–29.
Tov, "Textual   E. Tov. "Criteria for Textual Evaluation of the Biblical
    Evaluation"   Versions." *Beth Mikra* 30 (1985) 112–32. [Hebrew]
Tsafrir, "Suez Region"   Y. Tsafrir. "History of the Suez Region." *Qadmoniot* 6
                          (1973) 91–97. [Hebrew]
Tcherikover, "History of A. Tcherikover. "History of Jerusalem in the Time of the
    Jerusalem"   Second Temple." Pp. 221–51 in *The Book of Jerusalem*, ed.
                          M. Avi-Yonah. Jerusalem, 1956. [Hebrew]
Tuell, *First and Second S. S. Tuell. *First and Second Chronicles*. Interpretation.
    Chronicles*   Louisville, 2001.
Tuland, "Josephus"   C. G. Tuland. "Josephus, *Antiquities* Book XI: Correction
                          or Confirmation of Biblical Post-exilic Records?" *Andrews
                          University Seminary Studies* 4 (1966) 176–92.
Tur-Sinai, "Historical   N. H. Tur-Sinai. "On Some Historical References in the
    References"   Bible." *Eretz-Israel* 5 (B. Mazar Volume; 1958) 74–79.
Tur-Sinai, *Lachish   N. H. Tur-Sinai. *Lachish Ostraca: Letters from the Time of
    Ostraca*   Jeremiah*. Jerusalem, 1940. [Hebrew]
Tur-Sinai, *Peshutô*   N. H. Tur-Sinai. *Vol. 2: The Books of Former Prophets*;
                          vol. 4: The Books of Psalms and Proverbs of *Peshutô shel
                          Mikra*. Jerusalem, 1964–67.

Tur-Sinai, "To the Chief Musician"   N. H. Tur-Sinai. "To the Chief Musician: A Psalm of the Sons of Korah." Pp. 335–50 in vol. 2 of Tur-Sinai, *The Language and the Book*. 2nd ed. Jerusalem, 1959. [Hebrew]

Uffenheimer, *Bible and Jewish History*   B. Uffenheimer (ed.). *Bible and Jewish History: Studies in Bible and Jewish History Dedicated to the Memory of Jacob Liver*. Tel Aviv, 1971.

Uffenheimer, *Visions of Zechariah*   B. Uffenheimer. *The Visions of Zechariah: From Prophecy to Apocalyptic*. Jerusalem, 1961. [Hebrew]

Ulrich, *Qumran Text*   E. C. Ulrich. *The Qumran Text of Samuel and Josephus*. Harvard Semitic Monographs 19. Chico, California, 1978.

Unger, *Israel and the Arameans*   M. F. Unger. *Israel and the Arameans of Damascus*. Grand Rapids, Michigan, 1957.

Ussishkin, *Conquest of Lachish*   D. Ussishkin. *The Conquest of Lachish by Sennacherib*. Tel Aviv, 1982.

Ussishkin, "Lachish"   D. Ussishkin. "Lachish in the Days of the Kingdom of Judah: The Recent Archaeological Excavations." *Qadmoniot* 15 (1982) 42–56. [Hebrew]

Ussishkin, "*Short Inscription*"   D. Ussishkin. "On the *Short Inscription from the Tomb of* '. . . *YAHU Who Is over the Household*." *Lešonénu* 33 (1968–69) 297–303.

Van Grol, "Servants We Are"   H. W. M. Van Grol. "Indeed, Servants We Are: Ezra 9, Nehemiah 9 and 2 Chronicles 12 Compared." Pp. 209–27 in *The Crisis of Israelite Religion: Transformation of Religious Tradition in Exilic and Post-exilic Times*. Oudtestamentische Studiën 42. Leiden, 1999.

Vannutelli, *Libri Synoptici*   P. Vannutelli. *Libri Synoptici Veteris Testamenti seu Librorum Regum et Chronicorum Loci Paralleli*. Rome, 1931–34.

de Vaux, *Ancient Israel*   R. de Vaux. *Ancient Israel: Its Life and Institutions*. New York, 1961.

Watson, "Chiastic Patterns"   W. G. E. Watson. "Chiastic Patterns in Biblical Hebrew Poetry." Pp. 118–68 in Welch (ed.), *Chiasmus in Antiquity*.

Watson, *Hebrew Poetry*   W. G. E. Watson. *Classical Hebrew Poetry*. Journal for the Study of the Old Testament Supplements 26. Sheffield, 1984.

Watts, *Isaiah*   J. D. W. Watts. *Isaiah 1–33*. Word Biblical Commentary. Waco, Texas, 1985.

Weinfeld, "Molech Worship"   M. Weinfeld. "Molech Worship in Israel and Its Background." Pp. 37–61, 152 in vol. 1 of *Proceedings of the Fifth World Congress of Jewish Studies*. Jerusalem, 1969. [Hebrew]

Weiser, *Introduction*   A. Weiser. *Introduction to the Old Testament*. London, 1961.

Weiss, "Because Three . . . and Because Four"   M. Weiss. "Because Three . . . and Because Four (Amos, I–II)." *Tarbiz 36* (1967) 307–18 (= pp. 13–26 in *Scriptures in Their Own Light: Collected Essays*. Jerusalem, 1988). [Hebrew]

Weiss, *Bible from Within*   M. Weiss. *The Bible from Within: The Method of Total Interpretation*. Jerusalem, 1984.

Weiss, "Chiasm in the Bible" — R. Weiss. "Chiasm in the Bible." Pp. 259–73 in Weiss, *Text and Language.*

Weiss, "The Language of Chronicles" — R. Weiss. "The Language of Chronicles." Pp. 96–98 in Weiss, *Mashot beMikra.* Jerusalem, 1976. [Hebrew]

Weiss, "*Negative* לא" — R. Weiss. "*On the Use of the Negative* לא *in the Bible.*" Pp. 20–45 in Weiss, *Text and Language.*

Weiss, "On Chiasmus" — R. Weiss. "On Chiasmus in the Bible." *Beth Mikra* 7 (1962) 46–51. [Hebrew]

Weiss, "On Ligatures in the Bible" — R. Weiss. "On Ligatures in the Bible." Pp. 3–19 in Weiss, *Text and Language.*

Weiss, "Synonymous Variants" — R. Weiss. "Synonymous Variants in Divergences between the Samaritan and Massoretic Texts of the Pentateuch." Pp. 63–189 in Weiss, *Text and Language.*

Weiss, *Text and Language* — R. Weiss. *Studies in the Text and Language of the Bible.* Jerusalem, 1981. [Hebrew]

Weiss, "Textual Notes" — R. Weiss. "Textual Notes." Pp. 55–59 in Weiss, *Text and Language.*

Weissbach, *Keilinschriften* — F. H. Weissbach. *Die Keilinschriften der Achämeniden.* Leipzig, 1911.

Welch, *Chronicler* — A. C. Welch. *The Work of the Chronicler: Its Purpose and Its Date.* London, 1939.

Welch, *Judaism* — A. C. Welch. *Post-exilic Judaism.* Edinburgh, 1935.

Welch, *Chiasmus in Antiquity* — J. W. Welch (ed.). *Chiasmus in Antiquity: Structures, Analyses, Exegesis.* Hildesheim, 1981.

Wellhausen, *Composition des Hexateuchs* — J. Wellhausen. *Die Composition des Hexateuchs und der historischen Bücher des Alten Testaments.* 4th ed. Berlin, 1963.

Wellhausen, *Prolegomena* — J. Wellhausen. *Prolegomena zur Geschichte Israels.* Berlin, 1878. [ET, *Prolegomena to the History of Israel.* Gloucester, Massachusetts, 1973]

Welten, *Geschichte* — P. Welten. *Geschichte und Geschientsdarstellung in den Chronikbüchern.* Neukirchen-Vluyn, 1973.

Wenham, "David's Sons" — G. J. Wenham. "Were David's Sons Priests?" *Zeitschrift für die alttestamentliche Wissenschaft* 87 (1975) 79–82.

de Wette, *Beiträge* — W. M. L. de Wette. "Historisch-kritische Untersuchung über die Bücher der Chronik." Pp. 1–132 in part 1 of *Beiträge zur Einleitung in das Alte Testament.* Halle, 1806.

de Wette, *Critical and Historical Introduction* — W. M. L. de Wette. *A Critical and Historical Introduction to the Canonical Scriptures of the Old Testament.* Vol. 2, trans. and enlarged T. Parker. 3rd ed. Boston, 1859.

de Wette, *Lehrbuch* — W. M. L. de Wette. *Lehrbuch der historisch-kritischen Einleitung in die kanonischen und apokryphischen Bücher des Alten Testaments.* Vol. 1. 6th ed. Berlin, 1845.

Wevers, "Double Readings" — J. W. Wevers. "Double Readings in the Book of Kings." *Journal of Biblical Literature* 65 (1946) 307–10.

Whitehouse, "Uzziah (Azariah)" — O. C. Whitehouse. "Uzziah (Azariah)." Pp. 843–45 in *Dictionary of the Bible*, ed. J. Hastings. Edinburgh, 1902.

Whybray, *Succession Narrative* — R. N. Whybray. *The Succession Narrative.* London, 1968.

Wilda, *Königsbild*   G. Wilda. *Das Königsbild des Chronistischen Geschichtswerks.* Bonn, 1954.

Wildberger, *Jesaja*   H. Wildberger. *Jesaja 28–39.* Biblischer Kommentar, Altes Testament. Neukirchen-Vluyn, 1982.

Willi, *Chronik*   T. Willi. *Die Chronik als Auslegung: Untersuchungen zur literarischen Gestaltung der historischen Überlieferung Israel.* Forschungen zur Religion und Literatur des Alten und Neuen Testaments 106. Göttingen, 1972.

Willi, "Die Freiheit Israels"   T. Willi. "Die Freiheit Israels." Pp. 531–46 in *Festschrift Walter Zimmerli,* ed. H. Donner, R. Hanhart, and R. Smend. Göttingen, 1977.

Williamson, "Accession of Solomon"   H. G. M. Williamson. "The Accession of Solomon in the Books of Chronicles." *Vetus Testamentum* 26 (1976) 351–64.

Williamson, *Chronicles*   H. G. M. Williamson. *1 and 2 Chronicles.* New Century Bible Commentary. Grand Rapids, Michigan, 1982.

Williamson, "Genealogy of Judah"   H. G. M. Williamson. "Sources and Redaction in the Chronicler's Genealogy of Judah." *Journal of Biblical Literature* 98 (1979) 351–59.

Williamson, *Israel*   H. G. M. Williamson. *Israel in the Books of Chronicles.* Cambridge, 1977.

Williamson, "We Are Yours"   H. G. M. Williamson. "We Are Yours, O David: The Setting and Purpose of 1 Chronicles XII 1–23." *Oudtestamentische Studiën* 21 (1981) 164–76.

Wiseman, *Chronicles of Chaldean*   D. J. Wiseman. *Chronicles of Chaldean Kings.* London, 1956.

Woolley, *Carchemish*   C. L. Woolley. *Carchemish: Report on the Excavations at Jerablus on Behalf of the British Museum.* Part 2. Oxford, 1921.

Wright, "Structure of the Book of Wisdom"   A. G. Wright. "The Structure of the Book of Wisdom." *Biblica* 48 (1967) 165–84.

Würthwein, *Text of OT*   E. Würthwein. *The Text of the Old Testament.* Grand Rapids, Michigan, 1979.

Yadin, *Art of Warfare*   Y. Yadin. *The Art of Warfare in Biblical Lands.* London, 1963.

Yadin, "Dial of Ahaz"   Y. Yadin. "The Dial of Ahaz." *Eretz-Israel* 5 (B. Mazar Volume; 1958) 91–96.

Yadin, "Goliath's Javelin"   Y. Yadin. "Goliath's Javelin and the 'Menor Orgim.'" *Eretz-Israel* 4 (Y. Ben-Zvi Volume; 1956) 68–73.

Yadin, "Strategy"   Y. Yadin. "Some Aspects of the Strategy of Ahab and David (I Kings 20; II Sam. 11)." *Biblica* 36 (1955) 332–51.

Yaron, "Coptus Decree"   R. Yaron. "The Coptus Decree and 2 Sam xii 14." *Vetus Testamentum* 9 (1959) 89–91.

Yeivin, "Administration"   S. Yeivin. "Administration." Pp. 147–71, 308–11 in vol. 2 of Malamat (ed.), *The Age of the Monarchies.*

Yeivin, "Bath-Sheba"   S. Yeivin. "Bath-Sheba." Pp. 379–80 in vol. 2 of *Encyclopaedia Biblica.* Jerusalem, 1965. [Hebrew]

Yeivin, "David"   S. Yeivin. "David." Pp. 629–43 in vol. 2 of *Encyclopaedia Biblica.* Jerusalem, 1965. [Hebrew]

Yeivin, "The Divided Kingdom" S. Yeivin. "The Divided Kingdom: Rehoboam-Ahas / Jeroboam-Pekah." Pp. 126–79, 330–40 in vol. 1 of Malamat (ed.), *The Age of the Monarchies*.

Yeivin, "Marginal Glosses" S. Yeivin. "Marginal Glosses." *Tarbiz* 40 (1971) 395–98. [Hebrew]

Yeivin, "Solomon" S. Yeivin. "Solomon." Pp. 693–99 in vol. 7 of *Encyclopaedia Biblica*. Jerusalem, 1976. [Hebrew]

Yeivin, "Son of the King" S. Yeivin. "*Ben haMelech* (= 'Son of the King')." P. 160 in vol. 2 of *Encyclopaedia Biblica*. Jerusalem, 1965. [Hebrew]

Yeivin, "Uzziah" S. Yeivin. "Uzziah, Uzziahu." Pp. 126–31 in vol. 6 of *Encyclopaedia Biblica*. Jerusalem, 1971. [Hebrew]

Yeivin, "Wars of David" S. Yeivin. "The Wars of David." Pp. 149–65 in Liver (ed.), *Military History*.

Yellin, "Allusion" D. Yellin. "Allusion." Pp. 210–13 in Yellin, *Biblical Studies*. Jerusalem, 1983. [Hebrew]

Yellin, "Simile" D. Yellin. "Simile." Pp. 223–40 in Yellin, *Biblical Studies*. Jerusalem, 1983. [Hebrew]

Young, *Introduction* E. J. Young. *An Introduction to the Old Testament*. London, 1964.

Zadok, "Origin of the Name Shinar" R. Zadok. "The Origin of the Name Shinar." *Zeitschrift für Assyriologie* 74 (1984) 240–44.

Zakovitch, "Assimilation" Y. Zakovitch. "Assimilation in Biblical Narrative." Pp. 175–96 in *Empirical Models for Biblical Criticism*, ed. J. H. Tigay. Philadelphia, 1985.

Zakovitch, *Three–Four* Y. Zakovitch. *The Pattern of the Numerical Sequence Three–Four in the Bible*. Ph.D. dissertation. Hebrew University of Jerusalem, 1977. [Hebrew]

Zalewski, *Solomon* S. Zalewski. *Solomon's Ascension to the Throne: Studies in the Books of Kings and Chronicles*. Jerusalem, 1981. [Hebrew]

Zawadzki, "Death of Sennacherib" S. Zawadzki. "Oriental and Greek Tradition about the Death of Sennacherib." *State Archives of Assyria Bulletin* 4 (1990) 69–72.

Zenger, "Judith/ Judithbuch" E. Zenger. "Judith/Judithbuch." Pp. 406–7 in vol. 17 of *Theologische Realenzyklopädie*, ed. G. Krause and G. Müller. Berlin, 1988.

Zucker, "Solution of Thirty-Two *Midot*" M. Zucker. "The Solution of Thirty-Two *Midot* and the 'Mishnah' of Rabbi Eliezer." *Proceedings of the American Academy of Jewish Research* 23 (1954) 1–39. [Hebrew]

Zunz, *Vorträge der Juden* L. Zunz. *Die gottesdienstlichen Vorträge der Juden: Historisch entwickelt*. 2nd ed. Frankfurt am Main, 1892.

Indexes

Index of Authors

Abarbanel, I.   3, 393, 408
Abramsky, S.   45, 103,
  136, 143–144, 302, 305
Ackroyd, P. R.   8–9, 14,
  139, 339, 407
Aharoni, Y.   20, 35, 112,
  269–270
Aḥituv, S.   119, 364, 401
Albright, W. F.   86, 108,
  152, 277, 318
Allegro, J. M.   192
Allen, L. C.   361
Alt, A.   394
Amit, Y.   373
Aquila   111
Ashbel, D.   86
Auerbach, E.   145
Augustin, M.   1
Auld, A. G.   4
Avigad, N.   218, 397–398
Avishur, Y.   129, 272, 274

Barag, D.   184
Bar-Efrat, S.   275, 295,
  349–350, 356
Bar-Kochva, B.   393
Barnes, W. E.   305
Barthélemy, D.   366
Batten, L. W.   182
Becker, J.   7
Begrich, J.   139, 225, 263,
  307
Ben-Barak, Z.   55
Bendavid, A.   1–2, 411
Ben-Porat, Z.   194
Ben-Yashar, M.   105
Benzinger, I.   55, 58, 97,
  111, 134, 263, 320–321,
  323, 370, 377, 392
Bergman, A.   52
Bertheau, E.   3, 277, 302,
  323
Bertholdt, D. L.   3
Bickerman, E.   41–42
Biran, A.   16
  see also Bergman, A.

Blau, J.   244
Blenkinsopp, J.   9, 65
Borger, R.   53, 100, 204,
  396, 411
Braun, R. L.   9, 14–15, 75,
  139, 365
Breasted, J. H.   394
Briggs, C. A.   58, 132
Briggs, E. G.   58, 132
Bright, J.   20, 35
Brin, G.   11, 14, 106, 233,
  399
Brunet, A. M.   14
Buber, M. M.   356
Budde, K.   15, 51, 72, 161
Buhl, F.   132
Burney, C. F.   113–114,
  121, 148, 296, 377
Burns, J. B.   1
Bury, J. B.   53
Butzer, K. W.   401
Buzriya, J. (rabbi)   158

Cassuto, U.   72, 113, 367
Chapman, A. T.   411
Childs, B. S.   28
Clements, R. E.   135
Cogan, M.   21–22, 24, 30,
  49, 102, 113, 207, 213,
  244, 296, 397, 403, 411–
  412
Coggins, R. J.   54, 94, 102,
  105, 199
Cohen, C.   387
Conder, C. R.   80
Cook, S. A.   106
Cowley, A.   8, 184
Crenshaw, J. L.   134
Cross, F. M.   6, 9, 12, 14,
  169, 201, 236, 245, 406
Curtis, E. L.   1, 4, 13, 15,
  19, 27, 39, 42, 44–45,
  48, 51, 54, 57, 61, 65–66,
  77, 97, 100, 102–103,
  · 105, 107, 113–114, 125,
  128, 130, 134–135, 150,

  153, 155, 183, 188, 194,
  199, 204, 207, 217, 263,
  266, 271, 276, 281, 283,
  287, 293, 297, 302–303,
  305, 312, 323, 333, 341–
  342, 360, 370–371, 383,
  385, 389–390, 401–402,
  406

Dahood, M.   295
Day, J.   78
De Vries, S. J.   40
Deboys, D. G.   196
Delcor, M.   10
Delitzsch, F.   107, 207, 284
Demsky, A.   103, 135,
  389–390
Di Marco, A.   216–217
Dietrich, M.   394
Dillard, R. B.   196, 212,
  217, 223
Dillmann, A.   4
Diodorus Siculus   78, 185
Diringer, D.   106
Dirksen, P. B.   39
Donner, H.   80, 101, 115,
  397
Dothan, M.   50
Driver, G. R.   51, 136, 296,
  302
Driver, S. R.   1, 122, 135,
  146, 161

Ebeling, E.   398
Ehrlich, A. B.   23, 25, 41,
  58, 61, 65, 72, 108, 139,
  148, 152, 197, 200, 207,
  244, 271, 276, 279–281,
  314, 327, 342, 397
Eichhorn, J. G.   3
Eichrodt, W.   145
Eissfeldt, O.   407
Elat, M.   119, 332, 393–
  396, 401
Eliezer (rabbi)   68
Ellenbogen, M.   177

Elliger, K. 97
Elmslie, W. A. L. 1, 9, 13, 23, 102, 111, 134, 148, 199, 266, 281, 305, 380, 383, 390, 401
Endres, J. C. 1
Eph‘al, I. 18, 25, 33, 44, 80, 89, 100, 110, 184
Eupolemus 40
Eusebius 8
Evenari, H. 61

Falkenstein, A. 386
Fallon, F. 40
Farnakh (rabbi) 387
Feigin, S. I. 65
Fensham, F. C. 40, 265
Fenton, T. L. 89
Finkelstein, I. 145
Finkelstein, L. 157
Fox, M. V. 134
Fraenkel, L. 325
Freedman, D. N. 216, 406
Friedman, R. E. 146

Gabriel, I. 7
Galling, K. 155, 392
Garsiel, M. 20, 35, 103, 233
Geiger, A. 243
Gelston, A. 10
Gerleman, G. 5–6, 13–14, 154
Gershon, L. ben (rabbi) 9, 120, 340, 387
Gesenius, W. 68
Gibson, J. C. L. 80, 86
Gilad, H. 21
Ginsberg, H. L. 113
Ginzberg, L. 395
Glueck, N. 401
Goedicke, H. 287
Goethe, J. W. 404
Goettsberger, J. 42
Goitein, S. D. 145
Golan, D. 53
Goldstein, J. A. 393
Gooding, D. W. 366
Gordon, C. H. 72, 113, 239, 367, 399
Graetz, H. 113
Graf, K. H. 5, 321, 341
Gramberg, C. P. W. 5
Gray, G. B. 52
Gray, J. 12, 49, 56, 95, 108, 111, 113–114, 121, 146, 204, 276

Grayson, A. K. 82, 90–91, 100
Greenfield, J. C. 377, 399
Grintz, Y. M. 9, 145, 155, 184
Gunneweg, A. H. J. 153

Hänel, J. 84, 94, 97, 147, 292, 323, 330
Ha-Gelilee, Y. (rabbi) 68
Halevi, J. (rabbi) 68
Halevy, J. 86
Hanson, P. D. 9
Haran, M. 9, 57, 82, 146, 152, 308
Harper, R. F. 87, 355
Harrison, R. K. 8–9
Hauer, C. E. 20, 35
Haupt, P. 86, 113
Havenick, H. A. C. 4
Hayes, J. H. 45
Herner, S. 269–270
Herodotus 79, 109, 401
Hertzberg, H. W. 145
Hill, A. E. 217
Hobbs, T. R. 113
Hoenig, S. B. 394–396
Hoffman, M. Z. 57
Hoffman, Y. 233, 373
Homer 37
Horn, S. H. 394
Horovitz, H. S. 158, 210
Hummel, H. 239
Hurowitz, V. (A.) 148, 181, 399
Hurvitz, A. 1, 53, 87, 133, 249, 269, 272–273, 278

ibn Ezra, A. (rabbi) 68, 120, 216, 275, 369
Isaiah of Teranni (rabbi) 69
Ishida, T. 54
Ishmael (rabbi) 369

Japhet, S. 2, 6, 9–10, 20–21, 26, 40–43, 48, 67, 73, 94, 96, 102, 118, 129, 138, 147, 160, 162–163, 174, 188–189, 200, 207–208, 212, 230, 244, 266, 285, 320, 336, 341, 343–344, 346, 352, 355, 359–360, 365, 373, 376–377, 381, 390, 392, 405–406, 411
Jawitz, W. 57
Jepsen, A. 43, 55, 199

Johnson, D. M. 217, 406
Joines, K. 126
Jones, G. H. 111, 121
Josephus 8, 13, 15, 33, 36–38, 42, 46, 57, 67, 74, 89–90, 100, 103, 113, 120, 141, 153, 155, 185, 326, 328, 351, 367, 382, 391, 393, 395

Kalimi, I. 1, 3, 7–9, 12, 15–16, 22, 35, 65, 67, 75, 83, 92, 99–100, 120, 153, 168, 178, 201–202, 250, 253, 289, 308, 320, 355, 363, 367, 383–384, 405, 407, 409
Kallai, Z. 136, 402
Kaplan, J. 80
Karmon, Y. 116
Kasowski, C. J. 278, 400
Kassis, H. E. 112
Katzenstein, H. J. 40, 42, 80, 287, 382, 397–398
Kaufman, A. S. 280
Kaufmann, Y. 141–142
Kautzsch, E. 68, 239
Keel, Y. 296
Kegler, J. 1
Keil, C. F. 1–3, 7, 77, 406
Kelly, B. E. 39, 118
Kimhi, D. (rabbi) 3, 26, 51, 57–58, 68, 71, 107, 120, 153, 155, 199, 287, 293, 326, 340, 384, 387
Kitchen, K. A. 394
Kittel, R. 1, 43, 108, 147, 197, 320, 349
Klein, S. 57, 97, 382
Klostermann, A. 15, 51, 111, 113, 121
Knoppers, G. N. 365
Koch, K. 10
König, E. 9, 217, 295
Kogut, S. 216
Kosovsky, B. 278
Kraeling, E. G. H. 87
Krašovec, J. 325
Kropat, A. 1, 269, 278
Kuhl, C. 275
Kutscher, E. Y. 87, 245

Langdon, S. 33
Lemaire, A. 20
Lemke, W. E. 6, 14–15, 155, 277
Levin, L. D. 18, 411
Licht, J. S. 78

Lieberman, S. 37, 111, 155
Liver, J. 9, 40–41, 43, 55, 105, 146, 199, 323, 406
Loewenstamm, S. E. 30, 72, 187, 216, 296
Loretz, O. 394
Luckenbill, D. D. 16, 25, 52–53, 102, 187, 204, 360, 389, 403
Lund, N. W. 216
Lust, J. 366
Luzzatto, S. D. 135

Machinist, P. 184
Madsen, A. A. 1, 4, 13, 15, 19, 27, 39, 42, 44–45, 48, 51, 54, 57, 61, 65–66, 77, 97, 100, 102–103, 105, 107, 113–114, 125, 128, 130, 134–135, 150, 153, 155, 183, 188, 194, 199, 204, 207, 217, 263, 266, 271, 276, 281, 283, 287, 293, 297, 302–303, 305, 312, 323, 333, 341–342, 360, 370–371, 383, 385, 389–390, 401–402, 406
Maisler, B. 80, 269, 396
    see also Mazar, B.
Malamat, A. 45–46, 82, 85, 108–109, 112, 190, 357, 368, 394
Mantel, H. D. 185
Markoe, G. E. 394, 396
Mayerhofer, M. 377
Mazar, A. 120, 136
Mazar, B. 9, 30–32, 35, 89, 97, 101, 103–104, 106, 136, 279, 287, 406
    see also Maisler, B.
McCarter, P. K. 12, 65–66, 70, 73, 93, 112, 152–153, 155, 161, 312, 367, 402
McKenzie, S. L. 4, 6, 9, 12, 15, 58, 119, 155, 169, 245–246, 406, 409
Meek, T. J. 106
Meiggs, R. 53
Meissner, B. 398
Melammed, E. Z. 57, 69, 71, 216
Mettinger, T. N. D. 153, 266, 397–398
Michel, E. 16
Millar, W. R. 1

Miller, J. M. 45
Montgomery, J. A. 24, 27, 30, 49, 56, 81, 92, 95, 105, 108–109, 111, 114, 183, 199, 204, 276, 284, 383
Moore, C. A. 184
Moran, W. L. 347
Mortara, M. H. 9
Mosca, P. G. 78
Moscati, S. 397
Mosiman, S. K. 1
Mosis, R. 7, 94, 210, 294, 328, 330–331, 363, 390–392, 406
Movers, F. C. 9
Muffs, Y. 221
Myers, J. M. 19, 42, 54, 81, 163, 217, 355, 368, 388, 390, 406

Na'aman, N. 279, 281
Naor, M. 66, 148
Naveh, J. 16, 270
Naville, E. 394
Newsome, J. D. 9, 406
Nicholas of Damascus 37
Noordtzij, A. 42
North, C. R. 143
Noth, M. 7, 11, 20, 40, 55, 75, 97, 111, 121, 368, 389, 407, 409
Noy, D. 149, 367

Oded, B. 20, 32, 112, 119, 193, 201, 214, 332, 335
Öttli, S. 323
Olmstead, A. T. 13
Oppenheim, A. L. 355
Oren, A. 153–154
Ornan, U. 15, 350

Page, S. 102
Paran, M. 216, 295
Parpola, S. 33, 87, 90, 109
Paul, S. M. 264
Peretz, Y. 173
Pisano, S. 15
Pitard, W. T. 85–87, 95, 357
Plutarch 53, 78
Polzin, R. 1, 269–270, 278
Porter, J. R. 9
Poulssen, N. 143
Pritchard, J. B. 16, 25, 52–53, 80, 86, 90–91, 100, 102, 187, 350, 360, 367, 389, 403

Pseudo-Hieronymus 42
Pseudo-Philo 74
Pseudo-Scylax 80
Purvis, J. D. 142

Rabin, I. A. 158, 210
Rad, G. von 6, 141, 159, 195, 212, 392
Radak (rabbi) 94
    see also Kimhi, D.
Radday, Y. T. 216, 218
Rainey, A. F. 103, 109, 112
Rashi (rabbi) 26, 51, 69, 94, 107, 120, 154–155, 210, 275
    attributed to 23, 71, 199, 266, 326, 340, 383
Redford, D. B. 177
Redmount, C. A. 402
Rehm, M. 15, 100, 111
Reviv, H. 32, 35, 54, 119, 332, 336
Roberts, B. J. 11
Röllig, W. 80, 101, 115, 397
Rofé, A. 72, 274–275
Rosenzweig, F. 356
Rost, L. 363
Rothstein, J. W. 84, 94, 97, 147, 292, 323, 330
Rudolph, W. 6–9, 15, 25, 41–43, 46, 54, 58, 71, 84, 94, 97, 100, 103, 113, 126, 134, 136, 139, 155, 158, 163, 174, 187, 189, 194, 199–200, 207, 225, 265–266, 277–278, 281, 284, 292, 300, 302–303, 305, 307, 320, 323–324, 330, 338, 341–342, 355, 363–364, 368, 372, 377, 389–390, 392, 401, 407

Šanda, A. 43, 55, 111, 377, 390
Sanmartín, J. 394
Sappan, R. 216
Sarfati, G. B. A. 367
Sarna, N. M. 132
Schley, D. G. 145, 238–239
Schmoldt, H. 275
Schoors, A. 55
Schramm, W. 411
Schunk, K. D. 145
Scott, R. B. Y. 280

Seeligmann, I. L.   9, 11,
  39, 102, 105, 111–112,
  155, 158, 273, 276, 279
Segal, M. Z.   6, 8–9, 57, 59,
  61, 69, 71–72, 94, 97,
  111, 120, 122, 135–136,
  152–153, 155, 161, 295,
  312, 321, 346, 367, 400
Seidel, M.   232–233
Selms, A. van   42
Shaver, J. R.   392
Shenkel, J. D.   13
Shinan, A.   228
Smelik, K. A. D.   334
Smend, R.   7, 10, 265
Smith, F. R.   217
Smith, H. P.   15, 20, 51,
  55, 72, 122, 135
Snaith, N. H.   78, 204, 212
Soden, W. von   352, 386
Spalinger, A.   411
Sperber, A.   16, 109, 111,
  235, 318
Spinoza, B. de   408
Stade, B.   42, 111, 113–
  114, 121, 148, 377
Stager, L. E.   78
Stern, E.   42, 80, 109, 273,
  280
Stern, M.   185
Steuernagel, C.   195, 409
Sukenik, E. L.   106
Sukenik, Y.   120
  see also Yadin, Y.

Tadmor, H.   8, 22, 24, 30,
  32, 44, 49, 89, 102, 113,
  207, 296, 389, 397, 403,
  411
Tacitus   50
Täckholm, U.   394
Talmon, S.   6, 14, 54, 114,
  139–140, 235–237, 239,
  247, 295, 349, 354
Talshir, Z.   272

Tcherikover, A.   184–185
Thenius, O.   15, 111, 113,
  136, 148, 390
Thiel, W.   382
Thompson, J. A.   11
Thompson, S.   363
Thomson, I. H.   215
Throntveit, M. A.   196
Torrey, C. C.   13
Tov, E.   11, 13–14, 124,
  366
Tsafrir, Y.   402
Tuell, S. S.   10
Tuland, C. G.   37
Tur-Sinai, N. H.   69, 111–
  112, 121, 132, 195, 254

Uffenheimer, B.   9, 406
Ulrich, E. C.   6, 12, 245–
  246
Unger, M. F.   86
Ussishkin, D.   25, 397

Van Grol, H. W. M.   279
Vannutelli, P.   1
Vaux, R. de   153, 335,
  397–398, 406

Watson, W. G. E.   68, 195,
  216, 350, 356
Watts, J. D. W.   135
Weinfeld, M.   78
Weiss, M.   232–233, 362,
  404
Weiss, R.   123, 139, 150,
  200, 216–217, 229–230,
  237
Weissbach, F. H.   402
Welch, A. C.   9, 143, 157–
  158, 406
Welch, J. W.   215–218
Wellhausen, J.   5, 140,
  146, 183, 276, 340, 363
Welten, P.   9, 405
Wenham, G. J.   153

Wette, W. M. L. de   4, 7
Wevers, J. W.   225
Whitehouse, O. C.   106
Whybray, R. W.   363
Wilda, G.   143
Wildberger, H.   135
Willi, T.   6–7, 42, 49, 113,
  153, 194, 210, 279, 351,
  400, 407
Williamson, H. G. M.   6, 9,
  14–15, 19, 21, 23, 27,
  42, 47–50, 62, 82, 97,
  100, 102, 107, 112, 135–
  136, 143, 152–153, 158,
  165, 183, 194, 199, 204,
  211–212, 217, 228, 255,
  284, 297, 302–303, 312,
  330–332, 338, 342, 353,
  368, 382, 388, 390, 406
Wiseman, D. J.   82, 90–91,
  100
Woolley, C. L.   82
Wright, A. G.   218
Würthwein, E.   11

Yadin, Y.   84, 120, 206, 351
  see also Sukenik, Y.
Yaron, R.   210
Yeivin, S.   20, 35, 46, 106,
  198, 298, 332, 360, 364,
  399
Yellin, D.   195, 350
Yohanan (rabbi)   387
Yoshajah (rabbi)   158
Young, E. J.   57

Zadok, R.   55–56, 99, 151
Zakovitch, Y.   75, 228, 311,
  362–367
Zalewski, S.   46, 352
Zawadzki, S.   33
Zenger, E.   184
Zucker, M.   71
Zunz, L.   1, 9

Index of Scripture

Page numbers printed in bold type refer to a Scripture passage that has been cited in a specific example of the Chronicler's techniques. All citations in the index are according to Hebrew versification.

Genesis
3:16 **252**
4:8 286, 384
6:1–6 351
6:4 237
6:7–9 295
6:10–12 295
6:13–15 295
7:1 309
8:21 **235**
9:1 295
9:2–6 295
9:4 70
9:5 369
9:6 187
9:7 295
10:4 16
10:4–5 396
10:22 74
10:23 60
11:2 100
11:10–26 66
11:27 66
12:1 195
12:2 353
12:7 195
12:10–20 195
12:16 352
13:16 353
14:2 66
14:3 66
14:5 52
14:7 67
14:8 66
14:17 67
14:18 67
15:1 24
15:7 211
15:10 352
15:17 195
17:5 66
18:8 141, 205
18:18 353
19:8 97
19:25 97
20:1–18 195
20:3 54

Genesis (cont.)
21 363
21:18 326
21:21 75
22:1 24
22:1–14 202
22:2 83, 202
22:14 83
22:15–18 195
22:17 211, 352
22:20 24
23:9 311
24:7 195
24:12–22 326
24:27 132
25 254
25:1 58
25:1–4 **254**
25:12–16 **254**
25:13 323
25:34 349
26:2–5 195
26:3 97
26:4 97
26:7–11 195
27:3 369
27:13–15 195
28:14 352–353
31:10–13 54
31:21 88
31:24 195
31:29 195
32:3 104, 354
35:5 156
35:9–13 195
35:10 **235**
35:16 152
35:19 152
35:22 209
35:29 190
36:1 104
36:10 323
36:26 16, 396
36:40 104
36:43 104–105
37:1–3 99
38 208, 220, 383

Genesis (cont.)
38:2 75
38:2–5 319
38:2–30 **319**
38:10 319
38:12 75
38:24 50
39:7 24
40 327
40:1 24
40:13 327
40:20 327
41:1 304
41:38 156
42:23 207
43:6 99
43:8 99
43:11 99
43:20 68
45:25 99
45:27 99
45:28 99
46:1 99
46:2 99
46:3 353
46:8 323
46:9 **293**
46:12 **319**
46:13 **322**
46:17 75
48:1 24
48:5 209
48:7 152
48:22 209
49:3–4 209
49:8 209

Exodus
1:1 9, 323
1:7 349
1:10 210
1:15–16 291
1:21 191
2:5 74
2:15 74
3:2 248
4:10 68

Exodus (cont.)
4:10–17 363
4:22 264
6:7 **264**
6:10–12 275
6:12 275
6:13 295
6:13–28 275
6:14–25 295
6:21 76–77
6:24 152–153
6:26–27 265, 295
6:29–30 275
6:30 275
7:19 369
9:30 68
10:15 266
12 157
12:3 156
12:5 156, 376
12:6 281
12:8 158
12:9 158
12:21 156
13:4 38
13:15 68
14:4 68
14:13–14 **254**
15:26 125
16:12 281
17:7 216
18:21 156
18:24–26 142
19:22 150
20:3 156
20:18 38
21:12 187
21:23–25 187
23:8 233
23:14–17 63–64
23:19 141
23:31 110
25:14 149
26:31 **390**
26:31–35 390
28:20 394
29:1 212
29:7 55
29:21 55
29:30 386
29:37 386
29:38–41 312
29:39 281
29:41 281
30:12 199, 327
30:18 15
30:22–29 55
30:28 15
30:30 55

Exodus (cont.)
31:2–5 252
31:9 15
32:11 333
32:20 **134**
34:13 128
34:18–24 64, 369
34:23 63
34:24 63
34:26 141
35:4–29 221
35:30–33 252
35:32 391
36:17 270
36:25 **390–391**
36:35 **390**
36:35–36 390
39:13 394
39:32 72
40:2 72
40:6 72
40:29 72
40:34 72
40:35 226

Leviticus
1:2 369
2:13 355
4:27 397
5:1 68
7:13 312
7:35–36 153
8:11 55
8:12 55
8:33 386
9:12 **248**
9:18 **248**
10:5 154
13:46 113
16:1–2 291
16:16 145
17:7 212
17:8–9 143–144
17:10–14 70
18:15 383
18:23 **235**
18:27 97
19:31 140, 328
20:2 397
20:4 397
20:6 140, 328
20:12 383
20:14–25 50
20:27 328
21:9 50
21:14 93
23:5 281
23:26–32 386
23:33–36 147, 386

Leviticus (cont.)
24:17–22 187
24:19 186
25:32–34 211
26:12 **264**
26:34 314
26:34–35 161
26:46 125

Numbers
1:2 327
1:3 211
1:8 76
1:50 149, 152
1:50–51 152
2:5 76
3:5–9 152
3:10 152
3:19 152
3:28–31 56
3:31 149
4:1–15 149
4:4–15 56
5:1–4 113
7:9 149
7:10 386
7:10–88 386
7:18 76
7:23 76
9:3 281
9:14 318
9:17–18 72
10:15 76
10:17 149
11:15 210
12:6–8 54
12:10–15 113
15:8–9 312
15:40 275
16:14 210
16:15 154
17:1–5 153
17:1–28 153
18:1–7 153
18:2–4 152
18:4 152
18:19 355
18:22–23 152
20:14–21 212
21:24 108
21:26–28 52
21:30 84
21:39 52
23:10 352
25:7 75
25:13 153
26:5 293
26:5–7 293
26:19 319

Numbers (cont.)
26:19–20   319
26:23–24   **322**
28–29   147
28:4   281
28:12–13   312
29:7–11   386
29:12   147
29:12–34   386
29:35–36   147
32:41   52, 154
32:42   52
33:3   84
34:5   260
35:1–5   211
35:25   183
35:28   183

Deuteronomy
1:9–18   142
1:21   274
2:2–8   212
2:9   212
2:18–19   212
3:14   52, 154
4:8   125
4:42   97
5:7   156
5:28   125
6:14   156
6:18   24, 124
7:4   156, 326
7:5   126–128, 154
7:22   97
7:25   140, 154–155, 346
8:2   385
10:8   56, 149, 151
11:24   110
11:32   125
12:3   126, 128, 140, 154
12:4–14   140
12:8   142
12:10–11   38, 180
12:16   70
12:23–25   70
12:25   125
12:28   24, 124
12:31   78
13:2   54
13:2–3   206
13:4   54
13:6   54
13:19   125
14:1   264
14:21   141
14:26   369
15:23   70
16:1   38
16:2   156–157

Deuteronomy (cont.)
16:7   158
16:13–15   147, 386
16:16   63–64
16:19   233
17:9   149
17:18   149
17:20   46
18:1   149
18:9–12   128
18:10   129, 243
18:10–11   140
18:11   140, 328
19:5   62
19:11   97
19:16–21   187
20:19   68
21:17   209
21:27   129
23:4–5   383
24:8   149
25:19   38
26:15   263
26:17   125
26:17–18   **264**
27:9   149
27:15–26   58
28:15–68   58
28:24   352
28:68   179
29:12   **264**
29:19   58
29:19–28   58
29:21–27   129
29:22   355
29:24–25   129
29:27   129
31:8   274
31:9   149
32:6   264
32:11   244
34:10   **235**

Joshua
1:4   110
1:9   48
6:26   159
7   208
7:1   318
7:8   22
7:15   50
7:18   318
7:24   208
7:26   208
8:1   274
9   84
9:1   **241**
9:16   22
9:17   56

Joshua (cont.)
10:10–11   135
10:25   274
10:29   43
10:31   43
10:41   110
11:1   103
11:1–3   **241**
12:20   103
13:3   56, 260
13:16   84
15:4   260
15:9   65
15:60   65
16:3   110
18:1   145
18:8–10   145
18:14   65
18:28   64
19:1–9   102
19:15   103
19:25   124
19:45   57
20:6   183
21:2   145
21:5–42   211
21:11–13   **231**
21:17   382
21:18   **254**
21:24   57
21:33   **271**
21:44   38
21:45   159
22:11   145
23:1   22, 38
23:14–16   159
24:2   110
24:3   110
24:4   216
24:11   65
24:14   110
24:15   110
24:20   22

Judges
1:6–7   186
1:7   186
1:10   67
2:1   75
2:2   128
5:4   104
6–8   135
6:28   128
6:30–32   128
9   65
9:51   65
10:3–5   154
11:15–26   212
11:33   110

Judges (cont.)
  11:36   22
  12:5   152
  13:3   74
  15:10–11   186
  17   74
  17:6   125
  19:10   64–65
  19:11   64
  19:16   74
  19:20   74
  19:23   22
  20:5   65
  20:10   104
  21:19   145
  21:25   125

1 Samuel
  1–2   14, 153
  1–3   55
  1–4   145
  1:1   152–153
  1:23   242
  1:24   312
  2:11   151
  2:18   151
  3:3   151, 278
  3:15   151
  4   145
  4–6   146
  4:12   74
  6:14   311
  6:18   110
  6:21–7:2   66
  7:1   382
  7:1–2   382
  8:2   152
  8:5–6   397
  9:16   55
  10:1   55
  11:1–11   51, 347
  11:3   326
  13   210
  13:13–14   209
  13:16   104
  14:49   364
  15   209
  15:5   65
  15:24   329
  15:28   201
  15:33   186–187
  16–17   365–366
  16:1–13   160, 201, 363
  16:4   304
  16:6–9   75, 365–366
  16:6–10   366
  16:6–13   75
  16:7   366
  16:10   366

1 Samuel (cont.)
  16:10–11   366–367
  16:11   365–366
  16:11–13   366
  16:13   55, 304
  16:14   132
  16:20   68
  17   274, 366
  17:4   60
  17:7   60, 351
  17:11   274, 366
  17:12   75, 152, 366–367
  17:13   75, 218
  17:13–14   365–366
  17:17–18   365
  17:24–25   366
  17:28   365–366
  17:49–51   366
  18:12   132
  18:13   132
  18:14–27   36
  18:25   36
  18:27   36
  18:29   329
  19:12   349
  20:15   132, 389
  20:16   384
  21:10   203
  22:4–5   34
  22:6–23   328
  23:12   65
  23:13   21
  23:14   34
  25:2–43   93
  25:14   93
  25:22   210
  25:38   340
  27   36
  27:1–7   210
  27:2–3   21
  27:3   93
  27:5–11   36
  27:8   21
  28   209
  28–30   4
  28:1–2   210
  28:5   329
  28:6   54, 327–328
  28:6–7   251
  28:7   139–140, 209
  28:8   304
  28:15   54, 327–328
  28:16   328
  28:16–19   310
  28:17   209
  28:18   209, 310
  28:18–19   310, 328
  28:19   329
  28:20   329

1 Samuel (cont.)
  28:25   304
  29:1–11   210
  29:2   21
  29:4   210, **247**
  30:5   93
  31   4, 18, 139, 310, 339
  31:1   309, 329
  31:1–5   309
  31:1–13   209
  31:2   **262**, 309, 389
  31:3   329
  31:3–4   328
  31:4   309
  31:4–5   309
  31:5   309
  31:6   309–**310**, 331, 389
  31:7   329
  31:9   156, 326, 330
  31:10   203, 330
  31:12   326
  31:12–13   50
  31:13   **237**, 326

2 Samuel
  1–4   18
  1:1   74
  1:5   74
  1:6   74
  1:12   327, 349
  1:13   74
  2–4   96, 389
  2–5   20
  2:1   4
  2:1–4   18
  2:2   93
  2:3   21
  2:4   19, 55
  2:8–10   18
  2:8–4:12   310
  2:10   19
  2:11   19
  2:18   354
  3:1–5   331
  3:2   **316–317**
  3:2–5   4, 315–316
  3:3   93, 107
  3:5   **316–317**, 399
  3:12–39   18
  3:35   327
  4   18
  5   20, 135, 228
  5:1   19, 21
  5:1–2   160
  5:1–3   4, 18–20, 283
  5:1–10   228
  5:2   136–**137**
  5:3   19–20, 55, 201, **255**
  5:4–5   19–20

2 Samuel (cont.)

5:5 19, 96, **219**, 258, 315–**317**, 382
5:6 21, 64, 69, 119–**120**, 171
5:6–7 **121**
5:6–9 19–20, 52, 101, 119
5:6–10 283
5:7 34, 65
5:8 120, 245
5:9 34, 53
5:10 20
5:11 192, **236**, 347
5:11–12 22, 331
5:12 **248**
5:13 4, **235**
5:13–16 22
5:14–16 315, **317**, 330, 362–**363**
5:17 19, 34–35, 329, 331
5:17–18 35
5:17–21 154
5:17–25 19, 22, 34, 134–135, 195, 330, 345–346
5:18 35
5:19 35, 330, 345
5:19–20 **162–163**, 327
5:19–25 **345**
5:20 134–136, 345–346
5:21 140, 154–155, 330, 345
5:22 136
5:22–25 103, 135, 327, 345
5:23 330
5:24 **164**
5:25 103, 135–136, **164**
6 146
6:1–11 150
6:1–12 22
6:2 65–66, 171
6:3 150–151, 382
6:5 60–62, 267–268
6:6 73, **248**
6:7 150
6:10 244, **248**
6:10–11 56
6:11 340
6:13–14 150
6:14 61
6:14–17 **306**
6:15 60–**61**, 268, 307
6:16 4, 310, 389
6:17 56, 146, **251**, 307
6:20–23 4

2 Samuel (cont.)

7:1 38–39, 180–181, 192–193, 246
7:1–2 181
7:1–3 180
7:2 181
7:2–3 180
7:3 181
7:4 182
7:5 182, 191, 257
7:6 71–72
7:7 71
7:8 201, **257**
7:8–9 161
7:9 **137**
7:11 38, 161, 191, 309
7:12 38, 192, 264
7:12–13 **248**
7:13 159, 264
7:13–14 **264**
7:14 94, 264
7:14–15 **94**
7:15 131
7:18–29 28
7:20 **234**
7:23 212
7:24 264
7:25 137–**138**
7:27 **249**
8:1 39, 162
8:1–2 112, 392
8:2 **258**
8:3 85–**86**
8:3–8 38
8:6 **258**
8:7 204
8:8 14, 260
8:10 **273**–274
8:10–12 211
8:11 274
8:11–12 204, 369
8:12 85
8:13 104
8:16–18 153, **265**
8:18 153
9 389
9–20 363
10 38, 347
10:1–2 **249**
10:1–3 348
10:1–5 89
10:2 346
10:2–3 **348**
10:3 **251**, 347–348
10:4–5 347
10:6 84–85, 377–378, 402
10:8 378
10:9 **237**, 248

2 Samuel (cont.)

10:11 **238**
10:12 **238**
10:13 **238**
10:16–17 402
10:17 402
10:19 **234**
11:1 14, 38
11:2–24:25 14
11:3 362
11:27 363
12:10 187
12:14 210
12:15 363
12:15–19 363
12:24–25 363
12:26–31 26, 38
12:27 84
13:1 315, **317**
13:1–21:17 26
15:16 315, **317**
15:19 56
17:27 347
18:3 361
18:17 131
19:31 22
20:1 130–**131**
20:2 131
20:15 42
20:16 75
20:23 265
20:26 154
21 389
21:2–3 328
21:6 146
21:9 146
21:12 65
21:15–17 26
21:15–21 97
21:18 26
21:18–21 97
21:19 60, 131, 350–351
21:20 59
21:22 97
22:17 73
23 97, 228
23:7 60
23:8 292
23:8–17 97
23:8–23 97
23:8–29 97
23:8–39 228, 283
23:9 69–70
23:13–14 34
23:15–17 70
23:16 70
23:17 **70–71**
23:18–23 97
23:20 265

2 Samuel (cont.)
23:20–23 60
23:21 **59**–60, **351**
23:23 265
23:24 97
23:24–39 97
23:39 97
24 15, 146, 166, 170, 202, 211
24:1 167
24:2 167, 170–171, **273**
24:3 167–168, **249**
24:4 167, 169, **235**
24:5–7 91, 122
24:6 122
24:8 91, 171
24:9 167, 344
24:10 167
24:11 167
24:11–12 168
24:12 167
24:13 167, 341
24:14 167
24:15 171
24:16 72, **245**
24:17 167, 350
24:18 167–168, **236**
24:18–19 147
24:19 167–168
24:20 167
24:21 167, 170, 311
24:22 167, 311
24:22–23 **312**
24:23 167, 312
24:24 167–168, 269, 311
24:25 16, 167, 170

1 Kings
1 180, 363
1–2 363
1:2 93
1:11 181
1:23 181
1:25 181
1:27 181
1:33 181
1:34 55
1:39 55–56
1:45 55
2:11 96, 259, 382
2:11–12 196, 285–287
2:39–41 112, 392
3 53, 143–144
3:2 142
3:2–3 144
3:3 142
3:4 142, 146, **246**, **280**, 304

1 Kings (cont.)
3:4–15 285–286, 297, 304–**305**
3:5 53, **251**, 304
3:5–15 **54**, 304
3:7 46
3:8 351–352
3:9 **249**, 353
3:11 133, 219–**220**, **312–313**
3:11–14 133
3:13 41, 133, **238**, **313**
3:14 45–46
3:15 53, 142, 144, 304
4:1 297
4:6 397
4:11 382
4:13 154
4:20 352
4:21 110
4:24 110
5 301, 370
5:1 44–45, 108, 110
5:4 109–110
5:6 298
5:9 372
5:9–14 46
5:11 318
5:15 301, 347
5:15–9:25 82
5:16–26 347
5:16–32 **301–302**
5:16–36 301
5:16–9:9 202
5:16–10:25 **298**
5:16–10:29 297
5:17–18 39
5:18 38, 193
5:18–19 180
5:20 377
5:21 290–**291**, 371–**372**
5:21–23 290
5:22 377
5:22–23 **79**
5:23 62, 79
5:24–25 62–**63**
5:25 62, **271**
5:27–28 39, 68
5:29–30 40, 67–**68**, 201, 369–**370**
5:30 **262**
6:1 83, 114–**115**, 202, **247**, 289–**290**, 295, **373**
6:2 73, **271**, 278, **280**
6:2–36 295
6:3 **272**
6:14 390
6:19 278

1 Kings (cont.)
6:20 **272**
6:21 390
6:23 **270**
6:23–28 390
6:24 **272**, 307
6:24–25 307, 378–**379**
6:27 307, 378–**379**
6:31–32 390–391
6:37 115, 295
7 392
7:12 278
7:15 139, **271**
7:16 **271**
7:18 139
7:23 138
7:24–25 270
7:26 **271**
7:27 138
7:38 15, 138, **271**, 278
7:40 138
7:40–45 260
7:41 271
7:45 138
7:46 107
7:48 138
7:50 390–391
7:51 138
7:51–8:2 385
7:63 385
8:1 65
8:3 149
8:4 146, 149
8:5 314, 352
8:9 212, 270, 384
8:10 224–**226**, 299
8:10–11 **225**, 299–300
8:10–53 **299**
8:11 224–**226**
8:12–53 28, 299
8:16 201, 212
8:20 159, **262**
8:22 276
8:22–23 **276–277**
8:23 263, 276
8:24 159
8:25 263
8:26 101, 137–**138**
8:29 **239**–240
8:30 263
8:33 263, 266
8:35 263
8:37 266
8:37–39 266–**267**
8:39 **240**, **263**
8:52 129–**130**
8:54 276
8:56 159
8:58 126

1 Kings (cont.)
8:59   240
8:62–63   313–**314**
8:63   386
8:65   **236, 240, 260–261**, 386–387
8:65–66   147–**148**, 385
9:1   286
9:2–3   **285**
9:3   110, 284–285
9:4   126
9:5   **249**, 384
9:6   **240**
9:6–7   129
9:6–9   129
9:7   129
9:8   110
9:9   212
9:10   369
9:10–14   40, 42
9:10–21   40
9:11   40, 42
9:11–14   40
9:14   271
9:17   27
9:17–18   27, **240**
9:18   41
9:20   **241**
9:20–22   39, 68
9:21   39
9:24   24, 27, 63
9:24–25   **241**
9:25   27, 63–64, 121–**122**, 371
9:26–28   27, 396, 401
9:27   116
9:27–28   **242**
10:3   **236**
10:5   **235**
10:6   **261**
10:9   143, **261**, 290, 344
10:10   270
10:11   116, 377, 396
10:11–12   52
10:12   377
10:14   **227**
10:14–15   227, 307–**308**
10:17   203
10:21   41
10:22   116, 274, 393–395
10:25   274
10:26–28   297–**298**
10:26–29   238–239
10:27   41, 297, 351
10:28   **238**, 259–**260**
10:29   **239**
11   94

1 Kings (cont.)
11:1   203
11:1–13   46
11:4   46
11:14–24   45
11:14–25   45
11:17   287
11:23   16, 85–86
11:25   45
11:26   152
11:26–28   211
11:26–41   45
11:28   39
11:29–30   160
11:38   125
11:41   196
11:41–43   297
11:42   46
12:4   130
12:12–14   130
12:15   160, **242**
12:16   130–**131**, **242**
12:18   **249**–250
12:24   160
12:26–33   211
12:28   212
12:31   212
12:32   212
12:32–33   147
12:32–13:34   95
13:1–32   159
13:33   211–212
14:6–16   159
14:20   340
14:21   190, 383
14:22–24   190
14:22–28   **191**
14:25   278
14:25–26   **279**
14:25–28   190
14:26   44, 279
14:26–28   204
14:29   196
14:29–30   190
15:1   340
15:2   340
15:3   190, 344
15:7   196, 372
15:8   343
15:9   340
15:10   340
15:11   124
15:13   134, **236**
15:17–22   342
15:18   44, 86–**87**
15:20   107
15:22   104
15:23   **250**
15:24   237

1 Kings (cont.)
15:29   159
16:1–4   159
16:9   397–398
16:11–12   159
16:21   357
16:24   103
16:29–33   23
16:30–34   357
16:32   95
16:32–33   95
16:34   159, 335
17:17   24
18:3   397–398
18:6   398
18:30–32   140
19:10   140
19:14   140
19:15–16   55
20   95, 357
20:15   42
20:26–34   95
20:34   356
21:1   24
21:19   187
22   116, 118, 203, 356
22:1   95
22:1–2   95
22:1–3   357
22:2   84, 95, **358–359**
22:3   357–**359**
22:4   **242, 358–359**
22:9   336
22:10   84
22:17   164, 337, 350
22:17–19   275
22:19–28   357
22:20–23   358
22:22   383
22:26   399
22:27   336
22:28   336–337
22:30   23, 357–358
22:32   29, **358–359**, 373–**374**
22:33   **358–359**
22:34   358
22:34–35   336
22:35   164, 358
22:36   164
22:37   336
22:43   **242**, 357
22:49   116, 393–394, 396
22:49–50   116–**117**, 119, 233, **287**
22:50   116, 118
22:52–54   118

2 Kings

1:1　44
1:6　159
1:17　159
2:1–5　335
2:15–22　335
3:24　44
3:25　101
4:36　326
5:18　92
6:17–18　275
7:3　113
8:13　24
8:16–24　**303–304**
8:17　303
8:18　203, 381
8:18–22　303
8:20　22, 43, 295
8:20–21　295
8:20–22　42–**43**
8:21　44
8:22　43, 295
8:24　198, 281–282
8:24–26　**282**
8:25　282
8:26　203, 282, 381
8:26–29　203
9:1–6　55
9:1–10　203
9:1–26　203
9:6–8　203
9:21　203
10:3　124
10:10　159
10:13–14　48
10:27　92
10:31–34　30
10:32–33　30
11　171, 173
11–12　182
11:1　**249**, 382
11:2　49
11:4　76–77, 114, 182
11:6　114
11:8　204, **243**
11:9　182
11:10　173, 203–204
11:11　114
11:12　56, 174
11:13　114, 233
11:14　114
11:14–20　397
11:15　171
11:17　**243**
11:18　173, 182
11:19　107
12　172, 174–175, 399
12–13　34
12:1　175

2 Kings (cont.)

12:2　172, 175
12:3　31, 47, 125, 172,
　　174–175
12:4　182
12:5　175
12:6　172, 400
12:6–9　399
12:7　30, 175
12:7–9　**400**
12:7–17　30
12:8　172, 175, 182–**183**
12:10　172
12:11　172, 183–184
12:12　172, 175
12:12–15　379
12:13　399–400
12:13–14　380
12:14　172
12:14–15　**379**
12:15　172
12:17　172
12:18　88, 188
12:18–19　30, 32, 87–
　　90, 188
12:19　88, 175, 188
12:20　175–**177**, 190,
　　198
12:20–22　31, 177
12:20–24　189
12:21　49, 175–**177**, 188,
　　337
12:21–22　30
12:22　171–172, **176–
　　177**, 198
12:25　172
13:1　29
13:2–3　29
13:3　30
13:5–6　190
13:10　29
13:10–11　296
13:12–13　295–296
13:14–14:14　295
13:20　287
13:25　29
14:1　29
14:3　47, 125
14:5　190, 198
14:5–6　47
14:7　104, **250**
14:8　359
14:8–10　331
14:11　331, 361
14:13　331
14:15–16　295–296
14:20　100
14:21　54, 105
14:22　401

2 Kings (cont.)

15　402
15:1　105
15:3　125
15:5　112, 332, **396**–398
15:6　105, 196
15:7　105, 396
15:8　105
15:11　24
15:17　105
15:19　99, 403
15:23　105
15:27　105
15:29　99, 201, 403
15:30　105
15:32　105, 396
15:33　302
15:33–35　302
15:33–36　302
15:33–38　**303**
15:34　125, 332
15:36　195
16:2　335
16:3　78, **243**–244, 333,
　　350
16:7　361
16:9　361
16:10　245
16:20　101
17　201
17:6　403
17:13　338
17:14　355
17:24　102
17:24–33　102
17:26　102
17:31　244
18–19　44
18:3　124
18:4　**126**–127, **250**
18:11　403
18:13　24–25, 34
18:17　88–**89**, 91–**92**,
　　388
18:18　397–398
18:19　89, 387
18:21　48
18:22　244
18:23–24　48
18:28　387
19:2　28
19:4　28
19:7　33, **161**
19:9　48, 89
19:9–35　89
19:12　52
19:14　205
19:15–19　27, 205
19:15–35　29

2 Kings (cont.)

19:16–18 353–**354**
19:20–34 28
19:22 353
19:23 353
19:32 246, 388
19:32–33 28, 388
19:35 28–29, 33
19:35–36 32
19:36 26, 92, 337
19:36–37 161
19:37 32, 87, 90, 338, 369
20:1–11 205–208
20:3 25, 206–207
20:5 207
20:5–6 206–207
20:8 206–207
20:8–11 206
20:12 207–208
20:12–19 207–208
20:13 60
20:20 388
21:2 128, 350
21:3 95, 127
21:6 78, 128, 243–244, 328, 333
21:8 125
21:9 333
21:10 197
21:10–16 159
21:16–17 281
21:17 197
21:18 50
21:20–21 **250, 334**
21:22 334
21:23 **250**
21:24 54, 397
21:26 50
22 132
22:1 22–23
22:2 125
22:3 22
22:3–5 370
22:4 183, **200**
22:5 200, 399
22:6 **237**
22:7 **251**
22:8 183
22:9 200, 370–**371**
22:10 156, 184
22:10–13 199
22:12 184
22:13 199, **263**
22:14 184
22:14–16 57
22:16 81, 132–133, 156
22:19 132–133, 283–**284**

2 Kings (cont.)

22:20 81, 132
23 102
23:2 153, **273**
23:4 184
23:6 **134**, 308
23:8 128
23:10 78, 243
23:12 128
23:15 128
23:15–20 96, 102, 159
23:16 96, 159, 308–**309**
23:19 102
23:21 157
23:22 47
23:23 22, 200
23:24 184, 328
23:24–27 23
23:25 23
23:26–27 23
23:28 23, 82
23:28–30 31
23:29 22, 81–82, 90, 178–179, **245**
23:29–30 31
23:29–24:7 177
23:30 45, 54, 56, 105, 397
23:30–24:17 364
23:31–34 91
23:33 105, 178–179
23:34 45, 105, 178–179
23:34–35 45
23:35 178–179, 397
23:36–24:6 91
24:2–3 159
24:5 48
24:6 49–50
24:7 91, 179
24:9 48
24:17 105, 175
24:19 47, 202
24:20 202, **251**
24:21 175
24:29 81
25 233
25:3 397
25:7 233, 244
25:18 182–183
25:19 397
25:22 397
25:27 327

Isaiah

1:1 106
1:12 278
2:4 204
2:16 393, 395
4:3 99

Isaiah (cont.)

5:12 63
7:3 92
7:5 107, 198
7:7–9 342
7:8 107
7:9 107
7:17 107
8:19 140, 328
9:3 135
9:4 62
10:26 135
10:28–32 25
10:32 99
11:11 100
11:15 110
12:12 396
13:1 199
15:1 65, 101, 199
16:7 101
16:11 101
17:1 199
19:1 199
19:3 328
19:18 111
20:1 89
21:1 199
21:11 199
21:13 199
21:19 199
22:8–11 388
22:15 397
22:21–22 398
23:1 393
23:3 260
23:8 287
27:12 110
28:21 103, 134–135, 195
29:3 140
30:21 89
30:33 50
33:22 397
36–37 44
36:1 24, 34
36:2 91
36:3 397–398
36:4 89, 387
36:6 48
36:7 244
36:8–9 48
36:13 387
37:2 28
37:4 28
37:7 33, 161
37:9 48, 89
37:9–36 89
37:12 52
37:14 205

Isaiah (cont.)
37:15–20   27, 205
37:15–36   29
37:17–24   353
37:21–35   28
37:32   246
37:33   246, 388
37:33–34   388
37:33–35   28
37:36–37   32
37:37   26, 92, 337
37:37–38   161
37:38   32, 87, 90, 338, 369
38:1–8   205
38:3   25, 206
38:5–6   206
38:7–8   206
38:21–22   205
38:22   206
39:1   207
39:1–8   207
39:2   60
40:9   99
40:27   99
41:6   333
41:7   346
41:8   58
43:1   99
43:3   245
43:27   207
44:9–20   346
45:4   58
46:5–7   346
48:12   99
49:5   106
49:6   262
52:14   110
53:8   114
60:21   338
61:10–11   244
62:1   99
62:8   234
63:3   287
63:16   58
65:10   208

Jeremiah
2:18   260
2:27   237
3:9   237
4:20   287
7:10   266
7:12   145
7:14   145
7:31   78
10   246
10:9   396
14:17   **239**–240

Jeremiah (cont.)
15:7   84
19:5   78
19:5–6   78
21:1   77
21:9   293
22   177
22:10   179
22:11   105
22:13–17   48
22:19   49
23:4   274
23:25–32   54
24:27   264
25:11–12   161
26   111
26:6   145
26:14   124
26:18   111, 317
26:20–23   48, 111
26:21   112
26:22   111
27:7   161
29:10   314
30:10   99
30:22   264
31:1   264
31:8   264
31:33   264
32:35   78
32:38   264
34:5   51
36:26   399
37:2   202
37:13   293
37:14   293
38:6   399
38:15   202
38:20–21   202
39:3   89
39:4   251
39:6   244
39:9   293
40:4   124
40:7   397
44:30   178
46   82
46:2   81–82, 91, 178
48:31   101
48:36   101
49:17   111
49:29   154
50:11   287
52   233
52:2   47, 202
52:3   251
52:6   397
52:7   251
52:10   234, 244

Jeremiah (cont.)
52:15   293
52:24   182–183

Ezekiel
2:6   274
3:9   274
11:20   265
12:6   281
14:11   265
14:17   266
14:21   266
16:3   **241**
16:45   **241**
17:11–21   202
17:13–15   202
17:19   202
20:26   244
20:40   199
22:11   383
23:10   266
27:9   399
27:12   396
27:23   52
27:25   393
29:19   154
33:2   397
36:28   265
37:23   264
37:27   265
39:13   397
40:5   280
43:13   280
43:14   277
43:17   277
43:20   277
44:22   93
45:19   277
45:25   147

Hosea
1:1   106
1:9   265
2:17   208
2:25   265
5:3   107
5:5   107
7:1   102, 107
7:7   397
11:1   265

Joel
1:6–7   266
3:1   54
3:3   216

Amos
1:1   106
1:5   52

Amos (cont.)
2:1   50
2:3   397

Jonah
1:3   396

Micah
1:8–16   25
3:12   99, 111
4:3   204
4:14   397
5:1   152
7:3   397
7:20   58

Habakkuk
2:14   244

Zephaniah
2:15   111

Haggai
1:1   184
1:12   184
1:14   184
2:2   184
2:4   184

Zechariah
2:12   210
3:1   184
3:8   184
4:10   **253**
5:11   100
6:11   184
8:8   265
8:10   **253**
14:5   106

Malachi
1:9   **253**

Psalms
2:7   264
2:10   397
8:2   295
8:2–9   295
8:10   295
9:16   187
18:16   111
18:17   73
19:8   111
21:13   68
23:2   338
31:17–18   337
35:13–14   327
42   240
42:2   244

Psalms (cont.)
42:4   **239**–240
45:10   396
48:8   116, 393
50:13   111
60:2   104
76:3   67
78:27   352
78:43   206
78:60   72, 145
83:15–16   244
83:17–18   337
89   132, 192
89:1   111
89:5   192
89:27–28   264
89:31–34   94
89:34   132
96:1   217
96:10–11   **253**
97:7   337
103:1–22   295
103:1   295
103:22   295
104   295
105:1   217
105:2   217
105:6   58
105:8–11   195
105:8–15   195
105:10   58
105:12–15   195
105:13   71
105:15   217, 231
105:27   206
107:1   217
115:2–11   346
123:2   244
130:2   130
132:8–10   299
132:10   **253**
135:5–14   346
135:15–20   346
144:7   73
145:18   328

Job
7:2–3   244
9:7   111
16:7   110
27:16   352
28:16   396
31:9–10   187
33:14–18   54
33:23   207
39:27–28   34
40:30   287
42:17   190

Proverbs
3:16   46
8:16   397
13:24   94
15:3   253
21:13   187
23:13   94
26:27   187
31:24   287

Ruth
1:2   152
1:22   275
4:11   152
4:18–22   153
4:20–22   368
4:22   218

Canticles
2:8–9   354
5:7   154
8:14   354

Qoheleth
5:18   134
6:2   134
10:8   187

Lamentations
2:15   111

Esther
2:1   24
2:2   93
2:6   317
2:7   66
2:14   281
3:1   24
5:6   63
5:14   187
7:2   63
7:7   63
7:8   63
7:9–10   187

Daniel
1:2   99
1:3   89
1:5   63
1:8   63
1:16   63
5:2   273
5:7   255
5:12   101
5:16   255
5:29   255
5:30   101
9:12   397
10:21   255

Ezra
2:20   103
2:55   321
2:58   321
3:7   62–**63**, 79, 81
4:7   8, 37
4:8   8
4:10   109
4:11   8, 109
4:17   109
4:20   109
5:2   184
7:1   8, 24
7:5   182
7:28   333
8:1   8
8:36   109
9–10   141
9:12   326
10:21   106
10:22   76

Nehemiah
1:3   200
1:6   129–**130**
1:11   129
2:1   8
3:1   184
3:2   335
5:14   8
7:4–5   320
7:25   103
7:36   335
7:57   321
7:60   321
8–10   141
8:1–3   392
8:9   66
8:9–10   291
8:14   147
8:18   149
9:7   66
10:12   85
10:30   125, 141
11:1–2   320
11:3   321, 323
11:3–19   9, 320–**321**
11:4   320–321
11:9   76
11:12   77
11:30   273
12:10–11   8
12:17   76–77
12:21   76
12:22   8, 77
12:27   62
12:36   76
13:6   8
13:20   307

1 Chronicles
1   66, 292–293
1–2   292
1–9   7, 406
1:1–2 Chr 36:23   10
1:6   16
1:7   396
1:19   16
1:29–31   **254**
1:32–33   **254**
1:41   16, 396
1:51   104
2–8   323
2:1   **323**
2:1–2   **323**
2:1–8   323
2:1–8:40   323
2:3   75
2:3–4   208, **220**, 318–**319**
2:3–4:43   **323**
2:4   383
2:4–15   153
2:10–4:23   217
2:6   318
2:7   208
2:10–12   367
2:13   218
2:13–15   75, 366
2:15   73, 367
2:22–23   154
2:25–33   **322**
2:38   77
3   87, 292–293
3:1   93, 107, 315–**316**
3:1–4   315
3:1–8   315
3:1–9   **315, 317**
3:3   399
3:4   19–20, 96, 219, 258–259, 315–**316**, 383
3:5   296, 316, 362–364
3:5–8   315, 330, 362–**363**
3:6–8   363
3:8   316
3:9   315
3:12   105
3:15   105, 364
3:19   1
3:22   297
3:22–24   324
3:24   367
4:5–6   **323**
4:9   **252**
4:24–43   102
5   292
5:1   **229**

1 Chronicles (cont.)
5:1–2   208
5:1–3   **228, 293**
5:1–26   **323**
5:2–3   **229**
5:3   293
5:6   403
5:10   230
5:13   324
5:18–22   230
5:22   **255**
5:24   237, 321
5:25   75
5:25–26   323
5:26   198, 403
5:27–6:66   **323**
5:35   77
5:35–37   76
5:40   76
6:1–12   55
6:7–13   152
6:8–12   153
6:9   106
6:12   76
6:17   72, 146
6:21   76, 106
6:39–66   211
6:40–41   **231**
6:42   297
6:45   **254**
6:47   **271**
7:1   **322**
7:1–5   **323**
7:6–12   **323**
7:7   321
7:8   **323**
7:9   321
7:10–11   **323**
7:13   **323**
7:14–19   **323**
7:15–16   **220**
7:20–29   **323**
7:30–40   **323**
7:40   321
8–9   389–390
8:1–40   **323**
8:19   76
8:22   77
8:23   76
8:27   76
8:28   321
8:33   **262**, 364, 389
8:34–40   389
8:38   296, **322**
8:39–40   310
9   320
9:1   **323**
9:2   323
9:2–17   9, 320

1 Chronicles (cont.)
9:3   320–321
9:3–34   **321**
9:8   76
9:9   321
9:11   76
9:12   77
9:15   76–77
9:17–34   321
9:34   321
9:39   **262**, 364, 389
9:39–44   310
9:40–44   389
9:44   217, 296, **322**
10   4, 18, 51, 194, 390
10:1   329
10:1–12   209
10:1–14   19
10:2   **262**, 389
10:3   329
10:3–4   328
10:4   310
10:5   328
10:6   309–**310**, 328,
   331, 389
10:7   328–329
10:9   156, 326, 330
10:10   203, 326, 330
10:11–12   310
10:12   51, **237**, 326
10:13   51, 209, **263**,
   328, 377
10:13–14   20, 139–140,
   220, 229, 251, 310,
   328, 331, **339**
10:14   19, 96, 310, 328,
   330
11   21
11–12   228, 361
11:1   19, 21
11:1–3   4, 18–21, 160,
   282–283
11:1–9   228
11:2   136–**137**
11:3   19, 201, **255**, 283,
   292
11:4   21, 64, **120**, 171
11:4–5   120
11:4–7   101
11:4–8   20
11:4–9   21, 283
11:5   65, 69, **121**
11:6   53, **120**
11:7   53
11:9–12:41   21
11:10   160, 201, **255**,
   283, 286, 292
11:10–11   **292**
11:10–47   228

1 Chronicles (cont.)
11:10–12:47   282–283
11:11   292, 385
11:11–18   98
11:11–41   97
11:13   70
11:15–16   34
11:16   361
11:18   70
11:19   70–**71**
11:20–25   98
11:22   265
11:22–25   60
11:23   59–60, **351**
11:24   265
11:26   97
11:28   361
11:41   97
11:41–47   97
12   21
12:1   210, 361
12:1–8   228
12:1–23   406–407
12:3   361
12:7   361
12:8   77
12:9   354
12:9–16   228
12:10   361
12:15–16   406
12:17–19   228
12:18   361
12:19   **220**, 361
12:20   **247**, 294, 361
12:20–21   **221**
12:20–22   210
12:20–23   228, 293–**294**
12:21   210
12:22   361
12:23   255, 354, 361
12:24   160, 201
12:24–38   228
12:34   361
12:39   361
12:39–41   22, 228
13   22
13–15   361
13:2   200, 361
13:5   66, 194, **260–261**
13:6   65–66, 171
13:7   150–151, 382
13:8   60–**61**, 267–268
13:9   73, **248**
13:11   150, 361
13:13   57, 244, **248**
13:13–14   56
13:14   340
13:20   237
14   22

1 Chronicles (cont.)
14:1   192, **236**
14:1–2   22, 331
14:2   **248**
14:3   4, **235**
14:3–7   22, 362
14:4   362
14:4–7   317, 330
14:8   329, 331
14:8–16   195, 345–346
14:8–17   22, 330
14:10   330, 345
14:10–11   **162–163**, 327
14:10–16   **345**
14:11   134, 136, 345,
   361
14:12   155–156, 330,
   345–346
14:13   22, 136
14:13–16   327, 345
14:14   330
14:15   **164**
14:16   103, 136, 163–
   164
14:17   330, 338
15   150, 382
15–16   22, 61
15:1   307
15:1–16:1   306
15:2   150
15:2–16   7
15:3   307
15:11–12   150
15:13   150, 361
15:14–15   151
15:15   151
15:16   62, 267–268,
   375, 378
15:18   57, 77, 307
15:18–24   57
15:19   62
15:19–21   **268**
15:19–24   268
15:19–28   268
15:20   62, 77
15:21   57, 62
15:24   57, 62, 75, **268**
15:26–27   150
15:28   60–62, **268**
15:29   4, 310, 389
16   217
16:1   146, **251**, 307
16:4–5   57
16:8   217
16:9   217
16:13   58
16:15–18   195
16:15–22   195
16:17   58

1 Chronicles (cont.)

16:19–22 195
16:20 71
16:22 217, 231
16:23 217
16:30–31 **253**–254
16:34 217
16:38 57
16:39–40 143, 145
16:42 **378**
17:1 39, 192, 246
17:1–2 180
17:4 191, 257
17:5 71
17:7 **137**, 201, **257**
17:10 162, 191, 309
17:11 192
17:11–12 **248**
17:12 159, 264
17:12–13 **264**
17:13 **94**, 131
17:16–27 28
17:18 **234**
17:21 212
17:22 264
17:23 **137–138**
17:25 **249**
18:1 112, 162, 392
18:2 **258**
18:3 16, **85–86**
18:5 16, 85–86
18:6 86, **258**
18:7 204
18:7–10 16, 85
18:8 14, 260
18:10 **273**–274
18:10–11 204
18:11 15, 154, 273–
    274, 369
18:12 104
18:15 **265**
18:17 153, **265**
19 347, 349
19:1–5 89
19:2 **249**, 346–**347**
19:2–3 **348**
19:3 **251**, 347–349
19:4–5 347
19:6–7 378
19:7 84, 402
19:9 378
19:10 **237**, 248
19:12 **238**
19:13 **238**
19:14 **238**
19:16 16, 85
19:16–17 **402**
19:19 85, **234**
20:1–3 26

1 Chronicles (cont.)

20:4 26
20:4–7 97
20:5 60, 131, 350–351
20:6 59
20:8 97
21 91, 122, 170
21:1 167
21:1–27 390
21:1–22:1 167, 202, 211
21:2 167, 170–171, **273**
21:3 167–168, **249**
21:4 91, 167, 169, 171,
    235
21:5 167
21:6 167, 211
21:8 167, 217
21:9 167
21:9–10 168
21:10 167
21:11 167
21:12 341
21:13 167
21:14 171
21:15 72
21:16 167, 169, **245–**
    246
21:17 167, 169, 341,
    350
21:18 167–168, **236**
21:18–19 147
21:19 167–168
21:20 312
21:21 167, 169
21:22 167, 170, 311
21:23 167, **312**
21:24 154, 168, 311
21:25 167
21:26 167, 170
21:27 286
21:27–30 146
21:28 167, 169
21:28–30 390
21:28–22:1 15
21:29 143, 145
21:30 147, 167, 169
22 288
22:1 15, 83, 167, 169,
    390
22:2 16, 67, 201, 237
22:3 237
22:4 79, 237
22:5 46, 288
22:8 39, **255**
22:9 246, 338
22:9–10 39, 143
22:10 249, **264**
22:11 **262**, 286, 288
22:11–12 372

1 Chronicles (cont.)

22:13 126, 274
22:14 217, 237, 270–
    271, 273
22:14–15 237, 288
22:16 237, 273, 286
23–27 406
23:1 46
23:2 217
23:2–27:34 7
23:3–32 217
23:4–5 270
24:6 75
24:7 217, **219**
24:22–23 389
25:4 106
25:9 **219**
25:18 106
26:1–5 57
26:3 77
26:5 340
26:25 76–77
26:26–27 211
26:26–28 96, 315
27:5 182
27:5–6 265
27:16 76
27:22 77
27:23–24 211
27:34 **265**
28 365
28:1 **376**
28:3 39, **255**, 365
28:4 201
28:4–5 **365**
28:5 143, 344
28:5–16 365
28:6 365
28:6–7 **264**
28:7 249
28:8 126
28:9 193, 327
28:10 143, 365
28:20 274
29 221
29:1 46, 365
29:2 273
29:3 273, 385
29:4 396
29:5 273
29:7 270
29:9 221
29:10–19 28
29:14–16 **221**
29:19 126
29:20–24 285–**286**
29:20–25 287
29:21 236
29:22–25 46

1 Chronicles (cont.)
29:23 143, 286
29:23–24 286
29:25 286
29:26 19, 96
29:26–27 259
29:26–28 286–287
29:26–30 285–**286**
29:27 19, 96, 259, 383
29:29 196

2 Chronicles
1 46
1–9 223
1:1 286, 305
1:1–7 224
1:1–13 297, **305–306**
1:2–3 286, 384
1:2–13 285
1:3 143, 145, 280, 305
1:3–6 144
1:4 146
1:5 143, 145, 280
1:6 143, 145, **246**, 280
1:7 **251**, 304
1:7–12 **54**
1:9 137, 352
1:10 **249**, 353
1:11 219–**220, 312–313**
1:11–12 133, **238**
1:12 41, **223, 313**
1:13 143–145, 280, 297,
    304–305
1:14 297
1:14–16 297–298
1:15 41, 273, 351
1:16 **238**, 259–**260**, 298
1:17 **239, 298**
2 39, 370
2:1 **262**, 301–302
2:1–17 224, 301–**302**
2:2 282, 384
2:3 285
2:6 252, 255, 273, 285,
    391
2:7 377
2:9 62–**63**, 256, **271**
2:10–11 **261**, 290–**291**
2:10–15 290
2:11 261, 371–**372**
2:12–13 255
2:13 **252**, 273, 391
2:14 62–63, 256
2:15 79, 81, 377
2:16 201, 369
2:16–17 40, 67–**68**,
    369–**370**
2:17 **262**, 301, 369
3:1 83, 202, 289, 372

2 Chronicles (cont.)
3:1–2 **247, 289–290,**
    373
3:1–5:1 224
3:2 114–**115**, 289
3:3 73, **271**, 278, 280
3:4 **258, 272**
3:8 **272**, 278
3:10 **270**
3:10–13 390
3:11 **272**, 307
3:11–13 **378–379**
3:12 272
3:13 255, 307
3:14 255, 390–392
3:15 139, **271**
3:16 139
4:1 139
4:2 139
4:3–4 270
4:5 **271**
4:6 15, 139, **271**, 278
4:9 277–278
4:11 139
4:11–16 260
4:12 271
4:13 139
4:16 139
4:17 107
4:19 139
4:22 391–392
5:1 273
5:2 65
5:2–14 224
5:2–7:10 224
5:4 149
5:5 146, 149
5:6 314, 352
5:10 212, 270, 384
5:11 **225**, 300
5:11–13 299
5:11–7:3 **299–300**
5:13 224–**226**, 300
5:13–14 **225**, 299–300
5:14 224–226, 300
5:17 226
6:1–11 224
6:1–40 299
6:1–42 28
6:5 212, 224
6:5–6 201
6:6–11 224
6:10 159, **262**
6:12 276–277
6:12–14 **276–277**
6:12–42 224
6:13 270, 276–278
6:14 276
6:16–17 224

2 Chronicles (cont.)
6:17 101, **137–138**
6:18 145
6:20 130, **239**–240
6:20–21 224
6:21 **263**
6:24 266
6:26–28 284–285
6:28 266
6:28–30 266–**267**
6:30 **240, 263**
6:32 263
6:34 263
6:39` 263
6:40 129–**130**, 285
6:41–42 299
6:42 **253**
6:43 263
6:45 263
7:1 **226**, 300
7:1–2 226–**227**, 299–
    300
7:1–3 300
7:1–10 224
7:2 225–**226**, 300
7:3 299–300
7:4 313
7:4–5 **313–314**
7:5 313, 386
7:8 **236, 240, 260–261**
7:8–10 148, 386
7:9 147–148, 386–387
7:10 147
7:11 286
7:11–22 224
7:12 284
7:12–16 **285**
7:12–18 224
7:13 266–**267**
7:13–15 284
7:13–16 224
7:14 284
7:15 130
7:16 110, 285
7:17 126
7:17–18 224
7:18 **249**, 384
7:19 **240**
7:19–21 224
7:19–22 224
7:20 129
7:21 112
7:22 212, 224
8 27
8:1–2 42
8:1–6 42
8:1–16 224
8:2 41–42
8:3–4 41

2 Chronicles (cont.)
8:4–6 **240**
8:7 **241**
8:7–8 40
8:7–9 39, 68
8:8 39
8:11 27
8:12 121–**122**
8:12–13 **63**–64, **241**, 371
8:12–16 27
8:17–18 396, 401
8:17–9:12 224
8:18 116, **242**
8:65 148
9:2 **236**
9:4 **235**
9:5 **261**
9:8 143, **261**, 290, 344
9:9 270, 338
9:10 377, 396
9:10–11 52
9:11 377
9:13 **227**
9:13–14 227, **307–308**
9:13–28 224
9:14 273
9:16 204
9:20 41
9:21 273–274, **394**–395
9:24 273
9:25 274, 298
9:25–28 297–**298**
9:26 45, 108–110
9:27 41, 351
9:28 259–**260**, 298
9:29 196
9:29–31 297
9:30 46
10 107
10:4 130
10:12–14 130
10:15 118, 160, **242**
10:16 130–**131**, **242**
10:18 **249**–250
11:4 160
11:13–15 211
11:13–17 190
11:17–23 331, 340
11:21 270
12:1 107, 190
12:1–12 **191**, 279
12:2 278–279
12:2–4 190
12:2–8 279
12:2–9 **279**
12:5 178, 188, 191
12:5–6 **221**
12:7 118, 178

2 Chronicles (cont.)
12:9 44, 278–279
12:9–11 204
12:12 118, **256**, 284
12:13 46, 286, 383
12:15 196
12:25 **249**
13 344, 374
13:1–14 150
13:2 340, 372
13:2–19 340
13:3 **223**, 344, 372
13:3–20 196, 372
13:4–12 118, 196
13:5 354
13:6 211
13:7 46
13:8 344
13:8–9 212, **343**
13:8–11 **221**
13:10 334, 384
13:10–11 196, **343**
13:13 374
13:14 344
13:14–15 29
13:15–17 344
13:16–17 334
13:18 118, 196, 335, 344
13:19 335
13:20 340, 384
13:20–21 340–341
13:21 286, **340**
13:22 196
13:23 343
14:1 24, 124
14:5 193, 343
14:5–6 193
14:5–7 342
14:6 118, 193, 338, 343
14:7–8 344
14:7–14 342
14:10 **343**, 384
14:11–14 **375**
15 193
15–20 **374–375**
15:1 **256**
15:2 193, 327
15:4 193
15:5 **253**
15:8–15 **288–289**
15:9 102–103, 288, 293
15:9–10 320
15:10 288
15:12–15 221
15:14 237
15:14–15 193
15:15 118, 328, 338
15:16 134, **236**

2 Chronicles (cont.)
15:18 273
16:1–6 342
16:2 44, **86–87**, 273
16:3 273
16:4 107
16:6 **104**
16:7 343
16:7–8 **342**
16:9 **253**, 343
16:10–12 26
16:12 **250**
16:14 51
17:1 286
17:1–5 **229**
17:3–4 217, 229, 311
17:3–5 **339**
17:5 357
17:6 76, 357
17:7 76
17:8 217
17:10–11 338
17:11 264
18 118, 164, 203, 357–358
18–19:1 336
18:1 203, 357–**359**
18:2 84, 95, 357–**359**
18:3 **242**, 358–**359**
18:9 84
18:10–11 211
18:16 164, 337, 350
18:18–27 357
18:19–22 358
18:25 399
18:26 336
18:27 336–337
18:29 357–358
18:31 29, 357–**359**, 373–**374**
18:32 **358–359**
18:32–34 336
18:33 358
18:34 164, 358
19:1 165, 336, 357
19:1–3 118
19:3 **256**, 357
19:4 273
19:11 182
20:1 332
20:1–13 28
20:2 66
20:3 88
20:5–13 266
20:9 29, **266–267**
20:10–11 212
20:14 **256**
20:14–17 28
20:14–18 **230**

2 Chronicles (cont.)

20:15 230, **254–255**, 274
20:17 230, **254**, 274
20:23 341
20:29 338
20:30 193, 338
20:32 **242**
20:34 117
20:35 118
20:35–36 116, 119, 287
20:35–37 26, 116–119, 233, 287
20:36 395
20:36–37 119, **394**–395
20:37 117–118, 384
21:1–20 **303–304**
21:3 **127**, 273
21:4 107, 286
21:5 303
21:6 203, 382
21:6–10 303
21:8 43, 295
21:8–9 295
21:8–10 **43**
21:9 43
21:10 43, 217, 295
21:11–19 303
21:14 256
21:14–15 22
21:16–17 22, 198
21:17 48, 256
21:18 22, 340
21:19 51
21:20 282, 303
21:20–22:2 **282**
21:24 167
21:32 357
22 203
22:1 198, 281–282
22:2 203, 281–282, 382
22:2–6 203
22:7 55, 203
22:7–8 203
22:7–9 118
22:8 48
22:9 384
22:10 203, 382
22:10–12 172
22:11 49
23–24 182
23:1 **76**, 182
23:6 77, 182
23:7 77, **243**
23:9 173, 204
23:10–21 171, 173
23:11 56, 174
23:12 114, 233
23:14 171

2 Chronicles (cont.)

23:15 182
23:16 **243**
23:18 173, 182
23:20 107
23:24 321
24 31, 34, 172, 174–175, 399
24:1 175
24:1–2 172
24:2 125, 174–175, 182
24:3 171–172, 175, 182, 198
24:4 175
24:4–14 172
24:5 400
24:5–6 **400**
24:5–14 199
24:6 172, 175, **182–183**, 199
24:7 199, 380
24:8 175
24:9 199
24:10 221
24:11 172, 175, 183, 199
24:12 173, 175, 199, 400
24:12–14 379
24:14 171, 173, 175, 273, **379–380**
24:14–16 337
24:15 171, 175, 190
24:16 171
24:17 173, 175
24:17–18 376
24:17–22 31, 174
24:18 47, 171, 187, 337
24:19 376
24:19–20 **376**
24:20 172, 175, 187–189, **256**, 376
24:20–22 47, 171
24:21 171, 176, 189, 337
24:21–22 189
24:22 172, 175–176
24:23 31–32, 86
24:23–24 88, 176
24:23–25 32, **90**
24:24 175, 187–188
24:24–25 31, 49
24:25 49, 171, 175, 188–189, 337
24:25–27 **176–177**
24:26 198
24:27 198
25 107
25:1 317

2 Chronicles (cont.)

25:2 47, 125
25:3 190, 198
25:3–4 47
25:6 107
25:6–10 118
25:7 107
25:9 107
25:11 104, **250**
25:14 104, 360
25:14–16 47, 359–360
25:15 360
25:16 360–361
25:17 359
25:17–19 331
25:17–24 360
25:20 104, 331, 360–361, 385
25:23 331
25:24 57, 273
25:27 118
25:28 65, 100–101
26:1 54, 105
26:3 105
26:4 125
26:5 332
26:5–8 332
26:6–8 332
26:7 105
26:8 105, 332–333, 338
26:9 105
26:11 105
26:14 105
26:15–16 333
26:16 332–333
26:18 105
26:19 105
26:20 182
26:21 105, 113, 397
26:22 105, 196
26:23 105, 396
27:1 302, 396
27:1–4 302
27:1–9 303
27:2 105, 125, 332
27:3 **222**
27:5 196, **223, 314–315**, 333
27:5–6 302
27:6 196, 333
27:6–7 196
27:7 196, 302
27:8 302–303
28 213, 349
28:1 335
28:3 **78, 243**–244, 333, 350
28:3–11 213
28:5 86, 335, 377

2 Chronicles (cont.)
28:5–8 213
28:5–15 335
28:6 213
28:6–7 377
28:7 76
28:8 213, 335, 377
28:9 214, 335
28:10 335
28:11 335
28:12–27 213
28:15 335, 349
28:16 361
28:17 213–214
28:17–19 335
28:18 214
28:19 213
28:20 286, 403
28:20–21 361
28:22 213, 333
28:22–23 361
28:23 86
28:24 213
28:24–25 **222**
28:27 **101**
29–32 207
29:1 207
29:2 124
29:3 213, 412
29:4–11 213
29:6 213
29:7 213
29:8–9 213–214
29:9 213
29:11 151
29:23 344
30 47
30:1–7 201
30:5 273
30:6 192, 200
30:8 355
30:9 192, **253**
30:13 315
30:18–19 27
30:24 157, 270
30:25 67
30:27 **263**
31:1 126–**127**, 201,
    250, 320
31:10 182
31:20 24, 124, 207
32 48, 200, 205
32:1 23–26, 34, 124,
    200, 207

2 Chronicles (cont.)
32:2–5 388
32:6–8 48, 388
32:7 274
32:7–8 217
32:8 339
32:9 **88–89**, 91–**92**,
    317, 388
32:10 387
32:10–11 388
32:11 387
32:12 244
32:15 338
32:17 **222**, 338, 353–
    354
32:18–19 354
32:20 27–28, **205**, 207
32:20–21 28
32:21 26, 28, 33, 87,
    161, 337–338
32:21–22 200
32:22 338
32:23 26, 338
32:24 205–**206**, 208
32:27 273
32:31 206–208, 385
33:2 128, 350
33:3 95, 127, 197
33:4–5 197
33:6 **78**, 243–244, 333
33:7 197
33:8 125
33:9 333
33:11–13 179
33:12 197, 333–334
33:12–13 197
33:12–16 334
33:18 197
33:18–19 197
33:19 197
33:20 197
33:22 **250**, **334**
33:23 202, 334
33:24 **250**
33:25 54
34 96, 132
34:1 22–23
34:2 125
34:3 308
34:3–5 **308–309**
34:4 134, 155
34:5 308
34:5–6 102
34:6 103, 320

2 Chronicles (cont.)
34:6–7 201
34:7 128, 155
34:8 22, 308
34:9 200
34:10 399–400
34:11 **237**
34:12 **251**, 371
34:16 370
34:16–17 **370–371**
34:17 200
34:18 156, 370
34:21 199, **263**
34:24 58, 132, 156
34:27 132, 283–**284**
34:28 132, 383
34:30 153, **273**
35 156
35:7 157, **376**
35:7–8 **222**
35:7–9 156–157
35:8–9 157
35:9 76
35:13 157–158, **222**
35:18 47, 200
35:19 22
35:20 22–23, 81–82,
    90, 178–179, **245**
35:20–36 177
35:21–22 23
35:22 178–179
35:22–24 23
35:26–27 23
36 160
36:1 45, 54, 105, 320
36:1–10 364
36:2 105
36:3 178–179
36:3–4 105
36:3–8 91
36:4 45, 105, 178–179
36:6 50
36:7 99
36:8 48, 50
36:9 48
36:10–11 320
36:12 47, 202
36:13 158, 202, **251**
36:18 320
36:19 **223**
36:21 160, **222**, **314**
36:22 9
36:22–23 1

Deuterocanonical Literature

Apocrypha

1 Esdras
  1:23 81
  1:32 55
  1:40 50
  9:21 106

Judith
  4:6 184
  11:14 184
  15:8 184

1 Maccabees
  1:22 391
  1:29 393
  2:28 57

1 Maccabees (cont.)
  3:13 393
  3:14 393
  4:51 391
  6:1–2 204
  16:19 100

2 Maccabees
  5:24 393

Sirach
  44:20 385
  47:13 385
  50:1 400

Tobit
  4:7 187

Pseudepigrapha

Jubilees
  2:19–20 265
  4:33 74
  7:13–16 74
  8:1 74
  19:29 265
  34:20 74
  47:5 74
  49:13 158

Pseudo-Philo, L.A.B.
  44:1, 2 74
  45:2 74
  65:4 74

New Testament

Matthew
  7:2 186
  27:51 391

Luke
  23:45 391

Index of Ancient Sources

Ancient Bible Versions

1. Dead Sea Scrolls

1QGenAp 67
4QSam^a 13

4QSam^a
1 Samuel
  1:24 312
  17:4 60
2 Samuel
  3:3 93
  5:6 119
  5:8 119
  5:11 236–37
  6:2 65, 66
  6:6 73
4QSam^a on the verse
  after 2 Sam 24:16
    169, 245

The *pesher* on 2 Sam 7:11
  (4QFlorilegium)
  191–92

1QIsa^a
Isaiah
  15:1 65, 101
  16:7 101
  20:1 89
  28:21 135
  37:32 246
  37:33 246
  43:3 245
  49:5 106
  49:6 262

1QIsa^b
  62:8 234

4QJer^b
  Jer 10 246

4QChr / 4Q118
2 Chronicles
  28:27 12
  29:1–3 12

*2. The Samaritan
  Pentateuch* 14

Genesis
  8:21 235
  35:10 235

Exodus
  3:2 248
  13:4 38
  18:24–26 142
  20:18 38

Leviticus
  18:23 235

Numbers
  23:10 352

Deuteronomy
  1:9–18 142
  6:18 124
  7:5 126–27
  34:10 235

3. Septuagint (LXX)

Genesis
  4:8 384
  10:23 60
  11:2 100

Numbers
  21:24 108
  23:10 352

Deuteronomy
  6:18 124
  16:7 158

Joshua
  11:1 103
  12:20 103
  18:28 64
  19:15 103

Samuel
  Codex Vaticanus (B)
    13

1 Samuel
  1:1 – 2 Sam 11:1 14
  1:24 312
  7:1 382
  17 366
  17:4 60
  25:22 210
  27:3 93
  28:19 328–29

2 Samuel
  3:3 93
  5:8 120
  5:21 154–55, 345
  5:25 136

2 Samuel (cont.)
  6:2 65
  6:5 61
  6:6 73
  7:11 191–92
  7:15 131
  8:3 85
  8:8 14
  8:12 211
  8:18 153
  10:3 348–49
  11:2–24:25 14
  21:6 146
  23:16 70
  23:17 70–71
  23:21 59–60, 351
  24:16–17 169
  24:25 16

1 Kings
  2^{46k} 109
  4:6 397
  4:11 382
  5:20 377
  5:24 62
  5:30 302
  6:2 73, 272
  7:15 131, 139
  8:11 225
  8:29 239
  8:65 148
  8:66 147
  9:8 111
  9:14 41
  9:20 241
  9:25 122
  9:26 401
  10:22 395
  10:27 297
  15:22 104
  22:27 336

2 Kings
  11:4a 77
  11:10 204
  11:12 56
  11:13 114
  13:12 295–96
  15:5 113
  18:17 92
  21:3 95
  21:6 128
  22:19 284
  22:20 133

Isaiah
2:16 395
11:11 100

Jeremiah
10 246

Zechariah
5:11 100

Ezra
  Codex Alexan-
    drinus (A) 8

Chronicles
  Codex Vaticanus
    (B) 13

1 Chronicles
2:6 318
3:5 362
7:1 322
8:38 297
9:44 297
10:9 326
10:12 326
11:4 21
14:4 362
14:11 163
16:13 58
17:5 72
18:3, 5, 7–10 16
18:17 92, 153
19:3 348

2 Chronicles
1:13 305
3:1 83, 372
3:2 115
3:13 305, 307
4:5 271
5:13 225
6:17 137
7:13 266
15:16 134
16:7 342
21:9 43
21:17 281
22:2 281
23:1 77
24:18 187
24:25 189
25:28 100
26:1 54
26:8 332
26:21 113
27:7 196
28:3 243
28:27 101
32:22 338
32:24 206
32:31 207

2 Chronicles (cont.)
33:19 197
34:21 263–64
34:24 58
34:27 283–84
36:1 55
36:4 45
36:8 50

4. Targum Onkelos

Genesis
14:18 67

**5. Targum Jonathan
(Tg. Jonathan)**

1 Samuel
3:3 278
17:7 60
31:12–13 51

2 Samuel
5:6 120
5:21 155
6:6 73
8:18 153
10:3 348–49
20:26 154
23:17 70

1 Kings
5:1 109–10
5:11 318
9:8 111

2 Kings
15:5 113

Isaiah
1:12 278
2:15 395
19:18 111

**6. Targum Yerushalmi
(Pseudo-Jonathan)**

Genesis
14:18 67
21:21 74–75
46:17 75

7. Targum of Job
40:30 287

8. Targum of Chronicles

1 Chronicles
2:6 318
3:1 107
17:5 71
18:17 265

2 Chronicles
2:9 62
3:1 83
3:13 305, 307
10:16 242
13:3 223
20:36 395
21:17 281
28:3 243
32:31 207

9. Peshiṭta

Deuteronomy
6:18 124

Joshua
18:28 64

2 Samuel
6:6 73
7:15 131
8:12 211
8:18 153
20:1 131
23:17 70
23:21 59

1 Kings
5:1 109–10
6:2 73, 272
9:8 111
9:14 41

2 Kings
11:10 204
18:17 92

Psalms
89:34 132

Ezra 8

1 Chronicles
2:6 318
3:5 362
7:1 322
8:38 297
9:44 297
10:14 139
14:11 163
16:13 58
17:5 71
18:17 265

2 Chronicles
2:9 62
3:1 83, 372
3:2 115
6:17 137
10:16 242
13:3 223
15:16 134

2 Chronicles (cont.)
21:6 382
21:17 281
22:2 281
24:27 198–99
28:3 243
33:6 128
33:8 125
34:21 263–64

10. Vetus Latina / Old Latin

Joshua
11:1 103
12:20 103
19:15 103

2 Samuel
20:1 131

1 Kings
9:8 111

2 Chronicles
1:13 305
10:16 242

11. Vulgate

Joshua
11:1 103
12:20 103

Joshua (cont.)
18:28 64
19:15 103

1 Samuel
27:3 93

2 Samuel
5:8 120
6:6 73
7:15 131
20:1 131
23:17 70
23:21 59

1 Kings
5:1 109–10
6:2 73, 272
9:14 41
22:27 336

2 Kings
11:10 204
15:5 113
18:17 92

Psalms
89:34 132

1 Chronicles
2:6 318
7:1 322
14:11 163

1 Chronicles (cont.)
18:17 265

2 Chronicles
1:13 305
2:9 62
3:1 83, 372
3:2 115
3:13 305, 307
10:16 242
13:3 223
15:16 134
24:25 189
24:27 198–99
32:22 338
32:31 207

12. Hexapla

1 Kings
5:1 109–10

13. Aquila

1 Kings
9:8 111

14. Ethiopian Text

2 Chronicles
24:27 198–99

Ancient Near Eastern Sources

1. Aramaic Inscriptions and Letters

Aramaic Inscription of Tell Dan
  Biran/Naveh, *IEJ* 43 (1993) 87 16
  Biran/Naveh, *IEJ* 45 (1995) 9 16
Aramaic Mosaic Inscription from the
  En-Gedi Synagogue (line 13) 253
Elephantine Papyri
  Cowley, *Aramaic Papyri*,
    no. 30, lines 18–19, 30 8, 184
    no. 31, lines 17–18, 29 8, 184
Melqart-Stele of Bar-Hadad
  Albright, *BASOR* 87 (1942) 25–26 86
  Pitard, *Ancient Damascus*, 139–41 86
Tombstone of King Uzziah
  Sukenik, *Tarbiz* 2 (1931) 290,
    pls. 1–2 106, 341

2. Egyptian Sources

Hatshepsut, Queen
  Breasted, *Records of Egypt*, 2.109,
    §265 394
  Naville, *Temple of Deir el Bahari*,
    Part 3, pls. 69–79 394

Seal Ring of Psamtik I
  Wooly, *Charchemish*, pl. 26c no. 8 82
Wen-Amon scroll 287

3. Hebrew Coin, Ostraca, Seal, and Tomb Inscriptions

Coin Inscriptions
Coins of Hezekiah, the governor 184
Silver coin of Johana[n], the priest
  Barag, *INJ* 9 (1986/87) 4–21 184

Ostraca
Arad Ostraca
  Aharoni, *Arad*
    no. 1, line 3 269
    no. 4, line 3 270
    no. 6, line 4 270
    no. 8, line 5 270
    no. 9, line 3 270
    no. 10, line 2 270
Lachish Ostraca
  Tur-Sinai, *Lachish*
    no. 3, lines 8–9 69, 111
    no. 6, line 10 111

Tell Qasile Ostraca
  Maisler (= Mazar), "Tell Qasile," 67,
    no. 2   269, 396

Seal Inscriptions
Seal of Abijah
  Diringer, *Le iscrizioni antico-ebraiche
    palestinesi*, 223   106
Seals from the Collection of Dr. Hecht
  Avigad, *Hebrew Seals*, 123–24   398
Seal of Gedaliahu from Lachish
  Moscati, *L'epigrafia ebraica*,
    No. 30   397
Seal of Jezebel
  Avigad, *IEJ* 14 (1964) 274–76,
    pl. 56   218
Seal of Shebaniah
  Diringer, *Le iscrizioni antico-ebraiche
    palestinesi*, 221   106
Three Seals from the Time of Jeremiah
  Avigad, *Hebrew Bullae*, 21–23   398

Tomb inscription
Tomb Inscription of ". . .]iahu, who was
  over the household"
  Donner-Röllig, *KAI*, no. 191B   342, 397

4. *Moabite Inscription*

Mesha Stele
  Donner-Röllig, *KAI*, no. 181,
    lines 10–12   101
  Donner-Röllig, *KAI*, no. 181,
    lines 17–18   360

5. *Phoenician Inscriptions*

Inscription of Eshmunᶜazar, king of the
  Sidonians
  Donner-Röllig, *KAI*, no. 14
    line 1   115
  Donner-Röllig, *KAI*, no. 14
    lines 18–19   80
Inscription from Idalion
  Donner-Röllig, *KAI*, no. 38, line 1   115
Inscription from Kition
  Donner-Röllig, *KAI*, no. 32, line 1   115

6. *Sumerian, Hittite, Assyrian, Babylonian,
and Persian Texts and Inscriptions*

Historical Texts
Adad-nirari III
  Tell al-Rimah Stele (Page, *Iraq* 30
    [1968] 142)   102
Ashurbanipal
  Luckenbill, *ARAB*, vol. 2, §795   187
Babylonian Chronicles
  B.M. 21901, rev. 61–67 (Wiseman,
    Chronicles of Chaldean, 62–63;
    Grayson, *ABC*, 95–96)   90

B.M. 21906, rev. 66–78 (Wiseman,
  Chronicles of Chaldean, 62–75; Gray-
  son, *ABC*, 95–96)   82
B.M. 21946, obv. 1–8 (Wiseman,
  Chronicles of Chaldean, 66–69; Gray-
  son, *ABC*, 99)   82, 91
B.M. 21946, rev. 11–13 (Wiseman,
  Chronicles of Chaldean, 72–73; Gray-
  son, *ABC*, 102)   100
Darius I Stele
  Gewicht-Inschriften, Dar. Pond. 9.
    (Weissbach, *Keilinschriften*,
    102–5)   401–2
Esarhaddon
  Borger, *Asarhaddon*, Prism A, I,
    p. 48   53
  Borger, *Asarhaddon*, Prism Ninive A,
    V 55, 60   100
  Borger, *Asarhaddon*, 86, no. 57:10–
    11   396
  Luckenbill, *ARAB*, vol. 2,
    §§527–28   53
  Pritchard, *ANET*, 289a   350
Gudea
  Cylinder Inscription of Gudea, King of
    Lagash (Falkenstein and von Soden,
    Hymnen und Gebete, 180)   386
Mursili I
  The Hittite "Telepinus
    Declaration"   99
Nabonidus
  Langdon, *Neubabylonischen*, 270–72,
    I.7–40   33
  Cyrus Cylinder
    Pritchard, *ANET*, 315a   350
Sargon II
  Luckenbill, *ARAB*, vol. 2, §173   204
Sennacherib
  Chicago Oriental Institute Prism
    Inscription   44, 200
  Col. III, 18–23; Luckenbill, *Annals of
    Sennacherib*, 32–33   25
  Col. III, 27–30; Luckenbill, *Annals of
    Sennacherib*, 33   350, 388–89
  Luckenbill, *ARAB*, vol. 2, §237   52
Shalmaneser III
  Kurkh Monolith Inscription   52, 85
  Michel, *WO* 1 (1947–52) 257,
    259   16
  Luckenbill, *ARAB*, vol. 1, §608   16
  Luckenbill, *ARAB*, vol. 1, §610   52,
    360
Tiglath-Pileser III
  Luckenbill, *ARAB*, vol. 1, §772   102,
    403
  Luckenbill, *ARAB*, vol. 1,
    §§815–19   403

Letters
Assyrian and Babylonian
  Harper, *ABL*
    Part 7, nos. 4–10   355
    Part 11, no. 1091   87
  Parpola, *Correspondence of Sargon*,
    160, no. 204, line 10   109
Tell El-Amarna
  Knudtzon, *El-Amarna Tafeln*, vol. 1,
    no. 6, lines 8–16   347

7. Ugaritic Texts

2 Aqht, V 31–33   72
Dietrich-Loretz-Sanmartín, *Die Keil-
  alphabetischen Texte aus Ugarit*, 202,
  §4.81   394
Gordon, *Ugaritic Textbook*, 173, text
  51:17–19, VII   399
Gordon, *Ugaritic Textbook*, 179, text 67:
  V 15 (= F AB V 15; IIAB viii 7   113
Gordon, *Ugaritic Textbook*, 195, text 128,
  III 18–19   72
KRT, II 23–24   367

***Greek, Jewish-Hellenistic,
and Latin Sources***

Diodorus Siculus
  20.14.4–7   78
  40.3   185

Eupolemus   40

Hecataeus of Abdera
  Stern, *Greek and Latin
  Authors*, 1.26–28   185

Herodotus, *Histories*
  2.158   401
  3.89   109
  4.42   401
  7.98   79
  8.67   79

Josephus

  Against Apion (Ag. Ap.)
    1.8   8

  Jewish Antiquities (Ant.)
    1.73   351
    1.180   67
    1.197   141
    1.245   326
    1.246   326
    2.224   74
    6.18   382
    6.171   60
    6.197   36
    6.201   36
    6.203   36
    6.323   36
    6.378   328
    7.61–64   120
    7.77   155
    7.83   57, 382
    7.106   15
    7.110   153
    8.5   42

8.181   395
8.211   46
9.227   113
10.4   89
10.21–22   33
10.74   90
11.21–22   37
11.325–339   185
12.271   57
12.288   393
13.229   100
13.230   100
13.231   100
13.233   100
13.235   100
14.8–9   37
14.76   67
19.343   67

  Jewish War (J.W.)
    1.6.2   37
    2.1.3   100
    2.1.4   100
    2.1.8   100
    5.5.5–6   391

Plutarch
  Alexander 9.1   53
  Moralia 171C–D   78
  Moralia 175A   78

Pseudo-Philo, *Bib. Ant.*   74

Pseudo-Scylax, codex
  Parisinus 443   80

Tacitus, *History* 5.5   50–51

Rabbinic Sources

1. Halakhic Midrashim

Mekilta de Rabbi
  Ishmael, *Masechta de
  Pasaḥ*, §6   158

Mekilta de Rabbi
  Ishmael, *Masechta de
  Shira*, §6   210
Sifra (*Torat Kohanim*)
  1.3   369
Sifre
  Numbers, *Naso*,
    23.21   206
  Deuteronomy, *Reʾeh*,
    16.2   157

2. Mishnah (m.)

  Maʿaśerot (Maʿaś.)
    2:3   307
  Meʿilah 9:2   400
  Middot (Mid.) 5:1   278
  Roš Haššanah (Roš Haš.)
    2:2–4   155
  Šeqalim (Šeqal.)
    4:2   400
    5:4   400
  Soṭah 1:7   186
  Yoma 5:1   391

3. Tosefta (t.)

  *ʿAbodah Zarah (ʿAbod.
    Zar.)* 3.19   154
  Sanhedrin (Sanh.)
    7.11   369
  Soṭah 4.1   186

4. Jerusalem Talmud (y.)

  *ʿAbodah Zarah (ʿAbod.
    Zar.)* 3.3 (42d)   154
  Moʿed Qaṭan (Moʿed Qaṭ.)
    1.7 (6a)   386
  Nedarim (Ned.)
    6.1 (19b)   158
  Yebamot (Yebam.)
    16.3 (82b)   340

5. Babylonian Talmud (b.)

'Abodah Zarah ('Abod.
  Zar.)
  11a 51
  44a 154
Baba Qamma (B. Qam.)
  36b 307
Baba Batra (B. Bat.)
  14b–15a 9
  15a 8
  91a 74
Berakot (Ber.)
  4a 107
  7a 210
'Erubin ('Erub.)
  63a 154
Giṭṭin (Giṭ.)
  33a 307
  67a 307
Ketubbot (Ketub.)
  106b 379
Megillah (Meg.) 13a 3,
  74
Mo'ed Qaṭan (Mo'ed
  Qaṭ.) 9a 386, 388
Nedarim (Ned.) 32a 186
Sanhedrin (Sanh.)
  64b 244
  90a 186
  93a 68
  93b 8
  94b 26
Šabbat (Šabb.)
  105b 186
Soṭah 11a 210
Yoma
  16b 278
  69a 185

6. Aggadic Midrashim

Genesis Rabbah
  (Gen. Rab.)
  9:7 186
  9:11 186
  35:3 388
  43:7 67
  65:16 340
  94:6 75

Leviticus Rabbah
  (Lev. Rab.)
  1:1 75
  1:3 3
  26:7 328
  29:11 367
  33:5 340

Numbers Rabbah
  (Num. Rab.)
  10:5 74

Ruth Rabbah
  2:1 3

Lamentations Rabbati,
  Pethihta 30 29

Psalms Shocher–Tov
  7:2 74
  9:11 367

Proverbs 31:15 74

Yalqut Shimeoni (Yal.)
  2.146 94
  2.193 386–87

7. Other Rabbinic Sources

Aboth de Rabbi Nathan
  A, 37 369
Beraitha of Thirty-Two
  Midot 68, 71
Pirqe de Rabbi Eliezer
  (Pirqe R. El.)
  36 120
  48 74
Seder Olam Rabbah
  20 75

Jewish Medieval Exegesis

Rashi, Commentary on
  1 Samuel
    31:12–13 51
  2 Samuel
    3:3 107
    5:8 120
    7:14 94
    5:21 154, 155

A Commentary Ascribed
  to Rashi, on
  1 Chronicles
    10:12 326
    17:5 71
  2 Chronicles
    13:21 340
    24:27 198–99

Rabbi Abraham ibn Ezra,
  Commentary on
  Gen 43:20 68
  Exod 4:10 68
  Deut 20:19 68

Rabbi David Kimhi,
  Commentary on
  1 Samuel
    31:12–13 51
    31:13 326

2 Samuel
  3:3 107
  5:6 120
  5:8 120
  5:21 155
  7:14 94
  8:18 153
Psalms
  21:13 68
Chronicles (introduc-
  tion to) 3
1 Chronicles
  3:1 107
  5:3 293
  13:13 57
  16:13 58
  17:5 71
2 Chronicles
  7:9 387
  13:21 340
  20:35–36 287
  20:37 384
  24:27 198–99

Rabbi Moshe ben Naḥ-
  man (Naḥmanides),
  Commentary on
  Exod 1:1 9

Rabbi Levi ben Gershon
  (Gershonides),
  Commentary on
  2 Samuel
    5:8 120
  2 Chronicles
    13:21 340
    36:22 9, 120, 387

Rabbi Yeshayahu of
  Trani, Commentary
  on
  2 Sam 5:21 155

Don Isaac Abarbanel,
  Commentary on
  Samuel (introduction
  to) 3, 408
  1 Kgs 10:22 393

Christian Sources

Eusebius 8

Hieronymus 395

Pseudo-Hieronymus 42